ACTS
OF READING

ACTS
OF READING

Patricia Harkin

Purdue University

Prentice Hall
Upper Saddle River, New Jersey 07458

Library of Congress Cataloging-in-Publication Data

Harkin, Patricia
    Acts of reading / Patricia Harkin.
      p.   cm.
    Includes index.
    ISBN 0-13-042938-4 (pbk.)
    1. College readers. I. Title.
PE1122.H36   1999
808'.0427—dc21   98-37097
                             CIP

Editorial director: Charlyce Jones Owen
Executive editor: Leah Jewell
Acquisitions editor: Carrie Brandon
Editorial/production supervision and interior design: Mary Araneo
Senior managing editor: Bonnie Biller
Buyer: Mary Ann Gloriande
Editorial assistant: Gianna Caradonna
Permission specialist: Diane Kraut
Development editor: Julie Nord
Photo researchers: Francelle Carapetzan and Beth Boyd
Photo research supervisor: Melinda Reo
Image permission supervisor: Kay Dellosa
Cover art director: Jayne Conte
Cover designer: Kiwi Design
Cover art: Henri Matisse, "Ivy in Flower" 1953/Dallas Museum of Arts

Credits appear beginning on page 741, which constitutes a continuation of this page.

This book was set in 10/12 Janson by A & A Publishing Services, Inc.
and was printed and bound by Courier Companies, Inc. The cover
was printed by Phoenix Color Corp.

    © 1999 by Prentice-Hall, Inc.
    Simon & Schuster/A Viacom Company
    Upper Saddle River, New Jersey 07458

Printed in the United States of America

10 9 8 7 6 5 4 3 2 1

ISBN 0-13-042938-4

PRENTICE-HALL INTERNATIONAL (UK) LIMITED, *London*
PRENTICE-HALL OF AUSTRALIA PTY. LIMITED, *Sydney*
PRENTICE-HALL CANADA INC., *Toronto*
PRENTICE-HALL HISPANOAMERICANA, S.A., *Mexico*
PRENTICE-HALL OF INDIA PRIVATE LIMITED, *New Delhi*
PRENTICE-HALL OF JAPAN, INC., *Tokyo*
SIMON & SCHUSTER ASIA PTE. LTD., *Singapore*
EDITORA PRENTICE-HALL DO BRASIL, LTDA., *Rio de Janeiro*

For James J. Sosnoski

Contents

CHAPTER TWO
Gaps: How Texts Invite Us to Read Them   55

SECOND ACTS: USING THE TEXT'S STRATEGIES TO BUILD YOUR READING   225

CHAPTER FOUR
How Language Guides Us to Configure Meaning   227

CHAPTER FIVE
Generic Expectations: How Readers of Narrative Know What to Expect   283

CHAPTER EIGHT
Conventions of Shared Readings: How Readers Talk with One Another about Texts

Preface

What do we do when we read? In more than twenty years of teaching, I have asked my students that questions many times. Nearly always, they respond that when we read, we "try to figure out what the author was trying to say."

Let's think for a moment about that answer. It emerges, I think, from several assumptions:

1. To read is to be on the receiving end of a communication. Someone—the "author"—has a message to communicate. And someone else—the "reader"—has to decipher that message.
2. Some messages are "easier" to decipher than others. "Ordinary" texts, like an account of the Super Bowl in the newspaper or instructions for changing a tire, are easier to decipher than are "literary" texts, such as poems, stories, and plays, because authors of literary texts are deliberately obscure.
3. Reading is figuring. Like a problem in mathematics, the text we are reading (especially when it's a literary text) can seem like a puzzle that needs to be solved. Part of the puzzlement has to do with figural language, language that configures experience in ways that can be problematic.
4. Reading is "trying." And, it is trying in both senses of the word: it is *difficult* because it is an *attempt* to come to terms with the language, the thoughts, the culture of another.

How do these assumptions affect you as a reader and as a student? I believe that they are disabling. Many students believe that good readers, especially English teachers, already know how to solve the puzzles. They may even believe that this ability is somehow innate, that good readers are born, not made. Such students may often feel that they simply don't possess these instincts, that they don't know, and can't learn, "what the author was trying to say." So, they are silent in English classes.

That's unfortunate, because although these assumptions are more or less accurate, they don't tell enough of the story of reading within the context of culture. Reading certainly is (in part) figuring out what the author was trying to say. However, readers are certainly not always successful in their attempts to understand something—a text—that comes from outside themselves. It is true that cultures distinguish "literary" from "nonliterary" texts. And, figural language, because it asks us to look at the ordinary in an extraordinary way, can certainly be troublesome.

But on the other hand, how can anyone ever know what another is "trying to say"? Suppose, for example, that we could call an author on the telephone and simply ask her about the meaning of a text. Could we be sure that she would tell us the truth? And would the "truth" be what she intended when she started to write or what she understood when she finished? Could she have changed her mind in the time that elapsed between the writing and the telephone conversation, or even forgotten what she intended? Could a text mean something that its author did *not* intend? If I—or you—find a different meaning from the one the author intended, are we wrong? Is the author the only one who has the right to say what a poem or story means?

Most people have experienced confusion about the meaning of conversations even with close friends and family, situations in which they communicated—or understood—more, or less, or something completely different from what was consciously intended. You pass a friend in the corridor and say, "nice sweater." A moment later, she says "What was that supposed to mean?" If it is difficult to know the intentions of our own friends and family, is it not even more difficult to know what Shakespeare intended more than five hundred years ago in a social and spiritual context completely different from ours? Or, what an author whose race, gender, ethnicity, or sexual orientation differs from yours might intend today? When students use the phrase "trying to say," they acknowledge that this whole issue is problematic, and that authors and readers have to try very hard to communicate.

As for figural language, we use it all the time. Whenever we say that the structure of a DNA molecule is "like a spiral staircase," that the truck we drive is "like a rock," or that the Princess of Wales was "England's rose," we ask our audience to configure experience in a different way.

In this book, I try to make reading less trying for you by beginning with assumptions that demystify its processes. I assume, first of all, that the author's intention is not the *only* meaning of the text, that meaning emerges from a transaction between an author (who is certainly trying to say something) and a reader (who is usually trying to figure it out). So, instead of concentrating on the author's intention (something that we really cannot know), I ask you to focus on something that we can know at least a little about: what we do when we read.

Theorists of reading, from disciplines such as philosophy, psychology, sociology, and literary studies, have described certain processes, or acts, in which readers engage as they make meaning from a text. This book will describe those processes to you and give you an opportunity to practice them. In **First Acts: Entering the Text** (Chapters One through Three), we shall consider how and why readings differ. Every reader brings to a text a unique combination of personality, culture, habits of speech, values, expectations, and assumptions—all of which play into how that reader reacts. One of the most important premises of this book is that, just as authors have many different reasons for writing, readers have different reasons for reading. In their differing reading acts, readers make meaning. Acts of reading differ as persons differ, because of their race, gender, economic or social class; because of their regional, religious, or cultural background; or because of their sexual orientation or other, even more subtle, kinds of diversity. The chapters, examples, and exercises in this book will help you see how these differences matter.

In **Second Acts: Using the Text's Strategies to Build Your Reading** (Chapters Four through Eight), we shall raise a more puzzling question: why are readings so often similar? How is it that in spite of all the different feelings and memories and all the diversity of social, racial, and gendered backgrounds we bring to our reading, we still find that readers often *agree* about meaning? One answer is that *texts contain guidelines about how readers might read them.* Merely by being alive and alert, we learn to follow these guidelines because they are part of the thousands of cultural messages we send and receive every day. Authors learn how to write texts and readers learn how to read them by attending to the messages that cultures constantly send and receive: prayers, songs, commercials, fairy tales, myths, news, history, stories, poems, and plays. Every kind of discourse carries the codes that shape our understanding.

Although readers' diversity can produce differing readings, interpretations, or understandings of a text's meaning, it is still possible to describe, in very general terms, certain processes in which virtually all readers may be said to engage. You already know and use those processes. You in fact possess all the skills you need. At every moment of your life so far, your culture has been teaching you how to read. You read TV shows, music videos, political campaign commercials, and films every day, using exactly the same kinds of skills that literary texts call for.

The same culture that occasions and fosters the differences that seem so "trying," therefore, may also be seen to contain and limit those differences through these common signals. An individual reader may not "get" all of a text's signals, she may resist some of them, and she may even find some that the author did not intend. Still, readers do seem to attend to what they perceive as guidelines for making meaning. In this book, we shall look at some of these guidelines.

I assume, therefore, not that literary texts are different in kind from other texts but rather that different texts call for different kinds of reading acts. This book will describe these *acts of reading*, show how they work on some poems, plays, and stories, and ask you to become more conscious of the skills you already possess, refine them, and try them out on some of the "trying" texts that used to trouble you.

Patricia Harkin

Acknowledgments

Many generous persons have helped this book along on its unusually long road to completion. I first conceived the notion of writing about theory for undergraduates when Wolfgang Iser and Fredric Jameson prompted me to see that exciting ideas should not be withheld from first-year students. William J. Gracie at Miami University, Dominic Consolo at Denison, and Eric Birdsall, Robert Holland, Bruce Holland, and Janet Marting at the University of Akron gave me the opportunity to try my approach in the classroom. Jinny Marting's institutional and personal support was absolutely essential. Without her, this book would not be. Joan Mullin, at the University of Toledo, did stupendously what Writing Center Directors are supposed to do: in her, the role of facilitator rises to that of muse.

The University of Toledo and Purdue University provided institutional support. Matt Carey, Kurt Kearcher, Mike Donnelly, and Brenda Wyatt at the University of Toledo, and Cynthia Fortner, Bryan Kopp, and Jeff Schneider at Purdue lent their enthusiasm and expertise as teachers and as friends. Matt drafted many questions for the "Constructing a Reading" sections, Cynthia, Bryan, and Jeff co-authored the *Instructor's Manual*.

David R. Shumway at Carnegie Mellon University, Susan Jarratt, John Heyda, and Jacqueline Wallace at Miami University, and David Downing at Indiana University of Pennsylvania read drafts and made helpful suggestions. Randolph L. Wadsworth offered encouragement and a wonderful reading of "Good Country People"; Sallie Wadsworth shared her home and her grace. The Women's Writing Group at Purdue—Margie Berns, Reade Dornan, Margaret Finders, Muriel Harris, Janice Lauer, Patricia Sullivan, and, particularly,

Shirley K. Rose—read large sections of the manuscript with the candor and laughter that can only come from caring colleagues who are very smart. To Shirley, especially, I am grateful for a shrewdness that never deviates into cynicism.

Gregor Joseph Sosnowski and Linda Stine offered postmodern irony throughout the long process of manuscript preparation. Jonathan Hugh Daniel and Susan Romanik-Daniel shared their concerns about the fate of the whales, the fortunes of the Devil Rays, and the future of philosophic inquiry—while they taught me what it really means to teach.

The following Prentice Hall reviewers gave insightful suggestions: Sandra K. Fischer, SUNY at Albany; Cheryl Forbes, Hobart & William Smith Colleges; Marjorie Roemer, Rhode Island College; Hephzibah Roskelly, University of North Carolina; James Seitz, University of Pittsburgh; William E. Sheidley, University of Southern Colorado; and Melissa Sprenkle, University of Tennessee.

Nancy Perry believed in this book even when I doubted it. Megan Abshire knew exactly what was needed. Julie Nord has been a countess among development editors—knowing, forgiving, and wise. Mary Araneo completed production on time and in good humor; Diane Kraut expedited permissions.

James J. Sosnoski—spouse, colleague, teacher, friend, chef, inventor, and finder of lost keys, buried insights, and unimagined options—has consistently invoked the magic of technology to help this project proceed more quickly. I am more grateful, though, for the ways in which he slowed it down—by raising difficult questions. To him this work is faithfully dedicated.

ACTS
OF READING

FIRST ACTS
Entering the Text

CHAPTER ONE

First Impressions:
Reader Meets Text

The poem that follows tells a story.

Long Distance

Howard Nemerov

Here on the phone is Miss Patricia Mitchell
Of Nacogdoches, Texas, who is writing her term paper
About a poem of mine she wants to ask about.
"It's such a privilege, Mr. N," she says,
Just to pick up the phone and talk to you.

"The others in the class are writing theirs
On Wm B Yeats and Emily Dickinson,
And they can't just call up and talk to them,
Now can they?" "No, Patricia," I reply,
"Now that you mention it, I guess they can't."

I've rarely felt so grateful to be in the Book
As I am talking with Miss Patricia Mitchell
Far out in faraway Texas, and not to be
Cut off and isolate, like William Y
and Emily D with their unlisted numbers.

STUDENT CALLING POET & ASKING OF WRITING PROCESS

Let's look together at the story this poem tells as we think about the topic of this book: what happens when people read. While you think about *what it says to you*, about your responses to the poet and the student, the man and the

3

woman, the author and the reader, I'll tell you *how I read it*. In other words, I'll tell you how and why I make meaning from this text.

HOW READERS MAKE MEANING

First, I notice that our text, "Long Distance," has two characters: the speaker (a poet) and Miss Patricia Mitchell (a student). The *speaker* is, in this case, the "I" of the poem, the one who is telling the story, the one from whose perspective the poem is written. I assume that the speaker here is also the author, Howard Nemerov, or at least some part of his professional identity that he has chosen for this occasion. In this story, the speaker (let's call him "Nemerov" to distinguish him from the man Howard Nemerov) describes how he feels when a student calls to ask him about one of his poems.

When "Nemerov" describes Ms. Mitchell's phone call from his own perspective, he invites me to share that perspective on the situation. I know Patricia Mitchell, therefore, only through "Nemerov's" view of her. He describes her only as a function in his story: a caller who "wants to ask about" one of his poems.

What does she want to ask? "Nemerov" does not say. He has left a *gap* in the story—an omission that causes me to want more information than the text has given. This gap makes me curious. Therefore, I speculate.

Perhaps Patricia Mitchell is wondering how "Nemerov" felt when he wrote his poem, or what he had been dreaming just before, or what was happening in the world as he composed it, or how many drafts he wrote before he was satisfied. On the basis of my experience as a teacher and as a reader of poems, I am inclined to think that she called to ask what the poem *means*. Like my own students whom I described in the Preface, she considers "Nemerov," as the author of the poem, the ultimate authority. Ordinarily, readers do not have direct access to the author's intention, and that is what makes this case so special. Miss Mitchell can just call "Nemerov" on the phone and ask him.

On the basis of this assumption, I encounter a new gap: why does "Nemerov" seem to ignore Ms. Mitchell's efforts to "read" him? He does not even tell us what question she asked, let alone how he answered. Again, I speculate: Perhaps he feels a certain annoyance: Perhaps he thinks that the complex meaning of his poetic work cannot be reduced to a sentence or two in a long-distance phone conversation with a student. Perhaps he values the power and mystery that come with being the author, and he doesn't want to share this privilege with anyone else. All of these guesses make the poem make sense to me. They are also consistent with one another. That is, "Nemerov" might be annoyed by the interruption *and* protective of his authorial privilege *and* unwilling to simplify his meaning: one interpretation does not cancel or negate the others. Since I have no particular reason to prefer or to eliminate any of them, I assume all three explanations, and go on.

I notice that resistance is not the only response "Nemerov" seems to have to the phone call. In spite of the interruption and his feelings about it, *gap* "Nemerov" says "I have rarely felt so grateful to be in the Book." Here is another gap. What book? One possible answer is the phone book; "Nemerov" is glad that he is able to answer phone calls and to reflect on his own motivations and feelings. But I think he is also happy to be in the canon, "the Book" of texts that are perceived by a culture as valuable enough to be assigned to students as the topic of term papers in literature classes. These conjectures, though there could be many others, help me to continue to make sense of this text, so I assume them.

But then I pause again for another gap. Why does "Nemerov" bring Yeats and Dickinson into his story? Again, on the basis of my experience, I look for a *gap* reason that is consistent with the meaning I've made so far: my sense that the Book means both the phone book and the canon. "Nemerov," I note, is in both books but Dickinson and Yeats are in only one—the canon. They have earned immortality through their poetry. But they are dead! They aren't in the phone book; their numbers are "unlisted," and Patricia Mitchell can't call them.

As he reflects on Mitchell's phone call, therefore, "Nemerov" has a new set of emotions about himself and his art. He is glad to be alive and in the Book, even if life does entail answering troublesome and intrusive questions about meaning. Life—for a poet or any other person—is never without such interruptions. I interpret this poem to mean that being a poet and being alive involves accepting and even celebrating these disturbances because, as we've just seen, they are the stuff of life. Moreover, as I believe Nemerov demonstrates, they are the stuff of poetry.

It should be clear that what I've been doing here is *constructing*, or *making*, a meaning from Nemerov's poem, rather than "finding" the "definitive" meaning he has buried there. It is an assumption of this book that this is how reading really works; this is why I say that we *make* meaning, and why most of this book's exercises are called "Constructing a Reading."

How Readers' Interests Shape Their Readings

I have no way of proving that what I've just written is what Nemerov intended when he wrote this poem. Unlike Ms. Mitchell, I haven't called Mr. Nemerov. (He died in 1991.) I have no special access to his mind.

My reading—my construction of meaning—is based on *my experiences* with life and with texts. I decided that Patricia Mitchell called to ask about meaning because, as an English teacher, I know that my students are generally more concerned about meaning than about other issues and that they tend to equate meaning with "what the author was trying to say." Because I become annoyed when strangers telephone me at home, I assume that "Nemerov" does, too. Because I believe that life is a series of interruptions, I think that "Nemerov" does, too. I've interpreted by projecting my own feelings, real or imagined, onto the speaker.

My reading is also based on my interests. I use the word *interest* in two senses:

- Because of who we are and what we believe, some things attract our attention and others do not. As an English teacher, I am interested in poetry and in how students feel about reading it.
- We tend to be attracted by things that serve our *interests:* things or activities from which we can gain in economic or other ways. My interests in writing this textbook are served by this poem: it illustrates some of the points I want to make and, because it features a student who is writing about poetry, I think it might interest you. Your being interested serves my interests.

Suppose, for example, you are "interested" in rock music and you share that interest with your friends: you talk with them about sound and lyrics; you go to concerts together; you listen and dance to the music you like at parties. The music that captures your interest, therefore, also serves your interests by giving you and your friends something in common.

That *readers read according to their interests* is one of the most important premises of this book. Your interest in this poem, for example, might be affected by your position as a student. Because you yourself will be required, before long, to write papers about poems, you might sympathize with Patricia Mitchell instead of "Nemerov." Perhaps, in other words, you decline "Nemerov's" invitation to assume his perspective on Ms. Mitchell, or perhaps you assume it but then reject it. Let's try thinking about this story from the perspective of another author, Patricia Mitchell, "who is writing her term paper."

As the author of a paper, Mitchell has a job to do. I assume, again, that she plans to write about the meaning of Nemerov's poetry and that for Ms. Mitchell, meaning equals "what 'Nemerov' was trying to say." She therefore telephones "Nemerov" to find out. Congratulating herself on having chosen a living poet whom she can call, she shares her pleasure in this self-actualizing behavior with "Nemerov." She feels sympathy for students who are writing about Emily Dickinson or William Butler Yeats because those authors cannot answer questions. Unfortunately, in spite of Ms. Mitchell's care and good intentions, it seems that "Nemerov" merely uses her as an opportunity to ponder his own importance. Instead of answering her questions, he turns her phone call into a stimulus for meditation about his poetry and his life. If our interests are similar to hers, we may feel irritated not by her phoning "Nemerov," but by his apparent lack of interest in helping her. We may wonder whether she was hurt or frustrated, and whether the phone call was helpful at all to her writing.

What I intend to demonstrate with these readings of "Long Distance" is that *readers' interests affect their constructions of meaning*. I'm defining *meaning* as the sense we make of texts in the context of our interests. The word *text* will mean anything from which we make meaning—a poem, a story, a play, a film, a cartoon, a TV show, a style of clothing, a painting, a sculpture, even an incident.

CONSTRUCTING A READING

In your journal, ponder what we've just done together by answering these questions.

1. Which of my two readings of "Long Distance" do you think is closer to Nemerov's intention? Why?
2. Does my reading the poem from Patricia Mitchell's perspective seem strange to you? Do you think I'm joking? Why?
3. Think of an alternative reading to the two I've given, write it in your journal, and share it with the class.

How Readers Thematize

Now let's look at another poem, one that also describes relations between a student and a teacher, but this time from the student's perspective. This poem tells a story about some feelings that many African American students—and other student authors—probably share.

Theme for English B

Langston Hughes

The instructor said,

> *Go home and write*
> *a page tonight.*
> *And let that page come out of you—*
> *Then, it will be true.*

I wonder if it's that simple?
I am twenty-two, colored, born in Winston-Salem.
I went to school there, then Durham, then here
to this college on the hill above Harlem.
I am the only colored student in my class.
The steps from the hill lead down into Harlem,
through a park, then I cross St. Nicholas,
Eighth Avenue, Seventh, and I come to the Y,
the Harlem Branch Y, where I take the elevator
up to my room, sit down, and write this page:

It's not easy to know what is true for you or me
at twenty-two, my age. But I guess I'm what
I feel and see and hear, Harlem, I hear you:
hear you, hear me—we two—you, me, talk on this page.
(I hear New York, too.) Me—who?

Well, I like to eat, sleep, drink, and be in love.
I like to work, read, learn, and understand life.
I like a pipe for a Christmas present,
or records—Bessie, bop, or Bach.
I guess being colored doesn't make me *not* like
the same things other folks like who are other races.
So will my page be colored that I write?
Being me, it will not be white.
But it will be
a part of you, instructor.
You are white—
yet a part of me, as I am a part of you.
That's American.
Sometimes perhaps you don't want to be a part of me.
Nor do I often want to be a part of you.
But we are, that's true!
As I learn from you,
I guess you learn from me—
although you're older—and white—
and somewhat more free.

This is my page for English B.

CONSTRUCTING A READING

1. What do you imagine the speaker of Hughes's poem was thinking as he prepared the assignment? What were his "interests"?
2. What do you think the professor would have thought of this piece of writing if Hughes's speaker turned it in?
3. What meaning do you make from the speaker's assertion that "sometimes perhaps you don't want to be a part of me. Nor do I often want to be a part of you"? Do you think these emotions characterize African Americans and/or other "minorities"? Are they limited to such minorities? Why? In what way(s)?

I have brought these two poems together because I see in them a common theme: students facing troublesome writing assignments. I use the word *theme* to mean the reader's generalization about what the text is about. "Students facing troublesome assignments . . ." is a more general statement—at a higher level of abstraction—than "Mitchell calls Nemerov to ask about a poem" or "African American student worries about writing assignment." To *thematize*, then, to find or make a theme as a part of your reading of a text, is a process of generalizing.

Notice, though, that in naming my theme—students facing troublesome writing assignments—I'm relying on *my own readings* of the two texts. In this respect I differ from critics who tend to think of theme as something that is in the text, put there by the author. Instead, *I'm finding theme in readers' thoughts and responses*. Notice, too, that the theme I described serves my interests as a teacher writing to you, a student, who will soon be facing troublesome writing assignments yourself. I've served my interests by sharing my perceptions with you to advance our discussion of how readers make meaning.

And, more importantly, to define theme from the reader's perspective rather than the author's allows for different readers to find different themes, or the same reader to find different themes at different times. "Students facing troublesome assignments," then, is not the only way of thematizing these two texts. Surely you can imagine a situation in which a reader might link "Theme from English B" with other texts about the experiences of African Americans or read the Nemerov poem together with other poems about poets reflecting on their art. *Theme*, then, as I'll use the term in this book, *reflects the interests of the reader who finds or makes it*. Since different readers have different interests, themes vary.

TERMS WE'LL BE USING IN THIS TEXT

In my readings of Hughes' and Nemerov's poems, I've introduced some of the terms that you will need to use throughout this book: *gap*, *theme*, and *text*. I'll review them briefly here.

Gap is a place or moment in an act of reading when a reader feels the need for more information than the text has provided. Sometimes readers experience gaps simply because they are unfamiliar with the text's language. For example, a reader who had never heard of a composer named Bach or a singer named Bessie Smith would experience a gap in her reading of "Theme for English B." But other gaps are specifically intended by the author—for example, when Howard Nemerov does not reveal what Patricia Mitchell asked in her phone call. (Chapter Two will explore gaps in more detail.)

Theme is a generalization we make about a text that reflects, or makes it fit, our interests. We make a text coherent, we make its primary meaning, by *thematizing*. A theme can be a topic—for example, when we speak of writing a "theme" in first-year writing course. Theme can also be an idea or abstraction, such as "art" or "life" or "the experience of being marginalized." In any case, theme is a generalization through which readers bring the disparate aspects of their reading acts together.

Text is anything from which we make meaning. In this sense, a conversation can be a text, or a film, a TV program, a magazine advertisement, a painting, even a building.

CONSTRUCTING A READING

Write a page or two in your journal about one or more of the questions that follow. Don't try to answer all of them, but rather select the ones in which you have the most interest.

1. Relate an incident in which you worried about not understanding something important. Your story should be about interpreting something, but it need not be about interpreting a literary work. You might write about not understanding what to do in a social situation, or about being unable to fathom what was going on between people you care about (divorcing parents, for example). Or, you might tell about a time when you misunderstood another person's signals. Then, comment on your story as Nemerov or Hughes has.

2. Write about how (or whether) Langston Hughes's and Howard Nemerov's poems intersect with your own thoughts and feelings. For instance, have you ever wished that you could simply telephone an author to ask about the meaning of a literary work? Have you ever felt that your experiences were so different from those of your teachers and classmates that you had difficulty doing an assignment? Write about that experience.

3. Describe a typical incident from a high school or other college English class that shows how you have been taught to think about reading literature. For example, in your prior experiences in literature classes, were you encouraged to offer your own interpretations of texts? Were you expected to focus on the author's intention?

4. What kinds of reading do you do for your own interest or pleasure? Would you call what you read "literature?" Why or why not? Do you think that "reading" TV commercials, film, newspapers, or magazines involves the same kinds of activities as reading literature? Give examples of how you think the two compare (or contrast).

5. Why do you think authors write literary works?

HOW READERS' DIVERSITY LEADS THEM TO MAKE DIFFERENT MEANINGS

In reading "Long Distance," I suggested that readers' interests affect the meanings they make. In this section, I'll ask you to consider the diversity of those interests. The term *diversity* refers to variety in class or kind. African American, Native American, Hispanic American, Asian American, European American, and Canadian; male and female; rich and poor, homosexual and heterosexual; married and single; and rural, urban, and suburban students and their teachers are all reading this book. Their readings reflect their interests, feelings, backgrounds, class, race, and gender. That's diversity. Most colleges and universities strive to attract students of diverse races, religions, and national origins, and they shape their curricula to reflect diverse beliefs, customs, and values.

Difference comes into play when we begin to try to describe the effects that diverse interests have on our reading of texts. In my discussion of "Long Distance," I stipulated that I don't know what Howard Nemerov intended in his poem. Nonetheless, I read it and shared my reading with you. There is probably a difference between what he intended in the poem and how I read it. There is almost certainly a difference between how I read a text and how you read it and between how you read it and how other students in your class read it. If, tomorrow or next year, you read Nemerov's poem again, there will be a difference between your own two (or more) readings. African American students probably read "Theme for English B" with differing interests from those of white students, and any reader who is a student will probably read both poems differently from any reader who is not a student. A reader's ability or desire to assume a poet's or speaker's perspective reflects that reader's interests. Our diversity of interests causes us to read in various ways. Those various ways make *difference*.

Because of that difference, we cannot talk about *determinate*—that is, certain, or unchangeable—meaning. No one can say with certainty that "the text means this and only this." It is not possible ever to say which reading is "correct," because in the context of difference, no stable, single meaning can be found. But, even as we realize that we cannot stipulate one definitive meaning, we still try to read better, more carefully, more attentively than we have before. Perhaps our growing awareness of difference motivates us to work harder at making meaning, in the hope that we can bridge the distances between us, that we can communicate in spite of them. It's as though we were striving for determinate meaning even though we know we can't ever reach it. In that sense, meaning is put off, saved for later, deferred. Diversity leads to different readings that in turn defer meaning.

Difference operates within texts themselves as well as between texts and their readers. "Nemerov's" perspective, for example, differs from Patricia Mitchell's because their social and political standing and gender differ. Because Langston Hughes is an African American, he experiences another type of difference. Hughes's speaker worries that his difference will not contribute to a healthy diversity but rather alienate him from his teacher and the other students. Neither text "resolves" that opposition: that is, "Long Distance" does not mean that "Nemerov" is right and Patricia Mitchell is wrong; "Theme for English B" does not mean that Hughes's speaker is right and his teacher is wrong—or vice versa. Both poems (as I read them) ask their readers to consider the difference *within the text*—such that the difference itself becomes the meaning.

Also, both speakers' perspectives seem to *differ within themselves*. "Nemerov" is both pleased and annoyed by Patricia's call; Hughes's speaker both wants and does not want to belong to the white establishment.

difference "Nemerov" needs to be both famous and undisturbed; Hughes's speaker desires to be both different and the same, both inside and outside. The difference within texts evokes the differences within readers; in other words, readers who look carefully for the difference within the texts they read can learn to see the ways in which they themselves are divided by contradictory needs and desires. In the poem that follows, Linda Hogan asks her reader to see how that difference within affects her making of texts.

Heritage

Linda Hogan

From my mother, the antique mirror
where I watch my face take on her lines.
She left me the smell of baking bread
to warm fine hairs in my nostrils,
she left the large white breasts that weigh down
my body.

From my father I take his brown eyes,
the plague of locusts that leveled our crops,
they flew in formation like buzzards.

From my uncle the whittled wood
that rattles like bones

and is white
and smells like all our old houses
that are no longer there. He was the man
who sang old chants to me, the words
my father was told not to remember.

From my grandfather who never spoke
I learned to fear silence.
I learned to kill a snake
when begging for rain.

And grandmother, blue-eyed woman
whose skin was brown,
she used snuff.
When her coffee can full of black saliva
spilled on me
it was like the brown cloud of grasshoppers
that leveled her fields.
It was the brown stain
that covered my white shirt.
That sweet black liquid like the food

she chewed up and spit into my father's mouth
when he was an infant.

It was the brown earth of Oklahoma
stained with oil.
She said tobacco would purge your body of poisons.
It has more medicine than stones and knives
against your enemies.
That tobacco is the dark night that covers me.

She said it is wise to eat the flesh of deer
so you will be swift and travel over many miles.
She told me how our tribe has always followed a stick
that pointed west
that pointed east.
From my family I have learned the secrets
of never having a home.

CONSTRUCTING A READING

1. Do you understand the speaker in this poem to be Linda Hogan or (as I suggested about the speaker in Howard Nemerov's "Long Distance") an aspect of the author's "self" or an entirely invented person? Do you perceive a difference in Hogan's and Nemerov's speakers in terms of their "closeness" to their material? Discuss your answer, and the reasons for it, with your group members. → resemblance / behaviors

2. In what ways are our parents a mirror? Do you think that "mirroring" is particularly important for Native Americans and other minorities? Why or why not? How so? AnyBody - wants piece of culture w/ them

3. How do you read Hogan's emotional attitude toward her "large white breasts"? Do you perceive the feelings as positive, negative, ambiguous? How does your gender affect your response? understanding

4. More then half of this poem is devoted to describing Hogan's (speaker's) heritage from her grandmother. How do you respond to the description of the "coffee can full of black saliva" when you first encounter it? Did your response change as a result of reading the series of comparisons to "a cloud of grasshoppers," "the brown stain," "the food she chewed up and spit into my father's mouth when he was an infant," "brown earth" "dark night"? How so?

5. Do you think that "the secrets of never having a home" are peculiar to Native Americans? Why or why not?

6. What are the secrets of never having a home?

7. Write a poem about the ways in which you see yourself in the mirror of your family.

How Readers Differ from One Another

People—and readers—differ in far more ways than we can easily describe. We can define *difference* in terms of race, gender, class, nationality, and sexual orientation. There are even subtler differences, however, between, for example, a sister and brother, divorced spouses, roommates of the same gender, roommates of different genders, a white male hunter and a white male environmentalist, members of fraternities and sororities, a person who inherited money and a person who earns high fees for endorsing athletic shoes, and even "me" today and "me" yesterday.

To talk and think about the many unstable ways in which people differ one from another, we need to develop temporary, situational language—terminology that we create to serve our needs in a unique situation. At one moment, or in a certain kind of situation, we might be inclined to notice difference in gender; at another, the distinction between teachers and students might be more meaningful. In some kinds of discussions, it is helpful to mark differences between gay people and straight people, and so forth.

In view of all these differences, we might expect every reading to be dissimilar from every other one. When you think of it, it is surprising that readers ever agree about anything. Nonetheless we often find similarities in readings. This book will examine not only reasons why readings differ but also reasons why reading acts often tend to be remarkably similar.

How Readers' Differences Shape What They Perceive

Many psychologists believe that our differing interests actually affect what we perceive. To investigate this hypothesis, look at a poem that I haven't already "read" for you. Like both "Long Distance" and "Theme from English B," Robert Frost's "Home Burial" tells a story, but its narrative is longer and more complex than those of the other two poems.

Home Burial

Robert Frost

He saw her from the bottom of the stairs
Before she saw him. She was starting down,
Looking back over her shoulder at some fear.
She took a doubtful step and then undid it
To raise herself and look again. He spoke
Advancing toward her: 'What is it you see
From up there always—for I want to know.'
She turned and sank upon her skirts at that,
And her face changed from terrified to dull.
He said to gain time: 'What is it you see,'
Mounting until she cowered under him.

'I will find out now—you must tell me, dear.'
She, in her place, refused him any help
With the least stiffening of her neck and silence.
She let him look, sure that he wouldn't see,
Blind creature; and a while he didn't see.
But at last he murmured, 'Oh,' and again, 'Oh.'

'What is it-what?' she said.

                    'Just that I see.'

'You don't,' she challenged. 'Tell me what it is.'

'The wonder is I didn't see at once.
I never noticed it from here before.
I must be wonted to it—that's the reason.
The little graveyard where my people are!
So small the window frames the whole of it.
Not so much larger than a bedroom, is it?
There are three stones of slate and one of marble,

Broad-shouldered little slabs there in the sunlight
On the sidehill. We haven't to mind *those*.
But I understand: it is not the stones,
But the child's mound—'

        'Don't, don't, don't, don't,' she cried.

She withdrew shrinking from beneath his arm
That rested on the banister, and slid downstairs;
And turned on him with such a daunting look,
He said twice over before he knew himself:
'Can't a man speak of his own child he's lost?'

'Not you! Oh, where's my hat? Oh, I don't need it!
I must get out of here. I must get air.
I don't know rightly whether any man can.'

'Amy! Don't go to someone else this time.
Listen to me. I won't come down the stairs.'
He sat and fixed his chin between his fists.
'There's something I should like to ask you, dear.'

'You don't know how to ask it.'

                    'Help me, then.

Her fingers moved the latch for all reply.

'My words are nearly always an offence.
I don't know how to speak of anything
So as to please you. But I might be taught
I should suppose. I can't say I see how.
A man must partly give up being a man
With women-folk. We could have some arrangement

By which I'd bind myself to keep hands off
Anything special you're a-mind to name.
Though I don't like such things 'twixt those that love.
Two that don't love can't live together without them.
But two that do can't live together with them.'
She moved the latch a little. 'Don't—don't go.
Don't carry it to someone else this time.
Tell me about it if it's something human.
Let me into your grief. I'm not so much
Unlike other folks as your standing there
Apart would make me out. Give me my chance.
I do think, though, you overdo it a little.
What was it brought you up to think it the thing
To take your mother-loss of a first child
So inconsolably—in the face of love.
You'd think his memory might be satisfied—'

'There you go sneering now!'

                    'I'm not, I'm not!
You make me angry. I'll come down to you.
God, what a woman! And it's come to this,
A man can't speak of his own child that's dead.'

'You can't because you don't know how to speak.
If you had any feelings, you that dug
With your own hand—how could you?—his little grave;
I saw you from that very window there,
Making the gravel leap and leap in air,
Leap up, like that, like that, and land so lightly
And roll back down the mound beside the hole.
I thought, Who is that man? I didn't know you.
And I crept down the stairs and up the stairs

To look again, and still your spade kept lifting.
Then you came in. I heard your rumbling voice
Out in the kitchen, and I don't know why,
But I went near to see with my own eyes.
You could sit there with the stains on your shoes
Of the fresh earth from your own baby's grave
And talk about your everyday concerns.
You had stood the spade up against the wall
Outside there in the entry, for I saw it.'

'I shall laugh the worst laugh I ever laughed.
I'm cursed. God, if I don't believe I'm cursed.'

'I can repeat the very words you were saying.
'Three foggy mornings and one rainy day
Will rot the best birch fence a man can build.'
Think of it, talk like that at such a time!
What had how long it takes a birch to rot
To do with what was in the darkened parlour.
You *couldn't* care! The nearest friends can go
With anyone to death, comes so far short
They might as well not try to go at all.
No, from the time when one is sick to death,
One is alone, and he dies more alone.
Friends make pretence of following to the grave,
But before one is in it, their minds are turned
And making the best of their way back to life
And living people, and things they understand.
But the world's evil. I won't have grief so
If I can change it. Oh, I won't, I won't!'

'There, you have said it all and you feel better.
You won't go now. You're crying. Close the door.
    The heart's gone out of it: why keep it up.
Amy! There's someone coming down the road!'

'*You*—oh, you think the talk is all. I must go—
Somewhere out of this house. How can I make you—'

'If—you—do!' She was opening the door wider.
'Where do you mean to go? First tell me that.
I'll follow and bring you back by force. I *will!*—'

[handwritten margin note: TEST (Ending of Poem – Side I am on)]

CONSTRUCTING A READING

1. After you have read this poem carefully, retell it in your own words (paraphrase it) as though you were telling the story to someone else who has not read it. Write as much as you can. Your paraphrase should be about as long as the poem itself.
2. Discuss your paraphrases in groups. Designate someone to lead the discussion and make sure that every voice is heard. Someone else should keep a record of everyone's comments.
3. As you read or listen to each paraphrase, notice whether this reader notices something that other readers haven't, "adds" details that are not in the text, or leaves something out.
4. Try, as a group, to discover and describe the feelings that seem to dominate each reader's response. What does that response tell you about yourself and about one another?

5.   Share your group's responses with the rest of the class. As you listen to other students' narratives about this poem, speculate about why they see what they see and why they don't see some things that you saw. Do the responses seem to vary by gender, for example? Do they vary by experience, depending on whether the reader is a parent or a spouse, or whether the reader has experienced the death of a close friend or family member?

EXPLAINING DIFFERENCES AMONG READERS: THE ROLE OF FEELINGS

How do readers' differing feelings explain their different readings? The first and most obvious reason, of course, is that texts evoke complex emotions and that these emotions vary from reader to reader. To show you how these processes work, I've chosen two texts about war, a topic that often evokes strong emotions. As you read them, pay close attention to your feelings, marking places in the text that particularly affect you.

Dulce et Decorum Est

Wilfred Owen

Bent double, like old beggars under sacks,
Knock-kneed, coughing like hags, we cursed through sludge,
Till on the haunting flares we turned our backs
And towards our distant rest began to trudge.
Men marched asleep. Many had lost their boots
But limped on, blood-shod. All went lame; all blind;
Drunk with fatigue; deaf even to the hoots
Of tired, outstripped Five-Nines that dropped behind.

Gas! GAS! Quick, boys! — An ecstasy of fumbling,
Fitting the clumsy helmets just in time;
But someone still was yelling out and stumbling,
And flound'ring like a man in fire or lime . . .
Dim, through the misty panes and thick green light,
As under a green sea, I saw him drowning.

In all my dreams, before my helpless sight,
He plunges at me, guttering, choking, drowning.

If in some smothering dreams you too could pace
Behind the wagon that we flung him in,
And watch the white eyes writhing in his face,
His hanging face, like a devil's sick of sin;

If you could hear, at every jolt, the blood
Come gargling from the froth-corrupted lungs,
Obscene as cancer, bitter as the cud
Of vile, incurable sores on innocent tongues, —
My friend, you would not tell with such high zest
To children ardent for some desperate glory,
The old Lie: Dulce et decorum est
Pro patria mori.

The Soldier

Rupert Brooke

If I should die, think only this of me:
　　That there's some corner of a foreign field
That is for ever England. There shall be
　　In that rich earth a richer dust concealed;
A dust whom England bore, shaped, made aware,
　　Gave, once, her flowers to love, her ways to roam,
A body of England's, breathing English air,
　　Washed by the rivers, blest by suns of home.

And think, this heart, all evil shed away,
　　A pulse in the eternal mind, no less
　　　　Gives somewhere back the thoughts by England given;
Her sights and sounds; dreams happy as her day;
　　And laughter, learnt of friends; and gentleness,
　　　　In hearts at peace, under an English heaven.

CONSTRUCTING A READING

Write a page or two in response to one of the following questions, referring
carefully to the text as you write.
1. How do you feel when you finish reading each text? Describe your emo-
    tional response as fully and clearly as you can. For example, name one or
    more emotions—fear, sympathy, revulsion, pride, pity—and explain what
    exactly in the text evoked it and why you feel it.
2. Do you like the speakers of the poems? Why or why not? Do you share
    the speaker's feelings, beliefs, desires, gender, or politics?
3. Do you think that your own personal or family history—whether, for
    example, you or a relative has experienced combat—affects your
    response? How?
4. Do your feelings change during your reading of the work? If so, try to
    point to the place or places in the text where the change occurs or begins
    to occur. If not, try to explain why.

The Role of Memories, Associations, and Beliefs

Readers differ because they bring various memories to their readings. Our particular store of *memories* has a deep impact on the *beliefs* we carry through life and on how we respond to new *experiences*—depending on whether those memories stir painful or pleasant *associations*. Memories of childhood, of ethnic and social heritage, of the values our parents established for us, and of our own acceptance or rejection of those values, have much to do with our responses to the texts we read. The story that follows may evoke some memories for you. As you read, ask yourself whether you can share the speaker's experience but look also for diversity that leads to difference. That is, are this speaker's memories gendered, racial, class-based? How or how not? If you don't share the speaker's gender or race, can you still experience the emotion?

from *Hope Mills*

Constance Pierce

That summer, the summer of 1959, the sun moved into the sky quickly, and for the rest of the day, it was hidden behind the white shoot of its own light. Nights were black, but illuminated fitfully by heat lightning, and sometimes there were a few hot drops of rain. Along the unpaved streets near the Mill, the parsimonious rainfall left its mark in thin layers on the locusts and sourwoods, the scraggly hawthorns and sweet gums, mottling the dust on the leaves until it looked like they had blight.

Several miles out of town, where the new Interstate met up with the old four-lane for a while before swinging out to by-pass it, nobody had thought to put up a caution light, and a crew of migrant cotton workers had been killed when a tractor-trailer plowed into the back of their bus. It had happened—significantly, Tollie thought—on the very last day of spring. The pictures had been on the front pages of the newspaper, twenty bodies, some covered and some not, spread out on the new asphalt's bone-white lines, and all around was the debris of the tractor-trailer's load: coconuts, dark and haired-over, round as heads. Tollie had thought they look like large stones too, like they'd been there a long time. Gathering moss.

It was the first time she'd seen pictures of dead people in the newspaper, and they'd given her a quick nauseating shock, as if an important tribal taboo had been broken. She hadn't talked to anybody about it yet, not even Lily, her best friend (she guessed). Especially not Lily. She wanted to tell the old Lily all about it, but the new Lily was suffering from delusions of grandeur about how things were going to be when she got out of high school and Hope Mills and got to Hollywood or New York. The new Lily wouldn't understand the first thing about being dead on a highway.

The blurry photographs were worse in their effects than older, clearer pictures Tollie had seen in her stepfather Les's magazines, though often these involved many more dead people. The magazines had names like *Argosy*, *True*, and *Stag*, and as you got nearer the bottom of the old footlocker where Les kept them: *Male, Man's Conquest, For Men Only,* and *Impact: Bold True Action for Men*. The footlocker was in a room that had been the baby's, but now it was just "the little room," empty except for the footlocker and a gun rack on the wall with zero to three hunting rifles, depending on how many Les had at the pawn shop, and a small wardrobe where Les kept his clothes. The crib and bathinette had been sold to a couple down the street.

Les's magazines had articles on sports and hunting and on the true-life adventures of regular soldiers and soldiers-of-fortune, usually in exotic locales. There were photographs and drawings from the War, and of things that had been found after the War, all mixed in with half-naked women, often bound hand and foot, but sometimes carrying a whip or a knife themselves. The articles had names like "Fishing in the High Chapparel," "Displaying Your Guns," and "Heroes of the Coral Sea," but also "The Adventurer Who Raped a Nation," "Sex-Starved SS Women," and "Bloodbath on the Isle of Hate." What interested Tollie most was the arrangement of pictures and photographs. It made her dizzy; the movement from naked skinny bodies stacked up like pick-up stix to curvy half-naked cartoon women bound hand and foot; from drawings of men that looked like Steve Canyon, letting a little buck-tooth Oriental in pajamas have it with a bayonet, to watercolors of beautiful hooked fish, suspended large and mournful in the air, and photographs of deer hanging from tree-limbs, their bodies opened in long, dark slits.

She was compelled to the footlocker, she wasn't sure why. It seemed like there was an important code in the arrangement of pictures that she couldn't decipher. It frustrated her, and yet she went back for more: Was she a glutton for punishment, as her mother used to say she was, back when Janice noticed things? The magazines gave Tollie something like the creeps. Not the real creeps, because the drawings were made-up and the photographs were of things that had happened, like in her mother's favorite song, "Long Ago and Far Away," not like the dead migrants, who were right now and right here. Their pictures gave her the real creeps. The magazines weren't meant for her, but for men like Les, to see or not see. The front page of the newspaper was for everybody.

Every day on the radio the disk jockey, Jack McLaurin—a.k.a. Big Mack—had been filling up the time between records with remarks on the weather, going on in a fake pitch about how it was the hottest summer in twenty years. "We're going out in a swelter folks," he kept saying, his voice ranging several dangerous-animal sounds. Tollie was lying on the bed in her room, where she had sneaked a couple of the magazines. She had just finished "The White Woman and the Headhunter" and "The Blonde Queen of the Comanches," which she'd been able to concentrate on as long as Big Mack played music, but his voice was a real distraction. She didn't need him reminding her about the heat, either. She had heat rash between her new breasts and between her legs and all around her waist, like the measles. She powered herself all day long with cornstarch, which she shook from a large container that had been used for her baby brother's diaper rash before he died. At night, before going out with Ramirez, she would bathe and sneak some Chanel No. 5 bath powder from a box which was over fifteen years old and still half-full. Someone had given it to Janice before Tollie was born, and Janice had rationed it out like it was gold dust. The great cotton puff was so matted up by now there was no puffiness about it, but the powder still smelled good. In the evening, Tollie would rush past her mother and out the door, hoping Janice wouldn't pick up a whiff.

Not that her mother was noticing *anything* these days, Tollie thought, as she thought all the time now. She flipped past "Chewed to Bits by Giant Tropical Sea Turtles" and "The South Sea Harem of Sgt. Red Wirkus." Actually it was always a little depressing when, undetected, she sniffed the powder on her way to Ramirez's car. These days Janice didn't seem to notice enough to be alive.

But then there would be the car, idling in the driveway, distracting Tollie from Janice and Les. A hardtop-convertible with all its windows rolled down, looking cool in every way, except for the real rabbit's foot dangling from the rearview mirror on a short brassy chain.

Listening to Big Mack *trying* to be cool in the afternoons—but not able to talk about anything but the heat, the weather!—Tollie imagined him at the radio station, wiping the sweat off his forehead with a handkerchief and then running it, sopping wet, back under his collar. He should be sweating. He was screwing Lily every afternoon during something he'd made up just for the occasion, Platters Without Chatter, A Solid Hour of Rock 'n' Roll. Four to five o'clock, his voice would come on the air only once, to croak out the time and the heat "at the bottom of the hour." Then it was the absence of his voice that kept Tollie from concentrating. He should be sweating an ocean about Statutory Rape, something else she'd found mention of in the newspaper.

She'd seen Big Mack in the newspaper too, in the Sunday section called Living, which also included the Obituaries, though she'd noticed there weren't any for the dead migrants. He was about Les's age and he was heavy like Les used to be, but he wore his hair in a D.A. Les wore a short G.I. cut, though he'd never been in the service. During the War, he'd been turned down because of something in his lungs. In the picture, beside him on a couch at the radio station, were Big Mack's pretty wife and two little cotton-headed kids. Tollie wondered if it was the same couch where he was screwing Lily. It was so shiny it looked painted, unreal. No wonder he kept talking about the heat, she thought; that plastic was probably pulling the skin off his knees, the creep.

Fraud from the word Go. Not that you could tell Lily anything.

At night, when there was some choice, Tollie tuned Mack out in favor of the real disk jockeys far away, the ones he tried to imitate. She could hear them howling and whooping and growling from the Clear Channel stations in big cities everywhere east of the Rockies. She guessed they were doing the same thing on the other side of the Rockies too. She'd seen a big burly man from California growling like a wildcat on Dave Garroway. She didn't like the real deejays much better than she liked Big Mack, but at least one of them had to be the original. There must be a hundred phonies stretching out between the original in some bright faraway city and the phoney of phonies, Big Mack of Hope Mills.

Hopeless Mills. That's what people were beginning to call it.

She skimmed "Masculine Inadequacies Drive Women Nuts" and "Wyatt Earp, Hero or Heel?" Then she settled for a minute on "Five Places Where You Can Buy a Slave Girl." The five places were Saudi Arabia, India, Mangalore, the Marquesas Islands, and "the hot, savage jungles of the Mato Grosso." *For a 9mm Mauser,* she read, *a pocket knife, $10 Brazilian and a Primus Stove, I received a 16-year-old Quemada Virgin who came to me the way she came into the world. . . .*

Tollie reached for the Funk and Wagnalls, an old dictionary, 1939, that had belonged to her grandfather, one of Janice's few heirlooms from long ago and faraway Whiteville. She checked for Mauser, Primus, and Quemada, with no luck. Which she'd expected: They were all capitalized. Still, you never knew. She didn't let many new words go by her. That was a habit she'd got from her mother, who had an immense collection of words, even if she had more or less stopped talking by now.

Tollie put the dictionary back on the nightstand. For a moment she was wistful, remembering all the fun she and her mother used to have: Scrabble, crosswords. Wordgames in the car, back when Janice would get in a car. . . . Her mother had taught her the alphabet before she'd even gone to school, by singing "A You're Adorable," right up in Tollie's face. Giving her a quality for every letter, A to Z. Smiling. Tickling, kissing.

Tollie longed for the days when she and Janice had laughed over things in the newspaper, which they'd always divided and read together in the living room, even back when Tollie had just been interested in comics. Janice would poke fun at President Eisenhower, Estes Kefauver in his coonskin hat, the dumb sayings of John Foster Dulles, things like The Distant Early Warning System. She'd kidded Tollie that the two of them were "Commie-conspirators." Janice didn't do any of that anymore. She just leaves me to my own devices, Tollie thought with a little surge of anger. Which aren't worth a poot!

Junk. She passed by "Beware of Broadway B-Girls," and then closed the magazine. She got up and gathered the magazines in a neat pile, like Les kept them in, and then sneaked them back into the footlocker in the little room— dark as a grave! Tollie hurried out and shut the door. She went back to her room and got the radio.

In her mother's bedroom, she plugged in the radio and the iron and then opened the large plastic bag of sprinkled clothes. The inside of the bag smelled of mildew. Lately Janice would sprinkle down the clothes and roll them up, then let them stay in the bag until they mildewed or soured. From within the rolls of Les's khaki work pants and shirts and Janice's faded house-dresses, Tollie took out one of her two bright white pleated skirts and sniffed it. It smelled like Purex. Her skirts didn't get a chance to sour. She wore one of them every night, washed one of them every day. She took out the skirt and spread it on the ironing board, then wet her finger and tested the iron. She turned on the radio and waited. "Thank Heaven for Little Girls," an oldie-and-baddie, "Tears on My Pillow" (half-goodie), a weather report, then "Broken-Hearted Melody," a definite goodie.

She thought about the dead migrants and her heat rash and Lily screwing herself silly, without a rubber. Something was going to happen. She could feel it in the air, though she didn't have a bit of patience with people who said they could feel things in the air. Maybe it *was* the heat. Everybody seemed in a fever. Trying to set themselves off from something, by howling and growling or whatever it took. Big Mack was always rhyming and calling attention to his own name, like he was now, breaking into the last bit of "Broken-Hearted Melody." "Settle back, Jack, cut Mack some slack, don't gimme no flak, Mack's putting on a stack. . . ."

It was awful. She turned the dial and found the Negro station. She listened a few seconds until she determined that they weren't playing music but preaching, and when the ad came on for the services of Madame Lucretia— "Palm-Reader, Advisor, The Future Foretold: she hope me, she'll hope you"— Tollie turned the dial back to big Mack in defeat. She'd never waste a dime on somebody like Madame Lucretia. The Future Foretold! In Hope Mills, as any fool knew, you just had to put up with whatever came along. Big Mack. Crazy Mammas. Speeding trucks.

Tollie looked out the window at the stunted dusty trees. Why was it they were building Interstates for people to ride on when some people still *lived* on dirt streets? Lily was always saying, "Why don't y'all get somebody to pave that dirt road before I ruin every stitch of clothes I've got?" Who? Tollie wondered. Who and how? She wanted to live on a paved street more than Lily wanted her to. The sand-colored dirt rose in knee-high clouds each time a car passed, covering the shrubs and grass, and when the wind blew or a large truck went roaring by on its way to or from the Mill, the dust would find its way to the house itself, coming to rest in little drifts on the window-panes, like in drawings she'd seen of snow.

The new Lily was a case, in and unto herself, Tollie thought, testing the iron again and then beginning to work on her pleats. Dramatic. Melo-dramatic. Sometimes Lily wore a leather dog collar for a necklace, with a small metal heart-shaped tag engraved with "L & M," Lily & Mack.

"I feel like if I don't do something," Lily had said earlier in the week, lazing around on Tollie's bed while Tollie was powdering her rash—wrinkling the spread, which Tollie was going to have to re-iron herself—"If I don't do something real special, a big old wave of sameness is going to wash over the *land*."

From sea to shining sea, Tollie had thought, pulling out the elastic on her cotton underpants, and filling them up with cornstarch. That would suit her fine: a great bland wave rising up on one coast and rolling to a crest out where the radio stations switched from "W" to "K," and then crashing into the ocean on the other side. Washing the country cool and clean and leaving everything and everybody on an equal footing—comfortable, calm, and right as rain.

That would suit me finer than fine, she'd thought. But wasn't that just like Lily lately: "If *I* don't do something . . . a wave will wash over the *land*!"

"I feel like I got to do something real different or I'm going to get caught up in that old wave and lost," Lily had said, getting up, suddenly giving Tollie a look of pure venom. "Stop dusting that goddam stuff around. You're strangling me. And get yourself some grown-up panties, while you're at it!" Then she'd flounced out of the room, and inch of pink crinoline showing beneath her new low-cut sundress, her silvery page-boy bobbing in its crescent at her shoulders. She'd gone back into the living room to sit with Janice, who, Tollie knew, was the real reason for the new Lily's visits.

"You might at least straighten up the bed," Tollie had yelled after her. "You're not in this world by yourself."

Everybody was acting weird. Tollie sprinkled water on her skirt from a sprinkler screwed into the neck of a Coke bottle, set the iron in motion and let the hot smell of cotton blast her in the face, trying to pretend she was having a facial at one of the fancy beauty shops she'd read about in Lily's *Movie Star* and *Photoplay*. Acting like they were fighting for their lives. Everybody trying to be different, just like everybody else, and in all the same ways. If everybody weren't so caught up in that junk, she thought, half-drunk on cotton-vapors, half-blinded by sweat, maybe somebody would have had the sense to put first things first and remembered to put a caution light out at that intersection. You could fight for your life on the side.

Janice said everybody was just tired of President Eisenhower, though Janice called him General Eisenhower. "They're tired of toeing the line and minding their P's and Q's twenty-four hours a day," she'd say, without energy. "Three-hundred-and-sixty-five days a year, year in and year out, lest somebody thinks they're a Communist. Or a whore."

Tollie carefully pointed the iron's nose down a long stretch of pleat, accelerated, then sped toward the hem before the pleat got away from her. Yes, the summer was speeding by, and the decade, and even high school, and then what? She knew she was wasting time. You could waste time, but you couldn't save it. Time wasn't money, like Lily's father was always saying. Daylight Savings Time didn't even save time. It just got Management out of the Mill in time to get in some golf after work, like Les was always saying. She didn't believe much else Les said, but you could walk by the golf course if you were dumb enough to get out in the heat after supper and see the Managers knocking golf balls around, carrying big glasses of what she guessed was liquor and melted ice from hole to hole.

She wished she had a summer job, something more steady than babysitting. In her neighborhood, women couldn't afford to use a babysitter very often, even at fifty cents an hour. None of the stores were hiring girls her age. The weather was so dry there probably wouldn't be enough crops for anyone to hire extra pickers. Even Mr. Faircloth, who had the biggest produce farm in the county, probably wouldn't be hiring extra this year. Sometimes a person's prospects could look pretty dim, even when that person wanted to help herself.

Tollie tried hard to concentrate on her ironing, on the iron itself. She hoped she'd remember to unplug it after she turned it off. Janice worried all the time about unplugging things. She'd unplugged just about everything in the house before she'd gone to the Winn-Dixie, even. Once, not long after the baby had died, they'd gone to the beach for a week, the only time Les had ever taken them on a vacation. Before they left, Janice had been turning off and unplugging everything and she had reached for the toaster plug and unplugged the refrigerator by mistake. When they got back, the whole house had smelled like a cabbage that had rotted in the Hydrator and a black mold had been growing on everything inside the appliance. It had smelled like somebody had died in their kitchen.

"That just goes to show what happens when you go off," Les had said.

That was back when Janice still went out of the house. Now she almost never went anywhere except downtown on the bus to window shop, maybe once a week. She always came back looking exhausted. She let Les go to the Winn-Dixie on Friday nights, after he got paid. Les loved to spend the money himself, though he didn't have anything to show for it that Tollie could see. "Better spend it while I can," he always said, though he never gave her a dime, hardly gave Janice a dime either, especially now. Les said the Mill was going to start laying off. "Cotton's going out of style," he said. "Everything's going to be Easy-Care." Good, Tollie had thought. Maybe it'll stay pleated.

She thought the same thing now! She set the iron on end and tried to get better control of a pleat that kept slipping away from her. Ironing pleats was complicated, a science *and* an art. The bedroom was so hot she was beginning to feel weak. Between the heat and the pleats and the general atmosphere of 1959, she'd better watch out or she'd end up on a Prescription, like her mother.

She needed a rest. She left the skirt hanging on the ironing board and sat down on her mother's bed, fixing her eyes on the bottle of pills on the nightstand. The label on Janice's prescription said "Miltown." Tollie picked up the bottle and shook it. She thought "Miltown" said something about why Janice lay around the house: taking pills all day and half the night, watching Les sleep on the couch, the tv going to snow—watching Les, even though, or maybe because, she'd taken off her wedding band and put it in the drawer with her underwear, like it was something porn-o-graphic! Miltown. . . .

That was one of the things Tollie had begun to notice: that names seemed to know more, on their own, than whatever people had in mind when they named things There was Mil-town, and *Les* who was less, and *Jan*, like the month, + *ice*. And *Lily*, who worried all the time about who was white and who wasn't. There seemed to be an all-knowing Something behind it all, invisible but real and true. It was what she counted on, now that she'd given up Sunday school and revival. But it all moved in mysterious ways. There was, after all, *Hope* Mills. That didn't make any sense at all!

"Hot as . . . Haaaades," Big Mack said. "But that's allrrriiight! Look what's coming atcha now, ol' Mack's fave—"

Oh, no, Tollie thought, jumping up from the bed. She grabbed the iron and lit into a pleat, ironing faster. Already the guitar was rocking in the familiar sounds. All summer long, over and over, Big Mack had been playing "I Don't Wanna Hang Up My Rock 'n' Roll Shoes."

CONSTRUCTING A READING

In your journal or as your teacher directs, write a page or two in response to these questions.

1. If this story evokes childhood memories for you of any kind—listening to your own music, escaping your parents, dealing with uncertainties about relationships, perhaps even suffering the loss of a sibling—describe that memory and explain why the story made you think about it.
2. If you cannot respond to the story with memories of your own, write a page or two about why. If, for example, the dissimilarities between Tollie's adolescence and yours are too great for you to sympathize with her, describe the difference and explain how it makes you unsympathetic.
3. Tollie describes herself as "compelled to the footlocker. . . . It seemed like there was an important code in the arrangement of pictures that she couldn't decipher." Write for a few minutes about the code that Tollie can't read. What do you think this illegible code is about? How does it work? Why does she find it so compelling? Can you read it?
4. What about Constance Pierce's code in this story? Can you decipher what she is telling you about Tollie?
5. Why do you think Tollie's mother behaves as she does? How does that behavior affect Tollie? Why?
6. Even if you don't recognize any of the songs Big Mack plays, you probably recall songs that were important for you when you were fifteen. Why and how were they important? Compare your experiences to Tollie's and try by analogy to understand how they work for her.
7. Linda Hogan's and Langston Hughes's poems placed particular emphasis on their ethnicity. Do you read "Hope Mills" as placing emphasis on the ethnicity of its speaker? How so?

SHARING A READING

1.   Choose one of the texts in this chapter or a TV show you watch frequently or a film you viewed recently. Freewrite about the emotions and memories the text evokes in you. Describe, as best you can, the ways in which you see the text handling diversity and difference. Compare your response with those of your classmates. Next, write an essay in which you explain the concept of difference to someone who knows the text but who does not know your classmates.

2.   Describe to your classmates, from your own experience, one or more ways in which categories like "race" and "gender" are too broad to allow us to account for the kinds of difference we need to encounter and study. For example, you might recount an instance, like arriving at college for the first time, or joining a new social group, or going to work, or visiting a new friend's family, in which persons of the same race or gender had significantly divergent views of a situation, or in which an apparently minor diversity made a big difference in the interpretation of an event. What differences did you confront as you tried to make sense of the experience and how did you handle them?

3.   Interview one other student in your class about reading. Find out what your interviewee thinks about reading, why she or he reads, what he or she likes to read, and why. In thinking about your questions and answers, you both may want to return to the journal writing you did at the beginning of this chapter. Think of yourself as an inquiring journalist: be as perceptive as you can. Try to think of reasons for reading preferences that your subject might not be aware of. Try, in other words, to explain why she or he has the preferences and dislikes that you find out about. Then write a paper that introduces that student to your classmates. In your paper, try to make your classmates understand what makes your interviewee different and how that difference affects his or her reading preferences. Give—and explain—as many differences as you can. If you have difficulty, try looking at and thinking about published interviews with celebrities in magazines or TV shows. What kinds of questions do those interviewers ask? How do they follow up? How do they use the information they gather?

TEXTS FOR FURTHER READING

Exploring Readings and Feelings

CONSTRUCTING A READING

All of the texts that follow are, like "Dulce et Decorum Est" and "The Soldier," concerned with war. Read them carefully. After you have finished, choose one or two that you liked or that evoked particular feelings in you and freewrite about your response. The "Constructing a Reading" questions throughout this chapter will help you get started.

To Lucasta, Going to the Wars
Richard Lovelace

Tell me not, sweet, I am unkind
That from the nunnery
Of thy chaste breast and quiet mind
To war and arms I fly.

True, a new mistress now I chase
The first foe in the field;
And with a stronger faith embrace
A sword, a horse, a shield.

But this inconstancy is such
As you too shall adore;
I could not love thee, dear, so much,
Loved I not honor more.

Patterns
Amy Lowell

I walk down the garden paths,
And all the daffodils
Are blowing, and the bright blue squills.
I walk down the patterned garden paths
In my stiff, brocaded gown.
With my powdered hair and jewelled fan,
I too am a rare
Pattern. As I wander down
The garden paths.

My dress is richly figured,
And the train
Makes a pink and silver stain
On the gravel, and the thrift
Of the borders.
Just a plate of current fashion,
Tripping by in high-heeled, ribboned shoes.
Not a softness anywhere about me,
Only whalebone and brocade.
And I sink on a seat in the shade
Of a lime tree. For my passion
Wars against the stiff brocade.
The daffodils and squills
Flutter in the breeze
As they please.
And I weep;
For the lime-tree is in blossom
And one small flower has dropped upon my bosom.

And the plashing of waterdrops
In the marble fountain
Comes down the garden paths.
The dripping never stops.
Underneath my stiffened gown
Is the softness of a woman bathing in a marble basin,
A basin in the midst of hedges grown
So thick, she cannot see her lover hiding,
But she guesses he is near,
And the sliding of the water
Seems the stroking of a dear
Hand upon her.
What is Summer in a fine brocaded gown!
I should like to see it lying in a heap upon the ground.
All the pink and silver crumpled up on the ground.

I would be the pink and silver as I ran along the paths,
And he would stumble after,
Bewildered by my laughter.
I should see the sun flashing from his sword-hilt and the buckles on his shoes.
I would choose
To lead him in a maze along the patterned paths,
A bright and laughing maze for my heavy-booted lover.
Till he caught me in the shade.
And the buttons of his waistcoat bruised my body as he clasped me,
Aching, melting, unafraid.
With the shadows of the leaves and the sundrops,
And the plopping of the waterdrops,
All about us in the open afternoon—

I am very like to swoon
With the weight of this brocade,
For the sun sifts through the shade.

Underneath the fallen blossom
In my bosom,
Is a letter I have hid.
It was brought to me this morning by a rider from the Duke.
'Madam, we regret to inform you that Lord Hartwell
Died in action Thrusday se'nnight.'
As I read it in the white, morning sunlight,
The letters squirmed like snakes.
'Any answer, Madam,' said my footman.
'No,' I told him.
'See that the messenger takes some refreshment.
No, no answer.'
And I walked into the garden,
Up and down the patterned paths,
In my stiff, correct brocade.

The blue and yellow flowers stood up proudly in the sun,
Each one.
I stood upright too,
Held rigid to the pattern
By the stiffness of my gown.
Up and down I walked,
Up and down.

In a month he would have been my husband.
In a month, here, underneath this lime,
We would have broke the pattern;
He for me, and I for him,
He as Colonel, I as Lady,
On this shady seat.
He had a whim
That sunlight carried blessing.
And I answered, 'It shall be as you have said.'
Now he is dead.

In Summer and in Winter I shall walk
Up and down
The patterned garden paths
In my stiff, brocaded gown.
The squills and daffodils
Will give place to pillared roses, and to asters, and to snow.
I shall go
Up and down,
In my gown.

Gorgeously arrrayed,
Boned and stayed.
And the softness of my body will be guarded from embrace
By each button, hook, and lace.
For the man who should loose me is dead,
Fighting with the Duke in Flanders,
In a pattern called a war.
Christ! What are patterns for?

To a Child Born in Time of Small War

Helen Sorrels

Child, you were conceived in my upstairs room,
my girlhood all around. Later I spent
nights there alone imploring the traitor moon
to keep me childless still. I never meant
to bear you in this year of discontent.
You were there in your appointed place,
remnant of leaving, of a sacrament.
Child, if I loved you then, it was to trace
on a cold sheet your likeness to his absent face.

In May we were still alone. That month your life
stirred in my dark, as if my body's core
grew quick with wings. I turned away, more wife
than mother still, unwilling to explore
the fact of you. There was an orient shore,
a tide of hurt, that held my heart and mind.
It was as if you lived behind a door
I was afraid to open, lest you bind
my breaking. Lost in loss, I was not yours to find.

I swelled with summer. You were hard and strong
making me know you were there. When the mail
brought me no letter, and the time was long
between the war's slow gains, and love seemed frail,
I fought you. You were error, judgment, jail.
Without you, there were ways I, too, could fight
a war. Trapped in your growing, I would rail
against your grotesque carriage, swollen, tight.
I would have left you, and I did in dreams of flight.

Discipline of the seasons brought me round.
Earth comes to term and so, in time, did we.
You are a living thing of sight and sound.

Nothing of you is his, you are all of me:
your sex, gray eye, the struggle to be free
that made your birth like death, but I awake
for that caught air, your cry. I try to see
but cannot, the same lift his eyebrows take.
Child, if I love you now, it is for your own sake.

War

Luigi Pirandello

The passengers who had left Rome by the night express had had to stop until dawn at the small station of Fabriano in order to continue their journey by the small old-fashioned "local" joining the main line with Sulmona.

At dawn, in a stuffy and smoky second-class carriage in which five people had already spent the night, a bulky woman in deep mourning, was hoisted in—almost like a shapeless bundle. Behind her—puffing and moaning, followed her husband—a tiny man, thin and weakly, his face death-white, his eyes small and bright and looking shy and uneasy.

Having at last taken a seat he politely thanked the passengers who had helped his wife and who had made room for her; then he turned round to the woman trying to pull down the collar of her coat and politely enquired:

"Are you all right, dear?"

The wife, instead of answering, pulled up her collar again to her eyes, so as to hide her face.

"Nasty world," muttered the husband with a sad smile.

And he felt it his duty to explain to his travelling companions that the poor woman was to be pitied for the war was taking away from her her only son, a boy of twenty to whom both had devoted their entire life, even breaking up their home at Sulmona to follow him to Rome where he had to go as a student, then allowing him to volunteer for war with an assurance, however, that at least for six months he would not be sent to the front and now, all of a sudden, receiving a wire saying that he was due to leave in three days' time and asking them to go and see him off.

The woman under the big coat was twisting and wriggling, at times growling like a wild animal, feeling certain that all those explanations would not have aroused even a shadow of sympathy from those people who—most likely—were in the same plight as herself. One of them, who had been listening with particular attention, said:

"You should thank God that your son is only leaving now for the front. Mine has been sent there the first day of the war. He has already come back twice wounded and been sent back again to the front."

"What about me? I have two sons and three nephews at the front," said another passenger.

"Maybe, but in our case it is our *only* son," ventured the husband.

"What difference can it make? You may spoil your only son with excessive attentions, but you cannot love him more than you would all your other children if you had any. Paternal love is not like bread that can be broken into pieces and spilt amongst the children in equal shares. A father gives *all* his love to each one of his children without discrimination, whether it be one or ten, and if I am suffering now for my two sons, I am not suffering half for each of them but double. . . ."

"True . . . true . . ." sighed the embarrassed husband, "but suppose (of course we all hope it will never be your case) a father has two sons at the front and he loses one of them, there is still one left to console him . . . while . . ."

"Yes," answered the other, getting cross, "a son left to console him but also a son left for whom he must survive, while in the case of the father of an only son if the son dies the father can die too and put an end to his distress. Which of the two positions is the worse? Don't you see how my case would be worse than yours?"

"Nonsense," interrupted another traveller, a fat, red-faced man with bloodshot eyes of the palest grey.

He was panting. From his bulging eyes seemed to spurt inner violence of an uncontrolled vitality which his weakened body could hardly contain.

"Nonsense," he repeated, trying to cover his mouth with his hand so as to hide the two missing front teeth. "Nonsense. Do we give life to our children for our own benefit?"

The other travellers stared at him in distress. The one who had had his son at the front since the first day of the war sighed: "You are right. Our children do not belong to us, they belong to the Country. . . ."

"Bosh," retorted the fat traveller. "Do we think of the Country when we give life to our children? Our sons are born because . . . well, because they must be born and when they come to life they take our own life with them. This is the truth. We belong to them but they never belong to us. And when they reach twenty they are exactly what we were at their age. We too had a father and mother, but there were so many other things as well . . . girls, cigarettes, illusions, new ties . . . and the Country, of course, whose call we would have answered—when we were twenty—even if father and mother had said no. Now, at our age, the love of our Country is still great, of course, but stronger than it is the love for our children. Is there any one of us here who wouldn't gladly take his son's place at the front if he could?"

There was a silence all round, everybody nodding as to approve.

"Why then," continued the fat man, "shouldn't we consider the feelings of our children when they are twenty? Isn't it natural that at their age they should consider the love for their Country (I am speaking of decent boys, of course) even greater than the love for us? Isn't it natural that it should be so, as after all they must look upon us as upon old boys who cannot move any more and must stay at home? If Country exists, if Country is a natural necessity like bread, of which each of us must eat in order not to die of hunger, somebody must go to defend it. And our sons go, when they are twenty, and they don't want tears, because if they die, they die inflamed and happy (I am speaking, of course, of decent boys). Now, if one dies young and happy, without having the ugly sides of life, the boredom of it, the pettiness, the bitterness of disillusion . . . what more can we ask for him? Everyone should stop crying: everyone should laugh, as I do . . . or at least thank God—as I do—because my son, before dying, sent me a message saying that he was dying satisfied at having ended his life in the best way he could have wished. That is why, as you see, I do not even wear mourning. . . ."

He shook his light fawn coat as to show it; his livid lip over his missing teeth was trembling, his eyes were watery and motionless and soon after he ended with a shrill laugh which might well have been a sob.

"Quite so . . . quite so . . ." agreed the others.

The woman who, bundled in a corner under her coat, had been sitting and listening had—for the last three months—tried to find in the words of her husband and her friends something to console her in her deep sorrow, something that might show her how a mother should resign herself to send her son not even to death but to a probable danger of life. Yet not a word had she found amongst the many which had been said . . . and her grief had been greater in seeing that nobody——as she thought—could share her feelings.

But now the words of the traveller amazed and almost stunned her. She suddenly realized that it wasn't the others who were wrong and could not understand her but herself who could not rise up to the same height of those fathers and mothers willing to resign themselves, without crying, not only to the departure of their sons but even to their death.

She lifted her head, she bent over from her corner trying to listen with great attention to the details which the fat man was giving to his companions about the way his son had fallen as a hero, for his King and his Country, happy and without regrets. It seemed to her that she had stumbled into a world she had never dreamt of, a world so far unknown to her and she was so pleased to hear everyone joining in congratulating that brave father who could so stoically speak of his child's death.

Then suddenly, just as if she had heard nothing of what had been said and almost as if waking up from a dream, she turned to the old man, asking him:

"Then . . . is your son really dead?"

Everybody stared at her. The old man, too, turned to look at her, fixing his great, bulging, horribly watery light grey eyes, deep in her face. For some little time he tried to answer, but words failed him. He looked and looked at her, almost as if only then—at that silly, incongruous question—he had suddenly realized at last that his son was really dead . . . gone for ever . . . for ever. His face contracted, became horribly distorted, then he snatched in haste a handkerchief from his pocket and, to the amazement of everyone, broke into harrowing, heart-rending, uncontrollable sobs.

In Another Country

Ernest Hemingway

In the fall the war was always there, but we did not go to it any more. It was cold in the fall in Milan and the dark came very early. Then the electric lights came on, and it was pleasant along the streets looking in the windows. There was much game hanging outside the shops, and the snow powdered in the fur of the foxes and the wind blew their tails. The deer hung stiff and heavy and empty, and small birds blew in the wind and the wind turned their feathers. It was a cold fall and the wind came down from the mountains.

We were all at the hospital every afternoon, and there were different ways of walking across the town through the dusk to the hospital. Two of the ways were alongside canals, but they were long. Always, though, you crossed a bridge across a canal to enter the hospital. There was a choice of three bridges. On one of them a woman sold roasted chestnuts. It was warm, standing in front of her charcoal fire, and the chestnuts were warm afterward in your pocket. The hospital was very old and very beautiful, and you entered through a gate and walked across a courtyard and out a gate on the other side. There were usually funerals starting from the courtyard. Beyond the old hospital were the new brick pavilions, and there we met every afternoon and were all very polite and interested in what was the matter, and sat in the machines that were to make so much difference.

The doctor came up to the machine where I was sitting and said: "What did you like best to do before the war? Did you practice a sport?"

I said: "Yes, football."

"Good," he said. "You will be able to play football again better than ever."

My knee did not bend and the leg dropped straight from the knee to the ankle without a calf, and the machine was to bend the knee and make it move as in riding a tricycle. But it did not bend yet, and instead the machine lurched when it came to the bending part. The doctor said: "That will all pass. You are a fortunate young man. You will play football again like a champion."

In the next machine was a major who had a little hand like a baby's. He winked at me when the doctor examined his hand, which was between two leather straps that bounced up and down and flapped the stiff fingers, and said: "And will I, too, play football, captain-doctor?" He had been a very great fencer, and before the war the greatest fencer in Italy.

The doctor went to his office in a back room and brought a photograph which showed a hand that had been withered almost as small as the major's, before it had taken a machine course, and after was a little larger. The major held the photograph with his good hand and looked at it very carefully. "A wound?" he asked.

"An industrial accident," the doctor said.

"Very interesting, very interesting," the major said, and handed it back to the doctor.

"You have confidence?"

"No," said the major.

There were three boys who came each day who were about the same age I was. They were all three from Milan, and one of them was to be a lawyer, and one was to be a painter, and one had intended to be a soldier, and after we were finished with the machines, sometimes we walked back together to the Café Cova, which was next door to the Scala. We walked the short way through the Communist quarter because we were four together. The people hated us because we were officers, and from a wineshop someone would call out, "*A basso gli ufficiali!*" as we passed. Another boy who walked with us sometimes and made us five wore a black silk handkerchief across his face because he had no nose then and his face was to be rebuilt. He had gone out to the front from the military academy and been wounded within an hour after he had gone into the front line for the first time. They rebuilt his face, but he came from a very old family and they could never get the nose exactly right. He went to South America and worked in a bank. But this was a long time ago, and then we did not any of us know how it was going to be afterward. We only knew then that there was always the war, but that we were not going to it any more.

We all had the same medals, except the boy with the black silk bandage across his face, and he had not been at the front long enough to get any medals. The tall boy with a very pale face who was to be a lawyer had been a lieutenant of Arditi and had three medals of the sort we each had only one of. He had lived a very long time with death and was a little detached. We were all a little detached, and there was nothing that held us together except that we met every afternoon at the hospital. Although, as we walked to the Cova through the tough part of town, walking in the dark, with light and singing coming out of the wineshops, and sometimes having to walk into the street when the men and women would crowd together on the sidewalk so that we would have had to jostle them to get by, we felt held together by there being something that had happened that they, the people who disliked us, did not understand.

We ourselves all understood the Cova, where it was rich and warm and not too brightly lighted, and noisy and smoky at certain hours, and there were always girls at the tables and the illustrated papers on a rack on the wall. The girls at the Cova were very patriotic, and I found that the most patriotic people in Italy were the cafe girls—and I believe they are still patriotic.

The boys at first were very polite about my medals and asked me what I had done to get them. I showed them the papers, which were written in very beautiful language and full of *fratellanza* and *abnegazione*, but which really said, with the adjectives removed, that I had been given the medals because I was an American. After that their manner changed a little toward me, although I was their friend against outsiders. I was a friend, but I was never really one of them after they had read the citations, because it had been different with them and they had done very different things to get their medals. I had been wounded, it was true; but we all knew that being wounded, after all, was really an accident. I was never ashamed of the ribbons, though, and sometimes, after the cocktail hour, I would imagine myself having done all the things they had done to get their medals; but walking home at night through the empty streets with the cold wind and all the shops closed, trying to keep near the streetlights, I knew that I would never have done such things, and I was very much afraid to die, and often lay in bed at night by myself, afraid to die and wondering how I would be when I went back to the front again.

The three with the medals were like hunting-hawks; and I was not a hawk, although I might seem a hawk to those who had never hunted; they, the three, knew better and so we drifted apart. But I stayed good friends with the boy who had been wounded his first day at the front, because he would never know now how he would have turned out; so he could never be accepted either, and I liked him because I thought perhaps he would not have turned out to be a hawk either.

The major, who had been the great fencer, did not believe in bravery and spent much time while we sat in the machines correcting my grammar. He had complimented me on how I spoke Italian, and we talked together very easily. One day I had said that Italian seemed such an easy language to me that I could not take a great interest in it; everything was so easy to say. "Ah, yes," the major said. "Why, then, do you not take up the use of grammar?" So we took up the use of grammar, and soon Italian was such a difficult language that I was afraid to talk to him until I had the grammar straight in my mind.

The major came very regularly to the hospital. I do not think he ever missed a day, although I am sure he did not believe in the machines. There was a time when none of us believed in the machines, and one day the major said it was all nonsense. The machines were new then and it was we who were to prove them. It was an idiotic idea, he said, "a theory, like another." I had not learned my grammar, and he said I was a stupid impossible disgrace, and he was a fool to have bothered with me. He was a small man and he sat straight up in his chair with his right hand thrust into the machine and looked straight ahead at the wall while the straps thumped up and down with his fingers in them.

"What will you do when the war is over if it is over?" he asked me. "Speak grammatically!"

"I will go to the States."

"Are you married?"

"No, but I hope to be."

"The more of a fool you are," he said. He seemed very angry. "A man must not marry."

"Why, Signor Maggiore?"

"Don't call me 'Signor Maggiore.'"

"Why must not a man marry?"

"He cannot marry. He cannot marry," he said angrily. "If he is to lose everything, he should not place himself in a position to lose that. He should not place himself in a position to lose. He should find things he cannot lose."

He spoke very angrily and bitterly, and looked straight ahead while he talked.

"But why should he necessarily lose it?"

"He'll lose it," the major said. He was looking at the wall. Then he looked down at the machine and jerked his little hand out from between the straps and slapped it hard against his thigh. "He'll lose it," he almost shouted. "Don't argue with me!" Then he called to the attendant who ran the machines. "Come and turn this damned thing off."

He went back into the other room for the light treatment and the massage. Then I heard him ask the doctor if he might use his telephone and he shut the door. When he came back into the room, I was sitting in another machine. He was wearing his cape and had his cap on, and he came directly toward my machine and put his arm on my shoulder.

"I am so sorry," he said, and patted me on the shoulder with his good hand. "I would not be rude. My wife has just died. You must forgive me.

"Oh—" I said, feeling sick for him. "I am so sorry.

He stood there, biting his lower lip. "It is very difficult," he said. "I cannot resign myself."

He looked straight past me and out through the window. Then he began to cry. "I am utterly unable to resign myself," he said and choked. And then crying, his head up looking at nothing, carrying himself straight and soldierly, with tears on both his cheeks and biting his lips, he walked past the machines and out the door.

The doctor told me that the major's wife, who was very young and whom he had not married until he was definitely invalided out of the war, had died of pneumonia. She had been sick only a few days. No one expected her to die. The major did not come to the hospital for three days. Then he came at the usual hour, wearing a black band on the sleeve of his uniform. When he came back, there were large framed photographs around the wall, of all sorts of wounds before and after they had been cured by the machines. In front of the machine the major used were three photographs of hands like his that were completely restored. I do not know where the doctor got them. I always understood we were the first to use the machines. The photographs did not make much difference to the major because he only looked out of the window.

i sing of Olaf glad and big

e e cummings

i sing of Olaf glad and big
whose warmest heart recoiled at war:
a conscientious object-or

his wellbelovéd colonel(trig
westpointer most succinctly bred)
took erring Olaf soon in hand;
but—though an host of overjoyed
noncoms(first knocking on the head
him)do through icy waters roll
that helplessness which others stroke
with brushes recently employed
anent this muddy toiletbowl,
while kindred intellects evoke
allegiance per blunt instruments—
Olaf(being to all intents
a corpse and wanting any rag
upon what God unto him gave)
responds,without getting annoyed
"I will not kiss your fucking flag"

straightway the silver bird looked grave
(departing hurriedly to shave)

but—though all kinds of officers
(a yearning nation's blueeyed pride)
their passive prey did kick and curse
until for wear their clarion
voices and boots were much the worse,
and egged the firstclassprivates on
his rectum wickedly to tease
by means of skilfully applied
bayonets roasted hot with heat—
Olaf(upon what were once knees)
does almost ceaselessly repeat
"there is some shit I will not eat"

our president,being of which
assertions duly notified
threw the yellowsonofabitch
into a dungeon,where he died

Christ(of His mercy infinite)
i pray to see;and Olaf,too

preponderatingly because
unless statistics lie he was
more brave than me:more blond than you.

The Loneliness of the Military Historian
Margaret Atwood

Confess: it's my profession
that alarms you.
This is why few people ask me to dinner,
though Lord knows I don't go out of my way to be scary.
I wear dresses of sensible cut
and unalarming shades of beige,
I smell of lavender and go to the hairdresser's:
no prophetess mane of mine
complete with snakes, will frighten the youngsters.
If my eyes roll and I mutter,
if my arms are gloved in blood right up to the elbow,
if I clutch at my heart and scream in horror
like a third-rate actress chewing up a mad scene,
I do it in private and nobody sees
but the bathroom mirror.

In general I might agree with you:
women should not contemplate war,
should not weigh tactics impartially,
or evade the word *enemy*,
or view both sides and denounce nothing.
Women should march for peace,
or hand out white feathers to inspire bravery,
spit themselves on bayonets
to protect their babies,
whose skulls will be split anyway,

or, having been raped repeatedly,
hang themselves with their own hair.
These are the functions that inspire general comfort.
That, and the knitting of socks for the troops
and a sort of moral cheerleading.
Also: mourning the dead.
Sons, lovers, and so forth.
All the killed children.

Instead of this, I tell
what I hope will pass as truth.
A blunt thing, not lovely.
The truth is seldom welcome,

especially at dinner,
though I am good at what I do.
My trade is in courage and atrocities.
I look at them and do not condemn.
I write things down the way they happened,
as near as can be remembered.
I don't ask *why* because it is mostly the same.
Wars happen because the ones who start them
think they can win.
In my dreams there is glamour.
The Vikings leave their fields
each year for a few months of killing and plunder,
much as the boys go hunting.
In real life they were farmers.
They come back loaded with splendor.
The Arabs ride against Crusaders
with scimitars that could sever
silk in the air.
A swift cut to the horse's neck
and a hunk of armor crashes down
like a tower. Fire against metal.
A poet might say: romance against banality.
When awake, I know better.

Despite the propaganda, there are no monsters
or none that can be finally buried.
Finish one off and circumstances
and the radio create another.
Believe me: whole armies have prayed fervently
to God all night and meant it,
and been slaughtered anyway.
Brutality wins frequently,
and large outcomes have turned on the invention
of a mechanical device, viz. radar.

True, sometimes valor counts for something,
as at Thermopylae. Sometimes being right,
though ultimate virtue by agreed tradition
is decided by the winner.
Sometimes men throw themselves on grenades
and burst like paper bags of guts
to save their comrades.
I can admire that.
But rats and cholera have won many wars.
Those, and potatoes
or the absence of them.
It's no use pinning all those medals
across the chests of the dead.

Impressive, but I know too much.
Grand exploits merely depress me.

In the interests of research
I have walked on many battlefields
that once were liquid with pulped
men's bodies and spangled with burst
shells and splayed bone.
All of them have been green again
by the time I got there.
Each has inspired a few good quotes in its day.
Sad marble angels brood like hens
over the grassy nests where nothing hatches.
(The angels could just as well be described as *vulgar*,
  or *pitiless*, depending on camera angle.)
The word *glory* figures a lot on gateways.
Of course I pick a flower or two
from each, and press it in the hotel
Bible, for a souvenir.
I'm just as human as you.

But it's no use asking me for a final statement.
As I say, I deal in tactics.
Also statistics:
for every year of peace there have been four hundred
years of war.

Dien Bien Phu

Adrienne Rich

A nurse on the battlefield
wounded herself, but working

   dreams
        that each man she touches
        is a human grenade

                an anti-personnel weapon
                that can explode in her arms

   How long
        can she go on like this
        putting mercy
        ahead of survival

She is walking
in a white dress stained
with earth and blood

        down a road lined
        with fields long
        given up   blasted

    cemeteries of one name
    or two

A hand
juts out like barbed wire
it is terribly alone

if she takes it
        will it slash her wrists again

if she passes it by

        will she turn into a case
        of shell-shock, eyes
        glazed forever on the

            blank chart of
            amnesia

1973

Martial Choreograph

Maya Angelou

Hello young sailor.
You are betrayed and
do not know the dance of death.
Dandy warrior, swaying to
Rick James on your
stereo, you do not hear the
bleat of triumphant war, its
roar is not in
your ears, filled with Stevie Wonder.

"Show me how to do like you.
Show me how to do it."

You will be surprised that
trees grunt when torn from

their root sockets to fandango into dust,
and exploding bombs force a lively Lindy
on grasses and frail bodies.

Go galloping on, bopping,
in the airport, young sailor.
Your body, virgin
still, has not swung the bloody buck and wing.

Manhood is a newly delivered
message. Your eyes,
rampant as an open city,
have not yet seen life steal from
limbs outstretched and trembling
like the arms of dancers
and dying swans.

SHARING A READING

Choose one of the following questions as the topic of an essay in which you explain your reading of one of these texts on war to someone else. You should try to convey both how you respond to the text and why you think you respond that way.

1. Even though the texts are all, in some sense, about war, they certainly say different things about it, and they also address other concerns. Write about a theme that you perceive in two or more of these text—for example, "explorations of war and patriotism" or "war and its effect on families." Describe the theme you perceive to someone in your class.

2. Do you ever find that you experience emotions when you read these texts that are at odds with your beliefs or convictions? In other words, think about how these texts evoke a difference within you. If, for example, you believe that it is appropriate for nations to go to war to protect their interests and for citizens to fight in those wars, can you sympathetically read a text that is critical of war? Describe the experience to someone who shares your conviction.

3. Write an essay in which you describe your response to the ways in which two or more of these texts deal with the brutality of war. Does brutality occur only on the battlefield? Do these texts deal with brutality in more extensive terms? How and why do you respond to the depictions of brutality?

4. "To a Child Born in Time of Small War," "The Loneliness of the Military Historian," "Patterns," and "Dien Bien Phu" explore women's roles in relation to war, while "i sing of Olaf," "To Lucasta," and "In Another

Country" center on experiences that are usually male. Write an essay in which you explain your response to two or more of these texts in terms of gender. Assume that your reader knows the texts.

5.   Write an essay in which you explain your response to two or more of these poems in terms of race. Again, assume that your reader knows the texts.

Exploring Readings and Memories

Each of the texts that follow describes memories, and these memories are likely, in turn, to evoke some memories for you. Read them carefully and then answer the questions.

from *Nigger: An Autobiography*

Dick Gregory

I never learned hate at home, or shame. I had to go to school for that. I was about seven years old when I got my first big lesson. I was in love with a little girl named Helene Tucker, a light-complected little girl with pigtails and nice manners. She was always clean and she was smart in school. I think I went to school then mostly to look at her. I brushed my hair and even got me a little old handkerchief. It was a lady's handkerchief, but I didn't want Helene to see me wipe my nose on my hand. The pipes were frozen again, there was no water in the house, but I washed my socks and shirt every night. I'd get a pot, and go over to Mister Ben's grocery store, and stick my pot down into his soda machine. Scoop out some chopped ice. By evening the ice melted to water for washing. I got sick a lot that winter because the fire would go out at night before the clothes were dry. In the morning I'd put them on, wet or dry, because they were the only clothes I had.

Everybody's got a Helene Tucker, a symbol of everything you want. I loved her for her goodness, her cleanness, her popularity. She'd walk down my street and my brothers and sisters would yell, "Here comes Helene," and I'd rub my tennis sneakers on the back of my pants and wish my hair wasn't so nappy and the white folks' shirt fit me better. I'd run out on the street. If I knew my place and didn't come too close, she'd wink at me and say hello. That was a good feeling. Sometimes I'd follow her all the way home, and shovel the snow off her walk and try to make friends with her Momma and her aunts. I'd drop money on her stoop late at night on my way back from shining shoes in the taverns. And she had a Daddy, and he had a good job. He was a paper hanger.

I guess I would have gotten over Helene by summertime, but something happened in that classroom that made her face hang in front of me for the next twenty-two years. When I played the drums in high school it was for Helene and when I broke track records in college it was for Helene and when I started standing behind microphones and heard applause I wished Helene could hear it, too. It wasn't until I was twenty-nine years old and married and making money that I finally got her out of my system. Helene was sitting in that class-room when I learned to be ashamed of myself.

It was on a Thursday. I was sitting in the back of the room in a seat with a chalk circle drawn around it. The idiot's scat, the troublemaker's seat.

The teacher thought I was stupid. Couldn't spell, couldn't read, couldn't do arithmetic. Just stupid. Teachers were never interested in finding out that you couldn't concentrate because you were so hungry, because you hadn't had any breakfast. All you could think about was noontime, would it ever come? Maybe you could sneak into the cloakroom and steal a bite of some kid's lunch out of a coat pocket. A bite of something. Paste. You can't really make a meal of paste, or put it on bread for a sandwich, but sometimes I'd scoop a few spoon-fuls out of the big paste jar in the back of the room. Pregnant people get strange tastes. I was pregnant with poverty. Pregnant with dirt and pregnant with smells that made people turn away, pregnant with cold and pregnant with shoes that were never bought for me, pregnant with five other people in my bed and no Daddy in the next room, and pregnant with hunger. Paste doesn't taste too bad when you're hungry.

The teacher thought I was a troublemaker. All she saw from the front of the room was a little black boy who squirmed in his idiot's seat and made noises and poked the kids around him. I guess she couldn't see a kid who made noises because he wanted someone to know he was there.

It was on a Thursday, the day before the Negro payday. The eagle always flew on Friday. The teacher was asking each student how much his father would give to the Community Chest. On Friday night, each kid would get the money from his father, and on Monday he would bring it to the school. I decid-ed I was going to buy me a Daddy right then. I had money in my pocket from shining shoes and selling papers, and whatever Helene Tucker pledged for her Daddy I was going to top it. And I'd hand the money right in. I wasn't going to wait until Monday to buy me a Daddy.

I was shaking, scared to death. The teacher opened her book and started calling out names alphabetically.

"Helene Tucker?"

"My Daddy said he'd give two dollars and fifty cents."

"That's very nice, Helene. Very, very nice indeed."

That made me feel pretty good. It wouldn't take too much to top that. I had almost three dollars in dimes and quarters in my pocket. I stuck my hand in my pocket and held onto the money, waiting for her to call my name. But the teacher closed her book after she called everybody else in the class.

I stood up and raised my hand.

"What is it now?"

"You forgot me."

She turned toward the blackboard. "I don't have time to be playing with you, Richard."

"My Daddy said he'd . . ."

"Sit down, Richard, you're disturbing the class."

"My Daddy said he'd give . . . fifteen dollars."

She turned around and looked mad. "We are collecting this money for you and your kind, Richard Gregory. If your Daddy can give fifteen dollars you have no business being on relief."

"I got it right now, I got it right now, my Daddy gave it to me to turn in today, my Daddy said . . ."

"And furthermore," she said, looking right at me, her nostrils getting big and her lips getting thin and her eyes opening wide. "We know you don't have a Daddy."

Helene Tucker turned around, her eyes full of tears. She felt sorry for me. Then I couldn't see her too well because I was crying, too.

"Sit down Richard."

And I always thought the teacher kind of liked me. She always picked me to wash the blackboard on Friday, after school. That was a big thrill, it made me feel important. If I didn't wash it, come Monday the school might not function right.

"Where are you going, Richard?"

I walked out of school that day, and for a long time I didn't go back very often. There was shame there.

CONSTRUCTING A READING

1. This essay describes a memory in which Helene's face hangs in front of Richard for the next twenty-two years of his life. How do you respond to Gregory's text? Do you have similar memories? What emotions does Gregory's memory evoke in you? Compare your response to those of your group members.

2. Although he says, "the teacher thought I was stupid," he had thought the teacher liked him because she asked him to clean the blackboard. Do you think she likes Richard? If not, how does the difference between Richard's perspective on her feelings and your own affect your reading of the story?

Gains and Losses

Richard Rodriguez

Supporters of bilingual education today imply that students like me miss a great deal by not being taught in their family's language. What they seem not to recognize is that, as a socially disadvantaged child, I considered Spanish to be a private language. What I needed to learn in school was that I had the right— and the obligation—to speak the public language of *los gringos.* The odd truth is that my first-grade classmates could have become bilingual, in the conventional sense of that word, more easily than I. Had they been taught (as upper-middle-class children are often taught early) a second language like Spanish or French, they could have regarded it simply as that: another public language. In my case such bilingualism could not have been so quickly achieved. What I did not believe was that I could speak a single public language.

Without question, it would have pleased me to hear my teachers address me in Spanish when I entered the classroom. I would have felt much less afraid. I would have trusted them and responded with ease. But I would have delayed—for how long postponed?—having to learn the language of public society. I would have evaded—and for how long could I have afforded to delay?—learning the great lesson of school, that I had a public identity.

Fortunately, my teachers were unsentimental about their responsibility. What they understood was that I needed to speak a public language. So their voices would search me out, asking me questions. Each time I'd hear them, I'd look up in surprise to see a nun's face frowning at me. I'd mumble, not really meaning to answer. The nun would persist, 'Richard, stand up. Don't look at the floor. Speak up. Speak to the entire class, not just to me!' But I couldn't believe that the English language was mine to use. (In part, I did not want to believe it.) I continued to mumble. I resisted the teacher's demands. (Did I somehow suspect that once I learned public language my pleasing family life would be changed?) Silent, waiting for the bell to sound, I remained dazed, diffident, afraid.

Because I wrongly imagined that English was intrinsically a public language and Spanish an intrinsically private one, I easily noted the difference between classroom language and the language of home. At school, words were directed to a general audience of listeners. ('Boys and girls.') Words were meaningfully ordered. And the point was not self-expression alone but to make oneself understood by many others. The teacher quizzed: 'Boys and girls, why do we use that word in this sentence? Could we think of a better word to use there? Would the sentence change its meaning if the words were differently arranged? And wasn't there a better way of saying much the same thing?' (I couldn't say. I wouldn't try to say.)

Three months. Five. Half a year passed. Unsmiling, ever watchful, my teachers noted my silence. They began to connect my behavior with the difficult progress my older sister and brother were making. Until one Saturday morning three nuns arrived at the house to talk to our parents. Stiffly, they sat on the blue living room sofa. From the doorway of another room, spying the visitors, I noted the incongruity—the clash of two worlds, the faces and voices of school intruding upon the familiar setting of home. I overheard one voice gently wondering, 'Do your children speak only Spanish at home, Mrs. Rodriguez?' While another voice added, 'That Richard especially seems so timid and shy.'

That Rich-heard!

With great tact the visitors continued, 'Is it possible for you and your husband to encourage your children to practice their English when they are home?' Of course, my parents complied. What would they not do for their children's well-being? And how could they have questioned the Church's authority which those women represented? In an instant, they agreed to give up the language (the sounds) that had revealed and accentuated our family's closeness. The moment after the visitors left, the change was observed. '*Ahora*, speak to us *en inglés*,' my father and mother united to tell us.

At first, it seemed a kind of game. After dinner each night, the family gathered to practice 'our' English. (It was still then *inglés*, a language foreign to us, so we felt drawn as strangers to it.) Laughing, we would try to define words we could not pronounce. We played with strange English sounds. often over-anglicizing our pronunciations. And we filled the smiling gaps of our sentences with familiar Spanish sounds. But that was cheating, somebody shouted. Every-one laughed. In school, meanwhile, like my brother and sister, I was required to attend a daily tutoring session. I needed a full year of special attention. I also needed my teachers to keep my attention from straying in class by calling out; *Rich-heard*—their English voices slowly prying loose my ties to my other name, its three notes, *Ri-car-do.* Most of all I needed to hear my mother and father speak to me in a moment of seriousness in broken—suddenly heartbreaking— English. The scene was inevitable: One Saturday morning I entered the kitchen where my parents were talking in Spanish. I did not realize that they were talk-ing in Spanish however until, at the moment they saw me, I heard their voices change to speak English. Those *gringo* sounds they uttered startled me. Pushed me away. In that moment of trivial misunderstanding and profound insight, I felt my throat twisted by unsounded grief. I turned quickly and left the room. But I had no place to escape to with Spanish. (The spell was broken.) My brother and sisters were speaking English in another part of the house.

Again and again in the days following, increasingly angry, I was obliged to hear my mother and father: 'Speak to us *en inglés*.' *(Speak.)* Only then did I determine to learn classroom English. Weeks after, it happened: One day in school I raised my hand to volunteer an answer. I spoke out in a loud voice. And I did not think it remarkable when the entire class understood. That day, I moved very far from the disadvantaged child I had been only days earlier. The belief, the calming assurance that I belonged in public. had at last taken hold.

Shortly after, I stopped hearing the high and loud sounds of *los gringos*. A more and more confident speaker of English, I didn't trouble to listen to how strangers sounded, speaking to me. And there simply were too many English-speaking people in my day for me to hear American accents anymore. Conversations quickened. Listening to persons who sounded eccentrically pitched voices, I usually noted their sounds for an initial few seconds before I concentrated on *what* they were saying. Conversations became content-full. Transparent. Hearing someone's *tone* of voice—angry or questioning or sarcastic or happy or sad—I didn't distinguish it from the words it expressed. Sound and word were thus tightly wedded. At the end of a day, I was often bemused, always relieved, to realize how 'silent,' though crowded with words, my day in public had been. (This public silence measured and quickened the change in my life.)

At last, seven years old, I came to believe what had been technically true since my birth: I was an American citizen.

But the special feeling of closeness at home was diminished by then. Gone was the desperate, urgent, intense feeling of being at home; rare was the experience of feeling myself individualized by family intimates. We remained a loving family, but one greatly changed. No longer so close; no longer bound tight by the pleasing and troubling knowledge of our public separateness. Neither my older brother nor sister rushed home after school anymore. Nor did I. When I arrived home there would often be neighborhood kids in the house. Or the house would be empty of sounds.

Following the dramatic Americanization of their children, even my parents grew more publicly confident. Especially my mother. She learned the names of all the people on our block. And she decided we needed to have a telephone installed in the house. My father continued to use the word *gringo*. But it was no longer charged with the old bitterness or distrust. (Stripped of any emotional content, the word simply became a name for those Americans not of Hispanic descent.) Hearing him, sometimes, I wasn't sure if he was pronouncing the Spanish word *gringo* or saying gringo in English.

Matching the silence I started hearing in public was a new quiet at home. The family's quiet was partly due to the fact that, as we children learned more and more English, we shared fewer and fewer words with our parents. Sentences needed to be spoken slowly when a child addressed his mother or father. (Often the parent wouldn't understand.) The child would need to repeat himself. (Still the parent misunderstood.) The young voice, frustrated, would end up saying. 'Never mind'—the subject was closed. Dinners would be noisy with the clinking of knives and forks against dishes. My mother would smile softly between her remarks; my father at the other end of the table would chew and chew at his food, while he stared over the heads of his children.

My *mother!* My *father!* After English became my primary language, I no longer knew what words to use in addressing my parents. The old Spanish words (those tender accents of sound) I had used earlier—*mamá* and *papá*—I couldn't use anymore. They would have been too painful reminders of how much had changed in my life. On the other hand, the words I heard neighbor-hood kids call their parents seemed equally unsatisfactory. *Mother* and *Father;* *Ma, Papa, Pa, Dad, Pap* (how I hated the all-American sound of that last word especially)—all these terms I felt were unsuitable, not really terms of address for *my* parents. As a result, I never used them at home. Whenever I'd speak to my parents, I would try to get their attention with eye contact alone. In public conversations, I'd refer to 'my parents' or 'my mother and father.'

My mother and father, for their part, responded differently, as their chil-dren spoke to them less. She grew restless, seemed troubled and anxious at the scarcity of words exchanged in the house. It was she who would question me about my day when I came home from school. She smiled at small talk. She pried at the edges of my sentences to get me to say something more. (What?) She'd join conversations she overheard, but her intrusions often stopped her children's talking. By contrast, my father seemed reconciled to the new quiet. Though his English improved somewhat, he retired into silence. At dinner he spoke very little. One night his children and even his wife helplessly giggled at his garbled English pronunciation of the Catholic Grace before Meals. There-after he made his wife recite the prayer at the start of each meal, even on for-mal occasions, when there were guests in the house. Hers became the public voice of the family. On official business, it was she, not my father, one would usually hear on the phone or in stores, talking to strangers. His children grew so accustomed to his silence that, years later, they would speak routinely of his shyness. (My mother would often try to explain: Both his parents died when he was eight. He was raised by an uncle who treated him like little more than a menial servant. He was never encouraged to speak. He grew up alone. A man of few words.) But my father was not shy, I realized, when I'd watch him speak-ing Spanish with relatives. Using Spanish, he was quickly effusive. Especially when talking with other men, his voice would spark, flicker, flare alive with sounds. In Spanish, he expressed ideas and feelings he rarely revealed in Eng-lish. With firm Spanish sounds, he conveyed confidence and authority English would never allow him.

The silence at home, however, was finally more than a literal silence. Fewer words passed between parent and child, but more profound was the silence that resulted from my inattention to sounds. At about the time I no longer bothered to listen with care to the sounds of English in public, I grew careless about listening to the sounds family members made when they spoke. Most of the time I heard someone speaking at home and didn't distinguish his sounds from the words people uttered in public. I didn't even pay much atten-tion to my parents accented and ungrammatical speech. At least not at home. Only when I was with them in public would I grow alert to their accents. Though, even then, their sounds caused me less and less concern. For I was increasingly confident of my own public identity.

I would have been happier about my public success had I not sometimes recalled what it had been like earlier, when my family had conveyed its intimacy through a set of conveniently private sounds. Sometimes in public, hearing a stranger, I'd hark back to my past. A Mexican farmworker approached me downtown to ask directions to somewhere. "¿Hijito . . . ?" he said. And his voice summoned deep longing. Another time, standing beside my mother in the visiting room of a Carmelite convent, before the dense screen which rendered the nuns shadowy figures, 1 heard several Spanish-speaking nuns—their busy, singsong overlapping voices—assure us that yes, yes, we were remembered, all our family was remembered in their prayers. (Their voices echoed faraway family sounds.) Another day, a dark-faced old woman—her hand light on my shoulder—steadied herself against me as she boarded a bus. She murmured something I couldn't quite comprehend. Her Spanish voice came near, like the face of a never-before-seen relative in the instant before I was kissed. Her voice, like so many of the Spanish voices I'd hear in public, recalled the golden age of my youth. Hearing Spanish then, I continued to be a careful, if sad, listener to sounds. Hearing a Spanish-speaking family walking behind me, I turned to look. I smiled for an instant, before my glance found the Hispanic-looking faces of strangers in the crowd going by.

CONSTRUCTING A READING

1. How does language dictate private and public space for the speaker? How does education shift these spaces for him? What are the consequences of that shift for him? What are the consequences for his sense of cultural identity?
2. In what ways has your education affected your relations with your family members or friends?
3. What do you see as the gains and the losses in this story?
4. What is your response to the idea of a public language? What does the term imply for you? Have you ever had to encounter a shift in community which demanded the learning of public languages? Did you experience gains and losses?

SHARING A READING

1. Write to a person whom you knew as a child about an event that you remember from your own childhood (like those of Rodriguez, Gregory, or "Tollie"). Explain what that memory now means to you. In your writing, try to be clear about the connection between your gender, ethnicity, and/or social class and the importance of the memory.

CHAPTER TWO

Gaps:
How Texts Invite Us
to Read Them

Reading can be confusing. Poems sometimes seem to jump from one topic to another without connections; stories seem to stop without coming to a conclusion, leaving you checking to see whether any pages are missing from your book.

CLOSING GAPS TO BUILD A READING

Actually, a text in which every conceivable connection is spelled out for every conceivable reader would certainly be very long, not to mention very boring. In a sense, you (and all readers) *are* missing something at these difficult reading moments. As was mentioned in Chapter One, what happens is that we really do not have all the information we need to make sense of the text before us. But that is not the only reason those difficult reading moments, these *gaps*, should in fact be welcomed by readers. A *gap* is a moment of hesitation in a reading act when the reader experiences uncertainty about meaning. *Closing gaps* is a reading activity in which a reader tries to resolve that uncertainty by *imagining* connections among the bits of information that the text does provide. Finding or making gaps, bridging or closing them—and even deciding that a gap is unbridgeable—are crucial to any act of reading.

Many students think that being puzzled by a gap will mark them as bad readers. They suppose that it is somehow unsophisticated to encounter gaps—or to admit to encountering them. On the contrary, gaps are an ordinary part of reading, and it is a mark of sophistication to find many of them. Novice readers frequently ignore places in the text where they have difficulty con-

[handwritten margin note: finding meaning in text time to discuss and ponder]

55

structing meaning; they often say that they don't find any gaps in a text. Actually, though, the more experienced a reader is, the more gaps she or he is likely to find.

The more we imagine connections, and the more connections we imagine, the more we read "literarily." What makes a text literary is the kind of reading a reader gives to it, a consciousness of reading for gaps.

To illustrate, let's look at a passage from *The New York Times*, dated January 24, 1993:

> Thurgood Marshall, pillar of the civil rights revolution, architect of the legal strategy that ended the era of official segregation, and the first black justice of the Supreme Court, died today.

This sentence is the first line of a news story that you might skim over breakfast as you get ready for the day's activities. Although well written, it certainly does not seem to be particularly "literary." You read it to learn about Marshall's death, and to remind yourself of the events of his life.

But look what happens if I send a signal that this sentence is to be read as "literary" text by setting it as a poem.

January 24, Washington, D.C.

Thurgood Marshall,

Pillar
Of the civil rights revolution,

Architect
Of the legal strategy
That ended the era
Of official segregation

And the first
Black justice
Of the Supreme Court

Died
Today.

When you read this sentence as a poem, you make gaps: you ask "what do I have to imagine to make sense of this text?" As you raise and answer questions, closing gaps and making new ones as you read, you make meaning. You find places where the text seems to withhold stable meaning and to present unresolved questions instead. You see ambiguities and raise questions about them. You perceive (and create) different emphases than those of a news story.

> When we read a text as literary, we "look at the language in new ways," we see relevance in places we might ordinarily not notice, and we "subject the text to a different series of interpretive operations."
>
> Jonathan Culler, *Structuralist Poetics: Structuralism, Linguistics, and the Study of Literature*. Cornell University Press, 1975, p. 114.

The phrase "black justice," for example, seems to stand out, and call for interpretation. Does "black justice" mean an African American person who is Associate Justice of the Supreme Court, justice for black people, or perhaps even a special kind of justice—black justice, as opposed to white justice or Hispanic American justice? By reading *literarily*, rather than *literally*—by reading for gaps—you are able to raise that question. When you read for gaps, the word "today" gains emphasis, as though to underscore the fact that on January 24, 1993, even though African American citizens of the United States still have a long way to go before enjoying equality, Thurgood Marshall can no longer help them. You notice that "official segregation" (which is ended) seems to be differentiated from unofficial segregation, whose era is not yet over. You might construct parallels between "pillar" and "architect" and see a comparison or analogy between civil rights legislation and a building. Then you might notice that Thurgood Marshall is both the designer of that building and a structural part of it: as an African American lawyer who became an Associate Justice of the Supreme Court, he not only helped to write civil rights legislation, but also formed part of the class of persons for whom its protections were intended.

Most of the time, we already know whether a text we're reading is "literature" or not. Culture tells us. Literature appears in English textbooks; it is found in the "literature" sections of bookstores and libraries. When we have that clue, or invitation, to read a text as literature, we do so—by looking for gaps. However, when we read a science textbook, a business report, or a newspaper, we don't usually try to find gaps. We read the sports pages, for example, to get information about our favorite teams. In a newspaper account, such as the following excerpt from *The New York Times* for February 27, 1993, we want the text to give us the information we need as quickly and clearly as possible.

Pitchers Hope for Breaks and Slides Under the Sun

By Joe Sexton
Special to *The New York Times*

Port St. Lucie, Fla., Feb. 27 [1993]—The inspiration for pitching experimentation is varied: insecurity, injury, boredom, arrogance. The constant is that pitchers do it all the time. Here's a look through the window at the lab work being done by the Mets.

BRET SABERHAGEN'S SLIDER The right-hander has been addicted to the pitch since his first professional season, 1983. Club officials, though, have repeatedly advised him to drop the habit, mortified by the pitch's propensity for producing injury.

"I have always messed with it," said Saberhagen. And that's because "it" can always mess with the minds of batters. When one can throw 95 miles an hour, any off-speed pitch can be crippling. The slider gives Saberhagen, who also throws a mind-bendingly effective changeup and curve ball, one more option for buckling the knees and the nerve of the opposition.

But when we read the following text, we know we are reading a poem, so we make more of it, we study it for more complicated ideas. The exercise that follows will help us get started on this "literary" reading.

Pitcher

Robert Francis

His art is eccentricity, his aim
How not to hit the mark he seems to aim at,

His passion how to avoid the obvious,
His technique how to vary the avoidance.

The others throw to be comprehended. He
Throws to be a moment misunderstood.

Yet not too much. Not errant, arrant, wild,
But every seeming aberration willed.

Not to, yet still, still to communicate
Making the batter understand too late.

CONSTRUCTING A READING

1. Do you see gaps in the report from the sports pages? If it were the beginning of spring training for the 1993 baseball season, and you were a Mets fan, would you read it differently than you do now? Does the fact that it appears in this textbook about reading change the way you read it?
2. Try setting Joe Sexton's account of Saberhagen's pre-season efforts as a poem; rearrange or change the language if you like, or just insert line breaks.
3. Try setting the Robert Francis poem as an entry for "pitcher" in a baseball encyclopedia.

4. Many critics think that "Pitcher" is also (or "really") about a poet. Do you agree? Why or why not?

CONVENTIONS OF READING AND HOW THEY HELP US CLOSE GAPS

There are many ways of describing and accounting for gaps. Authors sometimes deliberately withhold information to spur a reader's imagination. At other times, readers may not understand the customs of the time, place, or culture in which a poem or story or play is set, especially when texts come from contexts that are very different from their own.

In this chapter, I shall concentrate on occasions when readers lack experience in the *conventions* of reading the kind of text at hand. A *convention* is a habitual expectation or way of behaving in a culture—of doing something, or seeing something or understanding something. Conventional behavior becomes so habitual that we don't even think about following it. However, since conventions vary in time and from culture to culture, what seems ordinary and unremarkable to one cultural group might seem odd to another. It is conventional in the west, for example, to shake hands with someone to whom one has just been introduced, whereas in many Asian countries the conventional greeting would be a bow. There are conventional ways of dressing at funerals that vary with religion and region. There are conventional ways of behaving at rock concerts, or baseball games, or business meetings. Notice that these conventions are not absolute rules: you certainly *can* wear your gym shorts to a funeral, or signify your approval at a rock concert by gently tapping your rolled-up program against your palm, or eat caviar instead of hot dogs at a baseball game—but that behavior would be unusual, unconventional.

Conventions of reading work in similar ways. Readers make meaning by finding or creating and then by closing or bridging the gaps that they perceive or even by deciding that the gaps in a text cannot or should not be closed. They are not absolute, inviolable rules of reading, but they are habits that readers have engaged in successfully for generations.

To illustrate a conventional way of reading, I'll begin with a visual, rather than a print text, one with which you are probably familiar—the "cuts" in a film or TV chase.

An outdoor shot shows a character running toward his car—a red Ferrari. Next, the camera is inside the car, and the shot shows the driver starting his engine. Then, another outside shot reveals the red Ferrari taking off in a cloud of dust. Next, we see two police officers entering their vehicle. Next, we see two cars—a Ferrari and a police car—careening down the Pacific Coast Highway, with the jagged rocks of the shore several hundred feet below. Next, the face of the Ferrari driver. Next, the face of the cops. A clock strikes the hour. Then, we see a domestic scene in which a woman tucks her baby daughter into bed. The rear of the Ferrari from the perspective of the police; the ocean; the two cars from above; the police, the hood of the Ferrari from the driver's perspective, and so on.

Chances are that you have no trouble following these cuts. You can make a story from them, making inferences about the relations among police, the Ferrari driver, and the woman. You understand what it means when the scene or even the camera angle changes, even though nobody in the film tells you what to think and even though all cuts don't "mean" the same thing. Sometimes, a cut indicates the passage of time between one scene and another. At other times, the shift indicates a change in the setting of the action. At still other moments, a cut could signify a change in point of view from one character to another. You have learned how to understand these clues, process them, and make meaning from them, just by living in your culture.

In just the same way, we rely on cultural conventions as we make meaning from gaps in verbal texts. Jokes are often conventional, for example. The essay that follows describes some ways in which the conventions of the "light-bulb joke" have changed to reflect the best and worst of humor in the United States. These jokes function to unify members of ethnic, racial, and social groups by opposing them to others, so they reveal racism, sexism, and classism. But because they change over time, they also reveal ways in which prejudice changes (and even possibly diminishes).

How Many Light-Bulb Jokes
Does It Take to Chart an Era?
Appliance Theory Applied

Daniel Harris

Unlike knock-knock jokes, dead-baby jokes, dumb-blonde jokes and why-did-the-chicken-cross-the-road jokes, the light-bulb joke is uniquely political. Not only does it make references to current events (how many Canadian separatists, how many Branch Davidians), it also summarizes, in epigrammatic form, the history of the second half of the 20th century, excoriating in virtually the same breath the illegal immigrant and the gainfully employed bureaucrat, big government and big business, homosexuals and homophobes, shrinks and paranoids. And because the light-bulb joke involves a piece of electrical equipment, it mirrors our ambivalent attitudes toward technology; which, ever since Thomas Edison invented the incandescent bulb in 1879, has become so complex that we can no longer install and repair our appliances without enlisting the services of price-gouging experts. In the light-bulb joke, the ancient literary genre of the riddle demonstrates its versatility and wickedly dissects the problems of the machine age.

The crux of the joke's humor lies in the words "how many," since in most instances changing a light bulb requires only one person—not the teeming hordes of support technicians and service providers who crowd around the ladder protesting unsafe working conditions and developing special bulb-insertion software. The light-bulb joke is, in spirit, both anticorporate and anti-Federal, providing a perfect vehicle for satirizing byzantine bureaucracies. It is the ideal joke of an era of upsizing, in which both large corporations and government agencies have bloated staffs that will allow the bulb to be changed only after the completion of environmental impact statements, ergonomic reports and Civil Service examinations conducted for the Light Bulb Administrator position. It is a deeply American joke, full of the rage of the Republican rebel who despises the social welfare state and advocates instead a pioneering philosophy of self-rule. At the risk of overstatement, you might suggest that the historical roots of the joke's libertarian agenda lie in the colonists' rejection of royalist tyranny and the 19th-century frontiersmen's love of personal initiative.

The light-bulb joke is also well suited to an age of consumer-protection campaigns and media exposés of the potentially life-threatening dangers of defective products, from exploding gas tanks to leaking silicone breast implants. It resonates with our suspicion of the rapaciousness of specialists eager to make a quick buck at the expense of both our pocketbooks and our physical safety; like the six garage mechanics, five of whom hold the ladder while the other gives the estimate at the end of the month. Within the context of its virtually infinite permutations, the joke transforms the light bulb into a kind of symbolic Every Commodity, whose purchase and installation is complicated by malfunctioning components and hidden costs. (How many I.B.M. PC owners? Only one, but the purchase of the light-bulb adapter card is extra.)

The joke is peculiarly modern because it makes sense only in an era in which the middle-class homeowner maintains his own property and is unable to afford the servants who, in a long-lost age of cheap immigrant labor, would have changed his bulbs for him. It is at once the epitaph for an obsolete class of household slaves and the patriotic battle hymn of the bedraggled housewife and the diligent handyman who cut their own lawns and unclog their own sinks. In the late 20th century, we are all bulb changers, participants in a pedestrian task that unites the rich with the poor.

The light bulb is a highly charged ideological object in our aging democracy—an emblem of normality, of a society that stigmatizes its exceptional citizens, reviling their lack of conformity and mechanical ineptitude as unpardonable evidence of their elitism. The ability to perform this simple household chore becomes a test of one's humanity, and those outcasts who fail are immediately interned in the menagerie of buffoons that the light-bulb joke so mercilessly pillories.

The joke singles out two contrasting groups in its role as an equal-opportunity leveler. On the one hand, it ridicules bungling minorities whose spatulate fingers are ill equipped to handle this fragile glass object, smashing the bulb with a hammer, cutting it in two with a chain saw or getting drunk until the room spins. On the other hand, it is increasingly used to satirize overeducated scientists who intellectualize a task that involves a mere twist of the wrist, compiling libraries of software documentation or defining Darkness™ as a new industry standard. Simultaneously snobbish and anti-elitist, the joke reflects an identity crisis occurring among angry white males. Hemmed in from below by destitute ethnic groups and from above by incomprehensible aristocracies of white-collar intellectuals, the average citizen holds himself up as the exemplar of common sense, which inevitably prevails over those who refuse to turn the bulb without first completing the software upgrade and drawing up forbiddingly complex contracts governing brownouts or pratfalls.

The fact that a single joke is used to belittle the supposed deficiencies of minorities and the esoteric skills of the intelligentsia suggests that, in some sense, we equate the tensions caused by ethnic conflicts with the tensions caused by the new hierarchies of knowledge. Both ethnic diversity and profound inequalities of information and know-how are contributing to social unrest, to the demoralizing feelings of inadequacy and competitiveness that are tearing apart a nation already fractured by intolerance. It is not an accident that the same joke is used to ridicule the homeboy and the software designer; both are viewed with distrust as members of subversive minorities.

One of the most surprising features of the light-bulb joke is how the lowly bulb has been used to make fun of the exalted computer, spawning scores of light-bulb jokes about Silicon Valley. (How many hardware engineers? Thirty— but of course just five years ago all it took was a couple of kids in a garage in Palo Alto.) Far from streamlining the modern environment, mechanization has made our lives more complex and has needlessly confused straightforward tasks like setting the clocks on our VCR's, paralyzing us with the cerebral intricacies of a chore it has turned into an indecipherable electronic puzzle. The joke catches the machine age in the nostalgic act of clarifying its original purpose—that of making things simpler, faster, easier to use.

The light-bulb joke reflects another form of social unrest. In the not too distant past, it was an uncensored forum for socially acceptable expressions of racism, homophobia, anti-Semitism and misogyny (How many feminists? Two—one to declare that the bulb has violated the socket and one to secretly wish that *she* were the socket.) In the 1990's, however, the joke is being turned against its traditional tellers by a gang of comic vigilantes bent on evening the score. It is a joke in turmoil, the battleground of a small civil war in which minorities, who for decades remained in tight-lipped silence as loudmouthed Archie Bunkers taunted them in public, are now talking back, lambasting such groups as homophobes, who change the bulb with sterile rubber gloves because it is possible that a gay person with AIDS just touched it. The scapegoats have been elevated from the butt of the joke to the joke tellers, a promotion that mirrors their increasing integration into society. While very little has been done from 1879 to the age of the politically incorrect to improve Edison's invention, the light-bulb joke has been constantly reinvented.

CONSTRUCTING A READING

1. With your group members, think of some other kinds of popular texts that reveal cultural values, e.g., TV commercials.
2. With your group members go through old magazines and newspapers to find conventional ways of invoking the cultural values that helped to defined an earlier era.

TYPES OF CONVENTIONS

Literary reading involves countless conventions, deeply embedded in culture, rarely spoken of, and operating continually in our "readings" of texts of all kinds: films, songs, TV shows, magazine advertisements, anything *to be interpreted*. What follows is by no means a complete account of them—there could be no such list because any act of reading—and any text—occurs in context, and context is limitless. Still, in spite of our individual feelings, associations, beliefs, and memories stemming from our varying backgrounds, readers tend to share cultural expectations that texts will have coherence, unity and significance.* These conventions tell us (more or less) what to do: we look for coherence, unity, and significance by asking questions like "what one thing is this text about? What is the unity here? How are all these aspects of the text related? How is this part of the text connected to that one? What statement does it make about life?" Our own associations and memories, however, tell us how to bridge the gaps we find and make sense of the texts we read.

The Convention of Unity

Readers tend to expect texts to be about something, and only one thing, and to offer a unified vision. The *convention of unity*, then, is a kind of instruction or assisted invitation to make sense of the text by finding or imagining that one thing. To see how this convention works, let's look at a text. Following is a riddle poem by Emily Dickinson, the poet with the unlisted number Nemorov mentions in "Long Distance," whom Patricia Mitchell's classmates couldn't reach.

---

*Jonathan Culler delineates these three conventions in *Structuralist Poetics*. London: Oxford University Press, 1976.

I Like to See it Lap the Miles

Emily Dickinson

I like to see it lap the Miles—
And lick the Valleys up—
And stop to feed itself at Tanks—
And then—prodigious step

Around a Pile of Mountains—
And supercilious peer
In Shanties—by the sides of Roads—
And then a Quarry pare

To fit its sides
And crawl between
Complaining all the while
In horrid—hooting stanza—
Then chase itself down Hill—

And neigh like Boanerges—
Then—prompter than a Star
Stop—docile and omnipotent
At its own stable door—

Riddles, conventionally, ask the question, "What am I?" So, that question will be our gap. The conventional way of closing this gap is to find the one "thing" (or word) that links all of the riddles' descriptions together and makes sense of them. To do so, we have to change the conventional riddle question, "What am I?" into one or more workable ones, as follows:

Q. What laps miles, licks valleys, steps around mountains, peers into shanties, etc.?

A. Some kind of creature, an animal perhaps.

Q. What kind?

A. An animal that neighs. A horse.

Q. OK, but this horse neighs like Boanerges. Who or what is Boanerges? (This poem presents the kind of gap that comes when a reader lacks information about the text's context. Look it up!)

A. *The Random House Dictionary* gives these definitions: 1. a surname given by Jesus to James and John. Mark 3:17. 2. (construed as sing.) a vociferous preacher or orator.
A Bible dictionary reveals that Boanerges means "Sons of Thunder."

This information does not immediately close our gap, but it does help us to make another one: this is clearly no ordinary horse. The animal we're dealing with is named for two disciples of Jesus and associated with vociferous preaching and thunder. Moreover, this horse is omnipotent and docile at the same time. And it accomplishes feats that would be impossible for ordinary horses—it can step around a pile of mountains, pare a quarry, and hoot complaints rhythmically, like stanzas of a poem.

The reader who solves this riddle will have to ask a series of gap questions directed toward finding an "it" that is like a horse but capable of all the feats that Dickinson describes. But such a reader also needs information about the context in which the poem was produced. A reader who knows that "iron horse" was a name for trains in the nineteenth century will probably decide, at last, that "it" is a train, but this reading still lacks an adequate explanation for the biblical reference to Boanerges. And so we have a new gap.

Q. How is a train like a vociferous preacher, like James and John?

A. Perhaps the iron horse could be understood as preaching noisily about progress by thunderously proclaiming its superiority to ordinary, nonmechanized forms of transportation.

There is, of course, no single answer. Readers may make their own individual unities, but the cultural expectation is that they will try to make *some* kind of unity. Although all readers experience gaps, they do not all experience the same ones, nor do they close them in the same ways. Some gaps are intended by the author: Emily Dickinson obviously wants you to guess what or whom her poem describes. Other gaps are occasioned by readers' inexperience, or cultural difference from the *world* of the text. (We will explore textual worlds in Chapter Three.) You might not know, for example, that Boanerges is the name that Jesus gave to James and John, or that "iron horse" is a nickname for a train—*whether or not Emily Dickinson expected you to.* Individual readers will arrive at their conclusions by way of different personal paths. And some readers may not get there at all—especially if they don't know that trains were once called iron horses. Our ability to make sense of literary texts comes, to a great extent, from what we already know about the culture from which the text emerges and from what we already know about reading texts, as well as from our own pattern of associations and memories.

Nor are we necessarily "finished" with our reading. We might, for example, go on to ask why Emily Dickinson chooses to compare a train to a horse and what that comparison says about her beliefs, or about the ideology from which the text emerged.

The Convention of Coherence

Here is another riddle.

Metaphors

Sylvia Plath

I'm a riddle in nine syllables,
An elephant, a ponderous house,
A melon strolling on two tendrils.
O red fruit, ivory, fine timbers!
This loaf's big with its yeasty rising.
Money's new-minted in this fat purse.
I'm a means, a stage, a cow in calf.
I've eaten a bag of green apples,
Boarded the train there's no getting off.

[handwritten margin notes: — pregnant woman — 9 syllables in each line]

The poem's title, "Metaphors," provides a hint about the kinds of gaps it will present to its readers: the word metaphor means an implied comparison or analogy between unlike things. (We shall attend to metaphor at greater length in Chapter Four.) And, because *I* is the only pronoun used in these comparisons, we might suspect that all of these descriptions refer to one person, the speaker. Notice that the poem (as a riddle) invites us to find only one answer to all of these questions—so that the answers to our gap questions need to be connected, not only with the "it" of the poem, but also with each other. We call this expectation the *convention of coherence:* readers expect that texts will be consistent with themselves, that a text will not wander off from its own main idea (which the convention of unity has prompted us to identify). In this case, we expect all of the poem to refer to the same condition of the same *I*. To construct a reading of this poem we need to formulate a gap-question: "what (one thing or person) might be described as (at one and the same time) a riddle, an elephant, a melon, etc.?" It may well seem that there could be no answer to this question, no way to bridge this particular gap. But because of the convention of coherence we are encouraged to look further.

[handwritten margin note: Everything connects w each other]

CONSTRUCTING A READING

1. Work with the kinds of associations or memories we discussed in the last chapter. What does the image of "a melon strolling on two tendrils" remind you of? Continue through each line, brainstorming and free associating until you arrive at a sense of the answer to this riddle.
2. When I teach this poem, the women in my classes frequently arrive at a reading before the men. On the basis of the discussion of diversity and difference in the last chapter, speculate about why this might be the case.

The Convention of Significance

Another convention, the *convention of significance*, suggests that our culture values poems, sees them as privileged and complicated texts that tend to make abstract statements about life in general. Readers expect poems to say something significant about life. The poem that follows invites its readers to invoke the convention of significance in its final line.

Nothing Gold Can Stay

Robert Frost

Nature's first green is gold,
Her hardest hue to hold.
Her early leaf's a flower;
But only so an hour.
Then leaf subsides to leaf.
So Eden sank to grief,
So dawn goes down to day.
Nothing gold can stay.

This poem presents many gaps. Let's begin with the first line, which invites the reader to make a connection.

Q. Why does the speaker equate nature's first green with gold?

On the surface, the proposition makes no sense, but the convention of unity leads us to expect that it *must* make sense in some way, so we begin to ask questions to help us figure out that sense. Let's try to make the gap question more precise.

Q. In what way is green like gold?

But before answering, we see that we need to ask another question:

Q. What does the speaker mean by gold—the metal or the color or both? And, what about "green"? The color, the part of a golf course? Money? Vegetation?

The second line gives us a clue and a temporary answer. Nature's first green, the color (hue) gold, does not last very long; it is nature's "hardest hue to hold." Our gap question now becomes,

Q. How is nature's first green something that is gold in color—but only briefly? In what sense could it make sense to say that?

One answer seems to come in the next line: "Her early leaf's a flower." Now we have two equations:

> Nature's first green = gold
> Nature's early leaf = a gold flower

The convention of coherence encourages us to think of these two equations as somehow equivalent, as saying the same thing.

> Nature's first green, which is a leaf, is a gold flower that does not last very long.

Now the speaker gives us more information about the situation being described.

> But only so an hour.
> Then leaf subsides to leaf.

But the new information comes with its own gap.

> **Q.** What does "so" mean?

From its position in the sentence, it would seem that here, "so," applied to the gold flower, means "like that." But then what? Knowing that "subsides" means to sink to a lower level or to become less active, we now can say that nature's first green, which is a gold flower, soon subsides into an ordinary green leaf.

So far, we seem to have a little poem about nature. But in the next lines, Frost complicates matters a bit and invites us to invoke the convention of significance.

> So Eden sank to grief,
> So dawn goes down to day.

We now have another equation: the statement that

> nature's first gold flowers turn to green leaves

is equal or analogous with the story of how

> Eden "sank to grief" when Adam and Eve were expelled from the Garden of Paradise to what we now call "mortal life"—

and those two propositions together equal the way

> dawn dwindles into an ordinary day.

Then comes the last line:

> Nothing gold can stay.

The convention of unity leads us to expect this last observation to explain the mysterious equations and tie the poem together somehow. The convention of significance leads us to expect that the connections we make will tell us something important about life in general. The text calls on us, in other words, to find a way in which each of these lines could be thought of as saying the same (important) thing about the conditions of our existence.

What link can we see among

- the seasons, in which nature's first green is gold,
- Adam and Eve's expulsion from the Garden of Eden
- the passage of an ordinary day, and
- the assertion that "nothing gold can stay"?

Looking now for a significant statement about life in general, I go back to reconsider my earlier questions and answers. By now, I suspect that this little poem is not just about flowers and plants, and so I rethink "gold" to mean not only the color of young plants, but also the value that culture attributes to young things, beginnings, innocence—all of them are rare and valuable like gold. In contemporary cultures, we often associate gold with value; we associate beginnings with innocence; we associate innocence with the kind of virtue Adam and Eve had in the garden, virtue that did not survive a test, virtue that did not last. Then I conclude that beautiful, natural moments, especially beginnings of all kinds, are transient, brief, and (therefore) valuable.

Let's think again about what we've done here. We have assumed that a text we call literary will present us with gaps, places where we know that we need to have more information. We have closed gaps by invoking conventions of unity, coherence, and significance. We have found or made unity, coherence and significance by using the processes of association and memory that we discussed in the last chapter, as we followed clues or responded to invitations that the text provided for us.

In the reading that I have just presented, "Nothing Gold Can Stay" becomes a poetic way of saying that life is the experience of transience. We may have arrived at different conclusions, but we have probably all participated in similar kinds of cognitive processes because those processes are deeply embedded in our culture. If your culture has not taught you to associate yellow flowers with Spring, or gold with value, you may not produce the meaning that the author intended, or the same meaning as other readers of these texts, but, if you take the trouble to make associations, you certainly will produce some meaning—your own.

HOW READERS (AND WRITERS) CAN PLAY WITH CONVENTIONS

Not every text yields itself easily to the three conventions I've just described. Some seem to abide by them strictly, some seem to fly in the face of them, and some seem to do both. Still, the conventions are useful to remember, both as a place to begin reading an unfamiliar text and as a baseline against which to measure a text's (or an author's) refusal to be bound by convention. Although the conventions will help you to make meaning of the text that follows, you may also see the text breaking them.

Living in Sin

Adrienne Rich

She had thought the studio would keep itself;
no dust upon the furniture of love.
Half heresy, to wish the taps less vocal,
the panes relieved of grime. A plate of pears,
a piano with a Persian shawl, a cat
stalking the picturesque amusing mouse
had risen at his urging.
Not that at five each separate stair would writhe
under the milkman's tramp; that morning light
so coldly would delineate the scraps
of last night's cheese and three sepulchral bottles;
that on the kitchen shelf among the saucers
a pair of beetle-eyes would fix her own—
envoy from some village in the moldings . . .
Meanwhile, he, with a yawn,
sounded a dozen notes upon the keyboard,
declared it out of tune, shrugged at the mirror,
rubbed at his beard, went out for cigarettes;
while she, jeered by the minor demons,
pulled back the sheets and made the bed and found
a towel to dust the table-top,
and let the coffee-pot boil over on the stove.
By evening she was back in love again,
though not so wholly but throughout the night
she woke sometimes to feel the daylight coming
like a relentless milkman up the stairs.

The story this poem tells presents several kinds of gaps, so it will be useful to begin by grouping them. One kind has to do with motivation.

Q. Why do the characters behave as they do?

Q. Why does the man play a few notes on the piano, declare it out of tune, and leave to get cigarettes?

Q. Why, after the man leaves, does the woman dust and make the bed and feel "jeered at by minor demons"?

Q. Who or what are these demons?

The conventions of coherence and significance would lead us to expect characters to behave in ways that are both internally consistent and idiomatic with the culture that the text represents. We expect that the man and the woman will be substantially the same characters at the end of the poem as they were at the beginning, and that they will behave in ways that are consistent with their culture. Let us begin then, by considering what the culture expected of men and women in the 1950s when this poem was written and first published.

> **Q.** What does (did) the title phrase, "Living in Sin," mean?
>
> **Q.** Do you use that term?
>
> **Q.** Do you know anyone who does?

If this couple is "living in sin," that is, living together without being married, at a time when such behavior is frowned upon, then we might say that the man and the woman believe that they love each other enough not to care what people think. They might have decided that they did not need a formal religious or civil marriage ceremony; they "feel married"; they "act married." Making that assumption helps me to see their behavior as consistent with the convention of unity. If they "act married," and "feel married," then they will both behave as married people conventionally do: for instance, they will both get irritable, he will leave to get cigarettes, and she will dust and worry about being a good "housewife."

The convention of significance then leads me to look for a statement about life in general.

> A couple "living in sin" will have the same kinds of experiences and feelings as a conventionally married couple.

However, many gaps remain—and, they seem not to be so easily bridged. The next group of gaps has to do with the descriptive details or imagery of the poem. The ways in which this studio apartment is described would seem to be telling us something, but what? In cases like this, where answers to gap-questions don't pop into our heads readily, it can be helpful to use freewriting. *Freewriting*, as you may know, is nonstop brainstorming on paper, just jotting down every associative responses that comes to mind when you think about, for instance:

> "dust upon the furniture of love,"
> "three sepulchral bottles,"
> "a pair of beetle eyes."

The idea is to let your mind wander, but also to think about conventions of coherence and significance. How are these descriptions appropriate? How not? Do they all "fit" with the reading so far?

> **Q.** What does the phrase "dust upon the furniture of love" make you think about?
>
> **Q.** How could a bottle be like a sepulchre? (If the word itself is unfamiliar to you, look it up in a dictionary!)
>
> **Q.** What kind of "beetle eyes" would be likely to appear "on a kitchen shelf among the saucers"?

Through attempting to answer these questions, you will probably begin building a sense of unity and coherence for the descriptive details. You might then think about confronting another gap: there seems to be an extraneous character here. What is the milkman doing in the story? Do you have any idea?

CONSTRUCTING A READING

1. Discuss the milkman with the members of your group and try, using the conventions of unity and coherence, to figure out what he is doing there.
2. Then, work together on a "group statement" about the meaning of the poem as a whole and share it with the rest of the class.
3. Discuss with the class the convention of coherence in the context of the poem's cultural milieu—the 1950s. Could this poem be written in today's sexual climate?

Poetry, of course, is not the only genre in which there are gaps. Sometimes the author of a story doesn't explain why characters do what they do, or how two different events in a narrative are connected, or how two ideas are like each other. In these cases, again, we close gaps by reading between the lines; we try to imagine what happens between the events the narrator does relate. The three conventions are still helpful. The convention of unity leads us to expect that everything in the story will be relevant to some unifying theme or idea; the convention of coherence suggests that characters will behave consistently; the convention of significance invites us to expect that the story will make some comment about existence. Try applying the conventions to Jean Rhys's story, "I Used To Live Here Once."

I Used to Live Here Once

Jean Rhys

She was standing by the river looking at the stepping stones and remembering each one. There was the round unsteady stone, the pointed one, the flat one in the middle—the safe stone where you could stand and look round. The next wasn't so safe for when the river was full the water flowed over it and even when it showed dry it was slippery. But after that it was easy and soon she was standing on the other side.

The road was much wider than it used to be but the work had been done carelessly. The felled trees had not been cleared away, and the bushes looked trampled. Yet it was the same road and she walked along feeling extraordinarily happy.

It was a fine day, a blue day. The only thing was that the sky had a glassy look that she didn't remember. That was the only word she could think of. Glassy. She turned the corner, saw that what had been the old pavé had been taken up, and there too the road was much wider, but it had the same unfin- ished look. {*Changes*}

She came to the worn stone steps that led up to the house and her heart began to beat. The screw pine was gone, so was the mock summer house called the ajoupa, but the clove tree was still there and at the top of the steps the rough lawn stretched away, just as she remembered it. She stopped and looked towards the house that had been added to and painted white. It was strange to see a car standing in front of it.

There were two children under the big mango tree, a boy and a little girl, and she waved to them and called "Hello" but they didn't answer her or turn their heads. Very fair children, as Europeans born in the West Indies so often are: as if the white blood is asserting itself against all odds.

The grass was yellow in the hot sunlight as she walked towards them. When she was quite close she called again, shyly: "Hello." Then, "I used to live here once," she said.

Still they didn't answer. When she said for the third time "Hello" she was quite near them. Her arms went out instinctively with the longing to touch them.

It was the boy who turned. His gray eyes looked straight into hers. His expression didn't change. He said: "Hasn't it gone cold all of a sudden. D'you notice? Let's go in." "Yes let's," said the girl.

Her arms fell to her sides as she watched them running across the grass to the house. That was the first time she knew. = *she's DEAD* · *GHOST*

CONSTRUCTING A READING

1. Make a brief list of two or three gap questions for this story and put them aside for a moment.
2. Then, write about your feelings and associations as you focus on the speaker of this story. Have you ever returned to a place you used to live or frequent, a place that is now occupied by someone else? What were your feelings?
3. Next, put yourself in the perspective of the children. Has anyone ever come to a place you now consider your own and described to you how

that place used to be? (Homecoming at your school, alumni returning to your dorm or sorority or fraternity house, a prior owner or resident returning to the place that you now call home?) What were your feelings?

4. Now return to your gap questions. Do you have any new thoughts about them? If so, reword or add to them, making any changes that now occur to you.

5. Share these gap questions with your group or class, paying particular attention to the three conventions. Can your group find answers for the gap questions that entail unity, metaphoric coherence, and significance?

6. Present your group's interpretation to the class.

7. After your discussions, are any gaps questions still left open? If so, would you say that these gaps are unbridgeable?

8. Then try to negotiate a "class statement" about the story's meaning— especially whether it's possible to close all the gaps and/or to agree upon closure.

Examining Conventions As a Group—Interpretive Communities

If you succeed in negotiating consensus in the foregoing exercise, you will have produced (or experienced) an *interpretive community*—a group of readers whose common interests explain why and how they tend to interpret a text's invitations in a similar way. These common interests might have to do with age, gender, race or ethnicity, social class, or with traits that are more difficult to perceive and categorize, such as occupation, religion, or political belief.

By reading and discussing the story that follows with your classmates, you will be preparing to see interpretive communities in action. An individual reader's responses to a text are almost always influenced by some sort of interpretive community—the community of the reader's classroom, family, race, or of the media, for instance. Think of how movie reviews influence the way we respond to movies. Reviews not only suggest to us whether we'll respond well to the film itself, they also encourage us to follow conventions in responding to it, conventions of unity and coherence, for instance. (We'll be talking in more detail about the conventions of reviews in Chapter Eight.)

Interpretive communities (such as moviegoers and reviewers) are often, of course, hotbeds of debate. The interests their members share do not in any way lead them to immediate agreement in their readings of texts. But through each community's debates some sort of consensus sometimes emerges, and that consensus often reveals a great deal about the community and its culture.

In reading the following story by John Updike, we can see how our own interpretive communities work, and how their "take" on a text like this one can change as a result of changes in their values, interests, histories, or politics.

A & P

John Updike

In walks these three girls in nothing but bathing suits. I'm in the third checkout slot, with my back to the door, so I don't see them until they're over by the bread. The one that caught my eye first was the one in the plaid green two-piece. She was a chunky kid, with a good tan and a sweet broad soft-looking can with those two crescents of white just under it, where the sun never seems to hit, at the top of the backs of her legs. I stood there with my hand on a box of HiHo crackers trying to remember if I rang it up or not. I ring it up again and the customer starts giving me hell. She's one of these cash-register-watchers, a witch about fifty with rouge on her cheekbones and no eyebrows, and I know it made her day to trip me up. She'd been watching cash registers for fifty years and probably never seen a mistake before.

By the time I got her feathers smoothed and her goodies into a bag—she gives me a little snort in passing, if she'd been born at the right time they would have burned her over in Salem—by the time I get her on her way the girls had circled around the bread and were coming back, without a pushcart, back my way along the counters, in the aisle between the checkouts and the Special bins. They didn't even have shoes on. There was this chunky one, with the two-piece—it was bright green and the seams on the bra were still sharp and her belly was still pretty pale so I guessed she just got it (the suit)—there was this one, with one of those chubby berry-faces, the lips all bunched together under her nose, this one, and a tall one, with black hair that hadn't quite frizzed right, and one of these sunburns right across under the eyes, and a chin that was too long—you know, the kind of girl other girls think is very "striking" and "attractive" but never quite makes it, as they very well know, which is why they like her so much—and then the third one, that wasn't quite so tall. She was the queen. She kind of led them, the other two peeking around and making their shoulders round. She didn't look around, not this queen, she just walked straight on slowly, on these long white primadonna legs. She came down a little hard on her heels, as if she didn't walk in bare feet that much, putting down her heels and then letting the weight move along to her toes as if she was testing the floor with every step, putting a little deliberate extra action into it. You never know for sure how girls' minds work (do you really think it's a mind in there or just a little buzz like a bee in a glass jar?) but you got the idea she had talked the other two into coming in here with her, and now she was showing them how to do it, walk slow and hold yourself straight.

She had on a kind of dirty-pink—beige maybe, I don't know—bathing suit with a little nubble all over it and, what got me, the straps were down. They were off her shoulders looped loose around the cool tops of her arms, and I guess as a result the suit had slipped a little on her, so all around the top of the cloth there was this shining rim. If it hadn't been there you wouldn't have known there could have been anything whiter than those shoulders. With the straps pushed off, there was nothing between the top of the suit and the top of her head except just *her*, this clean bare plane of the top of her chest down from the shoulder bones like a dented sheet of metal tilted in the light. I mean, it was more than pretty.

She had a sort of oaky hair that the sun and salt had bleached, done up in a bun that was unravelling, and a kind of prim face. Walking into the A & P with your straps down, I suppose it's the only kind of face you *can* have. She held her head so high her neck, coming up out of those white shoulders, looked kind of stretched, but I didn't mind. The longer her neck was, the more of her there was.

She must have felt in the corner of her eye me and over my shoulder Stokesie in the second slot watching, but she didn't tip. Not this queen. She kept her eyes moving across the racks, and stopped, and turned so slow it made my stomach rub the inside of my apron, and buzzed to the other two, who kind of huddled against her for relief, and then they all three of them went up the cat-and-dog-food-breakfast-cereal-macaroni-rice-raisins-seasonings-spreads-spaghetti-soft-drinks-crackers-and-cookies aisle. From the third slot I look straight up this aisle to the meat counter, and I watched them all the way. The fat one with the tan sort of fumbled with the cookies, but on second thought she put the package back. The sheep pushing their carts down the aisle—the girls were walking against the usual traffic (not that we have one-way signs or anything)—were pretty hilarious. You could see them, when Queenie's white shoulders dawned on them, kind of jerk, or hop, or hiccup, but their eyes snapped back to their own baskets and on they pushed. I bet you could set off dynamite in an A & P and the people would by and large keep reaching and checking oatmeal off their lists and muttering "Let me see, there was a third thing, began with A, asparagus, no, ah, yes, applesauce!" or whatever it is they do mutter. But there was no doubt, this jiggled them. A few house-slaves in pin curlers even looked around after pushing their carts past to make sure what they had seen was correct.

You know, it's one thing to have a girl in a bathing suit down on the beach, where what with the glare nobody can look at each other much anyway, and another thing in the cool of the A & P, under the fluorescent lights, against all those stacked packages, with her feet paddling along naked over our checker-board green-and-cream rubber-tile floor.

"Oh Daddy," Stokesie said beside me. "I feel so faint."

"Darling," I said. "Hold me tight." Stokesie's married, with two babies chalked up on his fuselage already, but as far as I can tell that's the only difference. He's twenty-two, and I was nineteen this April.

"Is it done?" he asks, the responsible married man finding his voice. I forgot to say he thinks he's going to be manager some sunny day, maybe in 1990 when it's called the Great Alexandrov and Petrooshki Tea Company or something.

What he meant was, our town is five miles from a beach, with a big summer colony out on the Point, but we're right in the middle of town, and the women generally put on a shirt or shorts or something before they get out of the car into the street. And anyway these are usually women with six children and varicose veins mapping their legs and nobody, including them, could care less. As I say, we're right in the middle of town, and if you stand at our front doors you can see two banks and the Congregational church and the newspaper store and three real-estate offices and about twenty-seven old freeloaders tearing up Central Street because the sewer broke again. It's not as if we're on the Cape; we're north of Boston and there's people in this town haven't seen the ocean for twenty years.

The girls had reached the meat counter and were asking McMahon something. He pointed, they pointed, and they shuffled out of sight behind a pyramid of Diet Delight peaches. All that was left for us to see was old McMahon patting his mouth and looking after them sizing up their joints. Poor kids, I began to feel sorry for them, they couldn't help it.

Now here comes the sad part of the story, at least my family says it's sad, but I don't think it's so sad myself. The store's pretty empty, it being Thursday afternoon, so there was nothing much to do except lean on the register and wait for the girls to show up again. The whole store was like a pinball machine and I didn't know which tunnel they'd come out of. After a while they come around out of the far aisle, around the light bulbs, records at discount of the Caribbean Six or Tony Martin Sings or some such gunk you wonder they waste the wax on, six-packs of candy bars, and plastic toys done up in cellophane that fall apart when a kid looks at them anyway. Around they come, Queenie still leading the way, and holding a little gray jar in her hand. Slots Three through Seven are unmanned and I could see her wondering between Stokes and me, but Stokesie with his usual luck draws an old party in baggy gray pants who stumbles up with four giant cans of pineapple juice (what do these bums do with all that pineapple juice? I've often asked myself) so the girls come to me. Queenie puts down the jar and I take it into my fingers icy cold. Kingfish Fancy Herring Snacks in Pure Sour Cream: 49¢. Now her hands are empty, not a ring or a bracelet, bare as God made them, and I wonder where the money's coming from. Still with that prim look she lifts a folded dollar bill out of the hollow at the center of her nubbled pink top. The jar went heavy in my hand. Really, I thought that was so cute.

Then everybody's luck begins to run out. Lengel comes in from haggling with a truck full of cabbages on the lot and is about to scuttle into that door marked MANAGER behind which he hides all day when the girls touch his eye.

Lengel's pretty dreary, teaches Sunday school and the rest, but he doesn't miss that much. He comes over and says, "Girls, this isn't the beach."

Queenie blushes, though maybe it's just a brush of sunburn I was noticing for the first time, now that she was so close. "My mother asked me to pick up a jar of herring snacks." Her voice kind of startled me, the way voices do when you see the people first, coming out so flat and dumb yet kind of tony, too, the way it ticked over "pick up" and "snacks." All of a sudden I slid right down her voice to her living room. Her father and the other men were standing around in ice-cream coats and bow ties and the women were in sandals picking up herring snacks on toothpicks off a big glass plate and they were all holding drinks the color of water with olives and sprigs of mint in them. When my parents have somebody over they get lemonade and if it's a real racy affair Schlitz in tall glasses with "They'll Do It Every Time" cartoons stencilled on.

"That's all right," Lengel said. "But this isn't the beach." His repeating this struck me as funny, as if it had just occurred to him, and he had been thinking all these years the A & P was a great big dune and he was the head lifeguard. He didn't like my smiling—as I say he doesn't miss much—but he concentrates on giving the girls that sad Sunday-school-superintendent stare.

Queenie's blush is no sunburn now, and the plump one in plaid, that I liked better from the back—a really sweet can—pipes up, "We weren't doing any shopping. We just came in for the one thing."

"That makes no difference," Lengel tells her, and I could see from the way his eyes went that he hadn't noticed she was wearing a two-piece before. "We want you decently dressed when you come in here."

"We *are* decent," Queenie says suddenly, her lower lip pushing, getting sore now that she remembers her place, a place from which the crowd that runs the A & P must look pretty crummy. Fancy Herring Snacks flashed in her very blue eyes.

"Girls, I don't want to argue with you. After this come in here with your shoulders covered. It's our policy." He turns his back. That's policy for you. Policy is what the kingpins want. What the others want is juvenile delinquency.

All this while, the customers had been showing up with their carts but, you know, sheep, seeing a scene, they had all bunched up on Stokesie, who shook open a paper bag as gently as peeling a peach, not wanting to miss a word. I could feel in the silence everybody getting nervous, most of all Lengel, who asks me, "Sammy, have you rung up their purchase?"

I thought and said "No" but it wasn't about that I was thinking. I go through the punches, 4, 9, GROC, TOT—it's more complicated than you think, and after you do it often enough, it begins to make a little song, that you hear words to, in my case "Hello (*bing*) there, you (*gung*) hap-py pee-pul (*splat*) "—the *splat* being the drawer flying out. I uncrease the bill, tenderly as you may imagine, it just having come from between the two smoothest scoops of vanilla

I had ever known there were, and pass a half and a penny into her narrow pink palm and nestle the herrings in a bag and twist its neck and hand it over, all the time thinking.

The girls, and who could blame them, are in a hurry to get out, so I say "I quit" to Lengel quick enough for them to hear, hoping they'll stop and watch me, their unsuspected hero. They keep right on going, into the electric eye; the door flies open and they flicker across the lot to their car, Queenie and Plaid and Big Tall Goony-Goony (not that as raw material she was so bad), leaving me with Lengel and a kink in his eyebrow.

"Did you say something, Sammy?"

"I said I quit."

"I thought you did."

"You didn't have to embarrass them."

"It was they who were embarrassing us."

I started to say something that came out "Fiddle-de-do." It's a saying of my grandmother's and I know she would have been pleased.

"I don't think you know what you're saying," Lengel said.

"I know you don't," I said. "But I do." I pull the bow at the back of my apron and start shrugging it off my shoulders. A couple of customers that had been heading for my slot begin to knock against each other like scared pigs in a chute.

Lengel sighs and begins to look very patient and old and gray. He's been a friend of my parents for years. "Sammy, you don't want to do this to your Mom and Dad," he tells me. It's true, I don't. But it seems to me that once you begin a gesture it's fatal not to go through with it. I fold the apron, "Sammy" stitched in red on the pocket and put it on the counter, and drop the bow tie on top of it. The bow tie is theirs. if you've ever wondered. "You'll feel this for the rest of your life." Lengel says, and I know that's true, too, but remembering how he made that pretty girl blush makes me so scrunchy inside I punch the No Sale tab and the machine whirs "pee-pul" and the drawer splats its out. One advantage to this scene taking place in summer, I can follow this up with a clean exit, there's no fumbling around getting your coat and galoshes, I just saunter into the electric eye in my white shirt that my mother ironed the night before, and the door heaves itself open, and outside the sunshine is skating around on the asphalt.

I look around for my girls, but they're gone, of course. There wasn't anybody but some young married screaming with her children about some candy they didn't get by the door of a powder-blue Falcon station wagon. Looking back in the big windows, over the bags of peat moss and aluminum lawn furniture stacked on the pavement, I could see Lengel in my place in the slot, checking the sheep through. His face was dark gray and his back stiff, as if he's just had an injection of iron, and my stomach kind of fell as I felt how hard the world was going to be to me hereafter.

CONSTRUCTING A READING

1.   Why does Sammy quit?
2.   What does Sammy mean when he says "I felt how hard the world was going to be to me hereafter"?
3.   How does Sammy view himself and his actions? Is there a gap between how you as a reader see him and how he sees himself? If so, how does this affect your reading of this story?
4.   Why do you think Updike shifts to the past tense in the last paragraph of the story?
5.   What sort of innocence has Sammy lost? Does his innocence seem like or unlike the sentiment in "Nothing Gold Can Stay" ("So Eden sank to grief")?
6.   Does the story evokes memories of your own adolescence? If so, write for a few minutes in your journal about the part or parts of the story that evoked your reminiscence. If not, write about how you do respond to the story.
7.   Discuss your responses to all these questions with your group, and compare them with others'. When there is agreement, can you identify a common interest that may have informed it?

How Readers Challenge Conventions: Reading against the Grain

"A & P" was first published in 1962. As I write about it and ask you to read it now, I feel uneasy about Sammy's attitudes toward the woman he calls Queenie and her friends. I suspect that many women (and men) who read "A & P" today might feel uncomfortable when Sammy muses about the white half-moons above Queenie's swimsuit top; or wonders how women's minds work "(do you really think it's a mind in there or just a little buzz like a bee in a glass jar?)" or compares a supermarket to a giant pinball machine in which the three young women become components of his game. I suspect, too, that some readers will see Sammy's gesture as foolish. Perhaps some older readers will see this story as evidence that young people will amount to no good because they are all obsessed with sex.

These responses are probably not the ones that Updike intended to evoke. (We can't know what Updike intended, of course, but I've just made an educated guess.) What are we to make of them? Are they wrong? No, they are not wrong. They are different—in the ways I described in Chapter One, and such differences are well worth examining. They happen when readers raise gap questions that emerge from their own, rather than the author's, worldview. When readers are offended by a character's actions or sentiments, or find the apparent significance of a poem or story to be at odds with their own ethical dispositions, or find themselves having any reading experience that they are fairly sure the author has not intended, they are *reading against the grain.* Such readings are among the most exciting aspects of literary studies today because they reveal some of the ways in which cultures establish value.

When Updike wrote this story in 1962, for example, the experience of gazing at another person, and through that gaze reducing the other to an object of pleasure, was considered the prerogative of heterosexual men in Western culture. Sammy's musings were typical of most men of his age and class. Now, however, readers are almost certainly aware of such changing attitudes as feminists' objections to male gazes like Sammy's and the putative cynicism of Gen X, and the conservative sexual ethic of the "religious right." And, many readers will think about these different responses whenever they read "A & P." To read this story against the grain is to see how literary texts reflect, challenge, and comment on the values of their times.

CONSTRUCTING A READING

1. "Sammy" (if he were real) would be in his late fifties now. Imagine that your uncle "Sammy" has just told you this story as you and he drive to the New England town where it is set. What would you say to him?

2. Imagine that a member of a feminist group at your school has objected to the inclusion of this story in your syllabus on the grounds that it is demeaning to women. On the basis of your reading of the story, write a letter to that person in which you agree or disagree with the position she or he takes.

3. With your group members, make a list of the aspects of this story that make it seem "dated."

4. Make another list of the aspects that are still relevant to young adults at the turn of the century.

The story that follows provides another opportunity to think about interpretive communities.

Butterflies

Patricia Grace

The grandmother plaited her granddaughter's hair and then she said, "Get your lunch. Put it in your bag. Get your apple. You come straight back after school, straight home here. Listen to the teacher," she said. "Do what she say."

Her grandfather was out on the step. He walked down the path with her and out onto the footpath. He said to a neighbor, "Our granddaughter goes to school. She lives with us now."

"She's fine," the neighbor said. "She's terrific with her two plaits in her hair."

"And clever," the grandfather said. "Writes every day in her book."

"She's fine," the neighbor said.

The grandfather waited with his granddaughter by the crossing and then he said, "Go to school. Listen to the teacher. Do what she say."

When the granddaughter came home from school her grandfather was hoeing around the cabbages. Her grandmother was picking beans. They stopped their work.

"You bring your book home?" the grandmother asked.

"Yes."

"You write your story?"

"Yes."

"What's your story?"

"About the butterflies."

"Get your book then. Read your story."

The granddaughter took her book from her schoolbag and opened it.

"I killed all the butterflies," she read. "This is me and this is all the butterflies."

"And your teacher like your story, did she?"

"I don't know"

"What your teacher say?"

"She said butterflies are beautiful creatures. They hatch out and fly in the sun. The butterflies visit all the pretty flowers, she said. They lay their eggs and then they die. You don't kill butterflies, that's what she said."

The grandmother and the grandfather were quiet for a long time, and their granddaughter, holding the book, stood quite still in the warm garden.

"Because you see," the grandfather said, "your teacher, she buy all her cabbages from the supermarket and that's why."

CONSTRUCTING A READING

1. With your group members, make a list of gap questions and do your best to answer them.
2. Speculate about the ethical position the story seems to invite you to take with respect to the little girl, her grandparents, and her teacher. Do you think that you are following the text's invitations or resisting them? Why?
3. Write a short account of a time in your childhood when you experienced a difference between the ethics of home and school.
4. Try to read this story against the grain. Write for a few minutes about what happens.

How Some Texts Challenge Conventions

The story that follows, Anne Leaton's "Like the Ant. Like the Praying Mantis," presents gaps that may be very difficult, and even impossible, to close.

Like the Ant. Like the Praying Mantis

Anne Leaton

She started the morning by killing an ant. It was a smooth, successful murder, with no evidence left at the scene. She deposited the segmented deep red and earth-brown carcass in the toilet bowl and flushed it away. The ant had been on the ceiling above her bed the night before, but when she woke, it was crawling up the counterpane towards her face. Perhaps it was a biting ant; how was she to know?

Then just before lunch the cat brought her a grass-green praying mantis, captured in the garden. She recoiled from it, while the cat stood swishing its tail and watching her, the insect held lightly in its jaws. Finally the cat dropped its prey at her feet, where it lay like a leaf. She picked it up between sheets of the morning newspaper, took it out to the back steps, and dropped a brick on it. She threw both the brick and the newspaper into the garbage bin. She felt rather sick. But it had probably nothing to do with the praying mantis. It was most likely the mushrooms she had eaten for breakfast; she sometimes found mushrooms indigestible.

She read a few recipes from the *Bouquet de France*. She had found these good against queasiness in the past, but today she was distracted by an image of Richard's face as it had looked when he told her—patiently, a little pained—that praying mantises were entirely harmless. 'You should have simply carried it out to the garden again and set it free. Why must you always kill these things?' She wouldn't tell him about today's praying mantis. It would be her secret, and the cat's.

Where was the cat? Only a moment ago she had seen it in the kitchen. She looked through the back windows into the garden and felt in her breast the usual curl of pleasure at the sight of her neat rows of clipped hedges and the raked paths through the middle of them and down the sides. There was a cluster of marigolds near the back wall, a few irises near the patio. A concession to Richard. She worked very hard in this garden, which she thought of as a large, tidy man, respectful of her in an eighteenth-century manner. He would never surprise her. Where she expunged, he would modestly retreat. Where she encouraged, he would gracefully, appropriately burgeon. The cat bothered her tidy man a little: its black flashed among the shrubbery like a glossy signal.

In the early afternoon she prepared a salad and sat on the small patio at the back of the house to eat it. I am not at all well, she thought, carefully chewing endive. My stomach. But she finished the salad and carried her plate inside.

'I am not afraid of him, not at all,' she said aloud, leaning against the kitchen sink. The pressure of the porcelain against her stomach soothed her. 'Not at all,' she repeated. 'Why should I be?'

The cat entered the kitchen through the open back door. It stood by the table looking at her with a wide green stare, as though it expected to be told something important. 'Go away,' she said. 'I'm ill. I don't want you here.' The cat stood so still it could have been black marble, a black marble cat to adorn her garden. 'You kill things,' she said. 'No one thinks anything of that.' The cat yawned, its eyes growing wild for a moment and its ears pointing backwards down its long head. It padded slowly back into the garden, dismissive. It's bored with me, she thought. Like Richard.

She boiled water and made herself a camomile tea, which she was sure would settle her stomach. Had she poisoned herself with a bad mushroom? She considered whether she should ring up Dr Taylor. He would want to see her before prescribing anything. It would be the next day before an appointment could be arranged. By then she would be all right again. The whole thing would be a waste of time. She disliked wasting time, doing things which had no effect, which came to no purpose.

Richard, she knew, was different. He loved doing things which led nowhere. He could sit for an hour on the patio playing with the cat, dangling a catnip mouse for the creature to jump at, swirling it around himself like a mata-dor's cape for the creature to chase. He would read part of a book and then part of another. Walk aimlessly around the garden with his hands in his pockets, stopping to stare up at the sky as though it were other than a perfect unbroken blue. She supposed it rested him, aimlessness, idleness. He was so busy, his work so burdensome. On such occasions she would leave the house and visit the nearby shops.

Finally, she lay down on the sunporch chaise. Her stomach churned, as though it were an ocean in a heavy wind. The nausea was worse; it pushed against her throat. She had nothing in the house to take for it. But rest, perhaps rest would help. She had slept poorly the night before.

After a moment she heard a soft murmur of laughter behind her, from the living room. Someone—a man—said, 'Never mind her, she sleeps like the dead.' Richard? The voice was familiar, but there was something disturbing in it. The simile, perhaps. Richard always spoke in a straightforward, declarative manner. Then a woman laughed. Unmistakably a woman: a tone like velvet, smooth and seductive. Who could she be? A business associate? He'd never spoken of a female business associate. She should get up at once and see if they needed anything. She heard the splash of liquid poured into glasses, the distur-bance of ice cubes in their metal container, their descent into the liquid. In the middle of the day? She thought. How unlike Richard.

She moved quietly to the living room door. 'But there's no need, is there?' the woman said. 'She's quite harmless, isn't she?'

The man said something in reply, but too softly for her to hear. Then they both laughed. She could see the shadow of his head on the door. She couldn't be sure it was Richard's head. If a strange man and a strange woman sat drinking in her living room, she should do something; she realised that. She should confront them. But she stood silently by the door, listening. She became aware that her heart was pounding furiously—she could see her blouse shaking above her left breast. Perhaps I shall faint, she thought. But why would I faint? Am I still so sick?

She entered the living room, moving slowly from behind the sofa towards the front, keeping her eyes fixed on the two heads tilted slightly towards each other, murmuring softly to each other. Was it Richard? There was hardly any sunlight coming through the window anymore. How could it have grown, suddenly, so dark? I must have slept without realising it, she thought.

'Richard?' she said, straining to see his face in the half-light.

'You mustn't worry about it,' the man said to the woman at his side. 'I'll take care of it. It's not for you to worry about.'

They must see me, she thought. They could not fail to see me now.

The woman leaned towards him, let the fingers of one hand drift from his hair to his mouth, kissed him passionately. He pressed against her, forcing her back against the sofa pillows.

'My God, Richard,' she said. 'Stop this! Stop this at once!'

He unlocked himself from the woman and turned his face towards her. His eyes were feverish and distant, his mouth drawn back into a grimace that distorted his face. But the face was, clearly, Richard's.

'What are you doing?' she said to him. 'What are you doing with this woman, in my house?'

He loosened his tie and drew it from around his neck. He began to unbutton his shirt. The woman said something indistinct to him, picked up her glass from the coffee table and swallowed the dregs.

'Don't think about it,' he said to her. 'She won't hear a thing. She won't even know we're in the house.'

'How could I not know you're in the house!' she said, and her voice vibrated comfortably in her head. 'Have you gone crazy? Who is this woman!'

The woman stood up and lifted her dress. She wore nothing underneath. She was as smooth and brown as caramel. Her laughter began as a whisper and became an aria that filled the room.

I am going to faint, she thought, feeling a buzzing whiteness encroaching upon her eyes. Then she straightened suddenly, alert. For Richard, snarling like an animal, had lunged at the woman's belly, his teeth seizing on her flesh. A red stream crawled towards her thigh. The woman hung limply in Richard's arms, pale, her eyes closed.

'Richard!' she screamed, moving back a step, raising her hands before her face. He turned his head towards her, not seeing her. It was a wide green stare, green as a plant, his mouth stretched tightly across his teeth, blood on his lips.

Something struck her on the chest, hard. My heart, she thought. It's killing me. She dropped one hand to her breast. It fell upon fur.

'You!' she screamed, rising from the chaise, grasping the cat with both hands and throwing it away from her violently. She stood in the half-dark sun-porch, shivering as though with a fatal chill. She clasped her arms about her body, swaying.

'Where are you?' she said. 'I'm going to kill you. Where are you hiding?' There was no movement in the room. The only sound was the rasp of her breath. Such a simple thing, she thought. Why haven't I done it before? Like the ant. Like the praying mantis. It's nothing. Only a cat. Where is it hiding?

She turned towards the windows. In the sun's last illumination she saw the cat vanishing into a hedge. It hesitated for a moment amid the foliage and stared towards the house, eyes green as a plant.

She heard Richard's key in the door and then his hesitation as he confronted the black interior of the house.

'Elizabeth?' he called. Then he switched on the overhead light in the foyer and shut the door behind him. 'Where the hell are you? Is something the matter?'

There was a muffled thump as he dropped his briefcase onto the table where it always rested until he moved it after dinner into his study. She heard him moving aimlessly around the living room. He was still for a moment; listening, she thought. Then he opened the liquor cabinet and poured himself a drink.

He'll be surprised, she thought. And then afraid. How will his face look when he's afraid? In ten years I've never seen that. It will be a new expression. Something completely different.

She sat out on the patio and looked over the garden: her large, tidy man, neatly barbered and respectful, lay sleeping in the moonlight. How lovely he is! she thought. Then just for a moment she thought she saw the flash of a black signal on the middle path. She grew tense and leaned forward in her chair. Then she remembered, and relaxed again, leaning back, smiling. Of course it wasn't the cat. Moonlight played tricks on her eyes. The cat was dead. In the living room. Lying next to the liquor cabinet, a glass overturned at the end of an out-stretched arm, a red stream crawling from his mouth and chest. It was such a simple thing, really. Why hadn't she thought of it before? Like the ant on the counterpane. Like the leaf-green praying mantis.

CONSTRUCTING A READING

1. Leaton's story seems deliberately to frustrate the conventions of reading. Write for a few moments about what happens when you try to find a single unifying idea or theme that ties its incidents together.

2.   Would you find it difficult to summarize this story to someone else? If so, describe the problem. If not, write the summary.

3.   What associations seem to form gaps for you as a reader? How, for example, is the garden "her tidy man?" Why do both Richard and the cat have stares that are "green as a plant"?

4.   How does the narration of this story affect your perceptions of its gaps?

5.   Make a list of other gap questions that occur to you or your group members. Try to separate your questions into categories. Are they about character or about significance or metaphoric coherence? Or do you need to create new categories? If so, how would you name them? Can all of your group's gaps be closed rationally?

The story that follows also challenges some of our conventional expectations. Try formulating some gap questions about *how* it does so, as you read.

What Did We Do Wrong?

Garrison Keillor

The first woman to reach the big leagues said she wanted to be treated like any other rookie, but she didn't have to worry about that. The Sparrows nicknamed her Chesty and then Big Numbers the first week of spring training, and loaded her bed at the Ramada with butterscotch pudding. Only the writers made a big thing about her being the First Woman. The Sparrows treated her like dirt.

Annie Szemanski arrived in camp fresh from the Federales League of Bolivia, the fourth second baseman on the Sparrows roster, and when Drayton stepped in a hole and broke his ankle Hemmie put her in the lineup, hoping she would break hers. "This was the front office's bright idea," he told the writers. "Off the record, I think it stinks." But when she got in she looked so good that by the third week of March she was a foregone conclusion. Even Hemmie had to admit it. A .346 average tells no lies. He disliked her purely because she was a woman—there was nothing personal about it. Because she *was* a woman, she was given the manager's dressing room, and Hemmie had to dress with the team. He was sixty-one, a heavy-weight, and he had a possum tattooed on his belly alongside the name "Georgene," so he was shy about taking his shirt off in front of people. He hated her for making it necessary. Other than that, he thought she was a tremendous addition to the team.

Asked how she felt being the first woman to make a major-league team, she said, "Like a pig in mud," or words to that effect, and then turned and released a squirt of tobacco juice from the wad of rum-soaked plug in her right cheek. She chewed a rare brand of plug called Stuff It, which she learned to chew when she was playing Nicaraguan summer ball. She told the writers, "They were so mean to me down there you couldn't write it in your newspaper. I took a gun everywhere I went, even to bed. *Especially* to bed. Guys were after me like you can't believe. That's when I started chewing tobacco—because no matter how bad anybody treats you, it's not as bad as this. This is the worst chew in the world. After this, everything else is peaches and cream." The writers elected Gentleman Jim, the Sparrows' P.R. guy, to bite off a chunk and tell them how it tasted, and as he sat and chewed it tears ran down his old sunburnt cheeks and he couldn't talk for a while. Then he whispered, "'You've been chewing this for two years? God, I had no idea it was so hard to be a woman."

When thirty-two thousand fans came to Cold Spring Stadium on April 4th for Opening Day and saw the scrappy little freckle-faced woman with tousled black hair who they'd been reading about for almost two months, they were dizzy with devotion. They chanted her name and waved Annie flags and Annie caps ($8.95 and $4.95) and held up handpainted bedsheets ("EVERY DAY IS LADIES' DAY," "A WOMAN'S PLACE—AT SECOND BASE," "E.R.A. & R.B.I." "THE GAME AIN'T OVER TILL THE BIG LADY BATS"), but when they saw No. 18 trot out to second with a load of chew as big as if she had the mumps it was a surprise. Then, bottom of the second, when she leaned over in the on-deck circle and dropped a stream of brown juice in the sod, the stadium experienced a moment of thoughtful silence.

One man in Section 31 said, "Hey, what's the beef? She can chew if she wants to. This is 1987. Grow up."

"I guess you're right," his next-seat neighbor said. "My first reaction was nausea, but I think you're right."

"Absolutely. She's a woman, but, more than that, she's a *person*."

Other folks said, "I'm with you on that. A woman can carry a quarter pound of chew in her cheek and spit in public, same as any man—why should there be any difference?"

And yet. Nobody wanted to say this, but the plain truth was that No. 18 was not handling her chew well at all. Juice ran down her chin and dripped onto her shirt. She's bit off more than she can chew, some people thought to themselves, but they didn't want to say that.

Arnie (the Old Gardener) Brixius mentioned it ever so gently in his "Hot Box" column the next day:

> It's only this scribe's opinion. but isn't it about time baseball cleaned up its act and left the tobacco in the locker? Surely big leaguers can go two hours without nicotine. Many a fan has turned away in disgust at the sight of grown men (and now a member her of the fair sex) with a faceful, spitting gobs of the stuff in full view of paying customers. Would Frank Sinatra do this on stage? Or Anne Murray? Nuff said.

End of April, Annie was batting .278, with twelve R.B.I.s, which for the miserable Sparrows was stupendous, and at second base she was surprising a number of people, including base runners who thought she'd be a pushover on the double play. A runner heading for second quickly found out that Annie had knees like ballpeen hammers and if he tried to eliminate her from the play she might eliminate him from the rest of the week. One night, up at bat against the Orioles, she took a step toward the mound after an inside pitch and yelled some things, and when the dugouts emptied she was in the thick of it with men who had never been walloped by a woman before. The home-plate ump hauled her off a guy she was pounding the cookies out of, and a moment later he threw her out of the game for saying things to him, he said, that he had never heard in his nineteen years of umpiring. ("Like what, for example?" writers asked. "Just tell us one thing." But he couldn't; he was too upset.)

The next week, the United Baseball Office Workers local passed a resolution in support of Annie, as did the League of Women Voters and the Women's Softball Caucus, which stated, "Szemanski is a model for all women who are made to suffer guilt for their aggressiveness, and we declare our solidarity with her heads-up approach to the game. While we feel she is holding the bat too high and should bring her hips into her swing more, we're behind her one hundred per cent."

Then, May 4th, at home against Oakland—seventh inning, two outs, bases loaded—she dropped an easy pop-up and three runs came across home plate. The fans sent a few light boos her way to let her know they were paying attention, nothing serious or overtly political, just some folks grumbling, but she took a few steps toward the box seats and yelled something at them that sounded like—well, something she shouldn't have said, and after the game she said some more things to the writers that Gentleman Jim pleaded with them not to print. One of them was Monica Lamarr, of the *Press*, who just laughed. She said, "Look, I spent two years in the Lifestyles section writing about motherhood vs. career and the biological clock. Sports is my way out of the gynecology ghetto, so don't ask me to eat this story. It's a hanging curve and I'm going for it. I'm never going to write about day care again." And she wrote it:

SZEMANSKI RAPS FANS
AS "SMALL PEOPLE"
AFTER DUMB ERROR GIVES
GAME TO A'S

FIRST WOMAN ATTRIBUTES BOOS
TO SEXUAL INADEQUACY IN STANDS

Jim made some phone calls and the story was yanked and only one truckload of papers went out with it, but word got around, and the next night, though Annie went three for four, the crowd was depressed, and even when she did great the rest of the home stand, and became the first woman to hit a major-league triple, the atmosphere at the ballpark was one of moodiness and deep hurt. Jim went to the men's room one night and found guys standing in line there, looking thoughtful and sad. One of them said, "She's a helluva ballplayer," and other guys murmured that yes, she was, and they wouldn't take anything away from her, she was great and it was wonderful that she had opened up baseball to women, and then they changed the subject to gardening, books, music, aesthetics, anything but baseball. They looked like men who had been stood up.

Gentleman Jim knocked on her door that night. She wore a blue chenille bathrobe flecked with brown tobacco-juice stains, and her black hair hung down in wet strands over her face. She spat into a Dixie cup she was carrying. "Hey! How the Fritos are you? I haven't seen your Big Mac for a while," she said, sort of. He told her she was a great person and a great ballplayer and that he loved her and wanted only the best for her, and he begged her to apologize to the fans.

"Make a gesture—anything. They *want* to like you. Give them a chance to like you."

She blew her nose into a towel She said that she wasn't there to be liked, she was there to play ball.

It was a good road trip. The Sparrows won five out of ten, lifting their heads off the canvas, and Annie raised her average to .291 and hit the first major-league home run ever by a woman, up into the left-field screen at Fenway. Sox fans stood and cheered for fifteen minutes. They whistled, they stamped, they pleaded, the Sparrows pleaded, umpires pleaded, but she refused to come out and tip her hat until the public-address announcer said, "No. 18, please come out of the dugout and take a bow. No. 18, the applause is for you and is not intended as patronizing in any way," and then she stuck her head out for 1.5 seconds and did not tip but only touched the brim. Later, she told the writers that just because people had expectations didn't mean she had to fulfill them— she used other words to explain this, but her general drift was that she didn't care very much about living up to anyone else's image of her, and if anyone thought she should, they could go watch wrist wrestling.

The forty thousand who packed Cold Spring Stadium June 6th to see the Sparrows play the Yankees didn't come for a look at Ron Guidry. Banners hung from the second deck: "WHAT DID WE DO WRONG?" and "ANNIE COME HOME" and "WE LOVE YOU, WHY DO YOU TREAT US THIS WAY?" and "IF YOU WOULD LIKE TO DISCUSS THIS IN A NON-CONFRONTATIONAL, MUTUALLY RESPECTFUL WAY, MEET US AFTER THE GAME AT GATE C." It was Snapshot Day, and all the Sparrows appeared on the field for photos with the fans except you know who. Hemmie begged her to go. "You owe it to them," he said.

"Owe?" she said. "*Owe?*"

"Sorry, wrong word," he said. "What if I put it this way: it's a sort of tradition."

"*Tradition?*" she said. "I'm supposed to worry about *tradition?*"

That day, she became the first woman to hit .300. A double in the fifth inning. The scoreboard flashed the message, and the crowd gave her a nice hand. A few people stood and cheered, but the fans around them told them to sit down. "She's not that kind of person," they said. "Cool it. Back off." The fans were trying to give her plenty of space. After the game, Guidry said, "I really have to respect her. She's got that small strike zone and she protects it well, so she makes you pitch to her." She said, "Guidry? Was that his name? I didn't know. Anyway, he didn't show me much. He throws funny, don't you think? He reminded me a little bit of a southpaw I saw down in Nicaragua, except she threw inside more."

All the writers were there, kneeling around her. One of them asked if Guidry had thrown her a lot of sliders.

She gave him a long, baleful look. "Jeez, you guys are out of shape," she said. "You're wheezing and panting and sucking air, and you just took the elevator *down* from the press box. You guys want to write about sports you ought to go into training. And then you ought to learn how to recognize a slider. Jeez, if you were writing about agriculture, would you have to ask someone if those were Holsteins?"

Tears came to the writer's eyes. "I'm trying to help," he said. "Can't you see that? Don't you know how much we care about you? Sometimes I think you put up this tough exterior to hide your own insecurity."

She laughed and brushed the wet hair back from her forehead. "It's no exterior," she said as she unbuttoned her jersey. "It's who I am." She peeled off her socks and stepped out of her cubicle a moment later, sweaty and stark naked. The towel hung from her hand. She walked slowly around them. "You guys learned all you know about women thirty years ago. That wasn't me back then, that was my mother." The writers bent over their notepads, writing down every word she said and punctuating carefully. Gentleman Jim took off his glasses. "My mother was a nice lady, but she couldn't hit the curve to save her Creamettes," she went on. "And now, gentlemen, if you'll excuse me, I'm going to take a shower." They pored over their notes until she was gone, and then they piled out into the hallway and hurried back to the press elevator.

Arnie stopped at the Shortstop for a load of Martinis before he went to the office to write the "Hot Box," which turned out to be about love:

> Baseball is a game but it's more than a game, baseball is people, dammit, and if you are around people you can't help but get involved in their lives and care about them and then you don't know how to talk to them or tell them how much you care and how come we know so much about pitching and we don't know squat about how to communicate? I guess that is the question.

The next afternoon, Arnie leaned against the batting cage before the game, hung over, and watched her hit line drives, fifteen straight, and each one made his head hurt. As she left the cage, he called over to her. "Later," she said. She also declined a pregame interview with Joe Garagiola, who had just told his NBC "Game of the Week" television audience, "This is a city in love with a little girl named Annie Szemanski," when he saw her in the dugout doing deep knee bends. "Annie! Annie!" he yelled over the air. "Let's see if we can't get her up here," he told the home audience. "Annie! Joe Garagiola!" She turned her back to him and went down into the dugout.

That afternoon, she became the first woman to steal two bases in one inning. She reached first on a base on balls, stole second, went to third on a sacrifice fly, and headed for home on the next pitch. The Catcher came out to make the tag, she caught him with her elbow under the chin, and when the dust cleared she was grinning at the ump, the catcher was sprawled in the grass trying to inhale, and the ball was halfway to the backstop.

The TV camera zoomed in on her, head down, trotting toward the dugout steps, when suddenly she looked up. Some out-of-town fan had yelled at her from the box seats. ("A profanity which also refers to a female dog," the News said.) She smiled and, just before she stepped out of view beneath the dugout roof, millions observed her right hand uplifted in a familiar gesture. In bars around the country, men looked at each other and said, "Did she do what I think I saw her do? She didn't do that, did she?" In the booth, Joe Garagiola was observing that it was a clean play, that the runner has a right to the base path, but when her hand appeared on the screen he stopped. At home, it sounded as if he had been hit in the chest by a rock. The screen went blank, then went to a beer commercial. When the show resumed, it was the middle of the next inning.

On Monday, for "actions detrimental to the best interests of baseball," Annie was fined a thousand dollars by the Commissioner and suspended for two games. He deeply regretted the decision, etc. "I count myself among her most ardent fans. She is good for baseball, good for the cause of equal rights, good for America." He said he would be happy to suspend the suspension if she would make a public apology, which would make him the happiest man in America.

Gentleman Jim went to the bank Monday afternoon and got the money, a thousand dollars, in a cashier's check. All afternoon, he called Annie's number over and over, waiting thirty and forty rings, then trying again. He called from a pay phone at the Stop 'N' Shop next door to the Cityview Apartments, where she lived, and between calls he sat in his car and watched the entrance, waiting for her to come out. Other men were parked there, too, in front, and some in back—men with Sparrows bumper stickers. After midnight, about eleven of them were left. "Care to share some onion chips and clam dip?" one guy said to another guy. Pretty soon all of them were standing around the trunk of the clam-dip guy's car, where he also had a case of beer.

"Here, let me pay you something for this beer," said a guy who had brought a giant box of pretzels.

"Hey, no. Really. It's just good to have other guys to talk to tonight," said the clam-dip owner.

"She changed a lot of very basic things about the whole way that I look at myself as a man," the pretzel guy said quietly.

"I'm in public relations," said Jim, "but even I don't understand all that she has meant to people."

"How can she do this to us?" said a potato-chip man. "All the love of the fans, how can she throw it away? Why can't she just play ball?"

Annie didn't look at it that way. "Pall Mall! I'm not going to crawl just because some Tootsie Roll says crawl, and if they don't like it, then Ritz, they can go Pepsi their Hostess Twinkies," she told the writers as she cleaned out her locker on Tuesday morning. They had never seen the inside of her locker before. It was stuffed with dirty socks, half unwrapped gifts from admiring fans, a set of ankle weights, and a small silver-plated pistol. "No way I'm going to pay a thousand dollars, and if they expect an apology—well, they better send out for lunch, because it's going to be a long wait. Gentlemen, goodbye and hang on to your valuable coupons." And she smiled her most winning smile and sprinted up the stairs to collect her paycheck. They waited for her outside the Sparrows office, twenty-six men, and then followed her down the ramp and out of Gate C. She broke into a run and disappeared into the lunchtime crowd on West Providence Avenue, and that was the last they saw of her—the woman of their dreams, the love of their lives, carrying a red gym bag, running easily away from them.

CONSTRUCTING A READING

1. The narrator reports that "Later, she told the writers that just because people had expectations didn't mean she had to fulfill them." Apply Annie's sentiments to Keillor's story.

2. Describe the tensions you perceive between Annie's sense of herself and the expectations of the fans, the organizations, the writers, and the other players. What expectations does the speaker seem to have?

3. Explore the way gender shapes these expectations for the characters, the speaker, and yourself as a reader. Consider, for instance, the various reactions of your class members.

4. This story first appeared in 1985. Do you think it still has something to say about the women's lives in sport, or women's lives in general? If so what? and how? Do you find its comment appropriate? Do you read it against the grain?

SHARING A READING

Write a short essay in which you explain how you closed (or tried to close, or somehow negotiated) the gaps you found in one of these three stories: "Butterflies," "Like the Ant. Like the Praying Mantis," and "What Did We Do Wrong?"

Assume that your reader is a fellow student who knows our terminology (gaps, conventions, difference, diversity, etc.) and the details of the story, but has been unable to come to terms with it. You need to explain how and why you arrived at your reading.

Remember that your project involves sharing a private experience (your reading of a literary work) with another person. One of your first problems, then, is to establish a common ground with your reader. Although you and your reader may both have read the same text, our discussion so far suggests that differences among reading perceptions and interpretive communities may be great enough to override that common experience. As we have learned in this chapter, different readers find different gaps and resolve them in different ways; sometimes too, readers may find they cannot close a gap, or simply choose not to.

One approach might be to explain why the gaps you have chosen to discuss are interesting or important to you. To get started, you might try an invention technique like freewriting, paraphrasing, or writing a response statement. If you can say why a question is important to you, you can probably arouse your reader's interest.

You will also need to think about shaping or organizing for this reader. You might, for example, explain in a narrative, organized chronologically, how you solved the problems that you isolated and came to your conclusions. Or, you might describe more than one reading, explaining how subsequent readings deepened your sense of the text. Or, you might decide to state your conclusion at the beginning of your paper and then explain why you think your reading makes sense. That paper would be organized as an argument, offering several reasons why your reader should agree that your reading is appropriate.

TEXTS FOR FURTHER READING

London

William Blake

I wander through each chartered street,
Near where the chartered Thames does flow
And mark in every face I meet
Marks of weakness, marks of woe.

In every cry of every man,
In every infant's cry of fear,
In every voice, in every ban,
The mind-forged manacles I hear.

How the chimney sweeper's cry
Every black'ning church appalls;
And the hapless soldier's sigh
Runs in blood down palace walls.

But most through midnight streets I hear
How the youthful harlot's curse
Blasts the newborn infant's tear,
And blights with plagues the marriage hearse.

CONSTRUCTING A READING

1. Look up the word "charter" in an unabridged dictionary. Then try to imagine what it might mean for a street to be chartered. Freewrite to try to find a way in which streets and rivers might be chartered.
2. Do you find a connection between the cries of the man and those of the infant in stanza two? Between the chimney sweep and the soldier in stanza three? Write a sentence or two in which you try to follow the text's invitation to find coherence among these descriptions.
3. We do not usually connect marriage and death. How do you explain the phrase "marriage hearse"? Can you think of any instances, consistent with the descriptions in the earlier stanzas, in which marriage might bring death and in which harlots could blast an infant's tear?
4. After you have thought about individual gaps and discussed them with your group, write a brief account of how you unify the poem.

Cathedral

Raymond Carver

This blind man, an old friend of my wife's, he was on his way to spend the night. His wife had died. So he was visiting the dead wife's relatives in Connecticut. He called my wife from his in-laws'. Arrangements were made. He would come by train, a five-hour trip, and my wife would meet him at the station. She hadn't seen him since she worked for him one summer in Seattle ten years ago. But she and the blind man had kept in touch. They made tapes and mailed them back and forth. I wasn't enthusiastic about his visit. He was no one I knew. And his being blind bothered me. My idea of blindness came from the movies. In the movies, the blind moved slowly and never laughed. Sometimes they were led by seeing-eye dogs. A blind man in my house was not something I looked forward to.

That summer in Seattle she had needed a job. She didn't have any money. The man she was going to marry at the end of the summer was in officers' training school. He didn't have any money, either. But she was in love with the guy, and he was in love with her, etc. She'd seen something in the paper: HELP WANTED—*Reading to Blind Man*, and a telephone number. She'd worked with this blind man all summer. She read stuff to him, case studies, reports, that sort of thing. She helped him organize his little office in the county social-service department. They'd become good friends, my wife and the blind man. How do I know these things? She told me. And she told me something else. On her last day in the office, the blind man asked if he could touch her face. She agreed to this. She told me he touched his fingers to every part of her face, her nose—even her neck! She never forgot it. She even tried to write a poem about it. She was always trying to write a poem. She wrote a poem or two every year, usually after something really important had happened to her.

When we first started going out together, she showed me the poem. In the poem, she recalled his fingers and the way they had moved around over her face. In the poem, she talked about what she had felt at the time, about what went through her mind when the blind man touched her nose and lips. I can remember I didn't think much of the poem. Of course, I didn't tell her that. Maybe I just don't understand poetry. I admit it's not the first thing I reach for when I pick up something to read.

Anyway, this man who'd first enjoyed her favors, the officer-to-be, he'd been her childhood sweetheart. So okay. I'm saying that at the end of the summer she let the blind man run his hands over her face, said goodbye to him, married her childhood etc., who was now a commissioned officer, and she moved away from Seattle. But they'd kept in touch, she and the blind man. She made the first contact after a year or so. She called him up one night from an Air Force base in Alabama. She wanted to talk. They talked. He asked her to send him a tape and tell him about her life. She did this. She sent the tape. On the tape, she told the blind man about her husband and about their life together in the military. She told the blind man she loved her husband but she didn't like it where they lived and she didn't like it that he was a part of the military-industrial thing. She told the blind man she'd written a poem and he was in it. She told him that she was writing a poem about what it was like to be an Air Force officer's wife. The poem wasn't finished yet. She was still writing it. The blind man made a tape. He sent her the tape. She made a tape. This went on for years. My wife's officer was posted to one base and then another. She sent tapes from Moody AFB, McGuire, McConnell, and finally Travis, near Sacramento, where one night she got to feeling lonely and cut off from people she kept losing in that moving-around life. She got to feeling she couldn't go it another step. She went in and swallowed all the pills and capsules in the medicine chest and washed them down with a bottle of gin. Then she got into a hot bath and passed out.

But instead of dying, she got sick. She threw up. Her officer—why should he have a name? he was the childhood sweetheart, and what more does he want?—came home from somewhere, found her, and called the ambulance. In time, she put it all on a tape and sent the tape to the blind man. Over the years, she put all kinds of stuff on tapes and sent the tapes off lickety-split. Next to writing a poem every year, I think it was her chief means of recreation. On one tape, she told the blind man she'd decided to live away from her officer for a time. On another tape, she told him about her divorce. She and I began going out, and of course she told her blind man about it. She told him everything, or so it seemed to me. Once she asked me if I'd like to hear the latest tape from the blind man. This was a year ago. I was on the tape, she said. So I said okay, I'd listen to it. I got us drinks and we settled down in the living room. We made ready to listen. First she inserted the tape into the player and adjusted a couple of dials. Then she pushed a lever. The tape squeaked and someone began to talk in this loud voice. She lowered the volume. After a few minutes of harmless chitchat, I heard my own name in the mouth of this stranger, this blind man I didn't even know! And then this: "From all you've said about him, I can only conclude—" But we were interrupted, a knock at the door, something, and we didn't ever get back to the tape. Maybe it was just as well. I'd heard all I wanted to.

Now this same blind man was coming to sleep in my house.

"Maybe I could take him bowling," I said to my wife. She was at the draining board doing scalloped potatoes. She put down the knife she was using and turned around.

"If you love me," she said, "you can do this for me. If you don't love me, okay. But if you had a friend, any friend, and the friend came to visit, I'd make him feel comfortable." She wiped her hands with the dish towel.

"I don't have any blind friends," I said.

"You don't have *any* friends," she said. "Period. Besides," she said, "god-damn it, his wife's just died! Don't you understand that? The man's lost his wife!"

I didn't answer. She'd told me a little about the blind man's wife. Her name was Beulah. Beulah! That's a name for a colored woman.

"Was his wife a Negro?" I asked.

"Are you crazy?" my wife said. "Have you just flipped or something?" She picked up a potato. I saw it hit the floor, then roll under the stove. "What's wrong with you?" she said. "Are you drunk?"

"I'm just asking," I said.

Right then my wife filled me in with more detail than I cared to know. I made a drink and sat at the kitchen table to listen. Pieces of the story began to fall into place.

Beulah had gone to work for the blind man the summer after my wife had stopped working for him. Pretty soon Beulah and the blind man had themselves a church wedding. It was a little wedding—who'd want to go to such a wedding in the first place?—just the two of them, plus the minister and the minister's wife. But it was a church wedding just the same. It was what Beulah had wanted, he'd said. But even then Beulah must have been carrying the cancer in her glands. After they had been inseparable for eight years—my wife's word, *inseparable*—Beulah's health went into a rapid decline. She died in a Seattle hospital room, the blind man sitting beside the bed and holding onto her hand. They'd married, lived and worked together, slept together—had sex, sure—and then the blind man had to bury her. All this without his having ever seen what the goddamned woman looked like. It was beyond my understanding. Hearing this, I felt sorry for the blind man for a little bit. And then I found myself thinking what a pitiful life this woman must have led. Imagine a woman who could never see herself as she was seen in the eyes of her loved one. A woman who could go on day after day and never receive the smallest compliment from her beloved. A woman whose husband could never read the expression on her face, be it misery or something better. Someone who could wear makeup or not—what difference to him? She could, if she wanted, wear green eye-shadow around one eye, a straight pin in her nostril, yellow slacks and purple shoes, no matter. And then to slip off into death, the blind man's hand on her hand, his blind eyes streaming tears—I'm imagining now—her last thought maybe this: that he never even knew what she looked like, and she on an express to the grave. Robert was left with a small insurance policy and half of a twenty-peso Mexican coin. The other half of the coin went into the box with her. Pathetic.

So when the time rolled around, my wife went to the depot to pick him up. With nothing to do but wait—sure, I blamed him for that—I was having a drink and watching the TV when I heard the car pull into the drive. I got up from the sofa with my drink and went to the window to have a look.

I saw my wife laughing as she parked the car. I saw her get out of the car and shut the door. She was still wearing a smile. Just amazing. She went around to the other side of the car to where the blind man was already starting to get out. This blind man, feature this, he was wearing a full beard! A beard on a blind man! Too much, I say. The blind man reached into the back seat and dragged out a suitcase. My wife took his arm, shut the car door, and, talking all the way, moved him down the drive and then up the steps to the front porch. I turned off the TV. I finished my drink, rinsed the glass, dried my hands. Then I went to the door.

My wife said, "I want you to meet Robert. Robert, this is my husband. I've told you all about him." She was beaming. She had this blind man by his coat sleeve.

The blind man let go of his suitcase and up came his hand.

I took it. He squeezed hard, held my hand, and then he let it go.

"I feel like we've already met," he boomed.

"Likewise," I said. I didn't know what else to say. Then I said, "Welcome. I've heard a lot about you." We began to move then, a little group, from the porch into the living room, my wife guiding him by the arm. The blind man was carrying his suitcase in his other hand. My wife said things like, "To your left here, Robert. That's right. Now watch it, there's a chair. That's it. Sit down right here. This is the sofa. We just bought this sofa two weeks ago.

I started to say something about the old sofa. I'd liked that old sofa. But I didn't say anything. Then I wanted to say something else, small-talk, about the scenic ride along the Hudson. How going *to* New York, you should sit on the right-hand side of the train, and coming *from* New York, the left-hand side.

"Did you have a good train ride?" I said, "Which side of the train did you sit on, by the way?"

"'What a question; which side!" my wife said. "What's it matter which side?" she said.

"I just asked," I said.

"Right side," the blind man said. "I hadn't been on a train in nearly forty years. Not since I was a kid. With my folks. That's been a long time. I'd nearly forgotten the sensation. I have winter in my beard now," he said. "So I've been told, anyway. Do I look distinguished, my dear?" the blind man said to my wife.

"You look distinguished, Robert," she said. "Robert," she said. "Robert, it's just so good to see you."

My wife finally took her eyes off the blind man and looked at me. I had the feeling she didn't like what she saw. I shrugged.

I've never met, or personally known, anyone who was blind. This blind man was late forties, a heavy-set, balding man with stooped shoulders, as if he carried a great weight there. He wore brown slacks, brown shoes, a light-brown shirt, a tie, a sports coat. Spiffy. He also had this full beard. But he didn't use a cane and he didn't wear dark glasses. I'd always thought dark glasses were a must for the blind. Fact was, I wished he had a pair. At first glance, his eyes looked like anyone else's eyes. But if you looked close, there was something different about them. Too much white in the iris, for one thing, and the pupils seemed to move around in the sockets without his knowing it or being able to stop it. Creepy. As I stared at his face, I saw the left pupil turn in toward his nose while the other made an effort to keep in one place. But it was only an effort, for that eye was on the roam without his knowing it or wanting it to be.

I said, "Let me get you a drink. What's your pleasure? We have a little of everything. It's one of our pastimes."

"Bub, I'm a Scotch man myself," he said fast enough in this big voice.

"Right," I said. Bub! "Sure you are. I knew it."

He let his fingers touch his suitcase, which was sitting alongside the sofa. He was taking his bearings. I didn't blame him for that.

"I'll move that up to your room," my wife said.

"No, that's fine," the blind man said loudly. "It can go up when I go up."

"A little water with the Scotch?" I said.

"Very little," he said.

"I knew it," I said.

He said, "Just a tad. The Irish actor, Barry Fitzgerald? I'm like that fellow. When I drink water, Fitzgerald said, I drink water. When I drink whiskey, I drink whiskey." My wife laughed. The blind man brought his hand up under his beard. He lifted his beard slowly and let it drop.

I did the drinks, three big glasses of Scotch with a splash of water in each. Then we made ourselves comfortable and talked about Robert's travels. First the long flight from the West Coast to Connecticut, we covered that. Then from Connecticut up here by train. We had another drink concerning that leg of the trip.

I remembered having read somewhere that the blind didn't smoke because, as speculation had it, they couldn't see the smoke they exhaled. I thought I knew that much and that much only about blind people. But this blind man smoked his cigarette down to the nubbin and then lit another one. This blind man filled his ashtray and my wife emptied it.

When we sat down at the table for dinner, we had another drink. My wife heaped Robert's plate with cube steak, scalloped potatoes, green beans. I buttered him up two slices of bread. I said, "Here's bread and butter for you." I swallowed some of my drink. "Now let us pray," I said, and the blind man lowered his head. My wife looked at me, her mouth agape. "Pray the phone won't ring and the food doesn't get cold," I said.

We dug in. We ate everything there was to eat on the table. We ate like there was no tomorrow. We didn't talk. We ate. We scarfed. We grazed that table. We were into serious eating. The blind man had right away located his foods, he knew just where everything was on his plate. I watched with admiration as he used his knife and fork on the meat. He'd cut two pieces of meat, fork the meat into his mouth, and then go all out for the scalloped potatoes, the beans next, and then he'd tear off a hunk of buttered bread and eat that. He'd follow this up with a big drink of milk. It didn't seem to bother him to use his fingers once in a while, either.

We finished everything, including half a strawberry pie. For a few moments, we sat as if stunned. Sweat beaded on our faces. Finally, we got up from the table and left the dirty plates. We didn't look back. We took ourselves into the living room and sank into our places again. Robert and my wife sat on the sofa. I took the big chair. We had us two or three more drinks while they talked about the major things that had come to pass for them in the past ten years. For the most part, I just listened. Now and then I joined in. I didn't want him to think I'd left the room, and I didn't want her to think I was feeling left out. They talked of things that had happened to them—to them!—these past ten years. I waited in vain to hear my name on my wife's sweet lips: "And then my dear husband came into my life"—something like that. But I heard nothing of the sort. More talk of Robert. Robert had done a little of everything, it seemed, a regular blind jack-of-all-trades. But most recently he and his wife had had an Amway distributorship, from which, I gathered, they'd earned their living, such as it was. The blind man was also a ham radio operator. He talked in his loud voice about conversations he'd had with fellow operators in Guam, in the Philippines, in Alaska, and even in Tahiti. He said he'd have a lot of friends there if he ever wanted to go visit those places. From time to time, he'd turn his blind face toward me, put his hand under his beard, ask me something. How long had I been in my present position? (Three years.) Did I like my work? (I didn't.) Was I going to stay with it? (What were the options?) Finally, when I thought he was beginning to run down, I got up and turned on the TV.

My wife looked at me with irritation. She was heading toward a boil. Then she looked at the blind man and said, "Robert, do you have a TV?"

The blind man said, "My dear, I have two TVs. I have a color set and a black-and-white thing, an old relic. It's funny, but if I turn the TV on, and I'm always turning it on, I turn on the color set. It's funny, don't you think?"

I didn't know what to say to that. I had absolutely nothing to say to that. No opinion. So I watched the news program and tried to listen to what the announcer was saying.

"This is a color TV," the blind man said. "Don't ask me how, but I can tell."

"We traded up a while ago," I said.

The blind man had another taste of his drink. He lifted his beard, sniffed it, and let it fall. He leaned forward on the sofa. He positioned his ashtray on the coffee table, then put the lighter to his cigarette. He leaned back on the sofa and crossed his legs at the ankles.

My wife covered her mouth, and then she yawned. She stretched. She said, "I think I'll go upstairs and put on my robe. I think I'll change into something else. Robert, you make yourself comfortable," she said.

"I'm comfortable," the blind man said.

"I want you to feel comfortable in this house," she said.

"I am comfortable," the blind man said.

After she'd left the room, he and I listened to the weather report and then to the sports roundup. By that time, she'd been gone so long I didn't know if she was going to come back. I thought she might have gone to bed. I wished she'd come back downstairs. I didn't want to be left alone with a blind man. I asked him if he wanted another drink, and he said sure. Then I asked if he wanted to smoke some dope with me. I said I'd just rolled a number. I hadn't, but I planned to do so in about two shakes.

"I'll try some with you," he said.

"Damn right," I said. "That's the stuff."

I got our drinks and sat down on the sofa with him. Then I rolled us two fat numbers. I lit one and passed it. I brought it to his fingers. He took it and inhaled.

"Hold it as long as you can," I said. I could tell he didn't know the first thing.

My wife came back downstairs wearing her pink robe and her pink slippers.

"'What do I smell?" she said.

"'We thought we'd have us some cannabis," I said.

My wife gave me a savage look. Then she looked at the blind man and said, "Robert, I didn't know you smoked."

He said, "I do now, my dear. There's a first time for everything. But I don't feel anything yet."

"This stuff is pretty mellow," I said. "This stuff is mild. It's dope you can reason with," I said. "It doesn't mess you up."

"Not much it doesn't, bub," he said, and laughed.

My wife sat on the sofa between the blind man and me. I passed her the number. She took it and toked and then passed it back to me. "Which way is this going?" she said. Then she said, "I shouldn't be smoking this. I can hardly keep my eyes open as it is. That dinner did me in. I shouldn't have eaten so much."

"It was the strawberry pie," the blind man said. "That's what did it," he said, and he laughed his big laugh. Then he shook his head.

"There's more strawberry pie," I said.

"Do you want some more, Robert?" my wife said.

"Maybe in a little while," he said.

We gave our attention to the TV. My wife yawned again. She said, "Your bed is made up when you feel like going to bed, Robert. I know you must have had a long day. When you're ready to go to bed, say so." She pulled his arm. "Robert?"

He came to and said, "I've had a real nice time. This beats tapes, doesn't it?"

I said, "Coming at you," and I put the number between his fingers. He inhaled, held the smoke, and then let it go. It was like he'd been doing it since he was nine years old.

"Thanks, bub," he said. "But I think this is all for me. I think I'm beginning to feel it," he said. He held the burning roach out for my wife.

"Same here," she said. "Ditto. Me, too." She took the roach and passed it to me. "I may just sit here for a while between you two guys with my eyes closed. But don't let me bother you, okay? Either one of you. If it bothers you, say so. Otherwise, I may just sit here with my eyes closed until you're ready to go to bed," she said. "Your bed's made up, Robert, when you're ready. It's right next to our room at the top of the stairs. We'll show you up when you're ready. You wake me up now, you guys, if I fall asleep." She said that and then she closed her eyes and went to sleep.

The news program ended. I got up and changed the channel. I sat back down on the sofa. I wished my wife hadn't pooped out. Her head lay across the back of the sofa, her mouth open. She'd turned so that her robe had slipped away from her legs, exposing a juicy thigh. I reached to draw her robe back over her, and it was then that I glanced at the blind man. What the hell! I flipped the robe open again.

"You say when you want some strawberry pie," I said.

"I will," he said.

I said, "Are you tired? Do you want me to take you up to your bed? Are you ready to hit the hay?"

"Not yet," he said. "No, I'll stay up with you, bub. If that's all right. I'll stay up until you're ready to turn in. We haven't had a chance to talk. Know what I mean? I feel like me and her monopolized the evening." He lifted his beard and he let it fall. He picked up his cigarettes and his lighter.

"That's all right," I said. Then I said, "I'm glad for the company."

And I guess I was. Every night I smoked dope and stayed up as long as I could before I fell asleep. My wife and I hardly ever went to bed at the same time. When I did go to sleep, I had these dreams. Sometimes I'd wake up from one of them, my heart going crazy.

Something about the church and the Middle Ages was on the TV. Not your run-of-the-mill TV fare. I wanted to watch something else. I turned to the other channels. But there was nothing on them, either. So I turned back to the first channel and apologized.

"Bub, it's all right," the blind man said. "It's fine with me. Whatever you want to watch is okay. I'm always learning something. Learning never ends. It won't hurt me to learn something tonight. I got ears," he said.

• • •

We didn't say anything for a time. He was leaning forward with his head turned at me, his right ear aimed in the direction of the set. Very disconcerting. Now and then his eyelids drooped and then they snapped open again. Now and then he put his fingers into his beard and tugged, like he was thinking about something he was leaning on the television.

On the screen, a group of men wearing cowls was being set upon and tormented by men dressed in skeleton costumes and men dressed as devils. The men dressed as devils wore devil masks, horns, and long tails. This pageant was part of a procession. The Englishman who was narrating the thing said it took place in Spain once a year. I tried to explain to the blind man what was happening.

"Skeletons," he said. "I know about skeletons," he said, and he nodded.

The TV showed this one cathedral. Then there was a long, slow look at another one. Finally, the picture switched to the famous one in Paris, with its flying buttresses and its spires reaching up to the clouds. The camera pulled away to show the whole of the cathedral rising above the skyline.

There were times when the Englishman who was telling the thing would shut up, would simply let the camera move around over the cathedrals. Or else the camera would tour the countryside, men in fields walking behind oxen. I waited as long as I could. Then I felt I had to say something. I said, "They're showing the outside of this cathedral now. Gargoyles. Little statues carved to look like monsters. Now I guess they're in Italy. Yeah, they're in Italy. There's paintings on the walls of this one church."

"Are those fresco paintings, bub?" he asked, and he sipped from his drink.

I reached for my glass. But it was empty. I tried to remember what I could remember. "You're asking me are those frescoes?" I said. "That's a good question. I don't know."

The camera moved to a cathedral outside Lisbon. The differences in the Portuguese cathedral compared with the French and Italian were not that great. But they were there. Mostly the interior stuff. Then something occurred to me, and I said, "Something has occurred to me. Do you have any idea what a cathedral is? What they look like, that is? Do you follow me? If somebody says cathedral to you, do you have any notion what they're talking about? Do you know the difference between that and a Baptist church, say?"

He let the smoke dribble from his mouth. "I know they took hundreds of workers fifty or a hundred years to build," he said. "I just heard the man say that, of course. I know generations of the same families worked on a cathedral. I heard him say that, too. The men who began their life's work on them, they never lived to see the completion of their work. In that wise, bub, they're no different from the rest of us, right?" He laughed. Then his eyelids drooped again. His head nodded. He seemed to be snoozing. Maybe he was imagining himself in Portugal. The TV was showing another cathedral now. This one was in Germany. The Englishman's voice droned on. "Cathedrals," the blind man said. He sat up and rolled his head back and forth. "If you want the truth, bub, that's about all I know. What I just said. What I heard him say. But maybe you could describe one to me? I wish you'd do it. I'd like that. If you want to know, I really don't have a good idea."

I stared hard at the shot of the cathedral on the TV. How could I even begin to describe it? But say my life depended on it. Say my life was being threatened by an insane guy who said I had to do it or else.

I stared some more at the cathedral before the picture flipped off into the countryside. There was no use. I turned to the blind man and said, "To begin with, they're very tall." I was looking around the room for clues. "They reach way up. Up and up. Toward the sky. They're so big, some of them, they have to have these supports. To help hold them up, so to speak. These supports are called buttresses. They remind me of viaducts, for some reason. But maybe you don't know viaducts, either? Sometimes the cathedrals have devils and such carved into the front. Sometimes lords and ladies. Don't ask me why this is," I said.

He was nodding. The whole upper part of his body seemed to be moving back and forth.

"I'm not doing so good, am I?" I said.

He stopped nodding and leaned forward on the edge of the sofa. As he listened to me, he was running his fingers through his beard. I wasn't getting through to him, I could see that. But he waited for me to go on just the same. He nodded, like he was trying to encourage me. I tried to think what else to say. "They're really big," I said. "They're massive. They're built of stone. Marble, too, sometimes. In those olden days, when they built cathedrals, men wanted to be close to God. In those olden days, God was an important part of everyone's life. You could tell this from their cathedral-building. I'm sorry," I said, "but it looks like that's the best I can do for you. I'm just no good at it."

"That's all right, bub," the blind man said. "Hey, listen. I hope you don't mind my asking you. Can I ask you something? Let me ask you a simple question, yes or no. I'm just curious and there's no offense. You're my host. But let me ask if you are in any way religious? You don't mind my asking?"

I shook my head. He couldn't see that, though. A wink is the same as a nod to a blind man. "I guess I don't believe in it. In anything. Sometimes it's hard. You know what I'm saying?"

"Sure, I do," he said.

"Right," I said.

The Englishman was still holding forth. My wife sighed in her sleep. She drew a long breath and went on with her sleeping.

"You'll have to forgive me," I said. "But I can't tell you what a cathedral looks like. It just isn't in me to do it. I can't do any more than I've done."

The blind man sat very still, his head down, as he listened to me.

I said, "The truth is, cathedrals don't mean anything special to me. Nothing. Cathedrals. They're something to look at on late-night TV. That's all they are."

It was then that the blind man cleared his throat. He brought something up. He took a handkerchief from his back pocket. Then he said, "I get it, bub. It's okay. It happens. Don't worry about it," he said. "Hey, listen to me. Will you do me a favor? I got an idea. Why don't you find us some heavy paper? And a pen. We'll do something. We'll draw one together. Get us a pen and some heavy paper. Go on, bub, get the stuff," he said.

So I went upstairs. My legs felt like they didn't have any strength in them. They felt like they did after I'd done some running. In my wife's room, I looked around. I found some ballpoints in a little basket on her table. And then I tried to think where to look for the kind of paper he was talking about.

Downstairs, in the kitchen, I found a shopping bag with onion skins in the bottom of the bag. I emptied the bag and shook it. I brought it into the living room and sat down with it near his legs. I moved some things, smoothed the wrinkles from the bag, spread it out on the coffee table.

The blind man got down from the sofa and sat next to me on the carpet.

He ran his fingers over the paper. He went up and down the sides of the paper. The edges, even the edges. He fingered the corners.

"All right," he said. "All right, let's do her."

He found my hand, the hand with the pen. He closed his hand over my hand. "Go ahead, bub, draw," he said. "Draw. You'll see. I'll follow along with you. It'll be okay. Just begin now like I'm telling you. You'll see. Draw," the blind man said.

So I began. First I drew a box that looked like a house. It could have been the house I lived in. Then I put a roof on it. At either end of the roof, I drew spires. Crazy.

"Swell," he said. "Terrific. You're doing fine," he said. "Never thought anything like this could happen in your lifetime, did you, bub? Well, it's a strange life, we all know that. Go on now. Keep it up."

I put in windows with arches. I drew flying buttresses. I hung great doors. I couldn't stop. The TV station went off the air. I put down the pen and closed and opened my fingers. The blind man felt around over the paper. He moved the tips of his fingers over the paper, all over what I had drawn, and he nodded.

"Doing fine," the blind man said.

I took up the pen again, and he found my hand. I kept at it. I'm no artist. But I kept drawing just the same.

My wife opened up her eyes and gazed at us. She sat up on the sofa, her robe hanging open. She said, "What are you doing? Tell me, I want to know."

I didn't answer her.

The blind man said, "We're drawing a cathedral. Me and him are working on it. Press hard," he said to me. "That's right. That's good," he said. "Sure. You got it, bub. I can tell. You didn't think you could. But you can, can't you? You're cooking with gas now. You know what I'm saying? We're going to really have us something here in a minute. How's the old arm?" he said. "Put some people in there now. What's a cathedral without people?"

My wife said, "What's going on? Robert, what are you doing? What's going on?"

"It's all right," he said to her. "Close your eyes now," the blind man said to me.

I did it. I closed them just like he said.

"Are they closed?" he said. "Don't fudge."

"They're closed," I said.

"Keep them that way," he said. He said, "Don't stop now. Draw."

So we kept on with it. His fingers rode my fingers as my hand went over the paper. It was like nothing else in my life up to now.

Then he said, "I think that's it. I think you got it," he said. "Take a look. What do you think?"

But I had my eyes closed. I thought I'd keep them that way for a little longer. I thought it was something I ought to do.

"Well?" he said. "Are you looking?"

My eyes were still closed. I was in my house. I knew that. But I didn't feel like I was inside anything.

"It's really something," I said.

CONSTRUCTING A READING

1. Formulate questions about the motivation of the characters in "Cathedral." Why, for example, does the wife attempt suicide? Why does she become so fond of the blind man? The convention of unity might lead us to expect that her actions will be explicable in terms of a desire or lack. Do you find that the convention of unity works here?

2. How does the speaker/husband's attitude toward the blind man change? Why?

3. Speculate about the importance of the title "Cathedral."

The Rocking-Horse Winner

D. H. Lawrence

There was a woman who was beautiful, who started with all the advantages, yet she had no luck. She married for love, and the love turned to dust. She had bonny children, yet she felt they had been thrust upon her, and she could not love them. They looked at her coldly, as if they were finding fault with her. And hurriedly, she felt she must cover up some fault in herself. Yet what it was that she must cover up, she never knew. Nevertheless, when her children were present, she always felt the centre of her heart go hard. This troubled her, and in her manner she was all the more gentle and anxious for her children, as if she loved them very much. Only she herself knew that at the centre of her heart was a hard little place that could not feel love, no, not for anybody. Everybody else said of her: "She is such a good mother. She adores her children." Only she herself, and her children themselves, knew it was not so. They read it in each other's eyes.

There was a boy and two little girls. They lived in a pleasant house with a garden, and they had discreet servants, and felt themselves superior to anyone in the neighbourhood.

Although they lived in style, they felt always an anxiety in the house. There was never enough money. The mother had a small income, and the father had a small income, but not nearly enough for the social position which they had to keep up. The father went in to town to some office. But though he had good prospects, these prospects never materialised. There was always the grinding sense of the shortage of money, though the style was always kept up.

At last the mother said: "I will see if *I* can't make something." But she did not know where to begin. She racked her brains, and tried this thing and the other, but could not find anything successful. The failure made deep lines come into her face. Her children were growing up, they would have to go to school. There must be more money, there must be more money. The father, who was always very handsome and expensive in his tastes, seemed as if he never *would* be able to do anything worth doing. And the mother, who had a great belief herself, did not succeed any better, and her tastes were just as expensive.

And so the house came to be haunted by the unspoken phrase: *There must be more money! There must be more money!* The children could hear it all the time, though nobody ever said it aloud. They heard it at Christmas, when the expensive and splendid toys filled the nursery. Behind the shining modern rocking-horse, behind the smart doll's house, a voice would start whispering: There *must* be more money! There *must* be more money! And the children would stop playing, to listen for a moment. They would look into each other's eyes, to see if they had all heard. And each one saw in the eyes of the other two, that they too had heard. "There *must* be more money! There must be more money."

It came whispering from the springs of the still-swaying rocking-horse, and even the horse, bending his wooden, champing head, heard it. The big doll, sitting so pink and smirking in her new pram, could hear it quite plainly, and seemed to be smirking all the more self-consciously because of it. The foolish puppy, too, that took the place of the teddy bear, he was looking so extraordinarily foolish for no other reason but that he heard the secret whisper all over the house: "There must be more money."

Yet nobody ever said it aloud. The whisper was everywhere, and therefore no-one spoke it. Just as no-one ever says: "We are breathing!", in spite of the fact that breath is coming and going all the time.

"Mother!" said the boy Paul one day. "Why don't we keep a car of our own? Why do we always use uncle's, or else a taxi?"

"Because we're the poor members of the family," said the mother.

"But why *are* we, Mother?"

"Well—I suppose—" she said slowly and bitterly—"it's because your father has no luck."

The boy was silent for some time.

"Is luck money, Mother?" he asked, rather timidly.

"No, Paul! Not quite. It's what causes you to have money."

"Oh!" said Paul vaguely. "I thought when Uncle Oscar said *filthy lucker* it meant money."

"*Filthy lucre* does mean money," said the mother. "But it's lucre, not luck."

"Oh!" said the boy. "Then what *is* luck, Mother?"

"It's what causes you to have money. If you're lucky you have money. That's why it's better to be born lucky than rich. If you're rich, you may lose your money. But if you're lucky, you will always get more money."

"Oh! Will you! And is father not lucky?"

"Very unlucky, I should say," she said bitterly.

The boy watched her with unsure eyes.

"Why?" he asked.

"I don't know. Nobody ever knows why one person is lucky and another unlucky."

"Don't they? Nobody at all? Does *nobody* know?"

"Perhaps God! But he never tells."

"He ought to then.—And aren't you lucky either, Mother?"

"I can't be, if I married an unlucky husband."

"But by yourself, aren't you?"

"I used to think I was, before I married. Now I think I am very unlucky indeed."

"Why?"

"Well—never mind! Perhaps I'm not really," she said.

The child looked at her, to see if she meant it. But he saw, by the lines at her mouth, that she was only trying to hide something from him.

"Well anyhow," he said stoutly, "I'm a lucky person."

"Why?" said his mother, with a sudden laugh.

He stared at her. He didn't even know why he had said it.

"God told me," he asserted, brazening it out.

"I hope he did, Dear!" she said, again with a laugh, but rather bitter.

"He did, Mother!"

"Excellent!" said the mother, using one of her husband's exclamations.

The boy saw she did not believe him: or rather, that she paid no attention to his assertion. This angered him somewhere, and made him want to compel her attention.

He went off by himself, vaguely, in a childish way, seeking for the clue to "luck." Absorbed, taking no heed of other people, he went about with a sort of stealth, seeking inwardly for luck. He wanted luck, he wanted it, he wanted it. When the two girls were playing dolls, in the nursery, he would sit on his big rocking horse, charging madly into space, with a frenzy that made the little girls peer at him uneasily. Wildly the horse careered, the waving dark hair of the boy tossed, his eyes had a strange glare in them. The little girls dared not speak to him.

When he had ridden to the end of his mad little journey, he climbed down and stood in front of his rocking-horse, staring fixedly into its lowered face. Its red mouth was slightly open, its big eye was wide and glassy bright.

"Now!" he would silently command the snorting steed. "Now take me to where there is luck! Now take me!"

And he would slash the horse on the neck with the little whip he had asked Uncle Oscar for. He *knew* the horse could take him to where there was luck, if only he forced it. So he would mount again, and start on his furious ride, hoping at last to get there. He knew he could get there.

"You'll break your horse, Paul!" said the nurse.

"He's always riding like that! I wish he'd leave off!" said his elder sister Joan.

But he only glared down at them in silence. Nurse gave him up. She could make nothing of him. Anyhow he was growing beyond her.

One day his mother and his Uncle Oscar came in when he was on one of his furious rides. He did not speak to them.

"Hello! you young jockey! Riding a winner?" said his Uncle.

"Aren't you growing too big for a rocking horse? You're not a very little boy any longer, you know," said his mother.

But Paul only gave a blue glare from his big, rather close-set eyes. He would speak to nobody when he was in full tilt. His mother watched him with a curious expression on her face.

At last he suddenly stopped forcing his horse into the mechanical gallop and slid down.

"Well I got there!" he announced fiercely, his blue eyes still flaring, and his sturdy long legs straddling apart.

"Where did you get to?" asked his mother.

"Where I wanted to go to," he flared back at her.

"That's right, Son!" said Uncle Oscar. "Don't you stop till you get there. —What's the horse's name?"

"He doesn't have a name," said the boy.

"Gets on without all right?" asked the Uncle.

"Well, he has different names. He was called Sansovino last week."

"Sansovino, eh? Won the Ascot. How did you know his name?"

"He always talks about horse-races with Bassett," said Joan.

The uncle was delighted to find that his small nephew was posted with all the racing news. Bassett, the young gardener who had been wounded in the left foot in the war, and had got his present job through Oscar Cresswell, whose batman he had been, was a perfect blade of the "turf." He lived in the racing events. And the small boy lived with him.

Oscar Cresswell got it all from Bassett.

"Master Paul comes and asks me, so I can't do more than tell him, Sir," said Bassett, his face terribly serious, as if he were speaking of religious matters.

"And does he ever put anything on a horse he fancies?"

"Well—I don't want to give him away—he's a young sport, a fine sport, Sir. Would you mind asking him himself? He sort of takes a pleasure in it, and perhaps he'd feel I was giving him away, Sir, if you don't mind."

Bassett was serious as a church.

The uncle went back to his nephew, and took him off for a ride in the car.

"Say, Paul, old man, do you ever put anything on a horse?" the uncle asked.

The boy watched the handsome man closely.

"Why, do you think I oughtn't to?" he parried.

"Not a bit of it! I thought perhaps you might give me a tip for the Lincoln."

The car sped on into the country, going down to Uncle Oscar's place in Hampshire.

"Honour bright?" said the nephew.

"Honour bright, Son!" said the Uncle.

"Well then, Daffodil."

"Daffodil! I doubt it, Sonny. What about Mirza?"

"I only know the winner," said the boy. "That's Daffodil!"

"Daffodil, eh?"

There was a pause. Daffodil was an obscure horse, comparatively.

"Uncle!"

"Yes Son!"

"You won't let it go any further, will you? I promised Bassett."

"Bassett be damned, old man! What's he got to do with it?"

"We're partners! We've been partners from the first! Uncle, he lent me my first five shillings which I lost. I promised him, honour bright, it was only between me and him: only you gave me that ten shilling note I started winning with, so I thought you were lucky. You won't let it go any further, will you?"

The boy gazed at his uncle from those big, hot blue eyes, set rather close together. The uncle stirred and laughed uneasily.

"Right you are, Son! I'll keep your tip private. Daffodil, eh?—How much are you putting on him?"

"All except twenty pounds," said the boy. "I keep that in reserve." The uncle thought it a good joke.

"You keep twenty pounds in reserve, do you, you young romancer? What are you betting, then?"

"I'm betting three hundred," said the boy gravely. "But it's between you and me, Uncle Oscar! Honour bright?"

The uncle burst into a roar of laughter.

"It's between you and me all right, you young Nat Gould,'" he said, laughing. "But where's your three hundred?"

"Bassett keeps it for me. We're partners.

"You are, are you! And what is Bassett putting on Daffodil?"

"He won't go quite as high as I do, I expect. Perhaps he'll go a hundred and fifty."

"What, pennies?" laughed the Uncle.

"Pounds," said the child, with a surprised look at his uncle. "Bassett keeps a bigger reserve than I do."

Between wonder and amusement, Uncle Oscar was silent. He pursued the matter no further, but he determined to take his nephew with him to the Lincoln races.

"Now Son," he said, "I'm putting twenty on Mirza, and I'll put five for you on any horse you fancy. What's your pick?"

"Daffodil, Uncle!"

"No, not the fiver on Daffodil!"

"I should if it was my own fiver," said the child.

"Good! Good! Right you are! A fiver for me and a fiver for you, on Daffodil."

The child had never been to a race-meeting before, and his eyes were blue fire. He pursed his mouth tight, and watched. A Frenchman just in front had put his money on Lancelot. Wild with excitement, he flayed his arms up and down, yelling *Lancelot! Lancelot!*—in his French accent.

Daffodil came in first, Lancelot second, Mirza third. The child, flushed and with eyes blazing, was curiously serene. His uncle brought him five five-pound notes: four to one.

"What am I to do with these?" he cried, waving them before the boy's eyes.

"I suppose we'll talk to Bassett," said the boy. "I expect I have fifteen hundred now: and twenty in reserve: and this twenty."

His uncle studied him for some moments.

"Look here, Son!" he said. "You're not serious about Bassett and that fifteen hundred, are you?"

"Yes, I am. But it's between you and me, Uncle! Honour bright!"

"Honour bright all right, Son! But I must talk to Bassett."

"If you'd like to be a partner. Uncle, with Bassett and me, we could all be partners. Only you'd have to promise, Honour bright, Uncle, not to let it go beyond us three. Bassett and I are lucky, and you must be lucky, because it was your ten shillings I started winning with— —"

Uncle Oscar took both Bassett and Paul into Richmond Park for an afternoon, and there they talked.

"It's like this, you see, Sir," Bassett said. "Master Paul would get me talking about racing events, spinning yarns you know, Sir. And he was always keen on knowing if I'd made or if I'd lost. It's about a year since, now, that I put five shillings on Blush of Dawn for him: and we lost. Then the luck turned, with that ten shillings he had from you, that we put on Singhalese. And since that time, it's been pretty steady, all things considering. What do you say, Master Paul?"

"We're all right when we're *sure*," said Paul. "It's when we're not quite sure that we go down."

"Oh, but we're careful then," said Bassett.

"But when are you *sure?*" smiled Uncle Oscar.

"It's Master Paul, Sir!" said Bassett, in a secret, religious voice. "It's as if he had it from heaven. Like Daffodil, now, for the Lincoln. That was as sure as eggs."

"Did you put anything on Daffodil?" asked Oscar Cresswell.

"Yes Sir! I made my bit."

"And my nephew?"

Bassett was obstinately silent, looking at Paul.

"I made twelve hundred, didn't I, Bassett? I told Uncle I was putting three hundred on Daffodil."

"That's right!" said Bassett, nodding.

"But where's the money?" asked the uncle.

"I keep it safe locked up, Sir. Master Paul, he can have it any minute he likes to ask for it."

"What, fifteen hundred pounds?"

"And twenty! And *forty*, that is, with the twenty he made on the course."

"It's amazing!" said the uncle.

"If Master Paul offers you to be partners, Sir, I would if I were you: if you'll excuse me," said Bassett.

Oscar Cresswell thought about it.

"I'll see the money," he said.

They drove home again, and sure enough, Bassett came round to the garden house with fifteen hundred pounds in notes. The twenty pounds reserve was left with Joe Glee, in the Turf Commission deposit.

"You see it's all right, Uncle, when I'm *sure!* Then we go strong, for all we're worth. Don't we, Bassett?"

"We do that, Master Paul."

"And when are you sure?" said the Uncle, laughing.

"Oh well, sometimes I'm *absolutely* sure, like about Daffodil," said the boy. "And sometimes I have an idea; and sometimes I haven't even an idea, do I Bassett? Then we're careful, because we mostly go down."

"You do, do you! And when you're sure, like about Daffodil, what makes you sure, Sonny?"

"Oh well, I don't know," said the boy uneasily. "I'm sure, you know, Uncle, that's all."

"It's as if he had it from heaven, Sir!" Bassett reiterated.

"I should say so!" said the uncle.

But he became a partner. And when the Leger was coming on, Paul was "sure" about Lively Spark, which was a quite inconsiderable horse. The boy insisted on putting a thousand on the horse, Bassett went for five hundred, and Oscar Cresswell two hundred. Lively Spark came in first, and the betting had been ten to one against him. Paul had made ten thousand.

"You see," he said, "I was absolutely sure of him." Even Oscar Cresswell had cleared two thousand.

"Look here, Son," he said. "This sort of thing makes me nervous."

"It needn't, Uncle! Perhaps I shan't be sure again for a long time."

"But what are you going to do with your money?" asked the uncle.

"Of course," said the boy, "I started it for mother. She said she had no luck, because father is unlucky, so I thought if *I* was lucky, it might stop whispering."

"What might stop whispering?"

"Our house! I *hate* our house for whispering."

"What does it whisper?"

"Why? Why?"—the boy fidgeted—"Why, I don't know! But it's always short of money, you know, Uncle."

"I know it, Son, I know it."

"You know people send mother Writs, don't you, Uncle?"

"I'm afraid I do," said the uncle.

"And then the house whispers like people laughing at you behind your back. It's awful, that is! I thought if I was lucky— — —"

"You might stop it—" added the uncle.

The boy watched him with big blue eyes, that had an uncanny cold fire in them, and he said never a word.

"Well then!" said the uncle. "What are we doing?"

"1 shouldn't like mother to know I was lucky," said the boy.

"Why not, Son?"

"She'd stop me."

"I don't think she would."

"Oh!"—and the boy writhed in an odd way. "I *don't* want her to know, Uncle."

"All right, Son! We'll manage it without her knowing."

They managed it very easily. Paul, at the other's suggestion, handed over five thousand pounds to his uncle, who deposited it with the family lawyer, who was then to inform Paul's mother that a relative had put five thousand pounds into his hands, which sum was to be paid out a thousand pounds at a time, on the mother's birthday, for the next five years.

"So she'll have a birthday present of a thousand pounds for five successive years," said Uncle Oscar. "I hope it won't make it all the harder for her later."

Paul's mother had her birthday in November. The house had been "whispering" worse than ever, lately, and even in spite of his luck, Paul could not bear up against it. He was very anxious to see the effect of the birthday letter, telling his mother about the thousand pounds.

When there were no visitors, Paul now took his meals with his parents, as he was beyond the nursery control. His mother went in to town nearly every day. She had discovered that she had an odd knack of sketching furs and dress materials, so she worked secretly in the studio of a friend who was the chief "artist" for the leading drapers. She drew the figures of ladies in furs and ladies in silk and sequins, for the newspaper advertisements. This young woman artist earned several thousand pounds a year, but Paul's mother only made several hundreds, and she was again dissatisfied. She so wanted to be first in something, and she did not succeed, even in making sketches for drapery advertisements.

She was down to breakfast on the morning of her birthday. Paul watched her face as she read her letters. He knew the lawyer's letter. As his mother read it, her face hardened and became more expressionless. Then a cold, determined look came on her mouth. She hid the letter under the pile of others, and said not a word about it.

"Didn't you have anything nice in the post, for your birthday, Mother?" said Paul.

"Quite moderately nice," she said, her voice cold and absent. She went away to town without saying more.

But in the afternoon Uncle Oscar appeared. He said Paul's mother had had a long interview with the lawyer, asking if the whole five thousand could not be advanced at once, as she was in debt.

"What do you think, Uncle?" said the boy.

"I leave it to you, Son."

"Oh, let her have it, then! We can get some more with the other," said the boy.

"A bird in the hand is worth two in the bush, Laddie!" said Uncle Oscar.

"But I'm sure to *know* for the Grand National: or the Lincoln: or else the Derby. I'm sure to know for *one* of them," said Paul.

So Uncle Oscar signed the agreement, and Paul's mother touched the whole five thousand. Then something very curious happened. The voices in the house suddenly went mad, like a chorus of frogs on a spring evening. There were certain new furnishings, and Paul had a tutor. He was really going to Eton, his father's school, in the following autumn. There were flowers in the winter, and a blossoming of the luxury Paul's mother had been used to. And yet the voices in the house, behind the sprays of mimosa and almond blossom, and from under the piles of iridescent cushions, simply trilled and screamed in a sort of ecstasy: "There *must* be more money! Oh-h-h! There must be more money! Oh now, now-w! now-w-w!—there must be more money!"—More than ever! More than ever!

It frightened Paul terribly. He studied away at his Latin and Greek, with his tutor. But his intense hours were spent with Bassett. The Grand National hid gone by: he had not "known," and had lost a hundred pounds. Summer was at hand. He was in agony, for the Lincoln. But even for the Lincoln, he didn't "know," and he lost fifty pounds. He became wild-eyed and strange, as if something were going to explode in him.

"Let it alone, Son! Don't you bother about it!" urged Uncle Oscar. But it was as if the boy couldn't really hear what his Uncle was saying.

"I've got to know for the Derby! I've *got* to know for the Derby!" the child re-iterated, his big blue eyes blazing with a sort of madness.

His mother noticed how overwrought he was.

"You'd better go to the seaside! Wouldn't you like to go now to the seaside, instead of waiting? I think you'd better!" she said, looking down at him anxiously, her heart curiously heavy because of him.

But the child lifted his uncanny blue eyes.

"I couldn't possibly go before the Derby, Mother!" he said. "I couldn't possibly!"

"Why not?" she said, her voice becoming heavy when she was opposed. "Why not? You can still go from the seaside to see the Derby, with your Uncle Oscar, if that's what you wish. No need for you to wait here.—Besides, I think you care too much about these races. It's a bad sign. My family has been a gambling family, and you won't know till you grow up how much damage it has done. But it has done damage. I shall have to send Bassett away, and ask Uncle Oscar not to talk racing to you, unless you promise to be reasonable about it: go away to the seaside and forget it. You're all nerves!"

"I'll do what you like, Mother, so long as you don't send me away till after the Derby," the boy said.

"Send you away from where? just from this house?"

"Yes!" he said, gazing at her.

"Why, you curious child, what makes you care about this house so much, suddenly? I never knew you loved it!"

He gazed at her without speaking. He had a secret within a secret, something he had not divulged, even to Bassett or to his Uncle Oscar.

But his mother, after standing undecided and a little bit sullen for some moments, said:

"Very well, then! Don't go to the seaside till after the Derby, if you don't wish it. But promise me you won't let your nerves go to pieces! Promise you won't think so much about horse-racing and *events*, as you call them!"

"Oh no!" said the boy, casually. "I won't think much about them, Mother. You needn't worry. I wouldn't worry, Mother, if I were you."

"If you were me and I were you," said his mother, "I wonder what we *should* do!"

"But you know you needn't worry, Mother, don't you?" the boy repeated.

"I should be awfully glad to know it," she said wearily.

"Oh well, you *can*, you know. I mean you *ought* to know you needn't worry!" he insisted.

"Ought I? Then I'll see about it," she said.

Paul's secret of secrets was his wooden horse, that which had no name. Since he was emancipated from a nurse and a nursery governess, he had had his rocking-horse removed to his own bedroom at the top of the house.

"Surely you're too big for a rocking horse!" his mother had remonstrated.

"Well, you see, Mother, till I can have a *real* horse, I like to have *some* sort of animal about," had been his quaint answer.

"Do you feel he keeps you company?" she laughed.

"Oh yes! He's very good, he always keeps me company, when I'm there," said Paul.

So the horse, rather shabby, stood in an arrested prance in the boy's bedroom.

The Derby was drawing near, and the boy grew more and more tense. He hardly heard what was spoken to him, he was very frail, and his eyes were really uncanny. His mother had sudden strange seizures of uneasiness about him. Sometimes, for half an hour, she would feel a sudden anxiety about him, that was almost anguish. She wanted to rush to him at once, and know he was safe.

Two nights before the Derby, she was at a big party in town, when one of her rushes of anxiety about her boy, her first-born, gripped her heart till she could hardly speak. She fought with the feeling, might and main, for she believed in common-sense. But it was too strong. She had to leave the dance and go downstairs to telephone to the country. The children's nursery governess was terribly surprised and startled at being rung up in the night.

"Are the children all right, Miss Wilmot?"

"Oh yes, they are quite all right."

"Master Paul? Is he all right?"

"He went to bed as right as a trivet. Shall I run up and look at him?"

"No!" said Paul's mother reluctantly. 'No! Don't trouble. It's all right. Don't sit up. We shall be home fairly soon." She did not want her son's privacy intruded upon.

"Very good!" said the governess.

It was about one o'clock when Paul's mother and father drove up to their house. All was still. Paul's mother went to her room and slipped off her white fur cloak. She had told her maid not to wait up for her. She heard her husband downstairs, mixing a whiskey and soda.

And then, because of the strange anxiety at her heart, she stole upstairs to her son's room. Noiselessly she went along the upper corridor. Was there a faint noise? What was it?

She stood with arrested muscles outside his door, listening. There was a strange, heavy and yet not loud noise. Her heart stood still. It was a soundless noise, yet rushing and powerful. Something huge, in violent, hushed motion.

What was it? What in God's name was it? She ought to know. She felt that she *knew* the noise. She knew what it was.

Yet she could not place it. She couldn't say what it was. And on and on it went, like a madness.

Softly, frozen with anxiety and fear, she turned the door-handle.

The room was dark. Yet in the space near the window, she heard and saw something plunging to and fro. She gazed in fear and amazement.

Then suddenly she switched on the light, and saw her son, in his green pyjamas, madly surging on his rocking-horse. The blaze of light suddenly lit him up, as he urged the wooden horse, and lit her up, as she stood, blonde, in her dress of pale green and crystal, in the doorway.

"Paul!" she cried. "Whatever are you doing?"

"It's Malabar!" he screamed, in a powerful strange voice. "It's Malabar!"

His eyes blazed at her for one strange and senseless second, as he ceased urging his wooden horse. Then he fell with a crash to the ground, and she, all her tormented motherhood flooding upon her, rushed to gather him up.

But he was unconscious, and unconscious he remained, with some brain fever. He talked and tossed, and his mother sat stonily by his side.

"Malabar? It's Malabar? Bassett, Bassett, I *know*: it's Malabar!"

So the child cried, trying to get up and urge the rocking-horse that gave him his inspiration.

"What does he mean by Malabar?" asked the heart-frozen mother.

"I don't know," said the father, stonily.

"What does he mean by Malabar?" she asked her brother Oscar. "It's one of the horses running for the Derby," was the answer. And in spite of himself, Oscar Cresswell spoke to Bassett, and himself put a thousand on Malabar: at fourteen to one.

The third day of the illness was critical: they were watching for a change. The boy, with his rather long, curly hair, was tossing ceaselessly on the pillow. He neither slept nor regained consciousness, and his eyes were like blue stones. His mother sat, feeling her heart had gone, turned actually into a stone.

In the evening, Oscar Cresswell did not come, but Bassett sent a message, saying could he come up for one moment, just one moment. Paul's mother was angry at the intrusion, but on second thoughts she agreed. The boy was the same. Perhaps Bassett might bring him to consciousness.

The gardener, a shortish fellow with a little brown moustache and sharp little brown eyes, tiptoed into the room, touched his imaginary cap to Paul's mother, and stole to the bedside, staring with glittering, smallish eyes at the tossing, dying child.

"Master Paul!" he whispered. "Master Paul! Malabar came in first all right, a clean win. I did as you told me. You've made over seventy thousand pounds, you have, you've got over eighty thousand. Malabar came in all right, Master Paul."

"Malabar! Malabar! Did I say Malabar, Mother? Did I say Malabar? Do you think I'm lucky, Mother? I knew Malabar, didn't I? Over eighty thousand pounds! I call that lucky, don't you, Mother? Over eighty thousand pounds! I knew, didn't I know I knew? Malabar came in all right! If I ride my horse till I'm sure, then I tell you, Bassett, you can go as high as you like. Did you go for all you were worth, Bassett?"

"I went a thousand on it, Master Paul."

"I never told you, Mother, that if I can ride my horse, and *get there*, then I'm absolutely sure—Oh absolutely! Mother, did I ever tell you? I *am* lucky!"

"No, you never did," said the mother.

But the boy died in the night.

And even as he lay dead, his mother heard her brother's voice saying to her: "My God, Hester, you're eighty-odd thousand to the good, and a poor devil of a son to the bad. But poor devil, poor devil, he's best gone out of a life where he rides his rocking-horse to find a winner."

CONSTRUCTING A READING

1. In a book called *Readings and Feelings*, (NCTE: 1975) one of the first and most important documents in "reader-response criticism," David Bleich describes asking his students to write about "the most important word" in "The Rocking-Horse Winner." Try, first, to do Bleich's assignment, writing for ten minutes about which word in this story you find most important. Then, with your group members, speculate about why Bleich made his assignment. What do you think a student would learn about this story, and about reading in general, by writing about "the most important word"?

2. We might say that stories like this one, which leave the reader uncertain whether the events are natural or supernatural, constitute special kinds of gaps. Write for a few minutes about how you explain the events of this narrative to yourself. Does your explanation seem to take account of the conventions we have been considering?

A Narrow Fellow in the Grass

Emily Dickinson

A narrow Fellow in the Grass
Occasionally rides—
You may have met Him—did you not
His notice sudden is—

The Grass divides as with a Comb—
A spotted shaft is seen—
And then it closes at your feet
And opens further on—

He likes a Boggy Acre
A Floor too cool for Corn—
Yet when a Boy, and Barefoot—
I more than once at Noon
Have passed, I thought, a Whip lash
Unbraiding in the Sun
When stooping to secure it
It wrinkled, and was gone—

Several of Nature's People
I know, and they know me—
I feel for them a transport
Of cordiality—

But never met this Fellow
Attended, or alone
Without a tighter breathing
And Zero at the Bone—

CONSTRUCTING A READING

1. What one "fellow"
    divides grass
    has a spotted shaft
    can disappear and then appear further on
    likes dark damp fields
    disappears quickly
    frightens a barefoot boy?
2. What does the phrase "His notice sudden is" mean to you? Think about
    alternative phrasings. Does it mean that the speaker notices "him" sud-
    denly or "he" notices the speaker suddenly? Or both? Why?
3. Why do you suppose Emily Dickinson chose explicitly to have a male
    speaker?
4. What does "Zero at the bone" mean to you?

The Red-Headed League

Sir Arthur Conan Doyle

I had called upon my friend, Mr. Sherlock Holmes, one day in the autumn of last year and found him in deep conversation with a very stout, florid-faced, elderly gentleman with fiery red hair. With an apology for my intrusion, I was about to withdraw when Holmes pulled me abruptly into the room and closed the door behind me.

"You could not possibly have come at a better time, my dear Watson," he said cordially.

"I was afraid that you were engaged."

"So I am. Very much so."

"Then I can wait in the next room."

"Not at all. This gentleman, Mr. Wilson, has been my partner and helper in many of my most successful cases, and I have no doubt that he will be of the utmost use to me in yours also."

The stout gentleman half rose from his chair and gave a bob of greeting, with a quick little questioning glance from his small, fat-encircled eyes.

"Try the settee," said Holmes, relapsing into his armchair and putting his finger-tips together, as was his custom when in judicial moods. "I know, my dear Watson, that you share my love of all that is bizarre and outside the conventions and hum-drum routine of everyday life. You have shown your relish for it by the enthusiasm which has prompted you to chronicle, and, if you will excuse my saying so, somewhat to embellish so many of my own little adventures."

"Your cases have indeed been of the greatest interest to me," I observed.

"You will remember that I remarked the other day, just before we went into the very simple problem presented by Miss Mary Sutherland, that for strange effects and extraordinary combinations we must go to life itself, which is always far more daring than any effort of the imagination."

"A proposition which I took the liberty of doubting."

"You did, Doctor, but none the less you must come round to my view, for otherwise I shall keep on piling fact upon fact on you until your reason breaks down under them and acknowledges me to be right. Now, Mr. Jabez Wilson here has been good enough to call upon me this morning, and to begin a narrative which promises to be one of the most singular which I have listened to for some time. You have heard me remark that the strangest and most unique things are very often connected not with the larger but with the smaller crimes, and occasionally, indeed, where there is room for doubt whether any positive crime has been committed. As far as I have heard it is impossible for me to say whether the present case is an instance of crime or not, but the course of events is certainly among the most singular that I have ever listened to. Perhaps, Mr. Wilson, you would have the great kindness to recommence your narrative. I ask you not merely because my friend Dr. Watson has not heard the opening part but also because the peculiar nature of the story makes me anxious to have every possible detail from your lips. As a rule, when I have heard some slight indication of the course of events, I am able to guide myself by the thousands of other similar cases which occur to my memory. In the present instance I am forced to admit that the facts are, to the best of my belief, unique."

The portly client puffed out his chest with an appearance of some little pride and pulled a dirty and wrinkled newspaper from the inside pocket of his great-coat. As he glanced down the advertisement column, with his head thrust forward and the paper flattened out upon his knee, I took a good look at the man and endeavoured, after the fashion of my companion, to read the indications which might be presented by his dress or appearance.

I did not gain very much, however, by my inspection. Our visitor bore every mark of being an average commonplace British tradesman, obese, pompous, and slow. He wore rather baggy gray shepherd's check trousers, a not over-clean black frock-coat, unbuttoned in the front, and a drab waistcoat with a heavy brassy Albert chain, and a square pierced bit of metal dangling down as an ornament. A frayed top-hat and a faded brown overcoat with a wrinkled velvet collar lay upon a chair beside him. Altogether, look as I would, there was nothing remarkable about the man save his blazing red head, and the expression of extreme chagrin and discontent upon his features.

Sherlock Holmes's quick eye took in my occupation, and he shook his head with a smile as he noticed my questioning glances. "Beyond the obvious facts that he has at some time done manual labour, that he takes snuff, that he is a Freemason, that he has been in China, and that he has done a considerable amount of writing lately, I can deduce nothing else."

Mr. Jabez Wilson started up in his chair, with his forefinger upon the paper, but his eyes upon my companion.

"How, in the name of good-fortune, did you know all that, Mr. Holmes?" he asked. "How did you know, for example, that I did manual labour? It's as true as gospel, for I began as a ship's carpenter."

"Your hands, my dear sir. Your right hand is quite a size larger than your left. You have worked with it, and the muscles are more developed."

"Well, the snuff, then, and the Freemasonry?"

"I won't insult your intelligence by telling you how I read that, especially as, rather against the strict rules of your order, you use an arc-and-compass breastpin."

"Ah, of course, I forgot that. But the writing?"

"What else can be indicated by that right cuff so very shiny for five inches, and the left one with the smooth patch near the elbow where you rest it upon the desk?"

"Well, but China?"

"The fish that you have tattooed immediately above your right wrist could only have been done in China. I have made a small study of tattoo marks and have even contributed to the literature of the subject. That trick of staining the fishes' scales of a delicate pink is quite peculiar to China. When, in addition, I see a Chinese coin hanging from your watch-chain, the matter becomes even more simple."

Mr. Jabez Wilson laughed heavily. "Well, I never!" said he. "I thought at first that you had done something clever, but I see that there was nothing in it, after all."

"I begin to think, Watson," said Holmes, "that I make a mistake in explaining. '*Omne ignotum pro magnifico,*' you know, and my poor little reputation, such as it is, will suffer shipwreck if I am so candid. Can you not find the advertisement, Mr. Wilson?"

"Yes, I have got it now," he answered with his thick red finger planted halfway down the column. "Here it is. This is what began it all. You just read it for yourself, sir."

I took the paper from him and read as follows:

To the Red-headed League:
    On account of the bequest of the late Ezekiah Hopkins, of Lebanon, Pennsylvania, U.S.A., there is now another vacancy open which entitles a member of the League to a salary of £4 a week for purely nominal services. All red-headed men who are sound in body and mind, and above the age of twenty-one years, are eligible. Apply in person on Monday, at eleven o'clock, to Duncan Ross, at the offices of the League, 7 Pope's Court, Fleet Street.

"What on earth does this mean?" I ejaculated after I had twice read over the extraordinary announcement

Holmes chuckled and wriggled in his chair, as was his habit when in high spirits. "It is a little off the beaten track, isn't it?" said he. "And now, Mr. Wilson, off you go at scratch and tell us all about yourself, your household, and the effect which this advertisement had upon your fortunes. You will first make a note, Doctor, of the paper and the date."

"It is *The Morning Chronicle* of April 27, 1890. Just two months ago."

"Very good. Now, Mr. Wilson?"

"Well, it is just as I have been telling you, Mr. Sherlock Holmes," said Jabez Wilson, mopping his forehead; "I have a small pawnbroker's business at Coburg Square, near the City. It's not a very large affair, and of late years it has not done more than just give me a living. I used to be able to keep two assistants, but now I only keep one; and I would have a job to pay him but that he is willing to come for half wages so as to learn the business."

"What is the name of this obliging youth?" asked Sherlock Holmes.

"His name is Vincent Spaulding, and he's not such a youth, either. It's hard to say his age. I should not wish a smarter assistant, Mr. Holmes; and I know very well that he could better himself and earn twice what I am able to give him. But, after all, if he is satisfied, why should I put ideas in his head?"

"Why, indeed? You seem most fortunate in having an employee who comes under the full market price. It is not a common experience among employers in this age. I don't know that your assistant is not as remarkable as your advertisement."

"Oh, he has his faults, too," said Mr. Wilson. "Never was such a fellow for photography. Snapping away with a camera when he ought to be improving his mind, and then diving down into the cellar like a rabbit into its hole to develop his pictures. That is his main fault, but on the whole he's a good worker. There is no vice in him."

"He is still with you, I presume?"

"Yes, sir. He and a girl of fourteen, who does a bit of simple cooking and keeps the place clean—that's all I have in the house, for I am a widower and never had any family. We live very quietly, sir, the three of us; and we keep a roof over our heads and pay our debts, if we do nothing more."

"The first thing that put us out was that advertisement. Spaulding, he came down into the office just this day eight weeks, with this very paper in his hand and he says:

"'I wish to the Lord, Mr. Wilson, that I was a red-headed man.'

"'Why that?' I asks.

"'Why,' says he, 'here's another vacancy on the League of the Red-headed Men. It's worth quite a little fortune to any man who gets it, and I understand that there are more vacancies than there are men, so that the trustees are at their wits' end what to do with the money. If my hair would only change colour, here's a nice little crib all ready for me to step into.'

"'Why, what is it, then?' I asked. You see, Mr. Holmes, I am a very stay-at-home man, and as my business came to me instead of my having to go to it, I was often weeks on end without putting my foot over the door-mat. In that way I didn't know much of what was going on outside, and I was always glad of a bit of news.'

"'Have you never heard of the League of the Red-headed Men?' he asked with his eyes open.

"'Never.'

"'Why, I wonder at that, for you are eligible yourself for one of the vacancies.'

"'And what are they worth?' I asked.

"'Oh, merely a couple of hundred a year, but the work is slight, and it need not interfere very much with one's other occupations.'

"'Well, you can easily think that that made me prick up my ears, for the business has not been over-good for some years, and an extra couple of hundred would have been very handy.'

"'Tell me all about it,' said I.

"'Well,' said he, showing me the advertisement, 'you can see for yourself that the League has a vacancy, and there is the address where you should apply for particulars. As far as I can make out, the League was founded by an American millionaire, Ezekiah Hopkins, who was very peculiar in his ways. He was himself red-headed, and he had a great sympathy for all red-headed men; so when he died it was found that he had left his enormous fortune in the hands of trustees, with instructions to apply the interest to the providing of easy berths to men whose hair is of that colour. From all I hear it is splendid pay and very little to do.'

"'But,' said I, 'there would be millions of red-headed men who would apply.'

"'Not so many as you might think,' he answered. 'You see it is really confined to Londoners, and to grown men. This American had started from London when he was young, and he wanted to do the old town a good turn. Then, again, I have heard it is no use your applying if your hair is light red, or dark red, or anything but real bright, blazing, fiery red. Now, if you cared to apply, Mr. Wilson, you would just walk in; but perhaps it would hardly be worth your while to put yourself out of the way for the sake of a few hundred pounds.'

"Now, it is a fact, gentlemen, as you may see for yourselves, that my hair is of a very full and rich tint, so that it seemed to me that if there was to be any competition in the matter I stood as good a chance as any man that I had ever met. Vincent Spaulding seemed to know so much about it that I thought he might prove useful, so I just ordered him to put up the shutters for the day and to come right away with me. He was very willing to have a holiday, so we shut the business up and started off for the address that was given us in the advertisement.

"I never hope to see such a sight as that again, Mr. Holmes. From north, south, east, and west every man who had a shade of red in his hair had tramped into the city to answer the advertisement. Fleet Street was choked with red-headed folk, and Pope's Court looked like a coster's orange barrow. I should not have thought there were so many in the whole country as were brought together by that single advertisement. Every shade of colour they were—straw, lemon, orange, brick, Irish-setter, liver, clay; but, as Spaulding said, there were not many who had the real vivid flame-coloured tint. When I saw how many were waiting, I would have given it up in despair; but Spaulding would not hear of it. How he did it I could not imagine, but he pushed and pulled and butted until he got me through the crowd, and right up to the steps which led to the office. There was a double stream upon the stair, some going up in hope, and some coming back dejected; but we wedged in as well as we could and soon found ourselves in the office."

"Your experience has been a most entertaining one," remarked Holmes as his client paused and refreshed his memory with a huge pinch of snuff. "Pray continue your very interesting statement."

"There was nothing in the office but a couple of wooden chairs and a deal table, behind which sat a small man with a head that was even redder than mine. He said a few words to each candidate as he came up, and then he always managed to find some fault in them which would disqualify them. Getting a vacancy did not seem to be such a very easy matter, after all. However, when our turn came the little man was much more favourable to me than to any of the others, and he closed the door as we entered, so that he might have a private word with us.

"'This is Mr. Jabez Wilson,' said my assistant, 'and he is willing to fill a vacancy in the League.'

"And he is admirably suited for it,' the other answered. 'He has every requirement. I cannot recall when I have seen anything so fine.' He took a step backward, cocked his head on one side, and gazed at my hair until I felt quite bashful. Then suddenly he plunged forward, wrung my hand, and congratulated me warmly on my success.'

"'It would be injustice to hesitate,' said he. 'You will, however, I am sure, excuse me for taking an obvious precaution.' With that he seized my hair in both his hands, and tugged until I yelled with the pain. 'There is water in your eyes,' said he as he released me. 'I perceive that all is as it should be. But we have to be careful, for we have twice been deceived by wigs and once by paint. I could tell you tales of cobbler's wax which would disgust you with human nature.' He stepped over to the window and shouted through it at the top of his voice that the vacancy was filled. A groan of disappointment came up from below, and the folk all trooped away in different directions until there was not a red-head to be seen except my own and that of the manager.

"'My name,' said he, 'is Mr. Duncan Ross, and I am myself one of the pensioners upon the fund left by our noble benefactor. Are you a married man, Mr. Wilson? Have you a family?'

"I answered that I had not.

"His face fell immediately.

"'Dear me!' he said gravely, 'that is very serious indeed! I am sorry to hear you say that. The fund was, of course, for the propagation and spread of the red-heads as well as for their maintenance. It is exceedingly unfortunate that you should be a bachelor.'

"My face lengthened at this, Mr. Holmes, for I thought that I was not to have the vacancy after all; but after thinking it over for a few minutes he said that it would be all right.

"'In the case of another,' said he, 'the objection might be fatal, but we must stretch a point in favour of a man with such a head of hair as yours. When shall you be able to enter upon your new duties?'

"'Well, it is a little awkward, for I have a business already,' said I.

"'Oh, never mind about that, Mr. Wilson!' said Vincent Spaulding. 'I should be able to look after that for you.'

"'What would be the hours?' I asked.

"'Ten to two.'

"Now a pawnbroker's business is mostly done of an evening, Mr. Holmes, especially Thursday and Friday evening, which is just before pay-day; so it would suit me very well to earn a little in the mornings. Besides, I knew that my assistant was a good man, and that he would see to anything that turned up.

"That would suit me very well,' said I. 'And the pay?'

"'Is £4 a week.'

"'And the work?'

"'Is purely nominal.'

"What do you call purely nominal?'

"'Well, you have to be in the office, or at least in the building, the whole time. If you leave, you forfeit your whole position forever. The will is very clear upon that point. You don't comply with the conditions if you budge from the office during that time.'

"'It's only four hours a day, and I should not think of leaving,' said I.

"'No excuse will avail,' said Mr. Duncan Ross; 'neither sickness nor business nor anything else. There you must stay, or you lose your billet.'

"'And the work?'

"'Is to copy out the Encyclopaedia Britannica. There is the first volume of it in that press. You must find your own ink, pens, and blotting-paper, but we provide this table and chair. Will you be ready tomorrow?'

"'Certainly,' I answered.

"'Then, good-bye, Mr. Jabez Wilson, and let me congratulate you once more on the important position which you have been fortunate enough to gain.' He bowed me out of the room, and I went home with my assistant, hardly knowing what to say or do, I was so pleased at my own good fortune.

"Well, I thought over the matter all day, and by evening I was in low spirits again; for I had quite persuaded myself that the whole affair must be some great hoax or fraud, though what its object might be I could not imagine. It seemed altogether past belief that anyone could make such a will, or that they would pay such a sum for doing anything so simple as copying out the Encyclopaedia Britannica. Vincent Spaulding did what he could to cheer me up, but by bedtime I had reasoned myself out of the whole thing. However, in the morning I determined to have a look at it anyhow, so I bought a penny bottle of ink, and with a quill-pen, and seven sheets of foolscap paper, I started off for Pope's Court.

"Well, to my surprise and delight, everything was as right as possible. The table was set out ready for me, and Mr. Duncan Ross was there to see that I got fairly to work. He started me off upon the letter A, and then he left me; but he would drop in from time to time to see that all was right with me. At two o'clock he bade me good-day, complimented me upon the amount that I had written, and locked the door of the office after me.

"This went on day after day, Mr. Holmes, and on Saturday the manager came in and planked down four golden sovereigns for my week's work. It was the same next week, and the same the week after. Every morning I was there at ten, and every afternoon I left at two. By degrees Mr. Duncan Ross took to coming in only once of a morning, and then, after a time, he did not come in at all. Still, of course, I never dared to leave the room for an instant, for I was not sure when he might come, and the billet was such a good one, and suited me so well, that I would not risk the loss of it.

"Eight weeks passed away like this, and I had written about Abbots and Archery and Armour and Architecture and Attica, and hoped with diligence that I might get on to the B's before very long. It cost me something in foolscap, and I had pretty nearly filled a shelf with my writings. And then suddenly the whole business came to an end."

'To an end?"

"Yes, sir. And no later than this morning. I went to my work as usual at ten o'clock, but the door was shut and locked, with a little square of card-board hammered on to the middle of the panel with a tack. Here it is, and you can read for yourself."

He held up a piece of white card-board about the size of a sheet of note-paper. It read in this fashion:

THE RED-HEADED LEAGUE

IS

DISSOLVED.

October 9, 1890.

Sherlock Holmes and I surveyed this curt announcement and the rueful face behind it, until the comical side of the affair so completely overtopped every other consideration that we both burst out into a roar of laughter.

"I cannot see that there is anything very funny," cried our client, flushing up to the roots of his flaming head. "If you can do nothing better than laugh at me, I can go elsewhere."

"No, no," cried Holmes, shoving him back into the chair from which he had half risen. "I really wouldn't miss your case for the world. It is most refreshingly unusual. But there is, if you will excuse my saying so, something just a little funny about it. Pray what steps did you take when you found the card upon the door?"

"I was staggered, sir. I did not know what to do. Then I called at the offices round, but none of them seemed to know anything about it. Finally, I went to the landlord, who is an accountant living on the ground-floor, and I asked him if he could tell me what had become of the Red-headed League. He said that he had never heard of any such body. Then I asked him who Mr. Duncan Ross was. He answered that the name was new to him.

"'Well,' said I, 'the gentleman at No. 4.'

"'What, the red-headed man?'

"'Yes.'

"'Oh,' said he, 'his name was William Morris. He was a solicitor and was using my room as a temporary convenience until his new premises were ready. He moved out yesterday.'

"'Where could I find him?'

"'Oh, at his new offices. He did tell me the address. Yes, 17 King Edward Street, near St. Paul's.'

"I started off, Mr. Holmes, but when I got to that address it was a manufactory of artificial knee-caps, and no one in it had ever heard of either Mr. William Morris or Mr. Duncan Ross."

"And what did you do then?" asked Holmes.

"I went home to Saxe-Coburg Square, and I took the advice of my assistant. But he could not help me in any way. He could only say that if I waited I should hear by post. But that was not quite good enough, Mr. Holmes. I did not wish to lose such a place without a struggle, so, as I had heard that you were good enough to give advice to poor folk who were in need of it, I came right away to you."

"And you did very wisely," said Holmes. "Your case is an exceedingly remarkable one, and I shall be happy to look into it. From what you have told me I think that it is possible that graver issues hang from it than might at first sight appear."

"Grave enough!" said Mr. Jabez Wilson. "Why, I have lost four pound a week."

"As far as you are personally concerned," remarked Holmes, "I do not see that you have any grievance against this extraordinary league. On the contrary, you are, as I understand, richer by some £30, to say nothing of the minute knowledge which you have gained on every subject which comes under the letter A. You have lost nothing by them."

"No, sir. But I want to find out about them, and who they are, and what their object was in playing this prank—if it was a prank—upon me. It was a pretty expensive joke for them, for it cost them two and thirty pounds."

"We shall endeavour to clear up these points for you. And, first, one or two questions, Mr. Wilson. This assistant of yours who first called your attention to the advertisement—how long had he been with you?"

"About a month then."

"How did he come?"

"In answer to an advertisement."

"Was he the only applicant?"

"No, I had a dozen."

"Why did you pick him?"

"Because he was handy and would come cheap."

"At half-wages, in fact"

"Yes."

"What is he like, this Vincent Spaulding?"

"Small, stout-built, very quick in his ways, no hair on his face, though he's not short of thirty. Has a white splash of acid upon his forehead."

Holmes sat up in his chair in considerable excitement. "I thought as much," said he. "Have you ever observed that his ears are pierced for earrings?"

"Yes, sir. He told me that a gypsy had done it for him when he was a lad."

"Hum!" said Holmes, sinking back in deep thought. "He is still with you?"

"Oh, yes, sir; I have only just left him."

"And has your business been attended to in your absence?"

"Nothing to complain of, sir. There's never very much to do of a morning."

"That will do, Mr. Wilson. I shall be happy to give you an opinion upon the subject in the course of a day or two. Today is Saturday, and I hope that by Monday we may come to a conclusion."

"Well, Watson," said Holmes when our visitor had left us, "what do you make of it all?"

"I make nothing of it," I answered frankly. "It is a most mysterious business."

"As a rule," said Holmes, "the more bizarre a thing is the less mysterious it proves to be. It is your commonplace, featureless crimes which are really puzzling, just as a commonplace face is the most difficult to identify. But I must be prompt over this matter."

"What are you going to do, then?" I asked.

"To smoke," he answered. "It is quite a three pipe problem, and I beg that you won't speak to me for fifty minutes." He curled himself up in his chair, with his thin knees drawn up to his hawk-like nose, and there he sat with his eyes closed and his black clay pipe thrusting out like the bill of some strange bird. I had come to the conclusion that he had dropped asleep, and indeed was nodding myself, when he suddenly sprang out of his chair with the gesture of a man who has made up his mind and put his pipe down upon the mantelpiece.

"Sarasate plays at the St. James's Hall this afternoon," he remarked. "What do you think, Watson? Could your patients spare you for a few hours?"

"I have nothing to do to-day. My practice is never very absorbing."

"Then put on your hat and come. I am going through the City first, and we can have some lunch on the way. I observe that there is a good deal of German music on the programme, which is rather more to my taste than Italian or French. It is introspective, and I want to introspect. Come along!"

We travelled by the Underground as far as Aldersgate; and a short walk took us to Saxe-Coburg Square, the scene of the singular story which we had listened to in the morning. It was a poky, little, shabby-genteel place, where four lines of dingy two-storied brick houses looked out into a small railed-in enclosure, where a lawn of weedy grass and a few clumps of faded laurel-bushes made a hard fight against a smoke-laden and uncongenial atmosphere. Three gilt balls and a brown board with "JABEZ WILSON" in white letters, upon a corner house, announced the place where our red-headed client carried on his business. Sherlock Holmes stopped in front of it with his head on one side and looked it all over, with his eyes shining brightly between puckered lids. Then he walked slowly up the street, and then down again to the corner, still looking keenly at the houses. Finally he returned to the pawnbroker's, and, having thumped vigorously upon the pavement with his stick two or three times, he went up to the door and knocked. It was instantly opened by a bright-looking, clean-shaven young fellow, who asked him to step in.

"Thank you," said Holmes, "I only wished to ask you how you would go from here to the Strand."

"Third right, fourth left," answered the assistant promptly, closing the door.

"Smart fellow, that," observed Holmes as we walked away. "He is, in my judgment, the fourth smartest man in London, and for daring I am not sure that he has not a claim to be third. I have known something of him before."

"Evidently," said I, "Mr. Wilson's assistant counts for a good deal in this mystery of the Red-headed League. I am sure that you inquired your way merely in order that you might see him."

"Not him."

"What then?"

"The knees of his trousers."

"And what did you see?"

"What I expected to see."

"Why did you beat the pavement?"

"My dear doctor, this is a time for observation, not for talk. We are spies in an enemy's country. We know something of Saxe-Coburg Square. Let us now explore the parts which lie behind it."

The road in which we found ourselves as we turned round the corner from the retired Saxe-Coburg Square presented as great a contrast to it as the front of a picture does to the back. It was one of the main arteries which conveyed the traffic of the City to the north and west. The roadway was blocked with the immense stream of commerce flowing in a double tide inward and outward, while the footpaths were black with the hurrying swarm of pedestrians. It was difficult to realize as we looked at the line of fine shops and stately business premises that they really abutted on the other side upon the faded and stagnant square which we had just quitted.

"Let me see," said Holmes, standing at the corner and glancing along the line, "I should like just to remember the order of the houses here. It is a hobby of mine to have an exact knowledge of London. There is Mortimer's, the tobacconist, the little newspaper shop, the Coburg branch of the City and Suburban Bank, the Vegetarian Restaurant, and McFarlane's carriage-building depot. That carries us right on to the other block. And now, Doctor, we've done our work, so it's time we had some play. A sandwich and a cup of coffee, and then off to violin-land, where all is sweetness and delicacy and harmony, and there are no red-headed clients to vex us with their conundrums."

My friend was an enthusiastic musician, being himself not only a very capable performer but a composer of no ordinary merit. All the afternoon he sat in the stalls wrapped in the most perfect happiness, gently waving his long, thin fingers in time to the music, while his gently smiling face and his languid, dreamy eyes were as unlike those of Holmes, the sleuth-hound, Holmes the relentless, keen-witted, ready-handed criminal agent, as it was possible to conceive. In his singular character the dual nature alternately asserted itself, and his extreme exactness and astuteness represented, as I have often thought, the reaction against the poetic and contemplative mood which occasionally predominated in him. The swing of his nature took him from extreme languor to devouring energy; and, as I knew well, he was never so truly formidable as when, for days on end, he had been lounging in his armchair amid his improvisations and his black-letter editions. Then it was that the lust of the chase would suddenly come upon him, and that his brilliant reasoning power would rise to the level of intuition, until those who were unacquainted with his methods would look askance at him as on a man whose knowledge was not that of other mortals. When I saw him that afternoon so enwrapped in the music at St. James's Hall I felt that an evil time might be coming upon those whom he had set himself to hunt down.

"You want to go home, no doubt, Doctor," he remarked as we emerged.

"Yes, it would be as well."

"And I have some business to do which will take some hours. This business at Coburg Square is serious."

"Why serious?"

"A considerable crime is in contemplation. I have every reason to believe that we shall be in time to stop it. But to-day being Saturday rather complicates matters. I shall want your help to-night."

"At what time?"

"Ten will be early enough."

"I shall be at Baker Street at ten."

"Very well. And, I say, Doctor, there may be some little danger, so kindly put your army revolver in your pocket." He waved his hand, turned on his heel, and disappeared in an instant among the crowd.

I trust that I am not more dense than my neighbours, but I was always oppressed with a sense of my own stupidity in my dealings with Sherlock Holmes. Here I had heard what he had heard, I had seen what he had seen, and yet from his words it was evident that he saw clearly not only what had happened but what was about to happen, while to me the whole business was still confused and grotesque. As I drove home to my house in Kensington I thought over it all, from the extraordinary story of the red-headed copier of the Encyclopaedia down to the visit to Saxe-Coburg Square, and the ominous words with which he had parted from me. What was this nocturnal expedition, and why should I go armed? Where were we going, and what were we to do? I had the hint from Holmes that this smooth-faced pawnbroker's assistant was a formidable man—a man who might play a deep game. I tried to puzzle it out, but gave it up in despair and set the matter aside until night should bring an explanation.

It was a quarter-past nine when I started from home and made my way across the Park, and so through Oxford Street to Baker Street. Two hansoms were standing at the door, and as I entered the passage I heard the sound of voices from above. On entering his room I found Holmes in animated conversation with two men, one of whom I recognized as Peter Jones, the official police agent, while the other was a long, thin, sad-faced man, with a very shiny hat and oppressively respectable frock-coat.

"Ha! our party is complete," said Holmes, buttoning up his pea-jacket and taking his heavy hunting crop from the rack. "Watson, I think you know Mr. Jones, of Scotland Yard? Let me introduce you to Mr. Merryweather, who is to be our companion in to-night's adventure."

"We're hunting in couples again, Doctor, you see," said Jones in his consequential way. "Our friend here is a wonderful man for starting a chase. All he wants is an old dog to help him to do the running down."

"I hope a wild goose may not prove to be the end of our chase," observed Mr. Merryweather gloomily.

"You may place considerable confidence in Mr. Holmes, sir," said the police agent loftily. "He has his own little methods, which are, if he won't mind my saying so, just a little too theoretical and fantastic, but he has the makings of a detective in him. It is not too much to say that once or twice, as in that business of the Sholto murder and the Agra treasure, he has been more nearly correct than the official force."

"Oh, if you say so, Mr. Jones, it is all right," said the stranger with deference. "Still, I confess that I miss my rubber. It is the first Saturday night for seven-and-twenty years that I have not had my rubber."

"I think you will find," said Sherlock Holmes, "that you will play for a higher stake to-night than you have ever done yet, and that the play will be more exciting. For you, Mr. Merryweather, the stake will be some £30,000; and for you, Jones, it will be the man upon whom you wish to lay your hands."

"John Clay, the murderer, thief, smasher, and forger. He's a young man, Mr. Merryweather, but he is at the head of his profession, and I would rather have my bracelets on him than on any criminal in London. He's a remarkable man, is young John Clay. His grandfather was a royal duke, and he himself has been to Eton and Oxford. His brain is as cunning as his fingers, and though we meet signs of him at every turn, we never know where to find the man himself. He'll crack a crib in Scotland one week, and be raising money to build an orphanage in Cornwall the next. I've been on his track for years and have never set eyes on him yet."

"I hope that I may have the pleasure of introducing you to-night. I've had one or two little turns also with Mr. John Clay, and I agree with you that he is at the head of his profession. It is past ten, however, and quite time that we started. If you two will take the first hansom, Watson and I will follow in the second."

Sherlock Holmes was not very communicative during the long drive and lay back in the cab humming the tunes which he had heard in the afternoon. We rattled through an endless labyrinth of gas-lit streets until we emerged into Farrington Street.

"We are close there now," my friend remarked. "This fellow Merryweather is a bank director, and personally interested in the matter. I thought it as well to have Jones with us also. He is not a bad fellow, though an absolute imbecile in his profession. He has one positive virtue. He is as brave as a bull-dog and as tenacious as a lobster if he gets his claws upon anyone. Here we are, and they are waiting for us."

We had reached the same crowded thoroughfare in which we had found ourselves in the morning. Our cabs were dismissed, and, following the guidance of Mr. Merryweather, we passed down a narrow passage and through a side door, which he opened for us. Within there was a small corridor, which ended in a very massive iron gate. This also was opened, and led down a flight of winding stone steps, which terminated at another formidable gate. Mr. Merryweather stopped to light a lantern, and then conducted us down a dark, earth-smelling passage, and so, after opening a third door, into a huge vault or cellar, which was piled all round with crates and massive boxes.

"You are not very vulnerable from above," Holmes remarked as he held up the lantern and gazed about him.

"Nor from below," said Mr. Merryweather, striking his stick upon the flags which lined the floor. "Why, dear me, it sounds quite hollow!" he remarked, looking up in surprise.

"I must really ask you to be a little more quiet!" said Holmes severely. "You have already imperilled the whole success of our expedition. Might I beg that you would have the goodness to sit down upon one of those boxes, and not to interfere?"

The solemn Mr. Merryweather perched himself upon a crate, with a very injured expression upon his face, while Holmes fell upon his knees upon the floor and, with the lantern and a magnifying lens, began to examine minutely the cracks between the stones. A few seconds sufficed to satisfy him, for he sprang to his feet again and put his glass in his pocket.

"We have at least an hour before us," he remarked, "for they can hardly take any steps until the good pawnbroker is safely in bed. Then they will not lose a minute, for the sooner they do their work the longer time they will have for their escape. We are at present, Doctor—as no doubt you have divined—in the cellar of the City branch of one of the principal London banks. Mr. Merryweather is the chairman of directors, and he will explain to you that there are reasons why the more daring criminals of London should take a considerable interest in this cellar at present."

"It is our French gold," whispered the director. "We have had several warnings that an attempt might be made upon it."

"Your French gold?"

"Yes. We had occasion some months ago to strengthen our resources and borrowed for that purpose 30,000 napoleons from the Bank of France. It has become known that we have never had occasion to unpack the money, and that it is still lying in our cellar. The crate upon which I sit contains 2,000 napoleons packed between layers of lead foil. Our reserve of bullion is much larger at present than is usually kept in a single branch office, and the directors have had misgivings upon the subject."

"Which were very well justified," observed Holmes. "And now it is time that we arranged our little plans. I expect that within an hour matters will come to a head. In the meantime, Mr. Merryweather, we must put the screen over that dark lantern."

"And sit in the dark?"

"I am afraid so. I had brought a pack of cards in my pocket, and I thought that, as we were a *partie carrée*, you might have your rubber after all. But I see that the enemy's preparations have gone so far that we cannot risk the presence of a light. And, first of all, we must choose our positions. These are daring men, and though we shall take them at a disadvantage, they may do us some harm unless we are careful. I shall stand behind this crate, and do you conceal yourselves behind those. Then, when I flash a light upon them, close in swiftly. If they fire, Watson, have no compunction about shooting them down."

I placed my revolver, cocked, upon the top of the wooden case behind which I crouched. Holmes shot the slide across the front of his lantern and left us in pitch darkness—such an absolute darkness as I have never before experienced. The smell of hot metal remained to assure us that the light was still there, ready to flash out at a moment's notice. To me, with my nerves worked up to a pitch of expectancy, there was something depressing and subduing in the sudden gloom, and in the cold dank air of the vault.

"They have but one retreat," whispered Holmes. "That is back through the house into Saxe-Coburg Square. I hope that you have done what I asked you, Jones?"

"I have an inspector and two officers waiting at the front door."

"Then we have stopped all the holes. And now we must be silent and wait."

What a time it seemed! From comparing notes afterwards it was but an hour and a quarter, yet it appeared to me that the night must have almost gone, and the dawn be breaking above us. My limbs were weary and stiff, for I feared to change my position; yet my nerves were worked up to the highest pitch of tension, and my hearing was so acute that I could not only hear the gentle breathing of my companions, but I could distinguish the deeper, heavier in-breath of the bulky Jones from the thin, sighing note of the bank director. From my position I could look over the case in the direction of the floor. Suddenly my eyes caught the glint of a light.

At first it was but a lurid spark upon the stone pavement. Then it lengthened out until it became a yellow line, and then, without any warning or sound, a gash seemed to open and a hand appeared; a white, almost womanly hand, which felt about in the centre of the little area of light. For a minute or more the hand, with its writhing fingers, protruded out of the floor. Then it was withdrawn as suddenly as it appeared, and all was dark again save the single lurid spark which marked a chink between the stones.

Its disappearance, however, was but momentary. With a rending, tearing sound, one of the broad, white stones turned over upon its side and left a square, gaping hole, through which streamed the light of a lantern. Over the edge there peeped a clean-cut, boyish face, which looked keenly about it, and then, with a hand on either side of the aperture, drew itself shoulder-high and waist-high, until one knee rested upon the edge. In another instant he stood at the side of the hole and was hauling after him a companion, lithe and small like himself, with a pale face and a shock of very red hair.

"It's all clear," he whispered. "Have you the chisel and the bags? Great Scott! Jump, Archie, jump, and I'll swing for it!"

Sherlock Holmes had sprung out and seized the intruder by the collar. The other dived down the hole, and I heard the sound of rending cloth as Jones clutched at his skirts. The light flashed upon the barrel of a revolver, but Holmes's hunting crop came down on the man's wrist, and the pistol clinked upon the stone floor.

"It's no use, John Clay," said Holmes blandly. "You have no chance at all."

"So I see," the other answered with the utmost coolness. "I fancy that my pal is all right, though I see you have got his coat-tails."

"There are three men waiting for him at the door," said Holmes.

"Oh, indeed! You seem to have done the thing very completely. I must compliment you."

"And I you," Holmes answered. "Your red-headed idea was very new and effective."

"You'll see your pal again presently," said Jones. "He's quicker at climbing down holes than I am. Just hold out while I fix the derbies."

"I beg that you will not touch me with your filthy hands," remarked our prisoner as the handcuffs clattered upon his wrists. "You may not be aware that I have royal blood in my veins. Have the goodness, also, when you address me always to say 'sir' and 'please.'"

"All right," said Jones with a stare and a snigger. "Well, would you please, sir, march upstairs, where we can get a cab to carry your Highness to the police-station?"

"That is better," said John Clay serenely. He made a sweeping bow to the three of us and walked quietly off in the custody of the detective.

"Really, Mr. Holmes," said Mr. Merryweather as we followed them from the cellar, "I do not know how the bank can thank you or repay you. There is no doubt that you have detected and defeated in the most complete manner one of the most determined attempts at bank robbery that have ever come within my experience."

"I have had one or two little scores of my own to settle with Mr. John Clay," said Holmes. 'I have been at some small expense over this matter, which I shall expect the bank to refund, but beyond that I am amply repaid by having had an experience which is in many ways unique, and by hearing the very remarkable narrative of the Red-headed League."

• • • •

"You see, Watson," he explained in the early hours of the morning as we sat over a glass of whisky and soda in Baker Street, "it was perfectly obvious from the first that the only possible object of this rather fantastic business of the advertisement of the League, and the copying of the Encyclopaedia, must be to get this not over-bright pawnbroker out of the way for a number of hours every day. It was a curious way of managing it, but, really, it would be difficult to suggest a better. The method was no doubt suggested to Clay's ingenious mind by the colour of his accomplice's hair. The £4 a week was a lure which must draw him, and what was it to them, who were playing for thousands? They put in the advertisement, one rogue has the temporary office, the other rogue incites the man to apply for it, and together they manage to secure his absence every morning in the week. From the time that I heard of the assistant having come for half wages, it was obvious to me that he had some strong motive for securing the situation."

"But how could you guess what the motive was?"

"Had there been women in the house, I should have suspected a mere vulgar intrigue. That, however, was out of the question. The man's business was a small one, and there was nothing in his house which could account for such elaborate preparations, and such an expenditure as they were at. It must, then, be something out of the house. What could it be? I thought of the assistant's fondness for photography, and his trick of vanishing into the cellar. The cellar! There was the end of this tangled clue. Then I made inquiries as to this mysterious assistant and found that I had to deal with one of the coolest and most daring criminals in London. He was doing something in the cellar—something which took many hours a day for months on end. What could it be, once more? I could think of nothing save that he was running a tunnel to some other building.

"So far I had got when we went to visit the scene of action. I surprised you by beating upon the pavement with my stick. I was ascertaining whether the cellar stretched out in front or behind. It was not in front. Then I rang the bell, and, as I hoped, the assistant answered it. We have had some skirmishes, but we had never set eyes upon each other before. I hardly looked at his face. His knees were what I wished to see. You must yourself have remarked how worn, wrinkled, and stained they were. They spoke of those hours of burrowing. The only remaining point was what they were burrowing for. I walked round the corner, saw the City and Surburban Bank abutted on our friend's premises, and felt that I had solved my problem. When you drove home after the concert I called upon Scotland Yard and upon the chairman of the bank directors, with the result that you have seen."

"And how could you tell that they would make their attempt to-night?" I asked.

"Well, when they closed their League offices that was a sign that they cared no longer about Mr. Jabez Wilson's presence—in other words, that they had completed their tunnel. But it was essential that they should use it soon, as it might be discovered, or the bullion might be removed. Saturday would suit them better than any other day, as it would give them two days for their escape. For all these reasons I expected them to come to-night."

"You reasoned it out beautifully," I exclaimed in unfeigned admiration. "It is as long a chain, and yet every link rings true."

"It saved me from ennui," he answered, yawning. "Alas! I already feel it closing in upon me. My life is spent in one long effort to escape from the commonplaces of existence. These little problems help me to do so."

"And you are a benefactor of the race," said I.

He shrugged his shoulders. "Well, perhaps, after all, it is of some little use," he remarked. "'*L'homme c'est rien—l'œuvre c'est tout*,' as Gustave Flaubert wrote to George Sand."

CONSTRUCTING A READING

1. It might be said that Arthur Conan Doyle gives Holmes and Watson some gaps to close. By placing the reader in the same position as Watson, Doyle invites us to try to figure out what Holmes sees as gaps and how he closes them. In groups, try tracing the process of Holmes's reasoning by making a list of the gaps he formulates and closes.

2. Doyle gives his readers gaps, too, of course. What, for example, do Holmes's deductions about Mr. Wilson's past contribute to the coherence of the story?

3. Do you like Sherlock Holmes? Why or why not?

CHAPTER THREE

How Readers Construct
the World of the Text

Texts have worlds of their own.

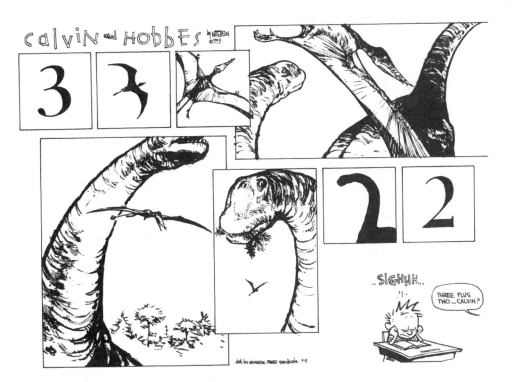

This cartoon shows us a world inside a child's imagination. In order to read this text, we need to grant a kind of existence to its world and live there for a moment. In the first eight panels, the cartoonist lets us see only what Calvin is imagining. Most readers recognize that the text is inviting them into a world where dinosaurs exist; they agree to enter that world without immediately imposing their own—without, that is, thinking to themselves, "Wait, dinosaurs are extinct; this can't be real!" Then readers begin to frame gap questions about how the dinosaurs connect with the numbers.

Only in the last panel does the cartoonist (and, hence, his readers) change perspectives. At that point, we see that the text has juxtaposed two conflicting worlds: the world of Calvin's imagination in which 3s and 2s take on the characteristics of prehistoric birds, and the world of the elementary school classroom in which Calvin has trouble with an arithmetic problem. The cartoon asks us to take a critical distance and realize that, in a child's imagination, not only is it more interesting to think about dinosaurs than about math, but an arithmetic problem can be as terrifying as a prehistoric monster. Perhaps we think for a moment about how a child's world is richer and more fun than our own, even though it is sometimes very frightening. But in order to make that meaning, we have to "be" Calvin for a moment, and then to stop being Calvin and play Calvin's world against the world of actuality; we have to enter his world, look at it critically, and then return, slightly changed, to our own.

WHAT IS "THE WORLD OF THE TEXT"?

I use the term *world* to designate all the ways in which the text describes or creates a context—all the things readers have to know or understand—or even momentarily grant for the sake of argument—in order to read a text.

These include, not only the historical and geographical places, events, and things to which a text refers, but also more subtle and more important ways in which texts invite us to read them. To read any text is *in some sense* to enter that text's world. As they make meaning from a text, readers encounter its system of values, its sense of logic, of cause and effect, of appropriate social and familial relations, and so forth. Before they can understand, and take a position on, the

---

Wolfgang Iser, on whose theories of reading much of this text is based, uses the term *repertoire* to name all of the "extratextual reality" to which the text refers. "This may be in the form of references to earlier works, or to social and historical norms, or to the whole culture from which the text has emerged."

Wolfgang Iser, *The Act of Reading: A Theory of Aesthetic Response.* The Johns Hopkins University Press, 1978.

conflict or problem the text asks them to consider, readers need to have some sense of how "things are supposed to be" in the world that the text represents.

How the World of the Text Differs from Its Setting

From your other courses, you may be familiar with more limiting conceptions of textual worlds. For example, the word *setting* has traditionally been used to indicate the time and place in which the events of a fiction take place. To see the difference between the formal idea of setting and the more complicated notion of world, think again about "In Another Country," the story by Ernest Hemingway we read in Chapter One. The *setting* for this story is an Italian military hospital during World War I, but its *world* is considerably more extensive. A reader alert to the text's world will remember that the United States did not enter the war until President Woodrow Wilson asked for a declaration of war on April 2, 1917, after more than three years of fighting in Europe had already occurred. Some Americans had, however, volunteered for noncombative duty in European armed forces long before that. European soldiers had somewhat ambivalent feelings about these Americans; on one hand, they knew that they needed the Americans' help, but on the other hand, this very fact was disconcerting, or even embarrassing. The world for this Hemingway text, then, includes beliefs about patriotism and manliness that might prompt a man to be ashamed of weeping, even at the death of his spouse, or of needing help, even if it is his country that needs it and he believes the cause is a good one. When we read Hemingway's text, we are invited to come to terms in some way with those beliefs, to see how they operate, and (importantly) to make some kind of judgment about them. These processes are far more complex—and far more relevant to our making sense of the story—than merely gathering information about Italian geography or World War I.

To enter the world of any text, therefore—to make meaning with it—we need complex and intricate information. We need to know at least a little, not only about a text's explicit historical and geographical setting, but also about the assumptions and beliefs of the people who live in the world it represents. By setting a text in a particular time or place, an author asks readers to recall what they already know about the setting (or to learn about it) and to perceive the text as making a comment of some kind about the world from which that setting emerges. To make these complex readings, we need to think (or learn) about what people thought and believed at the time and place the text represents and (if they differ) the time and place in which the text was produced.

READING FOR WORLD

The text that follows, Ursula Le Guin's "The Ones Who Walk Away from Omelas," uses its setting to guide readers toward raising questions about its worlds.

The Ones Who Walk Away from Omelas
(Variations on a theme by William James)

Ursula K. Le Guin

With a clamor of bells that set the swallows soaring, the Festival of Summer came to the city Omelas, bright-towered by the sea. The rigging of the boats in harbor sparkled with flags. In the streets between houses with red roofs and painted walls, between old moss-grown gardens and under avenues of trees, past great parks and public buildings, processions moved. Some were decorous: old people in long stiff robes of mauve and grey, grave master workmen, quiet, merry women carrying their babies and chatting as they walked. In other streets the music beat faster, a shimmering of gong and tambourine, and the people went dancing, the procession was a dance. Children dodged in and out, their high calls rising like the swallows' crossing flights over the music and the singing. All the processions wound towards the north side of the city, where on the great water-meadow called the Green Fields boys and girls, naked in the bright air, with mud-stained feet and ankles and long, lithe arms, exercised their restive horses before the race. The horses wore no gear at all but a halter without bit. Their manes were braided with streamers of silver, gold, and green. They flared their nostrils and pranced and boasted to one another; they were vastly excited, the horse being the only animal who has adopted our cere- monies as his own. Far off to the north and west the mountains stood up half encircling Omelas on her bay. The air of morning was so clear that the snow still crowning the Eighteen Peaks burned with white-gold fire across the miles of sunlit air, under the dark blue of the sky. There was just enough wind to make the banners that marked the racecourse snap and flutter now and then. In the silence of the broad green meadows one could hear the music winding through the city streets, farther and nearer and ever approaching, a cheerful faint sweetness of the air that from time to time trembled and gathered together and broke out into the great joyous clanging of the bells.

Joyous! How is one to tell about joy? How describe the citizens of Omelas?

They were not simple folk, you see, though they were happy. But we do not say the words of cheer much any more. All smiles have become archaic. Given a description such as this one tends to make certain assumptions. Given a description such as this one tends to look next for the King, mounted on a splendid stallion and surrounded by his noble knights, or perhaps in a golden litter borne by great-muscled slaves. But there was no king. They did not use swords, or keep slaves. They were not barbarians. I do not know the rules and laws of their society, but I suspect that they were singularly few. As they did without monarchy and slavery, so they also got on without the stock exchange, the advertisement, the secret police, and the bomb. Yet I repeat that these were not simple folk, not dulcet shepherds, noble savages, bland utopians. They were not less complex than us. The trouble is that we have a bad habit, encouraged by pedants and sophisticates, of considering happiness as something rather stupid. Only pain is intellectual, only evil interesting. This is the treason of the artist: a refusal to admit the banality of evil and the terrible boredom of pain. If you can't lick 'em, join 'em. If it hurts, repeat it. But to praise despair is to condemn delight, to embrace violence is to lose hold of everything else. We have almost lost hold; we can no longer describe a happy man, nor make any celebration of joy. How can I tell you about the people of Omelas? They were not naive and happy children—though their children were, in fact, happy. They were mature, intelligent, passionate adults whose lives were not wretched. 0 miracle! but I wish I could describe it better. I wish I could convince you. Omelas sounds in my words like a city in a fairy tale, long ago and far away, once upon a time. Perhaps it would be best if you imagined it as your own fancy bids, assuming it will rise to the occasion, for certainly I cannot suit you all. For instance, how about technology? I think that there would be no cars or helicopters in and above the streets; this follows from the fact that the people of Omelas are happy people. Happiness is based on a just discrimination of what is necessary, what is neither necessary nor destructive, and what is destructive. In the middle category, however—that of the unnecessary but undestructive, that of comfort, luxury, exuberance, etc.—they could perfectly well have central heating, subway trains, washing machines, and all kinds of marvelous devices not yet invented here, floating light-sources, fuelless power, a cure for the common cold. Or they could have none of that: it doesn't matter. As you like it. I inclined to think that people from towns up and down the coast have been coming in to Omelas during the last days before the Festival on very fast little trains and double-decked trams, and that the train station of Omelas is actually the handsomest building in town, though plainer than the magnificent Farmers' Market. But even granted trains, I fear that Omelas so far strikes some of you as goody-goody. Smiles, bells, parades, horses, bleh. If so, please add an orgy. If an orgy would help, don't hesitate. Let us not, however, have temples from which issue beautiful nude priests and priestesses already half in ecstasy and ready to copulate with any man or woman, lover or stranger, who desires union with the deep godhead of the blood, although that was my first idea. But really it would be better not to have any temples in Omelas—at least, not manned temples. Religion yes, clergy no. Surely the beautiful nudes can just wander about, offering themselves like divine soufflés to the hunger of the needy and the rapture of the flesh. Let them join the processions. Let tambourines be struck above the copulations, and the glory of desire be proclaimed upon the gongs, and (a not unimportant point) let the offering of these delightful rituals be beloved and looked after by all. One thing I know there is none of in Omelas is guilt. But what else should there be? I thought at first there were no drugs, but that is puritanical. For those who like it, the faint insistent sweetness of *drooz* may perfume the ways of the city, *drooz* which first brings a great lightness and brilliance to the mind and limbs, and then after some hours a dreamy languor, and wonderful visions at last of the very arcana and inmost secrets of the Universe, as well as exciting the pleasure of sex beyond all belief; and it is not habit-forming. For more modest tastes I think there ought to be beer. What else, what else belongs in the joyous city? The sense of victory, surely, the celebration of courage. But as we did without clergy, let us do without soldiers. The joy built upon successful slaughter is not the right kind of joy; it will not do; it is fearful and it is trivial. A boundless and generous contentment, a magnanimous triumph felt not against some outer enemy but in communion with the finest and fairest in the souls of all men everywhere and the splendor of the world's summer: this is what swells the hearts of the people of Omelas, and the victory they celebrate is that of life. I really don't think many of them need to take *drooz*.

Most of the processions have reached the Green Fields by now. A marvelous smell of cooking goes forth from the red and blue tents of the provisioners. The faces of small children are amiably sticky; in the benign grey beard of a man a couple of crumbs of rich pastry are entangled. The youths and girls have mounted their horses and are beginning to group around the starting line of the course. An old woman, small, fat, and laughing, is passing out flowers from a basket, and tall young men wear her flowers in their shining hair. A child of nine or ten sits at the edge of the crowd, alone, playing on a wooden flute. People pause to listen, and they smile, but they do not speak to him, for he never ceases playing and never sees them, his dark eyes wholly rapt in the sweet, thin magic of the tune.

He finishes, and slowly lowers his hands holding the wooden flute.

As if that little private silence were the signal, all at once a trumpet sounds from the pavilion near the starting line: imperious, melancholy, piercing. The horses rear on their slender legs, and some of them neigh in answer. Sober-faced, the young riders stroke the horses' necks and soothe them, whispering, "Quiet, quiet, there my beauty, my hope. . . ." They begin to form in rank along the starting line. The crowds along the racecourse are like a field of grass and flowers in the wind. The Festival of Summer has begun.

Do you believe? Do you accept the festival, the city, the joy? No? Then let me describe one more thing.

In a basement under one of the beautiful public buildings of Omelas, or perhaps in the cellar of one of its spacious private homes, there is a room. It has one locked door, and no window. A little light seeps in dustily between cracks in the boards, secondhand from a cobwebbed window somewhere across the cellar. In one corner of the little room a couple of mops, with stiff, clotted, foul-smelling heads, stand near a rusty bucket The floor is dirt, a little damp to the touch, as cellar dirt usually is. The room is about three paces long and two wide: a mere broom closet or disused tool room. In the room a child is sitting. It could he a boy or a girl. It looks about six but actually is nearly ten. It is feeble-minded. Perhaps it was born defective, or perhaps it has become imbecile through fear, malnutrition, and neglect It picks its nose and occasionally fumbles vaguely with its toes or genitals, as it sits hunched in the corner farthest from the bucket and the two mops. It is afraid of the mops. It finds them horrible. It shuts its eyes, but it knows the mops are still standing there; and the door is locked; and nobody will come. The door is always locked; and nobody ever comes, except that sometimes—the child has no understanding of time or interval—sometimes the door rattles terribly and opens, and a person, or several people, are there. One of them may come in and kick the child to make it stand up. The others never come close, but peer in at it with frightened, disgusted eyes. The food bowl and the water jug are hastily filled, the door is locked, the eyes disappear. The people at the door never say anything, but the child, who has not always lived in the tool room, and can remember sunlight and its mother's voice, sometimes speaks. "I will be good," it says. "Please let me out. I will be good!" They never answer. The child used to scream for help at night, and cry a good deal, but now it only makes a kind of whining, "eh-haa, eh-haa," and it speaks less and less often. It is so thin there are no calves to its legs; its belly protrudes; it lives on a half-bowl of corn meal and grease a day. It is naked. Its buttocks and thighs are a mass of festered sores, as it sits in its own excrement continually.

They all know it is there, all the people of Omelas. Some of them have come to see it, others are content merely to know it is there. They all know that it has to be there. Some of them understand why, and some do not, but they all understand that their happiness, the beauty of their city, the tenderness of their friendships, the health of their children, the wisdom of their scholars, the skill of their makers, even the abundance of their harvest and the kindly weathers of their skies, depend wholly on this child's abominable misery.

This is usually explained to children when they are between eight and twelve, whenever they seem capable of understanding; and most of those who come to see the child are young people, though often enough an adult comes, or comes back, to see the child. No matter how well the matter has been explained to them, these young spectators are always shocked and sickened at the sight. They feel disgust, which they had thought themselves superior to. They feel anger, outrage, impotence, despite all the explanations. They would like to do something for the child. But there is nothing they can do. If the child were brought up into the sunlight out of that vile place, if it were cleaned and fed and comforted, that would be a good thing, indeed; but if it were done, in that day and hour all the prosperity and beauty and delight of Omelas would wither and be destroyed. Those are the terms. To exchange all the goodness and grace of every life in Omelas for that single, small improvement: to throw away the happiness of thousands for the chance of the happiness of one: that would be to let guilt within the walls indeed.

The terms are strict and absolute; there may not even be a kind word spoken to the child.

Often the young people go home in tears, or in a tearless rage, when they have seen the child and faced this terrible paradox. They may brood over it for weeks or years. But as time goes on they begin to realize that even if the child could be released, it would not get much good of its freedom: a little vague pleasure of warmth and food, no doubt, but little more. It is too degraded and imbecile to know any real joy. It has been afraid too long ever to be free of fear. Its habits are too uncouth for it to respond to humane treatment. Indeed, after so long it would probably be wretched without walls about it to protect it, and darkness for its eyes, and its own excrement to sit in. Their tears at the bitter injustice dry when they begin to perceive the terrible justice of reality, and to accept it. Yet it is their tears and anger, the trying of their generosity and the acceptance of their helplessness, which are perhaps the true source of the splendor of their lives. Theirs is no vapid, irresponsible happiness. They know that they, like the child, are not free. They know compassion. It is the existence of the child, and their knowledge of its existence, that makes possible the nobility of their architecture, the poignancy of their music, the profundity of their science. It is because of the child that they are so gentle with children. They know that if the wretched one were not there snivelling in the dark, the other one, the flute-player, could make no joyful music as the young riders line up in their beauty for the race in the sunlight of the first morning of summer.

Now do you believe in them? Are they not more credible? But there is one more thing to tell, and this is quite incredible.

At times one of the adolescent girls or boys who go to see the child does not go home to weep or rage, does not, in fact, go home at all. Sometimes also a man or woman much older falls silent for a day or two, and then leaves home. These people go out into the street, and walk down the street alone. They keep walking, and walk straight out of the city of Omelas, through the beautiful gates. They keep walking across the farmlands of Omelas. Each one goes alone, youth or girl, man or woman. Night falls; the traveler must pass down village streets, between the houses with yellow-lit windows, and on out into the darkness of the fields. Each alone, they go west or north, towards the mountains. They go on. They leave Omelas, they walk ahead into the darkness, and they do not come back. The place they go towards is a place even less imaginable to most of us than the city of happiness. I cannot describe it at all. It is possible that it does not exist. But they seem to know where they are going, the ones who walk away from Omelas.

This story is set in "Omelas" during a ritual celebration. After describing the city's beauty and pleasures, Le Guin's narrator guides the reader to consider, not only setting, but also world: "Given a description such as this one tends to make certain assumptions."

To read this story for world, we need to make assumptions about the people who live in "a fairy tale" city where dreadful things happen. Although the narrator does not "know the rules and laws of their society," the details of the story show the effects of these rules and laws. The reader's job is to infer the "rules"—the beliefs and customs that obtain in Omelas—from their effects. How have its citizens achieved and maintained their "boundless and generous contentment"? Why do they not "say the words of cheer anymore"?

> They all know [the child] is there, the people of Omelas. . . . They all know it has to be there. Some of them understand why and some do not, but all understand that their happiness . . . depend[s] wholly on this child's abominable misery.

The world of this story, then, is one in which people know that the presence of happiness depends on the presence of unhappiness, wealth depends on poverty, health depends on sickness, and cleanliness depends on filth. The system that tortures the innocent little child cannot be dismantled without ruining the mechanisms that keep the whole culture prosperous and happy.

When I perceive this world, I begin to sympathize with the ones who walk away from Omelas. But from that emotion another gap emerges: I begin to wonder why they walk away. What must they be thinking, what must they believe, to leave this fantasy city? I conclude that the citizens leave because they abhor the fact that the culture's very existence relies on the torturous exploitation of a helpless child and that—even worse—the child is made to feel that she or he is somehow responsible for this plight. The ones who walk away, I infer, do not wish to be complicit in such a monstrous system any longer. Clearly, leaving such a place is moral and laudable. But then another gap presents itself: where do the ones who walk away from Omelas go? The story makes it appear that they go into some kind of wilderness, or unknown place. Another gap: what does *that* mean? Why don't they stay and help? But what could they do?

At some point during my attempts to infer the set of beliefs that make the world make sense to these fictional characters, I begin to associate their situation with my own. In my world, too, helpless and innocent victims of poverty and disease are somehow held responsible for their own misery by a system that cannot provide for them. That association leads me to draw other kinds of connections between Omelas and my world. My world, too, is built on such contradictions: in capitalist economies, wealth is possible because poverty exists. Then I have to ask myself how I can continue to live in such a world. Whose fault is it that the poor in my world live as they do? What should I do when I see their suffering? Should I blame them? Should I permit other people to blame them? Should they blame themselves? Should I walk away? Should I stay and try to do something about it? If I stay, what can or should I do, and how?

CONSTRUCTING A READING

1. Le Guin's narrator compares the values in Omelas with the values of those she addresses ("us"). What are the grounds of those comparisons? When, for example, the speaker says "[w]e have almost lost hold" and "we do not say the words of cheer much any more," does that "we" seem to

include you? Why or why not? To whom does it speak? For whom does it speak?

2.   Why might the speaker say, "Perhaps it would be best if you imagined it as your fancy bids, assuming it will rise to the occasion, for certainly I cannot suit you all?" What kind of real-world connections can you make with the imaginary Omelas? Is Omelas like a specific country or a group of countries?

3.   What would a city of happiness be for you? How do you think your vision compares to others?

4.   The subtitle, "Variations on a Theme by William James," refers to American philosopher and psychologist William James, who wrote about morality and the scapegoat figure. What does the story seem to say about scapegoats?

5.   Describe a scapegoat that you have noticed in your culture(s) and explain how the scapegoating process works.

6.   Why is the destination of the ones who walk away "even less imaginable to most of us than the city of happiness?" Why can't it be imagined? What does the narrator imply by saying that it might not exist?

DISTINGUISHING AMONG WORLDS

As you think about world, you will need to keep some distinctions in mind: Texts have worlds; texts refer to worlds; authors have worlds and, as we know, individual readers have worlds of their own.

Texts' Worlds

The _text's world_ includes the cultural, geographical, and historical context in which it was written—everything, in other words, to which it refers. The world of Le Guin's story, for example, includes both the imaginary place called Omelas and the United States in the 1970s. Omelas has "central heating, subway trains, washing machines," like the United States in the seventies, "and all kinds of marvelous devices not yet invented . . . floating light sources, fuelless power, a cure for the common cold."

Authors' Worlds

A text will inevitably contain certain aspects of its author's personal world. The _author's world_ can include individual life experiences as well as the broad cultural circumstances that combine to create a "world view." Writing about "The Ones Who Walk Away from Omelas" in _The Wind's Twelve Quarters_, the collection in which it appeared, Le Guin explains:

The central idea of this psychomyth, the scapegoat, turns up in Dostoyevsky's *Brothers Karamazov*, and several people have asked me, rather suspiciously, why I gave the credit to William James. The fact is, I haven't been able to re-read Dostoyevsky, much as I loved him, since I was twenty-five, and I'd simply forgotten he used the idea. But when I met it in James's "The Moral Philosopher and the Moral Life," it was with a shock of recognition. Here is how James puts it:

> Or if the hypothesis were offered us of a world in which Messrs. Fourier's and Bellamy's and Morris's utopias should all be outdone, and millions kept permanently happy on the one simple condition that a certain lost soul on the far-off edge of things should lead a life of lonely torment, what except a specifical and independent sort of emotion can it be which would make us immediately feel, even though an impulse arose within us to clutch at the happiness so offered, how hideous a thing would be its enjoyment when deliberately accepted as the fruit of such a bargain?

The dilemma of the American conscience can hardly be better stated. Dostoyevsky was a great artist, and a radical one, but his early social radicalism reversed itself, leaving him a violent reactionary. Whereas the American James, who seems so mild, so naïvely gentlemanly—look how he says "us," assuming all his readers are as decent as himself!—was, and remained, and remains, a genuinely radical thinker. Directly after the "lost soul" passage he goes on,

> All the higher, more penetrating ideals are revolutionary. They present themselves far less in the guise of effects of past experience than in that of probable causes of future experience, factors to which the environment and the lessons it has so far taught us must learn to bend.

The application of those two sentences to this story, and to science fiction, and to all thinking about the future, is quite direct. Ideals as "the probable causes of future experience"—that is a subtle and an exhilarating remark!

Of course I didn't read James and sit down and say, Now I'll write a story about that "lost soul." It seldom works that simply. I sat down and started a story, just because I felt like it, with nothing but the word "Omelas" in mind. It came from a road sign: Salem (Oregon) backwards. Don't you read road signs backwards? POTS. WOLS nerdlihc. Ocsicnarf Nas . . . Salem equals schelomo equels salaam equals Peace. Melas. O melas. Omelas. Homme hélas. "Where do you get your ideas from, Ms Le Guin?" From forgetting Dostoyevsky and reading road signs backwards, naturally. Where else?

The author's world is not the same as authorial intention, although they can contain common elements. As we defined the term in Chapter One, *authorial intention* is a product of a *conscious plan* on the part of the author. The author's world, though, can include elements of which she or he is not conscious. For example, Ursula Le Guin may have made an unconscious connection with the witch trials of Salem, Massachusetts, as she wrote this story about scapegoats. Perhaps, too, as this pacifist wrote during the early 1970s, her unconscious mind provided the war in Vietnam as a context for her narrator's assertion that "joy built upon successful slaughter is not the right kind of joy."

Readers' Worlds

Readers, too, come to the text with their own worlds. These worlds are neither simple nor consistent; nor are they even wholly available to us. The *reader's world* consists of all the kinds of differences that we discussed in Chapter One. It includes psychological backgrounds, social class, political and ethical beliefs, race, gender, and so forth. Moreover, since readers are constantly learning more about life (and texts), they are constantly changing their minds about issues that texts represent. Accordingly, the text will invoke different aspects of its readers' worlds each time it is read, and different readers will see different aspects of the text's world. They can all be different. They all change. None can ever be fully known.

Our ability to make meaning comes from convergences between our world(s) as readers and the world(s) of the text and author.

HOW TEXTUAL WORLDS RELATE TO CULTURAL VALUES

When we read for world, we often find that rather than merely representing the values that sustain their culture, texts question those values. James Thurber's story "The Greatest Man in the World" questions some of the ways in which cultures establish and honor their heroes. Because the story was written in 1937 but set in the 1950s, its world includes both the values of the time and place in which the text is set (as Thurber imagines them) and those of the author's world (in the 1930s). Certainly, too, it will evoke some of our own contemporary notions about heroes and heroism. As you read, look for ways in which the text questions its culture's values.

The Greatest Man in the World

James Thurber

Looking back on it now, from the vantage point of 1950, one can only marvel that it hadn't happened long before it did. The United States of America had been, ever since Kitty Hawk, blindly constructing the elaborate petard by which, sooner or later, it must be hoist. It was inevitable that some day there would come roaring out of the skies a national hero of insufficient intelligence, background, and character successfully to endure the mounting orgies of glory prepared for aviators who stayed up a long time or flew a great distance. Both Lindbergh and Byrd, fortunately for national decorum and international amity, had been gentlemen; so had our other famous aviators. They wore their laurels gracefully, withstood the awful weather of publicity, married excellent women, usually of fine family, and quietly retired to private life and the enjoyment of their varying fortunes. No untoward incidents, on a worldwide scale, marred the perfection of their conduct on the perilous heights of fame. The exception to the rule was, however, bound to occur and it did, in July, 1937, when Jack ("Pal") Smurch, erstwhile mechanic's helper in a small garage in Westfield,

Iowa, flew a second-hand, single-motored Bresthaven Dragon-Fly III mono-plane all the way around the world, without stopping.

Never before in the history of aviation had such a flight as Smurch's ever been dreamed of. No one had even taken seriously the weird floating auxiliary gas tanks, invention of the mad New Hampshire professor of astronomy, Dr. Charles Lewis Gresharn, upon which Smurch placed full reliance. When the garage worker, a slightly built, surly, unprepossessing young man of twenty-two, appeared at Roosevelt Field in early July, 1937, slowly chewing a great quid of scrap tobacco, and announced, "Nobody ain't seen no flyin' yet," the newspapers touched briefly and satirically upon his projected twenty-five-thou-sand-mile flight. Aeronautical and automotive experts dismissed the idea curtly, implying that it was a hoax, a publicity stunt. The rusty, battered, second-hand plane wouldn't go. The Gresham auxiliary tanks wouldn't work. It was simply a cheap joke.

Smurch, however, after calling on a girl in Brooklyn who worked in the flap-folding department of a large paper-box factory, a girl whom he later described as his "sweet patootie," climbed nonchalantly into his ridiculous plane at dawn of the memorable seventh of July, 1937, spit a curve of tobacco juice into the still air, and took off, carrying with him only a gallon of bootleg gin and six pounds of salami.

When the garage boy thundered out over the ocean the papers were forced to record, in all seriousness, that a mad, unknown young man—his name was vari-ously misspelled—had actually set out upon a preposterous attempt to span the world in a rickety, one-engined contraption, trusting to the long-distance refuelling device of a crazy schoolmaster. When, nine days later, without hav-ing stopped once, the tiny plane appeared above San Francisco Bay, headed for New York, spluttering and choking, to be sure, but still magnificently and miraculously aloft, the headlines, which long since had crowded everything else off the front page—even the shooting of the Governor of Illinois by the Vileti gang—swelled to unprecedented size, and the news stories began to run to twenty-five and thirty columns. It was noticeable, however, that the accounts of the epoch-making flight touched rather lightly upon the aviator himself. This was not because facts about the hero as a man were too meagre, but because they were too complete.

Reporters, who had been rushed out to Iowa when Smurch's plane was first sighted over the little French coast town of Serly-le-Mer, to dig up the story of the great man's life, had promptly discovered that the story of his life could not be printed. His mother, a sullen short-order cook in a shack restau-rant on the edge of a tourists' camping ground near Westfield, met all inquiries as to her son with an angry "Ah, the hell with him; I hope he drowns." His father appeared to be in jail somewhere for stealing spotlights and laprobes from tourists' automobiles; his young brother, a weak-minded lad, had but recently escaped from the Preston, Iowa, Reformatory and was already wanted in several Western towns for the theft of money-order blanks from post offices. These alarming discoveries were still piling up at the very time that Pal Smurch, the greatest hero of the twentieth century, blear-eyed, dead for sleep, half-starved, was piloting his crazy junk-heap high above the region in which the lamentable story of his private life was being unearthed, headed for New York and a greater glory than any man of his time had ever known.

The necessity for printing some account in the papers of the young man's career and personality had led to a remarkable predicament. It was of course impossible to reveal the facts, for a tremendous popular feeling in favor of the young hero had sprung up, like a grass fire, when he was halfway across Europe on his flight around the globe. He was, therefore, described as a modest chap, taciturn, blond, popular with his friends, popular with girls. The only available snapshot of Smurch, taken at the wheel of a phony automobile in a cheap photo studio at an amusement park, was touched up so that the little vulgarian looked quite handsome. His twisted leer was smoothed into a pleasant smile. The truth was, in this way, kept from the youth's ecstatic compatriots; they did not dream that the Smurch family was despised and feared by its neighbors in the obscure Iowa town, nor that the hero himself, because of numerous unsavory exploits, had come to be regarded in Westfield as a nuisance and a menace. He had, the reporters discovered, once knifed the principal of his high school—not mortally, to be sure, but he had knifed him; and on another occasion, surprised in the act of stealing an altar-cloth from a church, he had bashed the sacristan over the head with a pot of Easter lilies; for each of these offences he had served a sentence in the reformatory.

Inwardly, the authorities, both in New York and in Washington, prayed that an understanding Providence might, however awful such a thing seemed, bring disaster to the rutty, battered plane and its illustrious pilot, whose unheard-of flight had aroused the civilized world to hosannas of hysterical praise. The authorities were convinced that the character of the renowned aviator was such that the limelight of adulation was bound to reveal him to all the world as a congenital hooligan mentally and morally unequipped to cope with his own prodigious fame. "I trust," said the Secretary of State, at one of many secret Cabinet meetings called to consider the national dilemma, "I trust that his mother's prayer will be answered," by which he referred to Mrs. Emma Smurch's wish that her son might be drowned. It was however, too late for that—Smurch had leaped the Atlantic and then the Pacific as if they were millponds. At three minutes after two o'clock on the afternoon of July 17, 1937, the garage boy brought his idiotic plane into Roosevelt Field for a perfect three-point landing.

It had, of course, been out of the question to arrange a modest little reception for the greatest flier in the history of the world. He was received at Roosevelt Field with such elaborate and pretentious ceremonies as rocked the world.

Fortunately, however, the worn and spent hero promptly swooned, had to be removed bodily from his plane, and was spirited from the field without having opened his mouth once. Thus he did not jeopardize the dignity of this first reception, a reception illumined by the presence of the Secretaries of War and the Navy, Mayor Michael J. Moriarity of New York, the Premier of Canada, Governors Fanniman, Groves, McFeely, and Critchfield, and a brilliant array of European diplomats. Smurch did not, in fact, come to in time to take part in the gigantic hullabaloo arranged at City Hall for the next day. He was rushed to a secluded nursing home and confined to bed. It was nine days before he was able to get up, or to be more exact, before he was permitted to get up. Meanwhile the greatest minds in the country, in solemn assembly, had arranged a secret conference of city, state, and government officials, which Smurch was to attend for the purpose of being instructed in the ethics and behavior of heroism.

On the day that the little mechanic was finally allowed to get up and dress and, for the first time in two weeks, took a great chew of tobacco, he was permitted to receive the newspapermen—this by way of testing him out. Smurch did not wait for questions. "Youse guys," he said—and the *Times* man winced—"youse guys can tell the cock-eyed world dat I put it over on Lindbergh, see? Yeh—an' made an ass o' them two frogs." The "two frogs" was a reference to a pair of gallant French fliers who, in attempting a flight only halfway round the world, had, two weeks before, unhappily been lost at sea. The *Times* man was bold enough, at this point, to sketch out for Smurch the accepted formula for interviews in cases of this kind; he explained that there should be no arrogant statements belittling the achievements of other heroes, particularly heroes of foreign nations. "Ah, the hell with that," said Smurch. "I did it, see? I did it, an' I'm talkin' about it." And he did talk about it.

None of this extraordinary interview was, of course, printed. On the contrary, the newspapers, already under the disciplined direction of a secret directorate created for the occasion and composed of statesmen and editors, gave out to a panting and restless world that "Jacky," as he had been arbitrarily nicknamed, would consent to say only that he was very happy and that anyone could have done what he did. "My achievement has been, I fear, slightly exaggerated," the *Times* man's article had him protest, with a modest smile. These newspaper stories were kept from the hero, a restriction which did not serve to abate the rising malevolence of his temper. The situation was, indeed, extremely grave, for Pal Smurch was, as he kept insisting, "rarin' to go." He could not much longer be kept from a nation clamorous to lionize him. It was the most desperate crisis the United States of America had faced since the sinking of the *Lusitania*.

On the afternoon of the twenty-seventh of July, Smurch was spirited away to a conference-room in which were gathered mayors, governors, government officials, behaviorist psychologists, and editors. He gave them each a limp, moist paw and a brief unlovely grin. "Hah ya?" he said. When Smurch was seated, the Mayor of New York arose and, with obvious pessimism, attempted to explain what he must say and how he must act when presented to the world, ending his talk with a high tribute to the hero's courage and integrity. The Mayor was followed by Governor Fanniman of New York, who, after a touching declaration of faith, introduced Cameron Spottiswood, Second Secretary of the American Embassy in Paris, the gentleman selected to coach Smurch in the amenities of public ceremonies. Sitting in a chair, with a soiled yellow tie in his hand and his shirt open at the throat, unshaved, smoking a rolled cigarette, Jack Smurch listened with a leer on his lips. "I get ya, I get ya," he cut in, nastily. "Ya want me to ack like a softy, huh? Ya want me to ack like that —— —— baby-faced Lindbergh, huh? Well, nuts to that, see?" Everyone took in his breath sharply; it was a sigh and a hiss. "Mr. Lindbergh," began a United States Senator, purple with rage, "and Mr. Byrd—" Smurch, who was paring his nails with a jackknife, cut in again. "Byrd!" he exclaimed. "Aw fa God's sake, dat big—" Somebody shut off his blasphemies with a sharp word. A newcomer had entered the room. Everyone stood up, except Smurch, who, still busy with his nails, did not even glance up. "Mr. Smurch," said someone sternly, "the President of the United States!" It had been thought that the presence of the Chief Executive might have a chastening effect upon the young hero, and the former had been, thanks to the remarkable cooperation of the press, secretly brought to the obscure conference-room.

A great, painful silence fell. Smurch looked up, waved a hand at the President. "How ya comin'?" he asked, and began rolling a fresh cigarette. The silence deepened. Someone coughed in a strained way. "Gee; it's hot, ain't it?" said Smurch. He loosened two more shirt buttons, revealing a hairy chest and the tattooed word "Sadie" enclosed in a stencilled heart. The great and important men in the room, faced by the most serious crisis in recent American history, exchanged worried frowns. Nobody seemed to know how to proceed. "Come awn, come awn," said Smurch. "Let's get the hell out of here! When do I start cuttin' in on de parties, huh? And what's they goin' to be *in* it?" He rubbed a thumb and forefinger together meaningly. "Money!" exclaimed a state senator, shocked, pale. "Yeh, money," said Pal, flipping his cigarette out of a window. "An' big money." He began rolling a fresh cigarette. "Big money," he repeated, frowning over the rice paper. He tilted back in his chair, and leered at each gentleman, separately, the leer of an animal that knows its power, the leer of a leopard loose in a bird-and-dog shop. "Aw fa God's sake, let's get some place where it's cooler," he said. "I been cooped up plenty for three weeks!"

Smurch stood up and walked over to an open window, where he stood staring down into the street, nine floors below. The faint shouting of newsboys floated up to him. He made out his name. "Hot dog!" he cried, grinning, ecstatic. He leaned out over the sill. "You tell 'em, babies!" he shouted down. "Hot diggity dog!" In the tense little knot of men standing behind him, a quick, mad impulse flared up. An unspoken word of appeal, of command, seemed to ring through the room. Yet it was deadly silent. Charles K. L. Brand, secretary to the Mayor of New York City, happened to be standing nearest Smurch; he looked inquiringly at the President of the United States. The President, pale, grim, nodded shortly. Brand, a tall, powerfully built man, once a tackle at Rutgers, stepped forward, seized the greatest man in the world by his left shoulder and the seat of his pants, and pushed him out the window.

"My God, he's fallen out the window!" cried a quick-witted editor.

"Get me out of here!" cried the President. Several men sprang to his side and he was hurriedly escorted out of a door toward a side-entrance of the building. The editor of the Associated Press took charge, being used to such things. Crisply he ordered certain men to leave, others to stay; quickly he outlined a story which all the papers were to agree on, sent two men to the street to handle that end of the tragedy, commanded a Senator to sob and two Congressmen to go to pieces nervously. In a word, he skillfully set the stage for the gigantic task that was to follow, the task of breaking to a grief-stricken world the sad story of the untimely, accidental death of its most illustrious and spectacular figure.

The funeral was, as you know, the most elaborate, the finest, the solemnest, and the saddest ever held in the United States of America. The monument in Arlington Cemetery, with its clean white shaft of marble and the simple device of a tiny plane carved on its base, is a place for pilgrims, in deep reverence, to visit. The nations of the world paid lofty tributes to little Jacky Smurch, America's greatest hero. At a given hour there were two minutes of silence throughout the nation. Even the inhabitants of the small, bewildered town of Westfield, Iowa, observed this touching ceremony; agents of the Department of Justice saw to that. One of them was especially assigned to stand grimly in the doorway of a little shack restaurant on the edge of the tourists' camping ground just outside the town. There, under his stern scrutiny, Mrs. Emma Smurch bowed her head above two hamburger steaks sizzling on her grill—bowed her head and turned away, so that the Secret Service man could not see the twisted, strangely familiar, leer on her lips.

CONSTRUCTING A READING

1. In what ways does the title, "The Greatest Man in the World," apply to "Pal" Smurch? Is he a great man in any way that makes sense to you?

2. What do you understand from this story about how societies create heroes or public figures? What role does the press or media play in representing public figures, then and now?

3. How do you react to Smurch's death? What does it seem to say about, not just the creation, but the control of heroes?

4. Why do you think that aviators so often became public heroes in the 1930s? (You might look in an encyclopedia for an account of Charles

Lindbergh's flight across the Atlantic in 1936.) What other kinds of acts, professions, or careers seem to have produced heroes in the past? How do you think various notions of heroism in America have changed over the course of the twentieth century?

5. What role does heroism play in your experience of contemporary life? Describe some similarities and differences between Pal Smurch and contemporary public figures.

WORKING WITH UNFAMILIAR TEXTUAL WORLDS

The story that follows, "Clay," from James Joyce's collection *Dubliners*, presents a complex problem of worlds. Many readers find the story completely incomprehensible on first reading, and therefore many editors of textbooks like this one simply decide not to use it. I've decided to use it precisely *because* its world is probably unfamiliar to you, so that you can see how much we depend on reading for world when we try to make meaning from a text.

Clay

James Joyce

The matron had given her leave to go out as soon as the women's tea was over and Maria looked forward to her evening out. The kitchen was spick and span: the cook said you could see yourself in the big copper boilers. The fire was nice and bright and on one of the side-tables were four very big barmbracks. These barmbracks seemed uncut; but if you went closer you would see that they had been cut into long thick even slices and were ready to be handed round at tea. Maria had cut them herself.

Maria was a very, very small person indeed but she had a very long nose and a very long chin. She talked a little through her nose, always soothingly: *Yes, my dear,* and *No, my dear.* She was always sent for when the women quarrelled over their tubs and always succeeded in making peace. One day the matron had said to her:

—Maria, you are a veritable peace-maker!

And the sub-matron and two of the Board ladies had heard the compliment. And Ginger Mooney was always saying what she wouldn't do to the dummy who had charge of the irons if it wasn't for Maria. Everyone was so fond of Maria.

The women would have their tea at six o'clock and she would be able to get away before seven. From Ballsbridge to the Pillar, twenty minutes; from the Pillar to Drumcondra, twenty minutes; and twenty minutes to buy the things. She would be there before eight. She took out her purse with the silver clasps and read again the words *A Present from Belfast.* She was very fond of that purse because Joe had brought it to her five years before when he and Alphy had gone to Belfast on a Whit-Monday trip. In the purse were two half-crowns and some coppers. She would have five shillings clear after paying tram fare. What a nice evening they would have, all the children singing! Only she hoped that Joe wouldn't come in drunk. He was so different when he took any drink.

Often he had wanted her to go and live with them; but she would have felt herself in the way (though Joe's wife was ever so nice with her) and she had become accustomed to the life of the laundry. Joe was a good fellow. She had nursed him and Alphy too; and Joe used often say:

—Mamma is mamma but Maria is my proper mother.

After the break-up at home the boys had got her that position in the *Dublin by Lamplight* laundry, and she liked it. She used to have such a bad opinion of Protestants but now she thought they were very nice people, a little quiet and serious, but still very nice people to live with. Then she had her plants in the conservatory and she liked looking after them. She had lovely ferns and wax-plants and, whenever anyone came to visit her, she always gave the visitor one or two slips from her conservatory. There was one thing she didn't like and that was the tracts on the walls; but the matron was such a nice person to deal with, so genteel.

When the cook told her everything was ready she went into the women's room and began to pull the big bell. In a few minutes the women began to come in by twos and threes, wiping their steaming hands in their petticoats and pulling down the sleeves of their blouses over their red steaming arms. They settled down before their huge mugs which the cook and the dummy filled up with hot tea, already mixed with milk and sugar in huge tin cans. Maria superintended the distribution of the barmbrack and saw that every woman got her four slices. There was a great deal of laughing and joking during the meal. Lizzie Fleming said Maria was sure to get the ring and, though Fleming had said that for so many Hallow Eves, Maria had to laugh and say she didn't want any ring or man either; and when she laughed her grey-green eyes sparkled with disappointed shyness and the tip of her nose nearly met the tip of her chin. Then Ginger Mooney lifted up her mug of tea and proposed Maria's health while all the other women clattered with their mugs on the table, and said she was sorry she hadn't a sup of porter to drink it in. And Maria laughed again till the tip of her nose nearly met the tip of her chin and till her minute body nearly shook itself asunder because she knew that Mooney meant well though, of course, she had the notions of a common woman.

But wasn't Maria glad when the women had finished their tea and the cook and the dummy had begun to clear away the tea-things! She went into her little bedroom and, remembering that the next morning was a mass morning, changed the hand of the alarm from seven to six. Then she took off her working skirt and her house-boots and laid her best skirt out on the bed and her tiny dress-boots beside the foot of the bed. She changed her blouse too and, as she stood before the mirror, she thought of how she used to dress for mass on Sunday morning when she was a young girl; and she looked with quaint affection at the diminutive body which she had so often adorned. In spite of its years she found it a nice tidy little body.

When she got outside the streets were shining with rain and she was glad of her old brown raincloak. The tram was full and she had to sit on the little stool at the end of the car, facing all the people, with her toes barely touching the floor. She arranged in her mind all she was going to do and thought how much better it was to be independent and to have your own money in your pocket. She hoped they would have a nice evening. She was sure they would but she could not help thinking what a pity it was Alphy and Joe were not speaking. They were always falling out now but when they were boys together they used to be the best of friends: but such was life.

She got out of her tram at the Pillar and ferreted her way quickly among the crowds. She went into Downes's cakeshop but the shop was so full of people that it was a long time before she could get herself attended to. She bought a dozen of mixed penny cakes, and at last came out of the shop laden with a big bag. Then she thought what else would she buy: she wanted to buy something really nice. They would be sure to have plenty of apples and nuts. It was hard to know what to buy and all she could think of was cake. She decided to buy some plumcake but Downes's plumcake had not enough almond icing on top of it so she went over to a shop in Henry Street. Here she was along time in suiting herself and the stylish young lady behind the counter, who was evidently a little annoyed by her, asked her was it wedding-cake she wanted to buy. That made Maria blush and smile at the young lady; but the young lady took it all very seriously and finally cut a thick slice of plumcake, parcelled it up and said:

—Two-and-four, please.

She thought she would have to stand in the Drumcondra tram because none of the young men seemed to notice her but an elderly gentleman made room for her. He was a stout gentleman and he wore a brown hard hat; he had a square red face and a greyish moustache. Maria thought he was a colonel-looking gentleman and she reflected how much more polite he was than the young men who simply stared straight before them. The gentleman began to chat with her about Hallow Eve and the rainy weather. He supposed the bag was full of good things for the little ones and said it was only right that the youngsters should enjoy themselves while they were young. Maria agreed with him and favoured him with demure nods and hems. He was very nice with her, and when she was getting out at the Canal Bridge she thanked him and bowed, and he bowed to her and raised his hat and smiled agreeably; and while she was going up along the terrace, bending her tiny head under the rain, she thought how easy it was to know a gentleman even when he has a drop taken.

Everybody said: *O, here's Maria!* when she came to Joe's house. Joe was there, having come home from business, and all the children had their Sunday dresses on. There were two big girls in from next door and games were going on. Maria gave the bag of cakes to the eldest boy, Alphy, to divide and Mrs Donnelly said it was too good of her to bring such a big bag of cakes and made all the children say:

—Thanks, Maria.

But Maria said she had brought something special for papa and mamma, something they would be sure to like, and she began to look for her plumcake. She tried in Downes's bag and then in the pockets of her raincloak and then on the hallstand but nowhere could she find it. Then she asked all the children had any of them eaten it—by mistake, of course—but the children all said no and looked as if they did not like to eat cakes if they were to be accused of stealing. Everybody had a solution for the mystery and Mrs Donnelly said it was plain that Maria had left it behind her in the tram. Maria, remembering how confused the gentleman with the greyish moustache had made her, coloured with shame and vexation and disappointment. At the thought of the failure of her little surprise and of the two and fourpence she had thrown away for nothing she nearly cried outright.

But Joe said it didn't matter and made her sit down by the fire. He was very nice with her. He told her all that went on in his office, repeating for her a smart answer which he had made to the manager. Maria did not understand why Joe laughed so much over the answer he had made but she said that the manager must have been a very overbearing person to deal with. Joe said he wasn't so bad when you knew how to take him, that he was a decent sort so long as you didn't rub him the wrong way. Mrs Donnelly played the piano for the children and they danced and sang. Then the two next-door girls handed round the nuts. Nobody could find the nutcrackers and Joe was nearly getting cross over it and asked how did they expect Maria to crack nuts without a nut-cracker. But Maria said she didn't like nuts and that they weren't to bother about her. Then Joe asked would she take a bottle of stout and Mrs Donnelly said there was port wine too in the house if she would prefer that. Maria said she would rather they didn't ask her to take anything: but Joe insisted.

So Maria let him have his way and they sat by the fire talking over old times and Maria thought she would put in a good word for Alphy. But Joe cried that God might strike him stone dead if ever he spoke a word to his brother again and Maria said she was sorry she had mentioned the matter. Mrs Donnelly told her husband it was a great shame for him to speak that way of his own flesh and blood but Joe said that Alphy was no brother of his and there was nearly being a row on the head of it. But Joe said he would not lose his temper on account of the night it was and asked his wife to open some more stout. The two next-door girls had arranged some Hallow Eve games and soon everything was merry again. Maria was delighted to see the children so merry and Joe and his wife in such good spirits. The next-door girls put some saucers on the table and then led the children up to the table, blindfold. One got the prayer-book and the other three got the water; and when one of the next-door girls got the ring Mrs Donnelly shook her finger at the blushing girl as much as to say: *O, I know all about it!* They insisted then on blindfolding Maria and leading her up to the table to see what she would get; and, while they were putting on the bandage, Maria laughed and laughed again till the tip of her nose nearly met the tip of her chin.

They led her up to the table amid laughing and joking and she put her hand out in the air as she was told to do. She moved her hand about here and there in the air and descended on one of the saucers. She felt a soft wet substance with her fingers and was surprised that nobody spoke or took off her bandage. There was a pause for a few seconds; and then a great deal of scuffling and whispering. Somebody said something about the garden, and at last Mrs Donnelly said something very cross to one of the next-door girls and told her to throw it out at once: that was no play. Maria understood that it was wrong that time and so she had to do it over again: and this time she got the prayer-book.

After that Mrs Donnelly played Miss McCloud's Reel for the children and Joe made Maria take a glass of wine. Soon they were all quite merry again and Mrs Donnelly said Maria would enter a convent before the year was out because she had got the prayer-book. Maria had never seen Joe so nice to her as he was that night, so full of pleasant talk and reminiscences. She said they were all very good to her.

At last the children grew tired and sleepy and Joe asked Maria would she not sing some little song before she went, one of the old songs. Mrs Donnelly said *Do, please, Maria!* and so Maria had to get up and stand beside the piano. Mrs Donnelly bade the children be quiet and listen to Maria's song. Then she played the prelude and said *Now, Maria!* and Maria, blushing very much, began to sing in a tiny quavering voice. She sang *I Dreamt that I Dwelt*, and when she came to the second verse she sang again:

> *I dreamt that I dwelt in marble halls*
> *With vassals and serfs at my side*
> *And of all who assembled within those walls*
> *That I was the hope and the pride.*
> *I had riches too great to count, could boast*
> *Of a high ancestral name,*
> *But I also dreamt, which pleased me most,*
> *That you loved me still the same.*

But no one tried to show her her mistake; and when she had ended the song Joe was very much moved. He said that there was no time like the long ago and no music for him like poor old Balfe, whatever other people might say; and his eyes filled up so much with tears that he could not find what he was looking for and in the end he had to ask his wife to tell him where the corkscrew was.

Notes for "Clay"

1. A Barmbrack is a cake containing currants, usually sold only on Halloween.
2. The title "peacemaker" occurs in the Roman Catholic Mass for All Saints' Day, the day after Halloween. The phrase, "Blessed are the peacemakers, for they shall be called the children of God," (Matthew 5: 9) is part of the Beatitudes of the Sermon on the Mount (Matthew 5: 1-12). In the Litany of the Blessed Virgin Mary, the title "peacemaker" is applied to Mary, the mother of Jesus.
3. Board Ladies are members of the board that administers and decides policy for the laundry.
4. The "dummy" is evidently a deaf mute employed by the laundry.
5. "A Present from Belfast" indicates that Maria's purse (which holds her money) comes from the Protestant part of Ireland.
6. Whit-Monday—the Monday after the seventh Sunday after Easter (Pentecost Sunday). The day is a traditional holiday.
7. Dublin by Lamplight was a Protestant institution for women. In a letter to his brother Stanislaus, Joyce wrote that he thought that the laundry was "a Magdalene house," i.e., a place for former prostitutes, women with alcohol dependency, etc. The "cure" evidently took the form (in part) of periods of work and exercise during which the women had to listen to "tracts" or inspirational religious readings.
8. The "tracts on the walls" were Protestant religious writings.
9. "The ring" is part of a ritual celebration of Halloween. It is an ancient Celtic Halloween custom to place a ring, a prayer book, some water, and a bit of clay in each of four saucers. A blindfolded woman then chooses among the dishes to learn her fortune. If she chooses the ring, she will marry soon; if she chooses the prayer book, she will enter a religious community; if she chooses water, she will have continued life; but if she chooses clay, she will die. At the time of this story, when the custom had become a parlor game for happy occasions, most families simply omitted the clay.
10. "Porter" is a dark brown beer.
11. November 1, All Saints' Day, is a "mass morning," a holy day of obligation on which Roman Catholics must attend Mass.
12. "Two and four" is two shillings and fourpence—quite a bit of money for someone in Maria's position.
13. "A drop taken," is an Irish way of saying that a person has had too much to drink.
14. "I Dreamt that I Dwelt" is a song from Michael William Balfe's musical drama, "A Bohemian Girl."
15. Maria sings the first verse twice, omitting the second verse, which is about suitors and love. The correct lyrics for the second verse are:

    I dreamt that suitors besought my hand,
       That knights on bended knee,
    And with vows no maiden heart could withstand,
       That they pledged their faith to me.
    And I dreamt that one of this noble host
       Came forth my hand to claim;
    Yet I also dreamt, which charmed me most,
       That you lov'd me still the same.

16. Michael William Balfe is the composer of the song.

How Author's World and Reader's World Converge

Here is some background on the world of "Clay"'s author. James Joyce had profoundly ambivalent feelings toward his native country and its people. These feelings are partly like those of many young men as they mature and begin to develop their own senses of identity: parents, neighbors, and even friends become embarrassing. For Joyce, though, this rather ordinary process seems to have taken on unusual proportions. He was infuriated by the political situation in Ireland, and he believed that the Irish people either drank themselves into oblivion or let themselves be lulled into quiescence by pious belief in the teachings of the Roman Catholic Church, or both. He was often scornful of his birthplace because Ireland continued to live under British rule and because so many of his countrymen seemed (to him) simply not to care about improving their personal circumstances or those of their country.

Now, here is a reading of this story constructed by William York Tindall. He makes this meaning:

> Maria is like the Poor Old Woman or Ireland herself. That her particular figure serves as the traditional figure of Ireland is suggested by other circumstances. Like most in Ireland in her day, she works for the Protestants who control Ireland's purse. (Maria's purse is from Protestant Belfast.) Shopkeepers condescend to her; and when a British colonel is polite to her on the tram, she loses her cake. Distracted by colonels and condescended to by a nation of shopkeepers, Ireland has been losing her cake for several centuries. Moreover, Mother Ireland's sons, commonly drunk, are always quarreling among themselves . . . .*

Tindall has applied his knowledge of Joyce's complex world to the gaps he has constructed in this text. One of his moves has been to see Maria as a metaphor for Ireland. (We'll do more with metaphor in the next chapter.) Although your reading may be less fully developed than Tindall's, you are certainly not clueless about "Clay," so respond to the questions that follow.

CONSTRUCTING A READING

1. Joyce's narrator tells us three times that when Maria laughs, the tip of her nose nearly touches the tip of her chin. Try to draw that image. What does your drawing suggest about the characterization of Maria, especially in the context of Halloween, and in connection with the copper boilers that Maria tends at the Dublin by Lamplight laundry?
2. What do Maria's attitude toward her co-workers and family, toward the clerk in the bakery, and toward the man on the bus suggest to you about her beliefs about social class and social aspirations?

---

*William York Tindall, *A Reader's Guide to James Joyce.* New York: Noonday, 1959, p. 30.

3. What does the narrator's attitude toward Maria tell us about his ideology? Does the narrator share Maria's social values? How do you know? Cite examples of passages from the text to support your understanding of the narrator's view of Maria. On the basis of these passages, describe the narrator's ideological world.
4. Describe your emotional response when the woman in the bakery asks Maria if she is choosing wedding cake. Are you sympathetic with Maria or with the clerk? During Maria's encounter with the man who has "a drop taken," do you sympathize with Maria or with her interlocutor? On the basis of these responses to Maria's conduct, develop an account of how and why your world differs from Maria's.

See if you can discriminate author's world from reader's world, and from the world of the text in this play by a twentieth-century American author who lives in Toledo, Ohio.

Black Swamp
A Comedy in Ten Minutes

Christine Child

CHARACTERS

JENELLE: She is in her first year of teaching the third grade. She is twenty-three years old.

AMY: Jenelle's friend from college. She is also twenty-three.

HORACE: He is a twenty-eight-year-old black man. When he isn't reading, he is the custodian of Jenelle's school.

MISS HALE: The assistant principal of Jenelle's school, she is old far beyond her actual twenty-eight years.

NORIO: He is a Japanese businessman in his late twenties. This is his first visit to the United States.

TIME: The present. It is tornado season.

PLACE: The "multi-purpose" room of the Anthony Wayne Elementary School, in Northwest Ohio, on what used to be the Black Swamp.

SETTING: Part gymnasium and part cafeteria, the "multi-purpose" room is a large empty room. Up Center, a very large American flag hangs from the ceiling. Up Stage Right is a door to the outside. Up Stage Left is a door to the rest of the school. There are a few metal folding chairs leaning against a wall. There are no windows.

(LIGHTS UP on the inside of a "multi-purpose" room of an elementary school. ENTER JENELLE AND AMY from the door Up Left. They are casually, but fashionably, dressed.)

JENELLE: Hello? Hello, is anybody here?!

AMY: I don't care what you say, Jenelle, it's really creepy out there. The sky was all *green.*

JENELLE: Oh, it's going to storm. Forget it. Hello? Is anyone here?!

AMY: Storms turn the sky gray or black, not *green.* No, it's weird.

JENELLE: I've got to get into my classroom. Where the hell is Horace? He's supposed to be here on weekends.

AMY (to herself): The air even smells green. Kind of swampy.

JENELLE: Amy, it's probably a tornado, don't worry about it. HORACE!!

AMY: A TORNADO?!?!

JENELLE: I forget you're not from around here. Look, it's tornado season. It'll pass right by, they always do.

AMY: I'm terrified of tornados!!

(ENTER HORACE. He is carrying a book, and is very fashionably dressed. He glides silently up behind them.)

HORACE: Good afternoon, ladies.

AMY (screams): EEK!

JENELLE: Horace, thank goodness! Can you let me into my classroom, please? I've *got* to get my lesson plan. Miss Smoot wants it Monday.

HORACE: I would like to be of assistance but there may be an impediment in the guise of Miss Hale. Please introduce your charming companion.

HORACE: Horace, this is my friend Amy. Amy, this is Horace, the custodian of our school.

AMY: Hi. You're the *janitor?*

HORACE: The title "custodian" is perhaps more apt, as well as less demeaning. (TAKES HER HAND.) I feel I was fated to meet you.

JENELLE: Knock it off, Horace. Why can't you let me into my room? I've *got* to get in!

HORACE: Miss Hale might not approve. You see,—

JENELLE: What's she *doing* here?! It's Sunday!

(A School Fire Alarm sounds very loudly, as MISS HALE ENTERS. She runs in, carrying several metal buckets. She is wearing an *unfashionable* pastel dress.)

MISS HALE: HORACE!! HORACE!! I've sounded the alarm, now we must collect water in these buckets. Jenelle, what are you doing here? Well, take some buckets. We've all got to pull together.

JENELLE: What's the matter?

MISS HALE: A tornado warning! A funnel cloud was sighted fifteen miles from here and it's headed this way! I thought you were here for shelter.

AMY: A TORNADO!!

MISS HALE: Quickly! Quickly, girls! And Horace! We must collect as much water as we can, and then sit in the northwest corner of this room with no windows, holding a book over our heads. Quickly!

JENELLE: Miss Hale, I know that's what it says in the Teacher's Handbook, but since school isn't in session, maybe we could—

MISS HALE: As your vice principal, *I* am in charge in the absence of Miss Smoot. The buckets! The books!

HORACE (taking some buckets): Perhaps, Amy, I could show you the splendors of our boiler room.

AMY: A *tornado*.

(HE HANDS her a bucket, takes her hand. THEY EXIT.)

MISS HALE: Jenelle! Books, quickly. Large ones!!

(SHE claps her hands peremptorily. JENELLE EXITS.)

Miss Smoot couldn't have done it better. Northwest, let's see, Northwest.

(THUNDER, LOUD WIND SOUNDS. THE LIGHTS FLICKER, GO OUT, BACK-UP LIGHTS COME ON DIMLY. SHE SHUDDERS, as though she's had an electric shock.)

Oh my, oh my, and I'm wearing my apron too. I'm that distracted I never took it off. I can't go on. I thought I could but I can't go on. It's them chickens. I hurt like I thought I'd die when I buried my babies, my Billy, my Amy, but I said to myself, "They've gone right straight to heaven and they'll never have to work on a godforsaken Black Swamp Farm like their Ma." Then I lost my faith in God. I've lost my babies, and I've lost my faith in God, but I could go on if it wasn't for them chickens. They're creatures of the Devil, they are. I *hate* them chickens. If I didn't get good money for the eggs I'd kill every last one of them and LAUGH while I did it. Then I'd fry 'em all up and give 'em to the Indians. I don't know if Indians eat fried chicken. They're a darned sight too smart to try and *raise* the stupid things. *Hate* them chickens!

(ENTER JENELLE with an armful of picture books.)

JENELLE: Miss Hale? I've got some books, but really, I think I can make it home before the twister touches down and—Miss Hale, are you all right?

MISS HALE (sees her, is rapt): Amy!! Amy, you've come back!

JENELLE: I'm Jenelle. You remember me. I teach third grade. My friend's name is Amy. Where is she? Will she be all right with Horace?

MISS HALE (reaches out): Come here, child. Let a mother's arms embrace you!

JENELLE: The lights are out. Did anything happen to you when they went out? Would you like a glass of water?

MISS HALE: You look just like my Mama. Your grandmama. Lord, I wish she could of seen you just once. You're so pretty. My, but aren't you dressed funny, though?

JENELLE: Is there, uh, any medicine you're supposed to be taking?

MISS HALE: And to think I never thought there was an afterlife!

(ENTER HORACE AND AMY. They have painted their faces. They look like American Indians in ceremonial paint.)

JENELLE: Amy! You've got to—what's that on your face!?

AMY (to Horace): The Red, the Yellow, the White, the Black. Are you sure the White women will not call their men to harm us, Eagle Feather?

HORACE: We come in peace, Running Deer. That is all we can do.

MISS HALE: Welcome, Eagle Feather, Running Deer. My name is Fern Wilford and this is my daughter Amy.

JENELLE: STOP IT! It's not funny, whatever you're doing. It's not funny!

MISS HALE: Amy, don't be afraid. The Indians won't harm you. They come in peace, didn't you hear them? Amy hasn't seen many folks lately, not even white folks, leastways, I don't think she has, so I hope you'll forgive her.

JENELLE: *My name is Jenelle.*

HORACE: The ways of the White Man are not our ways, but we seek to live in harmony with all creatures. Running Deer, greet the White Woman Amy.

AMY: I greet you in the spirit of peace Amy. The Red, the Yellow, the Black and the White.

JENELLE (hisses): I'll kill you for this. I'll never forgive you. I'll leave you here in the tornado!

HORACE: The ways of the White Man are violent and bloody. Even their women talk of death and hatred. Amy, my brave tribe was wiped from the face of the earth by your forefathers before you were born. Now we are here for an accounting. Once again we come in peace.

MISS HALE: That's it! That's why I can see my Amy again! We're all in the future!! Well, if that don't beat all. Amy, honey, we're in the future. Don't be afraid.

(JENELLE has been sidling towards the door. She stops.)

HORACE: You cannot leave. The curtain that separates the past from the future has been torn asunder. Its manifestation is the vortex you call a funnel cloud. You cannot escape. We are here for an accounting.

JENELLE (frightened): "The curtain that separates the past from the future . . ."

AMY: The Red and the Yellow, the Black and the White.

MISS HALE: You know, Eagle Feather, you look mighty familiar. Did I know you before?

HORACE: I found you when you were lost in the Black Swamp. I returned you into the arms of your father. When you were a grown woman you gave my people food. And it was your man who with his firestick slew my son. I am here for an accounting.

MISS HALE: Oh, Eagle Feather, oh I am powerful sorry! I never forgot how kindly you was when I was lost, and to think William killed your son! Why, I don't hardly know where to look. I lost my son too, Billy, and there ain't no pain like it, but at least he warn't killed. Well, leastways it was the Swamp killed him, not a human being. Oh, Eagle Feather. (SHE TAKES his hands in hers.)

JENELLE: You're practicing for the school pageant. You're good, you're very convincing. For a moment, you had me scared. But now, there's a tornado on its way, and it's time to leave.

AMY: I gave you beads. You gave me lace. Do you remember?

JENELLE: I don't know what the hell you think you're doing, Amy, but it isn't very nice!

HORACE: Running Deer died in a fire the White Man set to clear the Swamp. Though she was fleet of foot, she could not flee -

JENELLE: Oh come on! Who writes your lines? Nobody will listen to this. STOP IT!

MISS HALE: I told them the fires was wrong. I told them and told them. I said, "You'll kill us all. You'll kill the animals we need to eat, and the Indians, and if that wind shifts, you'll burn us in our beds." William, he was crazy, he was like a man possessed. It was the Swamp did it to him. He couldn't get nowhere against it and it turned him mean. He couldn't kill the Swamp, so he killed the Indians. The Swamp wouldn't die so he burned us in our beds. Everything went when the wind shifted. But not me, not me and the damn chickens. I went and lay in the pond and I watched the barns burn and the house, and I could hear William scream and I thought, "If there is a God this is just the beginning of the flames for you!" I'm sorry, I can't recollect that time without getting weepy. But they're tears of rage, that's what they are.

JENELLE: That's awful!

MISS HALE: It was an awful bad time, honey. But I'm just tickled to see you again. I want to know how you been and what you been doing, but somehow, I'm scared to ask.

JENELLE: I'm not your daughter. My name is Jenelle. I teach the third grade. You're the assistant principal of the Anthony Wayne Elementary school. Your name is Miss Hale.

MISS HALE: I always wanted you to be a teacher, so's you wouldn't have to work on a farm. And now it turns out you are one. Or were one, or something. And this place is your school. If that don't beat all!

(LOUD THUNDER. UPSTAGE RIGHT DOOR FLIES OPEN. ENTER NORIO. He is in a conservative business suit, carrying an attache case.)

NORIO: Excuse me, please.

AMY: The Yellow! The Red and the Yellow, the White and the Black. All four peoples. The Earth will be saved!

(SHE CHANTS to herself, with her eyes closed, making circling motions with her arms.)

MISS HALE: I smell Swamp! Amy, honey, do you smell it?

NORIO: Please, if you would be so kind. I have lost my way, and I believe it is going to storm. Where, please, is Route 2?

HORACE: I take my directions from the path of the sun and the moon.

JENELLE (hostile): Are you looking for the Toyota plant?

NORIO: No, I have nothing to do with cars. Except to drive one, of course.

JENELLE (hostile): You're Japanese, aren't you?

NORIO: Yes, I'm Japanese.

MISS HALE: Why, it's a different kind of savage! I never saw anybody like him before! Did you, Amy, or you, Eagle Feather, Running Deer? Is he in the future too?

NORIO: I am *Japanese*. Excuse me for disturbing you. Please direct me to Route 2 and I will leave you at once.

MISS HALE: If there's a tornado out there, you'd better set for a spell, Mister, or it'll blow you into next week. I smell Swamp! Doesn't anybody else smell it?

NORIO: Tornado? Swamp? Please?

MISS HALE: You better set for a spell. A tornado is a real big old wind storm. Flattens everything in its path. We're waiting for one them right now. And Swamp, well, this whole place, miles and miles of it, used to be Swamp. Oh, I'm getting a real powerful feeling that I smell that Swamp *breathing* again. Can you smell it?

HORACE: The curtain between the past and the present has been torn asunder. Its manifestation is the vortex you call a funnel cloud. We are here for an accounting.

NORIO: You are businessmen?

JENELLE: They're pretending to be Indians!

NORIO: Where are their turbans?

JENELLE: Red Indians! I mean, Native Americans.

NORIO: Red Native Americans?

JENELLE: Look at them! She's *white*. He's *black*. They're *pretending* to be Native Americans!

NORIO: Why?

JENELLE: I DON'T KNOW!!

MISS HALE: I can't get that Swamp smell out of my nose. It's making me real nervous. When the Swamp killed Billy, and then Amy, I thought to myself, "It ain't natural for William not to cry." I wanted to pinch him or hit him or burn him to get him to cry. But his face was so set. I think all them tears he never cried backed up somehow and rose up in his head like a tide. He had Swamp inside and Swamp outside and it drove him right out of his skull.

NORIO: How does Swamp affect soybeans?

JENELLE: *What?*

NORIO: Soybeans are my business. Swamp is a soil condition, yes? How does it affect soybeans? Mommy soybeans. I am here to inspect the Mommy soybeans. My firm imports from Mommy.

MISS HALE: Amy, honey, why is that man calling you Mommy?

JENELLE: Maumee?

NORIO: Yes. Ma-a-u-m-e-e. Mommy. Mommy River Basin. We take those soybeans and make soy sauce and ink.

JENELLE: You really are greedy, aren't you? It's not enough for you to take over our industry, now you want our agriculture! You've got your own country. Why don't you stay there? Go away! Get out! We don't want you here!!!

NORIO (bows): I leave now, of course.

AMY (grabs his arm): You must stay!! The Earth is in danger. The Red, the Yellow, the Black, the White! The four peoples must join hands and save it!!

HORACE: How do you know this, Running Deer?

AMY: Since we arrived here, the Great Spirit has been singing in my veins. As the vortex whirls closer, I see the four peoples circling the earth, red hand in yellow hand, black hand in white hand, weaving a spell of safety around our Earth.

HORACE: Is this the answer? Will all be made plain to us? We are here for an accounting. The pieces are in place. Look closely at the White woman, Amy. Look at the Yellow man from far away.

MISS HALE: I just don't know what they're talking about. Do you, Amy? And I still smell Swamp. I wonder if I should open that door, so's I could see what was making that Swamp smell?

(HORACE WALKS IN A CIRCLE PATTERN AROUND NORIO AND JENELLE.)

JENELLE: Horace, I don't know what you think you're doing but I don't appreciate it!

NORIO: Excuse me, please, what are you doing?

HORACE: Running Deer, all has been revealed to me! The White Man has dispossessed us only to be dispossessed by the Yellow Man!! The circle turns, and turns again.

AMY: We must forgive the White Man! The White Man must forgive the Yellow Man! The Black Man must forgive the White Man. We must join hands, the Red, the Yellow, the Black, and the White, and weave a spell of safety for our Earth! The vortex whirls closer!

JENELLE: Amy and Horace, you've lost it! I've humored you as long as I can but this is dangerous stupid stuff you're saying! You know, Horace, Miss Smoot doesn't like those books you read. She thinks you don't understand your position here. And I like you, Horace, so I'm going to warn you about something else. It's not a good idea to be too friendly with these Japs. First off, you can't trust them, and anyway, people will turn on you if they think you like the Japs. Too many people in Ohio have lost their jobs to the Japs to make it safe to be real buddy-buddy with them. You understand I'm telling you this for your own good?

MISS HALE: I HEAR THE SWAMP BREATHING!! IT'S COMING BACK AND IT WANTS OUR BLOOD!!!

AMY: The vortex is upon us! We must join hands!

(SHE AND HORACE JOIN HANDS. MISS HALE IS WRINGING HER HANDS AND DOESN'T NOTICE THEM. NORIO PUTS HIS HANDS IN HIS POCKETS.)

NORIO: I think America is very strange place.

AMY: White woman Fern Wilford, you must help us. Join hands and chant with us.

MISS HALE (frenzied): The Swamp, the Swamp!

JENELLE: I hear a train! It's the tornado!!

(SHE GRABS a picture book, runs to the upstage wall, sits crosslegged with her back to the wall, her head down on her chest, and the book held over her head.)

MISS HALE: AMY!!

JENELLE: MY NAME ISN'T AMY, YOU OLD BAT!!

MISS HALE: My baby, my baby!

AMY (gently): You must help us save the Earth.

(AMY TAKES MISS HALE'S HAND. THEY MOVE IN A CIRCLE, WITH HORACE, CHANTING.)

HORACE, AMY, MISS HALE: The Red and the Yellow, the Black and the White, The Red and the Yellow, the Black and the White, The Red and the Yellow, the Black and the White—(THEY REPEAT THIS OVER AND OVER.)

(SOUND OF VIOLENT WIND, VERY CLOSE AND VERY LOUD. NORIO JOINS THE CIRCLE, CHANTS FERVENTLY WITH THEM. THUNDER RUMBLES, THEN THERE IS A LOUD OOZ-ING SQUELCHING NOISE. MASSES OF SMOKE BEGIN POUR-ING ONTO THE STAGE. THE LIGHTS FLICKER WILDLY. AS THE NOISE CRESCENDOES, SO DOES THEIR CHANTING. THE NOISE SUBSIDES. THEIR CHANTING BECOMES SOFTER AND SLOWER. THE SMOKE SUBSIDES. THEY STOP CHANTING AND CIRCLING.)

HORACE: The Evil came very close.

AMY: It was with us in this place.

NORIO: I never experience anything so disturbing.

MISS HALE (Screams): OOOOOOOOHHHHHHH!! THE SWAMP GOT AMY!!!

(THERE IS A BOOK ON THE FLOOR WHERE SHE WAS SIT-TING, BUT JENELLE IS GONE...)

BLACKOUT

THE END

CONSTRUCTING A READING:

1. Why do you suppose Christine Child has set this play in the cultural and historical world of northwest Ohio? Describe what the play tells you about one or more of these world references:
   Native North Americans
   African Americans
   rural life
   Japanese businesses
   tornadoes

2. How does the tornado open the door to the spirits of the past? Why do they appear? How do these characters both conform to and evade familiar stereotypes? Why do you think that is? What can you piece together about the Black Swamp and what went on there with the Wilfords? Why does Horace (Eagle Feather) say they have come for an accounting?

3. How do you relate to Amy as she experiences all this? Can you draw a connection between the character Amy and the spirit Amy/Jenelle? What issues about these relations does the play raise for you?

4. One important way in which texts comment on their worlds is by alluding to other literary texts. Often, one text comments on another by raising a similar question but providing a different answer. Do you think about the tornado in *The Wizard of Oz* when you read this text? If so, do you think that this text comments on any aspect of *The Wizard of Oz*?

5. Although this play is set in a Toledo, Ohio, suburb, it makes a point about ethnic prejudice that has more general application. Alone or with your classmates, write a short play or story set on your campus that addresses questions of diversity.

6. In an essay addressed to your classmates, describe the text's world, the author's position, and how you as a reader bring your history to bear on your experience of this play.

CULTURAL ICONS: SYMBOLS OF WORLDS

One way of understanding how textual worlds represent beliefs, values, and knowledge is to think about cultural icons. An *icon* is an image that represents or stands for something else. For example, icons on a computer interface usually represent the programs that a user can initiate or call up by clicking on them. In the word processing program I'm using as I write this book, an icon of a paper clip that looks like a man represents "help," a complex hypertext that provides information about the program. The "paper clip guy" on my screen can lead me to different kinds of help each time I click on him. Sometimes, for example, he tells me how to make boxes; at other times, he might show me how to arrange items in a numerical sequence. The paper clip guy always "means" help, but the "help" he brings is presented and understood in different ways at different times.

A cultural icon functions in similar ways to represent complex social formations and value systems. For example, most people recognize the image of the Empire State Building, the Statue of Liberty, Times Square, or Wall Street as icons for the city of New York. When people see these images during the opening moments of a film, they recognize New York as the setting. But they also recognize that the icon "stands for" the something that we might call the "New York experience"—the excitement, the sophistication, the aggression, the crowding, the affluence and poverty, the center of economy, the Broadway stage—everything that New York "means" or can mean to anyone who encounters the icon. Similarly, we think of the flag or the eagle as icon for the United States and the American experience. The Nike swoosh stands for a certain conception of energetic use of leisure time and disposable income. A specific face might be identified with a brand of cosmetics and the kind of life it implies. The image of an athlete could be an icon that associates a brand of sports equipment or clothing with a certain kind of goal-oriented striving.

Notice that we can recognize what an icon "means" even if we don't accept or agree with the values or ideas it represents. A person who has not experienced the pleasures and privileges of "the American Way of Life" can still recognize the eagle or the flag as icons. Further, the exact meaning of an icon is often unspecifiable.

Each of the texts that follow is "about" Marilyn Monroe as a cultural icon. As you read them, consider what the image of Marilyn Monroe "means" to each author and how that meaning might change in time or vary from person to person. You may find it useful to do research, either in the library or in more immediate and empirical ways like asking persons of differing sexes, ages, and ideologies what Marilyn means (or meant) to them. Think too about how you are being asked to see, understand, and feel about Marilyn. The feelings or understandings that these texts evoke reveal some of the ways in which culture calls upon us to think about women, their social roles, their intellectual capacity, their sexuality. Does Marilyn Monroe stand for sexuality? Beauty? Vulnerability? Intelligence? The victimization of women?

The Woman Who Will Not Die

Gloria Steinem

> I knew I belonged to the public and to the world, not because I was talented or even beautiful but because I had never belonged to anything or anyone else.
> —from the unfinished autobiography of Marilyn Monroe

It has been nearly a quarter of a century since the death of a minor American actress named Marilyn Monroe. There is no reason for her to be part of my consciousness as I walk down a midtown New York street filled with color and action and life. In a shop window display of white summer dresses, I see several huge photographs—a life-size cutout of Marilyn standing in a white halter dress, some close-ups of her vulnerable, please-love-me smile—but they don't look dated. Oddly, Marilyn seems to be just as much a part of this street scene as the neighboring images of models who could now be her daughters—even her granddaughters.

I walk another block and pass a record store featuring the hit albums of a rock star named Madonna. She has imitated Marilyn Monroe's hair, style, and clothes, but subtracted her vulnerability. Instead of using seduction to offer men whatever they want, Madonna uses it to get what she wants—a 1980s difference that has made her the idol of teenage girls. Nevertheless, her international symbols of femaleness are pure Marilyn.

A few doors away, a bookstore displays two volumes on Marilyn Monroe in its well-stocked window. The first is nothing but random photographs, one of many such collections that have been published over the years. The second is one of several recent exposés on the circumstances surrounding Monroe's 1962 death from an accidental or purposeful overdose of sleeping pills. Could organized crime, Jimmy Hoffa in particular, have planned to use her friendship with the Kennedys and her suicide—could Hoffa or his friends even have caused that suicide—in order to embarrass or blackmail Robert Kennedy, who was definitely a Mafia enemy and probably her lover? Only a few months ago, Marilyn Monroe's name made international headlines again when a British television documentary on this conspiracy theory was shown and a network documentary made in the United States was suppressed, with potential pressure from crime-controlled unions or from the late Robert Kennedy's family as rumored reasons.

As I turn the corner into my neighborhood, I pass a newsstand where the face of one more young Marilyn Monroe look-alike stares up at me from a glossy magazine cover. She is Kate Mailer, Norman Mailer's daughter, who was born the year that Marilyn Monroe died. Now she is starring in *Strawhead*, a "memory play" about Monroe written by Norman Mailer, who is so obsessed with this long-dead sex goddess that he had written one long biography and another work—half fact, half fiction—about her, even before casting his daughter in this part.

The next morning, I turn on the television and see a promotion for a show on film director Billy Wilder. The only clip chosen to attract viewers and represent Wilder's entire career is one of Marilyn Monroe singing a few breathless bars in *Some Like It Hot*, one of two films they made together.

These are everyday signs of a unique longevity. If you add her years of movie stardom to the years since her death, Marilyn Monroe has been part of our lives and imaginations for nearly four decades. That's a very long time for one celebrity to survive in a throwaway culture.

. . .

One simple reason for her life story's endurance is the premature end of it. Personalities and narrative projected onto the screen of our imaginations are far more haunting—and far more likely to be the stuff of conspiracies and conjecture—if they have not been allowed to play themselves out to their logical or illogical ends. . . .

When the past dies, there is mourning, but when the future dies our imaginations are compelled to carry it on.

Would Marilyn Monroe have become the serious actress she aspired to be? Could she have survived the transition from sex goddess to mortal woman that aging would impose? Could she have stopped her disastrous marriages to men whose images she wanted to absorb (Beloved American DiMaggio, Serious Intellectual Miller), and found a partner who loved and understood her as she really was? Could she have kicked her life-wasting habits of addiction and procrastination? Would she have had or adopted children? Found support in the growing strength of women or been threatened by it? Entered the world of learning or continued to be ridiculed for trying? Survived and even enjoyed the age of sixty she now would be?

Most important, could she finally have escaped her lifetime combination of two parts talent, one part victim, and one part joke? Would she have been "taken seriously," as she so badly wanted to be?

We will never know. Every question is as haunting as any of its possible answers.

But the poignancy of this incompleteness is not enough to explain Marilyn Monroe's enduring power. Even among brief public lives, few become parables. Those that endure seem to hook into our deepest emotions of hope or fear, dream or nightmare of what our own fates might be.

. . .

In an intimate way during her brief life, Marilyn Monroe hooked into both those extremes of emotion. She personified many of the secret hopes of men and many secret fears of women.

To men, . . . she . . . was the child-woman who offered pleasure without adult challenge; a lover who neither judged nor asked anything in return. Both the roles she played and her own public image embodied a masculine hope for a woman who is innocent and sensuously experienced at the same time. "In fact," as Marilyn said toward the end of her career, "my popularity seemed almost entirely a masculine phenomenon."

Since most men have experienced female power only in their childhoods, they associate it with a time when they themselves were powerless. This will continue as long as children are raised almost totally by women, and rarely see women in authority outside the home. That's why male adults, and some females too, experience the presence of a strong woman as a dangerous regression to a time of their own vulnerability and dependence. For men, especially, who are trained to measure manhood and maturity by their distance from the world of women, being forced back to that world for female companionship may be very threatening indeed. A compliant child-woman like Monroe loves this dilemma by offering sex *without* the power of an adult woman, much less of an equal. As a child herself, she allows men to feel both conquering and protective; to be both dominating and admirable at the same time.

For women, Monroe embodied kinds of fear that were just as basic as the hope she offered men: the fear of a sexual competitor who could take away men on whom women's identities and even livelihoods might depend; the fear of having to meet her impossible standard of always giving—and asking nothing in return; the nagging fear that we might share her feminine fate of being vulnerable, unserious, constantly in danger of becoming a victim.

. . .

Watching Monroe, . . . women were forced to worry about her vulnerability—and thus their own. They might feel like a black moviegoer watching a black actor play a role that was too passive, too obedient, or a Jew watching a Jewish character who was selfish and avaricious. In spite of some extra magic, some face-saving sincerity and humor, Marilyn Monroe was still close to the humiliating stereotype of a dumb blonde: depersonalized, sexual, even a joke. Though few women yet had the self-respect to object on behalf of their sex, as one would object on behalf of a race or religion, they still might be left feeling a little humiliated—or threatened—without knowing why.

"I have always had a talent for irritating women since I was fourteen," Marilyn wrote in her unfinished autobiography. "Sometimes I've been to a party where no one spoke to me for a whole evening. The men, frightened by their wives or sweeties, would give me a wide berth. And the ladies would gang up in a corner to discuss my dangerous character."

But all that was before her death and the revelations surrounding it. The moment she was gone, Monroe's vulnerability was no longer just a turn-on for many men and an embarrassment for many women. It was a tragedy. Whether that final overdose was suicide or not, both men and women were forced to recognize the insecurity and private terrors that had caused her to attempt suicide several times before.

Men who had never known her wondered if their love and protection might have saved her. Women who had never known her wondered if their empathy and friendship might have done the same. For both women and men, the ghost of Marilyn came to embody a particularly powerful form of hope: the rescue fantasy. Not only did we imagine a happier ending for the parable of Marilyn Monroe's life, but we also fantasized ourselves as the saviors who could have brought it about.

Still, women didn't seem quite as comfortable about going public with their rescue fantasies as men did. It meant admitting an identity with a woman who always had been a little embarrassing, and who had now turned out to be doomed as well. Nearly all of the journalistic eulogies that followed Monroe's death were written by men. So are almost all of the more than forty books that have been published about Monroe.

Just after Monroe's death, one of the few women to write with empathy was Diana Trilling, an author confident enough not to worry about being trivialized by association—and respected enough to get published. Trilling regretted the public's "mockery of Marilyn's wish to be educated," and her dependence on sexual artifice that must have left "a great emptiness where a true sexuality would have supplied her with a sense of herself as a person." She mourned Marilyn's lack of friends, "especially women, to whose protectiveness her extreme vulnerability spoke so directly."

"But we were the friends," as Trilling said sadly, "of whom she knew nothing."

In fact, the contagion of feminism that followed Monroe's death by less than a decade may be the newest and most powerful reason for the continuing strength of her legend. As women began to be honest in public, and to discover that many of our experiences were more societal than individual, we also realized that we could benefit more by acting together than by deserting each other. We were less likely to blame or be the victim, whether Marilyn or ourselves, and more likely to rescue ourselves and each other.

In 1972, the tenth anniversary of her death and the birth year of *Ms.*, the first magazine to be published by and for women, Harriet Lyons, one of its early editors, suggested that *Ms.* do a cover story about Marilyn called "The Woman Who Died Too Soon." As the writer of this brief essay about women's new hope of reclaiming Marilyn, I was astounded by the response to the article. It was like tapping an underground river of interest. For instance:

Marilyn had talked about being sexually assaulted as a child, though many of her biographers had not believed her. Women wrote in to tell their similar stories. It was my first intimation of what since has become a documented statistic: One in six adult women has been sexually assaulted in childhood by a family member. The long-lasting effects—for instance, feeling one has no value except a sexual one—seemed shared by these women and by Marilyn. Yet most were made to feel guilty and alone, and many were as disbelieved by the grown-ups around them as Marilyn had been.

Physicians had been more likely to prescribe sleeping pills and tranquilizers than to look for the cause of Monroe's sleeplessness and anxiety. They had continued to do so even after she had attempted suicide several times. Women responded with their own stories of being overmedicated, and of doctors who assumed women's physical symptoms were "all in their minds." It was my first understanding that women are more likely to be given chemical and other arm's-length treatment, and to suffer from the assumption that they can be chemically calmed or sedated with less penalty because they are doing only "women's work." Then, ads in medical journals blatantly recommended tranquilizers for depressed housewives, and even now the majority of all tranquilizer prescriptions are written for women.

Acting, modeling, making a living more from external appearance than from internal identity—these had been Marilyn's lifelines out of poverty and obscurity. Other women who had suppressed their internal selves to become interchangeable "pretty girls"—and as a result were struggling with both lack of identity and terror of aging—wrote to tell their stones.

To gain the seriousness and respect that was largely denied her, and to gain the fatherly protection she had been completely denied, Marilyn married a beloved American folk hero and then a respected intellectual. Other women who had tried to marry for protection or for identity as women often are encouraged to do, wrote to say how impossible and childlike this had been for them, and how impossible for the husbands who were expected to provide their wives' identities. But Marilyn did not live long enough to see a time in which women sought their own identities, not just derived ones.

During her marriage to Arthur Miller, Marilyn had tried to have a child—but suffered an ectopic pregnancy, a miscarriage—and could not. Letters poured in from women who also suffered from this inability and from a definition of womanhood so tied to the accident of the physical ability to bear a child—preferably a son, as Marilyn often said, though later she also talked of a daughter—that their whole sense of self had been undermined. "Manhood means many things," as one reader explained, "but womanhood means only one." And where is the self-respect of a woman who wants to give birth only to a male child, someone different from herself?

Most of all, women readers mourned that Marilyn had lived and died in an era when there were so few ways for her to know that these experiences were shared with other women, that she was not alone.

Now women and men bring the past quarter century of change and understanding to these poignant photographs taken in the days just before her death. It makes them all the more haunting.

I still see the self-consciousness with which she posed for a camera. It makes me remember my own teenage discomfort at seeing her on the screen, mincing and whispering and simply hoping her way into love and approval. By holding a mirror to the exaggerated ways in which female human beings are trained to act, she could be as embarrassing—and as sad and revealing—as a female impersonator.

Yet now I also see the why of it, and the woman behind the mask that her self-consciousness creates.

I still feel worried about her, just as I did then. There is something especially vulnerable about big-breasted women in this world concerned with such bodies, but unconcerned with the real person within. We may envy these women a little, yet we feel protective of them, too.

But in these photographs, the body emphasis seems more the habit of some former self. It's her face we look at. Now that we know the end of her story, it's the real woman we hope to find—looking out of the eyes of Marilyn.

In the last interview before her death, close to the time of these photographs, Patricia Newcomb, her friend and press secretary, remembers that Marilyn pleaded unsuccessfully with the reporter to end his article like this:

> What I really want to say: That what the world really needs is a real feeling of kinship. Everybody: stars, laborers, Negroes, Jews, Arabs. We are all brothers. Please don't make me a joke. End the interview with what I believe.

CONSTRUCTING A READING

1. View *The Seven-Year Itch* and *Body of Evidence*. Using these films as your examples, explain how you understand Steinem's analysis of what she calls "the homewrecker aspect of Marilyn Monroe" by comparing the extent to which Marilyn and Madonna threaten the male protagonist's marriage in their respective films.

2. How do you understand Steinem's assertion that Madonna has "imitated Marilyn's hair, style, and clothes, but subtracted her vulnerability." Do you agree? Support your position with reference to one or more films or videos that feature each artist.

3. Steinem writes that:

> For women, Monroe embodied kinds of fear that were just as basic as the hope she offered men: the fear of a sexual competitor who could take away men on whom women's identities and even livelihoods might depend; the fear of having to meet her impossible standards of always giving—and asking nothing in return; the nagging fear that we might share her feminine fate of being vulnerable, unserious, constantly in danger of becoming a victim.

---

from *Marilyn: A Biography*

Norman Mailer

[During the filming of *The Seven-Year Itch,*] Marilyn is plump, close to fat, her flesh is bursting out of every strap, her thighs look heavy, her upper arms give a hint that she will yet be massively fat if she ever grows old, she has a belly which protrudes like no big movie star's belly in many a year, and yet she is the living bouncing embodiment of pulchritude. It is her swan song to being a sexual object. . . . She proves once again that she is as good as the actors she works with, and she and Tom Ewell do a comic march through the movie. As The Girl upstairs, a TV model in New York for the summer from Colorado, she creates one last American innocent, a pristine artifact of the mid-Eisenhower years, an American girl who *believes* in the products she sells in TV commercials—she is as simple and healthy as the whole middle of the country, and there to be plucked. It is an unbelievable performance for an actress who is on the edge of separating from her husband, has two atrocious films behind her, is in psychoanalysis, drinking too much, and all the while thinking of, breaking her contract and beginning a new life in New York to make movies with a photographer who has never produced a film.

It is an impossible load for an ordinary woman. It is a next to unendurable strain for a strong woman of firm identity, but it is natural for Marilyn. There is one grace to possessing small identity—it is the ability to move from one kind of life to another with more pleasure than pain. If this lack of identity becomes a progressive burden in a static situation (for everyone else tends to build and prosper more than oneself), a lack of psychic density also offers quick intelligence in a new role. This is not to say that she is heaven on the set of *The Seven-Year Itch*. Usually she is several hours late and often keeps the company in irons while forgetting her lines, but she is resilient, how she is resilient in this film.

As if she has been picking the opportunity, she has a critical fight with DiMaggio while on location in New York. He has accompanied her after much debate, and is on the street with several thousand New Yorkers on the night she is filmed standing over a subway grating with Tom Ewell. As the trains go by underneath, her skirts billow up. It is so hot in the city she presumably loves the rush of air on her thighs. She plays it in innocent delight, a strapping blonde with a white skirt blown out like a spinnaker above her waist—a fifty-foot silhouette of her in just this scene will later appear over Times Square. . . . "Oh," she says in a Betty Boop voice, "I always keep my undies in the icebox."

Witness DiMaggio with these thousands of spectators crammed on hot New York night streets to get a glimpse of Marilyn in white panties and powerhouse thighs over a wind blower on a subway grating. The scene is more indecent to DiMaggio than he ever conceived. The sound of New York snickers takes his ear. It is a jargon, based on sewers, whoors, and delicatessen—"Look at that pastrami!" Unable to endure any more, he tries to get away. A group of newspapermen cut him off on the way to Toots Shor's. Toots is around the corner from where they are shooting! The aristocracy at Shor's will have their unsaid reaction. One of the reporters says it instead. "What do you think of Marilyn having to show more of herself than she's shown before, Joe?"

. . . DiMaggio gives no answer. He will have his war with Marilyn as soon as she gets home. A monster of jealousy all these years, he will not even trust her to smile at a bellhop. Hotel guests in nearby rooms hear shouting, scuffling, and weeping before the dawn. In the morning, DiMaggio is on his way to California.

Two weeks later, back in Los Angeles, she announces to the press they are getting a divorce. She is sick and can see no one. DiMaggio shoulders through newspapermen and leaves to drive to San Francisco with the friend who had been best man at his wedding, Reno Barsocchini. He takes with him "two leather suitcases and a bag of gold-handled golf clubs." The Associated Press reports, "the news hit Hollywood like an A-bomb."

A few days later, Marilyn is back at work on *The Seven-Year Itch*. Her work is faster and more concentrated than before. Sometimes Wilder, to his surprise, can cut and print on a first or second take. New identity. Good film. . . .

She continues to see DiMaggio from time to time. He will even months later be her escort to the premiere of *The Seven-Year Itch*, although they are reported to fight before the evening is out. It is like a calculus of partial derivatives. The lack of complete commitment to the marriage creates a lack of finality in the separation. It is as if they cannot excise what was never finished, and the conclusion returns that they were locked like sweethearts, egoistic, narcissistic, petulant, pained, unwillingly attracted, and finally together for sex. If Marilyn almost never gives a hint of this, and will indicate to many a friend that she was bored with him, poor Joe, it is hard to explain why when they saw each other again in 1961 she was quick to explain he was a companion. Nothing was happening with DiMaggio, she assured her friends, because she was "cured." It is not the way a woman speaks of a man to whom she was sexually indifferent. . . .

But then it is characteristic of her to play leapfrog in love and work. She will start with Miller, then go to DiMaggio, come back to Miller, and pick up again with DiMaggio, . . . just as she leaves Hollywood to live in New York to return to Hollywood to leave again and return to die. She is entering a period of her life when the weight of the past will make her as sluggish as a dinosaur's tail. She might as well be feeding a family within herself—those separate personalities of her past—and if her general lack of identity has enabled her to be an angel of nuance in one hour, and a public relations monster in the next (with the moronic glee of the emptiest ambition in her eye), if she has been mercurially quick and will be as quick again when need arises, still she is approaching the years of crisis that come to all men and women who have managed to survive with little sense of inner identity, a time when the psychic energies of early success begin to exhaust themselves, and the ability to change over radically for each new situation diminishes at the same time one's reputation for unreliability begins to grow—it is then that the backwater of foul and exaggerated bad legends begins to enter the reactions of strangers at the sound of the name.

So she is at a moment in her life when events do not force her decision— she is in the rare situation of being able to wait and choose, the worst of times for someone like herself, for the tendency (since she cannot concentrate long enough to clarify her thoughts) is to find all projects becoming polluted with ambivalence. If she is at a crossroads, she can be certain that the longer she waits, the muddier it will get. Yet what a choice to make! Her need for security is probably greater than ever, doubled by her divorce from DiMaggio. . . .

She can then hardly fail to be relieved when the studio, delighted with her latest work, starts to woo her with attentions she has never received before. There is talk (at last!) of tearing up her contract and giving her a better one—if it is, one may be certain, vastly inferior to what other stars are getting, still it is an improvement. To celebrate the finish of *The Seven-Year Itch*, her agent Charles Feldman (who has also been her co-producer) throws a party for her. . . . It is Hollywood's way of welcoming her to the Establishment.

CONSTRUCTING A READING

1. How do you respond to Mailer's physical descriptions of Marilyn as "plump, close to fat," with "powerhouse thighs"? What attitude toward Monroe and/or women in general does the description imply? What attitude toward weight does the description imply? What do you think Mailer means by "powerhouse thighs"?
2. How do you respond to Mailer's psychological description of Marilyn as "possessing small identity," "lack[ing] psychic density," "resilient"? What attitude toward Monroe and women in general does it imply?

from *The Fifties*
David Halberstam

She was so alive she seemed to jump off the screen to create a personal relationship with her growing audience. "The golden girl who was like champagne on the screen," one of her husbands, Arthur Miller, wrote of her. Even when she was a struggling starlet, photographers understood instantly that she was special and inevitably asked her to pose. She was, photographer Richard Avedon once said, more comfortable in front of the camera than away from it. The famed French photographer Henri Cartier Bresson described something vivid, fragile, and evanescent about her, something "that disappears quickly [and] that reappears again." . . . To the studio heads she was, at first, just another dumb blonde, part of the endless stream of young women who had been voted the best-looking girls in their high school classes. . . . Early on, she was perceived as being at once too desirable, too available, and too vulnerable. Watching the reaction of studio wives to her at an early Hollywood party, Evelyn Keyes, the actress, turned to Arthur Miller, who had only just met Miss Monroe, and said, "They'll eat her alive."

. . . She was a sex goddess but also so desperately needy and childlike that she aroused a powerful instinct on the part of audiences to protect her. "When you look at Marilyn on the screen, you don't want anything to happen to her. You really care that she should be all right," said Natalie Wood. She had, said

Laurence Olivier, who directed her near the end of her career, a rare ability "to suggest one moment that she is the naughtiest little thing, and the next that she's perfectly innocent."

She had a keen sense of her own abilities and of men's response to them. Cast inevitably by others as the dumb blonde, she was shrewder and smarter than most directors suspected, and she often managed to deliver considerably more in a part than they had reckoned for. . . .

She was a genuine original. Her success, which looked so easy from a distance, was virtually impossible to repeat, try though Hollywood might. . . . Whereas she played the naif who somehow knew the score down deep, her imitators often tended to be hard and brittle. . . .

The vulnerability she projected came from a nightmarish childhood; the naïveté, such as it was, came from shrewdly perceiving, however involuntarily, what men were like and what they really wanted from women. She operated on the edge: There was a very thin line between who she was in real life and the poignant, sexual figure she played on the screen. She took her strength as an actress from her real-life experiences; but as she became more and more successful, she always retained the fear of being abandoned, of being unloved. She was needy on the screen because she was needy in real life.

There was a strain of emotional instability that had run through her family for several generations. Her mother, Gladys Mortensen, had brought Marilyn, whose real name was Norma Jeane, into the world in 1926 in Los Angeles as an illegitimate child. Her husband seemed to have disappeared and was clearly not the father of the child. The man Marilyn believed to be her father, a co-worker of her mother's named C. Stanley Gifford, never accepted responsibility for her. That weighed heavily on her, and as an adult she put no little effort into trying to fight that rejection by pursuing Gifford and trying to make contact with him. But even as the most successful actress in the world, she found that her phone calls to him were still not accepted.

Her mother, always mentally unstable, was institutionalized when she was not yet eight. Norma Jeane was passed around to different families and moved in and out of orphanages. All of this was traumatic for a child. She knew she had a mother and somewhere out there was a father, so why was she being handed over to strangers? She pleaded, "But I'm not an orphan! I'm not an orphan!" Of the families paid by the state to take her in, she was abused by the head of at least one. Another was a harsh fundamentalist: "Jesus is supposed to be so forgiving, but they never mentioned that," she said later. "He was basically out to smack you in the head if you did something wrong." She was precocious physically, and given the rejections and insecurities of her childhood, it was hardly surprising that she soon decided that the world was not interested in her goodness or intelligence. That was particularly true in Hollywood, she decided: "In Hollywood a girl's virtue is much less important than her hair-do. You're judged on how you look, not by what you are."

As such she was always wary, for there were dangers everywhere, people who you thought you could count on who would let you down. "You'd catch glimpses," noted her first husband, James Dougherty, an airplane-factory worker she married at age sixteen as much to escape her life as anything else, "of someone who had been unloved for too long and unwanted for too many years."

Her dream had always been to become a movie star. . . . She wended her way inevitably toward the studios and was noticed by a variety of people on the fringes of Hollywood She made friends with a number of photographers who worked for the seedy, sex-oriented magazines of the time. She was well aware that the men who said they would help her might or might not: There was no doubt in her mind . . . that trading off physical favors was part of her early career requirements. "When I started modelling, it was like part of the job. . . . They weren't shooting all those sexy pictures just to sell peanut butter in an ad or get a layout in some picture magazine. They wanted to sample the merchandise, and if you didn't go along, there were 25 girls who would. It wasn't any big dramatic tragedy."

In 1949 she agreed to do a nude shoot for a photographer friend named Tom Kelley. He paid only fifty dollars, but she was living hand to mouth and she owed him a favor—he had lent her five dollars on an earlier occasion for cab fare. Besides, fifty dollars was precisely the amount of money she needed for the monthly payment on her secondhand car. She was not nervous about the nudity, only its potential effect on her career, and she signed the model release with the name Mona Monroe. In fact, Kelley noted that once she took her clothes off, she seemed more comfortable than before—in his words, "graceful as an otter, turning sinuously with utter naturalness. All her constraints vanished as soon as her clothes were off." Not long after, she was finally given a screen test and it was considered a stunning success by those who looked at the results. But she was also stereotyped: starlet; dumb-blonde category; keep her speaking lines to a minimum.

Later there were those who believed that the studio had invented her. Certainly, with studio help, her hair became blonder, and plastic surgery was used to make her more photogenic. Her teeth were straightened, some work was done on her nose to slim it down, and additional work was done to refinish the contours of her chin. But the studios did that with hundreds of other young women and lightning did not strike them. Her success was completely hers.

By the late forties, she began to appear in the background in a number of films. . . .

When she got a part in an old-fashioned crime film called *The Asphalt Jungle*, she was initially not even listed in the credits. But the early screening audiences responded so enthusiastically to her on the comment cards that the studio executives took notice and somewhat reluctantly included her name. . . . Her presence was electric. There she was, sexual, defenseless, with her potent body and her little-girl voice. . . .

With *The Asphalt Jungle* her career exploded. She made thirteen films in the next two years, few of them memorable. The studios seemed to have no real idea who she was, only that somehow there was something that worked. She was becoming, almost without anyone knowing exactly how, the first female superstar of the postwar years. . . . Her image was perfect for Hollywood, fighting new competition from television, which now offered free home entertainment. Hollywood was responding to the challenge by gradually allowing greater latitude in showing sexual matters on the screen. Her sexuality, so overt it might previously have been doomed by the censors (in such scenes as the famous blowing up of her skirt in *The Seven-Year Itch*, for example) was now not only permissible, it was desirable.

"The truth," she once said, "is that I've never fooled anyone. I've let men fool themselves. Men sometimes didn't bother to find out who I was, and what I was. Instead they would invent a character for me. I wouldn't argue with them. They were obviously loving someone I wasn't. When they found this out they would blame me for disillusioning them and fooling them."

Even as professional success came, her personal life remained in turmoil. Relationships began well but ended badly. In 1952 she was introduced by a friend to Joe DiMaggio, the greatest baseball player of his era, who had just retired. They went out intermittently, starting in March 1952, and in January 1954 they were finally married in the San Francisco city hall. The relationship thrilled the tabloid soul of America: the greatest athlete-hero of the nation going out with the greatest sex symbol. They were both shy; both had risen by dint of talent to social spheres in which they were often uncomfortable. DiMaggio was attractive but not particularly verbal. Friends noted their powerful mutual attraction but also his inability to talk to her. Her career was just taking off; his career (but not his fame) was to all intents and purposes finished. He saw her as a good and sweet girl and hated the idea that Hollywood perpetually cast her (to his mind) as a slut.

It was to be an uneasy marriage. For their honeymoon they went to Japan, where DiMaggio was doing a celebrity tour. Her passport read Norma Jean DiMaggio. On the way, though, she was asked by American military officers to entertain the troops still serving in Korea, a year after the war had finally ended. She did, though DiMaggio declined to accompany her. There were some 100,000 soldiers gathered enthusiastically in an outdoor instant amphitheater to hear her perform. Later, as Gay Talese wrote in a brilliant piece in *Esquire*, when she rejoined DiMaggio, she reported to him breathlessly, "Joe, you've never heard such cheering." "Yes I have," he answered.

Within months it was clear that the marriage was in trouble. She went to New York to film *The Seven-Year Itch*. DiMaggio decided reluctantly to go with her. They shot the scene of the air blowing her skirt up at 2 A.M. to avoid a crowd, but the word got out and several thousand people showed up. She stood over the subway grating, the wind blowing her skirt above her panties, the crowd cheering, applauding and shouting, *"Higher, higher."* DiMaggio, the child of Italian immigrants, a man who perhaps more than any athlete of his generation valued his *dignity*, watched from the corner, stone-faced and silent. That the movie was a marvelous celebration of her innocence did not matter; instead he saw it as exposing of her in *public* for financial exploitation. They had a bitter fight that night. The next day he flew back to California alone. The marriage was effectively over. In late 1954 they were divorced; the marriage had lasted a scant year. As DiMaggio packed his things and moved out of the house, a crowd of newspapermen gathered. Someone asked him where he was going. "Back to San Francisco. That's my home."

. . .

Her life eventually became so troubled that it began to have a serious impact on her career. Unsure of her abilities, needing reassurance, she moved to New York to be near Arthur Miller, with whom she had begun a burgeoning romance, and to be a part of the Actors Studio. She longed to be respected as a serious actress, but her work habits were becoming shakier and shakier. Miller was both father figure and intellectual legitimizer. But it wasn't long before he found that he too was failing her. In July 1956, she married Miller, but there was no peace or respite. "Nobody cares," she told her maid as her marriage to Miller was coming apart. "Nobody even knows me anymore. What good is it being Marilyn Monroe? Why can't I just be an ordinary woman. . . . Oh why do things have to work out so rotten?" By 1957, her mental health was deteriorating ever more quickly: She was using even more sleeping pills and starting the day with a Bloody Mary.

More than most actors and actresses, she was exploited by the studios and was significantly underpaid at the height of her career. The studio heads always seemed to resent her success and continued to see her as essentially the dumb blonde. . . .

In February 1952, just as her career was taking off, there was an anonymous phone call to Twentieth Century-Fox. The naked girl in a nude calendar, said the male caller, was its newest star, Marilyn Monroe. The caller demanded ten thousand dollars. Otherwise, he said, he would take his proof to the newspapers. The studio people were terrified by the call but decided not to pay, which, they decided, would only lead to more blackmail. But they did pressure her to deny that she was the girl. It was a terrible moment for her: She was sure that her career was over. But she also decided to tell the truth and to take the initiative by leaking the story herself to a friendly writer. It *was* her on the calendar, she said, and there was no sense lying about it "Sure, I posed," she said "I was hungry." The public rallied to support her.

CONSTRUCTING A READING

1. Halberstam writes that Monroe was "perceived as at once too desirable, too available, and too vulnerable." What might Halberstam mean by those terms and how might they be excessive? What does it mean, in

other words, for a woman to be "*too* desirable"? Why does Evelyn Keyes believe these attributes will cause the "studio wives" to "eat her alive"?

2. Halberstam quotes Marilyn as saying that she "let men fool themselves . . . they were obviously loving someone I wasn't. When they found this out they would blame me for disillusioning them and fooling them." On the basis of what you've read so far, do you think Joe DiMaggio was such a man? Norman Mailer? Halberstam? Why and/or why not?

3. Using two or three of her films as examples, explain whether and why you think Marilyn Monroe's film roles portray her as "too desirable, too available, and too vulnerable."

SHARING A READING

Choose one of the following as a writing project.

1. Find stories about Marilyn Monroe in fan magazines of the fifties and sixties. Describe the tone of these stories—the attitude the author takes toward Marilyn and what she represents. In an essay addressed either to the women or to the men in your class, explain at least one of the ways in which Marilyn Monroe represented the cultural values or fears of the United States during that time.

2. In what ways did Thurber's story, "The Greatest Man in the World" (which was set in the 1950s) accurately predict the ways in which celebrities like Elvis and Marilyn would be treated by their culture? In what ways was he inaccurate?

3. Write a letter to James Thurber in which you describe one of today's celebrity "personalities." Your job is to explain to Mr. Thurber, using Pal Smurch as a comparison, how and why your chosen celebrity gained her or his notoriety and/or fame.

4. Many people believe that the media play a part in, and frequently actually create, the world that they reflect or report on. On the basis of one or more texts from this chapter, take a position on this question and explain your point of view to someone of another generation.

5. Norman Mailer, David Halberstam, and Gloria Steinem all tell the story of Marilyn Monroe's break from Joe DiMaggio. Although they relate many of the same events, their tellings of the story differ. Write an essay in which you describe and speculate about these differences on the basis of what you now know and believe about Marilyn as well as about diversity and difference, especially with respect to gender and ethnicity.

6. In a letter written to one of your high school teachers or to your parents, explain how the idea of textual worlds would have made it easier for you to understand something important that they tried—and failed—to teach you.

7. Choose a magazine or TV advertisement that relies more on images than on words and explain its world as a set of values. Ads for clothing, cos-

metics, sports equipment, beer, cigarettes, insurance, and automobiles might be good places to start. In an essay, oral report, or hypertext for your classmates, describe the values and beliefs that are evoked but not named in the advertisement.

TEXTS FOR FURTHER READING

Hoosier-ettes

Jamie Barlowe

When I was fourteen
I was lanky,
and loved basketball;
but had to play girls' ball:
half-court;
underhand free throws.
They taught us
to doubt ourselves,
as we stood in our
faded green gym shorts:
we'd get too tired
full court;
we'd hurt ourselves
if we played hard—
maybe ruin our chances
for babies;
our arms were too weak
to throw overhand.
Strengthen them?
They'd sooner
see us die.

CONSTRUCTING A READING

1. What does this poem say about cultural norms, particularly about expectations for gender roles?
2. How would you describe the speaker's feelings as she looks back at the experience? How did it affect her?
3. In what ways did "they" teach "us to doubt ourselves?" Who are "they?"
4. Consider how your gender influenced your experience of growing up. Were you ever discouraged from something you loved? Were you encouraged? How did you respond?
5. Write your own poem about an experience in which you felt discrimination.

from *Herland*

Charlotte Perkins Gilman

It is no use for me to try to piece out this account with adventures. If the people who read it are not interested in these amazing women and their history, they will not be interested at all.

As for us—three young men to a whole handful of women—what could we do? We did get away, as described, and were peacefully brought back again without, as Terry complained, even the satisfaction of hitting anybody.

There were no adventures because there was nothing to fight. There were no wild beasts in the country and very few tame ones. Of these I might as well stop to describe the one common pet of the country. Cats, of course. But such cats!

What do you suppose these lady Burbanks had done with their cats? By the most prolonged and careful selection and exclusion they had developed a race of cats that did not sing! That's a fact. The most those poor dumb brutes could do was to make a kind of squeak when they were hungry or wanted the door open, and, of course, to purr, and make the various mother-noises to their kittens.

Moreover, they had ceased to kill birds. They were rigorously bred to destroy mice and moles and all such enemies of the food supply; but the birds were numerous and safe.

While we were discussing birds, Terry asked them if they used feathers for their hats, and they seemed amused at the idea. He made a few sketches of our women's hats, with plumes and quills and those various tickling things that stick out so far; and they were eagerly interested, as at everything about our women.

As for them, they said they only wore hats for shade when working in the sun; and those were big light straw hats, something like those used in China and Japan. In cold weather they wore caps or hoods.

"But for decorative purposes—don't you think they would be becoming?" pursued Terry, making as pretty a picture as he could of a lady with a plumed hat.

They by no means agreed to that, asking quite simply if the men wore the same kind. We hastened to assure her that they did not—drew for them our kind of headgear.

"And do no men wear feathers in their hats?"

"Only Indians," Jeff explained. "Savages, you know." And he sketched a war bonnet to show them.

"And soldiers," I added, drawing a military hat with plumes.

They never expressed horror or disapproval, nor indeed much surprise— just a keen interest. And the notes they made!—miles of them!

But to return to our pussycats. We were a good deal impressed by this achievement in breeding, and when they questioned us—I can tell you we were well pumped for information—we told of what had been done for dogs and horses and cattle, but that there was no effort applied to cats, except for show purposes.

I wish I could represent the kind, quiet, steady, ingenious way they questioned us. It was not just curiosity—they weren't a bit more curious about us than we were about them, if as much. But they were bent on understanding our kind of civilization, and their lines of interrogation would gradually surround us and drive us in till we found ourselves up against some admissions we did not want to make.

"Are all these breeds of dogs you have made useful?" they asked.

"Oh—useful! Why, the hunting dogs and watchdogs and sheepdogs are useful—and sleddogs of course!—and ratters, I suppose, but we don't keep dogs for their *usefulness*. The dog is 'the friend of man,' we say—we love them."

That they understood. "We love our cats that way. They surely are our friends, and helpers, too. You can see how intelligent and affectionate they are."

It was a fact. I'd never seen such cats, except in a few rare instances. Big, handsome silky things, friendly with everyone and devotedly attached to their special owners.

"You must have a heartbreaking time drowning kittens," we suggested. But they said, "Oh, no! You see we care for them as you do for your valuable cattle. The fathers are few compared to the mothers, just a few very fine ones in each town; they live quite happily in walled gardens and the houses of their friends. But they only have a mating season once a year."

"Rather hard on Thomas, isn't it?" suggested Terry.

"Oh, no—truly! You see, it is many centuries that we have been breeding the kind of cats we wanted. They are healthy and happy and friendly, as you see. How do you manage with your dogs? Do you keep them in pairs, or segregate the fathers, or what?"

Then we explained that—well, that it wasn't a question of fathers exactly; that nobody wanted a—a mother dog; that, well, that practically all our dogs were males—there was only a very small percentage of females allowed to live.

Then Zava, observing Terry with her grave sweet smile, quoted back at him: "Rather hard on Thomas, isn't it? Do they enjoy it—living without mates? Are your dogs as uniformly healthy and sweet-tempered as our cats?"

Jeff laughed, eyeing Terry mischievously. As a matter of fact we began to feel Jeff something of a traitor—he so often flopped over and took their side of things; also his medical knowledge gave him a different point of view somehow.

"I'm sorry to admit," he told them, "that the dog, with us, is the most diseased of any animal—next to man. And as to temper—there are always some dogs who bite people—especially children."

That was pure malice. You see, children were the—the *raison d'être* in this country. All our interlocutors sat up straight at once. They were still gentle, still restrained, but there was a note of deep amazement in their voices.

"Do we understand that you keep an animal—an unmated male animal—that bites children? About how many are there of them, please?"

"Thousands—in a large city," said Jeff, "and nearly every family has one in the country."

Terry broke in at this. "You must not imagine they are all dangerous—it's not one in a hundred that ever bites anybody. Why, they are the best friends of the children—a boy doesn't have half a chance that hasn't a dog to play with."

"And the girls?" asked Somel.

"Oh—girls—why they like them too," he said, but his voice flatted a little. They always noticed little things like that, we found later.

Little by little they wrung from us the fact that the friend of man, in the city, was a prisoner; was taken out for his meager exercise on a leash; was liable not only to many diseases but to the one destroying horror of rabies; and, in many cases, for the safety of the citizens, had to go muzzled. Jeff maliciously added vivid instances he had known or read of injury and death from mad dogs.

They did not scold or fuss about it. Calm as judges, those women were. But they made notes; Moadine read them to us.

"Please tell me if I have the facts correct," she said. "In your country—and in others too?"

"Yes," we admitted, "in most civilized countries."

"In most civilized countries a kind of animal is kept which is no longer useful—"

"They are a protection," Terry insisted. "They bark if burglars try to get in."

Then she made notes of "burglars" and went on: "because of the love which people bear to this animal."

Zava interrupted here. "Is it the men or the women who love this animal so much?"

"Both!" insisted Terry.

"Equally?" she inquired.

And Jeff said, "Nonsense, Terry—you know men like dogs better than women do—as a whole."

"Because they love it so much—especially men. This animal is kept shut up, or chained."

"Why?" suddenly asked Somel. "We keep our father cats shut up because we do not want too much fathering; but they are not chained—they have large grounds to run in."

"A valuable dog would be stolen if he was let loose," I said. "We put collars on them, with the owner's name, in case they do stray. Besides, they get into fights—a valuable dog might easily be killed by a bigger one."

"I see," she said. "They fight when they meet—is that common?" We admitted that it was.

"They are kept shut up, or chained." She paused again, and asked, "Is not a dog fond of running? Are they not built for speed?" That we admitted, too, and Jeff, still malicious, enlightened them further.

"I've always thought it was a pathetic sight, both ways—to see a man or a woman taking a dog to walk—at the end of a string."

"Have you bred them to be as neat in their habits as cats are?" was the next question. And when Jeff told them of the effect of dogs on sidewalk merchandise and the streets generally, they found it hard to believe.

You see, their country was as neat as a Dutch kitchen, and as to sanitation—but I might as well start in now with as much as I can remember of the history of this amazing country before further description.

And I'll summarize here a bit as to our opportunities for learning it. I will not try to repeat the careful, detailed account I lost; I'll just say that we were kept in that fortress a good six months all told, and after that, three in a pleasant enough city where—to Terry's infinite disgust—there were only "Colonels" and little children—no young women whatever. Then we were under surveillance for three more—always with a tutor or a guard or both. But those months were pleasant because we were really getting acquainted with the girls. That was a chapter!—or will be—I will try to do justice to it.

We learned their language pretty thoroughly—had to; and they learned ours much more quickly and used it to hasten our own studies.

Jeff, who was never without reading matter of some sort, had two little books with him, a novel and a little anthology of verse; and I had one of those pocket encyclopedias—a fat little thing, bursting with facts. These were used in our education—and theirs. Then as soon as we were up to it, they furnished us with plenty of their own books, and I went in for the history part—I wanted to understand the genesis of this miracle of theirs.

And this is what happened, according to their records:

As to geography—at about the time of the Christian era this land had a free passage to the sea. I'm not saying where, for good reasons. But there was a fairly easy pass through that wall of mountains behind us, and there is no doubt in my mind that these people were of Aryan stock, and were once in contact with the best civilization of the old world. They were "white," but somewhat darker than our northern races because of their constant exposure to sun and air.

The country was far larger then, including much land beyond the pass, and a strip of coast. They had ships, commerce, an army, a king—for at that time they were what they so calmly called us—a bi-sexual race.

What happened to them first was merely a succession of historic misfortunes such as have befallen other nations often enough. They were decimated by war, driven up from their coastline till finally the reduced population, with many of the men killed in battle, occupied this hinterland, and defended it for years, in the mountain passes. Where it was open to any possible attack from below they strengthened the natural defenses so that it became unscalably secure, as we found it.

They were a polygamous people, and a slave-holding people, like all of their time; and during the generation or two of this struggle to defend their mountain home they built the fortresses, such as the one we were held in, and other of their oldest buildings, some still in use. Nothing but earthquakes could destroy such architecture—huge solid blocks, holding by their own weight. They must have had efficient workmen and enough of them in those days.

They made a brave fight for their existence, but no nation can stand up against what the steamship companies call "an act of God." While the whole fighting force was doing its best to defend their mountain pathway, there occurred a volcanic outburst, with some local tremors, and the result was the complete filling up of the pass—their only outlet. Instead of a passage, a new ridge, sheer and high, stood between them and the sea; they were walled in, and beneath that wall lay their whole little army. Very few men were left alive, save the slaves; and these now seized their opportunity, rose in revolt, killed their remaining masters even to the youngest boy, killed the old women too, and the mothers, intending to take possession of the country with the remaining young women and girls.

But this succession of misfortunes was too much for those infuriated virgins. There were many of them, and but few of these would-be masters, so the young women, instead of submitting, rose in sheer desperation and slew their brutal conquerors.

This sounds like Titus Andronicus, I know, but that is their account. I suppose they were about crazy—can you blame them?

There was literally no one left on this beautiful high garden land but a bunch of hysterical girls and some older slave women.

That was about two thousand years ago.

At first there was a period of sheer despair. The mountains towered between them and their old enemies, but also between them and escape. There was no way up or down or out—they simply had to stay there. Some were for suicide, but not the majority. They must have been a plucky lot, as a whole, and they decided to live—as long as they did live. Of course they had hope, as youth must, that something would happen to change their fate.

So they set to work, to bury the dead, to plow and sow, to care for one another.

Speaking of burying the dead, I will set down while I think of it, that they had adopted cremation in about the thirteenth century, for the same reason that they had left off raising cattle—they could not spare the room. They were much surprised to learn that we were still burying—asked our reasons for it, and were much dissatisfied with what we gave. We told them of the belief in the resurrection of the body, and they asked if our God was not as well able to resurrect from ashes as from long corruption. We told them of how people thought it repugnant to have their loved ones burn, and they asked if it was less repugnant to have them decay. They were inconveniently reasonable, those women.

Well—that original bunch of girls set to work to clean up the place and make their living as best they could. Some of the remaining slave women rendered invaluable service, teaching such trades as they knew. They had such records as were then kept, all the tools and implements of the time, and a most fertile land to work in.

There were a handful of the younger matrons who had escaped slaughter, and a few babies were born after the cataclysm—but only two boys, and they both died.

For five or ten years they worked together, growing stronger and wiser and more and more mutually attached, and then the miracle happened—one of these young women bore a child. Of course they all thought there must be a man somewhere, but none was found. Then they decided it must be a direct gift from the gods, and placed the proud mother in the Temple of Maaia—their Goddess of Motherhood—under strict watch. And there, as years passed, this wonder-woman bore child after child, five of them—all girls.

I did my best, keenly interested as I have always been in sociology and social psychology, to reconstruct in my mind the real position of these ancient women. There were some five or six hundred of them, and they were harem-bred; yet for the few preceding generations they had been reared in the atmosphere of such heroic struggle that the stock must have been toughened somewhat. Left alone in that terrific orphanhood, they had clung together, supporting one another and their little sisters, and developing unknown powers in the stress of new necessity. To this pain-hardened and work-strengthened group, who had lost not only the love and care of parents, but the hope of ever having children of their own, there now dawned the new hope.

Here at last was Motherhood, and though it was not for all of them personally, it might—if the power was inherited—found here a new race.

It may be imagined how those five Daughters of Maaia, Children of the Temple, Mothers of the Future—they had all the titles that love and hope and reverence could give—were reared. The whole little nation of women surrounded them with loving service, and waited, between a boundless hope and an equally boundless despair, to see if they, too, would be mothers.

And they were! As fast as they reached the age of twenty-five they began bearing. Each of them, like her mother, bore five daughters. Presently there were twenty-five New Women, Mothers in their own right, and the whole spirit of the country changed from mourning and mere courageous resignation to proud joy. The older women, those who remembered men, died *off*; the youngest of all the first lot of course died too, after a while, and by that time there were left one hundred and fifty-five parthenogenetic women, founding a new race.

They inherited all that the devoted care of that declining band of original ones could leave them. Their little country was quite safe. Their farms and gardens were all in full production. Such industries as they had were in careful order. The records of their past were all preserved, and for years the older women had spent their time in the best teaching they were capable of, that they might leave to the little group of sisters and mothers all they possessed of skill and knowledge.

There you have the start of Herland! One family, all descended from one mother! She lived to a hundred years old; lived to see her hundred and twenty-five great-granddaughters born; lived as Queen-Priestess-Mother of them all; and died with a nobler pride and a fuller joy than perhaps any human soul has ever known—she alone had founded a new race!

The first five daughters had grown up in an atmosphere of holy calm, of awed watchful waiting, of breathless prayer. To them the longed-for motherhood was not only a personal joy, but a nation's hope. Their twenty-five daughters in turn, with a stronger hope, a richer, wider outlook, with the devoted love and care of all the surviving population, grew up as a holy sisterhood, their whole ardent youth looking forward to their great office. And at last they were left alone, the white-haired First Mother was gone, and this one family, five sisters, twenty-five first cousins, and a hundred and twenty-five second cousins, began a new race.

Here you have human beings, unquestionably, but what we were slow in understanding was how these ultra-women, inheriting only from women, had eliminated not only certain masculine characteristics, which of course we did not look for, but so much of what we had always thought essentially feminine.

The tradition of men as guardians and protectors had quite died out. These stalwart virgins had no men to fear and therefore no need of protection. As to wild beasts—there were none in their sheltered land.

The power of mother-love, that maternal instinct we so highly laud, was theirs of course, raised to its highest power; and a sister-love which, even while recognizing the actual relationship, we found it hard to credit.

Terry, incredulous, even contemptuous, when we were alone, refused to believe the story. "A lot of traditions as old as Herodotus—and about as trustworthy!" he said. "It's likely women—just a pack of women—would have hung together like that! We all know women can't organize—that they scrap like anything—are frightfully jealous."

"But these New Ladies didn't have anyone to be jealous of, remember," drawled Jeff.

"That's a likely story," Terry sneered.

"Why don't you invent a likelier one?" I asked him. "Here *are* the women—nothing but women, and you yourself admit there's no trace of a man in the country." This was after we had been about a good deal.

"I'll admit that," he growled. "And it's a big miss, too. There's not only no fun without 'em—no real sport—no competition; but these women aren't *womanly*. You know they aren't."

That kind of talk always set Jeff going; and I gradually grew to side with him. "Then you don't call a breed of women whose one concern is mother-hood—womanly?" he asked.

"Indeed I don't," snapped Terry. "What does a man care for mother-hood—when he hasn't a ghost of a chance at fatherhood? And besides—what's the good of talking sentiment when we are just men together? What a man wants of women is a good deal more than all this 'motherhood'!"

We were as patient as possible with Terry. He had lived about nine months among the "Colonels" when he made that outburst; and with no chance at any more strenuous excitement than our gymnastics gave us—save for our escape fiasco. I don't suppose Terry had ever lived so long with neither Love, Combat, nor Danger to employ his superabundant energies, and he was irritable. Neither Jeff nor I found it so wearing. I was so much interested intel-lectually that our confinement did not wear on me; and as for Jeff, bless his heart!—he enjoyed the society of that tutor of his almost as much as if she had been a girl—I don't know but more.

As to Terry's criticism, it was true. These women, whose essential distinc-tion of motherhood was the dominant note of their whole culture, were strik-ingly deficient in what we call "femininity." This led me very promptly to the conviction that those "feminine charms" we are so fond of are not feminine at all, but mere reflected masculinity—developed to please us because they had to please us, and in no way essential to the real fulfillment of their great process. But Terry came to no such conclusion.

"Just you wait till I get out!" he muttered.

Then we both cautioned him. "Look here, Terry, my boy! You be careful! They've been mighty good to us—but do you remember the anesthesia? If you do any mischief in this virgin land, beware of the vengeance of the Maiden Aunts! Come, be a man! It won't be forever."

To return to the history:

They began at once to plan and build for their children, all the strength and intelligence of the whole of them devoted to that one thing. Each girl, of course, was reared in full knowledge of her Crowning Office, and they had, even then, very high ideas of the molding powers of the mother, as well as those of education.

Such high ideals as they had! Beauty, Health, Strength, Intellect, Good-ness—for these they prayed and worked.

They had no enemies; they themselves were all sisters and friends. The land was fair before them, and a great future began to form itself in their minds.

The religion they had to begin with was much like that of old Greece—a number of gods and goddesses; but they lost all interest in deities of war and plunder, and gradually centered on their Mother Goddess altogether. Then, as they grew more intelligent, this had turned into a sort of Maternal Pantheism.

Here was Mother Earth, bearing fruit. All that they ate was fruit of motherhood, from seed or egg or their product. By motherhood they were born and by motherhood they lived—life was, to them, just the long cycle of motherhood.

But very early they recognized the need of improvement as well as of mere repetition, and devoted their combined intelligence to that problem—how to make the best kind of people. First this was merely the hope of bearing better ones, and then they recognized that however the children differed at birth, the real growth lay later—through education.

Then things began to hum.

As I learned more and more to appreciate what these women had accomplished, the less proud I was of what we, with all our manhood, had done.

You see, they had had no wars. They had had no kings, and no priests, and no aristocracies. They were sisters, and as they grew, they grew together—not by competition, but by united action.

We tried to put in a good word for competition, and they were keenly interested. Indeed, we soon found from their earnest questions of us that they were prepared to believe our world must be better than theirs. They were not sure; they wanted to know; but there was no such arrogance about them as might have been expected.

We rather spread ourselves, telling of the advantages of competition: how it developed fine qualities; that without it there would be "no stimulus to industry." Terry was very strong on that point.

"No stimulus to industry," they repeated, with that puzzled look we had learned to know so well. "*Stimulus? To Industry?* But don't you *like* to work?"

"No man would work unless he had to," Terry declared.

"Oh, no *man!* You mean that is one of your sex distinctions?"

"No, indeed!" he said hastily. "No one, I mean, man or woman, would work without incentive. Competition is the—the motor power, you see."

"It is not with us," they explained gently, "so it is hard for us to understand. Do you mean, for instance, that with you no mother would work for her children without the stimulus of competition?"

No, he admitted that he did not mean that. Mothers, he supposed, would of course work for their children in the home; but the world's work was different—that had to be done by men, and required the competitive element.

All our teachers were eagerly interested.

"We want so much to know—you have the whole world to tell us of, and we have only our little land! And there are two of you—the two sexes—to love and help one another. It must be a rich and wonderful world. Tell us—what is the work of the world, that men do—which we have not here?"

"Oh, everything," Terry said grandly. "The men do everything, with us." He squared his broad shoulders and lifted his chest. "We do not allow our women to work. Women are loved—idolized—honored—kept in the home to care for the children."

"What is 'the home'?" asked Somel a little wistfully.

But Zava begged: "Tell me first, do *no* women work, really?"

"Why, yes," Terry admitted. "Some have to, of the poorer sort."

"About how many—in your country?"

"About seven or eight million," said Jeff, as mischievous as ever.

CONSTRUCTING A READING

1. How does the fantasy setting of *Herland* provide a way of challenging the familiar?
2. What are some of the differences among the narrator, Terry, and Jeff? How do their values differ? How do they view this experience differently? How does this affect the clashing of values in Herland and the resulting satire?
3. Terry growls that "these women aren't 'womanly'." How does *Herland* question various conceptions of womanhood? How does it challenge motherhood and parenthood? How about issues of religion or work? What are some of the other values that are questioned?
4. The period during which Charlotte Perkins Gilman wrote *Herland* is often referred to as the Progressive period in American history—a time when American society struggled with the consequences of the industrial revolution and an emerging urban culture. How does this knowledge inform your reading of this story? What does Herland suggest about relations of gender, work, and progress?

The Eve of the Spirit Festival
Lan Samantha Chang

After the Buddhist ceremony, when our mother's spirit had been chanted to a safe passage and her body cremated, Emily and I sat silently on our living room carpet. She held me in her arms; her long hair stuck to our wet faces. We sat as stiffly as temple gods except for the angry thump of my sister's heart against my cheek.

Finally she spoke. "It's Baba's fault," she said. "The American doctors would have fixed her."

I was six years old—I only knew that our father and mother had decided against an operation. And I had privately agreed, imagining the doctors tearing a hole in her body. As I thought of this, and other things, I felt a violent sob pass through me.

"Don't cry, Baby," Emily whispered. "You're okay." I felt my tears dry to salt, my throat lock shut.

Then our father walked into the room.

He and Emily had become quite close in the past few months. Emily was eleven, old enough to visit my mother when it had become clear that the hospital was the only option. But now she refused to acknowledge him.

"First daughter—"he began.

"Go away, Baba," Emily said. Her voice shook. She put her hand on the back of my head and turned me away from him also. The evening sun glowed garnet red through the dark tent of her hair.

"You said she would get better," I heard her say. "Now you're burning paper money for her ghost. What good will that do?"

"I am sorry," our father said.

"I don't care."

Her voice burned. I squirmed beneath her hand, but she wouldn't let me look. It was between her and Baba. I watched his black wingtip shoes retreat to the door. When he had gone, Emily let go of me. I sat up and looked at her; something had changed. Not in the lovely outlines of her face—our mother's face—but in her eyes, shadow-black, lost in unforgiveness.

They say the dead return to us. But we never saw our mother again, though we kept a kind of emptiness waiting in case she might come back. I listened always, seeking her voice, the lost thread of a conversation I'd been too young to have with her. Emily rarely mentioned our mother, and soon my memories faded. I could not picture her. I saw only Emily's angry face, the late sun streaking red through her dark hair.

After the traditional forty-nine-day mourning period, Baba didn't set foot in the Buddhist temple. It was as if he had listened to Emily: what good did it do? Instead he focused on earthly ambitions, his research at the lab.

At that time he aspired beyond the position of lab instructor to the rank of associate professor, and he often invited his American colleagues over for "drinks." After our mother died, Emily and I were recruited to help. As we went about our tasks, we would sometimes catch a glimpse of our father standing in the corner, watching the American men and studying to become one.

But he couldn't get it right—our parties had an air of cultural confusion. We served potato chips on lacquered trays; Chinese landscapes bumped against watercolors of the Statue of Liberty, the Empire State Building.

Nor were Emily or I capable of helping him. I was still a child, and Emily didn't care. She had grown beyond us; she stalked around in blue jeans, seething with fury at everything to do with him.

"I hate this," she said, fiercely ripping another rag from a pair of old pajama bottoms. "Entertaining these jerks is a waste of time. Some chemists from Texas were visiting his department and he had invited them over for cocktails.

"I can finish it," I said. "You just need to do the parts I can't reach."

"It's not the dusting," she said. "It's the way he acts around them. 'Herro,

herro! Hi Blad, hi Warry! Let me take your coat! Howsa Giants game?'" she mimicked. "If he were smart he wouldn't invite people over on football afternoons in the first place."

"What do you mean?" I said, worried that something was wrong. Brad Delmonte was my father's boss. I had noticed Baba reading the sports page that morning—something he rarely did.

"Oh, forget it," Emily said. I felt as if she and I were utterly separate. Then she smiled. "You've got oil on your glasses, Claudia."

Baba walked in carrying two bottles of wine. "They should arrive in half an hour," he said, looking at his watch. "They won't be early. Americans are never early."

Emily looked up. "I'm going to Jodie's house," she said.

Baba frowned and straightened his tie. "I want you to stay while they're here. We might need something from the kitchen."

"Claudia can get it for them."

"She's barely tall enough to reach the cabinets."

Emily stood up, clenched her dustcloth. "I don't care," she said. "I hate meeting those men."

"They're successful American scientists. You'd be better off with them instead of running around with your teenage friends, these sloppy kids, these rich white kids who dress like beggars."

"You're nuts, Dad," Emily said—she had begun addressing him the way an American child does. "You're nuts if you think these bosses of yours are ever going to do anything for you or any of us." And she threw her dustcloth, hard, into our New York Giants wastebasket.

"Speak to me with respect."

"You don't deserve it!"

"You are staying in this apartment! That is an order!"

"I wish you'd died instead of Mama!" Emily cried, and ran out of the room. She darted past our father; her long braid flying behind her. He stared at her; his expression oddly slack, the way it had been in the weeks after the funeral. He stepped toward her; reached hesitantly at her flying braid, but she turned and saw him, cried out as if he had struck her. His hands dropped to his sides.

Emily refused to leave our room. Otherwise that party was like so many others. The guests arrived late and left early. They talked about buying new cars and the Dallas Cowboys. I served pretzels and salted nuts. Baba walked around emptying ashtrays and refilling drinks. I noticed that the other men also wore vests and ties, but that the uniform looked somehow different on my slighter, darker father.

"Cute little daughter you have there," said Baba's boss. He was a large bearded smoker with a sandy voice. He didn't bend down to look at me or the ashtray that I raised toward his big square hand.

I went into our room and found Emily sitting on one of our unmade twin beds. It was dusk. Through the window the dull winter sun had almost disappeared. She didn't look up when I came in, but after a moment she spoke.

"I'm going to leave," she said. "As soon as I turn eighteen, I'm going to leave home and never come back!" She burst into tears. I reached for her shoulder but her thin, heaving body frightened me. She seemed too grown up to be comforted. I thought about the breasts swelling beneath her sweater. Her body had become a foreign place.

Perhaps Emily had warned me that she would someday leave in order to start me off on my own. I found myself avoiding her; as though her impending desertion would matter less if I deserted her first. I discovered a place to hide while she and my father fought, in the living room behind a painted screen. I would read a novel or look out the window. Sometimes they forgot about me—from the next room I would hear one of them break off an argument and say, "Where did Claudia go?" "I don't know," the other would reply. After a silence, they would start again.

One of these fights stands out in my memory. I must have been ten or eleven years old. It was the fourteenth day of the seventh lunar month: the eve of Guijie, the Chinese Spirit Festival, when the living are required to appease and provide for the ghosts of their ancestors. To the believing, the earth was thick with gathering spirits; it was safest to stay indoors and burn incense.

I seldom thought about the Chinese calendar; but every year on Guijie I wondered about my mother's ghost. Where was it? Would it still recognize me? How would I know when I saw it? I wanted to ask Baba, but I didn't dare. Baba had an odd attitude toward Guijie. On one hand, he had eschewed all Chinese customs since my mother's death. He was a scientist, he said; he scorned the traditional tales of unsatisfied spirits roaming the earth.

But I cannot remember a time when I was not made aware, in some way, of Guijie's fluctuating lunar date. That year the eve of the Spirit Festival fell on a Thursday, usually his night out with the men from his department. Emily and I waited for him to leave, but he sat on the couch, calmly reading the *New York Times*.

Around seven o'clock, Emily began to fidget. She had a date that night and had counted on my father's absence. She spent half an hour washing and combing her hair, trying to make up her mind. Finally she asked me to give her a trim. I knew she'd decided to go out.

"Just a little," she said. "The ends are scraggly." We spread some newspapers on the living room floor. Emily stood in the middle of the papers with her hair combed down her back, thick and glossy, black as ink. It hadn't really been cut since she was born. Since my mother's death I had taken over the task of giving it the periodic touchup.

I hovered behind her with the shears, searching for the scraggly ends, but there were none.

My father looked up from his newspaper. "What are you doing that for? You can't go out tonight," he said.

"I have a date!"

My father put down his newspaper. I threw the shears onto a chair and fled to my refuge behind the screen.

Through a slit over the hinge I caught a glimpse of Emily near the foyer; slender in her denim jacket her black hair flooding down her back, her delicate features contorted with anger. My father's hair was disheveled, his hands clenched at his sides. The newspapers had scattered over the floor.

"Dressing up in boys' clothes, with paint on your face—"

"This is nothing! My going out on a few dates is nothing! You don't know what the hell you're talking about!"

"Don't shout." My father shook his finger. "Everyone in the building will hear you.

Emily raised her voice. "Who the hell cares? You're such a coward; you care more about what other people think than how I feel!"

"Acting like a loose woman in front of everybody, a streetwalker!" The floor shook under my sister's stamp. Though I'd covered my ears, I could hear her crying. The door slammed, and her footfalls vanished down the stairs.

Things were quiet for a minute. Then I heard my father walk toward my corner. My heart thumped with fear—usually he let me alone. I had to look up when I heard him move the screen away. He knelt down next to me. His hair was streaked with gray, and his glasses needed cleaning.

"What are you doing?" he asked.

I shook my head, nothing.

After a minute I asked him, "Is Guijie why you didn't go play bridge tonight, Baba?"

"No, Claudia," he said. He always called me by my American name. This formality, I thought, was an indication of how distant he felt from me. "I stopped playing bridge last week."

"Why?" We both looked toward the window, where beyond our reflections the Hudson River flowed in the darkness.

"It's not important," he said.

"Okay."

But he didn't leave. "I'm getting old," he said after a moment. "Someone ten years younger was just promoted over me. I'm not going to try to keep up with them anymore."

It was the closest he had ever come to confiding in me. After a few more minutes he stood up and went into the kitchen. The newspapers rustled under his feet. For almost half an hour I heard him fumbling through the kitchen cabinets, looking for something he'd probably put there years ago. Eventually he came out, carrying a small brass urn and some matches. When Emily returned home after midnight, the apartment still smelled of the incense he had burned to protect her while she was gone.

My father loved Emily more. I knew this in my bones: it was why I stayed at home every night and wore no makeup, why I studied hard and got good grades, why I eventually went to college at Columbia, right up the street. Jealously I guarded my small allotment of praise, clutching it like a pocket of precious stones. Emily snuck out of the apartment late at night; she wore high-heeled sandals with patched blue jeans; she twisted her long hair into graceful, complex loops and braids that belied respectability. She smelled of lipstick and perfume. So certain she was of my father's love. His anger was a part of it. I knew nothing I could ever do would anger him that way.

When Emily turned eighteen and did leave home, a part of my father disappeared. I wondered sometimes, where did it go? Did she take it with her? What secret charm had she carried with her as she vanished down the tunnel to the jet that would take her to college in California, steadily and without looking back, while my father and I watched silently from the window at the gate? The apartment afterward became quite still—it was only the two of us, mourning and dreaming through pale blue winter afternoons and silent evenings.

Emily called me, usually late at night after my father had gone to sleep. She sent me pictures of herself and people I didn't know, smiling on the sunny Berkeley campus. Sometimes after my father and I ate our simple meals or TV dinners I would go into our old room, where I had kept both of our twin beds, and take out Emily's pictures, trying to imagine what she must have been feeling, studying her expression and her swinging hair. But I always stared the longest at a postcard she'd sent me one winter break from northern New Mexico, a professional photo of a powerful, vast blue sky over faraway pink and sandy-beige mesas. The clarity and cleanness fascinated me. In a place like that, I thought, there would be nothing to search for, no reason to hide.

After college, she went to work at a bank in San Francisco. I saw her once when she flew to Manhattan on business. She skipped a meeting to have lunch with me. She wore an elegant gray suit and had pinned up her hair.

"How's Dad?" she said. I looked around, slightly alarmed. We were sitting in a bistro on the East Side, but I somehow thought he might overhear us.

"He's okay," I said. "We don't talk very much. Why don't you come home and see him?"

Emily stared at her water glass. "I don't think so."

"He misses you."

"I know. I don't want to hear about it."

"You hardly ever call him."

"There's nothing to talk about. Don't tell him you saw me, promise?"

"Okay."

During my junior year at Columbia, my father suffered a stroke. He was fifty-nine years old, and he was still working as a lab instructor in the chemistry department. One evening in early fall I came home from a class and found him on the floor near the kitchen telephone. He was wearing his usual vest and tie. I called the hospital and sat down next to him. His wire-rimmed glasses lay on the floor a foot away. One half of his face was frozen, the other half lined with sudden age and pain.

"They said they'll be right here," I said. "It won't be very long." I couldn't tell how much he understood. I smoothed his vest and straightened his tie. I folded his glasses. I knew he wouldn't like it if the ambulance workers saw him in a state of dishevelment. "I'm sure they'll be here soon," I said.

We waited. Then I noticed he was trying to tell me something. A line of spittle ran from the left side of his mouth. I leaned closer. After a while I made out his words: "Tell Emily," he said.

The ambulance arrived as I picked up the telephone to call California. That evening, at the hospital, what was remaining of my father left the earth.

Emily insisted that we not hold a Buddhist cremation ceremony. "I never want to think about that stuff again," she said. "Plus, all of his friends are Americans. I don't know who would come, except for us." She had reached New York the morning after his death. Her eyes were vague and her fingernails bitten down.

On the third day we scattered his ashes in the river. Afterward we held a small memorial service for his friends from work. We didn't talk much as we straightened the living room and dusted the furniture. It took almost three hours. The place was a mess. We hadn't had a party in years.

It was a cloudy afternoon, and the Hudson looked dull and sluggish from the living room window. I noticed that although she had not wanted a Buddhist ceremony, Emily had dressed in black and white according to Chinese mourning custom. I had asked the department secretary to put up a sign on the bulletin board. Eleven people came; they drank five bottles of wine. Two of his Chinese students stood in the corner eating cheese and crackers.

Brad Delmonte, paunchy and no longer smoking, attached himself to Emily. "I remember when you were just a little girl," I heard him say as I walked by with the extra crackers.

"I don't remember you," she said.

"You're still a cute little thing." She bumped his arm, and he spilled his drink.

Afterward we sat on the couch and surveyed the cluttered coffee table. It was past seven but we didn't talk about dinner.

"I'm glad they came," I said.

"I hate them." Emily looked at her fingernails. Her voice shook. "I don't know whom I hate more, them or him—for taking it."

"It doesn't matter anymore," I said.

"I suppose."

We watched the room grow dark.

"Do you know what?" Emily said. "It's the eve of the fifteenth day of the seventh lunar month."

"How do you know?" During college I had grown completely unaware of the lunar calendar.

"One of those chemistry nerds from China told me this afternoon."

I wanted to laugh, but instead felt myself make a strange whimpering sound, squeezed out from my tight and hollow chest.

"Remember the time Dad and I had that big fight?" she said. "You know that now, in my grownup life, I don't fight with anyone? I never had problems with anybody except him."

"No one cared about you as much as he did," I said.

"I don't want to hear about it." Her voice began to shake again. "He was a pain, and you know it. He got so strict after Mama died. It wasn't all my fault."

"I'm sorry," I said. But I was so angry with her that I felt my face turn red, my cheeks tingle in the dark. She'd considered our father a nerd as well, had squandered his love with such thoughtlessness that I could scarcely breathe to think about it. It seemed impossibly unfair that she had memories of my mother as well. Carefully I waited for my feelings to go away. Emily, I thought, was all I had.

But as I sat, a vision distilled before my eyes: the soft baked shades, the great blue sky of New Mexico. I realized that after graduation I could go wherever I wanted. Somewhere a secret, rusty door swung open and filled my mind with sweet freedom, fearful coolness.

"I want to do something," I said.

"Like what?"

"I don't know." Then I got an idea. "Emily, why don't I give you a haircut?"

We found newspapers and spread them on the floor. We turned on the lamps and moved the coffee table out of the way, took the wineglasses to the sink. Emily went to the bathroom, and I searched for the shears a long time before I found them in the kitchen. I glimpsed the incense urn in a cabinet and quickly shut the door. When I returned to the living room, it smelled of shampoo. Emily was standing in the middle of the papers with her wet hair down her back, staring at herself in the reflection from the window. The lamplight cast circles under her eyes.

"I had a dream last night," she said. "I was walking down the street. I felt a tug. He was trying to reach me, trying to pull my hair."

"I'll just give you a trim," I said.

"No," she said. "Why don't you cut it?"

"What do you mean?" I snapped a two-inch lock off the side. Emily looked down at the hair on the newspapers. "I'm serious," she said. "Cut my hair. I want to see two feet of hair on the floor."

"Emily, you don't know what you're saying," I said. But a strange, weightless feeling had come over me. I placed the scissors at the nape of her neck. "How about it?" I asked, and my voice sounded low and odd.

"I don't care." An echo of the past. I cut. The shears went *snack*. A long black lock of hair hit the newspapers by my feet.

The Chinese say that our hair and our bodies are given to us from our ancestors, gifts that should not be tampered with. My mother herself had never done this. But after the first few moments I enjoyed myself, pressing the thick black locks through the shears, heavy against my thumb. Emily's hair slipped to the floor around us, rich and beautiful, lying in long graceful arcs over my shoes. She stood perfectly still, staring out the window. The Hudson River flowed behind our reflections, bearing my father's ashes through the night.

When I was finished, the back of her neck gleamed clean and white under a precise shining cap. "You missed your calling," Emily said. "You want me to do yours?"

My hair, browner and scragglier, had never been past my shoulders. I had always kept it short, figuring the ancestors wouldn't be offended by my tampering with a lesser gift. "No," I said. "But you should take a shower. Some of those small bits will probably itch."

"It's already ten o'clock," she said. "We should go to sleep soon anyway." Satisfied, she glanced at the mirror in the foyer. "I look like a completely different person," she said. She left to take her shower. I wrapped up her hair in the newspapers and went into the kitchen. I stood next to the sink for a long time before throwing the bundle away.

The past sees through all attempts at disguise. That night I was awakened by a wrenching scream. I gasped and stiffened, grabbing a handful of blanket.

"Claudia," Emily cried from the other bed. "Claudia, wake up!"

"What is it?"

"I saw Baba." She hadn't called our father Baba in years. "Over there, by the door. Did you see him?"

"No," I said. I didn't see anything." My bones felt frozen in place. After a moment I opened my eyes. The full moon shone through the window, bathing our room in silver and shadow. I heard my sister sob and then fall silent. I looked carefully at the door, but I noticed nothing.

Then I understood that his ghost would never visit me. I was, one might say, the lucky daughter. But I lay awake until morning, waiting; part of me is waiting still.

CONSTRUCTING A READING

1. This story evokes at least two worlds: a particular one of Chinese American cultural relations and a more general one of death and loss. How do you see the two words interacting?

2.   Is the experience of adolescence "universal" in your view? What about the death of a parent? List and describe the aspects of these experiences that might be shared by many readers. Then list the aspects that are specific to Chinese American cultures. Do your two lists intersect?
3.   Do you think that readers who do not share the beliefs and practices of Asian American cultures can come to grips with the world(s) of this story? Why and how?
4.   In what sense is Claudia the "lucky" daughter?
5.   With your group members, compare the Chinese observance of the "Eve of the Spirits" in this story to the Irish celebration of Halloween in "Clay." How do the Irish characters compare with the Asian American ones with respect to following customs? What do the customs mean to them? Is Maria in any sense a "lucky" woman like Claudia? Report your discussions to your classmates.

Presleystroika

Kay Sloan

On a cool summer evening in Leningrad, I was watching young Russian couples dancing in a restaurant that must have been elegant once—at the turn of the century perhaps, when its chipped marble columns and fogged mirrors had been new. But now decay had set in, and the young people might as well have been Romans dancing among the ruins of a fallen empire. It had rained that afternoon, a chilly mid-August downpour, and the parquet floor glistened beneath the leaks in the glass roof.

A dark-haired man suddenly released his dance partner, and, folding his muscular arms and thrusting out his legs, began a spirited version of the Russian kazatska, all the while trying to avoid the rain puddles on the floor. One young woman had gotten drunk on vodka, and she kept beckoning to a British businessman sitting at a side table. From the way she was moving, she wanted him to join her in a version of the Watusi. He was minding his own business, doing his best to ignore her. He pulled a sheaf of leaflets from a black briefcase and began passing them out to the customers.

"Vlado: A Russian Elvis Extravaganza" read the leaflet, in blue lettering that looped across the boots of an Elvis look-alike. Vlado was wearing wraparound sunglasses and a red jumpsuit, jewelled in silver, with sideburns that swept out to the corners of his mouth. "August 11th-August 18th, 1991," it read. "Leningrad Music Hall." It was sponsored by "Elvisly Yours" in London, and that night, the Sunday before I was to be in Moscow, was the last show. What luck.

I'd once loved Elvis. I'd even gotten Elvis's autograph back before he was an international heartthrob, when he was mostly famous all over Mississippi, where I grew up. Back in 1956, Elvis had sung at the opening of Strahn's Shoe Store in Biloxi—an extravaganza, they'd called it, same as this Leningrad show—and I had been there, handing him my diary to autograph, wearing my poodle skirt and bobby socks. For a couple of years, when I wanted to make a date jealous, I'd tell him about how Elvis winked at me, and how it had been just like the movies.

But it was more than movies: Elvis was revolution, the Lenin of lust. Everybody knew it, especially the P.T.A. parents and the Baptist preachers. In Mississippi in 1956, he stood for everything good Southern girls weren't supposed to want, swiveling hips and rhythm that only black people were rumored to have. Elvis let the black cat out of the pink bag, and it was a slinky, sexy cat. When you danced to "Jailhouse Rock," you knew there was more to life than obeying laws. *Everybody in the whole cell block was dancin' to the jailhouse rock.* That curl on Elvis's lip sneered to the entire world that not all girls wanted to live a life of Betty Crocker cake mixes and crying babies and home permanents—their mothers' lives. Instead, we became romantic revolutionaries trying to shake, rattle and roll our futures, dreaming about Elvis, the ideal lover in an ideal world. He meant we didn't have to wax kitchen floors or change diapers or humor a beer-drinking husband. As long as we had Elvis, we had hope, and we clung to him.

That's why I was curious about this Vlado, this Russian Elvis. After all, I'd never thought that the sequined Las Vegas Elvis was all that different from the black leather Elvis who'd signed my diary in Biloxi in 1956. The plump women in halter tops in the Caesar's Palace audiences knew what he stood for, and it was more than adolescent lust. He was the prince in all the fairy tales our mothers had read us since we were babies. And people wonder why he's spotted working in a Sarasota gas station or in a Minnesota dairy farm! Of course we were going to raise him from the dead, even if it was in the form of Vlado. Elvis was our salvation.

Maybe listening to "Jailhouse Rock" so often emboldened me. I never did have a housewife's life. I fled to New Orleans when I was eighteen, then to New York's Greenwich Village, where there were too many folksingers and poetry readings to think about Elvis very much. I had left my 45's behind in Biloxi, abandoning Elvis for what I thought were better things. By then, at dull parties, I'd trot out my Elvis story like a joke, exaggerating how long he'd gazed at me, or how badly I'd blushed. People in New York were always incredulous. It was the one bit of information that could knock their sophisticated socks off, and they'd stare like I was from the moon, just like when I told them I'd been fully immersed when I was baptized. Meeting Elvis *had* felt like a baptism, a drowning in hormones that washed away my childhood.

In 1991, nearly three decades after I left Mississippi, I was in Russia, putting together an exhibition of Soviet photography for a gallery back in New York. I was taking my own photographs, too, haunted by the faces I'd seen on the Leningrad subway—sad, lined faces with shoulders hunched over a sack of cabbages or a bottle of vodka. I'd felt like weeping, feeling the eyes on my lizard skin boots and short leather skirt, and the soft purse filled with dollars and more rubles than they might earn in three months. I'd wanted a babushka for my head, or a sack of potatoes to carry. My camera suddenly felt like an invasive eye, a sign that told the Leningraders I was there to observe, to take rather than give. I had left it behind when I'd gone out for dinner on that Sunday evening.

On that soggy August night, I wondered what kind of Soviet women would go to hear a Russian Elvis. What did he mean to them? I bought a ticket on the spot, even though the British businessman was selling it at a good bit more than the price advertised on the pamphlet.

It was not quite dark when I crossed the Neva River to Park Lenina; from the bridge the sun cast its last light on the buildings lining the river, an uneven geometry of gold shining between the gray of water and sky. A half-arc of a rainbow was fading, the yellow and red barely visible against silver clouds. I found the Leningrad Music Hall inside an imposing modern building set in the park. I was late, having lingered at the sunset on the bridge. High-heeled showgirls were already prancing across the stage in beaded costumes so sheer it appeared they were wearing only the pearls stitched into the mesh at strategic places. Pink plumes adorned their heads, making them look like giant exotic birds.

But I was too busy looking at the audience to pay much attention to the showgirls on stage. In the seat before me, a middle-aged blonde woman beamed at the stage while she creased and re-creased the playbill in her lap. She kept whispering to a friend who was fanning herself with a photograph of Vlado. Periodically she would stop fanning to look at the picture, then wave it even more briskly through the air.

A low moaning sound came from the side of the stage, and then the tune took shape: "Fools Rush In." Vlado came striding out, microphone to his mouth, gold and silver glittering from his bellbottomed jumpsuit. The audience grew quiet, and I realized I'd been expecting a wild cheer to go up. But instead they watched cautiously as Vlado gyrated across the stage, pants flapping about his boots. He had a double chin and a fuzz of dark chest hair visible all the way down to his wide silver belt: the Vegas Elvis. My heart sank a little, it seemed more vulgar than I'd expected. But hadn't that always been part of the appeal, after all?

It had been a hot June day in Biloxi when Elvis opened Strahn's Shoe Store, and Oscar Strahn hadn't installed air-conditioning yet. His daughter, Karen Strahn, was a good friend of mine—we were in the Biloxi Debuteens together—so she called up as many Debuteens as she could find and smuggled a bunch of us in through the back door before her father had opened up the front. We had barely noticed how hot it was back there, packed into the store shoulder to shoulder, waiting for Elvis to show. It was the hair I saw first, a glimpse of slick black and I knew it was Elvis and let out a yelp. We heaved forward in one single movement while Oscar Strahn tried to stand between us and his star. After all, he'd paid Elvis good money to open his new store. "Show a little respect, girls," he kept telling us. "You're guests at Biloxi's first shopping center! Back off, now."

Elvis somehow got his guitar plugged in and began wailing away. The words were raw, but the voice was smooth. It was "Hound Dog," my favorite. He would swing the neck of his guitar around if we got too close, but it was a joy to be brushed by it, making us part of the music for a few seconds. When he sang the slow ones, he didn't have to move his guitar or swivel his hips. His voice was enough, deep and slow, like he could see right through your clothes.

I had been so excited when Karen called that I'd forgotten to put on my bra, and there I was, dancing so hard I was bouncing around beneath my blouse. Who cared? All I knew was that something wonderful was happening right in front of my eyes, a broken taboo that told me my parents and my Sunday School teacher were wrong when they said rock 'n roll was sinful. Brother Beeker at Second Baptist had even said Elvis might be a Communist, sent to Mississippi to try to subvert the family and brainwash innocent teenagers. "He might sound like one of us, but you look again." He had stood behind the pulpit, wagging a finger at us kids in the back row. When we giggled, he blushed, connecting his freckles into a single redness over his receding hairline. "You leave the looking to your parents. You don't even need to look once, girls, you hear?"

It was wonderful to see the way Elvis swivelled his hips and rolled about on his toes in Strahn's Shoe Store, the forbidden things Ed Sullivan's camera hadn't let us watch. That cute boy with the puffy lips, we called him. When Elvis finished his song, he winked at me. "That gum good?" he asked. I'd been chewing bubble gum so hard I couldn't answer him. All I could do was pop a big pink bubble and laugh. I was that happy.

Cryin' all the time . . .

That was what Vlado was singing now, the older songs from the fifties, crooning to us to love him tender, and never let him go. He swivelled his hips, and a terrible wave of sadness washed over me. His voice carried that same intimacy that Elvis always implied, the way he made you feel that he was alone with you, in whatever convertible or on whatever beach you wanted to imagine. I remembered Oscar Strahn in his shoe store and how he would grin when one of the "Elvis girls" would stop in for a pair of sandals or saddle oxfords.

"How's Elvis?" he would ask us. He made us feel as if we knew Elvis personally just because, on that one June day in Strahn's Shoe Store, Elvis had winked at us or shaken our hands or signed our diaries—the things that meant, at age fourteen, that our souls had touched.

Beside me in the Leningrad Music Hall, a woman in a fox fur jacket chewed loudly on gum that smelled like licorice. She applauded when Vlado finished, a polite smile on her face, and I wondered, how do you grow up without Elvis? Down in front, a group of Soviet sailors, their white caps streaming navy ribbons down their backs, had their dates with them, and the whole group of them were grinning and clapping.

After each song, the applause grew louder and louder until finally, when Vlado sang "I Can't Help Falling in Love With You," the crowd rose and women in front threw red carnations at his feet. Still singing, he stooped awkwardly, as if protecting a bad back, and gathered up a handful of flowers. I thought of the decaying Leningrad restaurant where I'd had dinner that night and the way the dancers, dressed in clothes that had been fashionable in the West several seasons ago, had whirled about the floor, ignoring the inelegance of rain puddles. Now, the audience ignored the obvious inelegance of Vlado's bad back.

All around me, the crowd had finally come alive. It seemed people everywhere shared a desperate impulse to invent gods, both in the consumer world of the West—how far away it seemed at that moment!—and there in the heart of the Communist world, where bronze statues and plaques celebrated Lenin at nearly every turn. The woman beside me wiped at her eyes with a handkerchief. I felt like weeping, too, but probably not for the same reasons. It was for the bewigged man on the stage with his fake sideburns and stiff back and for the Soviets in furs weeping into their handkerchiefs, still craving something that Vlado gave them a brief glimpse of—romance resurrected. Even if they'd been cast in gold, all the Lenin statues in Leningrad couldn't satisfy what these women wanted. Vlado meant they didn't have to wait in long lines for bread or cook cabbage for supper or humor a vodka-drinking husband—the lives their mothers had led, too.

So, Elvis was still just as subversive as Brother Bob Beeker had declared him in 1956, but nobody here would ever claim him for a Communist. That was the very thing he threatened—all those years of censorship and repression. There was something still forbidden about Vlado, a steady effort to confront something in the world outside. Vlado swung his wide hips in a style more like a waltz than like the wild thrusting that "Elvis the Pelvis" had done in the fifties, but my heart went out to him and I realized tears were in my eyes. He was letting the cat out of the bag, and it was a desperate, hungry cat.

I took the overnight express to Moscow, travelling on a train too stuffy to sleep well, and checked into my hotel room in time to have the complimentary breakfast. The dining room was strangely quiet. An Australian woman who'd arrived with me on the same sleeper train decided it was the difference between the people of Leningrad and Moscow.

"Look what a gloomy group these Muscovites are," she said, adjusting her glasses on her nose. "At least in Leningrad they had some spirit."

I thought she might be right. It was my first visit, after all. How could I have known what had transpired the night of August 18, 1991, while I had sat in Park Lenina listening to Vlado crooning old Elvis songs?

In silence, people helped themselves to the pastries and sausages and thick gruel, shooting odd looks at the loud Italian teenagers laughing at a far table, oblivious to the gloom. From a bulletin board, Vlado's face smiled at the diners. It was a poster announcing that his show would be having a run in Moscow, but I couldn't imagine these glum Muscovites twitching in their seats to "Jailhouse Rock." Their faces seemed chiseled with their terrible history, and the impassive way it had been received through the ages, not as something created but observed—events inexorable, changes that occurred outside the scope of human challenge. The poster advertising Vlado's show seemed a ludicrous acceptance of Western heroes and hopes.

It wasn't long before an old Soviet woman joined me at my table, carrying two plates piled high with small round cakes. When she thought no one was looking, she dumped them into a canvas bag beneath the table. For re-sale, probably. She nodded at me when I noticed, offering a quick grin that showed missing teeth.

I told her good day in my broken Russian, and she answered in English that was not much better.

"The president," she told me. "Is gone." She waved a plump hand at the glum diners around me. "Sad today."

"What?" I asked. "Gorbachev? Yeltsin? Who's gone?"

She waved a finger before her lips. "Is sick," she whispered. "Gorbachev. New men in Kremlin."

"Gorbachev is dying?" I asked, my voice climbing to a squeak.

A knowing look crossed her face and I thought of the Gypsy fortune-teller I'd seen reading palms on the Arbat early that morning. "Maybe dead."

The French couple sitting a couple of chairs away glanced up and the man leaned my way. "There's been a coup d'é'tat. The old-line Communists have taken over. Gorbachev is out."

I could feel my jaw drop, and I heard myself do something strange: I laughed, and the French couple looked at me oddly. But when I looked around at the grim faces in that steamy, cabbage-smelling dining hall, I knew something terrible and real had happened.

I had an appointment with a Russian photographer named Boris that morning. From Leningrad, I had arranged to meet him at one of the entrances to Red Square. Outside, as I turned the corner onto the broad avenue that ran into the city center, a column of tanks came rolling past, gun barrels pointing ahead, the faces of young soldiers peering out above the turrets. It was the sort of thing you see in photographs, but the camera never shows you how tanks leave tracks chewed into asphalt streets, or how they rumble like the sound of hundreds of New York garbage trucks.

Or how it feels like a fist in your stomach to see a sight like that. There was something familiar about the nauseated feeling that rose in my chest—it was how I'd reacted decades ago when I'd passed a Ku Klux Klan rally, back when I was still in high school in Biloxi, when I was still using Elvis to make dates jealous. The white hoods and burning cross had seemed just as ominous and anonymous as these tanks rolling by, full of the promise of violence.

My camera felt heavy around my neck, and I lifted it to shoot the picture. Clouds of exhaust hung over the line of tanks like gunsmoke. When a loud explosion suddenly rang in the air, I jumped and looked about quickly for the victim—and then realized that one of the tanks in the rear had backfired. A young woman paused beside me to stare at the tanks, disbelieving, then hurried away helplessly, clutching at the throat of her sweater as if she might shut out a chill in the air.

Not far away was the bridge over the Moskva River leading to the Russian Parliament Building. Further along was Red Square, where I hoped I could still find Boris. Everywhere, the faces passing by were frightened and sad, the lips tight, silent, as if to say the day began yet another epoch of history over which they had no power. A little boy clung to his mother's hand, his face upturned to frown at all the adults hurrying by. His mouth was frozen in a pout. Like Elvis, I thought, or Vlado.

Even at the demonstration just outside Red Square, the protesters seemed not so much angry as stoic observers of this new twist in history. A woman whose pale face matched the white of her sweater translated the speaker's words for me: Yeltsin was calling for a general strike. Early that morning, she said, protesters had stood in front of the Soviet tanks, blocking their path. Unable to reach the Russian Parliament Building or Red Square, the tanks had formed a ring around the city.

Just at my elbow, I heard an American voice complaining to the man with her: "Skin as chalky as that, she should never wear that colorless sweater." It was a tall woman with hair perfectly done up in a bun, and red lipstick that matched her silk blouse. I was about to trade notes with them, to see what they might have heard, but when I realized what she was saying, I turned away, embarrassed for her, at her own way of feeling powerful on that overwhelming day. In my mind, an old Elvis song started. The words were in Vlado's voice, warning people not to step on his blue suede shoes. It was a mantra to assure me I'd be safe, that the whole country would be all right, despite the tanks circling the city like sharks, waiting for the right moment to attack.

I finally found Boris near the entrance to Red Square where a line of buses filled with bored-looking soldiers barricaded the area. Beyond, the blue spires of St. Basil's Cathedral were barely visible above the buses, as if they had been grabbed tip in a giant fist. Boris was shooting a picture of some protesters who were talking to the soldiers, trying to persuade them to abandon the barricade, but most just stared back, expressionless.

"They are children," he told me, waving an arm at the soldiers. "They obey whoever is father today."

"Who *is* father today?" I asked.

He shrugged. "The hard-liners. Gorbachev was forcing them out, stepping all over them."

Blue suede shoes . . . I waved my hand through the air as if I could shoo away the annoying music in my head, and Boris turned to see who I was gesturing to. It was that kind of day: nerves.

We detoured a couple of blocks to the KGB Building, so Boris could show me the great complex where the coup had probably originated. In front of one of the large gray buildings, an old man in baggy pants bent over to sweep the sidewalk clear of the papers that had blown there. A handbill with Vlado's face printed on it was visible among the anti-coup leaflets that he deposited into a trash can. The old man didn't take time to read them; he went about his job as if nothing had happened.

"You see the old man?" asked Boris. "This is how the Soviet people are. Where are most of the people in Moscow today? They are at their jobs; they are afraid to be at Red Square."

Fools rush in . . . "Vlado," I said, pointing to a crumpled leaflet "I heard him last night in Leningrad. He's the Russian Elvis."

Boris snorted. "Yes, or they are paying good roubles to hear Vlado, trash from the West."

I didn't try to explain that Elvis had once triggered my own revolt in 1956, how he'd brought black rhythm and blues and sexuality to us and made it all okay. We headed toward the Russian Parliament Building, leaving Manezh Square behind, where a circle of soldiers kept gradually expanding pushing back the protesters. I focused my long-distance lens on a young soldier. He was staring straight ahead with a blank look, chewing the side of his inner lip so that his mouth puckered. An older man was trying to persuade him to leave his post.

"You shouldn't be so cynical," I told Boris.

He was aiming his camera up at a group of chefs who had appeared on a balcony to hear the talks, their white hats like a cluster of mushrooms. "Some people have tasted too much freedom to give it up," he said. "They see things on television, in movies. They want more."

I thought of the couples I'd seen dancing the kazatska in Leningrad the night before, avoiding the rain puddles on the floor.

When we arrived at the Parliament Building, a barricade of buses with deflated tires blocked off the bridge, preventing the Soviet tanks from reaching Yeltsin.

We stayed at the Parliament Building all afternoon, photographing the demonstrators and the pamphleteers as they came and went, distributing the latest news. On a post, an advertisement for Vlado's upcoming Moscow extravaganza had been partly covered with an anti-coup leaflet. Only Vlado's upper torso was visible, the microphone to his mouth, making it look as if he were broadcasting the revolutionary news himself.

Around the post, the protesters dragged metal posts, wooden spools, street signs—anything they could get their hands on—to strengthen the barricade around Yeltsin. Boris and I said little to each other, shooting roll after roll of film.

Just as the sun finally set, flaming blood-red in the west over the Moskva River, a stream of demonstrators poured by, chanting for Yeltsin. One of the leaders pounded a fist against the air; in the other hand he clutched a yellow umbrella. Carrying an umbrella to the revolution, I thought, as if this night might be a normal one with mundane concerns, where getting wet was the worst to be feared.

In the center of the march walked a balding, barrel-bellied man carrying a Russian flag on a homemade stick. He was tall, and the flag waved high above the marchers' heads. For an instant, I couldn't place why his face was familiar. He bent slowly, as if he had a bad back, to pick up a leaflet that had fallen, and then I realized it was Vlado, minus his Elvis wig and side-burns and sequined jumpsuit. Wearing an ordinary windbreaker and jeans, he could have been any other protester. I recognized his brown eyes, and the way his forehead extended into a slight ridge above them. He was chewing gum, casting an anxious gaze over the protesters in front, his large head rising like a periscope above the crowd. I could even hear his deep voice booming over the chants of the others: *Yeltsin, Yeltsin.*

"It's Vlado," I told Boris. "The Russian Elvis."

His eyes flickered over the crowd until they rested on the back of Vlado's head. "He's afraid they'll cancel his show." He shrugged. "He has a lot at stake."

"Cancel his show? You think that's why he's here?" I could see Vlado's fist in the air now, punctuating the chant.

"You think he is a new Lenin? You think he cares about Gorbachev? No. He cares for his career."

Rain had begun to glisten from the faces passing by. My face felt hot and my hands shook, remembering the vulnerable man on stage bending to protect his back, and now the balding man marching with a Russian flag, slowly disappearing in the distance.

A young woman went marching by just then, struggling to put up her umbrella at the same time she held a small Ukrainian flag. She looked about for a place to leave the flag, and, before I could even think, I stepped into the column and held it for her while she righted the umbrella. She smiled and marched on, leaving me with the splinter of wood that bore the flag.

I stood there for a few seconds, my heart fluttering like something bobbing in the middle of a stream. *Everybody in the whole cell block . . .* Then I waved to Boris and joined the river. *Yeltsin, Yeltsin.* The current swept me up, flowing down the streets already chewed by tanks, moving beyond a line of army trucks, then snaking through an opening in a barricade, swelling into a giant pool at the Russian Parliament Building. *Yeltsin, Yeltsin.* The sound was like a heartbeat, keeping the rhythm of the feet and fists of the single organism it seemed we'd become. Up ahead, I could still see Vlado, and I thought of Oscar Strahn's shoe store and how we'd sweated together waiting for Elvis to appear and change our lives, hoping he could make some difference. We had felt a thrill of danger at the way the world had grown a little larger that day in 1956.

An old man with two broken teeth behind his smile grabbed my arm and pointed to a Soviet tank, jerking its way down the street. A Russian flag flapped above it, waving the white, blue and red bars. It was approaching the Parliament Building with its guns turned away, pointing above the heads of the crowds who followed behind. They cheered the tank's defection, tossing the soldiers cigarettes and flowers as it lurched down the avenue to secure a position at the Parliament Building.

I cheered, too. . . . *is dancing to the jailhouse rock.* I'd run out of film long ago, but the song lyrics still ran through my mind. For an instant, I spotted Boris perched on the ledge of a low building, adjusting his lens. It looked as if he were focusing on Vlado, who had just thrown a package of cigarettes to the soldiers riding in the tank. It missed, and he went trotting to the tank to retrieve it, bending stiffly before the great tracks could roll over the cigarettes. Vlado handed the package up to the soldier, his face shining, probably with both sweat and rain, and with something else—admiration for the young man lurching there above him in the night. The soldier gave a tight smile and raised his arm in a brief fist as he rode his tank into a horribly uncertain future.

I followed behind the tank, waving the Ukrainian flag, swept up in the cheering of thousands of Soviets. "*Spa-see-ba!*" they changed, thanking the soldiers. I thought of the crowd the night before in Leningrad, cheering Vlado, singing along with Elvis's songs. *Everbody in the whole cell block is dancin' to the jailhouse rock . . .*

I thought of Elvis's face on black velvet canvases in countless truckstops, the lines of fans waiting to enter Graceland, and the busts of Elvis sold in bus stations across America. Here, in a country dotted with monumental Lenin statues, red enamel buttons with Lenin's profile, patient Soviets queuing up to see the embalmed body in Red Square, and endless plaques paying tribute to every minute event in Lenin's life—here's where he hid in a haystack, here's the doorway where he waited for a Bolshevik who didn't show up—the romance with power had been over a different sort of promise, an idol who had offered another utopian fantasy. A human being who'd become a god. But now the idols had aged and the monuments of past decades were falling. In only a few days, the statute of Dzherzhinsky, the founder of the KGB, would be toppled by workers wielding a giant crane.

Tomorrow, I imagined, the old man in front of the KGB Building would still be bending down with his small broom sweeping the sidewalk, pushing leaflets into a trash can—announcements of Vlado's extravaganza, pamphlets opposing the coup, hamburger wrappers from McDonald's—it would seem all the same to him. But that night, carrying the Ukrainian flag in my American hands, history was more than something that left debris to be swept into trash-bins. The only heroes of history were not would-be human gods but the people who destroyed them.

The renegade tank had found a position guarding the Parliament Building. A man lifted up his young son, wearing an outsized leather army helmet, and let him scramble onto the tank. The child stood there for a moment, gazing out over the adults gathered in a great mass, and, as if he had found an audience and a stage, he began to dance, the soles of his small rubber boots knocking rhythm against brown steel.

CONSTRUCTING A READING

1. This essay evokes several worlds, each of which has a different set of attitudes about Elvis. Describe, in a paragraph or two, the world of Biloxi, Mississippi, in 1956, the world of Kay Sloan as a professional woman who currently teaches and writes at an American university, and the world of late summer 1991, as the Soviet Union disintegrated and its commitment to communism changed. In what ways do these worlds interact in Sloan's essay?

2. What does Elvis represent in this story? How does he function as an icon for Kay Sloan's parents, for citizens of the Soviet Union in 1991, and for Sloan herself?

3. Is it difficult for you to think of communism as a comfortable set of ideas? Is it difficult for you to think of Elvis as threatening? If so, then you are seeing how texts can make our own worlds momentarily "strange." Describe your attitude toward Elvis Presley before and after you read Sloan's essay.

4. Write an essay about a kind of music, behavior, or dress that threatens a segment of your culture as early rock and roll threatened the culture of Kay Sloan's parents. Describe its "threatening" aspects and your response to them.

In the texts that follow, several poets, a student, a singer/songwriter, and a graphic artist work with Marilyn Monroe as an icon. Study their representations carefully and answer the questions as your teacher directs.

The Death
of Marilyn Monroe

Sharon Olds

The ambulance men touched her cold
body, lifted it, heavy as iron,
onto the stretcher, tried to close the
mouth, closed the eyes, tied the
arms to the sides, moved a caught
strand of hair, as if it mattered,
saw the shape of her breasts, flattened by
gravity, under the sheet,
carried her, as if it were she,
down the steps.

These men were never the same. They went out
afterwards, as they always did,
for a drink or two, but they could not meet
each other's eyes.

Their lives took
a turn—one had nightmares, strange
pains, impotence, depression. One did not
like his work, his wife looked
different, his kids. Even death
seemed different to him—a place where she
would be waiting,

and one found himself standing at night
in the doorway to a room of sleep, listening to a
woman breathing, just an ordinary
woman
breathing.

Candle in the Wind

Elton John

Goodbye Norma Jeane
Though I never knew you at all
You had the grace to hold yourself
While those around you crawled
They crawled out of the woodwork

And they whispered into your brain
They set you on the treadmill
And they made you change your name

And it seems to me you have lived your life
Like a candle in the wind
Never knowing who to cling to
When the rain set in
And I would have liked to know you
But I was just a kid
Your candle burned out long before
Your legend ever did

Loneliness was tough
The toughest role you ever played
Hollywood created a superstar
And pain was the price you paid
Even when you died
The press still hounded you
All the papers had to say
Was that Marilyn was found in the nude
Goodbye Norma Jeane
Though I never knew you at all
You had the grace to hold yourself
While those around you crawled

Goodbye Norma Jeane
From the young man in the 22nd row
Who sees you as something more than sexual
More than just our Marilyn Monroe.

CONSTRUCTING A READING

1. What is the effect of the speaker's addressing Norma Jeane rather than Marilyn Monroe?

2. How does "the young man in the 22nd row" see "more than just our Marilyn Monroe"? What does he see?

3. What is the effect of "our" in the last line? To whom does the speaker refer?

4. If you can, view the video of Elton John's performance of "Candle in the Wind." What if anything does the video add to the meaning you make of the lyric? What if anything does it detract?

Prayer for Marilyn Monroe

Ernesto Cardenal

Lord accept this girl
called Marilyn Monroe throughout the world
though that was not her name
(but you know her real name, that of the orphan raped at nine
the shopgirl who tried to kill herself when aged sixteen)
who now goes into your presence without make-up
without her Press Agent
without her photographs or signing autographs
lonely as an astronaut facing the darkness of outer space.

When a girl, she dreamed she was naked in a church
      (according to *Time*)
standing in front of a prostrate multitude, heads to the ground,
and had to walk on tiptoe to avoid the heads.
You know our dreams better than all psychiatrists.
Church, house or cave all represent the safety of the womb
but also something more . . .
The heads are admirers, so much is clear (that
mass of heads in the darkness below the beam to the screen)
but the temple isn't the studios of 20th-Century Fox.
The temple, of marble and gold, is the temple of her body
in which the Son of Man stands whip in hand
driving out the money-changers of 20th-Century Fox
who made your house of prayer a den of thieves.

CONSTRUCTING A READING

1. This poem is an elegy, a poem or song composed in memory of someone who has died. How might such a poem be expected to treat its subject? Describe the ways in which this poem meets or flaunts those expectations.
2. The speaker calls Marilyn's body a temple "of marble and gold?" How does the poet treat the Christian notion that the body is a temple?
3. Look up the story of Jesus's anger in the temple (Mark 11: 15-18). How does the poet use that imagery?
4. Why might the speaker think Marilyn Monroe needs a prayer? In some ways, this prayer is also a condemnation. Whom do you think the poet faults?
5. Describe the poem's language about Marilyn's body, her fears, her abuse, and her construction as property. How do you respond to this language? Do you find this kind of language used to describe women today? If so, where?
6. What does this poem add to or confirm about your sense of Marilyn Monroe as a cultural icon?

Another Poem for Marilyn Monroe
Eric Rapp

How many poems are written about you?
Countless words by the man in Connecticut
who listens to Elton John.
Or the English major
who reads Cardenal translated.
On telephones 976 we hear your voice.
In movies we see your moving.
So many moves
that anything might make anyone
think of you.
In the Foodtown check-out line
a blonde woman in a fire pink jacket.
Your picture on the cover of *The Star.*
A pink carnation between your teeth.
Simple brown dress
the same one worn by the housewife from Kansas
who was impregnated by aliens
and probably voted for Kennedy.
Seeing you, most might think
of telephones or candles.
I think of graveyards
filled with a thousand pink carnations
rooted down by a thousand stainless teeth.

CONSTRUCTING A READING

1. What does this poem imply about people who experience culture through telephone sex lines or supermarket magazines? Why is Marilyn Monroe important to the people whom the poem describes?
2. How is this poem concerned with the effects of Marilyn's image? How does the poet seem to feel about the trading of that image? What do you think the poet means by "Another poem for Marilyn Monroe?"
3. This poet was an "English major" when he wrote this text. Do you relate to this poem more fully or immediately because its author is a student like you? Describe your response to the text and its author/speaker.

Four Marilyns
Andy Warhol

CONSTRUCTING A READING

1. Do some research about Andy Warhol and "Pop Culture" in the library or on the net. Then explain how you respond to the multiple images of Marilyn.
2. Steinem writes that "[m]en who had never known [Marilyn Monroe] wondered if their love and protection might have saved her." Using Elton John, Ernesto Cardenal, and Eric Rapp as your evidence, agree or disagree with Steinem.
3. What does it mean to be taken seriously? What does Marilyn mean by this phrase? Carole Oles? Ernesto Cardenal? Elton John? Gloria Steinem? your group members? you?

SECOND ACTS

Using the Text's Strategies to Build Your Reading

CHAPTER FOUR

How Language Guides Us to Configure Meaning

THE ROLE OF TROPES

"What's in a name?" Shakespeare's Juliet asks;

> ". . . that which we call a rose
> By any other name would smell as sweet."

In one of the most familiar love stories in Western culture, Romeo frequently calls Juliet by names other than her given one:

> "But soft, what light through yonder window breaks?"

he asks himself rhetorically at one point, and then responds,

> "It is the East and Juliet is the sun."

Shakespeare's lovers address and speak of each other in *figurative language*, one of the most important and puzzling kinds of guidelines that texts offer readers. You may have heard figurative language referred to by some of its subcategories, like simile, metaphor, symbol, or image. All of these aspects of texts help us to figure them out—by giving us a figure—a concrete picture of some kind—that helps us to construct meaning.

In its most general sense, *figurative language* guides readers to perceive similarities or draw analogies between disparate experiences. If I say, "It's like

> James J. Sosnoski writes that a "configuration is a 'figuring out' [that] offers an analogy from one realm of experience to suggest the shape an interpersonal experience *might* take in another."
>
> _____
>
> *Token Professionals and Master Critics: A Critique of Orthodoxy in Literary Studies.* State University of New York Press, 1994, p. xxxi.

an oven outside," I offer you an oven as a **figure** for the summer's heat, an image that recalls for you an experience like the one I'm trying to describe.

Figurative language presents readers with a special kind of gap; it offers an analogy (the weather is like an oven) and invites them to figure out *how* the analogy works (it's hot!). This chapter will concentrate on the processes by which readers construct meaning from figurative language, or *tropes*. The term is derived from a greek word that means a turning. Figurative language asks us to *turn* away from the ordinary and experience a different way of seeing through a *turn of phrase*.

Simile

Here is a trope by Robert Burns that you may already know:

> My Luv is like a red red rose
> That's newly sprung in June

Perhaps you already recognize this trope as a *simile*, an expressed comparison that is signaled to us by the word "like" or "as." Robert Burns's invitation to see a woman as like a rose is so familiar that you might not even think about it.

But let's do think about it. Through the simile, Burns's speaker gives instructions about how to produce the meaning of his song. It is as though he said to his reader, "I know you've never met the woman I love, but I want you to know what she's like so that you will understand why I find her so attractive. Imagine her as like a rose in June."

Prompted by these guidelines, Burns's readers might think about the way roses look in June when the mornings are still cool (at least in Scotland) and the dew glistens on the flowers in the garden. This rose is "newly sprung" and "red." From those attributes, a reader might infer that the flower promises more and fuller beauty, and therefore more gratification, to the man who gazes. Burns's speaker apparently enjoys gazing at his beloved and admiring her beauty *just as* he enjoys the beauty of flowers; perhaps he also thinks about wanting to possess that beauty *just as* one plucks flowers and puts them in vases.

Tropes Are Cultural Conventions

Thus, readers are invited to think about ways in which, to the male consciousness of the speaker, women and roses are alike. Somehow we know, however, that Burns is not guiding us to think about women as having petals and thorns and pistils and stamens. Instead, the trope prompts its readers to select and compare certain aspects of roses to certain aspects of women, and to ignore or "deselect" certain others.

But *how* do we know that? How is it that readers seem to understand which attributes to select and which ones to ignore when they encounter configurations? And, more to the point for many puzzled readers of poetry, how can we even identify these instructions when they aren't explicit? What do we do when we don't know what to do?

The answer is complex. Culture teaches readers how to read, but it does so in ways that are complicated, often silent, sometimes contradictory, and sometimes (as with instructions to think of women as objects to be gazed at, possessed, or plucked) even alarming!

These cultural teachings are called *conventions*: they are not rules, exactly, but rather traditional ways of doing or seeing things. *Conventions*, as we shall use the term, are patterns of language or behavior to which members of a culture have become accustomed. For centuries, poets have been asking readers to compare women and roses, and so we accept this guideline as conventional. In one of his most delightful sonnets, Shakespeare looks whimsically at such similes.

Sonnet 130

William Shakespeare

My Mistress' eyes are nothing like the Sun;
Coral is far more red than her lips' red;
If snow be white, why then her breasts are dun;
If hairs be wires, black wires grow on her head.
I have seen Roses damask'd, red and white,
But no such Roses see I in her cheeks;
And in some perfumes is there more delight
Than in the breath that from my Mistress reeks.
I love to hear her speak, yet well I know
That Music hath a far more pleasing sound;
I grant I never saw a goddess go;
My Mistress, when she walks, treads on the ground:
   And yet, by heaven, I think my love as rare
   As any she belied with false compare.

CONSTRUCTING A READING

1. Make a list of the common tropes you find in this poem.
2. What comment is Shakespeare making about the use of these common tropes?
3. In the final two lines (the couplet), Shakespeare's speaker seems to promise that his discourse about his beloved will not rely on tropes. On the basis of what you have read so far, do you believe him? Why or why not?

Part of the humor of Shakespeare's sonnet is that the comparisons he mentions were already commonplace more than five hundred years ago. Readers (and listeners, and film and TV audiences) become accustomed to these instructions and internalize them as part of their native language. Of course, we are not all accustomed to every convention, and that is why many readers find it difficult to read literary texts. They are simply not accustomed to the particular conventions that the text employs. You can *become* accustomed to reading conventions, however, and as you do so, you'll find literary texts easier to read.

Moreover, unconventional configurations can also be surprising and entertaining. It's true that authors rarely point to similarities between women and zinnias, or stepladders, or locomotives, but they could. You might, for example, say "my love is like a microwave oven," or "reading poetry is like trying to solve a connect-the-dots puzzle without any numbers," or "life is like a hamburger." In each case, you are describing one *experience* in terms of another: you are saying: "this is what it's like to know my beloved;" "this is what it's like to read a poem."

How Figurative Language Pervades Culture

It is important to realize that literary texts are not the only kinds of texts that use tropes. Every imaginable kind of text uses figurative language in order to explain one experience in terms of another. Often, a trope works to configure an unfamiliar experience in terms of another, more familiar one. When scientists explaining the structure of the DNA molecule point out that it is like a spiral staircase, their figure draws an analogy between the experience of looking at a spiral staircase and the experience of looking at a strand of DNA. In choosing that figure, they assume that although their audience may not know very much about molecular structure, they probably do have experience with spiral staircases. An automobile advertised as "like a rock" configures our experience of solidity in both the car and the geological formation. When breath mints are configured as "like a mountain in springtime," the analogy is from one feeling to another.

How Tropes Affect Our Understanding

The way we configure, or "trope upon," a concept profoundly affects our understanding of it. Expressions like "You're *wasting* my time," or "This gadget will *save* you hours," or "I've *invested* a lot of time in her," reflect the trope "time is money," which in turn affects the way we understand our lives. If you think of your time as money, you are more likely to worry about "spending" too much of it in unproductive ways than you would be if you think of your time as a psychic space for experience. When newscasters compare a political election to a horse race, they focus their audience's attention more on the competition than on the issues. When physicians speak of a "war" on life-threatening or debilitating diseases, they focus our attention on the ways in which such disorders need to be "attacked," or "fought." In an essay called "Aids and Its Metaphors," Susan Sontag describes the effect of these figures:

> [W]ars against diseases are not just calls for more zeal, and more money to be spent on research. The metaphor implements the way particularly dreaded diseases are envisaged as an alien "other," as enemies are in modern war. . . . Military metaphors contribute to the stigmatizing of certain illnesses and, by extension, of those who are ill.[*]

Sontag's point is that tropes can have unintended effects: that is, a physician who speaks of attacking cancer or AIDS probably does not intentionally construe her patient as the enemy: rather it is the disease against which she "trains" her "weapons." But a person who has AIDS or cancer may feel that she herself is the enemy—someone who is to be eliminated along with her medical condition.

Many theorists believe that tropes are part of the very process of our thinking—not just optional ornaments of speaking and writing but the very fabric of our knowledge of the lives we lead. We simply cannot, in other words, separate or detach figurative language from "straight" or "literal" language.

CONSTRUCTING A READING

1. Think of an unconventional way of configuring a loved one (e.g., my love is like a computer monitor) and explain your analogy.
2. Think of tropes for some familiar experiences on your campus, for example student apathy, or the feelings engendered by your sports teams, the attitude of Greeks toward non-Greeks, or commuters toward non-commuters. Explain the analogy.
3. Listen to a news or sportscast and make a list of the configurations the

---

[*]Susan Sontag, *Illness as Metaphor and Aids and Its Metaphors.* New York: Anchor Books, nd, p. 99.

announcers use to guide your response to the events they describe. Share your list with your classmates as a chart or computer graphic.

4. Look in an introductory textbook for one of the courses you are taking and try to find one or more tropes that explain important conceptions in a discipline by offering analogies. Explain them to your classmates and teacher.

TYPES OF TROPES

Since tropes are fundamental and pervasive, it follows that you already know how to read them. The same competence that permits you to understand a magazine advertisement for cosmetics also lets you understand the tropes in poems and stories. Although few readers stop to think about tropes, we all learn to process them from listening to and living in our world. To help you understand how these cultural instructions work, and to see distinctions among kinds of tropes, you might think about one of the most ubiquitous figures in western culture, in which a woman is compared to a rose.

Each of the texts that follow asks you to make an analogy between women and roses. Specific guidelines vary, however, and different guidelines have different names. *Simile* is one of those names, and Kenneth Burke has defined four others—*metaphor, metonymy, synecdoche,* and *irony*—as the *master tropes.* Each asks a reader to see the world differently as a consequence of making a particular kind of analogy.

Metaphor

Metaphor, like simile, guides readers to connect two experiences and thereby to see both of them in a new way. The poem that follows asks you to take a new perspective on relations between a rose and a woman.

The Rose Family

Robert Frost

The rose is a rose,
And was always a rose.
But the theory now goes
That the apple's a rose,
And the pear is, and so's
The plum, I suppose.
The dear only knows
What will next prove a rose.
You, of course, are a rose—
But were always a rose.

> Kenneth Burke writes that "Metaphor is a device for seeing something in terms of something else. It brings out the thisness of a that, the thatness of a this. . . . to consider A from the point of view of B is, of course, to use B as a *perspective* upon A. . . . the seeing of something in terms of something else involves the 'carrying-over' of a term from one realm into another."
>
> ---
>
> *A Grammar of Motives.* University of California Press, 1969, pp. 503–4.

Notice that the words "like" or "as," the markers of simile, are absent from this poem. Notice, too, that this text is a bit more difficult to process than Burns's simple invitation to compare his beloved to a rose. Frost's speaker assures his beloved that

> You, of course, are a rose

but he doesn't tell her (or us) exactly how.

Frost's figure is an example of *metaphor*, a trope that guides its audience to see one thing in terms of another. A metaphor can be a comparison, an analogy, a juxtaposition, a tension, or a fusion, but it always asks its audience to transfer the characteristic(s) of one thing to another. To look at a woman as though she were a rose is to carry over some attribute from the realm of flowers to the realm of women. But what, we are left to wonder, is the attribute?

As I read Frost's poem, I think of scientific accounts of botanical categories. Apples, pears, and roses all have seeds and blossoms and reproduce by similar processes; from the perspective of science, then, it might be correct to say "the apple's a rose." But, for Frost's speaker, that understanding, both of roses and of fruits, seems inappropriate: he cannot see the "roseness" of an apple. Perhaps he thinks of fruits as ordinary ways of sustaining his physical being. By contrast, a rose would be an extraordinary way of sustaining his spiritual being. Therefore, the speaker can certainly see the "roseness" of the person he loves. To do so, he carries over an attribute of roses, such as sensuousness, beauty, or delicacy, into the realm of women.

Metonymy

In *metonymy*, a concrete thing stands for, or represents, an abstract thing. When we say, "you're breaking my heart," for example, we use a physical (or corporeal) part of the body, "the heart," as a metonymy for a host of complex incorporeal feelings. If a sportscaster wishes to convey the complexity of what it is to be a baseball pitcher—the timing, the strength, the ability to throw a variety of pitches, the sense of situations, the instinct for detecting motion on the bases—she might use the metonymy, "arm." Each of these examples in a sense *reduces* the whole of an intangible idea to a single image. But this "reduction"

> "For metonymy," Kenneth Burke writes, "we could substitute reduction. . . . The basic strategy in metonymy is . . . to convey some incorporeal or intangible state in terms of the corporeal or tangible. E.g., to speak of 'the heart' rather than of 'the emotions.'"
>
> ────────
>
> *A Grammar of Motives.* University of California Press, 1969, pp. 504–6.

does not diminish the person or idea to which it refers. Rather, metonymy is closer to the kind of reduction that takes place in cooking—in which a chef reduces or distills a large amount of liquid to a much smaller amount in order to make the flavor more intense. Metonymy makes the trope's thought or complexity more intense by "reducing" the whole of a very complex idea or set of circumstances to a single corporeal or physical part. Using metonymy, for example, a poet might reduce the incorporeal beauty or desirability of a woman to the physical image of a rose, as Ben Jonson does in the poem that follows:

Song: To Celia

Ben Jonson

Drink to me only with thine eyes,
  And I will pledge with mine;
Or leave a kiss but in the cup,
  And I'll not look for wine.
The thirst that from the soul doth rise
  Doth ask a drink divine:
But might I of Jove's nectar sup,
  I would not change for thine.
I sent thee, late, a rosy wreath,
  Not so much honoring thee,
As giving it a hope that there
  It could not withered be.
But thou thereon did'st only breathe,
  And sent'st it back to me;
Since when it grows, and smells, I swear,
  Not of itself, but thee.

Here, the woman, as reading audience, is asked to see herself reduced to a rose, and then to notice that the analogy works in reverse. It's not, the poet says, that she smells like a rose, but rather that the rose has borrowed her (superior) fragrance.

CONSTRUCTING A READING

1. What is Ben Jonson's speaker's purpose when he tells the woman that the rose now smells "not of itself, but thee"? How does the trope help him to accomplish this purpose?

2. Do you think Ben Jonson's compliment would have been effective with women in the seventeenth century? Effective at what? Why or why not?

Synecdoche

When newscasters speak of "the White House," "Buckingham Palace," "Wall Street," they are employing *synecdoche*, a trope that presents the container as a figure for the contained, the whole for the part, or the part for the whole. The building or place (the Pentagon or Baghdad) is the container that represents the military power or governmental authority contained within it. Often, too, synecdoche presents the place where something can be found as a figure for that something. When an astronaut says, "Houston, we have a problem," he constructs a synecdoche by which all the members of the support staff at the NASA headquarters are called "Houston."

In the poem that follows, the seventeenth century poet Edmund Waller uses synecdoche to begin a seduction.

Song
Edmund Waller

Go, lovely rose!
Tell her that wastes her time and me
    That now she knows,
When I resemble her to thee,
    How sweet and fair she seems to be.

Tell her that's young,
And shuns to have her graces spied,
    That hadst thou sprung
In deserts where no men abide,
    Thou must have uncommended died.

Small is the worth
Of beauty from the light retired;
    Bid her come forth,
Suffer herself to be desired.
    And not blush so to be admired.

Then die, that she
The common fate of all things rare
    May read in thee;
How small a part of time they share,
    That are so wondrous sweet and fair!

"For synecdoche," Burke writes, "we could substitute representation . . . with such meanings as part for the whole, whole for the part, container for the contained. Sign for the thing signified, material for the thing made . . . cause for effect, effect for cause, genus for species, species for genus, etc. All such conversions imply an integral relationship, a relationship of convertibility, between the two terms."

A Grammar of Motives. University of California Press, 1969, pp. 504–8.

Waller's figure guides us to make an analogy between the woman and the rose that is based on beauty and mutability (susceptibility to change). A rose's beauty is relatively short-lived. When the speaker sends a rose to his beloved, he reminds her that, like the rose, she will be beautiful for a short time, then change to a less attractive version of herself, and then, finally, die. When she looks at the rose before her, the woman who reads the poem is guided to associate herself with the flower as a *representation* of the beauty and mutability that they have in common. The woman and the rose are *in the same place*—literally and figuratively. Moreover, the rose, like the woman, *contains* its own mutability: Waller's synecdoche substitutes the container for the contained. Since her life of beauty will be short, the speaker urges the lady to take advantage of the time available and permit herself "to be admired" by him rather then rejecting his affection. This tactic, by the way, is a conventional poetic argument called *carpe diem*, Latin for "seize the day."

CONSTRUCTING A READING

1. Paraphrase this seventeenth-century poem in contemporary language, being careful to retain the guidelines in stanza 1 and the comparisons in stanza 2 and stanza 4.
2. Write for a few minutes about your response to Waller's trope. Do you experience this figure of speech as a friendly reminder or a hostile one? Explain how your gender, race, and class affect your response.

The poem that follows, from William Blake's *Songs of Experience*, uses the rose trope in a complex way:

The Sick Rose

William Blake

O Rose, thou art sick!
The invisible worm
That flies in the night,
In the howling storm,

Has found out thy bed
Of crimson joy;
And his dark secret love
Does thy life destroy.

We might say that Blake's rose is a metaphor for a kind of youthful feminine sexual innocence. Like a beautiful young woman, the rose is innocent in her "bed of secret joy." But her beauty attracts the worm (or male lover). When the worm/man "loves" the rose, he destroys her. But we could also read the rose as a metonymy in which the beauty and fragility of innocence is reduced or distilled into this one small but beautiful flower/woman. The speaker knows that neither the rose's beauty nor a young woman's innocence can survive. Eventually, they will be destroyed by the very pleasures of sexuality that their beauty evokes and attracts. Or, we could see this trope as a synecdoche in which this rose (like Waller's) contains in its beauty the seeds of its own destruction.

CONSTRUCTING A READING

1. Write a bit about how you respond to this poem. Do you, for example, find it frightening or threatening? Why or why not?
2. How do you see the "worm trope" working in this text?
3. Blake surely knew the tradition of rose tropes that we see exemplified in Jonson, Waller, and Shakespeare. What similarities and differences do you see between his poem (composed around 1789) and the love lyrics written more than a century earlier by Edmund Waller and Ben Jonson? Can you read Blake's poem as a commentary on the earlier ones? If so, how? If not, why not?

Irony

Irony, the last trope we consider, is an invitation to perceive two opposed situations or experiences simultaneously. We say, "it's ironic," for example, when a bride and groom are killed in an auto accident on their wedding night or when a sports franchise fails to retain the coach who led the players to multiple championships or when the audience of a play knows information that one of its characters does not have. The irony emerges from the sorrow that comes

"For irony," Burke writes, "we could substitute dialectic . . . [between] mutually related or interacting perspectives."

A Grammar of Motives. University of California Press, 1969, p. 503.

when joy was expected, or from apparent ingratitude when gratitude was expected, or from knowledge when ignorance was expected. The two perspectives—expectation and actuality—coexist and comment upon one another, and that commentary is known as irony.

Allen Ginsberg's poem, "To Aunt Rose," gives us a representation of the speaker's aunt through the interactions of several perspectives, including, I think, the entire poetic tradition of "rose tropes" we have just sampled. As you consider the complex ironies of this text, it might help if you think about your own childhood memories of an older person who was important to you. Over the years, as the person ages, you remember the younger person even while you speak to the elderly one.

To Aunt Rose

Allen Ginsberg

Aunt Rose—now—might I see you
with your thin face and buck tooth smile and pain
of rheumatism—and a long black heavy shoe
for your bony left leg
limping down the long hall in Newark on the running carpet
past the black grand piano
in the day room
where the parties were
and I sang Spanish loyalist songs
in a high squeaky voice
(hysterical) the committee listening
while you limped around the room
collected the money—
Aunt Honey, Uncle Sam, a stranger with a cloth arm
in his pocket
and huge young bald head
of Abraham Lincoln Brigade

—your long sad face
your tears of sexual frustration
(what smothered sobs and bony hips
under the pillows of Osborne Terrace)
—the time I stood on the toilet seat naked
and you powdered my thighs with Calomine
against the poison ivy—my tender
and shamed first black curled hairs
what were you thinking in secret heart then
knowing me a man already—
and I an ignorant girl of family silence on the thin pedestal
of my legs in the bathroom—Museum of Newark.

Aunt Rose
Hitler is dead, Hitler is in Eternity; Hitler is with
Tamburlane and Emily Brontë

Though I see you walking still, a ghost on Osborne Terrace
down the long dark hall to the front door
limping a little with a pinched smile
in what must have been a silken
flower dress
welcoming my father, the Poet, on his visit to Newark
—see you arriving in the living room
dancing on your crippled leg
and clapping hands his book
had been accepted by Liveright

Hitler is dead and Liveright's gone out of business
The Attic of the Past and *Everlasting Minute* are out of print
Uncle Harry sold his last silk stocking
Claire quit interpretive dancing school
Buba sits a wrinkled monument in Old
Ladies Home blinking at new babies

last time I saw you was the hospital
pale skull protruding under ashen skin
blue veined unconscious girl
in an oxygen tent
the war in Spain has ended long ago
Aunt Rose

Ginsberg's poem offers at least four perspectives for readers to juxtapose: Aunt Rose as a young woman; Aunt Rose as old and invalid; the speaker as an adolescent; and the speaker as a mature man. The older speaker remembers his aunt as a dynamic, passionate, and politically active woman who raised money for loyalists during the Spanish Civil war, read Emily Brontë and Shakespeare, and desired the love of men. When Ginsberg's speaker last saw Aunt Rose in "the hospital" she was evidently no longer able to discriminate past from present or imaginary events from actual ones. Patiently, the speaker reminds her that the persons she envisions are no longer as she remembers them—Claire quit interpretive dancing school, Buba [grandmother] is in a home for the elderly, and Hitler is dead. Aunt Rose seems to have confused "reality" (like the Spanish Civil War and the Liveright Publishing Company) with "fiction" (like Emily Brontë's novels and Shakespeare's play Tamburlane). And again the speaker tries to straighten her out. The speaker remembers significant aspects of his relationship with his aunt—what she meant to him and to others, what she cared about, how she lived her life. These reminiscences include the striking image of the adolescent speaker "on the toilet seat naked." The questions that follow guide you toward making meaning with this extraordinary configuration. As you respond to them, you are developing different perspectives from which to see Aunt Rose. Irony emerges as these perspectives play off against one another in your experience of the poem. Your sense of Aunt Rose will come from your having experienced these perspectives in dialectical relation to one another.

CONSTRUCTING A READING

1. With your group members, list the analogies you are being asked to draw in this complex configuration.
2. Again with your group members, try to work out the analogies. In what sense, for example, can an adolescent boy be both "a man already" and "an ignorant girl"? How are his legs like a pedestal? How is this bathroom like a museum?
3. How do these tropes explain the speaker's relation with Aunt Rose?
4. Did the speaker understand that relationship when he was an adolescent? Does he understand it now? What does she mean to him?
5. Speculate about thematic connections between "To Aunt Rose," and "Go, Lovely Rose." Both texts draw parallels between women and roses in the context of mutability and death. How do the texts differ in their treatment of both the trope and the theme? How are they similar?

HOW A TROPE CHANGES IN THE COURSE OF A TEXT

A trope can be carried throughout a text, changing in meaning as the text develops.

Snow-white and Rose-red

Brothers Grimm

A poor widow once lived in a little cottage with a garden in front of it, in which grew two rose trees, one bearing white roses and the other red. She had two children, who were just like the two rose trees; one was called Snow-white and the other Rose-red, and they were the sweetest and best children in the world, always diligent and always cheerful; but Snow-white was quieter and more gentle than Rose-red. Rose-red loved to run about the fields and meadows, and to pick flowers and catch butterflies; but Snow-white sat at home with her mother and helped her in the household, or read aloud to her when there was no work to do. The two children loved each other so dearly that they always walked about hand-in-hand whenever they went out together, and when Snow-white said: 'We will never desert each other,' Rose-red answered: 'No, not as long as we live;' and the mother added: 'Whatever one gets she shall share with the other.' They often roamed about in the woods gathering berries and no beast offered to hurt them; on the contrary, they came up to them in the most confiding manner; the little hare would eat a cabbage leaf from their hands, the deer grazed beside them, the stag would bound past them merrily, and the birds remained on the branches and sang to them with all their might. No evil ever befell them; if they tarried late in the wood and night overtook them, they lay down together on the moss and slept till morning, and their mother knew they were quite safe, and never felt anxious about them. Once, when they had slept the night in the wood and had been wakened by the morning sun, they perceived a beautiful child in a shining white robe sitting close to their resting-place. The figure got up, looked at them kindly, but said nothing, and vanished into the wood. And when they looked round about them they became aware that they had slept quite close to a precipice, over which they would certainly have fallen had they gone on a few steps further in the darkness. And when they told their mother of their adventure, she said what they had seen must have been the angel that guards good children.

Snow-white and Rose-red kept their mother's cottage so beautifully clean and neat that it was a pleasure to go into it. In summer Rose-red looked after the house, and every morning before her mother awoke she placed a bunch of flowers before the bed, from each tree a rose. In winter Snow-white lit the fire and put on the kettle, which was made of brass, but so beautifully polished that it shone like gold. In the evening when the snowflakes fell their mother said: 'Snow-white, go and close the shutters;' and they drew round the fire, while the mother put on her spectacles and read aloud from a big book and the two girls listened and sat and span. Beside them on the ground lay a little lamb, and behind them perched a little white dove with its head tucked under its wings.

One evening as they sat thus cosily together someone knocked at the door as though he desired admittance. The mother said: 'Rose-red, open the door quickly; it must be some traveller seeking shelter.' Rose-red hastened to unbar the door, and thought she was a poor man standing in the darkness outside; but it was no such thing, only a bear, who poked his thick black head through the door. Rose-red screamed aloud and sprang back in terror, the lamb began to bleat, the dove flapped its wings, and Snow-white ran and hid behind her mother's bed. But the bear began to speak, and said; 'Don't be afraid: I won't hurt you. I am half frozen, and only wish to warm myself a little.' 'My poor bear,' said the mother, 'lie down by the fire, only take care you don't burn your fur.' Then she called out; 'Snow-white and Rose-red, come out; the bear will do you no harm: he is a good, honest creature.' So they both came out of their hiding-places, and gradually the lamb and dove drew near too, and they all forgot their fear. The bear asked the children to beat the snow a little out of his fur, and they fetched a brush and scrubbed him till he was dry. Then the

beast stretched himself in front of the fire, and growled quite happily and comfortably. The children soon grew quite at their ease with him, and led their
helpless guest a fearful life. They tugged his fur with their hands, put their
small feet on his back, and rolled him about here and there, or took a hazel
wand and beat him with it; and if he growled they only laughed. The bear submitted to everything with the best possible good-nature, only when they went
too far he cried; 'Oh! children, spare my life!

> Snow-white and Rose-red,
> Don't beat your lover dead.'

When it was time to retire for the night, and the others went to bed, the
mother said to the bear; 'You can lie there on the hearth, in heaven's name; it
will be shelter for you from the cold and wet.' As soon as day dawned the children let him out, and he trotted over the snow into the wood. From this time
on the bear came every evening at the same hour, and lay down by the hearth
and let the children play what pranks they liked with him; and they got so
accustomed to him that the door was never shut till their black friend had made
his appearance.

When spring came, and all outside was green, the bear said one morning
to Snow-white: 'Now I must go away, and not return again the whole summer.'
'Where are you going to, dear bear?' asked Snow-white. 'I must go to the wood
and protect my treasure from the wicked dwarfs. In winter, when the earth is
frozen hard, they are obliged to remain underground, for they can't work their
way through; but now, when the sun has thawed and warmed the ground, they
break through and come up above to spy the land and steal what they can; what
once falls into their hands and into their caves is not easily brought back to
light.' Snow-white was quite sad over their friend's departure, and when she
unbarred the door for him, the bear, stepping out, caught a piece of his fur in
the door-knocker, and Snow-white thought she caught sight of glittering gold
beneath it, but she couldn't be certain of it; and the bear ran hastily away, and
soon disappeared behind the trees.

A short time after this the mother sent the children into the wood to collect fagots. They came in their wanderings upon a big tree which lay felled on
the ground, and on the trunk among the long grass they noticed something
jumping up and down, but what it was they couldn't distinguish. When they
approached nearer they perceived a dwarf with a wizened face and a beard a
yard long. The end of the beard was jammed into a cleft of the tree, and the little man sprang about like a dog on a chain, and didn't seem to know what he
was to do. He glared at the girls with his fiery red eyes, and screamed out:
'What are you standing there for? can't you come and help me?' 'What were
you doing, little man?' asked Rose-red. 'You stupid, inquisitive goose!' replied
the dwarf; 'I wanted to split the tree, in order to get little chips of wood for our
kitchen fire; those thick logs that serve to make fires for coarse, greedy people

like yourselves quite burn up all the little food we need. I had successfully driven in the wedge, and all was going well, but the cursed wood was so slippery that it suddenly sprang out, and the tree closed up so rapidly that I had no time to take my beautiful white beard out, so here I am stuck fast, and I can't get away; and you silly, smooth-faced, milk-and-water girls just stand and laugh! Ugh! what wretches you are!'

The children did all in their power, but they couldn't get the beard out; it was wedged in far too firmly. 'I will run and fetch somebody,' said Rose-red. 'Crazy blockheads!' snapped the dwarf; 'what's the good of calling anyone else? you're already two too many for me. Does nothing better occur to you than that?' 'Don't be so impatient,' said Snow-white, 'I'll see you get help;' and taking her scissors out of her pocket she cut the end off his beard. As soon as the dwarf felt himself free he seized a bag full of gold which was hidden among the roots of the tree, lifted it up, and muttered aloud: 'Curse these rude wretches, cutting off a piece of my splendid beard!' With these words he swung the bag over his back, and disappeared without as much as looking at the children again.

Shortly after this Snow-white and Rose-red went out to get a dish of fish. As they approached the stream they was something which looked like an enormous grasshopper, springing towards the water as if it were going to jump in. They ran forward and recognised their old friend the dwarf. 'Where are you going to?' asked Rose-red; 'you're surely not going to jump into the water?' 'I'm not such a fool,' screamed the dwarf. 'Don't you see that cursed fish is trying to drag me in?' The little man had been sitting on the bank fishing, when unfortunately the wind had entangled his beard in the line; and when immediately afterwards a big fish bit, the feeble little creature had no strength to pull it out; the fish had the upper fin, and dragged the dwarf towards him. He clung on with all his might to every rush and blade of grass, but it didn't help him much; he had to follow every movement of the fish, and was in great danger of being drawn into the water. The girls came up just at the right moment, held him firm, and did all they could to disentangle his beard from the line; but in vain, beard and line were in a hopeless muddle. Nothing remained but to produce the scissors and cut the beard, by which a small part of it was sacrificed.

When the dwarf perceived what they were about he yelled to them; 'Do you call that manners, you toadstools! to disfigure a fellow's face? it wasn't enough that you shortened my beard before, but you must now needs cut off the best bit of it. I can't appear like this before my own people. I wish you'd been at Jericho first.' Then he fetched a sack of pearls that lay among the rushes, and without saying another word he dragged it away and disappeared behind a stone.

It happened that soon after this the mother sent the two girls to the town to buy needles, thread, laces, and ribbons. Their road led over a heath where huge boulders of rock lay scattered here and there. While trudging along they saw a big bird hovering in the air, circling slowly above them, but always descending lower, till at last it settled on a rock not far from them. Immediately afterwards they heard a sharp, piercing cry. They ran forward, and saw with horror that the eagle had pounced on their old friend the dwarf, and was about to carry him off. The tender-hearted children seized a hold of the little man, and struggled so long with the bird that at last he let go his prey. When the dwarf had recovered from the first shock he screamed in his screeching voice; 'Couldn't you have treated me more carefully? you have torn my thin little coat all to shreds, useless, awkward hussies that you are!' Then he took a bag of precious stones and vanished under the rocks into his cave. The girls were accustomed to his ingratitude, and went on their way and did their business in town. On their way home, as they were again passing the heath, they surprised the dwarf pouring out his precious stones on an open space, for he had thought no one would pass by at so late an hour. The evening sun shone on the glittering stones, and they glanced and gleamed so beautifully that the children stood still and gazed on them. 'What are you standing there gaping for?' screamed the dwarf, and his ashen-grey face became scarlet with rage. He was about to go off with these angry words when a sudden growl was heard, and a black bear trotted out of the wood. The dwarf jumped up in a great fright, but he hadn't time to reach his place of retreat, for the bear was already close to him. Then he cried in terror: 'Dear Mr. Bear, spare me! I'll give you all my treasure. Look at those beautiful precious stones lying there. Spare my life! what pleasure would you get from a poor feeble little fellow like me? You won't feel me between your teeth. There, lay hold of these two wicked girls, they will be a tender morsel for you, as fat as young quails; eat them up, for heaven's sake.' But the bear, paying no attention to his words, gave the evil little creature one blow with his paw, and he never moved again.

The girls had run away, but the bear called after them: 'Snow-white and Rose-red, don't be afraid; wait, and I'll come with you.' Then they recognised his voice and stood still, and when the bear was quite close to them his skin suddenly fell off, and a beautiful man stood beside them, all dressed in gold. 'I am a king's son,' he said, 'and have been doomed by that unholy little dwarf, who had stolen my treasure, to roam about the woods as a wild bear till his death should set me free. Now he has got his well-merited punishment.'

Snow-white married him, and Rose-red his brother, and they divided the great treasure the dwarf had collected in his cave between them. The old mother lived for many years peacefully with her children; and she carried the two rose trees with her, and they stood in front of her window, and every year they bore the finest red and white roses.

CONSTRUCTING A READING

1. Many cultural theorists believe that fairy tales and folk tales instill patterns of behavior in the children who listen to them by providing examples of rewards and punishments. What instructions about behavior does

this story give to young girls? How does the rose trope figure in those instructions?

2. Speculate about the figurative function of some of the other aspects of this story: the bear, the dwarf, the treasure. Share your speculations with your group members.

3. With your group members, make a list of other fairy tales or children's stories that rely on figurative language. Present your list to the rest of the class (as a list or chart or computer graphic) in which you explain to your classmates how the tropes work.

Robert Frost's "After Apple-Picking" is another example of a sustained configuration.

After Apple-Picking
Robert Frost

My long two-pointed ladder's sticking through a tree
Toward heaven still,
And there's a barrel that I didn't fill
Beside it, and there may be two or three
Apples I didn't pick upon some bough.
But I am done with apple-picking now.
Essence of winter sleep is on the night,
The scent of apples: I am drowsing off.
I cannot rub the strangeness from my sight
I got from looking through a pane of glass
I skimmed this morning from the drinking trough
And held against the world of hoary grass.
It melted, and I let it fall and break.
But I was well
Upon my way to sleep before it fell,
And I could tell
What form my dreaming was about to take,
Magnified apples appear and disappear,
Stem end and blossom end,
And every fleck of russet showing clear.
My instep arch not only keeps the ache,
It keeps the pressure of a ladder-round.
I feel the ladder sway as the boughs bend.
And I keep hearing from the cellar bin
The rumbling sound
Of load on load of apples coming in.
For I have had too much
Of apple-picking: I am overtired

> Of the great harvest I myself desired.
> There were ten thousand thousand fruit to touch,
> Cherish in hand, lift down, and not let fall.
> For all
> That struck the earth,
> No matter if not bruised or spiked with stubble,
> Went surely to the cider-apple heap
> As of no worth.
> One can see what will trouble
> This sleep of mine, whatever sleep it is.
> Were he not gone,
> The woodchuck could say whether it's like his
> Long sleep, as I describe its coming on,
> Or just some human sleep.

Like "The Rose Family," this poem by Robert Frost withholds an explicit statement of the trope's "meaning." One of the gaps with which Frost presents his readers is to "figure out" the apples.

CONSTRUCTING A READING

1. With your group members, make a list of cultural associations with apples. Share your lists with the rest of the class.
2. Then, again with your group members, apply each of your associations to the poem. As you try each alternative, look for consistency. Does your reading of the apple make sense within its poetic phrase or line? Does it make sense within the poem as a whole? Does your reading of the apples help you to understand the other gaps in the poem—such as the two-pointed ladder? The cider-apple heap? The woodchuck?
3. As your group develops a sense of the figurative development of the poem, share your hypotheses with the rest of the class and discuss the relative merits of your different interpretations.

HOW A TROPE CHANGES FROM TEXT TO TEXT

Not every instance of the "rose trope" occurs in the writings of heterosexual white men. Here is Dorothy Parker's amusing variation.

One Perfect Rose

Dorothy Parker

A single flow'r he sent me, since we met.
　All tenderly his messenger he chose;
Deep-hearted, pure, with scented dew still wet
　One perfect rose.

I knew the language of the floweret;
　"My fragile leaves," it said, "his heart enclose."
Love long has taken for his amulet
　One perfect rose.

Why is it no one ever sent me yet
　One perfect limousine, do you suppose?
Ah no, it's always just my luck to get
　One perfect rose.

CONSTRUCTING A READING

1. Compare Dorothy Parker's speaker to Ben Jonson's.
2. Using the definitions of Burke's four master tropes that have been elaborated above, analyze Dorothy Parker's use(s) of tropes in this short poem. How many different figures can you find? Explain.
3. Do you find yourself liking or disliking the speaker in Parker's poem? Explain how the figures affect your response.

A Brown Girl Dead

Countee Cullen

With two white roses on her breasts,
　White candles at head and feet,
Dark Madonna of the grave she rests;
　Lord Death has found her sweet.

Her mother pawned her wedding ring
　To lay her out in white;
She'd be so proud she'd dance and sing
　To see herself tonight.

CONSTRUCTING A READING

1. Using Kenneth Burke's definition of irony, explain the function of the tropes of this poem.
2. Write a short comparison between this poem and one of the other texts that connect roses and women and death.

Lily and Rose
Barbara G. Walker

White and red sisters are well known in fairy tales, such as the story of Snow White and Rose Red. Here the sisters are transformed into husband and wife, for the benefit of a matricentric or female-governed nation.

The villain whose heart or soul resides outside of his body is also a convention of fairy tales, based on that most primitive of human beliefs, that a person may be hurt through magical aggression against a detached body part, such as hair, spittle, blood, fingernail clippings, and so forth. Many primitive cultures held that the placenta or umbilical cord was a newborn infant's other self, external soul, or blood-rich vital spirit, and great care must be taken with it. Such objects were ceremonially disposed of with assiduous charms to preserve the child from harm. Similarly, fairy tale monsters are often attacked by magic, through destruction of something external to their bodies. Such details indicate the true antiquity of the folklore embedded in these stories.

Once upon a time there was a poor peasant girl who was named Lily because she had lily white skin and silver blond hair. She was the only child of a wood-cutter living in the deep forest; Lily's mother died when she was quite young. Her father taught her to work felling trees, and cutting, trimming, splitting, trussing, and stacking wood for market.

Her father was a hard taskmaster, but his training made Lily stronger and stronger as she grew up. By the time she was full grown, she was well able to wield the heaviest ax, to chop trees or split kindling for hours at a time without tiring, or to carry a hundredweight of firewood on her back ten miles to the market town. She also learned to shape and carve wood and became a skillful artisan.

Lily might have been content with her rough but peaceful life, were it not for two disadvantages.

The first was her beauty, which Lily saw as a problem because it attracted all the rowdy youths for miles around. They teased her incessantly, waylaid her on the road to market, stole her wood, plucked at her clothes, pulled her hair, held her down and mauled her, and played dozens of crude tricks that they seemed to think would force her to pay attention to them, even to like them. In fact, they made Lily increasingly angry. Once or twice she lost her temper altogether and attacked her tormentors in earnest. Though outnumbered, she fought so effectively that she left one with broken teeth, another with a broken nose, a third with a broken arm (clubbed by a length of firewood), and two more internally injured from kicks in the belly. Naturally, this only escalated their malice.

Then came her father's misfortune. One day the woodcutter's right arm was caught and mangled by a falling tree, and he was unable to use it anymore. Thereafter, Lily had to do all the chopping and other heavy work. In his loneliness, frustration, and constant pain, the woodcutter took to drink. He spent half of their scanty earnings on liquor while Lily struggled alone to do the work of two woodcutters. Despite her best efforts, she and her father became poorer.

As time went on, her father became more subject to drunken rages, stupors, and fits of madness. He would berate Lily for not working harder, or he would accuse her of bewitching him. Sometimes he would wander away and not return for days or even weeks. Thus Lily's young womanhood became little more than incessant sorrow, backbreaking toil, and nagging irritations. She saw herself as unlucky and often wished she could he someone else.

One day while chopping, she noticed a warhorse in full regalia standing all alone in a forest stream, looking uncomfortable and puzzled. Lily waded into the water to investigate. She found that the horse was tethered by his rein to the hand of a dead knight-errant, who lay under the surface of the water. Lily guessed he had been wounded in a battle, had perhaps fainted, and had fallen from his horse into the stream, where, weighed down by his suit of armor, he had drowned in water only waist-deep.

Lily detached the horse from his master's corpse, led him out of the stream, and tethered him on the bank. Then she dragged out the knight's body. While she was wondering what to do next, the horse whinnied and gave her a nudge with his nose. Suddenly she understood that the horse was telling her to take the knight's place. Without hesitating to think, she set about doing so.

With difficulty she extracted the dead knight from his armor and clothing and gave him back to the stream in pristine nakedness. As he drifted away, she found a fortune indeed, in a well-filled purse tied to his belt. She left her own clothing by the stream and dressed herself in knightly armor, which fitted her tolerably well. The metal suit was so clumsy and heavy that she couldn't mount the horse until she found a huge boulder to climb on first. Once mounted, however, she felt transformed, more powerful than her former self. She said to the horse, "I shall call you Fortune."

Lily arranged her weapons, slinging her big woodsman's ax across her back, and settled herself in the saddle. "Go, Fortune," she said to the horse, and they rode out of the forest.

At first Lily had thought to go home and share her luck with her father. But then she reflected that he would only drink it all away. Moreover, what if she was suspected of having robbed and killed the knight? She would go to the gallows. Impelled by these thoughts, she rode by her father's cottage without stopping and threw down on the doorstep enough money to keep him in food and drink for a year. Then she set out to travel and see the world.

On the road to town, Lily encountered the same lads who were accustomed to tormenting her. Her heart sank. "They will report me," she thought desperately. Then she remembered that she was fully covered by the armor. The visor concealed her face. If she didn't speak, they would have no way to identify her. So she rode toward them boldly.

To her surprise, all the lads bowed down and obsequiously tugged their forelocks as she approached. She smiled inside her helmet. To the largest youth, who had manhandled her most rudely in the past, she gave a buffet with the flat of her sword that rolled him over in the mud. He hastily scrambled up to his knees, babbling, "Yes, sir! Thank you, sir!"

Again she smiled. "Now I am Sir Lily, respected by the country louts," she said to herself. "Cowardly toadies that they are, what different faces they show to a bearer of weapons!" She began to like the idea of masquerading permanently as a knight-errant.

She camped for several weeks in the hills and practiced using her weapons. With the sharp dagger, she chopped her hair short. She taught herself to speak in a low, masculine-sounding voice. During her leisure hours, she carved a lily out of wood and placed it as a crest on her helmet. When she felt ready, she rode forth in search of adventure.

One day she came to a castle that was still and silent. There were no knights on the battlements, no workers in the fields, no merchants passing in and out of the gate, no flags flying, no cattle or other animals. The only living thing to be seen was a pretty red-haired maiden penned in an iron cage beside the castle gate. She was weeping bitterly.

"What's the matter?" Lily asked her.

"Oh, Sir Knight, I am the most unfortunate creature in the world," wailed the maiden. "I am Princess Rose, the king's daughter. My parents have been taken hostage by a terrible ogre, who holds them captive in the castle and makes me live in this cage until I consent to marry him. I'll die first. He is hideous and cruel. He has killed all my father's knights and many of our servants. No one can fight him. The ogre is invulnerable."

"Why?" Lily asked.

"He has grown a huge magical tree in the castle courtyard. At the top of the tree is a chest, and in that chest the ogre's heart is hidden. As long as his heart is safe there, nothing can harm him."

"We'll see about that," said Lily, who felt that she had had enough of bullies to last her a lifetime. "I am Sir Lily, and I know how to deal with trees. Is there a secret way into the castle?"

Princess Rose told her of a waste pipe on the north side of the castle that led into the underground dungeons. "I used to play there as a child, until I was caught and forbidden. But surely a noble knight like yourself wouldn't enter a castle by so ignominious a route."

"Nothing that accomplishes its purpose is ignominious," Lily said.

Under cover of darkness, she rode around to the north side of the castle, tethered Fortune, and removed her armor. Carrying only her dagger and her ax, she crawled through the waste pipe and made her way into the castle courtyard. There stood the magic tree, huge and black against the night sky. Lily went to work with her ax and soon cut through the thick trunk. The tree tottered and fell with a tremendous crash!

The ogre, roused from sleep, came roaring out of the castle with a torch in each hand. He was a nightmarish creature, twice as tall as a man, with one eye in the middle of his forehead and long tusks sticking out of his mouth. He lunged at Lily, who deftly eluded him and darted to the fallen crest of the tree. There she found a wooden chest wedged among the branches. With one blow of her ax she broke the chest, exposing the ogre's heart, which was beating wildly. Lily plunged her dagger into it. Just as he was reaching out to seize her, the ogre pitched forward on his face and lay still.

Lily took a bunch of keys from the dead monster's belt and went off to free Princess Rose from her cage. When she was released, the princess threw her arms around Lily and kissed her. "You are my noble white knight, valiant Sir Lily," she cried. "You must come into the castle. My parents will want to meet you and make a celebratory feast for you."

The king and queen were released from their prison and reunited with their daughter amid much rejoicing. The dead ogre and his tree were cleared away, and all was made ready for a great feast. Additional servants were hired from neighboring estates. Soon the castle was a hive of activity, as preparations were made to celebrate the destruction of the ogre, who had oppressed the whole countryside for a long time.

The grateful king and queen presented Lily with a new velvet cloak to wear to the feast, and Princess Rose with her own hands embroidered a golden lily on it. At the banquet table the king arose and made a speech, praising Lily as the kingdom's bravest knight, even though "still a beardless youth." He went on to say that, true to kingly tradition, he intended to give Sir Lily half his kingdom and the hand of his daughter in marriage.

Lily choked on her mouthful of roast goose and had to drink a few hasty swallows of wine.

"My handsome white knight is becomingly modest," said Rose, kissing her tenderly.

Quite taken aback, Lily hardly knew what to say. She managed to rise to her feet and thank the king graciously enough. But after she sat down, she leaned over and whispered in Rose's ear, "We have to talk."

When they met together in a private room, Lily told Rose that she was a woman and revealed the whole story of her false knighthood. Princess Rose sat in silence for a few minutes. Then she began to laugh. She laughed and laughed, so infectiously that Lily had to join in.

"It's the best joke ever," Rose said, wiping her eyes. "All those proud warriors, outdone by a woman who chops wood. Lily, I love you anyway. We'll be married, you and I. It will be for the great good of the kingdom, which has been needing an efficient government for a long time. Eventually we'll be king and queen. I'll keep your secrets, and you'll keep mine."

Lily said doubtfully, "I'm not sure I can carry off this deception forever."

"Nonsense. You're adventurous, or you wouldn't have done what you did in the first place. Don't doubt yourself now. We'll have fun with this, you'll see."

In the end, Lily agreed. She was married to Princess Rose in a gorgeous ceremony, and they settled down to live together. The servants said they seemed very happy, because they always laughed a lot in their private apartments, behind closed doors.

When Lily and Rose took over rulership of the country, their subjects came to honor and love them very much. King Lily often rode among the people on his noble horse, Fortune, to visit with them in person and listen to their troubles, which he usually put right. Queen Rose was greatly praised for her common sense, her benevolence to the poor, and her many good works.

There were occasional whispers about their sexual proclivities, which were not always strictly orthodox. It was said that the queen took lovers from time to time, and so did the king when he was traveling abroad. It was even said that the king took male lovers, as had several other kings recorded by the histories. Unlike those others, however, King Lily chose men who had never showed homosexual tendencies before, nor did they afterward. It was puzzling. Nevertheless, not one of them could be induced to gossip about the king's sexual tastes.

Lily and Rose governed well and were beloved by their people. They raised two children, who were trained to govern after King Lily. On the whole, they lived happily ever after.

In the deep forest far away, a small bag of money was anonymously left once a month on the doorstep of a crippled old woodcutter, who soon used it to drink himself to death.

CONSTRUCTING A READING

1. What cultural instructions does Walker's fairy tale offer to young women? How does the name of Princess Rose figure in those instructions?

2. With your group members, make a list of the aspects of this story that you construe as figural—and why. Explain your list to the rest of the class.

3. Describe and explain one or more differences in figuration between "Lily and Rose" and "Snow-white and Rose-red."

Rose in Smoke
Robert Mapplethorpe

CONSTRUCTING A READING

1. With your group members, discuss the ways in which this rose might be thought of as a figure. What would it be a figure of?
2. Write a short essay about this photograph using "a rose is a rose is a rose" as the topic.
3. Do some research on the controversies surrounding Robert Mapplethorpe's photographs and write a short account of those controversies in the context of what you have learned about figuration in this chapter.

TEXTS FOR FURTHER READING

Minerva, Ohio

Thomas Dukes

Leaves haunt the way from school
for Amish children in Athena's town,
bright ghosts of autumn decorating

and descending into the smile
of walking home. These plainclothes
children do not snatch

testaments of color for home or scrapbook:
They would not mock the Lord
or disobey. But from bonneted

faces and boys' hat bands spring
flags of red oak and gold maple rebellion,
ecstasy riding the trail between schoolwork

and chores at home. As childhood slips
from the dyes of autumn into winter's
white farm labor, these sentries

of innocence march toward duty through
what they see of the changing world.

CONSTRUCTING A READING

1. Look up Minerva in a classical dictionary and on a map of Ohio. How does the name—of the goddess and of the town—function as a trope in Dukes's poem?
2. From what do these children rebel?
3. How are these children "sentries of innocence"?
4. How does the phrase "bright ghosts of autumn" work as a configuration? What does it configure?

Harlem

Langston Hughes

What happens to a dream deferred?

Does it dry up
Like a raisin in the sun?
Or fester like a sore—
And then run?
Does it stink like rotten meat?
Or crust and sugar over—
Like a syrupy sweet?

Maybe it just sags
Like a heavy load.

Or does it explode?

CONSTRUCTING A READING

1.   From your own knowledge of racial conflict in the United States during your lifetime, explain Hughes's tropes by imagining or describing historical examples of each of his alternatives.

SHARING A READING

1.   Write an essay in which you explain to another reader how the apple trope works in Frost's "After Apple-Picking."
2.   Imagine that you are an executive for an advertising firm that aspires to land the Caron account. Caron, you discover, is a venerable French company that manufactures and markets fragrances. Your job is to develop an ad campaign for a Caron fragrance named Fleurs de Rocailles. You consult your trusty French dictionary left over from college and discover that *rocaille* is a decorative landscaping that features pebbles and shells. The perfume's name, then, means roughly, "flowers from a rock garden." Your job is to develop an ad campaign that will increase sales in the United States. It goes without saying that you cannot change the perfume's name. You sniff the fragrance a few times. It's light (not overpowering) and flowery, rather like lilies of the valley: just the thing, you decide, for young and affluent working women to wear to the office. Assemble a team; find an image; use a trope; write the ad. Then write a memo to your immediate superior explaining your appeal and how and why you think it will work.
3.   For centuries, poets and other artists have compared women to roses. On the basis of what you now know about tropes and culture, speculate about

why this is the case. Why roses, specifically? And, why and how (again on the basis of your current knowledge) has the trope changed over time? You will need to find examples from several kinds of texts, literary and nonliterary, to support your position. Your audience is the rest of your class, persons who share your language and who are interested in this question.

4. Many cultural critics believe that figures like the ones we have just studied, accumulated over centuries, have profoundly affected the way a culture perceives women. What do you think? Do these tropes really affect the way you personally think about relations between men and women? Do you think they affect others' perceptions? Explain your conclusions to someone of another generation, a parent or grandparent or a son or daughter. In order to be clear to your reader, and to support your analysis, you'll need examples of how women have been "figured" in some texts (literary, nonliterary, visual, etc.) that you both know well.

5. Choose an advertisement that sells something (e.g., clothing, sports equipment, beer) by configuring an entire way of life in one image. Write an essay in which you describe and analyze the appeal. Remember that we perceive tropes through a process of making comparisons or analogies. In your essay, then, you'll need to describe very carefully the kinds of comparisons the advertisement asks you to make and how you make them. Does it call up any associations or memories that might be shared by other members of your culture? What exactly is being sold (for example, not just long distance telephone service, but a way of thinking about relationships)? Your reader is someone who knows our terminology, but who does not know your advertisement. Therefore, you should include the ad with your paper but also describe it in your writing.

6. Write a paragraph or two for an introductory textbook in your major that uses configuration to define an important concept. For example, a model in psychology is like a . . . ; a molecule in chemistry is like . . . ; a morpheme in linguistics is like a . . . ; net present value in accounting is like . . . etc. Use the trope you choose as a way to introduce the new conception by analogy to one with which you expect your first-year readers to be familiar.

7. Summarize a recent news story that uses a configuration to explain an event or a relationship. Explain to someone younger than you how the configuration might guide readers toward a specific attitude.

Fire and Ice

Robert Frost

Some say the world will end in fire,
Some say in ice.
From what I've tasted of desire
I hold with those who favor fire,
But if it had to perish twice,
I think I know enough of hate
To say that for destruction ice
Is also great
And would suffice.

CONSTRUCTING A READING

1. The poem "Fire and Ice," like Frost's "The Rose Family," considers relations between the languages of science and the languages of poetry. How would you paraphrase the poem and its conclusion?

Good Country People

Flannery O'Connor

Besides the neutral expression that she wore when she was alone, Mrs. Freeman had two others, forward and reverse, that she used for all her human dealings. Her forward expression was steady and driving like the advance of a heavy truck. Her eyes never swerved to left or right but turned as the story turned as if they followed a yellow line down the center of it. She seldom used the other expression because it was not often necessary for her to retract a statement, but when she did, her face came to a complete stop, there was an almost imperceptible movement of her black eyes, during which they seemed to be receding, and then the observer would see that Mrs. Freeman, though she might stand there as real as several grain sacks thrown on top of each other, was no longer there in spirit. As for getting anything across to her when this was the case, Mrs. Hopewell had given it up. She might talk her head off. Mrs. Freeman could never be brought to admit herself wrong on any point. She would stand there and if she could be brought to say anything, it was something like, "Well, I wouldn't of said it was and I wouldn't of said it wasn't," or letting her gaze range over the top kitchen shelf where there was an assortment of dusty bottles, she might remark, "I see you ain't ate many of them figs you put up last summer."

They carried on their most important business in the kitchen at breakfast. Every morning Mrs. Hopewell got up at seven o'clock and lit her gas heater and Joy's. Joy was her daughter, a large blonde girl who had an artificial leg. Mrs. Hopewell thought of her as a child though she was thirty-two years old and highly educated. Joy would get up while her mother was eating and lumber into the bathroom and slam the door, and before long, Mrs. Freeman would arrive at the back door. Joy would hear her mother call, "Come on in," and then they would talk for a while in low voices that were indistinguishable in the bathroom. By the time Joy came in, they had usually finished the weather report and were on one or the other of Mrs. Freeman's daughters, Glynese or Carramae. Joy called them Glycerin and Caramel. Glynese, a redhead, was eighteen and had many admirers; Carramae, a blonde, was only fifteen but already married and pregnant. She could not keep anything on her stomach. Every morning Mrs. Freeman told Mrs. Hopewell how many times she had vomited since the last report.

Mrs. Hopewell liked to tell people that Glynese and Carramae were two of the finest girls she knew and that Mrs. Freeman was a *lady* and that she was never ashamed to take her anywhere or introduce her to anybody they might meet. Then she would tell how she had happened to hire the Freemans in the first place and how they were a godsend to her and how she had had them four years. The reason for her keeping them so long was that they were not trash. They were good country people. She had telephoned the man whose name they had given as a reference and he had told her that Mr. Freeman was a good farmer but that his wife was the nosiest woman ever to walk the earth. "She's got to be into everything," the man said. "If she don't get there before the dust settles, you can bet she's dead, that's all. She'll want to know all your business. I can stand him real good," he had said, "but me nor my wife neither could have stood that woman one more minute on this place." That had put Mrs. Hopewell off for a few days.

She had hired them in the end because there were no other applicants but she had made up her mind before hand exactly how she would handle the woman. Since she was the type who had to be into everything, then, Mrs. Hopewell had decided, she would not only let her be into everything, she would *see to it* that she was into everything—she would give her the responsibility of everything, she would put her in charge. Mrs. Hopewell had no bad qualities of her own but she was able to use other people's in such a constructive way that she never felt the lack. She had hired the Freemans and she had kept them four years.

Nothing is perfect. This was one of Mrs. Hopewell's favorite sayings. Another was: that is life! And still another, the most important, was: well, other people have their opinions too. She would make these statements, usually at the table, in a tone of gentle insistence as if no one held them but her, and the large hulking Joy, whose constant outrage had obliterated every expression from her face, would stare just a little to the side of her, her eyes icy blue, with the look of someone who has achieved blindness by an act of will and means to keep it.

When Mrs. Hopewell said to Mrs. Freeman that life was like that, Mrs. Freeman would say, "I always said so myself." Nothing had been arrived at by anyone that had not first been arrived at by her. She was quicker than Mr. Freeman. When Mrs. Hopewell said to her after they had been on the place a while, "You know, you're the wheel behind the wheel," and winked, Mrs. Freeman had said, "I know it. I've always been quick. It's some that are quicker than others."

"Everybody is different," Mrs. Hopewell said.

"Yes, most people is," Mrs. Freeman said.

"It takes all kinds to make the world."

"I always said it did myself."

The girl was used to this kind of dialogue for breakfast and more of it for dinner; sometimes they had it for supper too. When they had no guest they ate in the kitchen because that was easier. Mrs. Freeman always managed to arrive at some point during the meal and to watch them finish it. She would stand in the doorway if it were summer but in the winter she would stand with one elbow on top of the refrigerator and look down on them, or she would stand by the gas heater, lifting the back of her skirt slightly. Occasionally she would stand against the wall and roll her head from side to side. At no time was she in any hurry to leave. All this was very trying on Mrs. Hopewell but she was a woman of great patience. She realized that nothing is perfect and that in the Freemans she had good country people and that if, in this day and age, you get good country people, you had better hang onto them.

She had had plenty of experience with trash. Before the Freemans she had averaged one tenant family a year. The wives of these farmers were not the kind you would want to be around you for very long. Mrs. Hopewell, who had divorced her husband long ago, needed someone to walk over the fields with her; and when Joy had to be impressed for these services, her remarks were usually so ugly and her face so glum that Mrs. Hopewell would say, "If you can't come pleasantly, I don't want you at all," to which the girl, standing square and rigid-shouldered with her neck thrust slightly forward, would reply, "If you want me, here I am—LIKE I AM."

Mrs. Hopewell excused this attitude because of the leg (which had been shot off in a hunting accident when Joy was ten). It was hard for Mrs. Hopewell to realize that her child was thirty-two now and that for more than twenty years she had had only one leg. She thought of her still as a child because it tore her heart to think instead of the poor stout girl in her thirties who had never danced a step or had any *normal* good times. Her name was really Joy but as soon as she was twenty-one and away from home, she had had it legally changed. Mrs. Hopewell was certain that she had thought and thought until she had hit upon the ugliest name in any language. Then she had gone and had the beautiful name, Joy, changed without telling her mother until after she had done it. Her legal name was Hulga.

When Mrs. Hopewell thought the name, Hulga, she thought of the broad blank hull of a battleship. She would not use it. She continued to call her Joy to which the girl responded but in a purely mechanical way.

Hulga had learned to tolerate Mrs. Freeman who saved her from taking walks with her mother. Even Glynese and Carramae were useful when they occupied attention that might otherwise have been directed at her. At first she had thought she could not stand Mrs. Freeman for she had found that it was not possible to be rude to her. Mrs. Freeman would take on strange resentments and for days together she would be sullen but the source of her displeasure was always obscure; a direct attack, a positive leer, blatant ugliness to her face—these never touched her. And without warning one day, she began calling her Hulga.

She did not call her that in front of Mrs. Hopewell who would have been incensed but when she and the girl happened to be out of the house together, she would say something and add the name Hulga to the end of it, and the big spectacled Joy-Hulga would scowl and redden as if her privacy had been intruded upon. She considered the name her personal affair. She had arrived at it first purely on the basis of its ugly sound and then the full genius of its fitness had struck her. She had a vision of the name working like the ugly sweating Vulcan who stayed in the furnace and to whom, presumably, the goddess had to come when called. She saw it as the name of her highest creative act. One of her major triumphs was that her mother had not been able to turn her dust into Joy, but the greater one was that she had been able to turn it herself into Hulga. However, Mrs. Freeman's relish for using the name only irritated her. It was as if Mrs. Freeman's beady steel-pointed eyes had penetrated far enough behind her face to reach some secret fact. Something about her seemed to fascinate Mrs. Freeman and then one day Hulga realized that it was the artificial leg. Mrs. Freeman had a special fondness for the details of secret infections, hidden deformities, assaults upon children. Of diseases, she preferred the lingering or incurable. Hulga had heard Mrs. Hopewell give her the details of the hunting accident, how the leg had been literally blasted off, how she had never lost consciousness. Mrs. Freeman could listen to it any time as if it had happened an hour ago.

When Hulga stumped into the kitchen in the morning (she could walk without making the awful noise but she made it—Mrs. Hopewell was certain—because it was ugly-sounding), she glanced at them and did not speak. Mrs. Hopewell would be in her red kimono with her hair tied around her head in rags. She would be sitting at the table, finishing her breakfast and Mrs. Freeman would be hanging by her elbow outward from the refrigerator, looking down at the table. Hulga always put her eggs on the stove to boil and then stood over them with her arms folded, and Mrs. Hopewell would look at her— a kind of indirect gaze divided between her and Mrs. Freeman—and would think that if she would only keep herself up a little, she wouldn't be so bad looking. There was nothing wrong with her face that a pleasant expression wouldn't help. Mrs. Hopewell said that people who looked on the bright side of things would be beautiful even if they were not.

Whenever she looked at Joy this way, she could not help but feel that it would have been better if the child had not taken the Ph.D. It had certainly not brought her out any and now that she had it, there was no more excuse for her to go to school again. Mrs. Hopewell thought it was nice for girls to go to school to have a good time but Joy had "gone through." Anyhow, she would not have been strong enough to go again. The doctors had told Mrs. Hopewell that with the best of care, Joy might see forty-five. She had a weak heart. Joy had made it plain that if it had not been for this condition, she would be far from these red hills and good country people. She would be in a university lecturing to people who knew what she was talking about. And Mrs. Hopewell could very well picture her there, looking like a scarecrow and lecturing to more of the same. Here she went about all day in a six-year-old skirt and a yellow sweat shirt with a faded cowboy on a horse embossed on it. She thought this was funny; Mrs. Hopewell thought it was idiotic and showed simply that she was still a child. She was brilliant but she didn't have a grain of sense. It seemed to Mrs. Hopewell that every year she grew less like other people and more like herself—bloated, rude, and squint-eyed. And she said such strange things! To her own mother she had said—without warning, without excuse, standing up in the middle of a meal with her face purple and her mouth half full—"Woman! do you ever look inside? Do you ever look inside and see what you are *not?* God!" she had cried sinking down again and staring at her plate, "Malebranche was right: we are not our own light. We are not our own light!" Mrs. Hopewell had no idea to this day what brought that on. She had only made the remark, hoping Joy would take it in, that a smile never hurt anyone.

The girl had taken the Ph.D. in philosophy and this left Mrs. Hopewell at a complete loss. You could say, "My daughter is a nurse," or "My daughter is a school teacher," or even, "My daughter is a chemical engineer." You could not say, "My daughter is a philosopher." That was something that had ended with the Greeks and Romans. All day Joy sat on her neck in a deep chair, reading. Sometimes she went for walks but she didn't like dogs or cats or birds or flowers or nature or nice young men. She looked at nice young men as if she could smell their stupidity.

One day Mrs. Hopewell had picked up one of the books the girl had just put down and opening it at random, she read, "Science, on the other hand, has to assert its soberness and seriousness afresh and declare that it is concerned solely with what-is. Nothing—how can it be for science anything but a horror and a phantasm? If science is right, then one thing stands firm: science wishes to know nothing of nothing. Such is after all the strictly scientific approach to Nothing. We know it by wishing to know nothing of Nothing." These words had been underlined with a blue pencil and they worked on Mrs. Hopewell like some evil incantation in gibberish. She shut the book quickly and went out of the room as if she were having a chill.

This morning when the girl came in, Mrs. Freeman was on Carramae. "She thrown up four times after supper," she said, "and was up twict in the night after three o'clock. Yesterday she didn't do nothing but ramble in the bureau drawer. All she did. Stand up there and see what she could run up on.

"She's got to eat," Mrs. Hopewell muttered, sipping her coffee, while she watched Joy's back at the stove. She was wondering what the child had said to the Bible salesman. She could not imagine what kind of a conversation she could possibly have had with him.

He was a tall gaunt hatless youth who had called yesterday to sell them a Bible. He had appeared at the door, carrying a large black suitcase that weighted him so heavily on one side that he had to brace himself against the door facing. He seemed on the point of collapse but he said in a cheerful voice, "Good morning, Mrs. Cedars!" and set the suitcase down on the mat. He was not a bad-looking young man though he had on a bright blue suit and yellow socks that were not pulled up far enough. He had prominent face bones and a streak of sticky-looking brown hair falling across his forehead.

"I'm Mrs. Hopewell," she said.

"Oh!" he said, pretending to look puzzled but with his eyes sparkling, "I saw it said 'The Cedars,' on the mailbox so I thought you was Mrs. Cedars!" and he burst out in a pleasant laugh. He picked up the satchel and under cover of a pant, he fell forward into her hall. It was rather as if the suitcase had moved first, jerking him after it. "Mrs. Hopewell!" he said and grabbed her hand. "I hope you are well!" and he laughed again and then all at once his face sobered completely. He paused and gave her a straight earnest look and said, "Lady, I've come to speak of serious things."

"Well, come in," she muttered, none too pleased because her dinner was almost ready. He came into the parlor and sat down on the edge of a straight chair and put the suitcase between his feet and glanced around the room as if he were sizing her up by it. Her silver gleamed on the two sideboards; she decided he had never been in a room as elegant as this.

"Mrs. Hopewell," he began, using her name in a way that sounded almost intimate, "I know you believe in Christian service."

"Well yes," she murmured.

"I know," he said and paused, looking very wise with his head cocked on one side, "that you're a good woman. Friends have told me."

Mrs. Hopewell never liked to be taken for a fool. "What are you selling?" she asked.

"Bibles," the young man said and his eye raced around the room before he added, "I see you have no family Bible in your parlor, I see that is the one lack you got!"

Mrs. Hopewell could not say, "My daughter is an atheist and won't let me keep the Bible in the parlor." She said, stiffening slightly, "I keep my Bible by my bedside." This was not the truth. It was in the attic somewhere.

"Lady," he said, "the word of God ought to be in the parlor."

"Well, I think that's a matter of taste," she began. "I think . . ."

"Lady," he said, "for a Chrustian, the word of God ought to be in every room in the house besides in his heart. I know you're a Christian because I can see it in every line of your face."

She stood up and said, "Well, young man, I don't want to buy a Bible and I smell my dinner burning."

He didn't get up. He began to twist his hands and looking down at them, he said softly, "Well lady, I'll tell you the truth—not many people want to buy one nowadays and besides, I know I'm real simple. I don't know how to say a thing but to say it. I'm just a country boy." He glanced up into her unfriendly face. "People like you don't like to fool with country people like me!"

"Why!" she cried, "good country people are the salt of the earth! Besides, we all have different ways of doing, it takes all kinds to make the world go 'round. That's life!"

"You said a mouthful," he said.

"Why, I think there aren't enough good country people in the world!" she said, stirred. "I think that's what's wrong with it!"

His face had brightened. "I didn't inraduce myself," he said. "I'm Manley Pointer from out in the country around Willohobie, not even from a place, just from near a place."

"You wait a minute," she said. "I have to see about my dinner." She went out to the kitchen and found Joy standing near the door where she had been listening.

"Get rid of the salt of the earth," she said, "and let's eat."

Mrs. Hopewell gave her a pained look and turned the heat down under the vegetables. "I can't be rude to anybody," she murmured and went back into the parlor.

He had opened the suitcase and was sitting with a Bible on each knee.

"You might as well put those up," she told him. "I don't want one."

"I appreciate your honesty," he said. "You don't see any more real honest people unless you go way out in the country."

"I know," she said, "real genuine folks!" Through the crack in the door she heard a groan.

"I guess a lot of boys come telling you they're working their way through college," he said, "but I'm not going to tell you that. Somehow," he said, "I don't want to go to college. I want to devote my life to Christian service. "See," he said, lowering his voice, "I got this heart condition. I may not live long. When you know it's something wrong with you and you may not live long, well then, lady . . ." He paused, with his mouth open, and stared at her.

He and Joy had the same condition! She knew that her eyes were filling with tears but she collected herself quickly and murmured, "Won't you stay for dinner? We'd love to have you!" and was sorry the instant she heard herself say it.

"Yes mam," he said in an abashed voice, "I would sher love to do that!"

Joy had given him one look on being introduced to him and then throughout the meal had not glanced at him again. He had addressed several remarks to her, which she had pretended not to hear. Mrs. Hopewell could not understand deliberate rudeness, although she lived with it, and she felt she had always to overflow with hospitality to make up for Joy's lack of courtesy. She urged him to talk about himself and he did. He said he was the seventh child of twelve and that his father had been crushed under a tree when he himself was eight year old. He had been crushed very badly, in fact, almost cut in two and was practically not recognizable. His mother had got along the best she could by hard working and she had always seen that her children went to Sunday School and that they read the Bible every evening. He was now nineteen years old and he had been selling Bibles for four months. In that time he had sold seventy-seven Bibles and had the promise of two more sales. He wanted to become a missionary because he thought that was the way you could do most for people. "He who losest his life shall find it," he said simply and he was so sincere, so genuine and earnest that Mrs. Hopewell would not for the world have smiled. He prevented his peas from sliding onto the table by blocking them with a piece of bread which he later cleaned his plate with. She could see Joy observing sidewise how he handled his knife and fork and she saw too that every few minutes, the boy would dart a keen appraising glance at the girl as if he were trying to attract her attention.

After dinner Joy cleared the dishes off the table and disappeared and Mrs. Hopewell was left to talk with him. He told her again about his childhood and his father's accident and about various things that had happened to him. Every five minutes or so she would stifle a yawn. He sat for two hours until finally she told him she must go because she had an appointment in town. He packed his Bibles and thanked her and prepared to leave, but in the doorway he stopped and wrung her hand and said that not on any of his trips had he met a lady as nice as her and he asked if he could come again. She had said she would always be happy to see him.

Joy had been standing in the road, apparently looking at something in the distance, when he came down the steps toward her, bent to the side with his heavy valise. He stopped where she was standing and confronted her directly. Mrs. Hopewell could not hear what he said but she trembled to think what Joy would say to him. She could see that after a minute Joy said something and that then the boy began to speak again, making an excited gesture with his free hand. After a minute Joy said something else at which the boy began to speak once more. Then to her amazement, Mrs. Hopewell saw the two of them walk off together, toward the gate. Joy had walked all the way to the gate with him and Mrs. Hopewell could not imagine what they had said to each other, and she had not yet dared to ask.

Mrs. Freeman was insisting upon her attention. She had moved from the refrigerator to the heater so that Mrs. Hopewell had to turn and face her in order to seem to be listening. "Glynese gone out with Harvey Hill again last night," she said. "She had this sty."

"Hill," Mrs. Hopewell said absently, "is that the one who works in the garage?"

"Nome, he's the one that goes to chiropracter school," Mrs. Freeman said. "She had this sty. Been had it two days. So she says when he brought her in the other night he says, 'Lemme get rid of that sty for you,' and she says, 'How?' and he says, 'You just lay yourself down acrost the seat of that car and I'll show you.' So she done it and he popped her neck. Kept on a-popping it several times until she made him quit. This morning," Mrs. Freeman said, "she ain't got no sty. She ain't got no traces of a sty."

"I never heard of that before," Mrs. Hopewell said.

"He ast her to marry him before the Ordinary," Mrs. Freeman went on, "and she told him she wasn't going to be married in no *office.*"

"Well, Glynese is a fine girl," Mrs. Hopewell said. "Glynese and Carramae are both fine girls."

"Carramae said when her and Lyman was married Lyman said it sure felt sacred to him. She said he said he wouldn't take five hundred dollars for being married by a preacher."

"How much would he take?" the girl asked from the stove.

"He said he wouldn't take five hundred dollars," Mrs. Freeman repeated.

"Well we all have work to do," Mrs. Hopewell said.

"Lyman said it just felt more sacred to him," Mrs. Freeman said. "The doctor wants Carramae to eat prunes. Says instead of medicine. Says them cramps is coming from pressure. You know where I think it is?"

"She'll be better in a few weeks," Mrs. Hopewell said.

"In the tube," Mrs. Freeman said. "Else she wouldn't be as sick as she is."

Hulga had cracked her two eggs into a saucer and was bringing them to the table along with a cup of coffee that she had filled too full. She sat down carefully and began to eat, meaning to keep Mrs. Freeman there by questions if for any reason she showed an inclination to leave. She could perceive her mother's eye on her. The first roundabout question would be about the Bible salesman and she did not wish to bring it on. "How did he pop her neck?" she asked.

Mrs. Freeman went into a description of how he had popped her neck. She said he owned a '55 Mercury but that Glynese said she would rather marry a man with only a '36 Plymouth who would be married by a preacher. The girl asked what if he had a '32 Plymouth and Mrs. Freeman said what Glynese had said was a '36 Plymouth.

Mrs. Hopewell said there were not many girls with Glynese's common sense. She said what she admired in those girls was their common sense. She said that reminded her that they had had a nice visitor yesterday, a young man selling Bibles. "Lord," she said, "he bored me to death but he was so sincere and genuine I couldn't be rude to him. He was just good country people, you know," she said, "—just the salt of the earth."

"I seen him walk up," Mrs. Freeman said, "and then later—I seen him walk off," and Hulga could feel the slight shift in her voice, the slight insinuation, that he had not walked off alone, had he? Her face remained expressionless but the color rose into her neck and she seemed to swallow it down with the next spoonful of egg. Mrs. Freeman was looking at her as if they had a secret together.

"Well, it takes all kinds of people to make the world go 'round," Mrs. Hopewell said. "It's very good we aren't all alike."

"Some people are more alike than others," Mrs. Freeman said.

Hulga got up and stumped, with about twice the noise that was necessary, into her room and locked the door. She was to meet the Bible salesman at ten o'clock at the gate. She had thought about it half the night. She had started thinking of it as a great joke and then she had begun to see profound implications in it. She had lain in bed imagining dialogues for them that were insane on the surface but that reached below to depths that no Bible salesman would be aware of. Their conversation yesterday had been of this kind.

He had stopped in front of her and had simply stood there. His face was bony and sweaty and bright, with a little pointed nose in the center of it, and his look was different from what it had been at the dinner table. He was gazing at her with open curiosity, with fascination, like a child watching a new fantastic animal at the zoo, and he was breathing as if he had run a great distance to reach her. His gaze seemed somehow familiar but she could not think where she had been regarded with it before. For almost a minute he didn't say anything. Then on what seemed an insuck of breath, he whispered, "You ever ate a chicken that was two days old?"

The girl looked at him stonily. He might have just put this question up for consideration at the meeting of a philosophical association. "Yes," she presently replied as if she had considered it from all angles.

"It must have been mighty small!" he said triumphantly and shook all over with little nervous giggles, getting very red in the face; and subsiding finally into his gaze of complete admiration, while the girl's expression remained exactly the same.

"How old are you?" he asked softly.

She waited some time before she answered. Then in a flat voice she said, "Seventeen."

His smiles came in succession like waves breaking on the surface of a little lake. "I see you got a wooden leg," he said. "I think you're real brave. I think you're real sweet."

The girl stood blank and solid and silent.

"Walk to the gate with me," he said. "You're a brave sweet little thing and I liked you the minute I seen you walk in the door."

Hulga began to move forward.

"What's your name?" he asked, smiling down on the top of her head.

"Hulga," she said.

"Hulga," he murmured, "Hulga. Hulga. I never heard of anybody name Hulga before. You're shy, aren't you, Hulga?" he asked.

She nodded, watching his large red hand on the handle of the giant valise.

"I like girls that wear glasses," he said. "I think a lot. I'm not like these people that a serious thought don't ever enter their heads. It's because I may die."

"I may die too," she said suddenly and looked up at him. His eyes were very small and brown, glittering feverishly.

"Listen," he said, "don't you think some people was meant to meet on account of what all they got in common and all? Like they both think serious thoughts and all?" He shifted the valise to his other hand so that the hand nearest her was free. He caught hold of her elbow and shook it a little. "I don't work on Saturday," he said. "I like to walk in the woods and see what Mother Nature is wearing. O'er the hills and far away. Pic-nics and things. Couldn't we go on a pic-nic tomorrow? Say yes, Hulga," he said and gave her a dying look as if he felt his insides about to drop out of him. He had even seemed to sway slightly toward her.

During the night she had imagined that she seduced him. She imagined that the two of them walked on the place until they came to the storage barn beyond the two back fields and there, she imagined, that things came to such a pass that she very easily seduced him and that then, of course, she had to reckon with his remorse. True genius can get an idea across even to an inferior mind. She imagined that she took his remorse in hand and changed it into a deeper understanding of life. She took all his shame away and turned it into something useful.

She set off for the gate at exactly ten o'clock, escaping without drawing Mrs. Hopewell's attention. She didn't take anything to eat, forgetting that food is usually taken on a picnic. She wore a pair of slacks and a dirty white shirt, and as an afterthought, she had put some Vapex on the collar of it since she did not own any perfume. When she reached the gate no one was there.

She looked up and down the empty highway and had the furious feeling that she had been tricked, that he had only meant to make her walk to the gate after the idea of him. Then suddenly he stood up, very tall, from behind a bush on the opposite embankment. Smiling, he lifted his hat which was new and wide-brimmed. He had not worn it yesterday and she wondered if he had bought it for the occasion. It was toast-colored with a red and white band around it and was slightly too large for him. He stepped from behind the bush still carrying the black valise. He had on the same suit and the same yellow socks sucked down in his shoes from walking. He crossed the highway and said, "I knew you'd come!"

The girl wondered acidly how he had known this. She pointed to the valise and asked, "Why did you bring your Bibles?"

He took her elbow, smiling down on her as if he could not stop. "You can never tell when you'll need the word of God, Hulga," he said. She had a moment in which she doubted that this was actually happening and then they began to climb the embankment. They went down into the pasture toward the woods. The boy walked lightly by her side, bouncing on his toes. The valise did not seem to be heavy today; he even swung it. They crossed half the pasture without saying anything and then, putting his hand easily on the small of her back, he asked softly, "Where does your wooden leg join on?"

She turned an ugly red and glared at him and for an instant the boy looked abashed. "I didn't mean you no harm," he said. "I only meant you're so brave and all. I guess God takes care of you."

"No," she said, looking forward and walking fast, "I don't even believe in God."

At this he stopped and whistled. "No!" he exclaimed as if he were too astonished to say anything else.

She walked on and in a second he was bouncing at her side, fanning with his hat. "That's very unusual for a girl," he remarked, watching her out of the corner of his eye. When they reached the edge of the wood, he put his hand on her back again and drew her against him without a word and kissed her heavily.

The kiss, which had more pressure than feeling behind it, produced that extra surge of adrenalin in the girl that enables one to carry a packed trunk out of a burning house, but in her, the power went at once to the brain. Even before he released her, her mind, clear and detached and ironic anyway, was regarding him from a great distance, with amusement but with pity. She had never been kissed before and she was pleased to discover that it was an unexceptional experience and all a matter of the mind's control. Some people might enjoy drain water if they were told it was vodka. When the boy, looking expectant but uncertain, pushed her gently away, she turned and walked on, saying nothing as if such business, for her, were common enough.

He came along panting at her side, trying to help her when he saw a root that she might trip over. He caught and held back the long swaying blades of thorn vine until she had passed beyond them. She led the way and he came breathing heavily behind her. Then they came out on a sunlit hillside, sloping softly into another one a little smaller. Beyond, they could see the rusted top of the old barn where the extra hay was stored.

The hill was sprinkled with small pink weeds. "Then you ain't saved?" he asked suddenly, stopping.

The girl smiled. It was the first time she had smiled at him at all. "In my economy," she said, "I'm saved and you are damned but I told you I didn't believe in God."

Nothing seemed to destroy the boy's look of admiration. He gazed at her now as if the fantastic animal at the zoo had put its paw through the bars and given him a loving poke. She thought he looked as if he wanted to kiss her again and she walked on before he had the chance.

"Ain't there somewheres we can sit down sometime?" he murmured, his voice softening toward the end of the sentence.

"In that barn," she said.

They made for it rapidly as if it might slide away like a train. It was a large two-story barn, cool and dark inside. The boy pointed up the ladder that led into the loft and said, "It's too bad we can't go up there."

"Why can't we?" she asked.

"Yer leg," he said reverently.

The girl gave him a contemptuous look and putting both hands on the ladder, she climbed it while he stood below, apparently awestruck. She pulled herself expertly through the opening and then looked down at him and said, "Well, come on if you're coming," and he began to climb the ladder, awkwardly bringing the suitcase with him.

"We won't need the Bible," she observed.

"You never can tell," he said, panting. After he had got into the loft, he was a few seconds catching his breath. She had sat down in a pile of straw. A wide sheath of sunlight, filled with dust particles, slanted over her. She lay back against a bale, her face turned away, looking out the front opening of the barn where hay was thrown from a wagon into the loft. The two pink-speckled hillsides lay back against a dark ridge of woods. The sky was cloudless and cold blue. The boy dropped down by her side and put one arm under her and the other over her and began methodically kissing her face, making little noises like a fish. He did not remove his hat but it was pushed far enough back not to interfere. When her glasses got in his way, he took them off of her and slipped them into his pocket.

The girl at first did not return any of the kisses but presently she began to and after she had put several on his cheek, she reached his lips and remained there, kissing him again and again as if she were trying to draw all the breath out of him. His breath was clear and sweet like a child's and the kisses were sticky like a child's. He mumbled about loving her and about knowing when he first seen her that he loved her, but the mumbling was like the sleepy fretting of a child being put to sleep by his mother. Her mind, throughout this, never stopped or lost itself for a second to her feelings. "You ain't said you loved me none," he whispered finally, pulling back from her. "You got to say that."

She looked away from him off into the hollow sky and then down at a black ridge and then down farther into what appeared to be two green swelling lakes. She didn't realize he had taken her glasses but this landscape could not seem exceptional to her for she seldom paid any close attention to her surroundings.

"You got to say it," he repeated. "You got to say you love me."

She was always careful how she committed herself. "In a sense," she began, "if you use the word loosely, you might say that. But it's not a word I use. I don't have illusions. I'm one of those people who see *through* to nothing."

The boy was frowning. "You got to say it. I said it and you got to say it," he said.

The girl looked at him almost tenderly. "You poor baby," she murmured. "It's just as well you don't understand," and she pulled him by the neck, face-down, against her. "We are all damned," she said, "but some of us have taken off our blindfolds and see that there's nothing to see. It's a kind of salvation."

The boy's astonished eyes looked blankly through the ends of her hair. "Okay," he almost whined, "but do you love me or don'tcher?"

"Yes," she said and added, "in a sense. But I must tell you something. There mustn't be anything dishonest between us." She lifted his head and looked him in the eye. "I am thirty years old," she said. "I have a number of degrees."

The boy's look was irritated but dogged. "I don't care," he said. "I don't care a thing about what all you done. I just want to know if you love me or don'tcher?" and he caught her to him and wildly planted her face with kisses until she said, "Yes, yes."

"Okay then," he said, letting her go. "Prove it."

She smiled, looking dreamily out on the shifty landscape. She had seduced him without even making up her mind to try. "How?" she asked, feeling that he should be delayed a little.

He leaned over and put his lips to her ear. "Show me where your wooden leg joins on," he whispered.

The girl uttered a sharp little cry and her face instantly drained of color. The obscenity of the suggestion was not what shocked her. As a child she had sometimes been subject to feelings of shame but education had removed the last traces of that as a good surgeon scrapes for cancer; she would no more have felt it over what he was asking than she would have believed in his Bible. But she was as sensitive about the artificial leg as a peacock about his tail. No one ever touched it but her. She took care of it as someone else would his soul, in private and almost with her own eyes turned away. "No," she said.

"I known it," he muttered, sitting up. "You're just playing me for a sucker."

"Oh no no!" she cried. "It joins on at the knee. Only at the knee. Why do you want to see it?"

The boy gave her a long penetrating look. "Because," he said, "it's what makes you different. You ain't like anybody else."

She sat staring at him. There was nothing about her face or her round freezing-blue eyes to indicate that this had moved her; but she felt as if her heart had stopped and left her mind to pump her blood. She decided that for the first time in her life she was face to face with real innocence. This boy, with an instinct that came from beyond wisdom, had touched the truth about her. When after a minute, she said in a hoarse high voice, "All right," it was like surrendering to him completely. It was like losing her own life and finding it again, miraculously, in his.

Very gently he began to roll the slack leg up. The artificial limb, in a white sock and brown flat shoe, was bound in a heavy material like canvas and ended in an ugly jointure where it was attached to the stump. The boy's face and his voice were entirely reverent as he uncovered it and said, "Now show me how to take it off and on."

She took it off for him and put it back on again and then he took it off himself, handling it as tenderly as if it were a real one. "See!" he said with a delighted child's face. "Now I can do it myself!"

"Put it back on," she said. She was thinking that she would run away with him and that every night he would take the leg off and every morning put it back on again. "Put it back on," she said.

"Not yet," he murmured, setting it on its foot out of her reach. "Leave it off for a while. You got me instead."

She gave a little cry of alarm but he pushed her down and began to kiss her again. Without the leg she felt entirely dependent on him. Her brain seemed to have stopped thinking altogether and to be about some other function that it was not very good at. Different expressions raced back and forth over her face. Every now and then the boy, his eyes like two steel spikes, would glance behind him where the leg stood. Finally she pushed him off and said, "Put it back on me now."

"Wait," he said. He leaned the other way and pulled the valise toward him and opened it. It had a pale blue spotted lining and there were only two Bibles in it. He took one of these out and opened the cover of it. It was hollow and contained a pocket flask of whiskey, a pack of cards, and a small blue box with printing on it. He laid these out in front of her one at a time in an evenly spaced row, like one presenting offerings at the shrine of a goddess. He put the blue box in her hand. THIS PRODUCT TO BE USED ONLY FOR THE PREVENTION OF DISEASE, she read, and dropped it. The boy was unscrewing the top of the flask. He stopped and pointed, with a smile, to the deck of cards. It was not an ordinary deck but one with an obscene picture on the back of each card. "Take a swig," he said, offering her the bottle first. He held it in front of her, but like one mesmerized, she did not move.

Her voice when she spoke had an almost pleading sound. "Aren't you," she murmured, "aren't you just good country people?"

The boy cocked his head. He looked as if he were just beginning to understand that she might be trying to insult him. "Yeah," he said, curling his lip slightly, "but it ain't held me back none. I'm as good as you any day in the week."

"Give me my leg," she said.

He pushed it farther away with his foot. "Come on now, let's begin to have us a good time," he said coaxingly. "We ain't got to know one another good yet."

"Give me my leg!" she screamed and tried to lunge for it but he pushed her down easily.

"What's the matter with you all of a sudden?" he asked, frowning as he screwed the top on the flask and put it quickly back inside the Bible. "You just a while ago said you didn't believe in nothing. I thought you was some girl!"

Her face was almost purple. "You're a Christian!" she hissed. "You're a fine Christian! You're just like them all—say one thing and do another. You're a perfect Christian, you're . . ."

The boy's mouth was set angrily. "I hope you don't think," he said in a lofty indignant tone, "that I believe in that crap! I may sell Bibles but I know which end is up and I wasn't born yesterday and I know where I'm going!"

"Give me my leg!" she screeched. He jumped up so quickly that she barely saw him sweep the cards and the blue box back into the Bible and throw the Bible into the valise. She saw him grab the leg and then she saw it for an instant slanted forlornly across the inside of the suitcase with a Bible at either side of its opposite ends. He slammed the lid shut and snatched up the valise and swung it down the hole and then stepped through himself.

When all of him had passed but his head, he turned and regarded her with a look that no longer had any admiration in it. "I've gotten a lot of interesting things," he said. "One time I got a woman's glass eye this way. And you needn't to think you'll catch me because Pointer ain't really my name. I use a different name at every house I call at and don't stay nowhere long. And I'll tell you another thing, Hulga," he said, using the name as if he didn't think much of it, "you ain't so smart. I been believing in nothing ever since I was born!" and then the toast-colored hat disappeared down the hole and the girl was left, sitting on the straw in the dusty sunlight. When she turned her churning face toward the opening, she saw his blue figure struggling successfully over the green speckled lake.

Mrs. Hopewell and Mrs. Freeman, who were in the back pasture, digging up onions, saw him emerge a little later from the woods and head across the meadow toward the highway. "Why, that looks like that nice dull young man that tried to sell me a Bible yesterday," Mrs. Hopewell said, squinting. "He must have been selling them to the Negroes back in there. He was so simple," she said, "but I guess the world would be better off if we were all that simple."

Mrs. Freeman's gaze drove forward and just touched him before he disappeared under the hill. Then she returned her attention to the evil-smelling onion shoot she was lifting from the ground. "Some can't be that simple," she said. "I know I never could."

CONSTRUCTING A READING

1. The names of Flannery O'Connor's characters (Mrs. Hopewell, Joy/Hulga, Manly Pointer, and Mrs. Freeman) are tropes in themselves.

How do they work? Analyze O'Connor's naming as an instance of figurative language and describe its effect on your reading of the story.

2. The figure of speech "without a leg to stand on" is often used to describe the persons on the losing side of an argument. If that configuration applies to Hulga at the end of the story, what is the argument about?

Separating

John Updike

The day was fair. Brilliant. All that June the weather had mocked the Maples' internal misery with solid sunlight—golden shafts and cascades of green in which their conversations had wormed unseeing, their sad murmuring selves the only stain in Nature. Usually by this time of the year they had acquired tans; but when they met their elder daughter's plane on her return from a year in England they were almost as pale as she, though Judith was too dazzled by the sunny opulent jumble of her native land to notice. They did not spoil her homecoming by telling her immediately. Wait a few days, let her recover from jet lag, had been one of their formulations, in that string of gray dialogues—over coffee, over cocktails, over Cointreau—that had shaped the strategy of their dissolution, while the earth performed its annual stunt of renewal unnoticed beyond their closed windows. Richard had thought to leave at Easter; Joan had insisted they wait until the four children were at last assembled, with all exams passed and ceremonies attended, and the bauble of summer to console them. So he had drudged away, in love, in dread, repairing screens, getting the mowers sharpened, rolling and patching their new tennis court.

The court, clay, had come through its first winter pitted and windswept bare of redcoat. Years ago the Maples had observed how often, among their friends, divorce followed a dramatic home improvement, as if the marriage were making one last effort to live; their own worst crisis had come amid the plaster dust and exposed plumbing of a kitchen renovation. Yet, a summer ago, as canary-yellow bulldozers gaily churned a grassy, daisy-dotted knoll into a muddy plateau, and a crew of pigtailed young men raked and tamped clay into a plane, this transformation did not strike them as ominous, but festive in its impudence; their marriage could rend the earth for fun. The next spring, waking each day at dawn to a sliding sensation as if the bed were being tipped, Richard found the barren tennis court—its net and tapes still rolled in the barn—an environment congruous with his mood of purposeful desolation, and the crumbling of handfuls of clay into cracks and holes (dogs had frolicked on the court in a thaw; rivulets had eroded trenches) an activity suitably elemental and interminable. In his sealed heart he hoped the day would never come.

Now it was here. A Friday. Judith was re-acclimated; all four children were assembled, before jobs and camps and visits again scattered them. Joan thought they should be told one by one. Richard was for making an announce-ment at the table. She said, "I think just making an announcement is a cop-out. They'll start quarrelling and playing to each other instead of focusing. They're each individuals, you know, not just some corporate obstacle to your freedom."

"O.K., O.K. I agree." Joan's plan was exact. That evening, they were giv-ing Judith a belated welcome-home dinner, of lobster and champagne. Then, the party over, they, the two of them, who nineteen years before would push her in a baby carriage along Fifth Avenue to Washington Square, were to walk her out of the house, to the bridge across the salt creek, and tell her, swearing her to secrecy. Then Richard Jr., who was going directly from work to a rock concert in Boston, would be told, either late when he returned on the train or early Saturday morning before he went off to his job; he was seventeen and employed as one of a golf-course maintenance crew. Then the two younger children, John and Margaret, could, as the morning wore on, be informed.

"Mopped up, as it were," Richard said.

"Do you have any better plan? That leaves you the rest of Saturday to answer any questions, pack, and make your wonderful departure."

"No," he said, meaning he had no better plan, and agreed to hers, though to him it showed an edge of false order, a hidden plea for control, like Joan's long chore lists and financial accountings and, in the days when he first knew her, her too-copious lecture notes. Her plan turned one hurdle for him into four—four knife-sharp walls, each with a sheer blind drop on the other side.

All spring he had moved through a world of insides and outsides, of barri-ers and partitions. He and Joan stood as a thin barrier between the children and the truth. Each moment was a partition, with the past on one side and the future on the other, a future containing this unthinkable *now*. Beyond four knifelike walls a new life for him waited vaguely. His skull cupped a secret, a white face, a face both frightened and soothing, both strange and known, that he wanted to shield from tears, which he felt all about him, solid as the sun-light. So haunted, he had become obsessed with battening down the house against his absence, replacing screens and sash cords, hinges and latches—a Houdini making things snug before his escape.

The lock. He had still to replace a lock on one of the doors of the screened porch. The task, like most such, proved more difficult than he had imagined. The old lock, aluminum frozen by corrosion, had been deliberately rendered obsolete by manufacturers. Three hardware stores had nothing that even approximately matched the mortised hole its removal (surprisingly easy) left. Another hole had to be gouged, with bits too small and saws too big, and the old hole fitted with a block of wood—the chisels dull, the saw rusty, his fingers thick with lack of sleep. The sun poured down, beyond the porch, on a world of neglect. The bushes already needed pruning, the windward side of the house was shedding flakes of paint, rain would get in when he was gone, insects, rot, death. His family, all those he would lose, filtered through the edges of his awareness as he struggled with screw holes, splinters, opaque instructions, minutiae of metal.

Judith sat on the porch, a princess returned from exile. She regaled them with stories of fuel shortages, of bomb scares in the Underground, of Pakistani workmen loudly lusting after her as she walked past on her way to dance school. Joan came and went, in and out of the house, calmer than she should have been, praising his struggles with the lock as if this were one more and not the last of their long succession of shared chores. The younger of his sons for a few minutes held the rickety screen door while his father clumsily hammered and chiseled, each blow a kind of sob in Richard's ears. His younger daughter, having been at a slumber party, slept on the porch hammock through all the noise—heavy and pink, trusting and forsaken. Time, like the sunlight, continued relentlessly; the sunlight slowly slanted. Today was one of the longest days. The lock clicked, worked. He was through. He had a drink; he drank it on the porch, listening to his daughter. "It was so sweet," she was saying, "during the worst of it, how all the butchers and bakery shops kept open by candlelight. They're all so plucky and cute. From the papers, things sounded so much worse here—people shooting people in gas lines, and everybody freezing."

Richard asked her, "Do you still want to live in England forever?" *Forever*: the concept, now a reality upon him, pressed and scratched at the back of his throat.

"No," Judith confessed, turning her oval face to him, its eyes still childishly far apart, but the lips set as over something succulent and satisfactory. "I was anxious to come home. I'm an American." She was a woman. They had raised her; he and Joan had endured together to raise her, alone of the four. The others had still some raising left in them. Yet it was the thought of telling Judith—the image of her, their first baby, walking between them arm in arm to the bridge—that broke him. The partition between his face and the tears broke. Richard sat down to the celebratory meal with the back of his throat aching; the champagne, the lobster seemed phases of sunshine; he saw them and tasted them through tears. He blinked, swallowed, croakily joked about hay fever. The tears would not stop leaking through; they came not through a hole that could be plugged but through a permeable spot in a membrane, steadily, purely, endlessly, fruitfully. They became, his tears, a shield for himself against these others—their faces, the fact of their assembly, a last time as innocents, at a table where he sat the last time as head. Tears dropped from his nose as he broke the lobster's back; salt flavored his champagne as he sipped it; the raw clench at the back of his throat was delicious. He could not help himself.

His children tried to ignore his tears. Judith, on his right, lit a cigarette, gazed upward in the direction of her too energetic, too sophisticated exhalation; on her other side, John earnestly bent his face to the extraction of the last morsels—legs, tail segments—from the scarlet corpse. Joan, at the opposite end of the table, glanced at him surprised, her reproach displaced by a quick grimace, of forgiveness, or of salute to his superior gift of strategy. Between them, Margaret, no longer called Bean, thirteen and large for her age, gazed from the other side of his pane of tears as if into a shopwindow at something she coveted—at her father, a crystalline heap of splinters and memories. It was not she, however, but John who, in the kitchen, as they cleared the plates and carapaces away, asked Joan the question: *"Why is Daddy crying?"*

Richard heard the question but not the murmured answer. Then he heard Bean cry, "Oh, no-oh!"—the faintly dramatized exclamation of one who had long expected it.

John returned to the table carrying a bowl of salad. He nodded tersely at his father and his lips shaped the conspiratorial words "She told."

"Told what?" Richard asked aloud, insanely.

The boy sat down as if to rebuke his father's distraction with the example of his own good manners. He said quietly, "The separation."

Joan and Margaret returned; the child, in Richard's twisted vision, seemed diminished in size, and relieved, relieved to have had the bogieman at last proved real. He called out to her—the distances at the table had grown immense—"You knew, you always knew," but the clenching at the back of his throat prevented him from making sense of it. From afar he heard Joan talking, levelly, sensibly, reciting what they had prepared: it was a separation for the summer, an experiment. She and Daddy both agreed it would be good for them; they needed space and time to think; they liked each other but did not make each other happy enough, somehow.

Judith, imitating her mother's factual tone, but in her youth off-key, too cool, said, "I think it's silly. You should either live together or get divorced."

Richard's crying, like a wave that has crested and crashed, had become tumultuous; but it was overtopped by another tumult, for John, who had been so reserved, now grew larger and larger at the table. Perhaps his younger sister's being, credited with knowing set him off. "Why didn't you *tell* us?" he asked, in a large round voice quite unlike his own. "You should have *told* us you weren't getting along."

Richard was startled into attempting to force words through his tears. "We do get along, that's the trouble, so it doesn't show even to us—" *That we do not love each* other was the rest of the sentence; he couldn't finish it.

Joan finished for him, in her style. "And we've always, *especially*, loved our children."

John was not mollified. "What do you care about *us*?" he boomed. "We're just little things you *had*." His sisters' laughing forced a laugh from him, which he turned hard and parodistic: "Ha ha *ha*." Richard and Joan realized simultaneously that the child was drunk, on Judith's homecoming champagne. Feeling bound to keep the center of the stage, John took a cigarette from Judith's pack, poked it into his mouth, let it hang from his lower lip, and squinted like a gangster.

"You're not little things we had," Richard called to him. "You're the whole point. But you're grown. Or almost."

The boy was lighting matches. Instead of holding them to his cigarette (for they had never seen him smoke; being "good" had been his way of setting himself apart), he held them to his mother's face, closer and closer, for her to blow out. Then he lit the whole folder—a hiss and then a torch, held against his mother's face. Prismed by tears, the flame filled Richard's vision; he didn't know how it was extinguished. He heard Margaret say, "Oh stop showing off," and saw John, in response, break the cigarette in two and put the halves entirely into his mouth and chew, sticking out his tongue to display the shreds to his sister.

Joan talked to him, reasoning—a fountain of reason, unintelligible. "Talked about it for years . . . our children must help us . . . Daddy and I both want . . ." As the boy listened, he carefully wadded a paper napkin into the leaves of his salad, fashioned a ball of paper and lettuce, and popped it into his mouth, looking around the table for the expected laughter. None came. Judith said, "Be mature," and dismissed a plume of smoke.

Richard got up from this stifling table and led the boy outside. Though the house was in twilight, the outdoors still brimmed with light, the lovely waste light of high summer. Both laughing, he supervised John's spitting out the lettuce and paper and tobacco into the pachysandra. He took him by the hand—a square gritty hand, but for its softness a man's. Yet, it held on. They ran together up into the field, past the tennis court. The raw banking left by the bulldozers was dotted with daisies. Past the court and a flat stretch where they used to play family baseball stood a soft green rise glorious in the sun, each weed and species of grass distinct as illumination on parchment. "I'm sorry, so sorry," Richard cried. "You were the only one who ever tried to help me with all the goddam jobs around this place."

Sobbing, safe within his tears and the champagne, John explained, "It's not just the separation, it's the whole crummy year, I *hate* that school, you can't make any friends, the history teacher's a scud."

They sat on the crest of the rise, shaking and warm from their tears but easier in their voices, and Richard tried to focus on the child's sad year—the weekdays long with homework, the weekends spent in his room with model airplanes, while his parents murmured down below, nursing their separation. How selfish, how blind, Richard thought; his eyes felt scoured. He told his son, "We'll think about getting you transferred. Life's too short to be miserable."

They had said what they could, but did not want the moment to heal, and talked on, about the school, about the tennis court, whether it would ever again be as good as it had been that first summer. They walked to inspect it and pressed a few more tapes more firmly down. A little stiltedly, perhaps trying now to make too much of the moment, Richard led the boy to the spot in the field where the view was best, of the metallic blue river, the emerald marsh, the scattered islands velvety with shadow in the low light, the white bits of beach far away. "See," he said. "It goes on being beautiful. It'll be here tomorrow."

"I know," John answered, impatiently. The moment had closed.

Back in the house, the others had opened some white wine, the champagne being drunk, and still sat at the table, the three females, gossiping. Where Joan sat had become the head. She turned, showing him a tearless face, and asked, "All right?"

"We're fine," he said, resenting it, though relieved, that the party went on without him.

In bed she explained, "I couldn't cry I guess because I cried so much all spring. It really wasn't fair. It's your idea, and you made it look as though I was kicking you out."

"I'm sorry," he said. "I couldn't stop. I wanted to but couldn't."

"You *didn't* want to. You loved it. You were having your way, making a general announcement."

"I love having it over," he admitted. "God, those kids were great. So brave and funny." John, returned to the house, had settled to a model airplane in his room, and kept shouting down to them, "I'm O.K. No sweat." "And the way," Richard went on, cozy in his relief, "they never questioned the reasons we gave. No thought of a third person. Not even Judith."

"That *was* touching," Joan said.

He gave her a hug. "You were great too. Very reassuring to everybody. Thank you." Guiltily, he realized he did not feel separated.

"You still have Dickie to do," she told him. These words set before him a black mountain in the darkness; its cold breath, its near weight affected his chest. Of the four children, his elder son was most nearly his conscience. Joan did not need to add, "That's one piece of your dirty work I won't do for you."

"I know. I'll do it. You go to sleep."

Within minutes, her breathing slowed, became oblivious and deep. It was quarter to midnight. Dickie's train from the concert would come in at one-fourteen. Richard set the alarm for one. He had slept atrociously for weeks. But whenever he closed his lids some glimpse of the last hours scorched them— Judith exhaling toward the ceiling in a kind of aversion, Bean's mute staring, the sunstruck growth in the field where he and John had rested. The mountain before him moved closer, moved within him; he was huge, momentous. The ache at the back of his throat felt stale. His wife slept as if slain beside him. When, exasperated by his hot lids, his crowded heart, he rose from bed and dressed, she awoke enough to turn over. He told her then, "Joan, if I could undo it all, I would."

"Where would you begin?" she asked. There was no place. Giving him courage, she was always giving him courage. He put on shoes without socks in the dark. The children were breathing in their rooms, the downstairs was hollow. In their confusion they had left lights burning. He turned off all but one, the kitchen overhead. The car started. He had hoped it wouldn't. He met only moonlight on the road; it seemed a diaphanous companion, flickering in the leaves along the roadside, haunting his rearview mirror like a pursuer, melting under his headlights. The center of town, not quite deserted, was eerie at this hour. A young cop in uniform kept company with a gang of T-shirted kids on the steps of the bank. Across from the railroad station, several bars kept open. Customers, mostly young, passed in and out of the warm night, savoring summer's novelty. Voices shouted from cars as they passed; an immense conversation seemed in progress. Richard parked and in his weariness put his head on the passenger seat, out of the commotion and wheeling lights. It was as when, in the movies, an assassin grimly carries his mission through the jostle of a carnival—except the movies cannot show the precipitous, palpable slope you cling to within. You cannot climb back down; you can only fall. The synthetic fabric of the car seat, warmed by his cheek, confided to him an ancient, distant scent of vanilla.

A train whistle caused him to lift his head. It was on time; he had hoped it would be late. The slender drawgates descended. The bell of approach tingled happily. The great metal body, horizontally fluted, rocked to a stop, and sleepy teenagers disembarked, his son among them. Dickie did not show surprise that his father was meeting him at this terrible hour. He sauntered to the car with two friends, both taller than he. He said "Hi" to his father and took the passenger's seat with an exhausted promptness that expressed gratitude. The friends got in the back, and Richard was grateful; a few more minutes' postponement would be won by driving them home.

He asked, "How was the concert?"

"Groovy," one boy said from the back seat.

"It bit," the other said.

"It was O.K.," Dickie said, moderate by nature, so reasonable that in his childhood the unreason of the world had given him headaches, stomach aches, nausea. When the second friend had been dropped off at his dark house, the boy blurted, "Dad, my eyes are killing me with hay fever! I'm out there cutting that mothering grass all day!"

"Do we still have those drops?"

"They didn't do any good last summer."

"They might this." Richard swung a U-turn on the empty street. The drive home took a few minutes. The mountain was here, in his throat. "Richard," he said, and felt the boy, slumped and rubbing his eyes, go tense at his tone, "I didn't come to meet you just to make your life easier. I came because your mother and I have some news for you, and you're a hard man to get ahold of these days. It's sad news."

"That's O.K." The reassurance came out soft, but quick, as if released from the tip of a spring.

Richard had feared that his tears would return and choke him, but the boy's manliness set an example, and his voice issued forth steady and dry. "It's sad news, but it needn't be tragic news, at least for you. It should have no practical effect on your life, though it's bound to have an emotional effect. You'll work at your job, and go back to school in September. Your mother and I are really proud of what you're making of your life; we don't want that to change at all."

"Yeah," the boy said lightly, on the intake of his breath, holding himself up. They turned the corner; the church they went to loomed like a gutted fort. The home of the woman Richard hoped to marry stood across the green. Her bedroom light burned.

"Your mother and I," he said, "have decided to separate. For the summer. Nothing legal, no divorce yet. We want to see how it feels. For some years now, we haven't been doing enough for each other, making each other as happy as we should be. Have you sensed that?"

"No," the boy said. It was an honest, unemotional answer: true or false in a quiz.

Glad for the factual basis, Richard pursued, even garrulously, the details. His apartment across town, his utter accessibility, the split vacation arrangements, the advantages to the children, the added mobility and variety of the summer. Dickie listened, absorbing. "Do the others know?"

"Yes."

"How did they take it?"

"The girls pretty calmly. John flipped out; he shouted and ate a cigarette and made a salad out of his napkin and told us how much he hated school."

His brother chuckled. "He did?"

"Yeah. The school issue was more upsetting for him than Mom and me. He seemed to feel better for having exploded."

"He did?" The repetition was the first sign that he was stunned.

"Yes. Dickie, I want to tell you something. This last hour, waiting for your train to get in, has been about the worst of my life. I hate this. *Hate it.* My father would have died before doing it to me." He felt immensely lighter, saying this. He had dumped the mountain on the boy. They were home. Moving swiftly as a shadow, Dickie was out of the car, through the bright kitchen. Richard called after him, "Want a glass of milk or anything?"

"No thanks."

"Want us to call the course tomorrow and say you're too sick to work?"

"No, that's all right." The answer was faint, delivered at the door to his room; Richard listened for the slam that went with a tantrum. The door closed normally, gently. The sound was sickening.

Joan had sunk into that first deep trough of sleep and was slow to awake. Richard had to repeat, "I told him."

"What did he say?"

"Nothing much. Could you go say goodnight to him? Please."

She left their room, without putting on a bathrobe. He sluggishly changed back into his pajamas and walked down the hall. Dickie was already in bed, Joan was sitting beside him, and the boy's bedside clock radio was murmuring music. When she stood, an inexplicable light—the moon?—outlined her body through the nightie. Richard sat on the warm place she had indented on the child's narrow mattress. He asked him, "Do you want the radio on like that?"

"It always is."

"Doesn't it keep you awake? It would me."

"No."

"Are you sleepy?"

"Yeah."

"Good. Sure you want to get up and go to work? You've had a big night."

"I want to."

Away at school this winter he had learned for the first time that you can go short of sleep and live. As an infant he had slept with an immobile, sweating intensity that had alarmed his babysitters. In adolescence he had often been the first of the four children to go to bed. Even now, he would go slack in the middle of a television show, his sprawled legs hairy and brown. "O.K. Good boy. Dickie, listen. I love you so much, I never knew how much until now. No matter how this works out, I'll always be with you. Really."

Richard bent to kiss an averted face but his son, sinewy, turned and with wet cheeks embraced him and gave him a kiss, on the lips, passionate as a woman's. In his father's ear he moaned one word, the crucial, intelligent word: "*Why?*"

Why. It was a whistle of wind in a crack, a knife thrust, a window thrown open on emptiness. The white face was gone, the darkness was featureless. Richard had forgotten why.

CONSTRUCTING A READING

1. How does the tennis court figure in this story?
2. How does the screen door lock work as a figure? The weather? The name, "Maples"? Hay fever?

CHAPTER FIVE

Generic Expectations:
How Readers of Narrative
Know What to Expect

What happens next? And then what? And why? One of Snoopy's problems as a novelist is finding a way of answering these questions. He knows, of course, that his readers will ask them. From the earliest moments of childhood in Western culture, people learn to listen to stories and wonder—"what happened next?" "And then what?" "And then what happened?" "Why?"

When readers ask these questions, they are following cultural guidelines about how to recognize and make meaning from stories. They expect, for example, that events will be interconnected and that later events will come as a result of earlier ones. (To Lucy, Snoopy's sentence sounds like the beginning of a story that describes the troubles that result from being called cute.) Readers expect a story to "close"—to come to a conclusion that answers the questions the story raises. If a mystery story begins with a murder, readers expect to know who committed that crime by the time the story ends; if a character is looking for something, readers expect her to find it; if a character sets off on an adventure, readers expect him to arrive somewhere. If a story tells us to expect trouble, we expect to learn what that trouble is.

Reading is propelled by a process of raising and answering questions. Readers in Western culture, having learned to expect that their questions will ultimately be answered, find it noteworthy and even frustrating when answers are withheld or unanticipated. This chapter is about how this question-and-answer process works—and about the kinds of stories that intentionally frustrate our expectations.

HOW WE RECOGNIZE A STORY

In the context of this book, it is useful to think of the questions "what happens next?" and "why?" as gaps in a story. In texts that readers recognize as stories, the gaps are predominantly—but not exclusively—about temporality (what happens next?) and causality (why?). Many theorists believe that gaps about causality and temporality actually *constitute* stories. In other words, we recognize a text as a story—a narrative—because it has gaps about temporality and causality.

I say "text" because, although we will look mostly at works of fiction in this chapter, any kind of text can be a story, can have a narrative. Plays, poems, paintings, TV commercials, print advertisements—these and many other texts

---

Shlomith Rimmon-Kenan defines *story* as a "series of events arranged in chronological order" and an *event* as a change from one state of affair to another. Gerald Prince sees a *minimal story* as consisting of a state of affairs, followed by an action, which causes another state of affairs that is the inverse of the first. Tsvetan Todorov considers *minimal narrative* to be a move from equilibrium through disequilibrium to a new equilibrium.

See the entries for "story" and "narrative" in Gerald Prince, *Dictionary of Narratology*. University of Nebraska Press, 1987.

often, though not always, have narrative elements. They are also just as influenced by the expectations of their own genres (comedy vs. drama, epic poetry vs. lyrical poetry, thirty-second TV commercial vs. thirty-page full-color magazine supplement) as fiction is by the narrative generic expectations we're discussing in this chapter. Finally, the interplay between generic expectation and reading acts is similar in all these genres; the more we recognize it when reading fiction, the more we can recognize it in reading other types of texts.

Narratology is the branch of literary theory that studies the definition and structure of stories. Although narratologists differ in their definitions of *story*, there is consensus on certain characteristics of *minimal story*—the set of features that signals readers to perceive a text as a narrative. First, stories involve change, a temporal phenomenon. Narratologists use the terms *state of affairs*, or *state of mind*, to designate that which changes in stories. A detective moving from a state of ignorance about a crime to the state of knowing "who dunnit" constitutes a story. But story also involves *causality*—a sense that later events occur *as a result of* earlier ones. A series of events—"John ate a hot dog and then Peter ate a hot dog and then Mary ate a hot dog"—is a chronology, but not a story. "Mary was dieting, but after both John and Peter ate a hot dog at the ball game, Mary decided that their hot dogs looked so good that she suspended her diet and she ate a hot dog too," however, is a series of *causally related events* and, therefore, a *story*.

Stories are, also, about someone: Peter, John, and Mary are the characters in their narrative. They perform the actions of the story; the story's events happen to them or at their bidding. We call the "someone" on whom the story centers the *protagonist*.

Because they expect changes in characters' states of being, readers of stories tend to raise gap questions about characters' motivation in order to learn the cause of the changes. (Mary ate the hot dog *because* John and Peter did, because it smelled good, because she wanted to.) When a narrator tells us that a shot rang out, we want to know why. Who fired the shot? Why? Was he or she angry? Insane? Criminal? If so, how did she or he get that way?

Finally, stories tend to resolve—or come to a recognizable conclusion that seems both to follow from the causal and temporal connections among their events and to restore equilibrium. Most stories in western culture end with some sort of restoration of equilibrium, or *closure*. For example, lovers meet; (and then, because of a misunderstanding) lovers separate; (but then, when the misunderstanding is cleared up) lovers find each other again. This form is very familiar to us, so deeply embedded in Western consciousness that we tend to feel uneasy when stories do not follow it, when they do not resolve. Many texts, however—especially recent, postmodern ones—deliberately play with or frustrate our expectations of closure, and a few such stories appear later in this chapter and elsewhere in this book. For now, though, we shall concentrate on charting the pattern from which such stories deviate.

ELEMENTS OF NARRATIVES

The Minimal Story

To illustrate these theoretical points, here is a story that you will probably recognize.

Minimal Story A
Event 1. Cinderella is sad [that's her initial state of mind] **because she cannot go to the Ball.**
And then,
Event 2. Her Fairy Godmother appears and gives her a beautiful gown and a dress and a coach. [so that she can go to the ball and be properly dressed, but the Fairy Godmother also introduces disequilibrium by requiring that Cinderella return before midnight.]
And then, [as a result]
Event 3. Cinderella goes to the ball and meets Prince Charming and she is happy [changed state of mind].
But then,

Minimal Story B
Event 1. Cinderella is sad because she expects never to see the Prince again.
But then,
Event 2. The prince searches for her by using her glass slipper as a test [thereby introducing disequilibrium into the situation again in the possibility that her sadness may change to happiness]
And then, [as a result]
Event 3. Cinderella and the Prince find each other and live happily ever after [their final state of mind].

Notice that each of these minimal stories involves a change from one state of affairs to another. Each goes from equilibrium through disequilibrium to equilibrium again. In each case, the events are causally and temporally related. The Cinderella story, as I have told it here, is composed of two minimal stories, but there could have been many more. I have deliberately left out the stepsisters, the pumpkin coach, and many other details of the traditional narrative, but they could be added on to the one I've just told. Even the most complex narratives can be broken down—and explained—as sequences of minimal stories.

Why, though, would anyone want to do that? What's the point of breaking up *War and Peace* into hundreds—or thousands—of minimal stories? The usefulness of this kind of analysis is that it reveals *the structure of narrative:* the relations of a story's parts at their most basic level. And that insight is important, according to many narrative theorists, because it allows us to see more clearly what it is that stories *do*, how they function in culture. For stories do much more than entertain us. Storytelling, narratologists believe, is one of the defining characteristics of human beings, like opposable thumbs and tool making. Cultures use their stories (like "Snow-white and Rose-red" in Chapter Four) to express, teach, and celebrate their values. Therefore, the ways in which a culture *fills in* the "bare bones" structure I have just described—the particular temporal and causal relations a culture's narratives involve, the kinds of protagonists they have, the types of closure they tend to feature—reveal quite a bit about that culture's values.

Cultural Implications

A look at the narratives we encounter in our daily lives can give us some examples of those inscribed cultural values. The Cinderella story, for example, suggests that the culture from which it emerged is one that encourages the belief that hard work and selflessness on the part of women will be rewarded with wealth and happiness. It would also seem to be a culture that values love—rather than equivalent net worth—as a basis for relationships. Finally, it encourages us to believe that those who marry for love live happily ever after. The minimal story that follows—or ones very much like it—is probably familiar to you. What does it reveal?

> **Event 1. Ryan is sad because he fears that his problem dandruff makes him unattractive to women** [disequilibrium].
>
> **Then,**
>
> **Event 2. His sister Brittany suggests that he use her dandruff shampoo.**
>
> **And then,** [as a result]
>
> **Event 3. Ryan has a date with a woman he admires** [Equilibrium restored. Brittany says "I told you so"].

Ryan has a sister instead of a Fairy Godmother, and she gives him advice instead of a magic pumpkin coach, but the resolution (restored self-esteem, happiness) certainly comes close to that of the Cinderella story. Narratologists would say that these two stories have the same structure and that both stories have the cultural impact of suggesting what to do if you want to live happily ever after. When we look at how the structure is filled in, though, we see that the culture that composed "Ryan's Dandruff" encourages its audiences to see the purchase of products as a way to solve problems of self-esteem and obtain love, whereas "Cinderella" promotes selflessness and duty—and the hope that a fairy godmother will reward these attributes magically and make all our dreams come true. In the commercial, the consumption of commodities takes the place of magic.

The poem that follows also illustrates the pattern. As you read, think about the cultural implications of Wordsworth's story.

I Wandered Lonely as a Cloud
William Wordsworth

I wandered lonely as a cloud
That floats on high o'er vales and hills,
When all at once I saw a crowd,
A host, of golden daffodils;
Beside the lake, beneath the trees,
Fluttering and dancing in the breeze.

Continuous as the stars that shine
And twinkle on the milky way,
They stretched in never-ending line
Along the margin of a bay:
Ten thousand saw I at a glance,
Tossing their heads in sprightly dance.

The waves beside them danced; but they
Out-did the sparkling waves in glee;
A poet could not but be gay,
In such a jocund company:
I gazed—and gazed—but little thought
What wealth the show to me had brought:

For oft, when on my couch I lie
In vacant or in pensive mood,
They flash upon that inward eye
Which is the bliss of solitude;
And then my heart with pleasure fills,
And dances with the daffodils.

Minimal Story A
First,
Event 1. The speaker was lonely.
Then,
Event 2. The speaker saw the daffodils.
Then, as a result,
Event 3. The poet was happy in their "jocund company."

Minimal Story B
First,
Event 1. The speaker had no idea "what wealth" the daffodil experience had brought him.
But then,
Event 2. He returned to his solitary life and lay "on [his] couch,"
And then, as a result [of recreating the daffodil scene in his "inward eye"],
Event 3. His heart fills with pleasure "and dances with the daffodils."

When I look at the ways in which this poem fills out its minimal story, I notice that the first state of affairs is "lonely" and the last one is "the bliss of solitude." What's the difference, I wonder, between loneliness and blissful solitude? The speaker is alone in both cases, so the change must be in his state of mind. What intervenes—what *causes the change* from one state to the other—is the vision of the daffodils, or, more precisely, two visions, one actual and the other imaginative. In the first minimal story, Wordsworth's speaker actually sees a field of daffodils. In the second one, the daffodils are in his "inward eye"—his imagination. The minimal story, then, is one in which the speaker's state changes as a consequence of imaginative activity. And it is in that aspect that the poem most interestingly (for me) reflects its culture's values. Wordsworth composed this poem in 1807, a time when many European philosophers, poets, and novelists had begun to value imagination and affection over reason as a way of knowing and establishing sympathy with other human beings. The Romantics, as these writers and thinkers were called, tended also to value what they called "natural" rather than artificial beauty—especially in the simple things of life. I also notice that the daffodils are described in terms—"dancing," "nodding their heads," forming a "crowd,"—that are more usually associated with people. I therefore take the daffodils to be a trope, a metaphor, for people than with flowers. Next, I wonder what Wordsworth wants to accomplish by asking me to see daffodils as people. What are the daffodil/people doing? Well, they're forming communities and evidently having a good time. I conclude that Wordsworth's apparently simple poem reveals something about the ways in which he hoped the natural world would encourage his readers to develop sympathy with their fellow human beings.

CONSTRUCTING A READING

1. With your classmates, apply the minimal story framework to some of the narratives you see, hear, or read every day, e.g., TV news, sitcoms, horror stories, sports contests, romance novels. You may wish to invent a visual way of sharing your findings with your classmates, by using videotapes, computer graphics, charts, or transparencies, for instance. In your

analysis of these minimal stories, point to the changes you perceive, describe the equilibrium and disequilibrium, and identify the protagonist. You may find some disagreement among class members. Make note of them—because they are important indications of culturally different readings—but it's not necessary for everyone to agree.

2. In your journal, make a list, as complete as possible, of the happenings in your day so far. Your list is a chronology; it shows temporal but not causal relations among the events of your day. Share your chronology with other members of your group. Together with them, talk about ways in which your chronologies may be made into stories through attention to causal relationships. (Save your list for later.)

Story, Discourse, and Plot

As you know, the Cinderella story involves many more elements than we mentioned in looking at its minimal story. All narratives are composed of a number of separate elements, which narratologists analyze.

For instance, we can distinguish *story*—the events of the narrative, what happens to whom—from *discourse*—how those events are described, by whom, to whom, and for what reason. *Plot* is the arrangement of events that keeps you reading, the result of the author's decision about which specific events to tell you about and when. Plot, then, is a technique by means of which readers' curiosity about what happens next and why is evoked—story and discourse contribute to sustaining that curiosity. Traditional narrative theory describes five elements or stages of plot: introduction, rising action or complication, climax or conflict, denouement (untangling, revelation) and conclusion. These stages are not present in all narratives, and they don't always occur sequentially, but they make useful signposts in our study.

Where Are You Going, Where Have You Been?
For Bob Dylan
Joyce Carol Oates

Her name was Connie. She was fifteen and she had a quick, nervous giggling habit of craning her neck to glance into mirrors or checking other people's faces to make sure her own was all right Her mother, who noticed everything and knew everything and who hadn't much reason any longer to look at her own face, always scolded Connie about it. "Stop gawking at yourself. Who are you? You think you're so pretty?" she would say. Connie would raise her eyebrows at these familiar old complaints and look right through her mother, into a shadowy vision of herself as she was right at that moment: she knew she was pretty and that was everything. Her mother had been pretty once too, if you could believe those old snapshots in the album, but now her looks were gone and that was why she was always after Connie.

"Why don't you keep your room clean like your sister? How've you got your hair fixed—what the hell stinks? Hair spray? You don't see your sister using that junk."

Her sister June was twenty-four and still lived at home. She was a secretary in the high school Connie attended, and if that wasn't bad enough—with her in the same building—she was so plain and chunky and steady that Connie had to hear her praised all the time by her mother and her mother's sisters. June did this, June did that, she saved money and helped clean the house and cooked and Connie couldn't do a thing, her mind was all filled with trashy daydreams. Their father was away at work most of the time and when he came home he wanted supper and he read the newspaper at supper and after supper he went to bed. He didn't bother talking much to them, but around his bent head Connie's mother kept picking at her until Connie wished her mother was dead and she herself was dead and it was all over. "She makes me want to throw up sometimes," she complained to her friends. She had a high, breathless, amused voice that made everything she said sound a little forced, whether it was sincere or not.

There was one good thing: June went places with girl friends of hers, girls who were just as plain and steady as she, and so when Connie wanted to do that her mother had no objections. The father of Connie's best girl friend drove the girls the three miles to town and left them at a shopping plaza so they could walk through the stores or go to a movie, and when he came to pick them up again at eleven he never bothered to ask what they had done.

They must have been familiar sights, walking around the shopping plaza in their shorts and flat ballerina slippers that always scuffed on the sidewalk, with charm bracelets jingling on their thin wrists; they would lean together to whisper and laugh secretly if someone passed who amused or interested them. Connie had long dark blond hair that drew anyone's eye to it, and she wore part of it pulled up on her head and puffed out and the rest of it she let fall down her back. She wore a pull-over jersey blouse that looked one way when she was at home and another way when she was away from home. Everything about her had two sides to it, one for home and one for anywhere that was not home: her walk, which could be childlike and bobbing, or languid enough to make anyone think she was hearing music in her head; her mouth, which was pale and smirking most of the time, but bright and pink on these evenings out; her laugh, which was cynical and drawling at home—"Ha, ha, very funny,"— but high-pitched and nervous anywhere else, like the jingling of the charms on her bracelet.

Sometimes they did go shopping or to a movie, but sometimes they went across the highway, ducking fast across the busy road, to a drive-in restaurant where older kids hung out. The restaurant was shaped like a big bottle, though squatter than a real bottle, and on its cap was a revolving figure of a grinning boy holding a hamburger aloft. One night in midsummer they ran across, breathless with daring, and right away someone leaned out a car window and invited them over, but it was just a boy from high school they didn't like. It made them feel good to be able to ignore him. They went up through the maze of parked and cruising cars to the bright-lit, fly-infested restaurant, their faces pleased and expectant as if they were entering a sacred building that loomed up out of the night to give them what haven and blessing they yearned for. They sat at the counter and crossed their legs at the ankles, their thin shoulders rigid with excitement, and listened to the music that made everything so good: the music was always in the background, like music at a church service; it was something to depend upon.

A boy named Eddie came in to talk with them. He sat backwards on his stool, turning himself jerkily around in semicircles and then stopping and turning back again, and after a while he asked Connie if she would like something to eat. She said she would so she tapped her friend's arm on her way out—her friend pulled her face up into a brave, droll look—and Connie said she would meet her at eleven across the way. "I just hate to leave her like that," Connie said earnestly, but the boy said that she wouldn't be alone for long. So they went out to his car, and on the way Connie couldn't help but let her eyes wander over the windshields and faces all around her, her face gleaming with a joy that had nothing to do with Eddie or even this place; it might have been the music. She drew her shoulders up and sucked in her breath with the pure pleasure of being alive, and just at that moment she happened to glance at a face just a few feet away from hers. It was a boy with shaggy black hair, in a convertible jalopy painted gold. He stared at her and then his lips widened into a grin. Connie slit her eyes at him and turned away, but she couldn't help glancing back and there he was, still watching her. He wagged a finger and laughed and said, "Gonna get you, baby," and Connie turned away again without Eddie noticing anything.

She spent three hours with him, at the restaurant where they ate hamburgers and drank Cokes in wax cups that were always sweating, and then down an alley a mile or so away, and when he left her off at five to eleven only the movie house was still open at the plaza. Her girl friend was there, talking with a boy. When Connie came up, the two girls smiled at each other and Connie said, "How was the movie?" and the girl said, "*You* should know." They rode off with the girl's father, sleepy and pleased, and Connie couldn't help but look back at the darkened shopping plaza with its big empty parking lot and its signs that were faded and ghostly now, and over at the drive-in restaurant where cars were still circling tirelessly. She couldn't hear the music at this distance.

Next morning June asked her how the movie was and Connie said, "So-so."

She and that girl and occasionally another girl went out several times a week, and the rest of the time Connie spent around the house—it was summer vacation—getting in her mother's way and thinking, dreaming about the boys she met. But all the boys fell back and dissolved into a single face that was not even a face but an idea, a feeling, mixed up with the urgent insistent pounding of the music and the humid night air of July. Connie's mother kept dragging her back to the daylight by finding things for her to do or saying suddenly, "What's this about the Pettinger girl?"

And Connie would say nervously, "Oh, her. That dope." She always drew thick clear lines between herself and such girls, and her mother was simple and kind enough to believe it. Her mother was so simple, Connie thought, that it was maybe cruel to fool her so much. Her mother went scuffling around the house in old bedroom slippers and complained over the telephone to one sister about the other, then the other called up and the two of them complained about the third one. If June's name was mentioned her mother's tone was approving, and if Connie's name was mentioned it was disapproving. This did not really mean she disliked Connie, and actually Connie thought that her mother preferred her to June just because she was prettier, but the two of them kept up a pretense of exasperation, a sense that they were tugging and strug-gling over something of little value to either of them. Sometimes, over coffee, they were almost friends, but something would come up—some vexation that was like a fly buzzing suddenly around their heads—and their faces went hard with contempt.

One Sunday Connie got up at eleven—none of them bothered with church—and washed her hair so that it could dry all day long in the sun. Her parents and sister were going to a barbecue at an aunt's house and Connie said no, she wasn't interested, rolling her eyes to let her mother know just what she thought of it. "Stay home alone then," her mother said sharply. Connie sat out back in a lawn chair and watched them drive away, her father quiet and bald, hunched around so that he could back the car out, her mother with a look that was still angry and not at all softened through the windshield, and in the back seat poor old June, all dressed up as if she didn't know what a barbecue was, with all the running yelling kids and the flies. Connie sat with her eyes closed in the sun, dreaming and dazed with the warmth about her as if this were a kind of love, the caresses of love, and her mind slipped over onto thoughts of the boy she had been with the night before and how nice he had been, how sweet it always was, not the way someone like June would suppose but sweet, gentle, the way it was in movies and promised in songs; and when she opened her eyes she hardly knew where she was, the back yard ran off into weeds and a fence-like line of trees and behind it the sky was perfectly blue and still. The asbestos "ranch house" that was now three years old startled her—it looked small. She shook her head as if to get awake.

It was too hot. She went inside the house and turned on the radio to drown out the quiet. She sat on the edge of her bed, barefoot, and listened for an hour and a half, to a program called XYZ Sunday Jamboree, record after record of hard, fast, shrieking songs she sang along with, interspersed by exclamations from "Bobby King": "An' look here, you girls at Napoleon's—Son and Charley want you to pay real close attention to this song coming up!"

And Connie paid close attention herself, bathed in a glow of slow-pulsed joy that seemed to rise mysteriously out of the music itself and lay languidly about the airless little room, breathed in and breathed out with each gentle rise and fall of her chest.

After a while she heard a car coming up the drive. She sat up at once, startled, because it couldn't be her father so soon. The gravel kept crunching all the way in from the road—the driveway was long—and Connie ran to the window. It was a car she didn't know. It was an open jalopy, painted a bright gold that caught the sunlight opaquely. Her heart began to pound and her fingers snatched at her hair, checking it, and she whispered, "Christ, Christ," wondering how she looked. The car came to a stop at the side door and the horn sounded four short taps, as if this were a signal Connie knew.

She went into the kitchen and approached the door slowly, then hung out the screen door, her bare toes curling down off the step. There were two boys in the car and now she recognized the driver: he had shaggy, shabby black hair that looked crazy as a wig and he was grinning at her.

"I ain't late, am I?" he said.

"Who the hell do you think you are?" Connie said.

"Toldja I'd be out, didn't I?"

"I don't even know who you are."

She spoke sullenly, careful to show no interest or pleasure, and he spoke in a fast, bright monotone. Connie looked past him to the other boy, taking her time. He had fair brown hair, with a lock that fell onto his forehead. His sideburns gave him a fierce, embarrassed look, but so far he hadn't even bothered to glance at her. Both boys wore sunglasses. The driver's glasses were metallic and mirrored everything in miniature.

"You wanta come for a ride?" he said.

Connie smirked and let her hair fall loose over one shoulder.

"Don'tcha like my car? New paint job," he said. "Hey."

"What?"

"You're cute."

She pretended to fidget, chasing flies away from the door.

"Don'tcha believe me, or what?" he said.

"Look, I don't even know who you are," Connie said in disgust.

"Hey, Ellie's got a radio, see. Mine broke down." He lifted his friend's arm and showed her the little transistor radio the boy was holding, and now Connie began to hear the music. It was the same program that was playing inside the house.

"Bobby King?" she said.

"I listen to him all the time. I think he's great."

"He's kind of great," Connie said reluctantly.

"Listen, that guy's *great*. He knows where the action is."

Connie blushed a little, because the glasses made it impossible for her to see just what this boy was looking at. She couldn't decide if she liked him or if he was a jerk, and so she dawdled in the doorway and wouldn't come down or go back inside. She said, "What's all that stuff painted on your car?"

"Can'tcha read it?" He opened the door very carefully, as if he were afraid it might fall off. He slid out just as carefully, planting his feet firmly on the ground, the tiny metallic world in his glasses slowing down like gelatine hardening, and in the midst of it Connie's bright green blouse. "This here is my name, to begin with," he said. ARNOLD FRIEND was written in tarlike black letters on the side, with a drawing of a round, grinning face that reminded Connie of a pumpkin, except it wore sunglasses. "I wanta introduce myself. I'm Arnold Friend and that's my real name and I'm gonna be your friend, honey, and inside the car's Ellie Oscar, he's kinda shy." Ellie brought his transistor radio up to his shoulder and balanced it there. "Now, these numbers are a secret code, honey," Arnold Friend explained. He read off the numbers 33, 19, 17 and raised his eyebrows at her to see what she thought of that, but she didn't think much of it. The left rear fender had been smashed and around it was written, on the gleaming gold background: DONE BY CRAZY WOMAN DRIVER. Connie had to laugh at that. Arnold Friend was pleased at her laughter and looked up at her. "Around the other side's a lot more—you wanta come and see them?"

"No."

"Why not?"

"Why should I?"

"Don'tcha wanta see what's on the car? Don'tcha wanta go for a ride?"

"I don't know."

"Why not?"

"I got things to do."

"Like what?"

"Things."

He laughed as if she had said something funny. He slapped his thighs. He was standing in a strange way, leaning back against the car as if he were balancing himself. He wasn't tall, only an inch or so taller than she would be if she came down to him. Connie liked the way he was dressed, which was the way all of them dressed: tight faded jeans stuffed into black, scuffed boots, a belt that pulled his waist in and showed how lean he was, and a white pull-over shirt that was a little soiled and showed the hard small muscles of his arms and shoulders. He looked as if he probably did hard work, lifting and carrying things. Even his neck looked muscular. And his face was a familiar face, somehow; the jaw and chin and cheeks slightly darkened because he hadn't shaved for a day or two, and the nose long and hawklike, sniffing as if she were a treat he was going to gobble up and it was all a joke.

"Connie, you ain't telling the truth. This is your day set aside for a ride with me and you know it," he said, still laughing. The way he straightened and recovered from his fit of laughing showed that it had been all fake.

"How do you know what my name is?" she said suspiciously.

"It's Connie."

"Maybe and maybe not."

"I know my Connie," he said, wagging his finger. Now she remembered him even better, back at the restaurant, and her cheeks warmed at the thought of how she had sucked in her breath just at the moment she passed him—how she must have looked to him. And he had remembered her. "Ellie and I come out here especially for you," he said. "Ellie can sit in back. How about it?"

"Where?"

"Where what?"

"Where're we going?"

He looked at her. He took off the sunglasses and she saw how pale the skin around his eyes was, like holes that were not in shadow but instead in light. His eyes were like chips of broken glass that catch the light in an amiable way. He smiled. It was as if the idea of going for a ride somewhere, to someplace, was a new idea to him.

"Just for a ride, Connie sweetheart."

"I never said my name was Connie," she said.

"But I know what it is. I know your name and all about you, lots of things," Arnold Friend said. He had not moved yet but stood still leaning back against the side of his jalopy. "I took a special interest in you, such a pretty girl, and found out all about you—like I know your parents and sister are gone somewheres and I know where and how long they're going to be gone, and I know who you were with last night, and your best girl friend's name is Betty. Right?"

He spoke in a simple lilting voice, exactly as if he were reciting the words to a song. His smile assured her that everything was fine. In the car Ellie turned up the volume on his radio and did not bother to look around at them.

"Ellie can sit in the back seat," Arnold Friend said. He indicated his friend with a casual jerk of his chin, as if Ellie did not count and she should not bother with him.

"How'd you find out all that stuff?" Connie said.

"Listen: Betty Schultz and Tony Fitch and Jimmy Pettinger and Nancy Pettinger," he said in a chant. "Raymond Stanley and Bob Hutter—"

"Do you know all those kids?"

"I know everybody."

"Look, you're kidding. You're not from around here."

"Sure.

"But—how come we never saw you before?"

"Sure you saw me before," he said. He looked down at his boots, as if he were a little offended. "You just don't remember."

"I guess I'd remember you," Connie said.

"Yeah?" He looked up at this, beaming. He was pleased. He began to mark time with the music from Ellie's radio, tapping his fists lightly together. Connie looked away from his smile to the car, which was painted so bright it almost hurt her eyes to look at it. She looked at that name, ARNOLD FRIEND. And up at the front fender was an expression that was familiar—MAN THE FLYING SAUCERS. It was an expression kids had used the year before but didn't use this year. She looked at it for a while as if the words meant something to her that she did not yet know.

"What're you thinking about? Huh?" Arnold Friend demanded. "Not worried about your hair blowing around in the car, are you?"

"No."

"Think I maybe can't drive good?"

"How do I know?"

"You're a hard girl to handle. How come?" he said. "Don't you know I'm your friend? Didn't you see me put my sign in the air when you walked by?"

"What sign?"

"My sign." And he drew an X in the air, leaning out toward her. They were maybe ten feet apart. After his hand fell back to his side the X was still in the air, almost visible. Connie let the screen door close and stood perfectly still inside it, listening to the music from her radio and the boy's blend together. She stared at Arnold Friend. He stood there so stiffly relaxed, pretending to be relaxed, with one hand idly on the door handle as if he were keeping himself up that way and had no intention of ever moving again. She recognized most things about him, the tight jeans that showed his thighs and buttocks and the greasy leather boots and the tight shirt, and even that slippery friendly smile of his, that sleepy dreamy smile that all the boys used to get across ideas they didn't want to put into words. She recognized all this and also the sing-song way he talked, slightly mocking, kidding, but serious and a little melancholy, and she recognized the way he tapped one fist against the other in homage to the perpetual music behind him. But all these things did not come together.

She said suddenly, "Hey, how old are you?"

His smile faded. She could see then that he wasn't a kid, he was much older—thirty, maybe more. At this knowledge her heart began to pound faster.

"That's a crazy thing to ask. Can'tcha see I'm your own age?"

"Like hell you are."

"Or maybe a coupla years older. I'm eighteen."

"Eighteen?" she said doubtfully.

He grinned to reassure her and lines appeared at the corners of his mouth. His teeth were big and white. He grinned so broadly his eyes became slits and she saw how thick the lashes were, thick and black as if painted with a black tarlike material. Then, abruptly, he seemed to become embarrassed and looked over his shoulder at Ellie. "*Him*, he's crazy," he said. "Ain't he a riot? He's a nut, a real character." Ellie was still listening to the music. His sunglasses told nothing about what he was thinking. He wore a bright orange shirt unbuttoned halfway to show his chest, which was a pale, bluish chest and not muscular like Arnold Friend's. His shirt collar was turned up all around and the very tips of the collar pointed out past his chin as if they were protecting him. He was pressing the transistor radio up against his ear and sat there in a kind of. daze, right in the sun.

"He's kinda strange," Connie said.

"Hey, she says you're kinda strange! Kinda strange!" Arnold Friend cried. He pounded on the car to get Ellie's attention. Ellie turned for the first time and Connie saw with shock that he wasn't a kid either—he had a fair, hairless face, cheeks reddened slightly as if the veins grew too close to the surface of his skin, the face of a forty-year-old baby. Connie felt a wave of dizziness rise in her at this sight and she stared at him as if waiting for something to change the shock of the moment, make it all right again. Ellie's lips kept shaping words, mumbling along with the words biasing in his ear.

"Maybe you two better go away," Connie said faintly.

"What? How come?" Arnold Friend cried. "We come out here to take you for a ride. It's Sunday." He had the voice of the man on the radio now. It was the same voice, Connie thought. "Don'tcha know it's Sunday all day? And honey, no matter who you were with last night, today you're with Arnold Friend and don't you forget it! Maybe you better step out here," he said, and this last was in a different voice. It was a little flatter, as if the heat was finally getting to him.

"No. I got things to do."

"Hey."

"You two better leave."

"We ain't leaving until you come with us."

"Like hell I am—"

"Connie, don't fool around with me. I mean—I mean, don't fool *around*," he said, shaking his head. He laughed incredulously. He placed his sunglasses on top of his head, carefully, as if he were indeed wearing a wig, and brought the stems down behind his ears. Connie stared at him, another wave of dizziness and fear rising in her so that for a moment he wasn't even in focus but was just a blur standing there against his gold car, and she had the idea that he had driven up the driveway all right but had come from nowhere before that and belonged nowhere and that everything about him and even about the music that was so familiar to her was only half real.

"If my father comes and sees you—"

"He ain't coming. He's at a barbecue."

"How do you know that?"

"Aunt Tillie's. Right now they're—uh—they're drinking. Sitting around," he said vaguely, squinting as if he were staring all the way to town and over to Aunt Tillie's back yard. Then the vision seemed to get clear and he nodded energetically. "Yeah. Sitting around. There's your sister in a blue dress, huh? And high heels, the poor sad bitch—nothing like you, Sweetheart! And your mother's helping some fat woman with the corn, they're cleaning the corn—husking the corn—"

"What fat woman?" Connie cried.

"How do I know what fat woman, I don't know every goddam fat woman in the world!" Arnold Friend laughed.

"Oh, that's Mrs. Hornsby. . . . Who invited her?" Connie said. She felt a little lightheaded. Her breath was coming quickly.

"She's too fat. I don't like them fat. I like them the way you are, honey," he said, smiling sleepily at her. They stared at each other for a while through the screen door. He said softly, "Now, what you're going to do is this: you're going to come out that door. You're going to sit up front with me and Ellie's going to sit in the back, the hell with Ellie, right? This isn't Ellie's date. You're my date. I'm your lover, honey."

"What? You're crazy—"

"Yes. I'm your lover. You don't know what that is but you will," he said. "I know that too. I know all about you. But look: it's real nice and you couldn't ask for nobody better than me, or more polite. I always keep my word. I'll tell you how it is, I'm always nice at first, the first time. I'll hold you so tight you won't think you have to try to get away or pretend anything because you'll know you can't. And I'll come inside you where it's all secret and you'll give in to me and you'll love me—"

"Shut up! You're crazy!" Connie said. She backed away from the door. She put her hands up against her ears as if she'd heard something terrible, something not meant for her. "People don't talk like that, you're crazy," she muttered. Her heart was almost too big now for her chest and its pumping made sweat break out all over her. She looked out to see Arnold Friend pause and then take a step toward the porch, lurching. He almost fell. But, like a clever drunken man, he managed to catch his balance. He wobbled in his high boots and grabbed hold of one of the porch posts.

"Honey?" he said. "You still listening?"

"Get the hell out of here!"

"Be nice, honey. Listen."

"I'm going to call the police—"

He wobbled again and out of the side of his mouth came a fast spat curse, an aside not meant for her to hear. But even this "Christ!" sounded forced. Then he began to smile again. She watched this smile come, awkward as if he were smiling from inside a mask. His whole face was a mask, she thought wildly, tanned down to his throat but then running out as if he had plastered makeup on his face but had forgotten about his throat.

"Honey—? Listen, here's how it is. I always tell the truth and I promise you this: I ain't coming in that house after you."

"You better not! I'm going to call the police if you—if you don't—"

"Honey," he said, talking right through her voice, "honey. I'm not coming in there but you are coming out here. You know why?"

She was panting. The kitchen looked like a place she had never seen before, some room she had run inside but that wasn't good enough, wasn't going to help her. The kitchen window had never had a curtain, after three years, and there were dishes in the sink for her to do—probably—and if you ran your hand across the table you'd probably feel something sticky there.

"You listening, honey? Hey?"

"—going to call the police—"

"Soon as you touch the phone I don't need to keep my promise and can come inside. You won't want that."

She rushed forward and tried to lock the door. Her fingers were shaking. "But why lock it," Arnold Friend said gently, talking right into her face. "It's just a screen door. It's just nothing." One of his boots was at a strange angle, as if his foot wasn't in it. It pointed out to the left, bent at the ankle. "I mean, anybody can break through a screen door and glass and wood and iron or anything else if he needs to, anybody at all, and specially Arnold Friend. If the place got lit up with a fire, honey, you'd come runnin' out into my arms, right into my arms an' safe at home—like you knew I was your lover and'd stopped fooling around. I don't mind a nice shy girl but I don't like no fooling around." Part of those words were spoken with a slight rhythmic lilt, and Connie somehow recognized them—the echo of a song from last year, about a girl rushing into her boy friend's arms and coming home again—

Connie stood barefoot on the linoleum floor, staring at him. "What do you want?" she whispered.

"I want you," he said.

"What?"

"Seen you that night and thought, that's the one, yes sir. I never needed to look anymore."

"But my father's coming back. He's coming to get me. I had to wash my hair first—" She spoke in a dry, rapid voice, hardly raising it for him to hear.

"No, your daddy is not coming and yes, you had to wash your hair and you washed it for me. It's nice and shining and all for me. I thank you sweetheart," he said with a mock bow, but again he almost lost his balance. He had to bend and adjust his boots. Evidently his feet did not go all the way down; the boots must have been stuffed with something so that he would seem taller. Connie stared out at him and behind him at Ellie in the car, who seemed to be looking off toward Connie's right, into nothing. Then Ellie said, pulling the words out of the air one after another as if he were just discovering them, "You want me to pull out the phone?"

"Shut your mouth and keep it shut," Arnold Friend said, his face red from bending over or maybe from embarrassment because Connie had seen his boots. "This ain't none of your business."

"What—what are you doing? What do you want?" Connie said. "If I call the police they'll get you, they'll arrest you—"

"Promise was not to come in unless you touch that phone, and I'll keep that promise," he said. He resumed his erect position and tried to force his shoulders back. He sounded like a hero in a movie, declaring something important. But he spoke too loudly and it was as if he were speaking to someone behind Connie. "I ain't made plans for coming in that house where I don't belong but just for you to come out to me, the way you should. Don't you know who I am?"

"You're crazy," she whispered. She backed away from the door but did not want to go into another part of the house, as if this would give him permission to come through the door. "What do you . . . you're crazy, you. . . ."

"Huh? What're you saying, honey?"

Her eyes darted everywhere in the kitchen. She could not remember what it was, this room.

"This is how it is, honey: you come out and we'll drive away, have a nice ride. But if you don't come out we're gonna wait till your people come home and then they're all going to get it."

"You want that telephone pulled out?" Ellie said. He held the radio away from his ear and grimaced, as if without the radio the air was too much for him.

"I toldja shut up, Ellie," Arnold Friend said "you're deaf, get a hearing aid, right? Fix yourself up. This little girl's no trouble and's gonna be nice to me, so Ellie keep to yourself, this ain't your date—right? Don't hem in on me, don't hog, don't crush, don't bird dog, don't trail me," he said in a rapid, meaningless voice, as if he were running through all the expressions he'd learned but was no longer sure which of them was in style, then rushing on to new ones, making them up with his eyes closed. "Don't crawl under my fence, don't squeeze in my chipmunk hole, don't sniff my glue, suck my popsicle, keep your own greasy fingers on yourself!" He shaded his eyes and peered in at Connie, who was backed against the kitchen table. "Don't mind him, honey, he's just a creep. He's a dope. Right? I'm the boy for you and like I said, you come out here nice like a lady and give me your hand, and nobody else gets hurt, I mean, your nice old bald-headed daddy and your mummy and your sister in her high heels. Because listen: why bring them in this?"

"Leave me alone," Connie whispered.

"Hey, you know that old woman down the road, the one with the chickens and stuff—you know her?"

"She's dead!"

"Dead? What? You know her?" Arnold Friend said.

"She's dead—"

"Don't you like her?"

"She's dead—she's—she isn't here any more—"

"But don't you like her, I mean, you got something against her? Some grudge or something?" Then his voice dipped as if he were conscious of a rudeness. He touched the sunglasses perched up on top of his head as if to make sure they were still there. "Now, you be a good girl."

"What are you going to do?"

"Just two things, or maybe three," Arnold Friend said. "But I promise it won't last long and you'll like me the way you get to like people you're close to. You will. It's all over for you here, so come on out. You don't want your people in any trouble, do you?"

She turned and bumped against a chair or something, hurting her leg, but she ran into the back room and picked up the telephone. Something roared in her ear, a tiny roaring, and she was so sick with fear that she could do nothing but listen to it—the telephone was clammy and very heavy and her fingers groped down to the dial but were too weak to touch it. She began to scream into the phone, into the roaring. She cried out, she cried for her mother, she felt her breath start jerking back and forth in her lungs as if it were something Arnold Friend was stabbing her with again and again with no tenderness. A noisy sorrowful wailing rose all about her and she was locked inside it the way she was locked inside this house.

After a while she could hear again. She was sitting on the floor with her wet back against the wall.

Arnold Friend was saying from the door, "That's a good girl. Put the phone back."

She kicked the phone away from her.

"No, honey. Pick it up. Put it back right."

She picked it up and put it back. The dial tone stopped.

"That's a good girl. Now, you come outside."

She was hollow with what had been fear but what was now just an emptiness. All that screaming had blasted it out of her. She sat, one leg cramped under her, and deep inside her brain was something like a pinpoint of light that kept going and would not let her relax. She thought, I'm not going to see my mother again. She thought, I'm not going to sleep in my bed again. Her bright green blouse was all wet.

Arnold Friend said, in a gentle-loud voice that was like a stage voice, "The place where you came from ain't there any more, and where you had in mind to go is cancelled out. This place you are now—inside your daddy's house—is nothing but a cardboard box I can knock down any time. You know that and always did know it. You hear me?"

She thought, I have got to think. I have got to know what to do.

"We'll go out to a nice field, out in the country here where it smells so nice and it's sunny," Arnold Friend said. "I'll have my arms tight around you so you won't need to try to get away and I'll show you what love is like, what it does. The hell with this house! It looks solid all right," he said. He ran his fingernail down the screen and the noise did not make Connie shiver, as it would have the day before. "Now, put your hand on your heart, honey. Feel that? That feels solid too but we know better. Be nice to me, be sweet like you can because what else is there for a girl like you but to be sweet and pretty and give in?—and get away before her people get back?"

She felt her pounding heart. Her hand seemed to enclose it. She thought for the first time in her life that it was nothing that was hers, that belonged to her, but just a pounding, living thing inside this body that wasn't really hers either.

"You don't want them to get hurt," Arnold Friend went on. "Now, get up, honey. Get up all by yourself."

She stood.

"Now, turn this way. That's right. Come over here to me.—Ellie, put that away, didn't I tell you? You dope. You miserable creepy dope," Arnold Friend said. His words were not angry but only part of an incantation. The incantation was kindly. "Now, come out through the kitchen to me, honey, and let's see a smile, try it, you're a brave, sweet little girl and now they're eating corn and hot dogs cooked to bursting over an outdoor fire, and they don't know one thing about you and never did and honey, you're better than them because not a one of them would have done this for you."

Connie felt the linoleum under her feet; it was cool. She brushed her hair back out of her eyes. Arnold Friend let go of the post tentatively and opened his arms for her, his elbows pointing in toward each other and his wrists limp, to show that this was an embarrassed embrace and a little mocking, he didn't want to make her self-conscious.

She put out her hand against the screen. She watched herself push the door slowly open as if she were back safe somewhere in the other doorway, watching this body and this head of long hair moving out into the sunlight where Arnold Friend waited.

"My sweet little blue-eyed girl," he said in a half-sung sigh that had nothing to do with her brown eyes but was taken up just the same by the vast sunlit reaches of the land behind him and on all sides of him—-so much land that Connie had never seen before and did not recognize except to know that she was going to it.

CONSTRUCTING A READING

1. With your group members see if you can mark the stages of plot in this story. It's not necessary for you to agree about every detail, but do try to see how Oates puts the narrative together.

2. This story might be called "suspenseful." If you agree, explain how Oates's plotting contributes to the building of suspense.

3. Look carefully at Oates's conclusion. What do you think happens after the last sentence of the story? How do you know?

4. How do you think Oates wants you to respond to Connie's predicament at the end of the story? How do you respond? How does your age and/or gender affect your response?

5. With your group members, make a list of the discursive details that Oates
    uses to characterize Connie and Arnold. What do you learn from these
    details, for example the way Connie wears her hair, the way Arnold
    dresses, the way Connie dresses, and so on?

Story Order and Discourse Order

One of the most important elements of narration is a distinction between *story order*, the events that are described in the story in chronological order, and *discourse order*, the order in which the events are actually told. "Babylon Revisited," by F. Scott Fitzgerald, illustrates the distinction. The story takes place over three days in 1931, during the great Depression that followed the stock market crash of October 1929. But in the course of the narration, the protagonist, Charles Wales, remembers and describes certain events of 1929 and 1930. An account of the three days in 1931, interrupted by the earlier episodes, constitutes this story's discourse order.

Babylon Revisited

F. Scott Fitzgerald

"And where's Mr. Campbell?" Charlie asked.

"Gone to Switzerland. Mr. Campbell's a pretty sick man, Mr. Wales."

"I'm sorry to hear that. And George Hardt?" Charlie inquired.

"Back in America, gone to work."

"And where is the Snow Bird?"

"He was in here last week. Anyway, his friend, Mr. Schaeffer, is in Paris."

Two familiar names from the long list of a year and a half ago. Charlie scribbled an address in his notebook and tore out the page.

"If you see Mr. Schaeffer, give him this," he said. "It's my brother-in-law's address. I haven't settled on a hotel yet."

He was not really disappointed to find Paris was so empty. But the stillness in the Ritz bar was strange and portentous. It was not an American bar any more—he felt polite in it, and not as if he owned it. It had gone back into France. He felt the stillness from the moment he got out of the taxi and saw the doorman, usually in a frenzy of activity at this hour, gossiping with a *chasseur* by the servants' entrance.

Passing through the corridor, he heard only a single, bored voice in the once-clamorous women's room. When he turned into the bar he traveled the twenty feet of green carpet with his eyes fixed straight ahead by old habit; and then, with his foot firmly on the rail, he turned and surveyed the room, encountering only a single pair of eyes that fluttered up from a newspaper in the corner. Charlie asked for the head barman, Paul, who in the latter days of the bull market had come to work in his own custom-built car—disembarking, however, with due nicety at the nearest corner. But Paul was at his country house today and Alix giving him information.

"No, no more," Charlie said, "I'm going slow these days."

Alix congratulated him: "You were going pretty strong a couple of years ago."

"I'll stick to it all right," Charlie assured him. "I've stuck to it for over a year and a half now."

"How do you find conditions in America?"

"I haven't been to America for months. I'm in business in Prague, representing a couple of concerns there. They don't know about me down there."

Alix smiled.

"Remember the night of George Hardt's bachelor dinner here?" said Charlie. "By the way, what's become of Claude Fessenden?"

Alix lowered his voice confidentially: "He's in Paris, but he doesn't come here any more. Paul doesn't allow it. He ran up a bill of thirty thousand francs, charging all his drinks and his lunches, and usually his dinner, for more than a year. And when Paul finally told him he had to pay, he gave him a bad check."

Alix shook his head sadly.

"I don't understand it, such a dandy fellow. Now he's all bloated up—" He made a plump apple of his hand.

Charlie watched a group of strident queens installing themselves in a corner.

"Nothing affects them," he thought. "Stocks rise and fall, people loaf or work, but they go on forever." The place oppressed him. He called for the dice and shook with Alix for the drink.

"Here for long, Mr. Wales?"

"I'm here for four or five days to see my little girl."

"Oh-h! You have a little girl?"

Outside, the fire-red, gas-blue, ghost-green signs shone smokily through the tranquil rain. It was late afternoon and the streets were in movement; the *bistros* gleamed. At the corner of the Boulevard des Capucines he took a taxi. The Place de la Concorde moved by in pink majesty; they crossed the logical Seine, and Charlie felt the sudden provincial quality of the left bank.

Charlie directed his taxi to the Avenue de l'Opera, which was out of his way. But he wanted to see the blue hour spread over the magnificent façade, and imagine that the cab horns, playing endlessly the first few bars of *Le Plus que Lent*, were the trumpets of the Second Empire. They were closing the iron grill in front of Brentano's Book-store, and people were already at dinner behind the trim little bourgeois hedge of Duval's. He had never eaten at a really cheap restaurant in Paris. Five course dinner, four francs fifty, eighteen cents, wine included. For some odd reason he wished that he had.

As they rolled on to the Left Bank and he felt its sudden provincialism, he thought, "I spoiled this city for myself. I didn't realize it, but the days came along one after another, and then two years were gone, and everything was gone, and I was gone."

He was thirty-five, and good to look at. The Irish mobility of his face was sobered by a deep wrinkle between his eyes. As he rang his brother-in-law's bell in the Rue Palatine, the wrinkle deepened till it pulled down his brows; he felt a cramping sensation in his belly. From behind the maid who opened the door darted a lovely little girl of nine who shrieked "Daddy!" and flew up, struggling like a fish, into his arms. She pulled his head around by one ear and set her cheek against his.

"My old pie," he said.

"Oh, daddy, daddy, daddy, daddy, dads, dads, dads!"

She drew him into the salon, where the family waited, a boy and a girl his daughter's age, his sister-in-law and her husband. He greeted Marion with his voice pitched carefully to avoid either feigned enthusiasm or dislike, but her response was more frankly tepid, though she minimized her expression of unalterable distrust by directing her regard toward his child. The two men clasped hands in a friendly way and Lincoln Peters rested his for a moment on Charlie's shoulder.

The room was warm and comfortably American. The three children moved intimately about, playing through the yellow oblongs that led to other rooms; the cheer of six o'clock spoke in the eager smacks of the fire and the sounds of French activity in the kitchen. But Charlie did not relax; his heart sat up rigidly in his body and he drew confidence from his daughter, who from time to time came close to him, holding in her arms the doll he had brought.

"Really extremely well," he declared in answer to Lincoln's question. "'There's a lot of business there that isn't moving at all, but we're doing even better than ever. In fact, damn well. I'm bringing my sister over from America next month to keep house for me. My income last year was bigger than it was when I had money. You see, the Czechs—"

His boasting was for a specific purpose; but after a moment, seeing a faint restiveness in Lincoln's eye, he changed the subject:

"Those are fine children of yours, well brought up, good manners."

"We think Honoria's a great little girl too."

Marion Peters came back from the kitchen. She was a tall woman with worried eyes, who had once possessed a fresh American loveliness. Charlie had never been sensitive to it and was always surprised when people spoke of how pretty she had been. From the first there had been an instinctive antipathy between them.

"Well, how do you find Honoria?" she asked.

"Wonderful. I was astonished how much she's grown in ten months. All the children are looking well."

"We haven't had a doctor for a year. How do you like being back in Paris?"

"It seems very funny to see so few Americans around."

"I'm delighted," Marion said vehemently. "Now at least you can go into a store without their assuming you're a millionaire. We've suffered like everybody, but on the whole it's a good deal pleasanter."

"But it was nice while it lasted," Charlie said. "We were a sort of royalty, almost infallible, with a sort of magic around us. In the bar this afternoon" he stumbled, seeing his mistake—"there wasn't a man I knew."

She looked at him keenly. "I should think you'd have had enough of bars."

"I only stayed a minute. I take one drink every afternoon, and no more."

"Don't you want a cocktail before dinner?" Lincoln asked.

"I take only one drink every afternoon, and I've had that."

"I hope you keep to it," said Marion.

Her dislike was evident in the coldness with which she spoke, but Charlie only smiled; he had larger plans. Her very aggressiveness gave him an advantage, and he knew enough to wait. He wanted them to initiate the discussion of what they knew had brought him to Paris.

At dinner he couldn't decide whether Honoria was most like them or her mother. Fortunate if she didn't combine the traits of both that had brought them to disaster. A great wave of protectiveness went over him. He thought he knew what to do for her. He believed in character; he wanted to jump back a whole generation and trust in character again as the eternally valuable element. Everything else wore out.

He left soon after dinner, but not to go home. He was curious to see Paris by night with clearer and more judicious eyes than those of other days. He bought a *strapontin* for the Casino and watched Josephine Baker go through her chocolate arabesques.

After an hour be left and strolled toward Montmartre, up the Rue Pigalle into the Place Blanche. The rain had stopped and there were a few people in evening clothes disembarking from taxis in front of cabarets, and *cocottes* prowling singly or in pairs, and many Negroes. He passed a lighted door from which issued music, and stopped with the sense of familiarity; it was Bricktop's, where he had parted with so many hours and so much money. A few doors farther on he found another ancient rendezvous and incautiously put his head inside. Immediately an eager orchestra burst into sound, a pair of professional dancers leaped to their feet and a maitre d'hotel swooped toward him, crying, "Crowd just arriving, sir!" But he withdrew quickly.

"You have to be damn drunk." he thought.

Zelli's was closed, the bleak and sinister cheap hotels surrounding it were dark; up in the Rue Blanche there was more light and a local, colloquial French crowd. The Poet's Cave had disappeared, but the two great mouths of the Café of Heaven and the Café of Hell still yawned—even devoured, as he watched, the meager contents of a tourist bus—a German, a Japanese, and an American couple who glanced at him with frightened eyes.

So much for the effort and ingenuity of Montmartre. All the catering to vice and waste was on an utterly childish scale, and he suddenly realized the meaning of the word "dissipate"—to dissipate into thin air; to make nothing out of something. In the little hours of the night every move from place to place was an enormous human jump, an increase of paying for the privilege of slower and slower motion.

He remembered thousand-franc notes given to an orchestra for playing a single number, hundred-franc notes tossed to a doorman for calling a cab.

But it hadn't been given for nothing.

It had been given, even the most wildly squandered sum, as an offering to destiny that he might not remember the things most worth remembering, the things that now he would always remember—his child taken from his control, his wife escaped to a grave in Vermont.

In the glare of a *brasserie* a woman spoke to him. He bought her some eggs and coffee, and then, eluding her encouraging stare, gave her a twenty-franc note and took a taxi to his hotel.

II

He woke upon a fine fall day—football weather. The depression of yesterday was gone and he liked the people on the streets. At noon he sat opposite Honoria at Le Grand Vatel, the only restaurant he could think of not reminiscent of champagne dinners and long luncheons that began at two and ended in a blurred and vague twilight

"Now, how about vegetables? Oughtn't you to have some vegetables?"

"Well, yes."

"Here's *épinards* and *chou-fleur* and carrots and *haricots*."

"I'd like *chou-fleur*."

"Wouldn't you like to have two vegetables?"

"I usually only have one at lunch."

The waiter was pretending to be inordinately fond of children. *"Qu'elle est mignonne la petite! Elle parle exactement comme une Française."*

"How about dessert? Shall we wait and see?"

The waiter disappeared. Honoria looked at her father expectantly.

"What are we going to do?"

"First, we're going to that toy store in the Rue Saint-Honoré and buy you anything you like. And then we're going to the vaudeville at the Empire."

She hesitated. "I like it about the vaudeville, but not the toy store."

"Why not?"

"Well, you brought me this doll." She had it with her. "And I've got lots of things. And we're not rich any more, are we?"

"We never were. But today you are to have anything you want."

"All right," she agreed resignedly.

When there had been her mother and a French nurse he had been inclined to be strict; now he extended himself, reached out for a new tolerance, he must be both parents to her and not shut any of her out of communication.

"I want to get to know you," he said gravely. "First let me introduce myself. My name is Charles J. Wales, of Prague."

"Oh, daddy!" her voice cracked with laughter.

"And who are you, please?" he persisted, and she accepted a rôle immediately: "Honoria Wales, Rue Palatine, Paris."

"Married or single?"

"No, not married. Single."

He indicated the doll. "But I see you have a child, madame."

Unwilling to disinherit it, she took it to her heart and thought quickly: "Yes, I've been married, but I'm not married now. My husband is dead."

He went on quickly, "And the child's name?"

"Simone. That's after my best friend at school."

"I'm very pleased that you're doing so well at school."

"I'm third this month," she boasted. "Elsie"—that was her cousin—"is only about eighteenth, and Richard is about at the bottom."

"You like Richard and Elsie, don't you?"

"Oh, yes. I like Richard quite well and I like her all right."

Cautiously and casually he asked: "And Aunt Marion and Uncle Lincoln—which do you like best?".

"Oh, Uncle Lincoln, I guess."

He was increasingly aware of her presence. As they came in, a murmur of ". . . adorable" followed them, and now the people at the next table bent all their silences upon her, staring as if she were something no more conscious than a flower.

"Why don't I live with you?" she asked suddenly. "Because mamma's dead?"

"You must stay here and learn more French. It would have been hard for daddy to take care of you so well."

"I don't really need much taking care of any more. I do everything for myself."

Going out of the restaurant, a man and a woman unexpectedly hailed him.

"Well, the old Wales!"

"Hello there, Lorraine. . . . Dunc."

Sudden ghosts out of the past: Duncan Schaeffer, a friend from college. Lorraine Quarrles, a lovely, pale blonde of thirty; one of a crowd who had helped them make months into days in the lavish times of three years ago.

"My husband couldn't come this year," she said, in answer to his question. "We're poor as hell. So he gave me two hundred a month and told me I could do my worst on that. . . . This your little girl?"

"What about coming back and sitting down?" Duncan asked.

"Can't do it." He was glad for an excuse. As always, he felt Lorraine's passionate, provocative attraction, but his own rhythm was different now.

"Well, how about dinner?" she asked.

"I'm not free. Give me your address and let me call you."

"Charlie, I believe you're sober," she said judicially. "I honestly believe he's sober, Dunc. Pinch him and see if he's sober."

Charlie indicated Honoria with his head. They both laughed.

"What's your address?" said Duncan skeptically.

He hesitated, unwilling to give the name of his hotel.

"I'm not settled yet. I'd better call you. We're going to see the vaudeville at the Empire."

"There! That's what I want to do," Lorraine said. "I want to see some clowns and acrobats and jugglers. That's just what we'll do, Dunc."

"We've got to do an errand first," said Charlie. "Perhaps we'll see you there."

"All right, you snob. . . . Good-by, beautiful little girl."

"Good-by."

Honoria bobbed politely.

Somehow, an unwelcome encounter. They liked him because he was functioning, because he was serious; they wanted to see him, because he was stronger than they were now, because they wanted to draw a certain sustenance from his strength.

At the Empire, Honoria proudly refused to sit upon her father's folded coat. She was already an individual with a code of her own, and Charlie was more and more absorbed by the desire of putting a little of himself into her before she crystallized utterly. It was hopeless to try to know her in so short a time.

Between the acts they came upon Duncan and Lorraine in the lobby where the band was playing.

"Have a drink?"

"All right, but not up at the bar. We'll take a table."

"The perfect father."

Listening abstractedly to Lorraine, Charlie watched Honoria's eyes leave their table, and he followed them wistfully about the room, wondering what they saw. He met her glance and she smiled.

"I liked that lemonade," she said.

What had she said? What had he expected? Going home in a taxi afterward, he pulled her over until her head rested against his chest.

"Darling, do you ever think about your mother?"

"Yes, sometimes," she answered vaguely.

"I don't want you to forget her. Have you got a picture of her?"

"Yes, I think so. Anyhow, Aunt Marion has. Why don't you want me to forget her?"

"She loved you very much."

"I loved her too."

They were silent for a moment.

"Daddy, I want to come and live with you," she said suddenly.

His heart leaped; he had wanted it to come like this.

"Aren't you perfectly happy?"

"Yes, but I love you better than anybody. And you love me better than anybody, don't you, now that mummy's dead?"

"Of course I do. But you won't always like me best, honey. You'll grow up and meet somebody your own age and go marry him and forget you ever had a daddy."

"Yes, that's true," she agreed tranquilly.

He didn't go in. He was coming back at nine o'clock and he wanted to keep himself fresh and new for the thing he must say then.

"When you're safe inside, just show yourself in that window."

"All right. Good-by, dads, dads, dads, dads."

He waited in the dark street until she appeared, all warm and glowing, in the window above and kissed her fingers out into the night.

III

They were waiting. Marion sat behind the coffee service in a dignified black dinner dress that just faintly suggested mourning. Lincoln was walking up and down with the animation of one who had already been talking. They were as anxious as he was to get into the question. He opened it almost immediately:

"'I suppose you know what I want to see you about—why I really came to Paris."

Marion played with the black stars on her necklace and frowned.

"I'm awfully anxious to have a home," he continued. "And I'm awfully anxious to have Honoria in it. I appreciate your taking in Honoria for her mother's sake, but things have changed now"—he hesitated and then continued more forcibly—"changed radically with me, and I want to ask you to reconsider the matter. It would be silly for me to deny that about three years ago I was acting badly—"

Marion looked up at him with hard eyes.

"—but all that's over. As I told you, I haven't had more than a drink a day for over a year, and I take that drink deliberately, so that the idea of alcohol won't get too big in my imagination. You see the idea?"

"No," said Marion succinctly.

"It's a sort of stunt I set myself. It keeps the matter in proportion."

"I get you," said Lincoln. "You don't want to admit it's got any attraction for you"

"Something like that. Sometimes I forget and don't take it. But I try to take it. Anyhow, I couldn't afford to drink in my position. The people I represent are more than satisfied with what I've done, and I'm bringing my sister over from Burlington to keep house for me, and I want awfully to have Honoria too. You know that even when her mother and I weren't getting along well we never let anything that happened touch Honoria. I know she's fond of me and I know I'm able to take care of her and—well, there you are. How do you feel about it?"

He knew that now he would have to take a beating. It would last an hour or two hours, and it would be difficult, but if he modulated his inevitable resentment to the chastened attitude of the reformed sinner, he might win his point in the end.

Keep your temper, he told himself. You don't want to be justified. You want Honoria.

Lincoln spoke first: "We've been talking it over ever since we got your letter last month. We're happy to have Honoria here. She's a dear little thing, and we're glad to be able to help her, but of course that isn't the question—"

Marion interrupted suddenly. "How long are you going to stay sober, Charlie?" she asked.

"Permanently, I hope."

"How can anybody count on that?"

"You know I never did drink heavily until I gave up business and came over here with nothing to do. Then Helen and I began to run around with—"

"Please leave Helen out of it. I can't bear to hear you talk about her like that."

He stared at her grimly; he had never been certain how fond of each other the sisters were in life.

"My drinking only lasted about a year and a half—from the time we came over until I—collapsed."

"It was time enough."

"It was time enough," he agreed.

"My duty is entirely to Helen," she said. "I try to think what she would have wanted me to do. Frankly, from the night you did that terrible thing you haven't really existed for me. I can't help that. She was my sister."

"Yes."

"When she was dying she asked me to look out for Honoria. If you hadn't been in a sanitarium then, it might have helped matters."

He had no answer.

"I'll never in my life be able to forget the morning when Helen knocked at my door, soaked to the skin and shivering, and said you'd locked her out."

Charlie gripped the sides of the chair. This was more difficult than he expected; he wanted to launch out into a long expostulation and explanation, but he only said: "The night I locked her out—" and she interrupted, "I don't feel up to going over that again."

After a moment's silence Lincoln said: "We're getting off the subject. You want Marion to set aside her legal guardianship and give you Honoria. I think the main point for her is whether she has confidence in you or not."

"I don't blame Marion," Charlie said slowly, "but I think she can have entire confidence in me. I had a good record up to three years ago. Of course, it's within human possibilities I might go wrong any time. But if we wait much longer I'll lose Honoria's childhood and my chance for a home." He shook his head. "I'll simply lose her, don't you see?"

"Yes, I see," said Lincoln.

"Why didn't you think of all this before?" Marion asked.

"I suppose I did, from time to time, but Helen and I were getting along badly. When I consented to the guardianship, I was flat on my back in a sanitarium and the market had cleaned me out. I knew I'd acted badly, and I thought if it would bring any peace to Helen, I'd agree to anything. But now it's different. I'm functioning, I'm behaving damn well, so far as—"

"Please don't swear at me," Marion said.

He looked at her, startled. With each remark the force of her dislike became more and more apparent. She had built up all her fear of life into one wall and faced it toward him. This trivial reproof was possibly the result of some trouble with the cook several hours before. Charlie became increasingly alarmed at leaving Honoria in this atmosphere of hostility against himself; sooner or later it would come out, in a word here, a shake of the head there, and some of that distrust would be irrevocably implanted in Honoria. But he pulled his temper down out of his face and shut it up inside him; he had won a point, for Lincoln realized the absurdity of Marion's remark and asked her lightly since when she had objected to the word "damn."

"Another thing," Charlie said: "I'm able to give her certain advantages now. I'm going to take a French governess to Prague with me. I've got a lease on a new apartment—"

He stopped, realizing that he was blundering. They couldn't be expected to accept with equanimity the fact that his income was again twice as large as their own.

"I suppose you can give her more luxuries than we can," said Marion. "When you were throwing away money we were living along watching every ten francs. . . . I suppose you'll start doing it again."

"Oh, no," he said. "I've learned. I worked hard for ten years, you know—until I got lucky in the market, like so many people. Terribly lucky. It didn't seem any use working any more, so I quit."

There was a long silence. All of them felt their nerves straining, and for the first time in a year Charlie wanted a drink. He was sure now that Lincoln Peters wanted him to have his child.

Marion shuddered suddenly; part of her saw that Charlie's feet were planted on the earth now, and her own maternal feeling recognized the naturalness of his desire; but she had lived for a long time with a prejudice—a prejudice founded on a curious disbelief in her sister's happiness, and which, in the shock of one terrible night, had turned to hatred for him. It had all happened at a point in her life where the discouragement of ill health and adverse circumstances made it necessary for her to believe in tangible villainy and a tangible villain.

"I can't help what I think!" she cried out suddenly. "How much you were responsible for Helen's death, I don't know. It's something you'll have to square with your own conscience."

An electric current of agony surged through him; for a moment he was almost on his feet, an unuttered sound echoing in his throat. He hung on to himself for a moment, another moment.

"Hold on there," said Lincoln uncomfortably. "I never thought you were responsible for that."

"Helen died of heart trouble," Charlie said dully.

"Yes, heart trouble." Marion spoke as if the phrase had another meaning for her.

Then, in the flatness that followed her outburst, she saw him plainly and she knew he had somehow arrived at control over the situation. Glancing at her husband, she found no help from him, and as abruptly as if it were a matter of no importance, she threw up the sponge.

"Do what you like!" she cried, springing up from her chair. "She's your child. I'm not the person to stand in your way. I think if it were my child I'd rather see her—" She managed to check herself. "You two decide it. I can't stand this. I'm sick. I'm going to bed."

She hurried from the room; after a moment Lincoln said:

"This has been a hard day for her. You know how strongly she feels." His voice was almost apologetic: "Where a woman gets an idea in her head."

"Of course."

"It's going to be all right. I think she sees now that you—can provide for the child, and so we can't very well stand in your way or Honoria's way."

"Thank you, Lincoln."

"I'd better go along and see how she is."

"I'm going."

He was still trembling when he reached the street, but a walk down the Rue Bonaparte to the *quais* set him up, and as he crossed the Seine, fresh and new by the *quai* lamps, he felt exultant. But back in his room he couldn't sleep. The image of Helen haunted him. Helen whom he had loved so until they had senselessly begun to abuse each other's love, tear it into shreds. On that terrible February night that Marion remembered so vividly, a slow quarrel had gone on for hours. There was a scene at the Florida, and then he attempted to take her home, and then she kissed young Webb at a table; after that there was what she had hysterically said. When he arrived home alone he turned the key in the lock in wild anger. How could he know she would arrive an hour later alone, that there would be a snowstorm in which she wandered about in slippers, too confused to find a taxi? Then the aftermath, her escaping pneumonia by a miracle, and all the attendant horror. They were "reconciled," but that was the beginning of the end, and Marion, who had seen with her own eyes and who imagined it to be one of many scenes from her sister's martyrdom, never forgot.

Going over it again brought Helen nearer, and in the white, soft light that steals upon half sleep near morning he found himself talking to her again. She said that he was perfectly right about Honoria and that she wanted Honoria to be with him. She said she was glad he was being good and doing better. She said a lot of other things—very friendly things—but she was in a swing in a white dress, and swinging faster and faster all the time, so that at the end he could not hear clearly all that she said.

IV

He woke up feeling happy. The door of the world was open again. He made plans, vistas, futures for Honoria and himself, but suddenly he grew sad, remembering all the plans he and Helen had made. She had not planned to die. The present was the thing—work to do and someone to love. But not to love too much, for he knew the injury that a father can do to a daughter or a mother to a son by attaching them too closely: afterward, out in the world, the child would seek in the marriage partner the same blind tenderness and, failing probably to find it, turn against love and life.

It was another bright, crisp day. He called Lincoln Peters at the bank where he worked and asked if he could count on taking Honoria when he left for Prague. Lincoln agreed that there was no reason for delay. One thing—the legal guardianship. Marion wanted to retain that a while longer. She was upset by the whole matter, and it would oil things if she felt that the situation was still in her control for another year. Charlie agreed, wanting only the tangible, visible child.

Then the question of a governess. Charles sat in a gloomy agency and talked to a cross Béarnaise and to a buxom Breton peasant, neither of whom he could have endured. There were others whom he would see tomorrow.

He lunched with Lincoln Peters at Griffons, trying to keep down his exultation.

"There's nothing quite like your own child," Lincoln said. "But you understand how Marion feels too."

"She's forgotten how hard I worked for seven years there," Charlie said. "She just remembers one night."

"There's another thing." Lincoln hesitated. "While you and Helen were tearing around Europe throwing money away, we were just getting along. I didn't touch any of the prosperity because I never got ahead enough to carry anything but my insurance. I think Marion felt there was some kind of injustice in it—you not even working toward the end, and getting richer and richer."

"It went just as quick as it came'" said Charlie

"Yes, a lot of it stayed in the hands of *chasseurs* and saxophone players and maîtres d'hôtel—well, the big party's over now. I just said that to explain Marion's feeling about those crazy years. If you drop in about six o'clock tonight before Marion's too tired, we'll settle the details on the spot."

Back at his hotel, Charlie found a *pneumatique* that had been redirected from the Ritz bar where Charlie had left his address for the purpose of finding a certain man.

> "DEAR CHARLIE: You were so strange when we saw you the other day that I wondered if I did something to offend you. If so, I'm not conscious of it. In fact, I have thought about you too much for the last year, and it's always been in the back of my mind that I might see you if I came over here. We *did* have such good times that crazy spring, like the night you and I stole the butcher's tricycle, and the time we tried to call on the president and you had the old derby rim and the wire cane. Everybody seems so old lately, but I don't feel old a bit. Couldn't we get together some time today for old time's sake? I've got a vile hangover for the moment, but will be feeling better this afternoon and will look for you about five in the sweat-shop at the Ritz.
>
> > "Always devotedly,
> > LORRAINE."

His first feeling was one of awe that he had actually, in his mature years, stolen a tricycle and pedaled Lorraine all over the Étoile between the small hours and dawn. In retrospect it was a nightmare. Locking out Helen didn't fit in with any other act of his life, but the tricycle incident did—it was one of many. How many weeks or months of dissipation to arrive at that condition of utter irresponsibility?

He tried to picture how Lorraine had appeared to him then—very attractive; Helen was unhappy about it, though she said nothing. Yesterday, in the restaurant, Lorraine had seemed trite, blurred, worn away. He emphatically did not want to see her, and he was glad Alix had not given away his hotel address. It was a relief to think, instead, of Honoria, to think of Sundays spent with her and of saying good morning to her and of knowing she was there in his house at night, drawing her breath in the darkness.

At five he took a taxi and bought presents for all the Peters—a piquant cloth doll, a box of Roman soldiers, flowers for Marion, big linen handkerchiefs for Lincoln.

He saw, when he arrived in the apartment, that Marion had accepted the inevitable. She greeted him now as though he were a recalcitrant member of the family, rather than a menacing outsider. Honoria had been told she was going; Charlie was glad to see that her tact made her conceal her excessive happiness. Only on his lap did she whisper her delight and the question "When?" before she slipped away with the other children.

He and Marion were alone for a minute in the room, and on an impulse he spoke out boldly:

"Family quarrels are bitter things. They don't go according to any rules. They're not like aches or wounds; they're more like splits in the skin that won't heal because there's not enough material. I wish you and I could be on better terms."

"Some things are hard to forget," she answered. "It's a question of confidence." There was no answer to this and presently she asked, "When do you propose to take her?"

"As soon as I can get a governess. I hoped the day after to-morrow."

"That's impossible, I've got to get her things in shape. Not before Saturday."

He yielded. Coming back into the room, Lincoln offered him a drink.

"I'll take my daily whisky," he said,

It was warm here, it was a home, people together by a fire. The children felt very safe and important; the mother and father were serious, watchful. They had things to do for the children more important than his visit here. A spoonful of medicine was, after all, more important than the strained relations between Marion and himself. They were not dull people, but they were very much in the grip of life and circumstances. He wondered if he couldn't do something to get Lincoln out of his rut at the bank.

A long peal at the door-bell; the *bonne á tout faire* passed through and went down the corridor. The door opened upon another long ring, and then voices, and the three in the salon looked up expectantly; Richard moved to bring the corridor within his range of vision, and Marion rose. Then the maid carne back along the corridor, closely followed by the voices, which developed under the light into Duncan Schaeffer and Lorraine Quarrles.

They were gay, they were hilarious, they were roaring with laughter. For a moment Charlie was astounded; unable to understand how they ferreted out the Peters' address.

"Ah-h-h!" Duncan waggad his finger roguishly at Charlie. "Ah-h-h!"

They both slid down another cascade of laughter. Anxious and at a loss, Charlie shook hands with them quickly and presented them to Lincoln and Marion. Marion nodded, scarcely speaking. She had drawn back a step toward the fire; her little girl stood beside her, and Marion put an arm about her shoulder.

With growing annoyance at the intrusion, Charlie waited for them to explain themselves. After some concentration Duncan said:

"We came to invite you out to dinner. Lorraine and I insist that all this chi-chi, cagy business 'bout your address got to stop."

Charlie came closer to them, as if to force them backward down the corridor.

"Sorry, but I can't. Tell me where you'll be and I'll phone you in half an hour."

This made no impression. Lorraine sat down suddenly on the side of a chair, and focusing her eyes on Richard, cried, "Oh, what a nice little boy! Come here, little boy." Richard glanced at his mother, but did not move. With a perceptible shrug of her shoulders, Lorraine turned back to Charlie:

"Come and dine. Sure your cousins won' mine. See you so sel'om. Or solemn."

"I can't," said Charlie sharply. "You two have dinner and I'll phone you."

Her voice became suddenly unpleasant. "All right, we'll go. But I remember once when you hammered on my door at four A.M. I was enough of a good sport to give you a drink. Come on, Dunc."

Still in slow motion, with blurred, angry faces, with uncertain feet they retired along the corridor.

"Good night," Charlie said.

"Good night!" responded Lorraine emphatically.

When he went back into the salon Marion had not moved, only now her son was standing in the circle of her other arm. Lincoln was still swinging Honoria back and forth like a pendulum from side to side.

"What an outrage!" Charlie broke out. "What an absolute outrage!"

Neither of them answered. Charlie dropped into an armchair, picked up his drink, set it down again and said:

"People I haven't seen for two years having the colossal nerve—"

He broke off. Marion had made the sound "Oh!" in one swift, furious breath, turned her body from him with a jerk and left the room.

Lincoln set down Honoria carefully.

"You children go in and start your soup," he said, and when they obeyed, he said to Charlie:

"Marion's not well and she can't stand shocks. That kind of people make her really physically sick."

"I didn't tell them to come here. They wormed your name out of somebody. They deliberately—"

"Well, it's too bad. It doesn't help matters. Excuse me a minute."

Left alone, Charlie sat tense in his chair. In the next room he could hear the children eating, talking in monosyllables, already oblivious to the scene between their elders. He heard a murmur of conversation from a farther room and then the ticking bell of a telephone receiver picked up, and in a panic he moved to the other side of the room and out of earshot.

In a minute Lincoln came back. "Look here, Charlie, I think we'd better call off dinner for tonight. Marion's in bad shape."

"Is she angry with me?"

"Sort of," he said, almost roughly. "She's not strong and—"

"You mean she's changed her mind about Honoria?"

"She's pretty bitter right now. I don't know. You phone me at the bank tomorrow."

"I wish you'd explain to her I never dreamed these people would come here. I'm just as sore as you are."

"I couldn't explain anything to her now."

Charlie got up. He took his coat and hat and started down the corridor. Then he opened the door of the dining room and said in a strange voice, "Good night, children."

Honoria rose and ran around the table to hug him.

"Good night, sweetheart," he said vaguely, and then trying to make his voice more tender, trying to conciliate something, "Good night, dear children."

V

Charlie went directly to the Ritz bar with the furious idea of finding Lorraine and Duncan, but they were not there, and he realized that in any case there was nothing he could do. He had not touched his drink at the Peters', and now he ordered a whisky-and-soda. Paul came over to say hello.

"It's a great change." he said sadly. "We do about half the business we did. So many fellows I hear about back in the States lost everything, maybe not in the first crash, but then in the second. Your friend George Hardt lost every cent, I hear. Are you back in the States?"

"No, I'm in business in Prague."

"I heard that you lost a lot in the crash."

"I did," and he added grimly, "but I lost everything I wanted in the boom."

"Selling short."

"Something like that."

Again the memory of those days swept over him like a nightmare—the people they had met travelling; then people who couldn't add a row of figures or speak a coherent sentence. The little man Helen had consented to dance with at the ship's party, who had insulted her ten feet from the table; the women and girls carried screaming with drink or drugs out of public places—

—The men who locked their wives out in the snow, because the snow of twenty-nine wasn't real snow. If you didn't want it to be snow, you just paid some money.

He went to the phone and called the Peters' apartment; Lincoln answered.

"I called up because this thing is on my mind. Has Marion said anything definite?"

"Marion's sick'" Lincoln answered shortly. "I know this thing isn't altogether your fault, but I can't have her go to pieces about it. I'm afraid we'll have to let it slide for six months; I can't take the chance of working her up to this state again."

"I see."

"I'm sorry, Charlie."

He went back to his table. His whisky glass was empty, but he shook his head when Alix looked at it questioningly. There wasn't much he could do now except send Honoria some things; he would send her a lot of things tomorrow. He thought rather angrily that this was just money—he had given so many people money. . . .

"No, no more," he said to another waiter. "What do I owe you?"

He would come back some day; they couldn't make him pay forever. But he wanted his child, and nothing was much good now, beside that fact. He wasn't young any more, with a lot of nice thoughts and dreams to have by himself. He was absolutely sure Helen wouldn't have wanted him to he so alone.

CONSTRUCTING A READING

1. With your group members, reconstruct all the events the narrative recounts in *chronological order*—the sequence in which they actually would have occurred.

2. Speculate about why Fitzgerald may have chosen his discourse order. Compare your answers with those of your classmates.

3. With your group members, consider how the discourse order affects your sympathy (or lack of it) for Charles Wales.

4. On the basis of what you know about alcoholism, are you persuaded by Charles Wales's assertion that he only takes one drink a day "deliberately, so that the idea of alcohol won't get too big in [his] imagination"? Consider your opinion in relation to discourse order. That is, think about the connection—if there is any—between the order in which the events are revealed to you, your sympathy with Charles, and your willingness to believe his account of his relation to alcohol.

5. At the end of the discourse and the story, Charlie shakes his head no when the bartender asks whether he wants a second drink. Then, he muses that he is absolutely sure Helen wouldn't have wanted him to be so alone. What do you think he will do next?

GENRE: NARRATIVE TYPES

Perhaps you remember a time in your childhood or adolescence when you were first able to predict the outcome of a film or TV program. In the course of many viewings over months and years, you learned, for example, that the Bradys would eventually settle their family squabbles; that Agents Scully and Mulder would probably not agree about extraterrestrial life, that Jerry Seinfeld would probably not marry, that detectives usually figure out who dunnit, and so forth. That ability to guess correctly how a story would turn out was an indication of your familiarity with its genre. A *genre* is a category or type of text—like poem, story, play, film, painting, song, etc. The Big Three literary genres are story (or narrative), poetry, and drama. But each genre has subgenres—adventure story, lyric poem, tragic play, *film noir,* folk song, etc. And each genre and subgenre has recognizable characteristics. The term *generic expectations* refers to a familiarity with those characteristics that allows you to predict—and that encourages you to expect—that certain characters will behave in certain ways, that certain plots will resolve in certain ways, that certain poems will rhyme in certain ways, that certain kinds of texts will have certain kinds of themes, and so on. In this chapter, I shall be concerned primarily with narrative genres—stories, narrative poems, TV, and film. Genres of poetry and drama will be discussed, as they become relevant, in this chapter and elsewhere in this book.

Turn on the TV in a foreign country and within a few minutes, you would probably figure out what kind of program you are watching—a sitcom, a mystery, a soap opera, a western, a science fiction story—even if you couldn't understand a word of the dialogue. Your generic expectations would have prompted you to recognize elements of discourse and story that you have seen before and to predict plot elements. Given a certain amount of experience with genre, audiences know what kinds of plot events to anticipate. They also have an idea of things that cannot happen—or at least are very unlikely. For example, sitcom audiences do not expect terrible things to happen to their characters, but in soap operas, characters are often murdered, raped, cheated on, possessed by the devil, kidnapped by aliens, or whatever.

Think of some genres about which you already have expectations as you consider how these guidelines work. A phrase like "it was a dark and stormy night," for example, signals a mystery/suspense narrative. "Once upon a time" promises a fairy tale. If a story begins "a long, long time ago, in a galaxy far away," you expect science fiction.

These are generic expectations about narrative events. But they are also expectations about how the story will be told—whether you will believe the events of the story are "really" happening or not. In a fairy tale, for example, we are not disconcerted when a puppet turns into a boy whose nose grows longer when he tells a lie, but we would be surprised if a realistic film showed a politician's nose lengthening during a press conference. In works of fantasy, we expect to encounter events (like the magical appearance of a pumpkin coach) and characters (like talking dinosaurs) that do not exist in nature. In more "realistic" works, we expect that events will be consistent with ordinary principles of physics and biology and that characters will behave like "ordinary" people.

How Genre Affects Theme

To get a sense of generic treatment of theme, let's look at how different genres treat the similar minimal stories. Here, again, is a poem by Robert Frost:

Design

Robert Frost

I found a dimpled spider, fat and white,
On a white heal-all, holding up a moth
Like a white piece of rigid satin cloth—
Assorted characters of death and blight
Mixed ready to begin the morning right,
Like the ingredients of a witches' broth—
A snow-drop spider, a flower like a froth,
And dead wings carried like a paper kite.

What had that flower to do with being white,
The wayside blue and innocent heal-all?
What brought the kindred spider to that height,
Then steered the white moth thither in the night?
What but design of darkness to appall?—
If design govern in a thing so small.

You've read this poem before, so you remember that it provides an account of a relatively unremarkable occurrence: a speaker observes and contemplates a spider killing a moth. This time, though, let's attend to the generic characteristics of Frost's poem. First, the text belongs to at least two genres: although it is a poem, "Design" also tells a story.

As a poem, "Design" is a sonnet, a kind of lyric poem that consists of fourteen lines in which each line rhymes with at least one other one. Sonnets have several possible rhyme schemes: this one is ABBAABBAACAACC. The fourteen lines are divided between an octet (the first eight lines) and a sextet (the last six). Frequently, the octet raises a question or establishes a situation. The sextet responds to the question or comments on the situation. An experienced reader of sonnets would expect to find these characteristics, and our poem delivers them.

Now, let us look at how "Design" works as a narrative text. I plot its minimal story in this way: First, the speaker is at ease. Then, he comes upon a white moth on a white heal-all—a plant that is commonly supposed to have medicinal benefits. Then, the speaker notices that a spider is in the process of killing the moth. Then, as a result, the speaker wonders whether these events were "designed." The speaker's disequilibrium comes as the result of the question(s) he asks himself. The last line conveys the speaker's attempt at a resolution; equilibrium more or less returns as the speaker realizes that he cannot understand the universe.

When I read Frost's poem, I feel uneasy about the violence in nature and puzzled about the metaphysical questions it raises. The same theme in a different genre, however, invites the reader to a very different response.

When I look at this cartoon, I chuckle—reacting completely differently than I do to "Design."

Yet, both texts tell the same story. A spider kills a moth. Nothing is inherently either funny or depressing about the events of the story. But the theme (let's say, questioning the reasons for violence in nature) is treated differently in two different genres. Generic expectations make the difference: experienced readers expect to laugh at a *New Yorker* cartoon, but to be provoked by Robert Frost's metaphysical questions.

How Genre Affects Gaps

The kinds of questions a story guides us to ask are what constitute its genre: gaps, in other words, are generic. To illustrate this premise, let's look together at "The Murders in the Rue Morgue," by Edgar Allen Poe, one of the prototypes of the detective story.

The Murders in the Rue Morgue
Edgar Allen Poe

What song the Syrens sang, or what name Achilles assumed when he hid himself among women, although puzzling questions are not beyond *all* conjecture.
—Sir Thomas Browne, Urn-Burial

The mental features discoursed of as the analytical, are, in themselves, but little susceptible of analysis. We appreciate them only in their effects. We know of them, among other things, that they are always to their possessor, when inordinately possessed, a source of the liveliest enjoyment. As the strong man exults in his physical ability, delighting in such exercises as call his muscles into action, so glories the analyst in that moral activity which *disentangles*. He derives pleasure from even the most trivial occupations bringing his talents into play. He is fond of enigmas, of conundrums, of hieroglyphics; exhibiting in his solutions of each a degree of *acumen* which appears to the ordinary apprehension preternatural. His results, brought about by the very soul and essence of method, have, in truth, the whole air of intuition. The faculty of re-solution is possibly much invigorated by mathematical study, and especially by that highest branch of it which, unjustly, and merely on account of its retrograde operations, has been called, as if *par excellence*, analysis. Yet to calculate is not in itself to analyze. A chess-player, for example, does the one without effort at the other. It follows that the game of chess, in its effects upon mental character, is greatly misunderstood. I am not now writing a treatise, but simply prefacing a somewhat peculiar narrative by observations very much at random; I will, therefore, take occasion to assert that the higher powers of the reflective intellect are more decidedly and more usefully tasked by the unostentatious game of draughts than by all the elaborate frivolity of chess. In this latter, where the pieces have different and *bizarre* motions, with various and variable values, what is only complex is mistaken (a not unusual error) for what is profound. The *attention* is here called powerfully into play. If it flag for an instant, an oversight is committed, resulting in injury or defeat. The possible moves being not only manifold but involute, the chances of such oversights are multiplied; and in nine cases out of ten it is the more concentrative rather than the more acute player who conquers. In draughts, on the contrary, where the moves are unique and have but little variation, the probabilities of inadvertence are diminished, and the mere attention being left comparatively unemployed, what advantages are obtained by either party are obtained by superior *acumen*. To be less abstract—Let us suppose a game of draughts where the pieces are reduced to four kings, and where, of course, no oversight is to be expected. It is obvious that here the victory can be decided (the players being at all equal) only by some *recherché* movement, the result of some strong exertion of the intellect. Deprived of ordinary resources, the analyst throws himself into the spirit of his opponent, identifies himself therewith, and not unfrequently sees thus, at a glance, the sole methods (sometimes indeed absurdly simple ones) by which he may seduce into error or hurry into miscalculation.

Whist has long been noted for its influence upon what is termed the calculating power; and men of the highest order of intellect have been known to take an apparently unaccountable delight in it, while eschewing chess as frivolous. Beyond doubt there is nothing of a similar nature so greatly tasking the faculty of analysis. The best chess-player in Christendom *may* be little more than the best player of chess; but proficiency in whist implies capacity for success in all these more important undertakings where mind struggles with mind. When I say proficiency, I mean that perfection in the game which includes a comprehension of *all* the sources whence legitimate advantage may be derived. These are not only manifold but multiform, and lie frequently among recesses of thought altogether inaccessible to the ordinary understanding. To observe attentively is to remember distinctly; and, so far, the concentrative chess-player will do very well at whist; while the rules of Hoyle (themselves based upon the mere mechanism of the game) are sufficiently and generally comprehensible. Thus to have a retentive memory, and to proceed by "the book," are points commonly regarded as the sum total of good playing. But it is in matters beyond the limits of mere rule that the skill of the analyst is evinced. He makes, in silence, a host of observations and inferences. So, perhaps, do his companions; and the difference in the extent of the information obtained, lies not so much in the validity of the inference as in the quality of the observation. The necessary knowledge is that of *what* to observe. Our player confines himself not at all; nor, because the game is the object, does he reject deductions from things external to the game. He examines the countenance of his partner, comparing it carefully with that of each of his opponents. He considers the mode of assorting the cards in each hand; often counting trump by trump, and honor by honor, through the glances bestowed by their holders upon each. He notes every variation of face as the play progresses, gathering a fund of thought from the differences in the expression of certainty, of surprise, of triumph, or chagrin. From the manner of gathering up a trick he judges whether the person taking it can make another in the suit. He recognizes what is played through feint, by the air with which it is thrown upon the table. A casual or inadvertent word; the accidental dropping or turning of a card, with the accompanying anxiety or carelessness in regard to its concealment; the counting of the tricks, with the order of their arrangement; embarrassment, hesitation, eagerness or trepidation—all afford, to his apparently intuitive perception, indications of the true state of affairs. The first two or three rounds having been played, he is in full possession of the contents of each hand, and thenceforward puts down his cards with as absolute a precision of purpose as if the rest of the party had turned outward the faces of their own.

The analytical power should not be confounded with simple ingenuity; for while the analyst is necessarily ingenious, the ingenious man is often remarkably incapable of analysis. The constructive or combining power, by which ingenuity is usually manifested, and to which the phrenologists (I believe erroneously) have assigned a separate organ, supposing it a primitive faculty, has been so frequently seen in those whose intellect bordered otherwise upon idiocy, as to have attracted general observation among writers on morals. Between ingenuity and the analytic ability there exists a difference far greater, indeed, than that between the fancy and the imagination, but of a character very strictly analogous. It will be found, in fact, that the ingenious are always fanciful, and the *truly* imaginative never otherwise than analytic.

The narrative which follows will appear to the reader somewhat in the light of a commentary upon the propositions just advanced.

Residing in Paris during the spring and part of the summer of 18—, I there became acquainted with a Monsieur C. Auguste Dupin. This young gentleman was of an excellent—indeed of an illustrious family, but, by a variety of untoward events, had been reduced to such poverty that the energy of his character succumbed beneath it, and he ceased to bestir himself in the world, or to care for the retrieval of his fortunes. By courtesy of his creditors, there still remained in his possession a small remnant of his patrimony; and, upon the income arising from this, he managed, by means of a rigorous economy, to procure the necessaries of life, without troubling himself about its superfluities. Books, indeed, were his sole luxuries, and in Paris these are easily obtained.

Our first meeting was at an obscure library in the Rue Montmartre, where the accident of our both being in search of the same very rare and very remarkable volume brought us into closer communion. We saw each other again and again. I was deeply interested in the little family history which he detailed to me with all that candor which a Frenchman indulges whenever mere self is the theme. I was astonished, too, at the vast extent of his reading; and, above all, I felt my soul enkindled within me by the wild fervor, and the vivid freshness of his imagination. Seeking in Paris the objects I then sought, I felt that the society of such a man would be to me a treasure beyond price; and this feeling I frankly confided to him. It was at length arranged that we should live together during my stay in the city; and as my worldly circumstances were somewhat less embarrassed than his own, I was permitted to be at the expense of renting, and furnishing in a style which suited the rather fantastic gloom of our common temper, a time-eaten and grotesque mansion, long deserted through superstitions into which we did not inquire, and tottering to its fall in a retired and desolate portion of the Faubourg St. Germain.

Had the routine of our life at this place been known to the world, we should have been regarded as madmen—although, perhaps, as madmen of a harmless nature. Our seclusion was perfect. We admitted no visitors. Indeed the locality of our retirement had been carefully kept a secret from my own former associates; and it had been many years since Dupin had ceased to know or be known in Paris. We existed within ourselves alone.

It was a freak of fancy in my friend (for what else shall I call it?) to be enamored of the Night for her own sake; and into this *bizarrerie*, as into all his others, I quietly fell; giving myself up to his wild whims with a perfect *abandon*. The sable divinity would not herself dwell with us always; but we could counterfeit her presence. At the first dawn of the morning we closed all the massy shutters of our old building; lighted a couple of tapers which, strongly perfumed, threw out only the ghastliest and feeblest of rays. By the aid of these we then busied our souls in dreams—reading, writing, or conversing, until warned by the clock of the advent of the true Darkness. Then we sallied forth into the streets, arm and arm, continuing the topics of the day, or roaming far and wide until a late hour, seeking, amid the wild lights and shadows of the populous city, that infinity of mental excitement which quiet observation can afford.

At such times I could not help remarking and admiring (although from his rich ideality I had been prepared to expect it) a peculiar analytic ability in Dupin. He seemed, too, to take an eager delight in its exercise—if not exactly in its display—and did not hesitate to confess the pleasure thus derived. He boasted to me, with a low chuckling laugh, that most men, in respect to himself, wore windows in their bosoms, and was wont to follow up such assertions by direct and very startling proofs of his intimate knowledge of my own. His manner at these moments was frigid and abstract; his eyes were vacant in expression; while his voice, usually a rich tenor, rose into a treble which would have sounded petulantly but for the deliberateness and entire distinctness of the enunciation. Observing him in these moods, I often dwelt meditatively upon the old philosophy of the Bi-Part Soul, and amused myself with the fancy of a double Dupin—the creative and the resolvent.

Let it not be supposed, from what I have just said, that I am detailing any mystery, or penning any romance. What I have described in the Frenchman, was merely the result of an excited, or perhaps of a diseased intelligence. But of the character of his remarks at the periods in question an example will best convey the idea.

We were strolling one night down a long dirty street, in the vicinity of the Palais Royal. Being both, apparently, occupied with thought, neither of us had spoken a syllable for fifteen minutes at least. All at once Dupin broke forth with these words:—

"He is a very little fellow, that's true, and would do better for the *Théâtre des Variétés.*"

"There can be no doubt of that," I replied unwittingly, and not at first observing (so much had I been absorbed in reflection) the extraordinary manner in which the speaker had chimed in with my meditations. In an instant afterward I recollected myself, and my astonishment was profound.

"Dupin," said I, gravely, "this is beyond my comprehension. I do not hesitate to say that I am amazed, and can scarcely credit my senses. How was it possible you should know I was thinking of ———?" Here I paused, to ascertain beyond a doubt whether he really knew of whom I thought

——— "of Chantilly," said he, "why do you pause? You were remarking to yourself that his diminutive figure unfitted him for tragedy."

This was precisely what had formed the subject of my reflections. Chantilly was a *quondam* cobbler of the Rue St. Denis, who, becoming stage-mad, had attempted the *rôle* of Xerxes, in Crébillon's tragedy so called, and been notoriously Pasquinaded for his pains.

"Tell me, for Heaven's sake," I exclaimed, "the method—if method there is—by which you have been enabled to fathom my soul in this matter." In fact I was even more startled than I would have been willing to express.

"It was the fruiterer," replied my friend, "who brought you to the conclusion that the mender of soles was not of sufficient height for Xerxes *et id genus omne.*"

"The fruiterer!——you astonish me—I know no fruiterer whomsoever."

"The man who ran up against you as we entered the street—it may have been fifteen minutes ago."

I now remembered that, in fact, a fruiterer, carrying upon his head a large basket of apples, had nearly thrown me down, by accident, as we passed from the Rue C—— into the thoroughfare where we stood; but what this had to do with Chantilly I could not possibly understand.

There was not a particle of *charlatanerie* about Dupin. "I will explain," he said, "and that you may comprehend all clearly, we will first retrace the course of your meditations, from the moment in which I spoke to you until that of the *recontre* with the fruiterer in question. The larger links of the chain run thus—Chantilly, Orion, Dr. Nichols, Epicurus, Stereotomy, the street stones, the fruiterer."

There are few persons who have not, at some period of their lives, amused themselves in retracing the steps by which particular conclusions of their own minds have been attained. The occupation is often full of interest; and he who attempts it for the first time is astonished by the apparently illimitable distance and incoherence between the starting-point and the goal. What, then, must have been my amazement when I heard the Frenchman speak what he had just spoken, and when I could not help acknowledging that he had spoken the truth. He continued:

"We had been talking of horses, if I remember aright, just before leaving the Rue C——. This was the last subject we discussed. As we crossed into this street, a fruiterer, with a large basket upon his head, brushing quickly past us, thrust you upon a pile of paving-stones collected at a spot where the causeway is undergoing repair. You stepped upon one of the loose fragments, slipped, slightly strained your ankle, appeared vexed or sulky, muttered a few words, turned to look at the pile, and then proceeded in silence. I was not particularly attentive to what you did; but observation has become with me, of late, a species of necessity.

"You kept your eyes upon the ground—glancing with a petulant expression, at the holes and ruts in the pavement, (so that I saw you were still thinking of the stones,) until we reached the little alley called Lamartine, which has been paved, by way of experiment, with the overlapping and riveted blocks. Here your countenance brightened up, and, perceiving your lips move, I could not doubt that you murmured the word 'stereotomy,' a term very affectedly applied to this species of pavement. I knew that you could not say to yourself 'stereotomy' without being brought to think of atomies, and thus of the theories of Epicurus; and since, when we discussed this subject not very long ago, I mentioned to you how singularly, yet with how little notice, the vague guesses of that noble Greek had met with confirmation in the late nebular cosmogony, I felt that you could not avoid casting your eyes upward to the great *nebula* in Orion, and I certainly expected that you would do so. You did look up; and I was now assured that I had correctly followed your steps. But in that bitter *tirade* upon Chantilly, which appeared in yesterday's *'Musée,'* the satirist, making some disgraceful allusions to the cobbler's change of name upon assuming the buskin, quoted a Latin line about which we have often conversed. I mean the line

   Perdidit antiquum litera prima sonum.

I had told you that this was in reference to Orion, formerly written Urion; and, from certain pungencies connected with this explanation, I was aware that you could not have forgotten it. It was clear, therefore, that you would not fail to combine the two ideas of Orion and Chantilly. That you did combine them I saw by the character of the smile which passed over your lips. You thought of the poor cobbler's immolation. So far, you had been stooping in your gait; but now I saw you draw yourself up to your full height. I was then sure that you reflected upon the diminutive figure of Chantilly. At this point I interrupted your meditations to remark that as, in fact, he *was* a very little fellow—that Chantilly—he would do better at the *Théâtree des Varietes."*

Not long after this, we were looking over an evening edition of the *Gazette des Tribunaux,* when the following paragraphs arrested our attention.

EXTRAORDINARY MURDERS.—This morning, about three o'clock, the inhabitants of the Quartier St. Roch were aroused from sleep by a succession of terrific shrieks, issuing, apparently, from the fourth story of a house in the Rue Morgue, known to be in the sole occupancy of one Madame L'Espanaye, and her daughter, Mademoiselle Camille L'Espanaye. After some delay, occasioned by a fruitless attempt to procure admission in the usual manner, the gateway was broken in with a crowbar, and eight or ten of the neighbors entered, accompanied by two *gendarmes.* By this time the cries had ceased; but, as the party rushed up the first flight of stairs, two or more rough voices, in angry contention, were distinguished, and seemed to proceed from the upper part of the house. As the second landing was reached, these sounds, also, had ceased, and everything remained perfectly quiet. The party spread themselves, and hurried from room to room. Upon arriving at a large back chamber in the fourth story, (the door of which, being found locked, with the key inside, was forced open,) a spectacle presented itself which struck every one present not less with horror than with astonishment.

"The apartment was in the wildest disorder—the furniture broken and thrown about in all directions. There was only one bedstead; and from this the bed had been removed, and thrown into the middle of the floor. On a chair lay a razor, besmeared with blood. On the hearth were two or three long and thick tresses of grey human hair, also dabbled in blood, and seeming to have been pulled out by the roots. Upon the floor were found four Napoleons, an ear-ring of topaz, three large silver spoons, three smaller of *métal d'Alger*, and two bags, containing nearly four thousand francs in gold. The drawers of a *bureau*, which stood in one corner, were open, and had been, apparently, rifled, although many articles still remained in them. A small iron safe was discovered under the *bed* (not under the bedstead). It was open, with the key still in the door. It had no contents beyond a few old letters, and other papers of little consequence.

"Of Madame L'Espanaye no traces were here seen; but an unusual quantity of soot being observed in the fire-place, a search was made in the chimney, and (horrible to relate!) the corpse of the daughter, head downward, was dragged therefrom; it having been thus forced up the narrow aperture for a considerable distance. The body was quite warm. Upon examining it, many excoriations were perceived, no doubt occasioned by the violence with which it had been thrust up and disengaged. Upon the face were many severe scratches, and, upon the throat, dark bruises, and deep indentations of finger nails, as if the deceased had been throttled to death.

"After a thorough investigation of every portion of the house, without farther discovery, the party made its way into a small paved yard in the rear of the building, where lay the corpse of the old lady, with her throat so entirely cut that, upon an attempt to raise her, the head fell off. The body, as well as the head, was fearfully mutilated—the former so much so as scarcely to retain any semblance of humanity.

"To this horrible mystery there is not as yet, we believe, the slightest clew."

The next day's paper had these additional particulars. "*The Tragedy in the Rue Morgue.* Many individuals have been examined in relation to this most extraordinary and frightful affair." [The word '*affaire*' has not yet, in France, the levity of import which it conveys with us,] "but nothing whatever has transpired to throw light upon it. We give below all the material testimony elicited.

"*Pauline Dubourg,* laundress, deposes that she has known both the deceased for three years, having washed for them during that period. The old lady and her daughter seemed on good terms—very affectionate towards each other. They were excellent pay. Could not speak in regard to their mode or means of living. Believed that Madame L. told fortunes for a living. Was reputed to have money put by. Never met any persons in the house when she called for the clothes or took them home. Was sure that they had no servant in employ. There appeared to be no furniture in any part of the building except in the fourth story.

"*Pierre Moreau,* tobacconist, deposes that he has been in the habit of selling small quantities of tobacco and snuff to Madame L'Espanaye for nearly four years. Was born in the neighborhood, and has always resided there. The deceased and her daughter had occupied the house in which the corpses were found, for more than six years. It was formerly occupied by a jeweller, who under-let the upper rooms to various persons. The house was the property of Madame L. She became dissatisfied with the abuse of the premises by her tenant, and moved into them herself, refusing to let any portion. The old lady was childish. Witness had seen the daughter some five or six times during the six years. The two lived an exceedingly retired life—were reputed to have money. Had heard it said among the neighbors that Madame L. told fortunes—did not believe it. Had never seen any person enter the door except the old lady and her daughter, a porter once or twice, and a physician some eight or ten times.

"Many other persons, neighbors, gave evidence to the same effect. No one was spoken of as frequenting the house. It was not known whether there were any living connexions of Madam L. and her daughter. The shutters of the front windows were seldom opened. Those in the rear were always closed, with the exception of the large back room, fourth story. The house was a good house—not very old.

"*Isidore Musèt, gendarme,* deposes that he was called to the house about three o'clock in the morning, and found some twenty or thirty persons at the gateway, endeavoring to gain admittance. Forced it open, at length, with a bayonet—not with a crowbar. Had but little difficulty in getting it open, on account of its being a double or folding gate, and bolted neither at bottom nor top. The shrieks were continued until the gate was forced—and then suddenly ceased. They seemed to be screams of some person (or persons) in great agony—were loud and drawn out, not short and quick. Witness led the way up stairs. Upon reaching the first landing, heard two voices in loud and angry contention—the one a gruff voice, the other much shriller—a very strange voice. Could distinguish some words of the former, which was that of a Frenchman. Was positive that it was not a woman's voice. Could distinguish the words '*sacré*' and '*diable.*' The shrill voice was that of a foreigner. Could not be sure whether it was the voice of a man or of a woman. Could not make out what was said, but believed the language to be Spanish. The state of the room and of the bodies was described by this witness as we described them yesterday.

"*Henri Duval,* a neighbor, and by trade a silversmith, deposes that he was one of the party who first entered the house. Corroborates the testimony of Musèt in general. As soon as they forced an entrance, they reclosed the door, to keep out the crowd, which collected very fast, notwithstanding the lateness of the hour. The shrill voice, the witness thinks, was that of an Italian. Was certain it was not French. Could not be sure that it was a man's voice. It might have been a woman's. Was not acquainted with the Italian language. Could not distinguish the words, but was convinced by the intonation that the speaker was an Italian. Knew Madame L. and her daughter. Had conversed with both frequently. Was sure that the shrill voice was not that of either of the deceased.

"—— *Odenheimer, restaurateur.* This witness volunteered his testimony. Not speaking French, was examined through an interpreter. Is a native of Amsterdam. Was passing the house at the time of the shrieks. They lasted for several minutes—probably ten. They were long and loud—very awful and distressing. Was one of those who entered the building. Corroborated the previous evidence in every respect but one. Was sure that the shrill voice was that of a man—of a Frenchman. Could not distinguish the words uttered. They were loud and quick—unequal—spoken apparently in fear as well as in anger. The voice was harsh—not so much shrill as harsh. Could not call it a shrill voice. The gruff voice said repeatedly *'sacré,' 'diable'* and once *'mon Dieu.'*

"*Jules Mignaud*, banker, of the firm of Mignaud et Fils, Rue Deloraine. Is the elder Mignaud. Madame L'Espanaye had some property. Had opened an account with his banking house in the spring of the year —— (eight years previously). Made frequent deposits in small sums. Had checked for nothing until the third day before her death, when she took out in person the sum of 4000 francs. This sum was paid in gold, and a clerk sent home with the money.

"*Adolphe Le Bon*, clerk to Mignaud et Fils, deposes that on the day in question, about noon, he accompanied Madame L'Espanaye to her residence with the 4000 francs, put up in two bags. Upon the door being opened, Mademoiselle L. appeared and took from his hands one of the bags, while the old lady relieved him of the other. He then bowed and departed. Did not see any person in the street at the time. It is a bye-street—very lonely.

"*Williem Bird*, tailor, deposes that he was one of the party who entered the house. Is an Englishman. Has lived in Paris two years. Was one of the first to ascend the stairs. Heard the voices in contention. The gruff voice was that of a Frenchman. Could make out several words, but cannot now remember all. Heard distinctly *'sacré'* and *'mon Dieu.'* There was a sound at the moment as if of several persons struggling—a scraping and scuffling sound. The shrill voice was very loud—louder than the gruff one. Is sure that it was not the voice of an Englishman. Appeared to be that of a German. Might have been a woman's voice. Does not understand German.

"Four of the above-named witnesses, being recalled, deposed that the door of the chamber in which was found the body of Mademoiselle L. was locked on the inside when the party reached it. Every thing was perfectly silent—no groans or noises of any kind. Upon forcing the door no person was seen. The windows, both of the back and front room, were down and firmly fastened from within. A door between the two rooms was closed, but not locked. The door leading from the front room into the passage was locked, with the key on the inside. A small room in the front of the house, on the fourth story, at the head of the passage, was open, the door being ajar. This room was crowded with old beds, boxes, and so forth. These were carefully removed and searched. There was not an inch of any portion of the house which was not carefully searched. Sweeps were sent up and down the chimneys. The house was a four story one, with garrets (*mansardes*). A trap-door on the roof was nailed down very securely—did not appear to have been opened for years. The time elapsing between the hearing of the voices in contention and the breaking open of the room door, was variously stated by the witnesses. Some made it as short as three minutes—some as long as five. The door was opened with difficulty.

"*Alfonzo Garcio*, undertaker, deposes that he resides in the Rue Morgue. Is a native of Spain. Was one of the party who entered the house. Did not proceed up stairs. Is nervous, and was apprehensive of the consequences of agitation. Heard the voices in contention. The gruff voice was that of a Frenchman. Could not distinguish what was said. The shrill voice was that of an Englishman—is sure of this. Does not understand the English language; but judges by the intonation.

"*Alberto Montani* confectioner, deposes that he was among the first to ascend the stairs. Heard the voices in question. The gruff voice was that of a Frenchman. Distinguished several words. The speaker appeared to be expostulating. Could not make out the words of the shrill voice. Spoke quick and unevenly. Thinks it the voice of a Russian. Corroborates the general testimony. Is an Italian. Never conversed with a native of Russia.

"Several witnesses, recalled, here testified that the chimneys of all the rooms on the fourth story were too narrow to admit the passage of a human being. By 'sweeps' were meant cylindrical sweeping-brushes, such as are employed by those who clean chimneys. These brushes were passed up and down every flue in the house. There is no back passage by which any one could have descended while the party proceeded up stairs. The body of Mademoiselle L'Espanaye was so firmly wedged in the chimney that it could not be got down until four or five of the party united their strength.

"*Paul Dumas*, physician, deposes that he was called to view the bodies about day-break. They were both then lying on the sacking of the bedstead in the chamber where Mademoiselle L. was found. The corpse of the young lady was much bruised and excoriated. The fact that it had been thrust up the chimney would sufficiently account for these appearances. The throat was greatly chafed. There were several deep scratches just below the chin, together with a series of livid spots which were evidently the impression of fingers. The face was fearfully discolored, and the eye-balls protruded. The tongue had been partially bitten through. A large bruise was discovered upon the pit of the stomach, produced, apparently, by the pressure of a knee. In the opinion of M. Dumas, Mademoiselle L'Espanaye had been throttled to death by some person or persons unknown. The corpse of the mother was horribly mutilated. All the bones of the right leg and arm were more or less shattered. The left *tibia* much splintered, as well as all the ribs of the left side. Whole body dreadfully bruised and discolored. It was not possible to say how the injuries had been inflicted. A heavy club of wood, or a broad bar of iron—a chair—any large, heavy, and obtuse weapon would have produced such results, if wielded by the hands of a very powerful man. No woman could have inflicted the blows with any weapon. The head of the deceased, when seen by witness, was entirely separated from the body, and was also greatly shattered. The throat had evidently been cut with some very sharp instrument—probably with a razor.

"*Alexandre Etienne*, surgeon, was called with M. Dumas to view the bodies. Corroborated the testimony, and the opinions of M. Dumas.

"Nothing farther of importance was elicited, although several other persons were examined. A murder so mysterious, and so perplexing in all its particulars, was never before committed in Paris—if indeed a murder has been committed at all. The police are entirely at fault—an unusual occurrence in affairs of this nature. There is not, however, the shadow of a clew apparent."

The evening edition of the paper stated that the greatest excitement still continued in the Quartier St. Roch—that the premises in question had been carefully researched, and fresh examinations of witnesses instituted, but all to no purpose. A postscript, however mentioned that Adolphe Le Bon had been arrested and imprisoned—although nothing appeared to criminate him, beyond the facts already detailed.

Dupin seemed singularly interested in the progress of this affair—at least so I judged from his manner, for he made no comments. It was only after the announcement that Le Bon had been imprisoned, that he asked me my opinion respecting the murders.

I could merely agree with all Paris in considering them an insoluble mystery. I saw no means by which it would be possible to trace the murderer.

"We must not judge of the means," said Dupin, "by this shell of an examination. The Parisian police, so much extolled for *acumen*, are cunning, but no more. There is no method in their proceedings, beyond the method of the moment. They make a vast parade of measures; but, not infrequently, these are so ill adapted to the objects proposed, as to put us in mind of Monsieur Jourdain's calling for his *robe-de-chambre—pour mieux entendre la musique*. The results attained by them are not unfrequently surprising, but, for the most part, are brought about by simple diligence and activity. When these qualities are unavailing, their schemes fail. Vidocq, for example, was a good guesser, and a persevering man. But, without educated thought, he erred continually by the very intensity of his investigations. He impaired his vision by holding the object too close. He might see, perhaps, one or two points with unusual clearness, but in so doing he, necessarily, lost sight of the matter as a whole. Thus there is such a thing as being too profound. Truth is not always in a well. In fact, as regards the more important knowledge, I do believe that she is invariably superficial. The depth lies in the valleys where we seek her, and not upon the mountain-tops where she is found. The modes and sources of this kind of error are well typified in the contemplation of the heavenly bodies. To look at a star by glances—to view it in a side-long way, by turning toward it the exterior portions of the *retina* (more susceptible of feeble impressions of light than the interior), is to behold the star distinctly—is to have the best appreciation of its lustre—a lustre which grows dim just in proportion as we turn our vision *fully* upon it. A greater number of rays actually fall upon the eye in the latter case, but, in the former, there is the more refined capacity for comprehension. By undue profundity we perplex and enfeeble thought; and it is possible to make even Venus herself vanish from the firmament by a scrutiny too sustained, too concentrated, or too direct.

"As for these murders, let us enter into some examinations for ourselves, before we make up an opinion respecting them. An inquiry will afford us amusement," [I thought this an odd term, so applied, but said nothing] "and, besides, Le Bon once rendered me a service for which I am not ungrateful. We will go and see the premises with our own eyes. I know G———, the Prefect of Police, and shall have no difficulty in obtaining the necessary permission."

The permission was obtained, and we proceeded at once to the Rue Morgue. This is one of those miserable thoroughfares which intervene between the Rue Richelieu and the Rue St. Roch. It was late in the afternoon when we reached it; as this quarter is at a great distance from that in which we resided. The house was readily found; for there were still many persons gazing up at the closed shutters, with an objectless curiosity, from the opposite site of the way. It was an ordinary Parisian house, with a gateway, on one side of which was a glazed watch-box, with a sliding panel in the window, indicating a *loge de concierge*. Before going in we walked up the street, turned down an alley, and then, again turning, passed in the rear of the building—Dupin, meanwhile, examining the whole neighborhood, as well as the house, with a minuteness of attention for which I could see no possible object.

Retracing our steps, we came again to the front of the dwelling, rang, and, having shown our credentials, were admitted by the agents in charge. We went up stairs—into the chamber where the body of Mademoiselle L'Espanaye had been found, and where both the deceased still lay. The disorders of the room had, as usual, been suffered to exist. I saw nothing beyond what had been stated in the *Gazette des Tribunaux*. Dupin scrutinized every thing—not excepting the bodies of the victims. We then went into the other rooms, and into the yard; a *gendarme* accompanying us throughout. The examination occupied us until dark, when we took our departure. On our way home my companion stopped in for a moment at the office of one of the daily papers.

I have said that the whims of my friend were manifold, and that *Je les menageais*:—for this phrase there is no English equivalent. It was his humor, now, to decline all conversation on the subject of the murder, until about noon the next day. He then asked me, suddenly, if I had observed any thing *peculiar* at the scene of the atrocity.

There was something in his manner of emphasizing the word "peculiar," which caused me to shudder, without knowing why.

"No, nothing *peculiar*," I said; "nothing more, at least, than we both saw stated in the paper."

"The *Gazette*," he replied, "has not entered, I fear, into the unusual horror of the thing. But dismiss the idle opinions of this print. It appears to me that this mystery is considered insoluble, for the very reason which should cause it to be regarded as easy of solution—I mean for the *outré* character of its features. The police are confounded by the seeming absence of motive—not for the murder itself—but for the atrocity of the murder. They are puzzled, too, by the seeming impossibility of reconciling the voices heard in contention, with the facts that no one was discovered up stairs but the assassinated Mademoiselle L'Espanaye, and that there were no means of egress without the notice of the party ascending. The wild disorder of the room; the corpse thrust, with the head downward, up the chimney; the frightful mutilation of the body of the old lady; these considerations, with those just mentioned, and others which I need not mention, have sufficed to paralyze the powers, by putting completely at fault the boasted *acumen*, of the government agents. They have fallen into the gross but common error of confounding the unusual with the abstruse. But it is by these deviations from the plane of the ordinary that reason feels its way, if at all, in its search for the true. In investigations such as we are now pursuing, it should not be so much asked 'what has occurred,' as 'what has occurred that has never occurred before.' In fact, the facility with which I shall arrive, or have arrived, at the solution of this mystery, is in the direct ratio of its apparent insolubility in the eyes of the police."

I stared at the speaker in mute astonishment

"I am now awaiting," continued he, looking toward the door of our apartment—"I am now awaiting a person who, although perhaps not the perpetrator of these butcheries, must have been in some measure implicated in their perpetration. Of the worst portion of the crimes committed, it is probable that he is innocent. I hope that I am right in this supposition; for upon it I build my expectation of reading the entire riddle. I look for the man here—in this room—every moment. It is true that he may not arrive; but the probability is that he will. Should he come, it will be necessary to detain him. Here are pistols; and we both know how to use them when occasion demands their use."

I took the pistols, scarcely knowing what I did, or believing what I heard, while Dupin went on, very much as if in a soliloquy. I have already spoken of his abstract manner at such times. His discourse was addressed to myself; but his voice, although by no means loud, had that intonation which is commonly employed in speaking to some one at a great distance. His eyes, vacant in expression, regarded only the wall.

"That the voices heard in contention," he said, "by the party upon the stairs, were not the voices of the women themselves, was fully proved by the evidence. This relieves us of all doubt upon the question whether the old lady could have first destroyed the daughter, and afterward have committed suicide. I speak of this point chiefly for the sake of method; for the strength of Madame L'Espanaye would have been utterly unequal to the task of thrusting her daughter's corpse up the chimney as it was found; and the nature of the wounds upon her own person entirely preclude the idea of self-destruction. Murder, then, has been committed by some third party; and the voices of this third party were those heard in contention. Let me now advert—not to the whole testimony respecting these voices—but to what was *peculiar* in that testimony. Did you observe anything peculiar about it?"

I remarked that, while all the witnesses agreed in supposing the gruff voice to be that of a Frenchman, there was much disagreement in regard to the shrill, or, as one individual termed it, the harsh voice.

"That was the evidence itself," said Dupin, "but it was not the peculiarity of the evidence. You have observed nothing distinctive. Yet there *was* something to be observed. The witnesses, as you remark, agreed about the gruff voice; they were here unanimous. But in regard to the shrill voice, the peculiarity is—not that they disagreed—but that, while an Italian, an Englishman, a Spaniard, a Hollander, and a Frenchman attempted to describe it, each one spoke of it as that *of a foreigner.* Each is sure that it was not the voice of one of his own countrymen. Each likens it—not to the voice of an individual of any nation with whose language he is conversant—but the converse. The Frenchman supposes it the voice of a Spaniard, and 'might have distinguished some words *had he been acquainted with the Spanish.*' The Dutchman maintains it to have been that of a Frenchman; but we find it stated that '*not understanding French this witness was examined through an interpreter.*' The Englishman thinks it the voice of a German, and '*does not understand German.*' The Spaniard 'is sure' that it was that of an Englishman, but 'judges by the intonation' altogether, '*as he has* no *knowledge of the English.*' The Italian believes it the voice of a Russian, but '*has never conversed with a native of Russia.*' A second Frenchman differs, moreover, with the first, and is positive that the voice was that of an Italian; but, not *being cognizant of that tongue,* is, like the Spaniard, 'convinced by the intonation.' Now, how strangely unusual must that voice have really been, about which such testimony as this *could* have been elicited!—in whose *tones,* even, denizens of the five great divisions of Europe could recognise nothing familiar! You will say that it might have been the voice of an Asiatic—of an African. Neither Asiatics nor Africans abound in Paris; but, without denying the inference, I will now merely call your attention to three points. The voice is termed by one witness 'harsh rather than shrill.' It is represented by two others to have been 'quick and *unequal.*' No word—no sounds resembling words—were by any witness mentioned as distinguishable.

"I know not," continued Dupin, "what impression I may have made, so far, upon your own understanding; but I do not hesitate to say that legitimate deductions even from this portion of the testimony—the portion respecting the gruff and shrill voices—are in themselves sufficient to engender a suspicion which should give direction to all farther progress in the investigation of the mystery. I said 'legitimate deductions;' but my meaning is not thus fully expressed. I designed to imply that the deductions are the *sole* proper ones, and that the suspicion arises *inevitably* from them as the single result. What the suspicion is, however, I will not say just yet. I merely wish you to bear in mind that, with myself, it was sufficiently forcible to give a definite form—a certain tendency—to my inquiries in the chamber.

"Let us now transport ourselves, in fancy, to this chamber. What shall we first seek here? The means of egress employed by the murderers. It is not too much to say that neither of us believe in praternatural events. Madame and Mademoiselle L'Espanaye were not destroyed by spirits. The doers of the deed were material, and escaped materially. Then how? Fortunately, there is but one mode of reasoning upon the point, and that mode *must* lead us to a definite decision.—Let us examine, each by each, the possible means of egress. It is clear that the assassins were in the room where Mademoiselle L'Espanaye was found, or at least in the room adjoining, when the party ascended the stairs. It is then only from these two apartments that we have to seek issues. The police have laid bare the floors, the ceilings, and the masonry of the walls, in every direction. No *secret* issues could have escaped their vigilance. But, not trusting to *their* eyes, I examined with my own. There were, then, *no* secret issues. Both doors leading from the rooms into the passage were securely locked, with the keys inside. Let us turn to the chimneys. These, although of ordinary width for some eight or ten feet above the hearths, will not admit, throughout their extent, the body of a large cat. The impossibility of egress, by means already stated, being thus absolute, we are reduced to the windows. Through those of the front room no one could have escaped without notice from the crowd in the street. The murderers *must* have passed, then, through those of the back room. Now, brought to this conclusion in so unequivocal a manner as we are, it is not our part, as reasoners, to reject it on account of apparent impossibilities. It is only left for us to prove that these apparent 'impossibilities' are, in reality, not such.

"There are two windows in the chamber. One of them is unobstructed by furniture, and is wholly visible. The lower portion of the other is hidden from view by the head of the unwieldy bedstead which is thrust close up against it. The former was found securely fastened from within. It resisted the utmost force of those who endeavored to raise it. A large gimlet-hole had been pierced in its frame to the left, and a very stout nail was found fitted therein, nearly to the head. Upon examining the other window, a similar nail was seen similarly fitted in it; and a vigorous attempt to raise this sash, failed also. The police were now entirely satisfied that egress had not been in these directions. And, *therefore*, it was thought a matter of supererogation to withdraw the nails and open the windows.

"My own examination was somewhat more particular, and was so for the reason I have just given—because here it was, I knew, that all apparent impossibilities *must* be proved to be not such in reality.

"I proceeded to think thus—*à posteriori*. The murderers *did* escape from one of these windows. This being so, they could not have refastened the sashes from the inside, as they were found fastened;—the consideration which put a stop, through its obviousness, to the scrutiny of the police in this quarter. Yet the sashes *were* fastened. They *must*, then, have the power of fastening themselves. There was no escape from this conclusion. I stepped to the unobstructed casement, withdrew the nail with some difficulty, and attempted to raise the sash. It resisted all my efforts, as I had anticipated. A concealed spring must, I now knew, exist; and this corroboration of my idea convinced me that my premises, at least, were correct, however mysterious still appeared the circumstances attending the nails. A careful search soon brought to light the hidden spring. I pressed it, and, satisfied with the discovery, forebore to upraise the sash.

"I now replaced the nail and regarded it attentively. A person passing out through this window might have reclosed it, and the spring would have caught—but the nail could not have been replaced. The conclusion was plain, and again narrowed in the field of my investigations. The assassins *must* have escaped through the other window. Supposing, then, the springs upon each sash to be the same, as was probable, there *must* be found a difference between the nails, or at least between the modes of their fixture. Getting upon the sacking of the bedstead, I looked over the head-board minutely at the second casement. Passing my hand down behind the board, I readily discovered and pressed the spring, which was, as I had supposed, identical in character with its neighbor. I now looked at the nail. It was as stout as the other, and apparently fitted in the same manner—driven in nearly up to the head.

"You will say that I was puzzled; but, if you think so, you must have misunderstood the nature of the inductions. To use a sporting phrase, I had not been once 'at fault.' The scent had never for an instant been lost. There was no flaw in any link of the chain. I had traced the secret to its ultimate result,—and that result was *the nail*. It had, I say, in every respect, the appearance of its fellow in the other window; but this fact was an absolute nullity (conclusive as it might seem to be) when compared with the consideration that here, at this point, terminated the clew. 'There *must* be something wrong,' I said, 'about the nail.' I touched it; and the head, with about a quarter of an inch of the shank, came off in my fingers. The rest of the shank was in the gimlet-hole, where it had been broken off. The fracture was an old one (for its edges were incrusted with rust), and had apparently been accomplished by the blow of a hammer, which had partially imbedded, in the top of the bottom sash, the head portion of the nail. I now carefully replaced this head portion in the indentation whence I had taken it, and the resemblance to a perfect nail was complete—the fissure was invisible. Pressing the spring, I gently raised the sash for a few inches; the head went up with it, remaining firm in its bed. I closed the window, and the semblance of the whole nail was again perfect.

"The riddle, so far, was now unriddled. The assassin had escaped through the window which looked upon the bed. Dropping of its own accord upon his exit (or perhaps purposely closed), it had become fastened by the spring; and it was the retention of this spring which had been mistaken by the police for that of the nail,—farther inquiry being thus considered unnecessary.

"The next question is that of the mode of descent. Upon this point I had been satisfied in my walk with you around the building. About five feet and a half from the casement in question there runs a lightning-rod. From this rod it would have been impossible for any one to reach the window itself, to say nothing of entering it. I observed, however, that the shutters of the fourth story were of the peculiar kind called by Parisian carpenters *ferrades*—a kind rarely employed at the present day, but frequently seen upon very old mansions at Lyons and Bordeaux. They are in the form of an ordinary door, (a single, not a folding door) except that the upper half is latticed or worked in open trellis— thus affording an excellent hold for the hands. In the present instance these shutters are fully three feet and a half broad. When we saw them from the rear of the house, they were both about half open—that is to say, they stood off at right angles from the wall. It is probable that the police, as well as myself, examined the back of the tenement; but, if so, in looking at these *ferrades* in the line of their breadth (as they must have done), they did not perceive this great breadth itself, or, at all events, failed to take it into due consideration. In fact, having once satisfied themselves that no egress could have been made in this quarter, they would naturally bestow here a very cursory examination. It was clear to me, however, that the shutter belonging to the window at the head of the bed, would, if swung fully back to the wall, reach to within two feet of the lightning-rod. It was also evident that, by exertion of a very unusual degree of activity and courage, an entrance into the window, from the rod, might have been thus effected.—By reaching to the distance of two feet and a half (we now suppose the shutter open to its whole extent) a robber might have taken a firm grasp upon the trellis-work. Letting go, then, his hold upon the rod, placing his feet securely against the wall, and springing boldly from it, he might have swung the shutter so as to close it, and, if we imagine the window open at the time, might even have swung himself into the room.

"I wish you to bear especially in mind that I have spoken of a *very* unusual degree of activity as requisite to success in so hazardous and so difficult a feat. It is my design to show you, first, that the thing might possibly have been accomplished:—but, secondly and *chiefly*, I wish to impress upon your understanding the *very extraordinary*—the almost præternatural character of that agility which could have accomplished it.

"You will say, no doubt, using the language of the law, that 'to make out my case' I should rather undervalue, than insist upon a full estimation of the activity required in this matter. This may be the practice in law, but it is not the usage of reason. My ultimate object is only the truth. My immediate purpose is to lead you to place in juxta-position that *very unusual* activity of which I have just spoken, with that *very peculiar* shrill (or harsh) and *unequal* voice, about whose nationality no two persons could be found to agree, and *in* whose utterance no syllabification could be detected."

At these words a vague and half-formed conception of the meaning of Dupin flitted over my mind. I seemed to be upon the verge of comprehension, without power to comprehend—as men, at times, find themselves upon the brink of remembrance, without being able, in the end, to remember. My friend went on with his discourse.

"You will see," he said, "that I have shifted the question from the mode of egress to that of ingress. It was my design to suggest that both were effected in the same manner, at the same point. Let us now revert to the interior of the room. Let us survey the appearances here. The drawers of the bureau, it is said, had been rifled, although many articles of apparel still remained within them. The conclusion here is absurd. It is a mere guess—a very silly one—and no more. How are we to know that the articles found in the drawers were not all these drawers had originally contained? Madame L'Espanaye and her daughter lived an exceedingly retired life—saw no company—seldom went out—had little use for numerous changes of habiliment. Those found were at least of as good quality as any likely to be possessed by these ladies. If a thief had taken any, why did he not take the best—why did he not take all? In a word, why did he abandon four thousand francs in gold to encumber himself with a bundle of linen? The gold *was* abandoned. Nearly the whole sum mentioned by Monsieur Mignaud, the banker, was discovered, in bags, upon the floor. I wish you, therefore, to discard from your thoughts the blundering idea of *motive*, engendered in the brains of the police by that portion of the evidence which speaks of money delivered at the door of the house. Coincidences ten times as remarkable as this (the delivery of the money, and murder committed within three days upon the party receiving it), happen to all of us every hour of our lives, without attracting even momentary notice. Coincidences, in general, are great stumbling-blocks in the way of that class of thinkers who have been educated to know nothing of the theory of probabilities—that theory to which the most glorious objects of human research are indebted for the most glorious of illustration. In the present instance, had the gold been gone, the fact of its delivery three days before would have formed something more than a coincidence. It would have been corroborative of this idea of motive. But, under the real circumstances of the case, if we are to suppose gold the motive of this outrage, we must also imagine the perpetrator so vacillating an idiot as to have abandoned his gold and his motive together.

"Keeping now steadily in mind the points to which I have drawn your attention—that peculiar voice, that unusual agility, and that startling absence of motive in a murder so singularly atrocious as this—let us glance at the butchery itself. Here is a woman strangled to death by manual strength, and thrust up a chimney, head downward. Ordinary assassins employ no such modes of murder as this. Least of all, do they thus dispose of the murdered. In the manner of thrusting the corpse up the chimney, you will admit that there was something *excessively outré*—something altogether irreconcilable with our common notions of human action, even when we suppose the actors the most depraved of men. Think, too, how great must have been that strength which could have thrust the body *up* such an aperture so forcibly that the united vigor of several persons was found barely sufficient to drag it *down!*

"Turn, now, to other indications of the employment of a vigor most marvellous. On the hearth were thick tresses—very thick tresses—of grey human hair. These had been torn out by the roots. You are aware of the great force necessary in tearing thus from the head even twenty or thirty hairs together. You saw the locks in question as well as myself. Their roots (a hideous sight!) were clotted with fragments of the flesh of the scalp—token of the prodigious power which had been exerted in uprooting perhaps half a million of hairs at a time. The throat of the old lady was not merely cut, but the head absolutely severed from the body: the instrument was a mere razor. I wish you also to look at the *brutal* ferocity of these deeds. Of the bruises upon the body of Madame L'Espanaye I do not speak. Monsieur Dumas, and his worthy coadjutor Monsieur Etienne, have pronounced that they were inflicted by some obtuse instrument; and so far these gentlemen are very correct. The obtuse instrument was clearly the stone pavement in the yard, upon which the victim had fallen from the window which looked in upon the bed. This idea, however simple it may now seem, escaped the police for the same reason that the breadth of the shutters escaped them—because, by the affair of the nails, their perceptions had been hermetically sealed against the possibility of the windows having ever been opened at all.

"If now, in addition to all these things, you have properly reflected upon the odd disorder of the chamber, we have gone so far as to combine the ideas of an agility astounding, a strength superhuman, a ferocity brutal, a butchery without motive, a *grotesquerie* in horror absolutely alien from humanity, and a voice foreign in tone to the ears of men of many nations, and devoid of all distinct or intelligible syllabification. What result, then, has ensued? What impression have I made upon your fancy?"

I felt a creeping of the flesh as Dupin asked me the question. "A madman," I said, "has done this deed—some raving maniac, escaped from a neighboring *Maison de Santé.*"

"In some respects," he replied, "your idea is not irrelevant. But the voices of madmen, even in their wildest paroxysms, are never found to tally with that peculiar voice heard upon the stairs. Madmen are of some nation, and their language, however incoherent in its words, has always the coherence of syllabification. Besides, the hair of a madman is not such as I now hold in my hand. I disentangled this little tuft from the rigidly clutched fingers of Madame L'Espanaye. Tell me what you can make of it."

"Dupin!" I said, completely unnerved; "this hair is most unusual—this is no *human* hair."

"I have not asserted that it is," said he; "but, before we decide this point, I wish you to glance at the little sketch I have here traced upon this paper. It is a *facsimile* drawing of what has been described in one portion of the testimony as 'dark bruises, and deep indentations of finger nails,' upon the throat of Mademoiselle L'Espanaye, and in another, (by Messrs. Dumas and Etienne,) as a 'series of livid spots, evidently the impression of fingers.'

"You will perceive," continued my friend, spreading out the paper upon the table before us, "that this drawing gives the idea of a firm and fixed hold.

There is no *slipping* apparent. Each finger has retained—possibly until the death of the victim—the fearful grasp by which it originally imbedded itself. Attempt, now, to place all your fingers, at the same time, in the respective impressions as you see them."

I made the attempt in vain.

"We are possibly not giving this matter a fair trial," he said. "The paper is spread out upon a plane surface; but the human throat is cylindrical. Here is a billet of wood, the circumference of which is about that of the throat. Wrap the drawing around it, and try the experiment again."

I did so; but the difficulty was even more obvious than before.

"This," I said, "is the mark of no human hand."

"Read now," replied Dupin, "this passage from Cuvier."

It was a minute anatomical and generally descriptive account of the large fulvous Ourang-Outang of the East Indian Islands. The gigantic stature, the prodigious strength and activity, the wild ferocity, and the imitative propensities of these mammalia are sufficiently well known to all. I understood the full horrors of the murder at once.

"The description of the digits," said I, as I made an end of reading, "is in exact accordance with this drawing. I see that no animal but an Ourang-Outang, of the species here mentioned, could have impressed the indentations as you have traced them. This tuft of tawny hair, too, is identical in character with that of the beast of Cuvier. But I cannot possibly comprehend the particulars of this frightful mystery. Besides, there were *two* voices heard in contention, and one of them was unquestionably the voice of a Frenchman."

"True; and you will remember an expression attributed almost unanimously, by the evidence, to this voice,—the expression, *'mon Dieu!'* This, under the circumstances, has been justly characterized by one of the witnesses (Montani, the confectioner,) as an expression of remonstrance or expostulation. Upon these two words, therefore, I have mainly built my hopes of a full solution of the riddle. A Frenchman was cognizant of the murder. It is possible—indeed it is far more than probable—that he was innocent of all participation in the bloody transactions which took place. The Ourang-Outang may have escaped from him. He may have traced it to the chamber; but, under the agitating circumstances which ensued, he could never have recaptured it. It is still at large. I will not pursue these guesses—for I have no right to call them more—since the shades of reflection upon which they are based are scarcely of sufficient depth to be appreciable by my own intellect, and since I could not pretend to make them intelligible to the understanding of another. We will call them guesses then, and speak of them as such. If the Frenchman in question is indeed, as I suppose, innocent of this atrocity, this advertisement, which I left last night, upon our return home, at the office of *Le Monde*, (a paper devoted to the shipping interest, and much sought by sailors,) will bring him to our residence."

He handed me a paper, and I read thus:

CAUGHT—*In the Bois de Boulogne, early in the morning of the —— inst;* (the morning of the murder,) *a very large Ourang-Outang of the Bornese species. The owner, (who is ascertained to be a sailor, belonging to a Maltese vessel,) may have the animal again, upon identifying it satisfactorily, and paying a few charges arising from its capture and keeping. Call at No. ——, Rue ——, Faubourg St. Germain—au troisième.*

"How was it possible," I asked, "that you should know the man to be a sailor, and belonging to a Maltese vessel?"

"I do *not* know it," said Dupin. "I am not *sure* of it. Here, however, is a small piece of ribbon, which from its form, and from its greasy appearance, has evidently been used in tying the hair in one of those long *queues* of which sailors are so fond. Moreover, this knot is one which few besides sailors can tie, and is peculiar to the Maltese. I picked the ribbon up at the foot of the lightning-rod. It could not have belonged to either of the deceased. Now if, after all, I am wrong in my induction from this ribbon, that the Frenchman was a sailor belonging to a Maltese vessel, still I can have done no harm in saying what I did in the advertisement. If I am in error, he will merely suppose that I have been misled by some circumstance into which he will not take the trouble to inquire. But if I am right, a great point is gained. Cognizant although innocent of the murder, the Frenchman will naturally hesitate about replying to the advertisement—about demanding the Ourang-Outang. He will reason thus:— 'I am innocent; I am poor; my Ourang-Outang is of great value—to one in my circumstances a fortune of itself—why should I lose it through idle apprehensions of danger? Here it is, within my grasp. It was found in the Bois de Boulogne—at a vast distance from the scene of that butchery. How can it ever be suspected that a brute beast should have done the deed? The police are at fault—they have failed to procure the slightest clew. Should they even trace the animal, it would be impossible to prove me cognizant of the murder, or to implicate me in guilt on account of that cognizance. Above all, *I am known*. The advertiser designates me as the possessor of the beast. I am not sure to what limit his knowledge may extend. Should I avoid claiming a property of so great value, which it is known that I possess, I will render the animal, at least, liable to suspicion. It is not my policy to attract attention either to myself or to the beast. I will answer the advertisement, get the Ourang-Outang, and keep it close until this matter has blown over.'"

At this moment we heard a step upon the stairs.

"Be ready," said Dupin, "with your pistols, but neither use them nor show them until at a signal from myself."

The front door of the house had been left open, and the visitor had entered, without ringing, and advanced several steps upon the staircase. Now, however, he seemed to hesitate. Presently we heard him descending. Dupin was moving quickly to the door, when we again heard him coming up. He did not turn back a second time, but stepped up with decision and rapped at the door of our chamber.

"Come in," said Dupin, in a cheerful and hearty tone.

A man entered. He was a sailor, evidently,—a tall, stout, and muscular-looking person, with a certain daredevil expression of countenance, not altogether unprepossessing. His face, greatly sunburnt, was more than half hidden by whisker and *mustachio*. He had with him a huge oaken cudgel, but appeared to be otherwise unarmed. He bowed awkwardly, and bade us "good evening," in French accents, which, although somewhat Neufchatelish, were still sufficiently indicative of a Parisian origin.

"Sit down, my friend," said Dupin. "I suppose you have called about the Ourang-Outang. Upon my word, I almost envy you the possession of him; a remarkably fine, and no doubt a very valuable animal. How old do you suppose him to be?"

The sailor drew a long breath, with the air of a man relieved of some intolerable burden, and then replied, in an assured tone:

"I have no way of telling—but he can't be more than four or five years old. Have you got him here?"

"Oh no; we had no conveniences for keeping him here. He is at a livery stable in the Rue Dubourg, just by. You can get him in the morning. Of course you are prepared to identify the property?"

"To be sure I am, sir."

"I shall be sorry to part with him," said Dupin.

"I don't mean that you should be at all this trouble for nothing, sir," said the man. "Couldn't expect it. Am very willing to pay a reward for the finding of the animal—that is to say, any thing in reason."

"Well," replied my friend, "that is all very fair, to be sure. Let me think!—what should I have? Oh! I will tell you. My reward shall be this. You shall give me all the information in your power about these murders in the Rue Morgue."

Dupin said the last words in a very low tone, and very quietly. Just as quietly, too, he walked toward the door, locked it, and put the key in his pocket. He then drew a pistol from his bosom and placed it, without the least flurry, upon the table.

The sailor's face flushed up as if he were struggling with suffocation. He started to his feet and grasped his cudgel; but the next moment he fell back into his seat, trembling violently, and with the countenance of death itself. He spoke not a word. I pitied him from the bottom of my heart.

"My friend," said Dupin, in a kind tone, "you are alarming yourself unnecessarily—you are indeed. We mean you no harm whatever. I pledge you the honor of a gentleman, and of a Frenchman, that we intend you no injury. I perfectly well know that you are innocent of the atrocities in the Rue Morgue. It will not do, however, to deny that you are in some measure implicated in them. From what I have already said, you must know that I have had means of information about this matter—means of which you could never have dreamed. Now the thing stands thus. You have done nothing which you could have avoided—nothing, certainly, which renders you culpable. You were not even guilty of robbery, when you might have robbed with impunity. You have nothing to conceal. You have no reason for concealment. On the other hand, you are bound by every principle of honor to confess all you know. An innocent man is now imprisoned, charged with that crime of which you can point out the perpetrator."

The sailor had recovered his presence of mind; in a great measure, while Dupin uttered these words; but his original boldness of bearing was all gone.

"So help me God," said he, after a brief pause, "I *will* tell you all I know about this affair;—but I do not expect you to believe one half I say—I would be a fool indeed if I did. Still, I *am* innocent, and I will make a clean breast if I die for it."

What he stated was, in substance, this. He had lately made a voyage to the Indian Archipelago. A party, of which he formed one, landed at Borneo, and passed into the interior on an excursion of pleasure. Himself and a companion had captured the Ourang-Outang. This companion dying, the animal fell into his own exclusive possession. After great trouble, occasioned by the intractable ferocity of his captive during the home voyage, he at length succeeded in lodging it safely at his own residence in Paris, where, not to attract toward himself the unpleasant curiosity of his neighbors, he kept it carefully secluded, until such time as it should recover from a wound in the foot, received from a splinter on board ship. His ultimate design was to sell it.

Returning home from some sailors' frolic on the night, or rather in the morning of the murder, he found the beast occupying his own bed-room, into which it had broken from a closet adjoining, where it had been, as was thought, securely confined. Razor in hand, and fully lathered, it was sitting before a looking-glass, attempting the operation of shaving, in which it had no doubt previously watched its master through the key-hole of the closet. Terrified at the sight of so dangerous a weapon in the possession of an animal so ferocious, and so well able to use it, the man, for some moments, was at a loss what to do. He had been accustomed, however, to quiet the creature, even in its fiercest moods, by the use of a whip, and to this he now resorted. Upon sight of it, the Ourang-Outang sprang at once through the door of the chamber, down the stairs, and thence, through a window, unfortunately open, into the street.

The Frenchman followed in despair; the ape, razor still in hand, occasionally stopping to look back and gesticulate at its pursuer, until the latter had nearly come up with it. It then again made off. In this manner the chase continued for a long time. The streets were profoundly quiet, as it was nearly three o'clock in the morning. In passing down an alley in the rear of the Rue Morgue, the fugitive's attention was arrested by a light gleaming from the open window of Madame L'Espanaye's chamber, in the fourth story of her house. Rushing to the building, it perceived the lightning-rod, clambered up with inconceivable agility, grasped the shutter, which was thrown fully back against the wall, and, by its means, swung itself directly upon the head-board of the bed. The whole feat did not occupy a minute. The shutter was kicked open again by the Ourang-Outang as it entered the room.

The sailor, in the meantime, was both rejoiced and perplexed. He had strong hopes of now recapturing the brute, as it could scarcely escape from the trap into which it had ventured, except by the rod, where it might be intercepted as it came down. On the other hand, there was much cause for anxiety as to what it might do in the house. This latter reflection urged the man still to follow the fugitive. A lightning-rod is ascended without difficulty, especially by a sailor; but, when he had arrived as high as the window, which lay far to his left, his career was stopped; the most that he could accomplish was to reach over so as to obtain a glimpse of the interior of the room. At this glimpse he nearly fell from his hold through excess of horror. Now it was that those hideous shrieks arose upon the night, which had startled from slumber the inmates of the Rue Morgue. Madame L'Espanaye and her daughter, habited in their night clothes, had apparently been arranging some papers in the iron chest already mentioned, which had been wheeled into the middle of the room. It was open, and its contents lay beside it on the floor. The victims must have been sitting with their backs toward the window; and, from the time elapsing between the ingress of the beast and the screams, it seems probable that it was not immediately perceived. The flapping-to of the shutter would naturally have been attributed to the wind.

As the sailor looked in, the gigantic animal had seized Madame L'Espanaye by the hair, (which was loose, as she had been combing it,) and was flourishing the razor about her face, in imitation of the motions of a barber. The daughter lay prostrate and motionless; she had swooned. The screams and struggles of the old lady (during which the hair was torn from her head) had the effect of changing the probably pacific purposes of the Ourang-Outang into those of wrath. With one determined sweep of its muscular arm it nearly severed her head from her body. The sight of blood inflamed its anger into phrenzy. Gnashing its teeth, and flashing fire from its eyes, it flew upon the body of the girl, and imbedded its fearful talons in her throat, retaining its grasp until she expired. Its wandering and wild glances fell at this moment upon the head of the bed, over which the face of its master, rigid with horror, was just discernible. The fury of the beast, who no doubt bore still in mind the dreaded whip, was instantly converted into fear. Conscious of having deserved punishment, it seemed desirous of concealing its bloody deeds, and skipped about the chamber in an agony of nervous agitation; throwing down and breaking the furniture as it moved, and dragging the bed from the bedstead. In conclusion, it seized first the corpse of the daughter, and thrust it up the chimney, as it was found; then that of the old lady, which it immediately hurled through the window headlong.

As the ape approached the casement with its mutilated burden, the sailor shrank aghast to the rod, and, rather gliding than clambering down it, hurried at once home—dreading the consequences of the butchery, and gladly abandoning, in his terror, all solicitude about the fate of the Ourang-Outang. The words heard by the party upon the staircase were the Frenchman's exclamations of horror and affright, commingled with the fiendish jabberings of the brute.

I have scarcely anything to add. The Ourang-Outang must have escaped from the chamber, by the rod, just before the breaking of the door. It must have closed the window as it passed through it. It was subsequently caught by the owner himself, who obtained for it a very large sum at the *Jardin des Plantes*. Le Bon was instantly released, upon our narration of the circumstances (with some comments from Dupin) at the *bureau* of the Prefect of Police. This functionary, however well disposed to my friend, could not altogether conceal his chagrin at the turn which affairs had taken, and was fain to indulge in a sarcasm or two, about the propriety of every person minding his own business.

"Let them talk," said Dupin, who had not thought it necessary to reply. "Let him discourse; it will ease his conscience. I am satisfied with having defeated him in his own castle. Nevertheless, that he failed in the solution of this mystery, is by no means that matter for wonder which he supposes it; for, in truth, our friend the Prefect is somewhat too cunning to be profound. In his wisdom is no *stamen*. It is all head and no body, like the pictures of the Goddess Laverna,—or, at best, all head and shoulders, like a codfish. But he is a good creature after all. I like him especially for one master stroke of cant, by which he has attained his reputation for ingenuity. I mean the way he has '*de nier ce qui est, et d'expliquer ce qui n'est pas.*'"*

CONSTRUCTING A READING

1. Using this story as your example, but remembering also "The Red Headed League" from Chapter Two and any other detective stories that you may know, begin to construct a list of the generic characteristics of detective stories by describing the kind of minimal story they usually tell.
2. What questions does the minimal story prompt you to ask?
3. Think next about the kinds of characters you find in both stories: the detective, his sidekick and at least one member of the police force. With your group members, describe each of them.
4. What questions, if any, do their characteristics lead you to raise?
5. Think next, again with your group, about relations between narrator and reader. What do you (as reader) know and when do you know it?
6. How about relations between the detective and the reader? With whom do you find yourself identifying and/or sympathizing?

---

*A quotation from Jean-Jacques Rousseau's *La Nouvelle Héloïse:* "to deny what *is* the case and to explain what is not the case."

7. Do you find that detective stories have a common theme? If so, what? If not, why?

Mixed Genres

The story that follows, "Young Goodman Brown," deliberately sends ambiguous generic signals. When (and if) you experience uncertainty about the events of this narrative, you'll be confronting Hawthorne's challenge to your generic expectations. I've annotated the text with some markers to help you.

Young Goodman Brown

Nathaniel Hawthorne

Young Goodman Brown came forth at sunset into the street at Salem village; but put his head back, after crossing the threshold, to exchange a parting kiss with his young wife. And Faith, as the wife was aptly named, thrust her own pretty head into the street, letting the wind play with the pink ribbons of her cap while she called to Goodman Brown.

> What do you think is the significance of Goodman Brown's wife's name, "Faith"?

"Dearest heart," whispered she, softly and rather sadly, when her lips were close to his ear, "prithee put off your journey until sunrise and sleep in your own bed tonight. A lone woman is troubled with such dreams and such thoughts that she's afeard of herself sometimes. Pray tarry with me this night, dear husband, of all the nights in the year."

> In the terms we have been using so far, Goodman Brown's departure introduces disequilibrium into the story: a disagreement between husband and wife. He is about to embark on a journey and his wife wants him to stay at home. At this point, do you take sides? As reader, do you want Goodman Brown to stay at home or do you want his wife to permit him to go without remonstrating? When Young Goodman Brown kisses his wife goodbye, what do you expect to happen?

"My love and my Faith," replied young Goodman Brown, "of all nights in the year, this one night must I tarry away from thee. My journey, as thou callest it, forth and back again, must needs be done 'twixt now and sunrise. What, my sweet, pretty wife, dost thou doubt me already, and we but three months married?"

"Then God bless you!" said Faith, with the pink ribbons; "and may you find all well when you come back."

"Amen!" cried Goodman Brown. "Say thy prayers, dear Faith, and go to bed at dusk, and no harm will come to thee."

> When Goodman Brown tells his wife that "no harm will come to" her, what do you expect to happen? If you expect that she will somehow be harmed, then you have learned to suspect that Goodman Brown's promises are not entirely trustworthy in this context. That suspicion is a generic expectation.

So they parted; and the young man pursued his way until, being about to turn the corner by the meetinghouse, he looked back and saw the head of Faith still peeping after him with a melancholy air, in spite of her pink ribbons.

"Poor little Faith!" thought he, for his heart smote him. "What a wretch am I to leave her on such an errand! She talks of dreams, too. Methought as she spoke there was trouble in her face, as if a dream had warned her what work is to be done tonight. But no, no; 't would kill her to think it. Well, she's a blessed angel on earth; and after this one night I'll cling to her skirts and follow her to heaven."

With this excellent resolve for the future, Goodman Brown felt himself justified in making more haste on his present evil purpose. He had taken a dreary road, darkened by all the gloomiest trees of the forest, which barely stood aside to let the narrow path creep through, and closed immediately behind. It was all as lonely as could be; and there is this peculiarity in such a solitude, that the traveller knows not who may be concealed by the innumerable trunks and the thick boughs overhead; so that with lonely footsteps he may yet be passing through an unseen multitude.

When Young Goodman Brown muses that his Faith "seemed troubled as if a dream had warned her what work will be done tonight," what do you expect to happen?

What do you suppose Brown's purpose is? Why does the narrator describe it as "evil"?

"There may be a devilish Indian behind every tree," said Goodman Brown to himself; and he glanced fearfully behind him as he added, "What if the devil himself should be at my very elbow!"

Techniques of characterization are generic conventions. What inference do you draw from this characterization of Native Americans?

His head being turned back, he passed a crook of the road, and looking forward again, beheld the figure of a man, in grave and decent attire, seated at the foot of an old tree. He arose at Goodman Brown's approach and walked onward side by side with him.

"You are late, Goodman Brown," said he. "The clock of the Old South was striking as I came through Boston, and that is full fifteen minutes agone."

"Faith kept me back a while," replied the young man, with a tremor in his voice, caused by the sudden appearance of his companion, though not wholly unexpected.

It was now deep dusk in the forest, and deepest in that part of it where these two were journeying. As nearly as could be discerned, the second traveller was about fifty years old, apparently in the same rank of life as Goodman Brown, and bearing a considerable resemblance to him, though perhaps more in expression than features. Still they might have been taken for father and son. And yet, though the elder person was as simply clad as the younger, and as simple in manner too, he had an indescribable air of one who knew the world, and

One of the ways in which Hawthorne characterizes is by the names of his characters. When Goodman Brown says that Faith detained him, what inference do you draw about the character of his spouse and his relationship with her?

who would not have felt abashed at the governor's dinner table or in King William's court, were it possible that his affairs should call him thither. But the only thing about him that could be fixed upon as remarkable was his staff, which bore the likeness of a great black snake, so curiously wrought that it might almost be seen to twist and wriggle itself like a living serpent. This, of course, must have been an ocular deception, assisted by the uncertain light.

"Come, Goodman Brown," cried his fellow-traveller, "this is a dull pace for the beginning of a journey. Take my staff, if you are so soon weary."

"Friend," said the other, exchanging his slow pace for a full stop, "having kept covenant by meeting thee here, it is my purpose now to return whence I came. I have scruples touching the matter thou wot'st of."

"Sayest thou so?" replied he of the serpent, smiling apart. "Let us walk on, nevertheless, reasoning as we go; and if I convince thee not thou shalt turn back. We are but a little way in the forest yet."

> What are your associations with serpents? What are your associations with reasoning? In the context of those associations, what do you expect will be the relations between Goodman Brown and the man with the serpentine staff?

"Too far! too far!" exclaimed the goodman, unconsciously resuming his walk. "My father never went into the woods on such an errand, nor his father before him. We have been a race of honest men and good Christians since the days of the martyrs; and shall I be the first of the name of Brown that ever took his path and kept—"

"Such company, thou wouds't say," observed the elder person, interpreting his pause. "Well said, Goodman Brown! I have been as well acquainted with your family as with ever a one among the Puritans; and that's no trifle to say. I helped your grandfather, the constable, when he lashed the Quaker woman so smartly through the streets of Salem; and it was I that brought your father a pitch pine knot, kindled at my own hearth, to set fire to the Indian village, in King Philip's war. They were my good friends, both; and many a pleasant walk have we had along this path, and returned merrily after midnight. I would fain be friends with you for their sake."

"If it be as thou sayest," replied Goodman Brown, "I marvel they never spoke of these matters; or, verily, I marvel not, seeing that the least rumor of the sort would have driven them from New England. We are a people of prayer, and good works to boot, and abide no such wickedness."

"Wickedness or not," said the traveller with the twisted staff, "I have a very general acquaintance here in New England. The deacons of many a church have drunk the communion wine with me; the selectmen of divers towns make me their chairman; and a majority of the Great and General Court are firm supporters of my interest. The governor and I, too,—But these are state secrets."

"Can this be so?" cried Goodman Brown, with a stare of amazement at his undisturbed companion. "Howbeit, I have nothing to do with the governor and council; they have their own ways, and are no rule for a simple husbandman like me. But, were I to go on with thee, how should I meet the eye of that good old man, our minister, at Salem village? Oh, his voice would make me tremble both Sabbath day and lecture day."

Thus far the elder traveller had listened with due gravity; but now burst into a fit of irrepressible mirth, shaking himself so violently that his snake-like staff actually seemed to wriggle in sympathy.

"Ha! ha! ha!" shouted he again and again; then composing himself. "Well, go on, Goodman Brown, go on; but prithee, don't kill me with laughing."

Why is the stranger laughing?

"Well, then, to end the matter at once," said Goodman Brown, considerably nettled, "there is my wife Faith. It would break her dear little heart; and I'd rather break my own."

"Nay, if that be the case," answered the other, "e'en go thy ways, Goodman Brown. I wold not for twenty old woman like the one hobbling before us that Faith should come to any harm."

As he spoke he pointed his staff at a female figure on the path, in whom Goodman Brown recognized a very pious and exemplary dame, who had taught him his catechism in youth, and was still his moral and spiritual advisor, jointly with the minister and Deacon Gookin.

"A marvel, truly, that Goody Cloyse should be so far in the wilderness at nightfall," said he. "But with your leave, friend, I shall take a cut through the woods until we have left this Christian woman behind. Being a stranger to you, she might ask whom I was consorting with and whiter I was going."

What is your response to the appearance of the old lady? Why do you suppose Goodman Brown wishes to avoid her?

"Be it so," said his fellow traveller. "Betake you to the woods, and let me keep the path."

Accordingly the young man turned aside, but took care to watch his companion, who advanced softly along the road until he had come within a staff's length of the old dame. She, meanwhile, was making the best of her way, with a singular speed for so aged a woman, and mumbling some indistinct words—a prayer, doubtless—as she went. The traveller put forth his staff and touched her withered neck with what seemed the serpent's tail.

"The devil!" screamed the pious old lady.

In your experience with other stories, what usually happens when someone meets the devil? What do you think will happen now in this story?

"Then Goody Cloyse knows her old friend?" observed the traveller, confronting her and leaning on his writhing stick.

"Ah, forsooth, and is it your worship indeed?" cried the good dame. "Yea, truly is it, and in the very image of my old gossip, Goodman Brown, the grandfather of the silly fellow that now is. But—would your worship believe it?—my broomstick hath strangely disappeared, stolen, as I suspect, by that unhanged witch, Goody Cory, and that, too, when I was all anointed with the juice of smallage, and cinquefoil, and wolf's bane—"

"Mingled with fine wheat and the fat of a newborn babe," said the shape of old Goodman Brown.

Ah, your worship knows the recipe," cried the old lady, cackling aloud. "So, as I was saying, being all ready for the meeting, and no horse to ride on, I made up my mind to foot it; for they tell me there is a nice young man to be taken into communion tonight. But now your good worship will lend me your arm, and we shall be there in a twinkling."

"That can hardly be," answered her friend. "I may not spare you my arm, Goody Cloyse; but here is my staff, if you will."

So saying, he threw it down at her feet, where, perhaps, it assumed life, being one of the rods which its owner had formerly lent to the Egyptian magi. Of this fact, however, Goodman Brown could not take cognizance. He had cast up his eyes in astonishment, and looking down again, beheld neither Goody Cloyse nor the serpentine staff, but his fellow-traveller alone, who waited for him as calmly as if nothing had happened.

Up until now, the story has been more or less realistic but now it suddenly seems to have supernatural events. When Goody Cloyse suddenly disappears, what is your response? Do you assume the story will eventually provide a rational explanation? Do you decide that this story is *about* the supernatural? Is there a sense in which you think both alternatives simultaneously?

"That old woman taught me my catechism," said the young man; and there was a world of meaning in this simple comment.

What world of meaning is in Goodman Brown's observation?

They continued to walk onward, while the elder traveller exhorted his companion to make good speed and persevere in the path, discoursing so aptly that his arguments seemed rather to spring up in the bosom of his auditor than to be suggested by himself. As they went, he plucked a branch of maple to serve for a walking stick, and began to strip it of the twigs and little boughs, which were wet with evening dew. The moment his fingers touched them they became strangely withered and dried up as with a week's sunshine. Thus the pair proceeded, at a good free pace, until suddenly, in a gloomy hollow of the road, Goodman Brown sat himself down on the stump of a tree and refused to go any farther.

At this point, the story elicits more than one set of generic expectations. On the one hand, it seems to be a realistic story about a young man who goes out at night on business. On the other, it would seem to be a fantasy about a witch and the devil. Describe your response to these contradictory guidelines.

"Friend," said he, stubbornly, "my mind is made up. Not another step will I budge on this errand. What if a wretched old woman do choose to go to the devil when I thought she was going to heaven: is that any reason why I should quit my dear Faith and go after her?"

Think again about the significance of Faith's name. What are you being led to expect?

"You will think better of this by and by," said his acquaintance, composedly. "Sit here and rest yourself a while; and when you feel like moving again, there is my staff to help you along."

Without more words, he threw his companion the maple stick, and was as speedily out of sight as if he had vanished into the deepening gloom. The young man sat a few moments by the roadside, applauding himself greatly, and thinking with how clear a conscience he should meet the minister in his morning walk, nor shrink from the eye of good old Deacon Gookin. And what calm sleep would be his that very night, which was to have been spent so wickedly, but so purely and sweetly now, in the arms of Faith! Amidst these pleasant and praiseworthy meditations, Goodman Brown heard the tramp of horses along the road, and deemed it advisable to conceal himself within the verge of the forest, conscious of the guilty purpose that had brought him thither, though now so happily turned from it.

On came the hoof tramps and the voices of the riders, two grave old voices, conversing soberly as they drew near. These mingled sounds appeared to pass along the road, within a few yards of the young man's hiding place; but, owing doubtless to the depth of the gloom at that particular spot, neither the travellers nor their steeds were visible. Though their figures brushed the small boughs by the wayside, it could not be seen that they intercepted, even for a moment, the faint gleam from the strip of bright sky athwart which they must have passed. Goodman Brown alternately crouched and stood on tiptoe, pulling aside the branches and thrusting forth his head as far as he durst without discerning so much as a shadow. It vexed him the more, because he could have sworn, were such a thing possible, that he recognized the voices of the minister and Deacon Gookin, jogging along quietly, as they were wont to do, when bound to some ordination or ecclesiastical council. While yet within hearing, one of the riders stopped to pluck a switch.

What was Goodman Brown's guilty purpose? Are you able to specify it yet?

"Of the two, reverend sir," said the voice like the deacon's, "I had rather miss an ordination dinner than tonight's meeting. They tell me that some of our community are to be here from Falmouth and beyond, and others from Connecticut and Rhode Island, besides several of the Indian powwows, who, after their fashion, know almost as much deviltry as the best of us. Moreover, there is a goodly young woman to be taken into communion."

What goodly young woman do you think it will be?

"Mighty well, Deacon Gookin!" replied the solemn old tones of the minister. "Spur up, or we shall be late. Nothing can be done, you know, until I get on the ground."

The hoofs clattered again; and the voices, talking so strangely in the empty air, passed on through the forest, where no church had ever been gathered or solitary Christian prayed. Wither, then, could these holy men be journeying so deep into the heathen wilderness? Young Goodman Brown caught hold of a tree for support, being ready to sink down on the ground, faint and overburdened with the heavy sickness of his heart. He looked up to the sky, doubting whether there really was a heaven above him. Yet there was the blue arch, and the stars brightening in it.

"With heaven above and Faith below, I will yet stand firm against the devil!" cried Goodman Brown.

By now the discourse has completely connected the character "Faith" with young Goodman Brown's religious beliefs. What is your response?

While he still gazed upward into the deep arch of the firmament and had lifted his hands to pray, a cloud, though no wind was stirring, hurried across the zenith and hid the brightening stars. The blue sky was still visible, except directly overhead, where this black mass of cloud was sweeping swiftly northward. Aloft in the air, as if from the depths of the cloud, came a confused and doubtful sound of voices. Once the listener fancied that he could distinguish the accents of townspeople of his own, men and women, both pious and ungodly, many of whom he had met at the communion table, and had seen others rioting at the tavern. The next moment, so indistinct were the sounds, he doubted whether he had heard aught but the murmur of the old forest, whispering without a wind. Then came a stronger swell of those familiar tones, heard daily in the sunshine at Salem village, but never until now from a cloud of night. There was one voice of a young woman, uttering lamentations, yet with an uncertain sorrow, and entreating for some favor, which perhaps, it would grieve her to obtain; and all the unseen multitude, both saints and sinners, seemed to encourage her onward.

"Faith!" shouted Goodman Brown, in a voice of agony and desperation; and the echoes of the forest mocked him, crying, "Faith! Faith!" as if bewildered wretches were seeking her all through the wilderness.

The cry of grief, rage, and terror was yet piercing the night, when the unhappy husband held his breath for a response. There was a scream, drowned immediately in a louder murmur of voices, fading into far-off laughter, as the dark cloud swept away, leaving the clear and silent sky above Goodman Brown. But something fluttered lightly down through the air and caught on the branch of a tree. The young man seized it, and beheld a pink ribbon.

"My Faith is gone!" cried he, after one stupefied moment. "There is no good on earth; and sin is but a name. Come, devil; for to thee is this world given."

And, maddened with despair, so that he laughed loud and long, did Goodman Brown grasp his staff and set forth again, at such a rate that he seemed to fly along the forest path rather than to walk or run. The road grew wilder and drearier and more faintly traced, and vanished at length, leaving him in the heart of the dark wilderness, still rushing onward with the instinct that guides mortal man to evil. The whole forest was peopled with frightful sounds—the creaking of the trees, the howling of wild beasts, and the yell of Indians; while sometimes the wind tolled like a distant church bell, and sometimes gave a broad roar around the traveller, as if all Nature were laughing him to scorn. But he was himself the chief horror of the scene, and shrank not from its other horrors.

"Ha! ha! ha!" roared Goodman Brown when the wind laughed at him. "Let us hear which will laugh loudest. Think not to frighten me with your deviltry. Come witch, come wizard, come Indian powwow, come devil himself, and here comes Goodman Brown. You may as well fear him as he fear you."

In truth, all through the haunted forest there could be nothing more frightful than the figure of Goodman Brown. On he flew among the black pines, brandishing his staff with frenzied gestures, now giving vent to an inspiration of horrid blasphemy, and now shouting forth such laughter as set all the echoes of the forest laughing like demons around him. The fiend in his own shape is less hideous than when he rages in the breast of man. Thus sped the demoniac on his course, until, quivering among the trees, he saw a red light before him, as when the felled trunks and branches of a clearing have been set on fire, and throw up their lurid blaze against the sky, at the hour of midnight. He paused, in a lull of the tempest that had driven him onward, and heard the swell of what seemed a hymn, rolling solemnly from a distance with the weight of many voices. He knew the tune; it was a familiar one in the choir of the village meeting-house. The verse died heavily away, and was lengthened by a chorus, not of human voices, but of all the sounds of the benighted wilderness pealing in awful harmony together. Goodman Brown cried out, and his cry was lost to his own ear by its unison with the cry of the desert.

In the interval of silence he stole forward until the light glared full upon his eyes. At one extremity of an open space, hemmed in by the dark wall of the forest, arose a rock, bearing some rude, natural resemblance either to an altar or a pulpit, and surrounded by four blazing pines, their tops aflame, their stems untouched, like candles at an evening meeting. The mass of foliage that had overgrown the summit of the rock was all on fire, blazing high into the night and fitfully illuminating the whole field. Each pendent twig and leafy festoon was in a blaze. As the red light arose and fell, a numerous congregation alternately shone forth, then disappeared in shadow, and again grew, as it were, out of the darkness, peopling the heart of the solitary woods at once.

"A grave and dark clad company," quoth Goodman Brown.

In truth they were such. Among them, quivering to and fro between gloom and splendor, appeared faces that would be seen next day at the council board of the province, and others which, Sabbath after Sabbath, looked devoutly heavenward, and benignantly over the crowded pews, from the holiest pulpits in the land. Some affirm that the lady of the governor was there. At least there were high dames well known to her, and wives of honored husbands, and widows, a great multitude, and ancient maidens, all of excellent repute, and fair young girls, who trembled lest their mothers should espy them. Either the sudden gleams of light flashing over the obscure field bedazzled Goodman Brown, or he recognized a score of the church members of Salem village famous for their especial sanctity. Good old Deacon Gookin had arrived, and waited at the skirts of that venerable saint, his revered pastor. But, irreverently consorting with these grave, reputable, and pious people, these elders of the church, these chaste dames and dewy virgins, there were men of dissolute lives and women of spotted fame, wretches given over to all mean and filthy vice, and suspected even of horrid crimes. It was strange to see that the good shrank not from the wicked, nor were the sinners abashed by the saints. Scattered also among their pale-faced enemies were the Indian priests, or powwows, who had often scared their native forest with more hideous incantations than any known to English witchcraft.

"But where is Faith?" thought Goodman Brown; and, as hope came into his heart, he trembled.

Another verse of the hymn arose, a slow and mournful strain, such as the pious love, but joined to words which expressed all that our nature can conceive of sin, and darkly hinted at far more. Unfathomable to mere mortals is the lore of fiends. Verse after verse was sung; and still the chorus of the desert swelled between like the deepest tone of a mighty organ; and with the final peal of that dreadful anthem there came a sound, as if the roaring wind, the rushing streams, the howling beasts, and every other voice of the unconcerted wilderness were mingling and according with the voice of guilty man in homage to the prince of all. The four blazing pines threw up a loftier flame, and obscurely discovered shapes and visages of horror on the smoke wreaths above the impious assembly. At the same moment the fire on the rock shot redly forth and formed a glowing arch above its base, where now appeared a figure. With reverence be it spoken, the figure bore no slight similitude, both in garb and manner, to some grave divine of the New England churches.

"Bring forth the converts!" cried a voice that echoed through the field and rolled into the forest.

At the word, Goodman Brown stepped forth from the shadow of the trees and approached the congregation, with whom he felt a loathful brotherhood by the sympathy of all that was wicked in his heart. He could have well nigh sworn that the shape of his own dead father beckoned him to advance, looking downward from a smoke wreath, while a woman, with dim features of despair, threw out her hand to warn him back. Was it his mother? But he had no power to retreat one step, nor to resist, even in thought, when the minister and good old Deacon Gookin seized his arms and led him to the blazing rock. Thither came also the slender form of a veiled female, led between Goody Cloyse, that pious teacher of the catechism, and Martha Carrier, who had received the devil's promise to be queen of hell. A rampant hag was she. And there stood the proselytes beneath the canopy of fire.

"Welcome, my children," said the dark figure, "to the communion of your race. Ye have found this young your nature and your destiny. My children, look behind you"

They turned; and flashing forth, as it were, in a sheet of flame, the fiend worshippers were seen; the smile of welcome gleamed darkly on every visage.

"There"; resumed the sable form, "are all whom ye have reverenced from youth. Ye deemed them holier than yourselves, and shrank from your own sin, contrasting it with their lives of righteousness and prayerful aspirations heavenward. Yet here are they all in my worshipping assembly. This night it shall be granted you to know their secret deeds: how hoary-bearded elders of the church have whispered wanton words to the young maids of their households; how many a woman, eager for widows' weeds, has given her husband a drink at bedtime and let him sleep his last sleep in her bosom; how beardless youths have made haste to inherit their fathers' wealth; and how fair damsels— blush not, sweet ones—have dug little graves in the garden, and bidden me, the sole guest to an infant's funeral. By the sympathy of your human hearts for sin ye shall scent out all the places—whether in church, bedchamber, street, field, or forest—where crime has been committed, and shall exult to behold the whole earth one stain of guilt, one mighty blood spot. Far more than this. It shall be yours to penetrate, in every bosom, the deep mystery of sin, the fountain of all wicked arts, and which inexhaustibly supplies more evil impulses than human power—than my power at its utmost—can make manifest in deeds. And now, my children, look upon each other."

They did so; and, by the blaze of the hell-kindled torches, the wretched man beheld his Faith, and the wife her husband, trembling before that unhallowed altar.

How would you describe and classify the "faith" trope in this story? How do you respond to Hawthorne's choice to use a woman as a figure for religious belief?

"Lo, there ye stand, my children," said the figure, in a deep and solemn tone, almost sad with its despairing awfulness, as if his once angelic nature could yet mourn for our miserable race. "Depending upon one another's hearts, ye had still hoped that virtue were not all a dream. Now are ye undeceived. Evil is the nature of mankind. Evil must be your only happiness. Welcome again, my children, to the communion of your race."

"Welcome," repeated the fiend worshippers, in one cry of despair and triumph.

And there they stood, the only pair, as it seemed, who were yet hesitating on the verge of wickedness in this dark world. A basin was hollowed, naturally, in the rock. Did it contain water, reddened by the lurid light? or was it blood? or, perchance, a liquid flame? Herein did the shape of evil dip his hand and prepare to lay the mark of baptism upon their foreheads, that they might be partakers of the mystery of sin, more conscious of the secret guilt of others, both in deed and thought, than they could now be of their own. The husband cast one look at his pale wife, and Faith at him. What polluted wretches would the next glance show them to each other, shuddering alike at what they disclosed and what they saw!

"Faith! Faith!" cried the husband, "look up to heaven, and resist the wicked one."

Whether Faith obeyed he knew not. Hardly had he spoken when he found himself amid calm night and solitude, listening to a roar of the wind which died heavily away through the forest. He staggered against the rock, and felt it chill and damp; while a hanging twig, that had been all on fire, besprinkled his cheek with the coldest dew.

The next morning young Goodman Brown came slowly into the street of Salem village, staring around him like a bewildered man.

> What is your response at this time to the color of Faith's ribbons? Is pink a usual color for a Puritan woman to wear?

The good old minister was taking a walk along the graveyard to get an appetite for breakfast and meditate his sermon, and bestowed a blessing, as he passed, on Goodman Brown. He shrank from the venerable saint as if to avoid an anathema. Old Deacon Gookin was at domestic worship, and the holy words of his prayer were heard through the open window. "What God doth the wizard pray to?" quoth Goodman Brown. Goody Cloyse, that excellent old Christian, stood in the early sunshine at her own lattice, catechizing a little girl who had brought her a pint of morning's milk. Goodman Brown snatched away the child as from the grasp of the fiend himself. Turning the corner by the meeting-house, he spied the head of Faith, with the pink ribbons, gazing anxiously forth, and bursting into such joy at sight of him that she skipped along the street and almost kissed her husband before the whole village. But Goodman Brown looked sternly and sadly into her face, and passed on without a greeting.

Had Goodman Brown fallen asleep in the forest and only dreamed a wild dream of a witch-meeting?

Be it so if you will; but, alas! it was a dream of evil omen for young

> Speculate about this question. Would the story have different meaning for you if the events in the forest were "only" a dream?

Goodman Brown. A stern, a sad, a darkly meditative, a distrustful, if not a desperate man did he become from the night of that fearful dream. On the Sabbath day, when the congregation were singing a holy psalm, he could not listen because an anthem of sin rushed loudly upon his ear and drowned all the blessed strain. When the minister spoke from the pulpit with power and fervid eloquence, and, with his hand on the open Bible, of the sacred truths of our religion, and of saint-like lives and triumphant deaths, and of future bliss or misery unutterable, then did Goodman Brown turn pale, dreading lest the roof should thunder down upon the gray blasphemer and his hearers. Often, waking suddenly at midnight, he shrank from the bosom of Faith; and at morning or eventide, when the family knelt down at prayer, he scowled and muttered to himself, and gazed sternly at his wife, and turned away. And when he had lived long, and was borne to his grave a hoary corpse, followed by Faith, an aged woman, and children and grandchildren, a goodly procession, besides neighbors not a few, they carved no hopeful verse upon his tombstone, for his dying hour was gloom.

C O N S T R U C T I N G   A   R E A D I N G

1. Compare your answers to the questions I've posed with those of your classmates. How do you account for differences?
2. Hawthorne's narrative hovers between realism and fantasy, leaving its readers uncertain whether its events are supernatural or rationally explicable. List some of the aspects of this story that leave you in such doubt. Speculate about Hawthorne's purpose in invoking the fantasy genre.
3. How do you think this story reflects its culture?

CHALLENGING GENERIC EXPECTATIONS

Earlier in this chapter, I noted that some stories deliberately reject or question the structures that narratologists describe. Ann Beattie's story, "The Working Girl," certainly seems to pose a problem for traditional narratology. In it, Beattie's storyteller has a conversation with someone else (another aspect of herself as storyteller? a reader?) about the kinds of generic expectations we have discussed in this chapter.

The Working Girl
Ann Beattie

This is a story about Jeanette, who is a working girl. She sometimes thinks of herself as a traveler, a seductress, a secret gourmet. She takes a one-week vacation in the summer to see her sister in Michigan, buys lace-edged silk underpants from a mail-order catalogue, and has improvised a way, in America, to make crème fraîche, which is useful on so many occasions.

Is this another story in which the author knows the main character too well?

Let's suppose, for a moment, that the storyteller is actually mystified by Jeanette, and only seems to stand in judgment because words come easily. Let's imagine that in real life there is, or once was, a person named Jeanette, and that from a conversation the storyteller had with her, it could be surmised that Jeanette has a notion of freedom, though the guilty quiver of the mouth when she says "Lake Michigan" is something of a giveaway about how she really feels. If the storyteller is a woman, Jeanette might readily confide that she is a seductress, but if the author is a man, Jeanette will probably keep quiet on that count. Crème fraîche is crème fraîche, and not worth thinking about. But back to the original supposition: Let's say that the storyteller is a woman, and that Jeanette discusses the pros and cons of the working life, calling a spade a spade, and greenbacks greenbacks, and if Jeanette is herself a good storyteller, Lake Michigan sounds exciting, and if she isn't, it doesn't. Let's say that Jeanette talks about the romance in her life, and that the storyteller finds it credible. Even interesting. That there are details: Jeanette's lover makes a photocopy of his hand and drops the piece of paper in her in-box; Jeanette makes a copy of her hand and has her trusted friend Charlie hang it in the men's room, where it is allowed to stay until Jeanette's lover sees it, because it means nothing to anyone else. If the storyteller is lucky, they will exchange presents small enough to be put in a breast pocket or the pocket of a skirt. Also a mini French-English/English-French dictionary (France is the place they hope to visit); a finger puppet; an ad that is published in the "personals" column, announcing, by his initials, whom he loves (her), laminated in plastic and made useful as well as romantic by its conversion into a keyring. Let's hope, for the sake of a good story, they are wriggling together in the elevator, sneaking kisses as the bubbles rise in the watercooler, and she is tying his shoelaces together at night, to delay his departure in the morning.

Where is the wife?

In North Dakota or Memphis or Paris, let's say. Let's say she's out of the picture even if she isn't out of the picture.

No no no. Too expedient. The wife has to be there: a presence, even if she's gone off somewhere. There has to be a wife, and she has to be either determined and brave, vile and addicted, or so ordinary that with a mere sentence of description, the reader instantly knows that she is a prototypical wife.

There is a wife. She is a pretty, dark-haired girl who married young, and who won a trip to Paris and is therefore out of town.

Nonsense. *Paris?*

She won a beauty contest.

But she can't be beautiful. She has to be ordinary.

It suddenly becomes apparent that she is extraordinary. She's quite beautiful, and she's in Paris, and although there's no reason to bring this up, the people who sponsored the contest do not know that she's married.

If this is what the wife is like, she'll be more interesting than the subject of the story.

Not if the working girl is believable, and the wife's exit has been made credible.

But we know how that story will end.

How will it end?

It will end badly—which means predictably—because either the beautiful wife will triumph, and then it will be just another such story, or the wife will turn out to be not so interesting after all, and by default the working girl will triumph.

When is the last time you heard of a working girl triumphing?

They do it every day. They are executives, not "working girls."

No, not those. This is about a real working girl. One who gets very little money or vacation time, who periodically rewards herself for life's injustices by buying cream and charging underwear she'll spend a year paying off.

All right, then. What is the story?

Are you sure you want to hear it? Apparently you are already quite shaken, to have found out that the wife, initially ordinary, is in fact extraordinary, and has competed in a beauty pageant and won a trip to Paris.

But this was to be a story about the working girl. What's the scoop with her?

This is just the way the people in the office think: the boss wants to know what's going on in his secretary's mind, the secretary wonders if the mail boy is gay, the mail boy is cruising the elevator operator, and every day the working girl walks into this tense, strange situation. She does it because she needs the money, and also because it's the way things are. It isn't going to be much different wherever she works.

Details. Make the place seem real.

In the winter, when the light disappears early, the office has a very strange aura. The ficus trees cast shadows on the desks. The water in the watercooler looks golden—more like wine than water.

How many people are there?

There are four people typing in the main room, and there are three executives, who share an executive secretary. She sits to the left of the main room.

Which one is the working girl in love with?

Andrew Darby, the most recently hired executive. He has prematurely gray hair, missed two days of work when his dog didn't pull through surgery, and was never drafted because of a deteriorating disc which causes him much pain, though it is difficult to predict when the pain will come on. Once it seemed to coincide with the rising of a bubble in the watercooler. The pain shot up his spine as though mimicking the motion of the bubble.

And he's married?

We just finished discussing his wife.

He's really married, right?

There are no tricks here. He's been married for six years.

Is there more information about his wife?

No. You can find out what the working girl thinks of her, but as far as judging for yourself, you can't, because she is in Paris. What good would it do to overhear a phone conversation between the wife and Andrew? None of us generalizes from phone conversations. Other than that, there's only a postcard. It's a close-up of a column, and she says on the back that she loves and misses him. That if love could be embodied in columns, her love for him would be Corinthian.

That's quite something. What is his reaction to that?

He receives the postcard the same day his ad appears in the "personals" column. He has it in his pocket when he goes to laminate the ad, punch a hole in the plastic, insert a chain, and make a keyring of it.

Doesn't he go through a bad moment?

A bit of one, but basically he is quite pleased with himself. He and Jeanette are going to lunch together. Over lunch, he gives her the keyring. She is slightly scandalized, amused, and touched. They eat sandwiches. He can't sit in a booth because of his back.

They sit at a table.

Ten years later, where is Andrew Darby?

Dead. He dies of complications following surgery. A blood clot that went to his brain.

Why does he have to die?

This is just reporting, now. In point of fact, he dies.

Is Jeanette still in touch with him when he dies?

She's his wife. Married men do leave their wives. Andrew Darby didn't have that rough a go of it. After a while, he and his former wife developed a fairly cordial relationship. She spoke to him on the phone the day he checked into the hospital.

What happened then?

At what point?

When he died.

He saw someone beckoning to him. But that isn't what you mean. What happened is that Jeanette was in a cab on her way to the hospital, and when she got there, one of the nurses was waiting by the elevator. The nurse knew that Jeanette was on her way, because she came at the same time every day. Also, Andrew Darby had been on that same floor, a year or so before, for surgery that was successful. That nurse took care of him then, also. It isn't true that the nurse you have one year will be gone the next.

This isn't a story about the working girl anymore.

It is, because she went right on working. She worked during the marriage and for quite a few years after he died. Toward the end, she wasn't working because she needed the money. She wanted the money, but that's different from needing the money.

What kind of a life did they have together?

He realized that he had something of a problem with alcohol and gave it up. She kept her figure. They went to Bermuda and meant to return, but never did. Every year she reordered perfume from a catalogue she had taken from the hotel room in Bermuda. She tried to find another scent that she liked, but always ended up reordering the one she was so pleased with. They didn't have children. He didn't have children with his first wife either, so that by the end it was fairly certain that the doctor had been right, and that the problem was with Andrew, although he never would agree to be tested. He had two dogs in his life, and one cat. Jeanette's Christmas present to him, the year he died, was a

Rolex. He gave her a certificate that entitled her to twenty free tanning sessions and a monthly massage.

What was it like when she was a working girl?

Before she met him, or afterwards?

Before and afterwards.

Before, she often felt gloomy, although she entertained more in those days, and she enjoyed that. Her charge card bills were always at the limit, and if she had been asked, even at the time, she would have admitted that a sort of overcompensation was taking place. She read more before she met him, but after she met him he read the same books, and it was nice to have someone to discuss them with. She was convinced that she had once broken someone's heart: a man she dated for a couple of years, who inherited his parents' estate when they died. He wanted to marry Jeanette and take care of her. His idea was to commute into New York from the big estate in Connecticut. She felt that she didn't know how to move comfortably into someone else's life. Though she tried to explain carefully, he was bitter and always maintained that she didn't marry him because she didn't like the furniture.

Afterwards?

You've already heard some things about afterwards. Andrew had a phobia about tollbooths, so when they were driving on the highway, he'd pull onto the shoulder when he saw the sign for a tollbooth, and she'd drive through it. On the Jersey Turnpike, of course, she just kept the wheel. They knew only one couple that they liked equally well—they liked the man as well as they liked the woman, that is. They tended to like the same couples.

What was it like, again, in the office?

The plants and the watercooler.

Besides that.

That's really going back in time. It would seem like a digression at this point.

But what about understanding the life of the working girl?

She turned a corner, and it was fall. With a gigantic intake of breath, her feet lifted off the ground.

Explain.

Nothing miraculous happened, but still things did happen, and life changed. She lost touch with some friends, became quite involved in reading the classics. In Bermuda, swimming, she looked up and saw a boat and remembered very distinctly, and much to her surprise, that the man she had been involved with before Andrew had inherited a collection of ships in bottles from his great-great-grandfather. And that day, as she came out of the water, she cut her foot on something. Whatever it was was as sharp as glass, if it was not glass. And that seemed to sum up something. She was quite shaken. She and Andrew sat in the sand, and the boat passed by, and Andrew thought that it was the pain alone that had upset her.

In the office, when the light dimmed early in the day. In the winter. Before they were together. She must have looked at the shadows on her desk and felt like a person lost in the forest.

If she thought that, she never said it.

Did she confide in Charlie?

To some extent. She and Charlie palled around together before she became involved with Andrew. Afterwards, too, a little. She was always consulted when he needed to buy a new tie.

Did Charlie go to the wedding?

There was no wedding. It was a civil ceremony.

Where did they go on their honeymoon?

Paris. He always wanted to see Paris.

But his wife went to Paris.

That was just coincidence, and besides, she wasn't there at the same time. By then she was his ex-wife. Jeanette never knew that his wife had been to Paris.

What things did he not know?

That she once lost two hundred dollars in a cab. That she did a self-examination of her breasts twice a day. She hid her dislike of the dog, which they had gotten at his insistence, from the pound. The dog was a chewer.

When an image of Andrew came to mind, what was it?

Andrew at forty, when she first met him. She felt sorry that he had a mole on his cheekbone, but later came to love it. Sometimes, after his death, the mole would fill the whole world of her dream. At least that is what she thought it was—a gray mass like a mountain, seen from the distance, then closer and closer until it became amorphous and she was awake, gripping the sheet. It was a nightmare, obviously, not a dream. Though she called it a dream.

Who is Berry McKenn?

A woman he had a brief flirtation with. Nothing of importance.

Why do storytellers start to tell one story and then tell another?

Life is a speeding train. Storytellers get derailed too.

What did Andrew see when he conjured up Jeanette?

Her green eyes. That startled look, as if the eyes had a life of their own, and were surprised to be bracketing so long a nose.

What else is there to say about their life together?

There is something of an anecdote about the watercooler. It disappeared once, and it was noticeably absent, as if someone had removed a geyser. The surprise on people's faces when they stared at the empty corner of the corridor was really quite astonishing. Jeanette went to meet Andrew there the day the repairman took it away. They made it a point, several times a day, to meet there as if by accident. One of the other girls who worked there—thinking Charlie was her friend, which he certainly was not: he was Jeanette's friend—had seen the watercooler being removed, and she whispered slyly to Charlie that it would be amusing when Jeanette strolled away from her desk, and Andrew left his office moments later with great purpose in his step and holding his blue pottery mug, because they would be standing in an empty corridor, with their prop gone and their cover blown.

What did Charlie say?

Jeanette asked him that too, when he reported the conversation. "They're in love," he said. "You might not want to think it, but a little thing like that isn't going to be a setback at all." He felt quite triumphant about taking a stand, though there's room for skepticism, of course. What people say is one thing, and what they later report they have said is another.

CONSTRUCTING A READING

1. When you read the sentence "but we know how that story will end," do you, in fact, know how the story you're reading will end? How? Why or why not?

2. With your group members, make a list of two or three moments in this narrative when Beattie appears to be playing with generic conventions (for example, the wife . . . is in "North Dakota or Memphis or Paris, let's say. Let's say she's out of the picture even if she isn't out of the picture."). Talk with your group members about the kinds of plot events that would occur if the wife were out of the picture. List them. Then discuss and list the kinds of plot events that would occur if the wife were *not* out of the picture. Do the same for the other moments. When you finish, talk with your group members about the generic expectations behind these plot predictions.

SHARING A READING

1. Return to the chronological list you made of the events in your day. Then, retell the events as a detective story, or as a fairy tale, or as a horror story, or as a TV sitcom. What does the genre lead you to add? What do you find yourself leaving out?

2. With your group, return to the list of familiar minimal stories (commercials, fairy tales, etc.) that you made earlier. Look for generic similarities in the texts you have chosen. Are there similar plots? Similar techniques of characterization? Similar themes? Make lists of similar characteristics on the chalkboard or on transparencies or computers. Give names to the genres of stories you have found (e.g., problem solution narrative, quest narrative, tragedy, etc.). Consider whether you find different kinds of stories in different venues. Are problem/solution stories only (or most often) found in commercials, for example? Are heroic quest narratives only

found in action/adventure films? If not, where else would you expect to find them? Where else do you find them?

3. Look back at some essays you've written in high school or college about summer vacations or trips during Spring Break, Proms, games, and so on. Do those writings qualify as *stories* under the definition we've established? Or are they merely chronological lists of happenings? Try rewriting one of them as a story with specific generic characteristics. Spring Break as a horror story? Prom as a TV commercial? The championship game as a tragedy?

4. Joyce Carol Oates described "Where Are You Going, Where Have You Been" as an instance of "psychological realism." What do you think she means by that term? On the basis of what you know about the kinds of people Oates's story represents, do you consider the story realistic? If so, describe the psychological patterns to which it is realistic. If not, explain why.

5. With your teacher's advice and help, form genre groups composed of people who read—or view—a particular genre. Together, describe to someone who is not familiar with it that genre's characteristics and explain how it reflects and/or functions in its culture.

6. Make an anthology of four or five instances of a genre you read or view frequently for an audience of people who also like that genre. Write an introduction to your anthology that both *describes* the characteristics of your genre (e.g., horror) and *explains* how it is mixed with others, (e.g., film, story, comic book, etc.).

7. Choose any story in this book so far and retell it in a different genre.

8. What are the genres of the three top-grossing films of the past year? Speculate about why these genres make the most money, giving careful attention to at least three generic characteristics.

A COLLABORATIVE ACTIVITY

Here is an experiment in recognizing generic expectations.

1. In your journal, write the name of a TV narrative program with which you are very familiar. (The program you choose must be a narrative: "Letterman" and "Monday Night Football" won't do.) Name the genre, (action, drama, sitcom, etc.), as precisely as possible. If you have trouble, ask yourself how *TV GUIDE* would classify it.

2. Next, answer these questions about how your narrative treats its story.
   a. Does each episode come to closure? (Is the story serialized, so that it never really ends? Is there a mixture, in which some stories close and others do not?)

    b. Does your TV program depict violence at all? (If so, how much violence? What kind? How explicit? Do you actually see the violence or is it merely referred to?)

    c. Does your TV program depict sex acts, allude to them, or omit mention of sex entirely? (If your story depicts sex, how explicit are the depictions? Are the sex acts heterosexual, homosexual, or both?)

    d. Does your TV show contain humor or comedy? (Is the comedy situational or the effect of one-liners? Or both? Does humor or comedy dominate the narrative or does it occur infrequently?)

    e. Does the narrative seem realistic to you? (Could the events actually happen? Does the dialogue sound real? Does the narrative seem fantastic? Are you encouraged to think that a rational explanation will be brought forward?)

    f. Do the characters change? (Can they surprise you? Are they stock characters?)

    g. What themes does your story depict? (Express the themes you find as sentences, like "Brady Bunch retains family values.")

3. Bring your list to class and form groups according to the genres you've named. Your class might, for example, have a sitcom group, an adventure group, a science fiction group, a fantasy group. Make a list of the programs in each genre group. Think and talk for a while about the similarities and differences among the instances of "your genre." Then, try to develop a list of the generic characteristics of the type of program you've chosen, taking account of the variations within them.

4. Next, at your teacher's direction, form new groups. This time, though, the groups should be formed around your responses to the first set of questions. Begin with the first question—about narrative closure—and divide the class into only three groups: those whose stories close, those whose stories are serialized, and those whose stories mix closure with serialization. How many different genres appear in your "closure group"? Next, regroup around the "violence" question, establishing your own criteria for degrees of difference. Next regroup on the basis of the sex question, and so on through the list.

5. Finally, as a class, consider these questions: Are you surprised to learn that characteristics "cross" genres? Is it possible to discover any one element that, by itself, serves as a sufficient or necessary characteristic of a genre?

TEXTS FOR FURTHER READING

As you read the following story, mark the places where you are surprised by its events.

Carried Away
Alice Munro

LETTERS

In the dining room of the Commercial Hotel, Louisa opened the letter that had arrived that day from overseas. She ate steak and potatoes, her usual meal, and drank a glass of wine. There were a few travellers in the room, and the dentist who ate there every night because he was a widower. He had shown an interest in her in the beginning but had told her he had never before seen a woman touch wine or spirits.

"It is for my health," said Louisa gravely.

The white tablecloths were changed every week and in the meantime were protected by oilcloth mats. In winter, the dining room smelled of these mats wiped by a kitchen rag, and of coal fumes from the furnace, and beef gravy and dried potatoes and onions—a smell not unpleasant to anybody coming in hungry from the cold. On each table was a little cruet stand with the bottle of brown sauce, the bottle of tomato sauce, and the pot of horseradish.

The letter was addressed to "The Librarian, Carstairs Public Library, Carstairs, Ontario." It was dated six weeks before—January 4, 1917.

Perhaps you will be surprised to hear from a person you don't know and that doesn't remember your name. I hope you are still the same Librarian though enough time has gone by that you could have moved on.

What has landed me here in Hospital is not too serious. I see worse all around me and get my mind off of all that by picturing things and wondering for instance if you are still there in the Library. If you are the one I mean, you are about of medium size or perhaps not quite, with light brownish hair. You came a few months before it was time for me to go in the Army following on Miss Tamblyn who had been there since I first became a user aged nine or ten. In her time the books were pretty much every which way, and it was as much as your life was worth to ask her for the least help or anything since she was quite a dragon. Then when you came what a change, it was all put into sections of Fiction and Non-Fiction and History and Travel and you got the magazines arranged in order and put out as soon as they arrived, not left to molder away till everything in them was stale. I felt gratitude but did not know how to say so. Also I wondered what brought you there, you were an educated person.

My name is Jack Agnew and my card is in the drawer. The last book I took out was very good—H. G. Wells, Mankind in the Making. *My education was to Second Form in High School, then I went into Douds as many did. I didn't join up right away when I was eighteen so you will not see me as a Brave Man. I am a person tending to have my own ideas always. My only relative in Carstairs, or anyplace, is my father Patrick Agnew. He works for Douds not at the factory but at the house doing the gardening. He is a lone wolf even more than me and goes out to the country fishing every chance he gets. I write him a letter sometimes but I doubt if he reads is.*

After supper Louisa went up to the Ladies' Parlor on the second floor, and sat down at the desk to write her reply.

I am very glad to hear you appreciated what I did in the Library though it was just the normal organization, nothing special.

I am sure you would like to hear news of home, but I am a poor person for the job, being an outsider here. I do talk to people in the Library and in the hotel. The travellers in the hotel mostly talk about how business is (it is brisk if you can get the goods) and a little about sickness, and a lot about the War. There are rumors on rumors and opinions galore, which I'm sure would make you laugh if they didn't make you angry I will not bother to write them down because I am sure there is a Censor reading this who would cut my letter to ribbons.

You ask how I came here. There is no interesting story My parents are both dead. My father worked for Eaton's in Toronto in the Furniture Department, and after his death my mother worked there too in Linens. And I also worked there for a while in Books. Perhaps you could say Eaton's was our Douds. I graduated from Jarvis Collegiate. I had some sickness which put me in hospital for a long time, but I am quite well now. I had a great deal of time to read and my favorite authors are Thomas Hardy, who is accused of being gloomy but I think is very true to life—and Willa Cather. I just happened to be in this town when I heard the Librarian had died and I thought, perhaps that is the job for me.

A good thing your letter reached me today as I am about to be discharged from here and don't know if it would have been sent on to where I am going. I am glad you did not think my letter was too foolish.

If you run into my father or anybody you do not need to say anything about the fact we are writing to each other. It is nobody's business and I know there are plenty of people would laugh at me writing to the Librarian as they did at me going to the Library even, why give them the satisfaction?

I am glad to be getting out of here. So much luckier than some I see that will never walk or have their sight and will have to hide themselves away from the world.

You asked where did I live in Carstairs. Well, it was not anyplace to be proud of. If you know where Vinegar Hill is and you turned off on Flowers Road it is the last house on the right, yellow paint once upon a time. My father grows potatoes, or did. I used to take them around town with my wagon, and every load I sold got a nickel to keep.

You mention favorite authors. At one time I was fond of Zane Grey, but I drifted away from reading fiction stories to reading History or Travel. I some-

times read books away over my head, I know, but I do get something out of them. H. G. Wells I mentioned is one and Robert Ingersoll who writes about religion. They have given me a lot to think about. If you are very religious I hope I have not offended you.

One day when I got to the Library is was a Saturday afternoon and you had just unlocked the door and were putting the lights on as is was dark and raining out. You had been caught out with no hat or umbrella and your hair had got wet. You took the pins out of it and let it come down. Is it too personal a thing to ask if you have is long still or have you cut is? You went over and stood by the radiator and shook your hair on it and the water sizzled like grease in the frying pan. I was sitting reading in the London Illustrated News *about the War. We exchanged a smile. (I didn't mean to say your hair was greasy when I wrote that!)*

I have not cut my hair though I often think about it. I do not know if it is vanity or laziness that prevents me.

I am not very religious.

I walked up Vinegar Hill and found your house. The potatoes are looking healthy. A police dog disputed with me, is he yours?

The weather is getting quite warm. We have had the flood on the river, which I gather is an annual Spring event. The water got into the hotel basement and somehow contaminated our drinking supply so that we were given free beer or ginger ale. But only if we lived or were staying there. You can imagine there were plenty of jokes.

I should ask if there is anything that I could send you.

I am not in need of anything particular. I get the tobacco and other bits of things the ladies in Carstairs do up for us. I would like to read some books by the authors you have mentioned but I doubt whether I would get the chance here.

The other day there was a man died of a heart attack. It was the News of all time. Did you hear about the man who died of a heart attack? That was all you heard about day and night here. Then everybody would laugh which seems hard-hearted but it just seemed so strange. It was not even a hot time so you couldn't say maybe he was scared. (As a matter of fact he was writing a letter at the time so I had better look out.) Before and after him others have died being shot up or blown up but he is the famous one, to die of a heart attack. Everybody is saying what a long way to come and a lot of expense for the Army to go to, for that.

The summer has been so dry the watering tank has been doing the streets every day, trying to lay the dust. The children would dance along behind it. There was also a new thing in town—a cart with a little bell that went along selling ice cream, and the children were pretty attentive to this as well. It was pushed by the man who had an accident at the factory—you know who I mean, though I can't recall his name. He lost his arm to the elbow. My room at the hotel, being on the third floor, it was like an oven, and I often walked about till after midnight. So did many other people, sometimes in pajamas. It was like a dream. There was still a little water in the river, enough to go out in a rowboat, and the Methodist minister did that on a Sunday in August. He was praying for rain in a public service. But there was a small leak in the boat and the water came in and wet his feet and eventually the boat sank and left him standing in the water, which did not nearly reach his waist. Was it an accident or a malicious trick? The talk was all that his prayers were answered but from the wrong direction.

I often pass the Douds' place on my walks. Your father keeps the lawns and hedges looking beautiful. I like the house, so original and airy-looking. But it may not have been cool even there, because I heard the voice of the mother and baby daughter late at night as if they were out on the lawn.

Though I told you there is nothing I need, there is one thing I would like. That is a photograph of you. I hope you will not think I am overstepping the bounds to ask for it. Maybe you are engaged to somebody or have a sweetheart over here you are writing to as well as me. You are a cut above the ordinary and it would not surprise me if some Officer had spoken for you. But now that I have asked I cannot take it back and will just leave it up to you to think what you like of me.

Louisa was twenty-five years old and had been in love once, with a doctor she had known in the sanitorium. Her love was returned, eventually, costing the doctor his job. There was some harsh doubt in her mind about whether he had been told to leave the sanitorium or had left of his own accord, being weary of the entanglement. He was married, he had children. Letters had played a part that time, too. After he left, they were still writing to one another. And once or twice after she was released. Then she asked him not to write anymore and he didn't. But the failure of his letters to arrive drove her out of Toronto and made her take the travelling job. Then there would be only the one disappointment in the week, when she got back on Friday or Saturday night. Her last letter had been firm and stoical, and some consciousness of herself as a heroine of love's tragedy went with her around the country as she hauled her display cases up and down the stairs of small hotels and talked about Paris styles and said that her sample hats were bewitching, and drank her solitary glass of wine. If she'd had anybody to tell, though, she would have laughed at just that notion. She would have said love was all hocus-pocus, a deception, and she believed that. But at the prospect she still felt a hush, a flutter along the nerves, a bowing down of sense, a flagrant prostration.

She had a picture taken. She knew how she wanted it to be. She would have liked to wear a simple white blouse, a peasant girl's smock with the string open at the neck. She did not own a blouse of that description and in fact had only seen them in pictures. And she would have liked to let her hair down. Or if it had to be up, she would have liked it piled very loosely and bound with strings of pearls.

Instead she wore her blue silk shirt-waist and bound her hair as usual. She thought the picture made her look rather pale, hollow-eyed. Her expression was sterner and more foreboding than she had intended. She sent it anyway.

I am not engaged, and do not have a sweetheart. I was in love once and it had to be broken off I was upset at the time but I knew I must bear it, and now I believe that it was all for the best.

She had wracked her brains, of course, to remember him. She could not remember shaking out her hair, as he said she had done, or smiling at any young man when the raindrops fell on the radiator. He might as well have dreamed all that, and perhaps he had.

She had begun to follow the war in a more detailed way than she had done previously. She did not try to ignore it anymore. She went along the street with a sense that her head was filled with the same exciting and troubling information as everybody else's. Saint-Quentin, Arras, Montdidier, Amiens, and then there was a battle going on at the Somme River, where surely there had been one before? She laid open on her desk the maps of the war that appeared as double-page spreads in the magazines. She saw in colored lines the German drive to the Marne, the first thrust of the Americans at Château-Thierry. She looked at the artist's brown pictures of a horse rearing up during an air attack, of some soldiers in East Africa drinking out of coconuts, and of a line of German prisoners with bandaged heads or limbs and bleak, sullen expressions. Now she felt what everybody else did—a constant fear and misgiving and at the same time this addictive excitement. You could look up from your life of the moment and feel the world crackling beyond the walls.

I am glad to hear you do not have a sweetheart though I know that is selfish of me. I do not think you and I will ever meet again. I don't say that because I've had a dream about what will happen or am a gloomy person always looking for the worst. It just seems to me it is the most probable thing to happen, though I don't dwell on it and go along every day doing the best I can to stay alive. I am not trying to worry you or get your sympathy either but just explain how the idea I won't ever see Carstairs again makes me think I can say anything I want. I guess it's like being sick with a fever. So I will say I love you. I think of you up on a stool at the Library reaching to put a book away and I come up and put my hands on your waist and lift you down, and you turning around inside my arms as if we agreed about everything.

Every Tuesday afternoon the ladies and girls of the Red Cross met in the Council Chambers, which was just down the hall from the Library. When the Library was empty for a few moments, Louisa went down the hall and entered the room full of women. She had decided to knit a scarf. At the sanitorium she had learned how to knit a basic stitch, but she had never learned or had forgotten how to cast on or off.

The older women were all busy packing boxes or cutting up and folding bandages from sheets of heavy cotton that were spread on the tables. But a lot of girls near the door were eating buns and drinking tea. One was holding a skein of wool on her arms for another to wind.

Louisa told them what she needed to know.

"So what do you want to knit, then?" said one of the girls with some bun still in her mouth.

Louisa said, a muffler. For a soldier.

"Oh, you'll want the regulation wool," another said, more politely, and jumped off the table. She came back with some balls of brown wool, and fished a spare pair of needles out of her bag, telling Louisa they could be hers.

"I'll just get you started," she said. "It's a regulation width, too."

Other girls gathered around and teased this girl, whose name was Corrie. They told her she was doing it all wrong.

"Oh, I am, am I?" said Corrie. "How would you like a knitting needle in your eye? Is it for a friend?" she said solicitously to Louisa. "A friend overseas?"

"Yes," said Louisa. Of course they would think of her as an old maid, they would laugh at her or feel sorry for her, according to whatever show they put on, of being kind or brazen.

"So knit up good and tight," said the one who'd finished her bun. "Knit up good and tight to keep him warm!"

One of the girls in this group was Grace Horne. She was a shy but resolute-looking girl, nineteen years old, with a broad face, thin lips often pressed together, brown hair cut in a straight hang, and an attractively mature body. She had become engaged to Jack Agnew before he went overseas, but they had agreed not to say anything about it.

SPANISH FLU

Louisa had made friends with some of the travellers who stayed regularly at the hotel. One of these was Jim Frarey, who sold typewriters and office equipment and books and all sorts of stationery supplies. He was a fair-haired, rather round-shouldered but strongly built man in his middle forties. You would think by the look of him that he sold something heavier and more important in the masculine world, like farm implements.

Jim Frarey kept travelling all through the Spanish flu epidemic, though you never knew then if stores would be open for business or not. Occasionally the hotels, too, would be closed, like the schools and movie houses and even— Jim Frarey thought this a scandal—the churches.

"They ought to be ashamed of themselves, the cowards," he said to

Louisa. "What good does it do anybody to lurk around home and wait for it to strike? Now you never closed the Library, did you?"

Louisa said only when she herself was sick. A mild case, hardly lasting a week, but of course she had to go to the hospital. They wouldn't let her stay in the hotel.

"Cowards," he said. "If you're going to be taken, you'll be taken. Don't you agree?"

They discussed the crush in the hospitals, the deaths of doctors and nurses, the unceasing drear spectacle of the funerals. Jim Frarey lived down the street from an undertaking establishment in Toronto. He said they still got out the black horses, the black carriage, the works, to bury such personages as warranted a fuss.

"Day and night they went on," he said. "Day and night." He raised his glass and said, "Here's to health, then. You look well yourself."

He thought that in fact Louisa was looking better than she used to. Maybe she had started putting on rouge. She had a pale-olive skin, and it seemed to him that her cheeks used to be without color. She dressed with more dash, too, and took more trouble to be friendly. She used to be very on-again, off-again, just as she chose. She was drinking whisky, now, too, though she would not try it without drowning it in water. It used to be only a glass of wine. He wondered if it was a boyfriend that had made the difference. But a boyfriend might perk up her looks without increasing her interest in all and sundry, which was what he was pretty sure had happened. It was more likely time running out and the husband prospects thinned out so dreadfully by the war. That could set a woman stirring. She was smarter and better company and better-looking, too, than most of the married ones. What happened with a woman like that? Sometimes just bad luck. Or bad judgment at a time when it mattered. A little too sharp and self-assured, in the old days, making the men uneasy?

"Life can't be brought to a standstill all the same," he said. "You did the right thing, keeping the Library open."

This was in the early winter of 1919, when there had been a fresh outbreak of flu after the danger was supposed to be past. They seemed to be all alone in the hotel. It was only about nine o'clock but the hotelkeeper had gone to bed. His wife was in the hospital with the flu. Jim Frarey had brought the bottle of whisky from the bar, which was closed for fear of contagion—and they sat at a table beside the window, in the dining room. A winter fog had collected outside and was pressing against the window. You could barely see the streetlights or the few cars that trundled cautiously over the bridge.

"Oh, it was not a matter of principle," Louisa said. "That I kept the Library open. It was a more personal reason than you think."

Then she laughed and promised him a peculiar story. "Oh, the whisky must have loosened my tongue," she said.

"I am not a gossip," said Jim Frarey.

She gave him a hard laughing look and said that when a person announced they weren't a gossip, they almost invariably were. The same when they promised never to tell a soul.

"You can tell this where and when you like just as long as you leave out the real names and don't tell it around here," she said. "That I hope I can trust you not to do. Though at the moment I don't feel as if I cared. I'll probably feel otherwise when the drink wears off. It's a lesson, this story. It's a lesson in what fools women can make of themselves. So, you say, what's new about that, you can learn it every day!"

She began to tell him about a soldier who had started writing letters to her from overseas. The soldier remembered her from when he used to go into the Library. But she didn't remember him. However, she replied in a friendly way to his first letter and a correspondence sprang up between them. He told her where he had lived in the town and she walked past the house so that she could tell him how things looked there. He told her what books he'd read and she gave some of the same kind of information. In short, they both revealed something of themselves and feelings warmed up on either side. On his side first, as far as any declarations went. She was not one to rush in like a fool. At first, she thought she was simply being kind. Even later, she didn't want to reject and embarrass him. He asked for a picture. She had one taken, it was not to her liking, but she sent it. He asked if she had a sweetheart and she replied truthfully that she did not. He did not send any picture of himself nor did she ask for one, though of course she was curious as to what he looked like. It would be no easy matter for him to have a picture taken in the middle of a war. Furthermore, she did not want to seem like the sort of woman who would withdraw kindness if looks did not come up to scratch.

He wrote that he did not expect to come home. He said he was not so afraid of dying as he was of ending up like some of the men he had seen when he was in the hospital, wounded. He did not elaborate, but she supposed he meant the cases they were just getting to know about now—the stumps of men, the blinded, the ones made monstrous with burns. He was not whining about his fate, she did not mean to imply that. It was just that he expected to die and picked death over some other options and he thought about her and wrote to her as men do to a sweetheart in such a situation.

When the war ended, it was a while since she had heard from him. She went on expecting a letter every day and nothing came. Nothing came. She was afraid that he might have been one of those unluckiest of soldiers in the whole war one of those killed in the last week, or on the last day, or even in the last hour. She searched the local paper every week, and the names of new casualties were still being printed there till after New Year's but his was not among them. Now the paper began to list as well the names of those returning home, often printing a photo with the name, and a little account of rejoicing. When the soldiers were returning thick and fast there was less room for these additions. And then she saw his name, another name on the list. He had not been killed, he had not been wounded—he was coming home to Carstairs, perhaps was already there.

It was then that she decided to keep the Library open, though the flu was raging. Every day she was sure he would come, every day she was prepared for him. Sundays were a torment. When she entered the Town Hall she always felt he might be there before her, leaning up against the wall awaiting her arrival. Sometimes she felt it so strongly she saw a shadow that she mistook for a man. She understood now how people believed they had seen ghosts. Whenever the door opened she expected to look up into his face. Sometimes she made a pact with herself not to look up till she had counted to ten. Few people came in, because of the flu. She set herself jobs of rearranging things, else she would have gone mad. She never locked up until five or ten minutes after closing time. And then she fancied that he might be across the street on the Post Office steps, watching her, being too shy to make a move. She worried of course that he might be ill, she always sought in conversation for news of the latest cases. No one spoke his name.

It was at this time that she entirely gave up on reading. The covers of books looked like coffins to her, either shabby or ornate, and what was inside them might as well have been dust.

She had to be forgiven, didn't she, she had to be forgiven for thinking, after such letters, that the one thing that could never happen was that he wouldn't approach her, wouldn't get in touch with her at all? Never cross her threshold, after such avowals? Funerals passed by her window and she gave no thought to them, as long as they were not his. Even when she was sick in the hospital her only thought was that she must get back, she must get out of bed, the door must not stay locked against him. She staggered to her feet and back to work. On a hot afternoon she was arranging fresh newspapers on the racks and his name jumped out at her like something in her feverish dreams.

She read a short notice of his marriage to a Miss Grace Horne. Not a girl she knew. Not a Library user.

The bride wore fawn silk crêpe with brown-and-cream piping, and a beige straw hat with brown velvet streamers.

There was no picture. Brown-and-cream piping. Such was the end, and had to be, to her romance.

But on her desk at the Library, a matter of a few weeks ago, on a Saturday night after everybody had gone and she had locked the door and was turning out the lights, she discovered a scrap of paper. A few words written on it. *I was engaged before I went overseas.* No name, not his or hers. And there was her photograph, partly shoved under the blotter.

He had been in the Library that very evening. It had been a busy time, she had often left the desk to find a book for somebody or to straighten up the papers or to put some books on the shelves. He had been in the same room with her, watched her, and taken his chance. But never made himself known.

I was engaged before I went overseas.

"Do you think it was all a joke on me?" Louisa said. "Do you think a man could be so diabolical?"

"In my experience, tricks like that are far more often indulged in by the women. No, no. Don't you think such a thing. Far more likely he was sincere. He got a little carried away. It's all just the way it looks on the surface. He was engaged before he went overseas, he never expected to get back in one piece but he did. And when he did, there is the fiancee waiting—what else could he do?"

"What indeed?" said Louisa.

"He bit off more than he could chew."

"Ah, that's so, that's so!" Louisa said. "And what was it in my case but vanity, which deserves to get slapped down!" Her eyes were glassy and her expression roguish. "You don't think he'd had a good look at me any one time and thought the original was even worse than that poor picture, so he backed off?"

"I do not!" said Jim Frarey. "And don't you so belittle yourself."

"I don't want you to think I am stupid," she said. "I am not so stupid and inexperienced as that story makes me sound."

"Indeed I don't think you are stupid at all."

"But perhaps you think I am inexperienced?"

This was it, he thought—the usual. Women after they have told one story on themselves cannot stop from telling another. Drink upsets them in a radical way, prudence is out the window.

She had confided in him once before that she had been a patient in a sanitorium. Now she told about being in love with a doctor there. The sanitorium was on beautiful grounds up on Hamilton Mountain, and they used to meet there along the hedged walks. Shelves of limestone formed the steps and in sheltered spots there were such plants as you do not commonly see in Ontario—azaleas, rhododendrons, magnolias. The doctor knew something about botany and he told her this was the Carolinian vegetation. Very different from here, lusher, and there were little bits of woodland, too, wonderful trees, paths worn under the trees. Tulip trees.

"Tulips!" said Jim Frarey. "Tulips on the trees!"

"No, no, it is the shape of their leaves!"

She laughed at him challengingly, then bit her lip. He saw fit to continue the dialogue, saying, "Tulips on the trees!" while she said no, it is the leaves that are shaped like tulips, no, I never said that, stop! So they passed into a state of gingerly evaluation—which he knew well and could only hope she did—full of small pleasant surprises, half-sardonic signals, a welling-up of impudent hopes, and a fateful sort of kindness.

"All to ourselves," Jim Frarey said. "Never happened before, did it? Maybe it never will again."

She let him take her hands, half lift her from her chair. He turned out the dining-room lights as they went out. Up the stairs they went, that they had so often climbed separately. Past the picture of the dog on his master's grave, and

High-land Mary singing in the field, and the old King with his bulgy eyes, his look of indulgence and repletion.

"It's a foggy, foggy night, and my heart is in a fright," Jim Frarey was half singing, half humming as they climbed. He kept an assured hand on Louisa's back. "All's well, all's well," he said as he steered her round the turn of the stairs. And when they took the narrow flight of steps to the third floor he said, "Never climbed so close to Heaven in this place before!"

But later in the night Jim Frarey gave a concluding groan and roused himself to deliver a sleepy scolding. "Louisa, Louisa, why didn't you tell me that was the way it was?"

"I told you everything," said Louisa in a faint and drifting voice.

"I got a wrong impression, then," he said. "I never intended for this to make a difference to you.

She said that it hadn't. Now without him pinning her down and steadying her, she felt herself whirling around in an irresistible way, as if the mattress had turned into a child's top and was carrying her off. She tried to explain that the traces of blood on the sheets could be credited to her period, but her words came out with a luxurious nonchalance and could not be fitted together.

ACCIDENTS

When Arthur came home from the factory a little before noon he shouted, "Stay out of my way till I wash! There's been an accident over at the works!" Nobody answered. Mrs. Feare, the housekeeper, was talking on the kitchen telephone so loudly that she could not hear him, and his daughter was of course at school. He washed, and stuffed everything he had been wearing into the hamper, and scrubbed up the bathroom, like a murderer. He started out clean, with even his hair slicked and patted, to drive to the man's house. He had had to ask where it was. He thought it was up Vinegar Hill but they said no, that was the father—the young fellow and his wife live on the other side of town, past where the Apple Evaporator used to be, before the war.

He found the two brick cottages side by side, and picked the left-hand one, as he'd been told. It wouldn't have been hard to pick which house, anyway. News had come before him. The door to the house was open, and children too young to be in school yet hung about in the yard. A small girl sat on a kiddie car, not going anywhere, just blocking his path. He stepped around her. As he did so an older girl spoke to him in a formal way—a warning.

"Her dad's dead. Hers!"

A woman came out of the front room carrying an armload of curtains, which she gave to another woman standing in the hall. The woman who received the curtains was gray-haired, with a pleading face. She had no upper teeth. She probably took her plate out, for comfort, at home. The woman who passed the curtains to her was stout but young, with fresh skin.

"You tell her not to get up on that stepladder," the gray-haired woman said to Arthur. "She's going to break her neck taking down curtains. She thinks we need to get everything washed. Are you the undertaker? Oh, no, excuse me! You're Mr. Doud. Grace, come out here! Grace! It's Mr. Doud!"

"Don't trouble her," Arthur said.

"She thinks she's going to get the curtains all down and washed and up again by tomorrow, because he's going to have to go in the front room. She's my daughter. I can't tell her anything."

"She'll quiet down presently," said a sombre but comfortable-looking man in a clerical collar, coming through from the back of the house. Their minister. But not from one of the churches Arthur knew. Baptist? Pentecostal? Plymouth Brethren? He was drinking tea.

Some other woman came and briskly removed the curtains.

"We got the machine filled and going," she said. "A day like this, they'll dry like nobody's business. Just keep the kids out of here."

The minister had to stand aside and lift his teacup high, to avoid her and her bundle. He said, "Aren't any of you ladies going to offer Mr. Doud a cup of tea?"

Arthur said, "No, no, don't trouble."

"The funeral expenses," he said to the gray-haired woman. "If you could let her know—"

"Lillian wet her pants!" said a triumphant child at the door. "Mrs. Agnew! Lillian peed her pants!"

"Yes. Yes," said the minister. "They will be very grateful."

"The plot and the stone, everything," Arthur said. "You'll make sure they understand that. Whatever they want on the stone."

The gray-haired woman had gone out into the yard. She came back with a squalling child in her arms. "Poor lamb," she said. "They told her she wasn't supposed to come in the house so where could she go? What could she do but have an accident!"

The young woman came out of the front room dragging a rug.

"I want this put on the line and beat," she said.

"Grace, here is Mr. Doud come to offer his condolences," the minister said.

"And to ask if there is anything I can do," said Arthur.

The gray-haired woman started upstairs with the wet child in her arms and a couple of others following.

Grace spotted them.

"Oh, no, you don't! You get back outside!"

"My mom's in here."

"Yes and your mom's good and busy, she don't need to be bothered with you. She's here helping me out. Don't you know Lillian's dad's dead?"

"Is there anything I can do for you?" Arthur said, meaning to clear out.

Grace stared at him with her mouth open. Sounds of the washing machine filled the house.

"Yes, there is," she said. "You wait here."

"She's overwhelmed," the minister said. "It's not that she means to be rude."

Grace came back with a load of books.

"These here," she said. "He had them out of the Library. I don't want to have to pay fines on them. He went every Saturday night so I guess they are due back tomorrow. I don't want to get in trouble about them."

"I'll look after them," Arthur said. "I'd be glad to."

"I just don't want to get in any trouble about them."

"Mr. Doud was saying about taking care of the funeral," the minister said to her, gently admonishing. "Everything including the stone. Whatever you want on the stone."

"Oh, I don't want anything fancy," Grace said.

On Friday morning last there occurred in the sawmill operation of Douds Factory a particularly ghastly and tragic accident. Mr. Jack Agnew, in reaching under the main shaft, had the misfortune to have his sleeve caught by a setscrew in an adjoining flunge, so that his arm and shoulder were drawn under the shaft. His head in consequence was brought in contact with the circular saw, that saw being about one foot in diameter. In an instant the unfortunate young man's head was separated from his body, being severed at an angle below the left ear and through the neck. His death is believed to have been instantaneous. He never spoke or uttered a cry so it was not any sound of his but by the spurt and shower of his blood that his fellow-workers were horribly alerted to the disaster.

This account was reprinted in the paper a week later for those who might have missed it or who wished to have an extra copy to send to friends or relations out of town (particularly to people who used to live in Carstairs and did not anymore). The misspelling of "flange" was corrected. There was a note apologizing for the mistake. There was also a description of a very large funeral, attended even by people from neighboring towns and as far away as Walley. They came by car and train, and some by horse and buggy. They had not known Jack Agnew when he was alive, but, as the paper said, they wished to pay tribute to the sensational and tragic manner of his death. All the stores in Carstairs were closed for two hours that afternoon. The hotel did not close its doors but that was because all the visitors needed somewhere to eat and drink.

The survivors were a wife, Grace, and a four-year-old daughter, Lillian. The victim had fought bravely in the Great War and had only been wounded once, not seriously. Many had commented on this irony.

The paper's failure to mention a surviving father was not deliberate. The editor of the paper was not a native of Carstairs, and people forgot to tell him about the father until it was too late.

The father himself did not complain about the omission. On the day of the funeral, which was very fine, he headed out of town as he would have done ordinarily on a day he had decided not to spend at Douds. He was wearing a felt hat and a long coat that would do for a rug if he wanted to take a nap. His overshoes were neatly held on his feet with the rubber rings from sealing jars. He was going out to fish for suckers. The season hadn't opened yet, but he always managed to be a bit ahead of it. He fished through the spring and early summer and cooked and ate what he caught. He had a frying pan and a pot hidden out on the riverbank. The pot was for boiling corn that he snatched out of the fields later in the year, when he was also eating the fruit of wild apple trees and grapevines. He was quite sane but abhorred conversation. He could not altogether avoid it in the weeks following his son's death, but he had a way of cutting it short.

"Should've watched out what he was doing."

Walking in the country that day, he met another person who was not at the funeral. A woman. She did not try to start any conversation and in fact seemed as fierce in her solitude as himself, whipping the air past her with long fervent strides.

The piano factory, which had started out making pump organs, stretched along the west side of town, like a medieval town wall. There were two long buildings like the inner and outer ramparts, with a closed-in bridge between them where the main offices were. And reaching up into the town and the streets of workers' houses you had the kilns and the sawmill and the lumberyard and storage sheds. The factory whistle dictated the time for many to get up, blowing at six o'clock in the morning. It blew again for work to start at seven and at twelve for dinnertime and at one in the afternoon for work to recommence, and then at five-thirty for the men to lay down their tools and go home.

Rules were posted beside the time clock, under glass. The first two rules were:

ONE MINUTE LATE IS FIFTEEN MINUTES PAY. BE PROMPT.
DON'T TAKE SAFETY FOR GRANTED. WATCH OUT
FOR YOURSELF AND THE NEXT MAN.

There had been accidents in the factory and in fact a man had been killed when a load of lumber fell on him. That had happened before Arthur's time. And once, during the war, a man had lost an arm, or part of an arm. On the day that happened, Arthur was away in Toronto. So he had never seen an accident—nothing serious, anyway. But it was often at the back of his mind now that something might happen.

Perhaps he did not feel so sure that trouble wouldn't come near him, as he had felt before his wife died. She had died in 1919, in the last flurry of the Spanish flu, when everyone had got over being frightened. Even she had not been frightened. That was nearly five years ago and it still seemed to Arthur like the end of a carefree time in his life. But to other people he had always seemed very responsible and serious—nobody had noticed much difference in him.

In his dreams of an accident there was a spreading silence, everything was shut down. Every machine in the place stopped making its customary noise and every man's voice was removed, and when Arthur looked out of the office window he understood that doom had fallen. He never could remember any particular thing he saw that told him this. It was just the space, the dust in the factory yard, that said to him *now*.

The books stayed on the floor of his car for a week or so. His daughter Bea said, "What are those books doing here?" and then he remembered.

Bea read out the titles and the authors. *Sir John Franklin and the Romance of the Northwest Passage*, by G. B. Smith. *What's Wrong with the World?*; G. K. Chesterton. *The Taking of Quebec*, Archibald Hendry. *Bolshevism: Practice and Theory*, by Lord Bertrand Russell.

"Bol-*shev*-ism," Bea said, and Arthur told her how to pronounce it correctly. She asked what it was, and he said, "It's something they've got in Russia that I don't understand so well myself. But from what I hear of it, it's a disgrace."

Bea was thirteen at this time. She had heard about the Russian Ballet and also about dervishes. She believed for the next couple of years that Bolshevism was some sort of diabolical and maybe indecent dance. At least this was the story she told when she was grown up.

She did not mention that the books were connected with the man who had had the accident. That would have made the story less amusing. Perhaps she had really forgotten.

The Librarian was perturbed. The books still had their cards in them, which meant they had never been checked out, just removed from the shelves and taken away.

"The one by Lord Russell has been missing a long time."

Arthur was not used to such reproofs, but he said mildly, "I am returning them on behalf of somebody else. The chap who was killed. In the accident at the factory."

The Librarian had the Franklin book open. She was looking at the picture of the boat trapped in the ice.

"His wife asked me to," Arthur said.

She picked up each book separately, and shook it as if she expected something to fall out. She ran her fingers in between the pages. The bottom part of her face was working in an unsightly way, as if she was chewing at the inside of her cheeks.

"I guess he just took them home as he felt like it," Arthur said.

"I'm sorry?" she said in a minute. "What did you say? I'm sorry."

It was the accident, he thought. The idea that the man who had died in such a way had been the last person to open these books, turn these pages. The thought that he might have left a bit of his life in them, a scrap of paper or a pipe cleaner as a marker, or even a few shreds of tobacco. That unhinged her.

"No matter," he said. "I just dropped by to bring them back."

He turned away from her desk but did not immediately leave the Library. He had not been in it for years. There was his father's picture between the two front windows, where it would always be.

A. V. Doud, founder of the Doud Organ Factory and Patron of this Library. A Believer in Progress, Culture, and Education. A True Friend of the Town of Carstairs and of the Working Man.

The Librarian's desk was in the archway between the front and back rooms. The books were on shelves set in rows in the back room. Green-shaded lamps, with long pull cords, dangled down in the aisles between. Arthur remembered years ago some matter brought up at the Council Meeting about buying sixty-watt bulbs instead of forty. This Librarian was the one who had requested that, and they had done it.

In the front room, there were newspapers and magazines on wooden racks, and some round heavy tables, with chairs, so that people could sit and read, and rows of thick dark books behind glass. Dictionaries, probably, and atlases and encyclopedias. Two handsome high windows looking out on the main street, with Arthur's father hanging between them. Other pictures around the room hung too high, and were too dim and crowded with figures for the person down below to interpret them easily. (Later, when Arthur had spent many hours in the Library and had discussed these pictures with the Librarian, he knew that one of them represented the Battle of Flodden Field, with the King of Scotland charging down the hill into a pall of smoke, one the funeral of the Boy King of Rome, and one the Quarrel of Oberon and Titania, from *A Midsummer Night's Dream*.)

He sat down at one of the reading tables, where he could look out the window. He picked up an old copy of the *National Geographic*, which was lying there. He had his back to the Librarian. He thought this the tactful thing to do, since she seemed somewhat wrought-up. Other people came in, and he heard her speak to them. Her voice sounded normal enough now. He kept thinking he would leave, but did not.

He liked the high bare window full of the light of the spring evening, and he liked the dignity and order of these rooms. He was pleasantly mystified by the thought of grown people coming and going here, steadily reading books. Week after week, one book after another, a whole life long. He himself read a book once in a while, when somebody recommended it, and usually he enjoyed it, and then he read magazines, to keep up with things, and never thought about reading a book until another one came along, in this almost accidental way.

There would be little spells when nobody was in the Library but himself and the Librarian.

During one of these, she came over and stood near him, replacing some newspapers on the rack. When she finished this, she spoke to him, with a controlled urgency.

"The account of the accident that was printed in the paper—I take it that was more or less accurate?"

Arthur said that it was possibly too accurate.

"Why? Why do you say that?"

He mentioned the public's endless appetite for horrific details. Ought the paper to pander to that?

"Oh, I think it's natural," the Librarian said. "I think it's natural to want to know the worst. People do want to picture it. I do myself. I am very ignorant of machinery. It's hard for me to imagine what happened. Even with the paper's help. Did the machine do something unexpected?"

"No," Arthur said. "It wasn't the machine grabbing him and pulling him in, like an animal. He made a wrong move or at any rate a careless move. Then he was done for."

She said nothing, but did not move away.

"You have to keep your wits about you," Arthur said. "Never let up for a second. A machine is your servant and it is an excellent servant, but it makes an imbecile master."

He wondered if he had read that somewhere, or had thought it up himself.

"And I suppose there are no ways of protecting people?" the Librarian said. "But you must know all about that."

She left him then. Somebody had come in.

The accident was followed by a rush of warm weather. The length of the evenings and the heat of the balmy days seemed sudden and surprising, as if this were not the way winter finally ended in that part of the country, almost every year. The sheets of floodwater shrank magically back into the bogs, and the leaves shot out of the reddened branches, and barnyard smells drifted into town and were wrapped in the smell of lilacs.

Instead of wanting to be outdoors on such evenings, Arthur found himself thinking of the Library, and he would often end up there, sitting in the spot he had chosen on his first visit. He would sit for half an hour, or an hour. He looked at the London *Illustrated News,* or the *National Geographic* or *Saturday Night* or *Collier's.* All of these magazines arrived at his own house and he could have been sitting there, in the den, looking out at his hedged lawns, which old Agnew kept in tolerable condition, and the flower beds now full of tulips of every vivid color and combination. It seemed that he preferred the view of the main street, where the occasional brisk-looking new Ford went by, or some stuttering older-model car with a dusty cloth top. He preferred the Post Office, with its clock tower telling four different times in four different directions— and, as people liked to say, all wrong. Also the passing and loitering on the side-walk. People trying to get the drinking fountain to work, although it wasn't turned on till the First of July.

It was not that he felt the need of sociability. He was not there for chat, though he would greet people if he knew them by name, and he did know most. And he might exchange a few words with the Librarian, though often it was only "Good evening" when he came in, and "Good night" when he went out. He made no demands on anybody. He felt his presence to be genial, reas-suring, and, above all, natural. By sitting here, reading and reflecting, here instead of at home, he seemed to himself to be providing something. People could count on it.

There was an expression he liked. *Public servant.* His father, who looked out at him here with tinted baby-pink cheeks and glassy blue eyes and an old man's petulant mouth, had never thought of himself so. He had thought of himself more as a public character and benefactor. He had operated by whims and decrees, and he had got away with it. He would go around the factory when business was slow, and say to one man and another, "Go home. Go on home now. Go home and stay there till I can use you again." And they would go. They would work in their gardens or go out shooting rabbits and run up bills for whatever they had to buy, and accept that it couldn't be otherwise. It was still a joke with them, to imitate his bark. *Go on home!* He was their hero more than Arthur could ever be, but they were not prepared to take the same treatment today. During the war, they had got used to the good wages and to being always in demand. They never thought of the glut of labor the soldiers had created when they came home, never thought about how a business like this was kept going by luck and ingenuity from one year to the next, even from one season to the next. They didn't like changes—they were not happy about the switch now to player pianos, which Arthur believed were the hope of the future. But Arthur would do what he had to, though his way of proceeding was quite the opposite of his father's. Think everything over and then think it over again. Stay in the background except when necessary. Keep your dignity. Try always to be fair.

They expected all to be provided. The whole town expected it. Work would be provided just as the sun would rise in the mornings. And the taxes on the factory raised at the same time rates were charged for the water that used to come free. Maintenance of the access roads was now the factory's responsibility instead of the town's. The Methodist Church was requesting a hefty sum to build the new Sunday school. The town hockey team needed new uniforms. Stone gateposts were being erected for the War Memorial Park. And every year the smartest boy in the senior class was sent to university, courtesy of Douds.

Ask and ye shall receive.

Expectations at home were not lacking either. Bea was agitating to go away to private school and Mrs. Feare had her eye on some new mixing apparatus for the kitchen, also a new washing machine. All the trim on the house was due to be painted this year. All that wedding-cake decoration that consumed paint by the gallon. And in the midst of this what had Arthur done but order himself a new car—a Chrysler sedan.

It was necessary—he had to drive a new car. He had to drive a new car, Bea had to go away to school, Mrs. Feare had to have the latest, and the trim had to be as fresh as Christmas snow. Else they would lose respect, they would lose confidence, they would start to wonder if things were going downhill. And it could be managed, with luck it could all be managed.

For years after his father's death, he had felt like an impostor. Not steadily, but from time to time he had felt that. And now the feeling was gone. He could sit here and feel that it was gone.

He had been in the office when the accident happened, consulting with a veneer salesman. Some change in noise registered with him, but it was more of an increase than a hush. It was nothing that alerted him—just an irritation. Because it happened in the sawmill, nobody would know about the accident immediately in the shops or in the kilns or in the yard, and work in some places continued for several minutes. In fact Arthur, bending over the veneer samples on his desk, might have been one of the last people to understand that there had been an intervention. He asked the salesman a question, and the salesman did not answer. Arthur looked up and saw the man's mouth open, his face frightened, his salesman's assurance wiped away.

Then he heard his own name being called—both "Mr. Doud!" as was customary and "Arthur, Arthur!" by such of the older men as had known him as a boy. Also he heard "saw" and "head" and "Jesus, Jesus, Jesus!"

Arthur could have wished for the silence, the sounds and objects drawing back in that dreadful but releasing way, to give him room. It was nothing like that. Yelling and questioning and running around, himself in the midst being propelled to the sawmill. One man had fainted, falling in such a way that if they had not got the saw turned off a moment before, it would have got him, too. It was his body, fallen but entire, that Arthur briefly mistook for the body of the victim. Oh, no, no. They pushed him on. The sawdust was scarlet. It was drenched, brilliant. The pile of lumber here was all merrily spattered, and the blades. A pile of work clothes soaked in blood lay in the sawdust and Arthur realized that it was the body, the trunk with limbs attached. So much blood had flowed as to make its shape not plain at first—to soften it, like a pudding.

The first thing he thought of was to cover that. He took off his jacket and did so. He had to step up close, his shoes squished in it. The reason no one else had done this would be simply that no one else was wearing a jacket.

"Have they gone a-get the doctor?" somebody was yelling. "Gone a-get the doctor!" a man quite close to Arthur said. "Can't sew his head back on—doctor. Can he?"

But Arthur gave the order to get the doctor; he imagined it was necessary. You can't have a death without a doctor. That set the rest in motion. Doctor, undertaker, coffin, flowers, preacher. Get started on all that, give them something to do. Shovel up the sawdust, clean up the saw. Send the men who had been close by to wash themselves. Carry the man who had fainted to the lunchroom. Is he all right? Tell the office girl to make tea.

Brandy was what was needed, or whisky. But he had a rule against it, on the premises.

Something still lacking. Where was it? There, they said. Over there. Arthur heard the sound of vomiting, not far away. All right. Either pick it up or tell somebody to pick it up. The sound of vomiting saved him, steadied him, gave him an almost lighthearted determination. He picked it up. He carried it delicately and securely as you might carry an awkward but valuable jug. Pressing the face out of sight, as if comforting it, against his chest. Blood seeped through his shirt and stuck the material to his skin. Warm. He felt like a wounded man. He was aware of them watching him and he was aware of himself as an actor must be, or a priest. What to do with it, now that he had it against his chest? The answer to that came, too. Set it down, put it back where it belongs, not of course fitted with exactness, not as if a seam could be closed. Just more or less in place, and lift the jacket and tug it into a new position.

He couldn't now ask the man's name. He would have to get it in some other way. After the intimacy of his services here, such ignorance would be an offense.

But he found he did know it—it came to him. As he edged the corner of his jacket over the ear that had lain and still lay upward, and so looked quite fresh and usable, he received a name. Son of the fellow who came and did the garden, who was not always reliable. A young man taken on again when he came back from the war. Married? He thought so. He would have to go and see her. As soon as possible. Clean clothes.

The Librarian often wore a dark-red blouse. Her lips were reddened to match, and her hair was bobbed. She was not a young woman anymore, but she maintained an eye-catching style. He remembered that years ago when they had hired her, he had thought that she got herself up very soberly. Her hair was not bobbed in those days—it was wound around her head, in the old style. It was still the same color—a warm and pleasant color, like leaves—oak leaves, say, in the fall. He tried to think how much she was paid. Not much, certainly. She kept herself looking well on it. And where did she live? In one of the boarding houses—the one with the schoolteachers? No, not there. She lived in the Commercial Hotel.

And now something else was coming to mind. No definite story that he could remember. You could not say with any assurance that she had a bad reputation. But it was not quite a spotless reputation, either. She was said to take a drink with the travellers. Perhaps she had a boyfriend among them. A boyfriend or two.

Well, she was old enough to do as she liked. It wasn't quite the same as the way it was with a teacher—hired partly to set an example. As long as she did her job well, and anybody could see that she did. She had her life to live, like everyone else. Wouldn't you rather have a nice-looking woman in here than a crabby old affair like Mary Tamblyn? Strangers might drop in, they judge a town by what they see, you want a nice-looking woman with a nice manner.

Stop that. Who said you didn't? He was arguing in his head on her behalf just as if somebody had come along who wanted her chucked out, and he had no intimation at all that that was the case.

What about her question, on the first evening, regarding the machines? What did she mean by that? Was it a sly way of bringing blame?

He had talked to her about the pictures and the lighting and even told her how his father had sent his own workmen over here, paid them to build the Library shelves, but he had never spoken of the man who had taken the books out without letting her know. One at a time, probably. Under his coat? Brought back the same way. He must have brought them back, or else he'd have had a houseful, and his wife would never stand for that. Not stealing, except temporarily. Harmless behavior, but peculiar. Was there any connection? Between thinking you could do things a little differently that way and thinking you could get away with a careless move that might catch your sleeve and bring the saw down on your neck?

There might be, there might be some connection. A matter of attitude.

"That chap—you know the one—the accident—" he said to the Librarian. "The way he took off with the books he wanted. Why do you think he did that?"

"People do things," the Librarian said. "They tear out pages. On account of something they don't like or something they do. They just do things. I don't know."

"Did he ever tear out some pages? Did you ever give him a lecture? Ever make him scared to face you?"

He meant to tease her a little, implying that she would not be likely to scare anybody, but she did not take it that way.

"How could I when I never spoke to him?" she said. "I never saw him. I never saw him, to know who he was."

She moved away, putting an end to the conversation. So she did not like to be teased. Was she one of those people full of mended cracks that you could only see close up? Some old misery troubling her, some secret? Maybe a sweetheart had been lost in the war.

• • • •

On a later evening, a Saturday evening in the summer, she brought the subject up herself, that he would never have mentioned again.

"Do you remember our talking once about the man who had the accident?"

Arthur said he did.

"I have something to ask you and you may think it strange."

He nodded.

"And my asking it—I want you to—it is confidential."

"Yes, indeed," he said.

"What did he look like?"

Look like? Arthur was puzzled. He was puzzled by her making such a fuss and secret about it—surely it was natural to be interested in what a man might look like, who had been coming in and making off with her books without her knowing about it—and because he could not help her, he shook his head. He could not bring any picture of Jack Agnew to mind.

"Tall," he said. "I believe he was on the tall side. Otherwise I cannot tell you. I am really not such a good person to ask. I can recognize a man easily but I can't ever give much of a physical description, even when it's someone I see on a daily basis.

"But I thought you were the one—I heard you were the one—" she said. "Who picked him up. His head."

Arthur said stiffly, "I didn't think that you could just leave it lying there." He felt disappointed in the woman, uneasy and ashamed for her. But he tried to speak matter-of-factly, keeping reproach out of his voice.

"I could not even tell you the color of his hair. It was all—all pretty much obliterated, by that time."

She said nothing for a moment or two and he did not look at her. Then she said, "It must seem as if I am one of those people—one of those people who are fascinated by these sorts of things."

Arthur made a protesting noise, but it did, of course, seem to him that she must be like that.

"I should not have asked you," she said. "I should not have mentioned it. I can never explain to you why I did. I would like just to ask you, if you can help it, never to think that that is the kind of person I am."

Arthur heard the word "never." She could never explain to him. He was never to think. In the midst of his disappointment he picked up this suggestion, that their conversations were to continue, and perhaps on a less haphazard basis. He heard a humility in her voice, but it was a humility that was based on some kind of assurance. Surely that was sexual.

Or did he only think so, because this was the evening it was? It was the Saturday evening in the month when he usually went to Walley. He was going there tonight, he had only dropped in here on his way, he had not meant to stay as long as he had done. It was the night when he went to visit a woman whose name was Jane MacFarlane. Jane MacFarlane lived apart from her husband, but she was not thinking of getting a divorce. She had no children. She earned her living as a dressmaker. Arthur had first met her when she came to his house to make clothes for his wife. Nothing had gone on at that time, and neither of them had thought of it. In some ways Jane MacFarlane was a woman like the Librarian—good-looking, though not so young, plucky and stylish and good at her work. In other ways, not so like. He could not imagine Jane ever presenting a man with a mystery, and following that up with the information that it would never be solved. Jane was a woman to give a man peace. The submerged dialogue he had with her—sensual, limited, kind—was very like the one he had had with his wife.

The Librarian went to the switch by the door, and turned out the main light. She locked the door. She disappeared among the shelves, turning out the lights there, too, in a leisurely way. The town clock was striking nine. She must think that it was right. His own watch said three minutes to.

It was time to get up, time for him to leave, time to go to Walley.

When she had finished dealing with the lights, she came and sat down at the table beside him.

He said, "I would never think of you in any way that would make you unhappy."

Turning out the lights shouldn't have made it so dark. They were in the middle of summer. But it seemed that heavy rain clouds had moved in. When Arthur had last paid attention to the street, he had seen plenty of daylight left: country people shopping, boys squirting each other at the drinking fountain, and young girls walking up and down in their soft, cheap, flowery summer dresses, letting the young men watch them from wherever the young men congregated—the Post Office steps, the front of the feed store. And now that he looked again he saw the street in an uproar from the loud wind that already carried a few drops of rain. The girls were shrieking and laughing and holding their purses over their heads as they ran to shelter, store clerks were rolling up awnings and hauling in the baskets of fruit, the racks of summer shoes, the garden implements that had been displayed on the sidewalks. The doors of the Town Hall banged as the farm women ran inside, grabbing on to packages and children, to cram themselves into the Ladies' Rest Room. Somebody tried the Library door. The Librarian looked over at it but did not move. And soon the rain was sweeping like curtains across the street, and the wind battered the Town Hall roof, and tore at the treetops. That roaring and danger lasted a few minutes, while the power of the wind went by. Then the sound left was the sound of the rain, which was now falling vertically and so heavily they might have been under a waterfall.

If the same thing was happening at Walley, he thought, Jane would know enough not to expect him. This was the last thought he had of her for a long while.

"Mrs. Feare wouldn't wash my clothes," he said, to his own surprise. "She was afraid to touch them."

The Librarian said, in a peculiarly quivering, shamed, and determined voice, "I think what you did—I think that was a remarkable thing to do."

The rain made such a constant noise that he was released from answering. He found it easy then to turn and look at her. Her profile was dimly lit by the wash of rain down the windows. Her expression was calm and reckless. Or so it seemed to him. He realized that he knew hardly anything about her—what kind of person she really was or what kind of secrets she could have. He could not even estimate his own value to her. He only knew that he had some, and it wasn't the usual.

He could no more describe the feeling he got from her than you can describe a smell. It's like the scorch of electricity. It's like burnt kernels of wheat. No, it's like a bitter orange. I give up.

He had never imagined that he would find himself in a situation like this, visited by such a clear compulsion. But it seemed he was not unprepared. Without thinking over twice or even once what he was letting himself in for, he said, "I wish—"

He had spoken too quietly, she did not hear him.

He raised his voice. He said, "I wish we could get married."

Then she looked at him. She laughed but controlled herself.

"I'm sorry," she said. "I'm sorry. It's just what went through my mind."

"What was that?" he said.

"I thought—that's the last I'll see of him."

Arthur said, "You're mistaken."

TOLPUDDLE MARTYRS

The passenger train from Carstairs to London had stopped running during the Second World War and even the rails were taken up. People said it was for the War Effort. When Louisa went to London to see the heart specialist, in the mid-fifties, she had to take the bus. She was not supposed to drive anymore.

The doctor, the heart specialist, said that her heart was a little wonky and her pulse inclined to be jumpy. She thought that made her heart sound like a comedian and her pulse like a puppy on a lead. She had not come fifty-seven miles to be treated with such playfulness but she let it pass, because she was already distracted by something she had been reading in the doctor's waiting room. Perhaps it was what she had been reading that had made her pulse jumpy.

On an inside page of the local paper she had seen the headline LOCAL MARTYRS HONORED, and simply to put in the time she had read further. She read that there was to be some sort of ceremony that afternoon at Victoria Park. It was a ceremony to honor the Tolpuddle Martyrs. The paper said that few people had heard of the Tolpuddle Martyrs, and certainly Louisa had not. They were men who had been tried and found guilty for administering illegal oaths. This peculiar offense, committed over a hundred years ago in Dorset,

England, had got them transported to Canada and some of them had ended up here in London, where they lived out the rest of their days and were buried without any special notice or commemoration. They were considered now to be among the earliest founders of the Trade Union movement, and the Trade Unions Council, along with representatives of the Canadian Federation of Labor and the ministers of some local churches, had organized a ceremony taking place today on the occasion of the hundred-and-twentieth anniversary of their arrest.

Martyrs is laying it on somewhat, thought Louisa. They were not executed, after all.

The ceremony was to take place at three o'clock and the chief speakers were to be one of the local ministers, and Mr. John (Jack) Agnew, a union spokesman from Toronto.

It was a quarter after two when Louisa came out of the doctor's office. The bus to Carstairs did not leave until six o'clock. She had thought she would go and have tea and something to eat on the top floor of Simpsons, then shop for a wedding present, or if the time fitted go to an afternoon movie. Victoria Park lay between the doctor's office and Simpsons, and she decided to cut across it. The day was hot and the shade of the trees pleasant. She could not avoid seeing where the chairs had been set up, and a small speakers' platform draped in yellow cloth, with a Canadian flag on the one side and what she supposed must be a Labor Union flag on the other. A group of people had collected and she found herself changing course in order to get a look at them. Some were old people, very plainly but decently dressed, the women with kerchiefs around their heads on the hot day, Europeans. Others were factory workers, men in clean short-sleeved shirts and women in fresh blouses and slacks, let out early. A few women must have come from home, because they were wearing summer dresses and sandals and trying to keep track of small children. Louisa thought that they would not care at all for the way she was dressed—fashionably, as always, in beige shantung with a crimson silk tam—but she noticed, just then, a woman more elegantly got up than she was, in green silk with her dark hair drawn tightly back, tied with a green-and-gold scarf. She might have been forty—her face was worn, but beautiful. She came over to Louisa at once, smiling, showed her a chair and gave her a mimeographed paper. Louisa could not read the purple printing. She tried to get a look at some men who were talking beside the platform. Were the speakers among them?

The coincidence of the name was hardly even interesting. Neither the first name nor the last was all that unusual.

She did not know why she had sat down, or why she had come over here in the first place. She was beginning to feel a faintly sickening, familiar agitation. She could feel that over nothing. But once it got going, telling herself that it was over nothing did no good. The only thing to do was to get up and get away from here before any more people sat down and hemmed her in.

The green woman intercepted her, asked if she was all right.

"I have to catch a bus," said Louisa in a croaky voice. She cleared her throat. "An out-of-town bus," she said with better control, and marched away, not in the right direction for Simpsons. She thought in fact that she wouldn't go there, she wouldn't go to Birks for the wedding present or to a movie either. She would just go and sit in the bus depot until it was time for her to go home.

Within half a block of the bus depot she remembered that the bus had not taken her there that morning. The depot was being torn down and rebuilt—there was a temporary depot several blocks away. She had not paid quite enough attention to which street it was on—York Street, east of the real depot, or King? At any rate, she had to detour, because both of these streets were being torn up, and she had almost decided she was lost when she realized she had been lucky enough to come upon the temporary depot by the back way. It was an old house—one of those tall yellow-gray brick houses dating from the time when this was a residential district. This was probably the last use it would be put to before being torn down. Houses all around it must have been torn down to make the large gravelled lot where the buses pulled in. There were still some trees at the edge of the lot and under them a few rows of chairs that she had not noticed when she got off the bus before noon. Two men were sitting on what used to be the veranda of the house, on old car seats. They wore brown shirts with the bus company's insignia but they seemed to be halfhearted about their work, not getting up when she asked if the bus to Carstairs was leaving at six o'clock as scheduled and where could she get a soft drink?

Six o'clock, far as they knew.

Coffee shop down the street.

Cooler inside but only Coke and orange left.

She got herself a Coca-Cola out of the cooler in a dirty little indoor waiting room that smelled of a bad toilet. Moving the depot to this dilapidated house must have thrown everyone into a state of indolence and fecklessness. There was a fan in the room they used as an office, and she saw, as she went by, some papers blow off the desk. "Oh, shit," said the office girl, and stamped her heel on them.

The chairs set up in the shade of the dusty city trees were straight-backed old wooden chairs originally painted different colors—they looked as if they had come from various kitchens. Strips of old carpet and rubber bathroom mats were laid down in front of them, to keep your feet off the gravel. Behind the first row of chairs she thought she saw a sheep lying on the ground, but it turned into a dirty-white dog, which trotted over and looked at her for a moment in a grave semiofficial way—gave a brief sniff at her shoes, and trotted away. She had not noticed if there were any drinking straws and did not feel like going back to look. She drank Coke from the bottle, tilting back her head and closing her eyes.

When she opened them, a man was sitting one chair away, and was speaking to her.

"I got here as soon as I could," he said. "Nancy said you were going to catch a bus. As soon as I finished with the speech, I took off. But the bus depot is all torn up.

"Temporarily," she said.

"I knew you right away," he said. "In spite of well, many years. When I saw you, I was talking to somebody. Then I looked again and you'd disappeared."

"I don't recognize you," said Louisa.

"Well, no," he said. "I guess not. Of course. You wouldn't."

He was wearing tan slacks, a pale-yellow short-sleeved shirt, a cream-and-yellow ascot scarf. A bit of a dandy, for a union man. His hair was white but thick and wavy, the sort of springy hair that goes in ripples, up and back from the forehead, his skin was flushed and his face was deeply wrinkled from the efforts of speechmaking and from talking to people privately, she supposed, with much of the fervor and persuasiveness of his public speeches. He wore tinted glasses, which he took off now, as if willing that she should see him better. His eyes were a light blue, slightly bloodshot and apprehensive. A good-looking man, still trim except for a little authoritative bulge over the belt, but she did not find these serviceable good looks—the careful sporty clothes, the display of ripply hair, the effective expressions—very attractive. She preferred the kind of looks Arthur had. The restraint, the dark-suited dignity that some people could call pompous, that seemed to her admirable and innocent.

"I always meant to break the ice," he said. "I meant to speak to you. I should have gone in and said goodbye at least. The opportunity to leave came up so suddenly."

Louisa did not have any idea what to say to this. He sighed. He said, "You must have been mad at me. Are you still?"

"No" she said, and fell back, ridiculously, on the usual courtesies. "How is Grace? How is your daughter? Lillian?"

"Grace is not so well. She had some arthritis. Her weight doesn't help it. Lillian is all right. She's married but she still teaches high school. Mathematics. Not too usual for a woman.

How could Louisa begin to correct him? Could she say, No, your wife Grace got married again during the war, she married a farmer, a widower. Before that she used to come in and clean our house once a week. Mrs. Feare had got too old. And Lillian never finished high school, how could she be a high-school teacher? She married young, she had some children, she works in the drugstore. She had your height and your hair, dyed blond. I often looked at her and thought she must be like you. When she was growing up, I used to give her my stepdaughter's outgrown clothes.

Instead of this, she said, "Then the woman in the green dress—that was not Lillian?"

"Nancy? Oh, no! Nancy is my guardian angel. She keeps track of where I'm going, and when, and have I got my speech, and what I drink and eat and have I taken my pills. I tend toward high blood pressure. Nothing too serious. But my way of life's no good. I'm on the go constantly. Tonight I've got to fly out of here to Ottawa, tomorrow I've got a tough meeting, tomorrow night I've got some fool banquet."

Louisa felt it necessary to say, "You knew that I got married? I married Arthur Doud."

She thought he showed some surprise. But he said, "Yes, I heard that. Yes."

"We worked hard, too," said Louisa sturdily. "Arthur died six years ago. We kept the factory going all through the thirties even though at times we were down to three men. We had no money for repairs and I remember cutting up the office awnings so that Arthur could carry them up on a ladder and patch the roof. We tried making everything we could think of. Even outdoor bowling alleys for those amusement places. Then the war came and we couldn't keep up. We could sell all the pianos we could make but also we were making radar cases for the Navy. I stayed in the office all through."

"It must have been a change," he said, in what seemed a tactful voice. "A change from the Library."

"Work is work," she said. "I still work. My stepdaughter Bea is divorced, she keeps house for me after a fashion. My son has finally finished university—he is supposed to be learning about the business, but he has some excuse to go off in the middle of every afternoon. When I come home at suppertime, I am so tired I could drop, and I hear the ice tinkling in their glasses and them laughing behind the hedge. Oh, Mud, they say when they see me, Oh, poor Mud, sit down here, get her a drink! They call me Mud because that was my son's name for me when he was a baby. But they are neither of them babies now. The house is cool when I come home—it's a lovely house if you remember, built in three tiers like a wedding cake. Mosaic tiles in the entrance hall. But I am always thinking about the factory, that is what fills my mind. What should we do to stay afloat? There are only five factories in Canada making pianos now, and three of them are in Quebec with the low cost of labor. No doubt you know all about that. When I talk to Arthur in my head, it is always about the same thing. I am very close to him still but it is hardly in a mystical way. You would think as you get older your mind would fill up with what they call the spiritual side of things, but mine just seems to get more and more practical, trying to get something settled. What a thing to talk to a dead man about."

She stopped, she was embarrassed. But she was not sure that he had listened to all of this, and in fact she was not sure that she had said all of it.

"What started me off—" he said. "What got me going in the first place, with whatever I have managed to do, was the Library. So I owe you a great deal."

He put his hands on his knees, let his head fall.

"Ah, rubbish," he said.

He groaned, and ended up with a laugh.

"My father," he said, "You wouldn't remember my father?"

"Oh, yes."

"Well. Sometimes I think he had the right idea."

Then he lifted his head, gave it a shake, and made a pronouncement.

"Love never dies."

She felt impatient to the point of taking offense. This is what all the speechmaking turns you into, she thought, a person who can say things like that. Love dies all the time, or at any rate it becomes distracted, overlaid—it might as well be dead.

"Arthur used to come and sit in the Library," she said. "In the beginning I was very provoked with him. I used to look at the back of his neck and think, Ha, what if something should hit you there! None of that would make sense to you. It wouldn't make sense. And it turned out to be something else I wanted entirely. I wanted to marry him and get into a normal life."

"A normal life," she repeated—and a giddiness seemed to be taking over, a widespread forgiveness of folly, alerting the skin of her spotty hand, her dry thick fingers that lay not far from his, on the seat of the chair between them. An amorous flare-up of the cells, of old intentions. *Oh, never dies.*

Across the gravelled yard came a group of oddly dressed folk. They moved all together, a clump of black. The women did not show their hair— they had black shawls or bonnets covering their heads. The men wore broad hats and black braces. The children were dressed just like their elders, even to the bonnets and hats. How hot they all looked in those clothes—how hot and dusty and wary and shy.

"The Tolpuddle Martyrs," he said, in a faintly joking, resigned, and compassionate voice. "Ah, I guess I'd better go over. I'd better go over there and have a word with them."

That edge of a joke, the uneasy kindness, made her think of somebody else. Who was it? When she saw the breadth of his shoulders from behind, and the broad flat buttocks, she knew who.

Jim Frarey.

Oh, what kind of a trick was being played on her, or what kind of trick was she playing on herself! She would not have it. She pulled herself up tightly, she saw all those black clothes melt into a puddle. She was dizzy and humiliated. She would not have it.

But not all black, now that they were getting closer. She could see dark blue, those were the men's shirts, and dark blue and purple in some of the women's dresses. She could see faces—the men's behind beards, the women's in their deep-brimmed bonnets. And now she knew who they were. They were Mennonites.

Mennonites were living in this part of the country, where they never used to be. There were some of them around Bondi, a village north of Carstairs. They would be going home on the same bus as she was.

He was not with them, or anywhere in sight.

A traitor, helplessly. A traveller.

Once she knew that they were Mennonites and not some lost unidentifiable strangers, these people did not look so shy or dejected. In fact they seemed quite cheerful, passing around a bag of candy, adults eating candy with the children. They settled on the chairs all around her.

No wonder she was feeling clammy. She had gone under a wave, which nobody else had noticed. You could say anything you liked about what had happened—but what it amounted to was going under a wave. She had gone under and through it and was left with a cold sheen on her skin, a beating in her ears, a cavity in her chest, and revolt in her stomach. It was anarchy she was up against—a devouring muddle. Sudden holes and impromptu tricks and radiant vanishing consolations.

But these Mennonite settlings are a blessing. The plop of behinds on chairs, the crackling of the candy bag, the meditative sucking and soft conversations. Without looking at Louisa, a little girl holds out the bag, and Louisa accepts a butterscotch mint. She is surprised to be able to hold it in her hand, to have her lips shape thank-you, then to discover in her mouth just the taste that she expected. She sucks on it as they do on theirs, not in any hurry, and allows that taste to promise her some reasonable continuance.

Lights have come on, though it isn't yet evening. In the trees above the wooden chairs someone has strung lines of little colored bulbs that she did not notice until now. They make her think of festivities. Carnivals. Boats of singers on the lake.

"What place is this?" she said to the woman beside her.

On the day of Miss Tamblyn's death it happened that Louisa was staying in the Commercial Hotel. She was a traveller then for a company that sold hats, ribbons, handkerchiefs and trimmings, and ladies' underwear to retail stores. She heard the talk in the hotel, and it occurred to her that the town would soon need a new Librarian. She was getting very tired of lugging her sample cases on and off trains, and showing her wares in hotels, packing and unpacking. She went at once and talked to the people in charge of the Library. A Mr. Doud and a Mr. Macleod. They sounded like a vaudeville team but did not look it. The pay was poor, but she had not been doing so well on commission, either. She told them that she had finished high school, in Toronto, and had worked in Eaton's Book Department before she switched to travelling. She did not think it necessary to tell them that she had only worked there five months when she was discovered to have t.b., and that she had then spent four years in a sanitorium. The t.b. was cured, anyway, her spots were dry.

The hotel moved her to one of the rooms for permanent guests, on the third floor. She could see the snow-covered hills over the rooftops. The town of Carstairs was in a river valley. It had three or four thousand people and a long main street that ran downhill, over the river, and uphill again. There was a piano and organ factory.

The houses were built for lifetimes and the yards were wide and the streets were lined with mature elm and maple trees. She had never been here when the leaves were on the trees. It must make a great difference. So much that lay open now would be concealed.

She was glad of a fresh start, her spirits were hushed and grateful. She had made fresh starts before and things had not turned out as she had hoped, but she believed in the swift decision, the unforeseen intervention, the uniqueness of her fate.

The town was full of the smell of horses. As evening came on, big blinkered horses with feathered hooves pulled the sleighs across the bridge, past the hotel, beyond the streetlights, down the dark side roads. Somewhere out in the country they would lose the sound of each other's bells.

CONSTRUCTING A READING

1. Try to describe the "surprises" you noted while reading as violations of generic expectations—that is, "when Jack died, I expected X to happen, but instead, Y happened." Share your list with your group members.
2. The story of Jack's death is told twice: once in the newspaper and once by the narrator. With your group members, discuss the differences in the two tellings. Do they constitute two genres within the story? How does the double telling affect you as reader? Are you more or less horrified by either one?
3. As the reader tries to piece together "what really happens" at the end of this story, several possibilities emerge. List them. With your group members, discuss the relative probability of each of your possible interpretations. Why do you suppose Munro establishes this ambiguity?
4. Do you read Jack's death as poetic retribution for his jilting of Louisa? Why or why not?
5. Do you see Louisa's wealth as a reward for hard work? As a consolation prize for losing Jack? Again, why or why not?
6. Do you think Jim Frarey seduced Louisa? Or did Louisa seduce him? Or do you have another view of the situation?
7. Some critics have given the name "magic realism" to stories like "Carried Away." On the basis of your reading of this story, describe the characteristics of "magic realism" as a genre.

The Two

Gloria Naylor

At first they seemed like such nice girls. No one could remember exactly when they had moved into Brewster. It was earlier in the year before Ben was killed—of course, it had to be before Ben's death. But no one remembered if it was in the winter or spring of that year that the two had come. People often came and went on Brewster Place like a restless night's dream, moving in and out in the dark to avoid eviction notices or neighborhood bulletins about the dilapidated condition of their furnishings. So it wasn't until the two were clocked leaving in the mornings and returning in the evenings at regular intervals that it was quietly absorbed that they now claimed Brewster as home. And Brewster waited, cautiously prepared to claim them, because you never knew about young women, and obviously single at that. But when no wild music or drunken friends careened out of the corner building on weekends, and especially, when no slightly eager husbands were encouraged to linger around that first-floor apartment and run errands for them, a suspended sigh of relief floated around the two when they dumped their garbage, did their shopping, and headed for the morning bus.

The women of Brewster had readily accepted the lighter, skinny one. There wasn't much threat in her timid mincing walk and the slightly protruding teeth she seemed so eager to show everyone in her bell-like good mornings and evenings. Breaths were held a little longer in the direction of the short dark one—too pretty, and too much behind. And she insisted on wearing those thin Qiana dresses that the summer breeze molded against the maddening rhythm of the twenty pounds of rounded flesh that she swung steadily down the street. Through slitted eyes, the women watched their men watching her pass, knowing the bastards were praying for a wind. But since she seemed oblivious to whether these supplications went answered, their sighs settled around her shoulders too. Nice girls.

And so no one even cared to remember exactly when they had moved into Brewster Place, until the rumor started. It had first spread through the block like a sour odor that's only faintly perceptible and easily ignored until it starts growing in strength from the dozen mouths it had been lying in, among clammy gums and scum-coated teeth. And then it was everywhere—lining the mouths and whitening the lips of everyone as they wrinkled up their noses at its pervading smell, unable to pinpoint the source or time of its initial arrival. Sophie could—she had been there.

It wasn't that the rumor had actually begun with Sophie. A rumor needs no true parent. It only needs a willing carrier, and it found one in Sophie. She had been there—on one of those August evenings when the sun's absence is a mockery because the heat leaves the air so heavy it presses the naked skin down on your body, to the point that a sheet becomes unbearable and sleep impossible. So most of Brewster was outside that night when the two had come in together, probably from one of those air-conditioned movies downtown, and had greeted the ones who were loitering around their building. And they had started up the steps when the skinny one tripped over a child's ball and the darker one had grabbed her by the arm and around the waist to break her fall. "Careful, don't wanna lose you now." And the two of them had laughed into each other's eyes and went into the building.

The smell had begun there. It outlined the image of the stumbling woman and the one who had broken her fall. Sophie and a few other women sniffed at the spot and then, perplexed, silently looked at each other. Where had they seen that before? They had often laughed and touched each other—held each other in joy or its dark twin—but where had they seen *that* before? It came to them as the scent drifted down the steps and entered their nostrils on the way to their inner mouths. They had seen that—done that—with their men. That shared moment of invisible communion reserved for two and hidden from the rest of the world behind laughter or tears or a touch. In the days before babies, miscarriages, and other broken dreams, after stolen caresses in barn stalls and cotton houses, after intimate walks from church and secret kisses with boys who were now long forgotten or permanently fixed in their lives—that was where. They could almost feel the odor moving about in their mouths, and they slowly knitted themselves together and let it out into the air like a yellow mist that began to cling to the bricks on Brewster.

So it got around that the two in 312 were *that* way. And they had seemed like such nice girls. Their regular exits and entrances to the block were viewed with a jaundiced eye. The quiet that rested around their door on the weekends hinted of all sorts of secret rituals, and their friendly indifference to the men on the street was an insult to the women as a brazen flaunting of unnatural ways.

Since Sophie's apartment windows faced theirs from across the air shaft, she became the official watchman for the block, and her opinions were deferred to whenever the two came up in conversation. Sophie took her position seriously and was constantly alert for any telltale signs that might creep out around their drawn shades, across from which she kept a religious vigil. An entire week of drawn shades was evidence enough to send her flying around with reports that as soon as it got dark they pulled their shades down and put on the lights. Heads nodded in knowing unison—a definite sign. If doubt was voiced with a "But I pull my shades down at night too," a whispered "Yeah, but you're not *that* way" was argument enough to win them over.

Sophie watched the lighter one dumping their garbage, and she went outside and opened the lid. Her eyes darted over the crushed tin cans, vegetable peelings, and empty chocolate chip cookie boxes. What do they do with all them chocolate chip cookies? It was surely a sign, but it would take some time to figure that one out. She saw Ben go into their apartment, and she waited and blocked his path as he came out, carrying his toolbox.

"What ya see?" She grabbed his arm and whispered wetly in his face.

Ben stared at her squinted eyes and drooping lips and shook his head slowly. "Uh, uh, uh, it was terrible."

"Yeah?" She moved in a little closer.

"Worst busted faucet I seen in my whole life." He shook her hand off his arm and left her standing in the middle of the block.

"You old sop bucket," she muttered, as she went back up on her stoop. A broken faucet, huh? Why did they need to use so much water?

Sophie had plenty to report that day. Ben had said it was terrible in there. No, she didn't know exactly what he had seen, but you can imagine—and they did. Confronted with the difference that had been thrust into their predictable world, they reached into their imaginations and, using an ancient pattern, weaved themselves a reason for its existence. Out of necessity they stitched all of their secret fears and lingering childhood nightmares into this existence, because even though it was deceptive enough to try and look as they looked, talk as they talked, and do as they did, it had to have some hidden stain to invalidate it—it was impossible for them both to be right. So they leaned back, supported by the sheer weight of their numbers and comforted by the woven barrier that kept them protected from the yellow mist that enshrouded the two as they came and went on Brewster Place.

Lorraine was the first to notice the change in the people on Brewster Place. She was a shy but naturally friendly woman who got up early, and had read the morning paper and done fifty sit-ups before it was time to leave for work. She came out of her apartment eager to start her day by greeting any of her neighbors who were outside. But she noticed that some of the people who had spoken to her before made a point of having something else to do with their eyes when she passed, although she could almost feel them staring at her back as she moved on. The ones who still spoke only did so after an uncomfortable pause, in which they seemed to be peering through her before they begrudged her a good morning or evening. She wondered if it was all in her mind and she thought about mentioning it to Theresa, but she didn't want to be accused of being too sensitive again. And how would Tee even notice anything like that anyway? She had a lousy attitude and hardly ever spoke to people. She stayed in that bed until the last moment and rushed out of the house fogged-up and grumpy, and she was used to being stared at—by men at least—because of her body.

Lorraine thought about these things as she came up the block from work, carrying a large paper bag. The group of women on her stoop parted silently and let her pass.

"Good evening," she said, as she climbed the steps.

Sophie was standing on the top step and tried to peek into the bag. "You been shopping, huh? What ya buy?" It was almost an accusation.

"Groceries." Lorraine shielded the top of the bag from view and squeezed past her with a confused frown. She saw Sophie throw a knowing glance to the others at the bottom of the stoop. What was wrong with this old woman? Was she crazy or something?

Lorraine went into her apartment. Theresa was sitting by the window, reading a copy of *Mademoiselle*. She glanced up from her magazine. "Did you get my chocolate chip cookies?"

"Why good evening to you, too, Tee. And how was my day? Just wonderful." She sat the bag down on the couch. "The little Baxter boy brought in a puppy for show-and-tell, and the damn thing pissed all over the floor and then proceeded to chew the heel off my shoe, but, yes, I managed to hobble to the store and bring you your chocolate chip cookies."

Oh, Jesus, Theresa thought, she's got a bug up her ass tonight.

"Well, you should speak to Mrs. Baxter. She ought to train her kid better than that." She didn't wait for Lorraine to stop laughing before she tried to stretch her good mood. "Here, I'll put those things away. Want me to make dinner so you can rest? I only worked half a day, and the most tragic thing that went down was a broken fingernail and that got caught in my typewriter."

Lorraine followed Theresa into the kitchen. "No, I'm not really tired, and fair's fair, you cooked last night. I didn't mean to tick off like that; it's just that . . . well, Tee, have you noticed that people aren't as nice as they used to be?"

Theresa stiffened. Oh, God, here she goes again. "What people, Lorraine? Nice in what way?"

"Well, the people in this building and on the street. No one hardly speaks anymore. I mean, I'll come in and say good evening—and just silence. It wasn't like that when we first moved in. I don't know, it just makes you wonder; that's all. What are they thinking?"

"I personally don't give a shit what they're thinking. And their good evenings don't put any bread on my table."

"Yeah, but you didn't see the way that woman looked at me out there. They must feel something or know something. They probably—"

"They, they, they!" Theresa exploded. "You know, I'm not starting up with this again, Lorraine. Who in the hell are they? And where in the hell are we? Living in some dump of a building in this God-forsaken part of town around a bunch of ignorant niggers with the cotton still under their fingernails because of you and your theys. They knew something in Linden Hills, so I gave up an apartment for you that I'd been in for the last four years. And then they knew in Park Heights, and you made me so miserable there we had to leave. Now these mysterious theys are on Brewster Place. Well, look out that window, kid. There's a big wall down that block, and this is the end of the line for me. I'm not moving anymore, so if that's what you're working yourself up to—save it!"

When Theresa became angry she was like a lump of smoldering coal, and her fierce bursts of temper always unsettled Lorraine.

"You see, that's why I didn't want to mention it." Lorraine began to pull at her fingers nervously. "You're always flying up and jumping to conclusions—no one said anything about moving. And I didn't know your life has been so miserable since you met me. I'm sorry about that," she finished tearfully.

Theresa looked at Lorraine, standing in the kitchen door like a wilted leaf, and she wanted to throw something at her. Why didn't she ever fight back? The very softness that had first attracted her to Lorraine was now a frequent cause for irritation. Smoked honey. That's what Lorraine had reminded her of, sitting in her office clutching that application. Dry autumn days in Georgia woods, thick bloated smoke under a beehive, and the first glimpse of amber honey just faintly darkened about the edges by the burning twigs. She had flowed just that heavily into Theresa's mind and had stuck there with a persistent sweetness.

But Theresa hadn't known then that this softness filled Lorraine up to the very middle and that she would bend at the slightest pressure, would be constantly seeking to surround herself with the comfort of everyone's goodwill, and would shrivel up at the least touch of disapproval. It was becoming a drain to be continually called upon for this nurturing and support that she just didn't understand. She had supplied it at first out of love for Lorraine, hoping that she would harden eventually, even as honey does when exposed to the cold. Theresa was growing tired of being clung to—of being the one who was leaned on. She didn't want a child—she wanted someone who could stand toe to toe with her and be willing to slug it out at times. If they practiced that way with each other, then they could turn back to back and beat the hell out of the world for trying to invade their territory. But she had found no such sparring partner in Lorraine, and the strain of fighting alone was beginning to show on her.

"Well, if it was that miserable, I would have been gone a long time ago," she said, watching her words refresh Lorraine like a gentle shower.

"I guess you think I'm some sort of a sick paranoid, but I can't afford to have people calling my job or writing letters to my principal. You know I've already lost a position like that in Detroit. And teaching is my whole life, Tee."

"I know," she sighed, not really knowing at all. There was no danger of that ever happening on Brewster Place. Lorraine taught too far from this neighborhood for anyone here to recognize her in that school. No, it wasn't her job she feared losing this time, but their approval. She wanted to stand out there and chat and trade makeup secrets and cake recipes. She wanted to be secretary of their block association and be asked to mind their kids while they ran to the store. And none of that was going to happen if they couldn't even bring themselves to accept her good evenings.

Theresa silently finished unpacking the groceries. "Why did you buy cottage cheese? Who eats that stuff?"

"Well, I thought we should go on a diet."

"If *we* go on a diet, then you'll disappear. You've got nothing to lose but your hair."

"Oh, I don't know. I thought that we might want to try and reduce our hips or something." Lorraine shrugged playfully.

"No, thank you. We are very happy with our hips the way they are," Theresa said, as she shoved the cottage cheese to the back of the refrigerator. "And even when I lose weight, it never comes off there. My chest and arms just get smaller, and I start looking like a bottle of salad dressing."

The two women laughed, and Theresa sat down to watch Lorraine fix dinner. "You know, this behind has always been my downfall. When I was coming up in Georgia with my grandmother, the boys used to promise me penny candy if I would let them pat my behind. And I used to love those jawbreakers—you know, the kind that lasted all day and kept changing colors in your mouth. So I was glad to oblige them, because in one afternoon I could collect a whole week's worth of jawbreakers."

"Really. That's funny to you? Having some boy feeling all over you."

Theresa sucked her teeth. "We were only kids, Lorraine. You know, you remind me of my grandmother. That was one straight-laced old lady. She had a fit when my brother told her what I was doing. She called me into the smokehouse and told me in this real scary whisper that I could get pregnant from letting little boys pat my butt and that I'd end up like my cousin Willa. But Willa and I had been thick as fleas, and she had already given me a step-by-step summary of how she'd gotten into her predicament. But I sneaked around to her house that night just to double-check her story, since that old lady had seemed so earnest. 'Willa, are you sure?' I whispered through her bedroom window. 'I'm tellin' ya, Tee,' she said. 'Just keep both feet on the ground and you home free.' Much later I learned that advice wasn't too biologically sound, but it worked in Georgia because those country boys didn't have much imagination."

Theresa's laughter bounced off of Lorraine's silent, rigid back and died in her throat. She angrily tore open a pack of the chocolate chip cookies. "Yeah," she said, staring at Lorraine's back and biting down hard into the cookie, "it wasn't until I came up north to college that I found out there's a whole lot of things that a dude with a little imagination can do to you even with both feet on the ground. You see, Willa forgot to tell me not to bend over or squat or—"

"Must you!" Lorraine turned around from the stove with her teeth clenched tightly together.

"Must I what, Lorraine? Must I talk about things that are as much a part of life as eating or breathing or growing old? Why are you always so uptight about sex or men?"

"I'm not uptight about anything. I just think it's disgusting when you go on and on about—"

"There's nothing disgusting about it, Lorraine. You've never been with a man, but I've been with quite a few—some better than others. There were a couple who I still hope to this day will die a slow, painful death, but then there were some who were good to me—in and out of bed."

"If they were so great, then why are you with me?" Lorraine's lips were trembling.

"Because—" Theresa looked steadily into her eyes and then down at the cookie she was twirling on the table. "Because," she continued slowly, "you can take a chocolate chip cookie and put holes in it and attach it to your ears and call it an earring, or hang it around your neck on a silver chain and pretend it's a necklace—but it's still a cookie. See—you can toss it in the air and call it a Frisbee or even a flying saucer, if the mood hits you, and it's still just a cookie. Send it spinning on a table—like this—until it's a wonderful blur of amber and brown light that you can imagine to be a topaz or rusted gold or old crystal, but the law of gravity has got to come into play, sometime, and it's got to come to rest—sometime. Then all the spinning and pretending and hoopla is over with. And you know what you got?"

"A chocolate chip cookie," Lorraine said.

"Uh-uh." Theresa put the cookie in her mouth and winked. "A lesbian." She got up from the table. "Call me when dinner's ready, I'm going back to read." She stopped at the kitchen door. "Now, why are you putting gravy on that chicken, Lorraine? You know it's fattening."

The Brewster Place Block Association was meeting in Kiswana's apartment. People were squeezed on the sofa and coffee table and sitting on the floor. Kiswana had hung a red banner across the wall, "Today Brewster—Tomorrow America!" but few understood what that meant and even fewer cared. They were there because this girl had said that something could be done about the holes in their walls and the lack of heat that kept their children with congested lungs in the winter. Kiswana had given up trying to be heard above the voices that were competing with each other in volume and length of complaints against the landlord. This was the first time in their lives that they felt someone was taking them seriously, so all of the would-be-if-they-could-be lawyers, politicians, and Broadway actors were taking advantage of this rare opportunity to display their talents. It didn't matter if they often repeated what had been said or if their monologues held no relevance to the issues; each one fought for the space to outshine the other.

"Ben ain't got no reason to be here. He works for the landlord."

A few scattered yeahs came from around the room.

"I lives in this here block just like y'all," Ben said slowly. "And when you ain't got no heat, I ain't either. It's not my fault 'cause the man won't deliver no oil."

"But you stay so zooted all the time, you never cold no way."

"Ya know, a lot of things ain't the landlord's fault. The landlord don't throw garbage in the air shaft or break the glass in them doors."

"Yeah, and what about all them kids that be runnin' up and down the halls."

"Don't be talking 'bout my kids!" Cora Lee jumped up. "Lot of y'all got kids, too, and they no saints."

"Why you so touchy—who mentioned you?"

"But if the shoe fits, steal it from Thom McAn's."

"Wait, please." Kiswana held up her hands. "This is getting us nowhere. What we should be discussing today is staging a rent strike and taking the landlord to court."

"What we should be discussin'," Sophie leaned over and said to Mattie and Etta, "is that bad element that done moved in this block amongst decent people."

"Well, I done called the police at least a dozen times about C. C. Baker and them boys hanging in that alley, smoking them reefers, and robbing folks," Mattie said.

"I ain't talkin' 'bout them kids—I'm talkin' 'bout those two livin' 'cross from me in 312."

"What about 'em?"

"Oh, you know, Mattie," Etta said, staring straight at Sophie. "Those two girls who mind their business and never have a harsh word to say 'bout nobody—them the two you mean, right, Sophie?"

"What they doin'—livin' there like that—is wrong, and you know it." She turned to appeal to Mattie. "Now, you a Christian woman. The Good Book say that them things is an abomination against the Lord. We shouldn't be havin' that here on Brewster and the association should do something about it."

"My Bible also says in First Peter not to be a busybody in other people's matters, Sophie. And the way I see it, if they ain't botherin' with what goes on in my place, why should I bother 'bout what goes on in theirs?"

"They sinning against the Lord!" Sophie's eyes were bright and wet.

"Then let the Lord take care of it," Etta snapped. "Who appointed you?"

"That don't surprise me comin' from *you*. No, not one bit!" Sophie glared at Etta and got up to move around the room to more receptive ears.

Etta started to go after her, but Mattie held her arm. "Let that woman be. We're not here to cause no row over some of her stupidness."

"The old prune pit," Etta spit out. "She oughta be glad them two girls are that way. That's one less bed she gotta worry 'bout pullin' Jess out of this year. I didn't see her thumpin' no Bible when she beat up that woman from Mobile she caught him with last spring."

"Etta, I'd never mention it in front of Sophie 'cause I hate the way she loves to drag other people's business in the street, but I can't help feelin' that what they're doing ain't quite right. How do you get that way? Is it from birth?"

"I couldn't tell you, Mattie. But I seen a lot of it in my time and the places I've been. They say they just love each other—who knows?"

Mattie was thinking deeply. "Well, I've loved women, too. There was Miss Eva and Ciel, and even as ornery as you can get, I've loved you practically all my life."

"Yeah, but it's different with them."

"Different how?"

"Well . . ." Etta was beginning to feel uncomfortable. "They love each other like you'd love a man or a man would love you—I guess."

"But I've loved some women deeper than I ever loved any man," Mattie was pondering. "And there been some women who loved me more and did more for me than any man ever did."

"Yeah." Etta thought for a moment. "I can second that, but it's still different, Mattie. I can't exactly put my finger on it, but . . ."

"Maybe it's not so different," Mattie said, almost to herself. "Maybe that's why some women get so riled up about it, 'cause they know deep down it's not so different after all." She looked at Etta. "It kinda gives you a funny feeling when you think about it that way, though."

"Yeah, it does," Etta said, unable to meet Mattie's eyes.

Lorraine was climbing the dark narrow stairway up to Kiswana's apartment. She had tried to get Theresa to come, but she had wanted no part of it. "A tenants' meeting for what? The damn street needs to be condemned." She knew Tee blamed her for having to live in a place like Brewster, but she could at least try to make the best of things and get involved with the community. That was the problem with so many black people—they just sat back and complained while the whole world tumbled down around their heads. And grabbing an attitude and thinking you were better than these people just because a lot of them were poor and uneducated wouldn't help, either. It just made you seem standoffish, and Lorraine wanted to be liked by the people around her. She couldn't live the way Tee did, with her head stuck in a book all the time. Tee didn't seem to need anyone. Lorraine often wondered if she even needed her.

But if you kept to yourself all the time, people started to wonder, and then they talked. She couldn't afford to have people talking about her, Tee should understand that—she knew from the way they had met. Understand. It was funny because that was the first thing she had felt about her when she handed Tee her application. She had said to herself, I feel that I can talk to this woman, I can tell her why I lost my job in Detroit, and she will understand. And she had understood, but then slowly all that had stopped. Now Lorraine was made to feel awkward and stupid about her fears and thoughts. Maybe Tee was right and she was too sensitive, but there was a big difference between being personnel director for the Board of Education and a first-grade teacher. Tee didn't threaten their files and payroll accounts but, somehow, she, Lorraine, threatened their children. Her heart tightened when she thought about that. The worst thing she had ever wanted to do to a child was to slap the spit out of the little Baxter boy for pouring glue in her hair, and even that had only been for a fleeting moment. Didn't Tee understand that if she lost this job, she wouldn't be so lucky the next time? No, she didn't understand that or anything else about her. She never wanted to bother with anyone except those weirdos at that club she went to, and Lorraine hated them. They were coarse and bitter, and made fun of people who weren't like them. Well, she wasn't like them either. W hy should she feel different from the people she lived around? Black people were all in the same boat—she'd come to realize this even more since they had moved to Brewster—and if they didn't row together, they would sink together.

Lorraine finally reached the top floor; the door to Kiswana's apartment was open but she knocked before she went in. Kiswana was trying to break up an argument between a short light-skinned man and some woman who had picked up a potted plant and was threatening to hit him in the mouth. Most of the other tenants were so busy rooting for one or the other that hardly anyone noticed Lorraine when she entered. She went over and stood by Ben.

"I see there's been a slight difference of opinion here," she smiled.

"Just nigger mess, miss. Roscoe there claim that Betina ain't got no right being secretary 'cause she owe three months' rent, and she say he owe more than that and it's none of his never mind. Don't know how we got into all this. Ain't what we was talkin' 'bout, no way. Was talkin' 'bout havin' a block party to raise money for a housing lawyer."

Kiswana had rescued her Boston Fern from the woman and the two people were being pulled to opposite sides of the room. Betina pushed her way out of the door, leaving behind very loud advice about where they could put their secretary's job along with the block association, if they could find the space in that small an opening in their bodies.

Kiswana sat back down, flushed and out of breath. "Now we need someone else to take the minutes."

"Do they come with the rest of the watch?" Laughter and another series of monologues about Betina's bad-natured exit followed for the next five minutes.

Lorraine saw that Kiswana looked as if she wanted to cry. The one-step-forward-two-steps-backwards progression of the meeting was beginning to show on her face. Lorraine swallowed her shyness and raised her hand. "I'll take the minutes for you."

"Oh, thank you." Kiswana hurriedly gathered the scattered and crumpled papers and handed them to her. "Now we can get back down to business."

The room was now aware of Lorraine's presence, and there were soft murmurs from the corners, accompanied by furtive glances while a few like Sophie stared at her openly. She attempted to smile into the eyes of the people watching her, but they would look away the moment she glanced in their direction. After a couple of vain attempts her smile died, and she buried it uneasily in the papers in her hand. Lorraine tried to cover her trembling fingers by pretending to decipher Betina's smudged and misspelled notes.

"All right," Kiswana said, "now who had promised to get a stereo hooked up for the party?"

"Ain't we supposed to vote on who we wants for secretary?" Sophie's voice rose heavily in the room, and its weight smothered the other noise. All of the faces turned silently toward hers with either mild surprise or coveted satisfaction over what they knew was coming. "I mean, can anybody just waltz in here and get shoved down our throats and we don't have a say about it?"

"Look, I can just go," Lorraine said. "I just wanted to help, I—"

"No, wait." Kiswana was confused. "What vote? Nobody else wanted to do it. Did you want to take the notes?"

"She can't do it," Etta cut in, "unless we was sitting here reciting the ABC's, and we better not do that too fast. So let's just get on with the meeting."

Scattered approval came from sections of the room.

"Listen here!" Sophie jumped up to regain lost ground. "Why should a decent woman get insulted and y'll take sides with the likes of them?" Her finger shot out like a pistol, which she swung between Etta and Lorraine.

Etta rose from her seat. "Who do you think you're talkin' to, you old hen's ass? I'm as decent as you are, and I'll come over there and lam you in the mouth to prove it!"

Etta tried to step across the coffee table, but Mattie caught her by the back of the dress; Etta turned, tried to shake her off, and tripped over the people in front of her. Sophie picked up a statue and backed up into the wall with it slung over her shoulder like a baseball bat. Kiswana put her head in her hands and groaned. Etta had taken off her high-heeled shoe and was waving the spiked end at Sophie over the shoulders of the people who were holding her back.

"That's right! That's right!" Sophie screamed. "Pick on me! Sure, I'm the one who goes around doin' them filthy, unnatural things right under your noses. Every one of you knows it; everybody done talked about it, not just me!" Her head moved around the room like a trapped animal's. "And any woman—any woman who defends that kind of thing just better be watched. That's all I gotta say—where there's smoke, there's fire, Etta Johnson!"

Etta stopped struggling against the arms that were holding her, and her chest was heaving in rapid spasms as she threw Sophie a look of wilting hate, but she remained silent. And no other woman in the room dared to speak as they moved an extra breath away from each other. Sophie turned toward Lorraine, who had twisted the meeting's notes into a mass of shredded paper. Lorraine kept her back straight, but her hands and mouth were moving with a will of their own. She stood like a fading spirit before the ebony statue that Sophie pointed at her like a crucifix.

"Movin' into our block causin' a disturbance with your nasty ways. You ain't wanted here!"

"What have any of you ever seen me do except leave my house and go to work like the rest of you? Is it disgusting for me to speak to each one of you that I meet in the street, even when you don't answer me back? Is that my crime?" Lorraine's voice sank like a silver dagger into their consciences, and there was an uneasy stirring in the room.

"Don't stand there like you a Miss Innocent," Sophie whispered hoarsely. "I'll tell ya what I seen!"

Her eyes leered around the room as they waited with a courtroom hush for her next words.

"I wasn't gonna mention something so filthy, but you forcin' me." She ran her tongue over her parched lips and narrowed her eyes at Lorraine. "You forgot to close your shades last night, and I saw the two of you!"

The silence in the room tightened into a half-gasp.

"There you was, standin' in the bathroom door, drippin' wet and as naked and shameless as you please . . ."

It had become so quiet it was now painful.

"Calling to the other one to put down her book and get you a clean towel. Standin' in that bathroom door with your naked behind. I saw it—I did!"

Their chests were beginning to burn from a lack of air as they waited for Lorraine's answer, but before the girl could open her mouth, Ben's voice snaked from behind her like a lazy breeze.

"Guess *you* get out the tub with your clothes on, Sophie. Must make it mighty easy on Jess's eyes."

The laughter that burst out of their lungs was such a relief that eyes were watery. The room laid its head back and howled in gratitude to Ben for allowing it to breathe again. Sophie's rantings could not be heard above the wheezing, coughing, and backslapping that now went on.

Lorraine left the apartment and grasped the stairway railing, trying to keep the bile from rising into her throat. Ben followed her outside and gently touched her shoulder.

"Miss, you all right?"

She pressed her lips tightly together and nodded her head. The lightness of his touch brought tears to her eyes, and she squeezed them shut.

"You sure? You look 'bout ready to keel over."

Lorraine shook her head jerkily and sank her nails deeply into her palm as she brought her hand to her mouth. I mustn't speak, she thought. If I open my mouth, I'll scream. Oh, God, I'll scream or I'll throw up, right here, in front of this nice old man. The thought of the churned up bits of her breakfast and lunch pouring out of her mouth and splattering on Ben's trouser legs suddenly struck her as funny, and she fought an overwhelming desire to laugh. She trembled violently as the creeping laughter tried to deceive her into parting her lips.

Ben's face clouded over as he watched the frail body that was so bravely struggling for control. "Come on now, I'll take you home." And he tried to lead her down the steps.

She shook her head in a panic. She couldn't let Tee see her like this. If she says anything smart to me now, I'll kill her, Lorraine thought. I'll pick up a butcher knife and plunge it into her face, and then I'll kill myself and let them find us there. The thought of all those people in Kiswana's apartment standing over their bleeding bodies was strangely comforting, and she began to breathe more easily.

"Come on now," Ben urged quietly, and edged her toward the steps.

"I can't go home." She barely whispered.

"It's all right, you ain't gotta—come on."

And she let him guide her down the stairs and out into the late September evening. He took her to the building that was nearest to the wall on Brewster Place and then down the outside steps to a door with a broken dirty screen. Ben unlocked the door and led her into his damp underground rooms.

He turned on the single light bulb that was hanging from the ceiling by a thick black cord and pulled out a chair for her at the kitchen table, which was propped up against the wall. Lorraine sat down, grateful to be able to take the weight off of her shaky knees. She didn't acknowledge his apologies as he took the half-empty wine bottle and cracked cup from the table. He brushed off the crumbs while two fat brown roaches raced away from the wet cloth.

"I'm makin' tea," he said, without asking her if she wanted any. He placed a blackened pot of water on the hot plate at the edge of the counter, then found two cups in the cabinet that still had their handles intact. Ben put the strong black tea he had brewed in front of her and brought her a spoon and a crumpled pound bag of sugar. Lorraine took three heaping teaspoons of sugar and stirred the tea, holding her face over the steam. Ben waited for her face to register the effects of the hot sweet liquid.

"I liked you from first off," he said shyly, and seeing her smile, he continued. "You remind me lots of my little girl." Ben reached into his hip pocket and took out a frayed billfold and handed her a tiny snapshot.

Lorraine tilted the picture toward the light. The face stamped on the celluloid paper bore absolutely no resemblance to her at all. His daughter's face was oval and dark, and she had a large flat nose and a tiny rounded mouth. She handed the picture back to Ben and tried to cover her confusion.

"I know what you thinkin'," Ben said, looking at the face in his hands. "But she had a limp—my little girl. Was a breech baby, and the midwife broke her foot when she was birthed and it never came back right. Always kinda cripped along—but a sweet child." He frowned deeply into the picture and paused, then looked up at Lorraine. "When I seen you—the way you'd walk up the street all timid-like and tryin' to be nice to these-here folks and the look on your face when some of 'em was just downright rude—you kinda broke up in here." He motioned toward his chest. "And you just sorta limped along inside. That's when I thought of my baby."

Lorraine gripped the teacup with both hands, but the tears still squeezed through the compressed muscles in her eyes. They slowly rolled down her face but she wouldn't release the cup to wipe them away.

"My father," she said, staring into the brown liquid, "kicked me out of the house when I was seventeen years old. He found a letter one of my girlfriends had written me, and when I wouldn't lie about what it meant, he told me to get out and leave behind everything that he had ever bought me. He said he wanted to burn them." She looked up to see the expression on Ben's face, but it kept swimming under the tears in her eyes. "So I walked out of his home with only the clothes on my back. I moved in with one of my cousins, and I worked at night in a bakery to put myself through college. I would send him a birthday card each year, and he always returned them unopened. After a while I stopped putting my return address on the envelopes so he couldn't send them back. I guess he burned those too." She sniffed the mucus up into her nose. "I still send those cards like that—without a return address. That way I can believe that, maybe, one year before he dies, he'll open them."

Ben got up and gave her a piece of toilet paper to blow her nose in.

"Where's your daughter now, Mr. Ben?"

"For me?" Ben sighed deeply. "Just like you—livin' in a world with no address."

They finished their tea in silence and Lorraine got up to go.

"There's no way to thank you, so I won't try."

"I'd be right hurt if you did." Ben patted her arm. "Now come back anytime you got a mind to. I got nothing, but you welcome to all of that. Now how many folks is that generous?"

Lorraine smiled, leaned over, and kissed him on the cheek. Ben's face lit up the walls of the dingy basement. He closed the door behind her, and at first her "Good night, Mr. Ben" tinkled like crystal bells in his mind. Crystal bells that grew larger and louder, until their sound was distorted in his ears and he almost believed that she had said "Good night, Daddy Ben"—no—"Mornin' Daddy Ben, mornin' Daddy Ben, mornin . . ." Ben's saliva began to taste like sweating tin, and he ran a trembling hand over his stubbled face and rushed to the corner where he had shoved the wine bottle. The bells had begun almost to deafen him and he shook his head to relieve the drumming pain inside of his ears. He knew what was coming next, and he didn't dare waste time by pouring the wine into a cup. He lifted the bottle up to his mouth and sucked at it greedily, but it was too late. *Swing Low, sweet chariot.* The song had started—the whistling had begun.

It started low, from the end of his gut, and shrilled its way up into his ears and shattered the bells, sending glass shards flying into a heart that should have been so scarred from old piercings that there was no flesh left to bleed. But the glass splinters found some minute, untouched place—as they always did—and tore the heart and let the whistling in. And now Ben would have to drink faster and longer, because the melody would now ride on his body's blood like a cancer and poison everywhere it touched. *Swing low, sweet chariot.* It mustn't get to his brain. He had a few more seconds before it got to his brain and killed him. He had to be drunk before the poison crept up his neck muscles, past his mouth, on the way to his brain. If he was drunk, then he could let it out—sing it out into the air before it touched his brain, caused him to remember. *Swing low, sweet chariot.* He couldn't die there under the ground like some animal. Oh,

God, please make him drunk. And he promised—he'd never go that long without a drink again. It was just the meeting and then that girl that had kept him from it this long, but he swore it would never happen again—just please, God, make him drunk.

The alcohol began to warm Ben's body, and he felt his head begin to get numb and heavy. He almost sobbed out his thanks for this redeeming answer to his prayers, because the whistling had just reached his throat and he was able to open his mouth and slobber the words out into the room. The saliva was dripping from the corners of his mouth because he had to take huge gulps of wine between breaths, but he sang on—drooling and humming—because to sing was salvation, to sing was to empty the tune from his blood, to sing was to unremember Elvira, and his daughter's "Mornin', Daddy Ben" as she dragged her twisted foot up his front porch with that song hitting her in the back.

Swing low

"Mornin', Ben. Mornin', Elvira."

Sweet chariot

The red pick-up truck stopped in front of Ben's yard.

Comin' for to carry me home

His daughter got out of the passenger side and began to limp toward the house.

Swing low

Elvira grinned into the creviced face of the white man sitting in the truck with tobacco stains in the corner of his mouth. "Mornin', Mr. Clyde. Right nice day, ain't it, sir?"

Sweet chariot

Ben watched his daughter come through the gate with her eyes on the ground, and she slowly climbed up on the porch. She took each step at a time, and her shoes grated against the rough boards. She finally turned her beaten eyes into his face, and what was left of his soul to crush was taken care of by the bell-like voice that greeted them. "Mornin', Daddy Ben. Mornin', Mama."

"Mornin', baby," Ben mumbled with his jaws tight.

Swing low

"How's things up at the house?" Elvira asked. "My little girl do a good job for you yesterday?"

Sweet chariot

"Right fine, Elvira. Got that place clean as a skinned rat. How's y'all's crops comin'?"

"Just fine, Mr. Clyde, sir. Just fine. We sure appreciate that extra land you done rented us. We bringin' in more than enough to break even. Yes, sir, just fine."

The man laughed, showing the huge gaps between his tobacco-rotted teeth. "Glad to do it. Y'all some of my best tenants. I likes keepin' my people happy. If you needs somethin', let me know."

"Sure will, Mr. Clyde, sir.

"Aw right, see y'all next week. Be by the regular time to pick up the gal."

"She be ready, sir."

The man started up the motor on the truck, and the tune that he whistled as he drove off remained in the air long after the dust had returned to the ground. Elvira grinned and waved until the red of the truck had disappeared over the horizon. Then she simultaneously dropped her arm and smile and turned toward her daughter. "Don't just stand there gawkin'. Get in the house—your breakfast been ready."

"Yes, Mama."

When the screen door had slammed shut, Elvira snapped her head around to Ben. "Nigger, what is wrong with you? Ain't you heard Mr. Clyde talkin' to you, and you standin' there like a hunk of stone. You better get some sense in you head 'fore I knock some in you!"

Ben stood with his hands in his pockets, staring at the tracks in the dirt where the truck had been. He kept balling his fists up in his overalls until his nails dug into his palms.

"It ain't right, Elvira. It just ain't right and you know it."

"What ain't right?" The woman stuck her face into his and he backed up a few steps. "That that gal work and earn her keep like the rest of us? She can't go to the fields, but she can clean house, and she'll do it! I see it's better you keep your mouth shut 'cause when it's open, ain't nothin' but stupidness comin' out." She turned her head and brushed him off as she would a fly, then headed toward the door of the house.

"She came to us, Elvira." There was a leaden sadness in Ben's voice. "She came to us a long time ago."

The thin woman spun around with her face twisted into an airless knot. "She came to us with a bunch of lies 'bout Mr. Clyde 'cause she's too damn lazy to work. Why would a decent widow man want to mess with a little black nothin' like her? No, anything to get out of work—just like you."

"Why she gotta spend the night then?" Ben turned his head slowly toward her. "Why he always make her spend the night up there alone with him?"

"Why should he make an extra trip just to bring her tail home when he pass this way every Saturday mornin' on the way to town? If she wasn't lame, she could walk it herself after she finish work. But the man nice enough to drop her home, and you want to bad-mouth him along with that lyin' hussy."

"After she came to us, you remember I borrowed Tommy Boy's wagon and went to get her that Friday night. I told ya what Mr. Clyde told me. 'She ain't finished yet, Ben.' Just like that—'She ain't finished yet.' And then standin' there whistlin' while I went out the back gate." Ben's nails dug deeper into his palms.

"So!" Elvira's voice was shrill. "So it's a big house. It ain't like this shit you got us livin' in. It take her longer to do things than most folks. You know that, so why stand there carryin' on like it mean more than that?"

"She ain't finished yet, Ben." Ben shook his head slowly. "If I was half a man I woulda—"

Elvira came across the porch and sneered into his face. "If you was half a man, you coulda given me more babies and we woulda had some help workin' this land instead of a half-grown woman we gotta carry the load for. And if you was even quarter a man, we wouldn't be a bunch of miserable sharecroppers on someone else's land—but we is, Ben. And I'll be damned if I see the little bit we got taken away 'cause you believe that gal's lowdown lies! So when Mr. Clyde come by here, you speak—hear me? And you act as grateful as your pitiful ass should be for the favors he done us."

Ben felt a slight dampness in his hands because his fingernails had broken through the skin of his palms and the blood was seeping around his cuticles. He looked at Elvira's dark braided head and wondered why he didn't take his hands out of his pockets and stop the bleeding by pressing them around it. Just lock his elbows on her shoulders and place one hand on each side of her temples and then in toward each other until the blood stopped. His big callused hands on the bones of her skull pressing in and in, like you would with a piece of dark cloth to cover the wounds on your body and clot the blood. Or he could simply go into the house and take his shotgun and press his palms around the trigger and handle, emptying the bullets into her sagging breasts just long enough— just pressing hard enough—to stop his palms from bleeding.

But the gram of truth in her words was heavy enough to weigh his hands down in his pockets and keep his feet nailed to the wooden planks in the porch, and the wounds healed over by themselves. Ben discovered that if he sat up drinking all night Friday, he could stand on the porch Saturday morning and smile at the man who whistled as he dropped his lame daughter home. And he could look into her beaten eyes and believe that she had lied.

The girl disappeared one day, leaving behind a note saying that she loved them very much, but she knew that she had been a burden and she understood why they had made her keep working at Mr. Clyde's house. But she felt that if she had to earn her keep that way, she might as well go to Memphis where the money was better.

Elvira ran and bragged to the neighbors that their daughter was now working in a rich house in Memphis. And she was making out awful well because she always sent plenty of money home. Ben would stare at the envelopes with no return address, and he found that if he drank enough every time a letter came, he could silence the bell-like voice that came chiming out of the open envelope—"Mornin' Daddy Ben, mornin' Daddy Ben, mornin' . . ." And then if he drank enough every day he could bear the touch of Elvira's body in the bed beside him at night and not have his sleep stolen by the image of her lying there with her head caved in or her chest ripped apart by shotgun shells.

But even after they lost the sharecropping contract and Elvira left him for a man who farmed near the levee and Ben went north and took a job on Brewster, he still drank—long after he could remember why. He just knew that whenever he saw a mailman, the crystal bells would start, and then that strange whistling that could shatter them, sending them on that deadly journey toward his heart.

He never dreamed it would happen on a Sunday. The mailman didn't run on Sundays, so he had felt safe. He hadn't counted on that girl sounding so much like the bells when she left his place tonight. But it was okay, he had gotten drunk in time, and he would never take such a big chance again. No, Lord, you pulled me through this time, and I ain't pressin' your mercy no more. Ben stumbled around his shadowy damp rooms, singing now at the top of his voice. The low, trembling melody of "Swing Low, Sweet Chariot" passed through his greasy windows and up into the late summer air.

Lorraine had walked home slowly, thinking about the old man and the daughter who limped. When she came to her stoop, she brushed past her neighbors with her head up and didn't bother to speak.

Theresa got off the uptown bus and turned the corner into Brewster Place. She was always irritable on Friday evenings because they had to do payroll inventories at the office. Her neck ached from bending over endless lists of computer printouts. What did that damn Board of Education think—someone in accounting was going to sneak one of their relatives on the payroll? The biggies had been doing that for years, but they lay awake at night, thinking of ways to keep the little guys from cashing in on it too. There was something else that had been turning uncomfortably in her mind for the last few weeks, and just today it had lain still long enough for her to pinpoint it—Lorraine was changing. It wasn't exactly anything that she had said or done, but Theresa sensed a firmness in her spirit that hadn't been there before. She was speaking up more—yes, that was it—whether the subject was the evening news or bus schedules or the proper way to hem a dress. Lorraine wasn't deferring to her anymore. And she wasn't apologizing for seeing things differently from Theresa.

Why did that bother her? Didn't she want Lorraine to start standing up for herself? To stop all that sniveling and handwringing every time Theresa raised her voice? Weren't things the way she had wanted them to be for the last five years? What nagged at Theresa more than the change was the fact that she was worrying about it. She had actually thought about picking a fight just to see how far she could push her—push her into what? Oh, God, I must be sick, she thought. No, it was that old man—that's what it was. Why was Lorraine spending so much time with that drunk? They didn't have a damn thing in common. What could he be telling her, doing for her, that was causing this? She had tried—she truly had—to get Lorraine to show some backbone. And now some ignorant country winehead was doing in a few weeks what she couldn't do for the last five years.

Theresa was mulling this over when a little girl sped past her on skates, hit a crack in the sidewalk, and fell. She went to walk around the child, who looked up with tears in her eyes and stated simply, "Miss, I hurt myself." She said it with such a tone of wonder and disappointment that Theresa smiled. Kids lived in such an insulated world, where the smallest disturbance was met with cries of protest. Oh, sweetheart, she thought, just live on and you'll wish many a day that the biggest problem in your life would be a scraped knee. But she was still just a little girl, and right now she wanted an audience for her struggle with this uninvited disaster.

Theresa bent down beside her and clucked her teeth loudly. "Oh, you did? Let's see." She helped her off the ground and made an exaggerated fuss over the scraped knee.

"It's bleeding!" The child's voice rose in horror.

Theresa looked at the tiny specks of blood that were beading up on the grimy knee. "Why, it sure is." She tried to match the note of seriousness in the child's tone. "But I think we have a little time before you have to worry about a transfusion." She opened her pocketbook and took out a clean tissue. "Let's see if we can fix it up. Now, I want you to spit on this for me and I'll wipe your knee."

The girl spit on the tissue. "Is it gonna hurt?"

"No, it won't hurt. You know what my grandma used to call spit? God's iodine. Said it was the best thing for patching anything up—except maybe a broken leg."

She steadied the girl's leg and gently dabbed at the dirty knee. "See, it's all coming off. I guess you're gonna live." She smiled.

The child looked at her knee with a solemn face. "I think it needs a Band-Aid."

Theresa laughed. "Well, you're out of luck with me. But you go on home and see if your mama has one for you—if you can remember which knee it was by then."

"What are you doing to her?" The voice pierced the air between the child and Theresa. She looked up and saw a woman rushing toward them. The woman grabbed the child to her side. "What's going on here?" Her voice was just half an octave too high.

Theresa stood up and held out the dirty and bloody tissue. "She scraped her knee." The words fell like dead weights. "What in the hell did you think I was doing?" She refused to let the woman avoid her eyes, enjoying every minute of her cringing embarrassment.

"Mama, I need a Band-Aid, you got a Band-Aid?" The child tugged on her arm.

"Yes, yes, honey, right away." The woman was glad to have an excuse to look down. "Thank you very much," she said, as she hurried the child away. "She's always so clumsy. I've told her a million times to be careful on those skates, but you know . . ."

"Yeah, right," Theresa said, watching them go. "I know." She balled the tissue in her hand and quickly walked into the building. She slammed the apartment door open and heard Lorraine running water in the bathroom.

"Is that you, Tee?"

"Yeah," she called out, and then thought, No, it's not me. It's not me at all. Theresa paced between the kitchen and living room and then realized that she still had the tissue. She threw it into the kitchen garbage and turned on the faucet to its fullest pressure and started washing her hands. She kept lathering and rinsing them, but they still felt unclean. Son-of-a-bitch, she thought, son-of-a-fucking-bitch! She roughly dried her hands with some paper towels and fought the impulse to wash them again by starting dinner early. She kept her hands moving quickly, chopping more onions, celery, and green peppers than she really needed. She vigorously seasoned the ground beef, jabbing the wooden spoon repeatedly into the red meat.

When she stopped to catch her breath and glanced toward the kitchen window, a pair of squinty black eyes were peering at her from the corner of a shade across the air shaft. "What the hell . . . ?" She threw down her spoon and ran over to the window.

"You wanna see what I'm doing?" The shade was pulled up with such force it went spinning on its rollers at the top of the window. The eyes disappeared from the corner of the shade across the air shaft.

"Here!" Theresa slammed the window up into its casing. "I'll even raise this so you can hear better. I'm making meat loaf, you old bat! Meat loaf!" She stuck her head out of the window. "The same way other people make it! Here, I'll show you!"

She ran back to the table and took up a handful of chopped onions and threw them at Sophie's window. "See, that's the onions. And here, here's the chopped peppers!" The diced vegetables hit against the windowpane. "Oh, yeah, I use eggs!" Two eggs flew out of the window and splattered against Sophie's panes.

Lorraine came out of the bathroom, toweling her hair. "What's all the shouting for? Who are you talking to?" She saw Theresa running back and forth across the kitchen, throwing their dinner out of the window. "Have you lost your mind?"

Theresa picked up a jar of olives. "Now, here's something *freaky* for you—olives! I put olives in my meat loaf! So run up and down the street and tell that!" The jar of olives crashed against the opposite building, barely missing Sophie's window.

"Tee, stop it!"

Theresa put her head back out the window. "Now olives are definitely weird, but you gotta take that one up with my grandmother because it's her recipe! Wait! I forgot the meat—can't have you think I would try to make meat loaf without meat." She ran back to the table and grabbed up the bowl.

"Theresa!!" Lorraine rushed into the kitchen.

"No, can't have you thinking that!" Theresa yelled as she swung back her arm to throw the bowl through Sophie's window. "You might feel I'm a *pervert* or something—someone you can't trust your damn children around!"

Lorraine caught her arm just as she went to hurl the bowl out of the window. She grabbed the bowl and shoved Theresa against the wall.

"Look," Lorraine said, pressing against the struggling woman, "I know you're pissed off, but ground sirloin is almost three dollars a pound!"

The look of sincere horror on Lorraine's face as she cradled the bowl of meat in her arm made Theresa giggle, and then slowly she started laughing and Lorraine nodded her head and laughed with her. Theresa laid her head back against the wall, and her plump throat vibrated from the full sounds passing through it. Lorraine let her go and put the bowl on the table. Theresa's sides were starting to ache from laughing, and she sat down in one of the kitchen chairs. Lorraine pushed the bowl a little further down the table from her, and this set them off again. Theresa laughed and rocked in the chair until tears were rolling down her cheeks. Then she crossed that fine line between laughter and tears and started to sob. Lorraine went over to her, cradled her head in her chest, and stroked her shoulders. She had no idea what had brought on all of this, but it didn't matter. It felt good to be the one who could now comfort.

The shade across the air shaft moved a fraction of an inch, and Sophie pressed one eye against her smeared and dripping windowpane. She looked at the two women holding each other and shook her head. "Um, um, um."

The next day Lorraine was on her way back from the supermarket, and she ran into Kiswana, who was coming out of their building, carrying an armful of books.

"Hi," she greeted Lorraine, "you sure have a full load there."

"Well, we ran out of vegetables last night." Lorraine smiled. "So I picked up a little extra today."

"You know, we haven't seen you at the meetings lately. Things are really picking up. There's going to be a block party next weekend, and we can use all the help we can get."

Lorraine stopped smiling. "Did you really think I'd come back after what happened?"

The blood rushed to Kiswana's face and she stared uncomfortably at the top of her books. "You know, I'm really sorry about that. I should have said something—after all, it was my house—but things just sort of got out of hand so quickly, I'm sorry, I . . ."

"Hey, look, I'm not blaming you or even that woman who made such a fuss. She's just a very sick lady, that's all. Her life must be very unhappy if she has to run around and try to hurt people who haven't done anything to her. But I just didn't want any more trouble, so I felt I ought to stay away."

"But the association is for all of us," Kiswana insisted, "and everyone doesn't feel the way she did. What you do is your own business, not that you're doing anything, anyway. I mean, well, two women or two guys can't live together without people talking. She could be your cousin or sister or something."

"We're not related," Lorraine said quietly.

"Well, good friends then," Kiswana stammered. "Why can't good friends just live together and people mind their own business. And even if you're not friends, even . . . well, whatever." She went on miserably, "It was my house and I'm sorry, I . . ."

Lorraine was kind enough to change the subject for her. "I see you have an armful yourself. You're heading toward the library?"

"No." Kiswana gave her a grateful smile. "I'm taking a few classes on the weekends. My old lady is always on my back about going back to school, so I enrolled at the community college." She was almost apologetic. "But I'm only studying black history and the science of revolution, and I let her know that. But it's enough to keep her quiet."

"I think that's great. You know, I took quite a few courses in black history when I went to school in Detroit."

"Yeah, which ones?"

While they were talking, C. C. Baker and his friends loped up the block. These young men always moved in a pack, or never without two or three. They needed the others continually near to verify their existence. When they stood with their black skin, ninth-grade diplomas, and fifty-word vocabularies in front of the mirror that the world had erected and saw nothing, those other pairs of tight jeans, suede sneakers, and tinted sunglasses imaged nearby proved that they were alive. And if there was life, there could be dreams of that miracle that would one day propel them into the heaven populated by their gods— Shaft and Superfly. While they grew old awaiting that transformation they moved through the streets, insuring that they could at least be heard, if not seen, by blasting their portable cassette players and talking loudly. They continually surnamed each other Man and clutched at their crotches, readying the equipment they deemed necessary to be summoned at any moment into Superfly heaven.

The boys recognized Kiswana because her boyfriend, Abshu, was director of the community center, and Lorraine had been pointed out to them by parents or some other adult who had helped to spread the yellow mist. They spotted the two women talking to each other, and on a cue from C. C., they all slowed as they passed the stoop. C. C. Baker was greatly disturbed by the thought of a Lorraine. He knew of only one way to deal with women other than his mother. Before he had learned exactly how women gave birth, he knew how to please or punish or extract favors from them by the execution of what lay curled behind his fly. It was his lifeline to that part of his being that sheltered his self-respect. And the thought of any woman who lay beyond the length of its power was a threat.

"Hey, Swana, better watch it talkin' to that dyke—she might try to grab a tit" C. C. called out.

"Yeah, Butch, why don't ya join the WACs and really have a field day."

Lorraine's arms tightened around her packages, and she tried to push past Kiswana and go into the building. "I'll see you later."

"No, wait." Kiswana blocked her path. "Don't let them talk to you like that. They're nothing but a bunch of punks." She called out to the leader, "C. C., why don't you just take your little dusty behind and get out of here. No one was talking to you.

The muscular tan boy spit out his cigarette and squared his shoulders. "I ain't got to do nothin'! And I'm gonna tell Abshu you need a good spankin' for taking up with a lesbo." He looked around at his reflections and preened himself in their approval. "Why don't ya come over here and I'll show ya what a real man can do." He cupped his crotch.

Kiswana's face reddened with anger. "From what I heard about you, C. C., I wouldn't even feel it."

His friends broke up with laughter, and when he turned around to them, all he could see mirrored was respect for the girl who had beat him at the dozens. Lorraine smiled at the absolutely lost look on his face. He curled his lips back into a snarl and tried to regain lost ground by attacking what instinct told him was the weaker of the two.

"Ya laughing at me, huh, freak? I oughta come over there and stick my fist in your cunt-eatin' mouth!"

"You'll have to come through me first, so just try it." Kiswana put her books on the stoop.

"Aw, Man, come on. Don't waste your time." His friends pulled at his arm. "She ain't nothing but a woman."

"I oughta go over there and slap that bitch in her face and teach her a lesson."

"Hey, Man, lay light, lay light," one whispered in his ear. "That's Abshu's woman, and that big dude don't mind kickin' ass."

C. C. did an excellent job of allowing himself to be reluctantly pulled away from Kiswana, but she wasn't fooled and had already turned to pick up her books. He made several jerky motions with his fist and forefinger at Lorraine.

"I'm gonna remember this, Butch!"

Theresa had watched the entire scene out of the window and had been ready to run out and help Kiswana if the boy had come up on the stoop. That was just like Lorraine to stand there and let someone else take up for her. Well, maybe she'd finally learned her lesson about these ignorant nothings on Brewster Place. They weren't ever going to be accepted by these people, and there was no point in trying.

Theresa left the window and sat on the couch, pretending to be solving a crossword puzzle when Lorraine came in.

"You look a little pale. Were the prices that bad at the store today?"

"No, this heat just drains me. It's hard to believe that we're in the beginning of October." She headed straight for the kitchen.

"Yeah," Theresa said, watching her back intently. "Indian Summer and all that."

"Mmm." Lorraine dumped the bags on the table. "I'm too tired to put these away now. There's nothing perishable in there. I think I'll take some aspirin and lay down."

"Do that," Theresa said, and followed her into the bedroom. "Then you'll be rested for later. Saddle called—he and Byron are throwing a birthday party at the club, and they want us to come over."

Lorraine was looking through the top dresser drawer for her aspirin. "I'm not going over there tonight. I hate those parties."

"You never hated them before." Theresa crossed her arms in the door and stared at Lorraine. "What's so different now?"

"I've always hated them." Lorraine closed the drawer and started searching in the other one. "I just went because you wanted to. They make me sick with all their prancing and phoniness. They're nothing but a couple of fags."

"And we're just a couple of dykes." She spit the words into the air.

Lorraine started as if she'd been slapped. "That's a filthy thing to say, Tee. You can call yourself that if you want to, but I'm not like that. Do you hear me? I'm not!" She slammed the drawer shut.

So she can turn on me but she wouldn't say a word to that scum in the streets, Theresa thought. She narrowed her eyes slowly at Lorraine. "Well, since my friends aren't good enough for the Duchess from Detroit," she said aloud, "I guess you'll go spend another evening with your boyfriend. But I can tell you right now I saw him pass the window just before you came up the block, and he's already stewed to the gills and just singing away. What do you two do down there in that basement—harmonize? It must get kinda boring for you, he only knows one song."

"Well, at least he's not a sarcastic bitch like some people." Theresa looked at Lorraine as if she were a stranger. "And I'll tell you what we do down there. We talk, Theresa—we really, really talk."

"So you and I don't talk?" Theresa's astonishment was turning into hurt. "After five years, you're going to stand there and say that you can talk to some dried-up wino better than you can to me?"

"You and I don't talk, Tee. You talk—Lorraine listens. You lecture—Lorraine takes notes about how to dress and act and have fun. If I don't see things your way, then you shout—Lorraine cries. You seem to get a kick out of making me feel like a clumsy fool."

"That's unfair, Lorraine, and you know it. I can't count the times I've told you to stop running behind people, sniveling to be their friends while they just hurt you. I've always wanted you to show some guts and be independent."

"That's just it, Tee! You wanted me to be independent of other people and look to you for the way I should feel about myself, cut myself off from the world, and join you in some crazy idea about being different. When I'm with Ben, I don't feel any different from anybody else in the world."

"Then he's doing you an injustice," Theresa snapped, "because we are different. And the sooner you learn that, the better off you'll be."

"See, there you go again. Tee the teacher and Lorraine the student, who just can't get the lesson right. Lorraine, who just wants to be a human being—a lousy human being who's somebody's daughter or somebody's friend or even somebody's enemy. But they make me feel like a freak out there, and you try to make me feel like one in here. That only place I've found some peace, Tee, is in that damp ugly basement, where I'm not different."

"Lorraine." Theresa shook her head slowly. "You're a lesbian—do you understand that word?—a butch, a dyke, a lesbo, all those things that kid was shouting. Yes, I heard him! And you can run in all the basements in the world, and it won't change that, so why don't you accept it?"

"I have accepted it!" Lorraine shouted. "I've accepted it all my life, and it's nothing I'm ashamed of. I lost a father because I refused to be ashamed of it—but it doesn't make me any *different* from anyone else in the world."

"It makes you damned different!"

"No!" She jerked open the bottom drawer of her dresser and took out a handful of her underwear. "Do you see this? There are two things that have been a constant in my life since I was sixteen years old—beige bras and oatmeal. The day before I first fell in love with a woman, I got up, had oatmeal for breakfast, put on a beige bra, and went to school. The day alter I fell in love with that woman, I got up, had oatmeal for breakfast, and put on a beige bra. I was no different the day before or after that happened, Tee."

"And what did you do when you went to school that next day, Lorraine? Did you stand around the gym locker and swap stories with the other girls about this new love in your life, huh? While they were bragging about their boyfriends and the fifty dozen ways they had lost their virginity, did you jump in and say, 'Oh, but you should have seen the one I gave it to last night?' Huh? Did you? Did you?"

Theresa was standing in front of her and shouting. She saw Lorraine's face crumple, but she still kept pushing her.

"You with your beige bras and oatmeal!" She grabbed the clothes from Lorraine's hand and shook them at her. "Why didn't you stand in that locker room and pass around a picture of this great love in your life? Why didn't you take her to the senior prom? Huh? Why? Answer me!"

"Because they wouldn't have understood," Lorraine whispered, and her shoulders hunched over.

"That's right! There go your precious 'theys' again. They wouldn't understand—not in Detroit, not on Brewster Place, not anywhere! And as long as they own the whole damn world, it's them and us, Sister—them and us. And that spells different!"

Lorraine sat down on the bed with her head in her hands, and heavy spasms shook her shoulders and slender back. Theresa stood over her and clenched her hands to keep herself from reaching out and comforting her. Let her cry. She had to smarten up. She couldn't spend the rest of her life in basements, talking to winos and building cardboard worlds that were just going to come crashing down around her ears.

Theresa left the bedroom and sat in the chair by the living room window. She watched the autumn sky darken and evening crystallize over the tops of the buildings while she sat there with the smugness of those who could amply justify their methods by the proof of their victorious ends. But even after seven cigarettes, she couldn't expel the sour taste in her mouth. She heard Lorraine move around in the bedroom and then go into the shower. She finally joined her in the living room, freshly clothed. She had been almost successful in covering the puffiness around her eyes with makeup.

"I'm ready to go to the party. Shouldn't you start getting dressed?"

Theresa looked at the black pumps and the green dress with black print. Something about the way it hung off of Lorraine's body made her feel guilty.

"I've changed my mind. I don't feel up to it tonight." She turned her head back toward the evening sky, as if the answer to their tangled lives lay in its dark face.

"Then I'm going without you." The tone of Lorraine's voice pulled her face unwillingly from the window.

"You won't last ten minutes there alone, so why don't you just sit down and stop it."

"I have to go, Tee." The urgency in her words startled Theresa, and she made a poor attempt of hiding it.

"If I can't walk out of this house without you tonight, there'll be nothing left in me to love you. And I'm trying, Theresa; I'm trying so hard to hold on to that."

Theresa would live to be a very old woman and would replay those words in her mind a thousand times and then invent a thousand different things she could have said or done to keep the tall yellow woman in the green and black dress from walking out of that door for the last time in her life. But tonight she was a young woman and still in search of answers, and she made the fatal mistake that many young women do of believing that what never existed was just cleverly hidden beyond her reach. So Theresa said nothing to Lorraine that night, because she had already sadly turned her face back to the evening sky in a mute appeal for guidance.

Lorraine left the smoky and noisy club and decided to walk home to stretch the time. She had been ready to leave from the moment she had arrived, especially after she saw the disappointment on everyone's face when she came in without Theresa. Theresa was the one who loved to dance and joke and banter with them and could keep a party going. Lorraine sat in a corner, holding one drink all night and looking so intimidated by the people who approached her that she killed even the most persistent attempts at conversation. She sensed a mood of quiet hysteria and self-mockery in that club, and she fled from it, refusing to see any possible connection with her own existence.

She had stuck it out for an hour, but that wasn't long enough. Tee would still be up, probably waiting at that window, so certain that she would be returning soon. She thought about taking a bus downtown to a movie, but she really didn't want to be alone. If she only had some friends in this city. It was then that she thought about Ben. She could come up the street in back of Brewster Place and cut through the alley to his apartment. Even if Tee was still in that window, she couldn't see that far down the block. She would just tap lightly on his door, and if he wasn't too drunk to hear her, then he wouldn't be too far gone to listen tonight. And she had such a need to talk to someone, it ached within her.

Lorraine smelled the claw-edged sweetness of the marijuana in the shadowy alley before she had gone more than fifty feet in. She stopped and peered through the leaden darkness toward the end and saw no one. She took a few more cautious steps and stopped to look again. There was still no one. She knew she would never reach Brewster like this; each time she stopped her senseless fears would multiply, until it would he impossible to get through them to the other side. There was no one there, and she would just have to walk through quickly to prove this to her pounding heart.

When she heard the first pair of soft thuds behind her, she willed herself not to stop and look back because there was no one there. Another thud and she started walking a little faster to reassure herself of this. The fourth thud started her to running, and then a dark body that had been pressed against the shadowy building swung into her path so suddenly she couldn't stop in time, and she bumped into it and bounced back a few inches.

"Can't you say excuse me, dyke?" C. C. Baker snarled into her face.

Lorraine saw a pair of suede sneakers flying down behind the face in front of hers and they hit the cement with a dead thump. Her bladder began to loosen, and bile worked its way up into her tightening throat as she realized what she must have heard before. They had been hiding up on the wall, watching her come up that back street, and they had waited. The face pushed itself so close to hers that she could look into the flared nostrils and smell the decomposing food caught in its teeth.

"Ain't you got no manners? Stepping on my foot and not saying you sorry?"

She slowly backed away from the advancing face, her throat working convulsively. She turned to run in the direction of the formless thuds behind her. She hadn't really seen them so they weren't there. The four bodies that now linked themselves across the alley hit her conscious mind like a fist, and she cried out, startled. A hand shot itself around her mouth, and her neck was jerked back while a hoarse voice whispered in her ear.

"You ain't got nothing to say now, huh? Thought you was real funny laughing at me in the streets today? Let's see if you gonna laugh now, dyke!" C. C. forced her down on her knees while the other five boys began to close in silently.

She had stepped into the thin strip of earth that they claimed as their own. Bound by the last building on Brewster and a brick wall, they reigned in that unlit alley like dwarfed warrior-kings. Born with the appendages of power, circumcised by a guillotine, and baptized with the steam from a million nonreflective mirrors, these young men wouldn't be called upon to thrust a bayonet into an Asian farmer, target a torpedo, scatter their iron seed from a B-52 into the wound of the earth, point a finger to move a nation, or stick a pole into the moon—and they knew it. They only had that three-hundred-foot alley to serve them as stateroom, armored tank, and executioner's chamber. So Lorraine found herself, on her knees, surrounded by the most dangerous species in existence—human males with an erection to validate in a world that was only six feet wide.

"I'm gonna show you somethin' I bet you never seen before." C. C. took the back of her head, pressed it into the crotch of his jeans, and jerkily rubbed it back and forth while his friends laughed. "Yeah, now don't that feel good? See, that's what you need. Bet after we get through with you, you ain't never gonna wanna kiss no more pussy."

He slammed his kneecap into her spine and her body arched up, causing his nails to cut into the side of her mouth to stifle her cry. He pushed her arched body down onto the cement. Two of the boys pinned her arms, two wrenched open her legs, while C. C. knelt between them and pushed up her dress and tore at the top of her pantyhose. Lorraine's body was twisting in convulsions of fear that they mistook for resistance, and C. C. brought his fist down into her stomach.

"Better lay the fuck still, cunt, or I'll rip open your guts."

The impact of his fist forced air into her constricted throat, and she worked her sore mouth, trying to form the one word that had been clawing inside of her—"Please." It squeezed through her paralyzed vocal cords and fell lifelessly at their feet. Lorraine clamped her eyes shut and, using all of the strength left within her, willed it to rise again.

"Please."

The sixth boy took a dirty paper bag lying on the ground and stuffed it into her mouth. She felt a weight drop on her spread body. Then she opened her eyes and they screamed and screamed into the face above hers—the face that was pushing this tearing pain inside of her body. The screams tried to break through her corneas out into the air, but the tough rubbery flesh sent them vibrating back into her brain, first shaking lifeless the cells that nurtured her memory. Then the cells went that contained her powers of taste and smell. The last that were screamed to death were those that supplied her with the ability to love—or hate.

Lorraine was no longer conscious of the pain in her spine or stomach. She couldn't feel the skin that was rubbing off of her arms from being pressed against the rough cement. What was left of her mind was centered around the pounding motion that was ripping her insides apart. She couldn't tell when they changed places and the second weight, then the third and fourth, dropped on her—it was all one continuous hacksawing of torment that kept her eyes screaming the only word she was fated to utter again and again for the rest of her life. Please.

Her thighs and stomach had become so slimy from her blood and their semen that the last two boys didn't want to touch her, so they turned her over, propped her head and shoulders against the wall, and took her from behind. When they had finished and stopped holding her up, her body fell over like an unstringed puppet. She didn't feel her split rectum or the patches in her skull where her hair had been torn off by grating against the bricks. Lorraine lay in that alley only screaming at the moving pain inside of her that refused to come to rest.

"Hey, C. C., what if she remembers that it was us?"

"Man, how she gonna prove it? Your dick ain't got no fingerprints." They laughed and stepped over her and ran out of the alley.

Lorraine lay pushed up against the wall on the cold ground with her eyes staring straight up into the sky. When the sun began to warm the air and the horizon brightened, she still lay there, her mouth crammed with paper bag, her dress pushed up under her breasts, her bloody pantyhose hanging from her thighs. She would have stayed there forever and have simply died from starvation or exposure if nothing around her had moved. There was no wind that morning, so the tin cans, soda bottles, and loose papers were still. There wasn't even a stray cat or dog rummaging in the garbage cans for scraps. There was nothing moving that early October morning—except Ben.

Ben had come out of the basement and was sitting in his usual place on an old garbage can he had pushed up against the wall. And he was singing and swaying while taking small sips from the pint bottle he kept in his back pocket. Lorraine looked up the alley and saw the movement by the wall. Side to side. Side to side. Almost in perfect unison with the sawing pain that kept moving inside of her. She crept up on her knees, making small grunting sounds like a wounded animal. As she crawled along the alley, her hand brushed a loose brick, and she clawed her fingers around it and dragged it along the ground toward the movement on Brewster Place. Side to side. Side to side.

Mattie left her bed, went to the bathroom, and then put on her tea kettle. She always got up early, for no reason other than habit. The timing mechanism that had been embedded in her on the farm wasn't aware that she now lived in a city. While her coffee water was heating up, she filled a pitcher to water her plants. When she leaned over the plants at the side of the apartment, she saw the body crawling up the alley. She raised the window and leaned out just to be sure the morning light wasn't playing tricks with her eyes. "Merciful Jesus!" She threw a coat over her night-gown, slipped on a pair of shoes, and tried to make her arthritic legs hurry down the steps.

Lorraine was getting closer to the movement. She raised herself up on her bruised and stiffened knees, and the paper bag fell out of her mouth. She supported herself by sliding against the wall, limping up the alley toward the movement while clawing her brick and mouthing her silent word. Side to side. Side to side. Lorraine finally reached the motion on top of the garbage can. Ben slowly started to focus her through his burgundy fog, and just as he opened his lips to voice the words that had formed in his brain—"My God, child, what happened to you?"—the brick smashed down into his mouth. His teeth crumbled into his throat and his body swung back against the wall. Lorraine brought the brick down again to stop the moving head, and blood shot out of his ears, splattering against the can and bottom of the wall. Mattie's screams went ricocheting in Lorraine's head, and she joined them with her own as she brought the brick down again, splitting his forehead and crushing his temple, rendering his brains just a bit more useless than hers were now.

Arms grabbed her around the waist, and the brick was knocked from her hand. The movement was everywhere. Lorraine screamed and clawed at the motions that were running and shouting from every direction in the universe. A tall yellow woman in a bloody green and black dress, scraping at the air, crying, "Please. Please."

CONSTRUCTING A READING

1. With your group members, discuss the effect of Naylor's discourse order. How would you have responded for example, if Naylor had recounted the confrontation between C. C., Kiswana, and Lucille at a different place in the narrative or not at all?

2. Overall, "The Two" would seem to be a tragic story of misunderstanding, violence, and death. But the story also contains some rather funny scenes—as for example the group's sarcastic banter during the block meeting. With your group members, discuss the effect of this mixture of generic characteristics. Do they detract from the overall effect? Intensify it? Make the story seem more or less realistic?

3. Again with your group members, discuss the ways in which Naylor works with (or on) your sympathy. How does she use plotting to do so? For example, does Naylor succeed in establishing sympathy for her lesbian protagonists even among readers who disapprove of their way of life? Why or why not and how?

4. What plot events work to enlist readers' emotions for and/or against

Ben? How does Naylor's arrangement of those plot events contribute to the effect?

5. Some of the details of this story might be disturbing to you. If so, write a page or two in your journal in which you identify the disturbing details and describe how they affect your reading of the story. Why do you think Naylor decided to be explicit about the details of the rape, rather than merely alluding to them?

Strung Out

Sara Paretsky

I

People born near the corner of 90th and Commercial used to have fairly predictable futures. The boys grew up to work in the mills; the girls took jobs in the bakeries or coffee shops. They married each other and scrimped to make a down payment on a neighborhood bungalow and somehow fit their large families into its small rooms.

Now that the mills are history, the script has changed. Kids are still marrying, still having families, but without the certainty of the steel industry to buoy their futures. The one thing that seems to stay the same, though, is the number who stubbornly cling to the neighborhood even now that the jobs are gone. It's a clannish place, South Chicago, and people don't leave it easily.

When Monica Larush got pregnant our senior year in high school and married football hero Gary Oberst, we all just assumed they were on their way to becoming another large family in a small bungalow. She wasn't a friend of mine, so I didn't worry about the possible ruin of her life. Anyway, having recently lost my own mother to cancer, I wasn't too concerned about other girls' problems.

Monica's and my lives only intersected on the basketball court. Like me, she was an aggressive athlete, but she clearly had a high level of talent as well. In those days, though, a pregnant girl couldn't stay in school, so she missed our championship winter. The team brought her a game ball. We found her, fat and pasty, eating Fritos in angry frustration in front of the TV in her mother's kitchen. When we left, we made grotesque jokes about her swollen face and belly, our only way of expressing our embarrassment and worry.

Gary and Monica rewrote their script, though. Gary got a job on the night shift at Inland Steel and went to school during the day. After the baby—Gary Junior—was born, Monica picked up her GED. The two of them scrimped, not for a down payment, but to make it through the University of Illinois's Chicago campus. Gary took a job as an accountant with a big Loop firm, Monica taught high school French, and they left the neighborhood. Moved north was what I heard.

And that was pretty much all I knew—or cared—about them before Lily Oberst's name and face started popping up in the papers. She was apparently mopping up junior tennis competition. Tennis boosters and athletic-apparel makers were counting the minutes until she turned pro.

I actually first heard about her from my old basketball coach, Mary Ann McFarlane. Mary Ann's first love had always been tennis. When she retired from teaching at sixty, she continued to act as a tennis umpire at local high school and college tournaments. I saw her once a year when the Virginia Slims came to Chicago. She worked as a linesperson there for the pittance the tour paid—not for the bucks, but for the excitement. I always came during the last few days and had dinner with her in Greek Town at the end of the finals.

"I've been watching Lily Oberst play up at the Skokie Valley club," Mary Ann announced one year. "Kid's got terrific stuff. If they don't ruin her too young she could be—well, I won't say another Martina. Martinas come once a century. But a great one.

"Lily Oberst?" I shook my head, fishing for why the name sounded familiar.

"You don't remember Monica? Didn't you girls keep in touch after your big year? Lily is her and Gary's daughter. I used to coach Monica in tennis besides basketball, but I guess that wasn't one of your sports."

After that I read the stories in detail and got caught up on twenty years of missing history. Lily grew up in suburban Glenview, the second of two children. The *Herald-Star* explained that both her parents were athletic and encouraged her and her brother to go out for sports. When a camp coach brought back the word that Lily might have some tennis aptitude, her daddy began working with her every day. She had just turned six then.

Gary put up a net for her in the basement and would give her an ice cream bar every time she could hit the ball back twenty-five times without missing.

"He got mad when it got too easy for me," Lily said, giggling, to the reporter. "Then he'd raise the net whenever I got to twenty-four."

When it became clear that they had a major tennis talent on their hands, Monica and Gary put all their energy into developing it. Monica quit her job as a teacher so that she could travel to camps and tournaments with Lily. Gary, by then regional director for a pharmaceutical firm, persuaded his company to put in the seed money for Lily's career. He himself took a leave of absence to work as her personal trainer. Even now that she was a pro Monica and Gary went with her everywhere. Of course Lily had a professional coach, but her day always started with a workout with Daddy.

Gary Junior didn't get much print attention. He apparently didn't share the family's sports mania. Five years older than Lily, he was in college studying for a degree in chemical engineering, and hoping to go off to Procter & Gamble in Cincinnati.

Lily turned pro the same year Jennifer Capriati did. Since Capriati was making history, joining the pros at thirteen, Lily, two years older, didn't get the national hoopla. But Chicago went wild. Her arrival in the Wimbledon quarterfinals that year was front-page news all over town. Her 6–2, 6–0 loss there to Monica Seles was shown live in every bar in the city. Fresh-faced and smiling under a spiky blond hairdo, she grinned through her braces and said it was just a thrill to be on the same court with players like Seles and Graf. The city fell in love.

So when it was announced that she was coming to Chicago to play in the Slims in February the tournament generated more publicity than it had ever known. After a year and a half on the pro circuit Lily was ranked eighth in the world, but the pictures of her arrival at the family home still showed an ingenuous grin. Her Great Dane, standing on his hind legs with his paws on her shoulders, was licking her face.

Mary Ann McFarlane called me a few days after the Obersts arrived back in town. "Want to come up to Glenview and watch the kid work out? You could catch up with Monica at the same time."

That sounded like a treat that would appeal to Monica about as much as it did to me. But I had never seen a tennis prodigy in the making. I agreed to drive out to Glenview on Friday morning. Mary Ann and I would have lunch with Monica after Lily's workout.

The Skokie Valley Tennis Club was just off the Edens Expressway at Dempster. Lily's workout started at eight but I hadn't felt the need to watch a sixteen-year-old, however prodigious, run laps. I arrived at the courts a little after ten.

When I asked a woman at the reception desk to direct me to Lily, she told me the star's workout was off-limits to the press today. I explained who I was. She consulted higher authority over the phone. Mary Ann had apparently greased the necessary skids: I was allowed past a bored guard lounging against a hall door. After showing him my driver's license, I was directed down the hall to the private court where Lily was practicing. A second guard there looked at my license again and then opened the door for me.

Lily had the use of three nets if she needed them. A small grandstand held only three people: Mary Ann and Monica and a young man in a workout suit with "Artemis" blazoned across the back. I recognized Monica from the newspaper photos, but they didn't do justice to her perfectly styled gold hair, the makeup enhancing her oval face, or the casual elegance of her clothes. I had a fleeting memory of her fat, pasty face as she sat eating Fritos twenty years ago. I would never have put those two images together. As the old bromide has it, living well is the best revenge.

Mary Ann squeezed my hand as I sat on her other side. "Good to see you, Vic," she whispered. "Monica—here's Vic."

We exchanged confused greetings across our old coach, me congratulating her on her daughter's success, she exclaiming at how I hadn't changed a bit. I didn't know if that was a compliment or not.

The man was introduced as Monte Allison, from Artemis Products' marketing department. Artemis supplied all of Lily's tennis clothes and shoes, as well as a seven-figure endorsement contract. Allison was just along to protect the investment, Mary Ann explained. The equipment maker heard her and ostentatiously turned his left shoulder to us.

On the court in front of us Lily was hitting tennis balls. A kid in white shorts was serving to her backhand. A dark man in shabby gray sweats stood behind her encouraging her and critiquing her stroke. And a third man in bright white clothes offered more forceful criticisms from the sidelines.

"Get into the shot, Lily. Come'n, honey, you're not concentrating."

"Gary," Mary Ann muttered at me. "That's Paco Callabrio behind her."

I don't know much about tennis, but even I'd heard of Callabrio. After dominating men's tennis in the sixties he had retired to his family home in Majorca. But five years ago he'd come out of seclusion to coach a few selected players. Lily had piqued his interest when he saw her at the French Open last year; Monica had leaped at the opportunity to have her daughter work with him. Apparently Gary was less impressed. As the morning wore on Gary's advice began clashing with Paco's more and more often.

In the midst of a heated exchange over Lily's upswing I sensed someone moving onto the bench behind me. I turned to see a young woman leaning at her ease against the bleacher behind her. She was dressed in loose-fitting trousers that accentuated the long, lean lines of her body.

Lily saw the newcomer at the same time I did. She turned very red, then very white. While Paco and Gary continued arguing, she signaled to the young man to start hitting balls to her again. She'd been too tired to move well a minute ago, but the woman's arrival infused her with new energy.

Mary Ann had also turned to stare. "Nicole Rubova," she muttered to me.

I raised my eyebrows. Another of the dazzling Czech players who'd come to the States in Martina's wake. She was part of the generation between Martina and Capriati, a year or so older than Graf but with time ahead of her still to fight for the top spots. Her dark, vivid beauty made her a mediagenic foil to Graf's and Lily's blondness, but her sardonic humor kept her from being really popular with the press.

"Gary's afraid she's going to rape his baby. He won't let Lily go out alone with any of the women on the circuit." Mary Ann continued to mutter at me.

I raised my brows again, this time amazed at Mary Ann's pithy remarks. She'd never talked so bluntly to me when she was my basketball coach.

By now Gary had also seen Rubova in the stands. Like Lily he changed color, then grew even more maniacal in his demands on his daughter. When Paco advised a rest around eleven-thirty, Gary shook his head emphatically.

"You can't spoil her, Paco. Believe me, I know this little girl. She's got great talent and a heart of gold, but she's lazy. You've got to drive her."

Lily was gray with exhaustion. While they argued over her she leaned over, her hands on her knees, and gasped for air.

"Mr. Oberst," Paco said, his chilly formality emphasizing his dislike, "you want Lily to be a great star. But a girl who plays when she is this fatigued will only injure herself, if she doesn't burn out completely first. I say the workout is over for the day."

"And I say she got to Wimbledon last year thanks to my methods," Gary yelled.

"And she almost had to forfeit her round of sixteen match because you were coaching her so blatantly from the seats," Paco shouted back. "Your methods stink, Oberst."

Gary stepped toward the Catalan, then abruptly turned his back on him and yelled at his daughter, "Lily, pick up your racket. Come on, girl. You know the rules."

"Really, Oberst," Monte Allison called tentatively down to the floor from the stands. "We can't injure Lily—that won't help any of us."

Monica nodded in emphatic agreement, but Gary paid no attention to either of them. Lily looked imploringly from Paco to Gary. When the coach said nothing else, she bent to pick up her racket and continued returning balls. She was missing more than she was hitting now and was moving leadenly around the court. Paco watched for about a minute, then turned on his heel and marched toward a door in the far wall. As he disappeared through it, Monica got up from Mary Ann's left and hurried after him.

I noticed a bright pink anorak with rabbit fur around the hood next to where she'd been sitting, and two furry leather mittens with rabbits embroidered on them.

"That's Lily's," Mary Ann said. "Monica must have forgotten she was holding them for her. I'll give them to the kid if she makes it through this session.

My old coach's face was set in angry lines. I felt angry, too, and kept half rising from my seat, wondering if I ought to intervene. Paco's departure had whipped Gary into a triumphant frenzy. He shooed the kid serving balls away and started hitting ground strokes to his daughter at a furious pace. She took it for about five minutes before collapsing on the floor in tears.

"I just can't do it anymore, Daddy. I just can't."

Gary put his own racket down and smiled in triumph.

A sharp clap came from behind me, making me jump. "Bravo, Gary!" Nicole cried. "What a man you are! Yes, indeed, you've proved you can frighten your little girl. Now the question is: Which matters more to you? That Lily become the great player her talent destines her to be? Or that you prove that you own her?"

She jumped up lightly from the bench and ran down to the court. She put an arm around Lily and said something inaudible to the girl. Lily looked from her to her father and shook her head, flushing with misery. Nicole shrugged. Before leaving the court she and Gary exchanged a long look. Only an optimist would have found the seeds of friendship in it.

II

The Slims started the next Monday. The events at the Skokie Valley Tennis Club made me follow the newspaper reports eagerly, but the tournament seemed to be progressing without any open fireworks. One or two of the higher seeds were knocked out early, but Martina, Rubova, Lily, and one of the Maleeva sisters were all winning on schedule, along with Zina Garrison. Indeed, Martina, coming off knee surgery, seemed to be playing with the energy of a woman half her age.

I called Mary Ann McFarlane Thursday night to make sure she had my pass to the quarterfinal matches on Friday. Lily was proving such a hit that tickets were hard to get.

"Oh, yes," she assured me. "We linespersons don't have much leverage, but I got Monica to leave a pass for you at the will-call window. Dinner Sunday night?"

I agreed readily. Driving down to the Pavilion on Friday, I was in good time for the noon match, which pitted Martina against Frederica Lujan.

Lujan was seeded twelfth to Martina's third in world rankings, but the gap between their games seemed much wider than those numbers. In fact, halfway through the first set Martina suddenly turned her game up a notch and turned an even match into a rout. She was all over the court, going down for shots that should have been unhittable.

An hour later we got the quarterfinal meeting the crowd had come to see: Lily against Nicole Rubova. When Lily danced onto the court, a vision in pink and white with a sweatband pulling her blond spikes back from her face, the stands roared with pleasure. Nicole got a polite round of applause, but she was only there to give their darling a chance to play.

A couple of minutes after they'd started their warm-up, Monica came in. She sat close to the court, about ten rows in front of me. The man she joined was Paco Callabrio. He had stood next to Lily on the court as she came out for her warmups, patted her encouragingly on the ass, and climbed into the stands. Monica must have persuaded him not to quit in fury last week.

At first I assumed Gary was boycotting the match, either out of dislike of Paco or for fear his overt coaching would cause Lily to forfeit. As play progressed, though, I noticed him on the far side of the court, behind the chair umpire, making wild gestures if Lily missed a close shot, or if he thought the linespersons were making bad calls.

When play began Rubova's catlike languor vanished. She obviously took her conditioning seriously, moving well around the court and playing the net with a brilliant ferocity. Mary Ann might be right—she might have designs on Lily's body—but it didn't make her play the youngster with any gentleness.

Lily, too, had a range of motion that was exciting to watch. She was big, already five ten, with long arms and a phenomenal reach. Whether due to Gary's drills or not, her backhand proved formidable; unlike most women on the circuit she could use it one handed.

Lily pushed her hard but Rubova won in three sets, earning the privilege of meeting Navratilova the next afternoon. It seemed to me that Lily suddenly began hitting the ball rather tentatively in the last few games of the final set. I wasn't knowledgeable enough to know if she had suddenly reached her physical limit, or if she was buckling under Rubova's attack.

The crowd, disappointed in their favorite's loss, gave the Czech only a lukewarm hand as she collected her rackets and exited. Paco, Monica, and Gary all disappeared from the stands as Lily left the court to a standing ovation.

Mary Ann had been a linesperson on the far sideline during the Rubova match. Neither of the players had given the umpire a hard time. Rubova at one point drew a line on the floor with her racket, a sarcastic indicator of where she thought Mary Ann was spotting Lily. Another time Lily cried out in frustration to the chair umpire; I saw Monica's shoulders tense and wondered if the prodigy was prone to tantrums. More likely she was worried by what Gary—turning puce on the far side—might do to embarrass her. Other than that the match had gone smoothly.

Doubles quarterfinals were on the agenda for late afternoon. I wasn't planning on watching those, so I wandered down to the court to have a word with Mary Ann before I left.

She tried to talk me into staying. "Garrison has teamed up with Rubova. They should be fun to watch—both are real active girls."

"Enough for me for one day. What'd you think of the kid in tournament play?"

Mary Ann spread her hands. "She's going to go a long way. Nicole out-played her today, but she won't forever. Although—I don't know—it looked to me in the last couple of games as though she might have been favoring her right shoulder. I couldn't be sure. I just hope Gary hasn't got her to injure herself with his hit-till-you-drop coaching methods. I'm surprised Paco's hanging on through it."

I grinned suggestively at her. "Maybe Monica has wonderful powers of persuasion."

Mary Ann looked at me calmly. "You're trying to shock me, Vic, but believe me, I was never a maiden aunt. And anyway, nothing on this circuit would shock me. . . They have free refreshments downstairs for players and crew. And press and hangers-on. Want to come have some coffee before you go? Some of the girls might even be there."

"And be a hanger-on? Sure, why not?" Who knows, maybe Martina would meet me and remember an urgent need for some detective work.

A freight elevator protected by guards carried the insiders to the lower depths. Mary Ann, in her linesperson's outfit, didn't need to show any identification. I came in for more scrutiny, but my player's-guest badge got me through.

The elevator decanted us onto a grubby corridor. Young people of both sexes hurried up and down its length, carrying clipboards at which they frowned importantly.

"PR staff," Mary Ann explained. "They feed all the statistics from the match to different wire services and try to drum up local interest in the tournament. Tie-ins with the auto show, that kind of thing."

Older, fatter people stood outside makeshift marquees with coffee and globular brownies. At the end of the hall I could see Paco and Monica huddled together. Gary wasn't in sight.

"Lily may have gone back in for a massage; I think she already did her press interview. Gary must be inside with her. He won't let her get a workover alone."

"Inside the locker room?" I echoed. "I know she's Daddy's darling, but don't the other women object to him being there while they're changing? And can she really stand having him watch her get massaged?"

"There's a lounge." Mary Ann shepherded me into the refreshment tent—really a niche roped off from the cement corridor with a rather pathetic plastic canopy overhead. "Friends and lovers of the stars can sit there while the girls dress inside. I don't expect he actually hangs around the massage table. Don't go picturing some fabulous hideaway, though. This is a gym at a relatively poor university. It's purely functional. But they do have a cement cubbyhole for the masseuse—that sets it apart from the normal school gym."

I suddenly realized I was hungry—it was long past lunchtime. The Slims catering was heavy on volume and carbohydrates. I rejected fried chicken wings and rice and filled a plastic bowl with some doubtful-looking chili. Mary Ann picked up a handful of cookies to eat with her coffee.

We settled at an empty table in the far corner and ate while Mary Ann pointed out the notables to me. Zina Garrison's husband was at the buffet next to Katarina Maleeva. The two were laughing together, trying to avoid a fat reporter who was unabashedly eavesdropping on them.

A well-groomed woman near the entrance to the marquee was Clare Rutland, the doyenne of the tour, Mary Ann explained. She had no formal title with the Slims, but seemed to be able to keep its temperamental stars happy, or at least functioning.

As I ate my chili, six or seven people stopped to talk to Rutland. They'd nod at her remarks and race off again. I imagined tennis stars' wishes, from lotus blossoms to Lotus racers, being satisfied at the wave of her hand.

Mary Ann, talking to acquaintances, began picking up some of the gossip buzzing the room: Lily might have strained her shoulder. Maybe torn her rotator cuff. In this kind of environment the worst scenarios are generated rapidly from the whiff of an idea. And Gary apparently had been thrown out of Lily's press conference and was now sulking in the women's lounge.

A collective cry from the group across the room made me jerk my head around. Nicole Rubova was sprinting down the hall, wet, a towel haphazardly draping her midriff.

"Clare," she gasped.

Clare Rutland was on her feet as soon as she heard the outcry, almost before Rubova came into view. She took off her cardigan and draped it across the player's shoulders. Rubova was too far from us for me to be able to hear her, but the reporters in the room crowded around her, tournament etiquette forgotten.

It only took a minute for Mary Ann to get the main point of the story from one of them: Gary Oberst was on the couch in the players' lounge. Someone had wrapped a string from a tennis racket around his neck a few times.

It was only later that everyone realized Lily herself had disappeared.

III

Clare Rutland curled one foot toward her chin and massaged her stockinged toes. Her face, rubbed free of makeup, showed the strain of the day in its sharply dug lines.

"This could kill the Slims," she remarked to no one in particular.

It was past midnight. I was in the windowless press room with her, Mary Ann, and a bunch of men, including Jared Brookings, who owned the PR firm handling the Slims in Chicago. Brookings had come in in person around nine, to see what could be done to salvage the tournament. He'd sent his fresh-faced minions packing long ago. They'd phoned him in terror when the police arrested Nicole Rubova, and clearly were not up to functioning in the crisis.

Arnold Krieger was there, too, with a handful of other reporters whose names I never learned. Krieger was the fat man who'd been listening in on Zina Garrison's husband earlier in the dining area. He covered tennis for one of the wire services and had made himself at home in the press room when the cops commandeered it for their headquarters.

"She'll be out on bond in the morning, right?" Krieger palmed a handful of nuts into his mouth as he started to talk, so his words came out clogged. "So she can play Martina at one, per the schedule."

Clare looked at him in dismay but didn't speak.

Brookings put his fingertips together. "It all depends, doesn't it? We can't be too careful. We've spent two decades building these girls up, but the whole fabric could collapse at any minute."

I could see Mary Ann's teacher instincts debating whether to correct his mixed metaphors and deciding against it. "The problem isn't just having one of the stars arrested for murder," she said bluntly. "Lily Oberst is a local heroine and now everyone is going to read that an evil lesbian who had designs on her killed her father because he stood between them. Chicago might rip Nicole apart. They certainly won't support the tournament."

"Besides," Clare Rutland added in a dull voice, "two of the top seeds withdrew when they heard about Rubova's arrest. They've gone off to locate a lawyer to handle the defense. The other Czechs may not play any more Slims this year if a cloud hangs over Rubova. Neither will Freddie Lujan. If they drop out, others may follow suit."

"If a cloud hangs over Rubova, it's over the whole tour," Monte Allison, the Artemis Products representative, spoke for the first time. "We may withdraw *our* sponsorship for the rest of the year—I can't speak for Philip Morris, of course. That's a corporate decision, naturally, not mine, but we'll be making it tomorrow or—no, tomorrow's Saturday. We'll make it Monday. Early."

I'd never yet known a corporation that could make an important decision early Monday just because one of its vice presidents said so in a forceful voice. But Allison was fretful because none of the tennis people was paying attention to him. Since Artemis also helped Philip Morris promote the tour, Allison was likely to urge that they withdraw their sponsorship just because he didn't like the way Clare Rutland kept snubbing him.

I muttered as much to Mary Ann.

"If they have to make a decision Monday, it gives you two days to solve the crime, Vic," she said loudly.

"You don't believe Rubova killed Oberst?" I asked her, still sotto voce.

"I believe the police wanted to arrest her because they didn't like her attitude," Mary Ann snapped.

The investigation had been handled by John McGonnigal, a violent crimes sergeant I know. He's a good cop, but a soignée, sardonic woman does not bring out the best in him. And by the time he'd arrived Nicole had dressed, in a crimson silk jumpsuit that emphasized the pliable length of her body, and withdrawn from shock into mockery.

When McGonnigal saw me slide into the interrogation room behind Rubova, he gave an exaggerated groan but didn't actively try to exclude me from his questioning sessions. Those gave me a sense of where everyone claimed to have been when Gary was killed, but no idea at all if McGonnigal was making a mistake in arresting Nicole Rubova.

Police repugnance at female-female sexuality might have helped ham interpret evidence so that it pointed at her. I hadn't been able to get the forensic data, but the case against Rubova seemed to depend on two facts: she was the only person known to be alone with Gary in the locker mom. And one of her rackets had a big section of string missing from it. This last seemed to be a rather slender thread to hang her on. It would have taken a good while to unthread enough string from a racket to have enough for a garrote. I didn't see where she'd had the time to do it.

McGonnigal insisted she'd spent Lily's press conference at it, dismissing claims from Frederica Lujan that she'd been talking to Nicole while it was going on. Some helpful person had told him that Frederica and Nicole had had an affair last year, so McGonnigal decided the Spanish player would say anything to help a friend.

None of the Slims people questioned my sitting in on the inquiry—they were far too absorbed in their woes over the tournament. The men didn't pay any attention to Mary Ann's comment to me now, but Clare Rutland moved slightly on the couch so that she was facing my old coach directly. "Who is this, Mary Ann?"

"V. I. Warshawski. About the best private investigator in the city." Mary Ann continued to speak at top volume.

"Is that why you came to the matches today?" The large hazel eyes looked at me with intense interest. I felt the power she exerted over tennis divas directed at me.

"I came because I wanted to watch Lily Oberst. I grew up playing basketball with her mother. Mary Ann here was our coach. After watching Gary train Lily last week I would have thought the kid might have killed him herself—he seemed extraordinarily brutal."

Clare smiled, for the first time since Nicole Rubova had come running down the hall in her towel ten hours ago. "If every tennis kid killed her father because of his brutal coaching, we wouldn't have any parents left on the circuit. Which might only improve the game. But Oberst was one of the worst. Only— why did she have to do it *here?* She must have known—only I suppose when you're jealous you don't think of such things."

"So you think Rubova killed the guy?"

Clare spread her hands, appealing for support. "You don't?"

"You know her and I don't, so I assume you're a better judge of her character. But she seems too cool, too poised, to kill a guy for the reason everyone's imputing to her. Maybe she was interested in Lily. But I find it impossible to believe she'd kill the girl's father because he tried to short-circuit her. She's very sophisticated, very smart, and very cool. If she *really* wanted to have an affair with Lily, she'd have figured out a way. I'm not sure she wanted to—I think it amused her to see Lily blush and get flustered, and to watch Gary go berserk. But if she did want to kill Gary she'd have done so a lot more subtly, not in a fit of rage in the locker room. One other thing: If—*if*—she killed him like that, on the spot, it must have been for some other reason than Lily."

"Like what?" Arnold Krieger had lost interest in Monte Allison and was eavesdropping on me, still chewing cashews.

I hunched a shoulder. "You guys tell me. You're the ones who see these prima donnas week in and week out."

Clare nodded. "I see what you mean. But then, who did kill Oberst?"

"I don't know the players and I don't have access to the forensic evidence. But—well, Lily herself would be my first choice."

A furious uproar started from Allison and Brookings, with Clare chiming in briefly. Mary Ann silenced them all with a coach's whistle—she still could put her fingers in her mouth and produce a sound like a steam engine.

"She must have been awfully tired of Gary sitting in her head," I continued when Mary Ann had shut them up. "She could hardly go to the bathroom without his permission. I learned today that he chose her clothes, her friends, ran her practice sessions, drove away her favorite coaches. You name it."

The police had found Lily quickly enough—she'd apparently had a rare fight with Gary and stormed away to Northwestern Hospital without telling Monica. Without her entourage it had taken her a while to persuade the emergency room that her sore shoulder should leap ahead of other emergencies. Once they realized who she was, though, they summoned their sports medicine maven at once. He swept her off in a cloud of solicitude for X rays, then summoned a limo to take her home to Glenview. There still would have been plenty of time for her to kill Gary before she left the Pavilion.

"Then there's Monica." I went on. "She and Paco Callabrio have been pretty friendly—several people hinted at it during their interviews this afternoon. She and Gary started dating when they were fifteen. That's twenty-four years with a bully. Maybe she figured she'd had enough."

"I don't like Paco for the spot very well. He's like Nicole—he's got a life, and an international reputation; he didn't need to ruin it by killing the father of one of his pupils. Although, apparently he came out of retirement because of financial desperation. So maybe he was worried about losing Lily as a client, and his affair with Monica deranged him enough that he killed Oberst."

"So you think it's one of those three?" Clare asked.

I shrugged. "Could be. Could be Allison here, worried about his endorsement contract. He watched Gary driving Lily to the breaking point. Artemis could lose seven, eight million dollars if Lily injured herself so badly she couldn't play anymore."

Allison broke off his conversation with Brookings when he heard his name. "What the hell are you saying? That's outrageous. We're behind Lily all the way. I could sue you—"

"Control yourself, Monte," Clare said coldly. "No one's accusing you of anything except high-level capitalism. The detective is just suggesting why someone besides Nicole might have killed Gary Oberst. Anything else?"

"The hottest outsider is Arnold Krieger here."

Two of the anonymous reporters snickered. Krieger muttered darkly but didn't say anything. The tale of Lily's interview with him had come out very early in McGonnigal's questioning.

Tennis etiquette dictates that the loser meet journalists first. The winner can then shower and dress at her leisure. After her match Lily had bounced out, surrounded by Paco, Gary, and Monica. She'd giggled with the press about her game, said she didn't mind losing to Nicole because Nicole was a great player, but she, Lily, had given the game her best, and anyway, she was glad to have a few extra days at home with Ninja, her Great Dane, before flying off to Palm Springs for an exhibition match. People asked about her shoulder. She'd said it was sore but nothing serious. She was going over to Northwestern for X rays just to be on the safe side.

Arnold Krieger then asked whether she felt she ever played her best against Rubova. "After all, most people know she's just waiting for the chance to get you alone. Doesn't that unnerve you?"

Lily started to giggle again, but Gary lost his temper and jumped Krieger on the spot. Security guards pried his hands from the journalist's throat; Gary was warned out of the press room. In fact, he was told that one more episode would get him barred from the tour altogether.

The cops loved that, but they couldn't find anyone who'd seen Krieger go into the locker room afterwards. In fact, most of us could remember his staying near the food, playing tag team with Garrison's husband.

"Don't forget, it was Rubova's racket the string was missing from," Krieger reminded me belligerently.

Clare eyed Krieger as though measuring him for an electric chair, then turned back to me. "What do you charge?"

"Fifty dollars an hour. Plus any unusual expenses—things above the cost of gas or local phone bills."

"I'm hiring you," Clare said briskly.

"To do what? Clear Nicole's name, or guarantee the tour can go on? I can only do the first—if she's not guilty. If it turns out to be Lily, or any of the other players, the Slims are going to be under just as much of a cloud as they are now."

Clare Rutland scowled, but she was used to being decisive. "Clear Nicole for me. I'll worry about the Slims after that. What do you need me to do to make it official?"

"I'll bring a contract by for you tomorrow, but right now what I really want is to take a look at the women's locker room."

"You can't do that," one of the anonymous reporters objected. "The police have sealed it."

"The police are through with it," I said. "They've made their arrest. I just need someone with a key to let me in."

Clare pinched the bridge of her nose while she thought about it. Maybe it was the objections the men kept hurling at her that made her decide. She stood up briskly, slipped her feet into their expensive suede pumps, and told me to follow her. Mary Ann and I left the press room in her wake. Behind us I could hear Allison shouting, "You can't do this."

IV

I tore the police seal without compunction. If they'd been in the middle of an investigation I would have honored it, but they'd had their chance, made their arrest.

The locker room was a utilitarian set of cement cubes. The attempt to turn the outermost cube into a lounge merely made it look forlorn. It held a few pieces of secondhand furniture, a large bottle of spring water, and a telephone.

Gary had been sitting on a couch plunked into the middle of the floor. Whoever killed him had stood right behind him, wrapping the racket string around his throat before he had time to react—the police found no evidence that he had been able even to lift a hand to try to pull it loose. A smear of dried blood on the back cushion came from where the string had cut through the skin of his neck.

Whoever had pulled the garrote must have cut her—or his—hands as well. I bummed a pad of paper from Clare and made a note to ask McGonnigal whether Nicole had any cuts. And whether he'd noticed them on anyone else. It was quite possible he hadn't bothered to look.

The lounge led to the shower room. As Mary Ann had warned, the place was strictly functional—no curtains, no gleaming fittings. Just standard brown tile that made my toes curl inside my shoes as I felt mold growing beneath them, and a row of small, white-crusted shower heads.

Beyond the showers was a bare room with hooks for coats or equipment bags and a table for the masseuse. A door led to the outer hall.

"It's locked at all times, though," Clare said.

"*All* the time? I expect someone has a key."

She took the notepad from me and scribbled on it. "I'll track that down for you in the morning."

A barrel of used towels stood between the showers and the massage room. For want of anything better to do I poked through them, but nothing unusual came to light.

"Normally all the laundry is cleared out at the end of the day, along with the garbage, but the maintenance crews couldn't come in tonight, of course," Clare explained.

The garbage bins were built into the wall. It was easy to lift the swinging doors off and pull the big plastic lining out. I took them over to the masseuse's corner and started emptying them onto the table piece by piece. I did them in order of room starting with the lounge. Police detritus—coffee cups, ashes, crumpled forms—made up the top layer. In the middle of the styrofoam and ash, I found two leather mittens with bunnies embroidered on them. The palms were cut to ribbons.

I went through the rest of the garbage quickly, so quickly I almost missed the length of nylon wrapped in paper towels. One end poked out as I perfunc-torily shook the papers; I saw it just as I was about to sweep everything off the massage table back into the bag.

"It's racket string," Mary Ann said tersely.

"Yes," I agreed quietly.

It was a piece about five inches long. I unrolled all the paper toweling and newsprint a sheet at a time. By the time I finished I had three more little pieces. Since the garrote that killed Gars had been deeply embedded in his throat, these might bave been cut from Nicole's racket to point suspicion at her.

"But the mittens . . ." My old coach couldn't bring herself to say more.

Clare Rutland was watching me, her face frozen. "The mittens are Lily's, aren't they? Her brother got them for her for Christmas. She showed them off to everyone on the tour when we had our first post-Christmas matches. Why don't you give them to me, Vic? The string should be enough to save Nicole."

I shook my head unhappily. "Could be. We'd have to have the lab make sure these pieces came from her racket. Anyway, I can't do that, Clare. I'm not Gary Oberst's judge and jury. I can't ignore evidence that I've found myself."

"But, Vic," Mary Ann said hoarsely, "how can you do that to Lily? Turn on her? I always thought you tried to help other women. And you saw yourself what her life was like with Gary. How can you blame her?"

I felt the muscles of my face distort into a grimace. "I don't blame her. But how can you let her go through her life without confronting herself? It's a good road to madness, seeing yourself as above and beyond the law. The special treatment she gets as a star is bound to make her think that way to some degree already. If we let her kill her father and get away with it, we're doing her the worst possible damage."

Mary Ann's mouth twisted in misery. She stared at me a long minute. "Oh, *damn* you, Vic!" she cried, and pushed her way past me out of the locker room.

The last vestiges of Clare Rutland's energy had fallen from her face, mak-ing her cheeks look as though they had collapsed into it. "I agree with Mary Ann, Vic. We ought to be able to work something out. Something that would be good for Lily as well as Nicole."

"No," I cried.

She lunged toward me and grabbed the mittens. But I was not only younger and stronger, my Nikes gave me an advantage over her high heels. I caught up with her before she'd made it to the shower-room door and gently took the mittens from her.

"Will you let me do one thing? Will you let me see Lily before you talk to the police?"

"What about Nicole?" I demanded. "Doesn't she deserve to be released as soon as possible?"

"If the lawyer the other women have dug up for her doesn't get her out, you can call Sergeant McGonnigal first thing in the morning. Anyway, go ahead and give him the string now. Won't that get her released?"

"I can't do that. I can't come with two separate pieces of evidence found in the identical place but delivered to the law eight hours apart. And no, I damned well will not lie about it for you. I'll do this much for you: I'll let you talk to Lily. But I'll be with you."

Anyway, once the cops have made an arrest they don't like to go back on it. They were just as likely to say that Nicole had cut the string out herself as part of an elaborate bluff.

Clare smiled affably. "Okay. We'll go first thing in the morning."

"No, Ms. Rutland. You're a hell of a woman, but you're not going to run me around the way you do the rest of the tour. If I wait until morning, you'll have been on the phone with Lily and Monica and they'll be in Majorca. We go tonight. Or I stick to you like your underwear until morning."

Her mouth set in a stubborn line, but she didn't waste her time fighting lost battles. "We'll have to phone first. They're bound to be in bed, and they have an elaborate security system. I'll have to let them know we're coming."

I breathed down her neck while she made the call, but she simply told Monica it was important that they discuss matters tonight, before the story made national headlines.

"I'm sorry, honey, I know it's a hell of an hour. And you're under a hell of a lot of strain. But this is the first moment I've had since Nicole found Gary. And we just can't afford to let it go till morning."

Monica apparently found nothing strange in the idea of a two A.M. discussion of Lily's tennis future. Clare told her I was with her and would be driving, so she turned the phone over to me for instructions. Monica also didn't question what I was doing with Clare, for which I was grateful. My powers of invention weren't very great by this point.

V

A single spotlight lit the gate at Nine Nightingale Lane. When I leaned out the window and pressed the buzzer, Monica didn't bother to check that it was really us: she released the lock at once. The gate swung in on well-oiled hinges.

Inside the gate the house and drive were dark. I switched my headlights on high and drove forward cautiously, trying to make sure I stayed on the tarmac. My lights finally picked out the house. The drive made a loop past the front door. I pulled over to the edge and turned off the engine.

"Any idea why the place is totally dark?" I asked Clare.

"Maybe Lily's in bed and Monica doesn't want to wake her up."

"Lily can't sleep just knowing there's a light on somewhere in the house? Try a different theory."

"I don't have any theories," Clare said sharply. "I'm as baffled as you are, and probably twice as worried. Could someone have come out here and jumped her, be lying in ambush for us?"

My mouth felt dry. The thought had occurred to me as well. Anyone could have lifted Lily's mittens from the locker room while she was playing. Maybe Arnold Krieger had done so. Gotten someone to let him in through the permanently locked end of the women's locker room, lifted the mittens, garroted Gary, and slipped out the back way again while Rubova was still in the shower. When he realized we were searching the locker room, he came to Glenview ahead of us. He'd fought hard to keep me from going into the locker room, now that I thought about it.

My gun, of course, was locked away in the safe in my bedroom. No normal person carries a Smith & Wesson to a Virginia Slims match.

"Can you drive a stick shift?" I asked Clare. "I'm going inside, but I want to find a back entrance, avoid a trap if I can. If I'm not out in twenty minutes, drive off and get a neighbor to call the cops. And lock the car doors. Whoever's in the house knows we're here: they released the gate for us."

The mittens were zipped into the inside pocket of my parka. I decided to leave them there. Clare might still destroy them in a moment of chivalry if I put them in the trunk for safekeeping.

I took a pencil flash from the glove compartment. Using it sparingly, I picked my way around the side of the house. A dog bayed nearby. Ninja, the Great Dane. But he was in the house. If Arnold Krieger or someone else had come out to get a jump on us, they would have killed the dog, or the dog would have disabled them. I felt the hair stand up on the back of my neck.

A cinder-block cube had been attached to the back of the house. I shone the flash on it cautiously. It had no windows. It dawned on me that they had built a small indoor court for Lily, for those days when she couldn't get to the club. It had an outside door that led to the garden. When I turned the knob, the door moved inward.

"I'm in here, Vic." Monica's voice came to me in the darkness. "I figured you'd avoid the house and come around the back."

"Are you all right?" I whispered loudly. "Who's inside with Lily?"

Monica laughed. "Just her dog. You worried about Paco interrupting us? He's staying downtown in a hotel. Mary Ann called me. She told me you'd found Lily's mittens. She wanted me to take Lily and run, but I thought I'd better stay to meet you. I've got a shotgun, Vic. Gary was obsessive about Lily's safety, except, of course, on the court. Where he hoped she'd run herself into early retirement."

"You going to kill me to protect your daughter? That won't help much. I mean, I'll be dead, but then the police will come looking, and the whole ugly story will still come out."

"You always were kind of a smart mouth. I remember that from our high school days. And how much I hated you the day you came to see me with the rest of the team when I was pregnant with little Gary." Her voice had a conversational quality. "No. I can persuade the cops that I thought my home was being invaded. Someone coming to hurt Lily on top of all she's already been through today. Mary Ann may figure it out, but she loves Lily too much to do anything to hurt her."

"Clare Rutland's out front with the car. She's going for help before too long. Her story would be pretty hard to discount."

"She's going to find the gate locked when she gets there. And even Clare, endlessly clever, will find it hard to scale a ten-foot electrified fence. No, it will be seen as a terrible tragedy. People will give us their sympathy. Lily's golden up here, after all."

I felt a jolt under my rib cage. "*You* killed Gary."

She burst out laughing. "Oh, my goodness, yes, Vic. Did you just figure that out, smart-ass that you are? I was sure you were coming up here to gun for me. Did you really think little Lily, who could hardly pee without her daddy, had some sudden awakening and strangled him?"

"Why, Monica? Because she may have hurt her shoulder? You couldn't just get him to lay off? I noticed you didn't even try at her practice session last week."

"I always hated that about you," she said, her tone still flat.

"Your goddamned high-and-mightiness. You don't—didn't—ever stop Gary from doing some damned thing he was doing. How do you think I got pregnant with little Gary? Because his daddy said lie down and spread your legs for me, pretty please? Get out of your dream world. I got pregnant the old-fashioned way: he raped me. We married. We fought—each other and everything around us. But we made it out of that hellhole down there just like you did. Only not as easily."

"It wasn't easy for me," I started to say, but I sensed a sudden movement from her and flung myself onto the floor. A tennis ball bounced off the wall behind me and ricocheted from my leg.

Monica laughed again. "I have the shotgun. But I kind of like working with a racket. I was pretty good once. Never as good as Lily, though. And when Lily was born—when we realized what her potential was—I saw I could move myself so far from South Chicago it would never be able to grab me again."

Another *thwock* came in the dark and another ball crashed past me.

"Then Gary started pushing her so hard, I was afraid she'd be like Andrea Jaeger. Injured and burned out before she ever reached her potential. I begged him, pleaded with him. We'd lose that Artemis contract and everything else. But Gary's the kind of guy who's always right."

This time I was ready for the swish of her racket in the dark. Under cover of the ball's noise, I rolled across the floor in her direction. I didn't speak, hoping the momentum of her anger would keep her going without prompting.

"When Lily came off the court today favoring her shoulder, I told him I'd had it, that I wanted him out of her career. That Paco knew a thousand times more how to coach a girl with Lily's talent than he did. But Mr. Ever-right just laughed and ranted. He finally said Lily could choose. Just like she'd chosen him over Nicole, she'd choose him over Paco."

I kept inching my way forward until I felt the net. One of the balls had stopped there; I picked it up.

Monica hadn't noticed my approach. "Lily came up just then and heard what he said. On top of the scene he'd made at her little press doohickey it was too much for her. She had a fit and left the room. I went down the hall to an alcove where Johnny Lombardy—the stringer—kept his spool. I just cut a length of racket string from his roll, went back to the lounge, and—God, it was easy."

"And Nicole's racket?" I asked hoarsely, hoping my voice would sound as though it was farther away.

"Just snipped a few pieces out while she was in the shower. She's another one like you—snotty know-it-all. It won't hurt her to spend some time in jail."

She fired another ball at the wall and then, unexpectedly, flooded the room with light. Neither of us could see, but she at least was prepared for the shock. It gave her time to locate me as I scrambled to my feet. I found myself tangled in the net and struggled furiously while she steadied the gun on her shoulder.

I wasn't going to get my leg free in time. Just before she fired, I hurled the ball I'd picked up at her. It hit her in the face. The bullet tore a hole in the floor inches from my left foot. I finally yanked my leg from the net and launched myself at her.

VI

"I'm sorry, Vic. That you almost got killed, I mean. Not that I called Monica—she needed me. Not just then, but in general. She never had your, oh, centeredness. She needed a mother."

Mary Ann and I were eating in Greek Town. The Slims had limped out of Chicago a month ago, but I hadn't felt like talking to my old coach since my night with Monica. But Clare Rutland had come to town to meet with one of the tour sponsors, and to hand me a check in person. And she insisted that the three of us get together. After explaining how she'd talked the Sponsors and players into continuing, Clare wanted to know why Mary Ann had called Monica that night.

"Everyone needs a mother, Mary Ann. That's the weakest damned excuse I ever heard for trying to help someone get away with murdering her husband."

Mary Ann looked at me strangely. "Maybe Monica is right about you, Victoria: too high-and-mighty. But it was Lily I was trying to help. I wouldn't have done it if I'd known Monica was going to try to kill you. But you can take care of yourself. You survived the encounter. She didn't."

"What do you mean?" I demanded. "All I did was bruise her face getting her not to shoot me. And no one's going to give her the death penalty. I'd be surprised if she served more than four years."

"You don't understand, Vic. She didn't have anything besides the . . . the scrappiness that got her and Gary out of South Chicago. Oh, she learned how to dress, and put on makeup, and what kinds of things North Shore people eat for dinner. Now that the fight's gone out of her she doesn't have anything inside her to get her through the bad times. You do."

Clare Rutland interrupted hastily. "The good news is that Lily will recover. We have her working with a splendid woman, psychotherapist, I mean. She's playing tennis as much as she wants, which turns out to be a lot. And the other women on the circuit are rallying around in a wonderful way. Nicole is taking her to Maine to spend the summer at her place near Bar Harbor with her."

"Artemis dropped their endorsement contract," I said. "It was in the papers here."

"Yes, but she's already made herself enough to get through the next few years without winning another tournament. Let's be honest. She could live the rest of her life on what she's made in endorsements so far. Anyway, I hear Nike and Reebok are both sniffing around. No one's going to do anything until after Monica's trial—it wouldn't look right. But Lily will be fine."

We dropped it there. Except for the testimony I had to give at Monica's trial I didn't think about her or Lily too much as time went by. Sobered by my old coach's comments, I kept my time on the stand brief. Mary Ann, who came to the trial every day, seemed to be fighting tears when I left the courtroom, but I didn't stop to talk to her.

The following February, though, Mary Ann surprised me by phoning me.

"I'm not working on the lines this year," she said abruptly. "I've seen too much tennis close up. But Lily's making her first public appearance at the Slims, and she sent me tickets for all the matches. Would you like to go?"

I thought briefly of telling her to go to hell, of saying I'd had enough tennis—enough of the Obersts—to last me forever. But I found myself agreeing to meet her outside the box office on Harrison the next morning.

CONSTRUCTING A READING

1. Can V. I. be said to solve this mystery? If so, how? If not, would you still count it as a detective story? Why or why not?
2. With your group members, compare V. I. to Sherlock Holmes and M. Dupin. Talk about the relative importance of the similarities and differences, and about which you like best.
3. Do you think that Paretsky might be making some kind of commentary on the male detectives? If so, what?

4. Paretsky sometimes uses the name of actual tennis players—Martina, Graf, Capriati—and sometimes fictional ones. How do you respond to this aspect of her discourse?

A Noiseless, Patient Spider
Walt Whitman

A noiseless patient spider,
I mark'd where on a little promontory it stood isolated,
Mark'd how to explore the vacant vast surrounding,
It launch'd forth filament, filament, filament, out of itself,
Ever unreeling them, ever tirelessly speeding them.

And you O my soul where you stand,
Surrounded, detached, in measureless oceans of space,
Ceaselessly musing, venturing, throwing, seeking the spheres to connect them,
Till the bridge you will need be form'd, till the ductile anchor hold,
Till the gossamer thread you fling catch somewhere, O my soul.

CONSTRUCTING A READING

1. Does this poem tell a story? How or how not?
2. Use this poem and "Design" to explain the conception of genre to someone who is not taking your class.
3. Use this poem and "Design" to explain the notion of figurative language to someone who is not in your class.

---

from Briar Rose
Robert Coover

He is surprised to discover how easy it is. The branches part like thighs, the silky petals caress his cheeks. His drawn sword is stained, not with blood, but with dew and pollen. Yet another inflated legend. He has undertaken this great adventure, not for the supposed reward—what is another lonely bedridden princess?—but in order to provoke a confrontation with the awful powers of enchantment itself. To tame mystery. To make, at last, his name. He'd have been better off trying for the runes of wisdom or the Golden Fleece. Even another bloody grail. As the briars, pillowy with a sudden extravagance of fresh blooms, their thorns decorously sheathed in the full moonlight, open up to receive him as a doting mother might, he is pricked only by chagrin. Yet he knows what it has cost others who have gone before him, he can smell their bodies caught in the thicket, can glimpse the pallor of their moon-bleached bones, rattling gently when the soft wind blows. That odor of decay is about the extent of his ordeal, and even it is assuaged by the fragrances of fresh tansy and camomile, roses, lilac and hyssop, lavender and savory, which encompass him affectionately—perhaps he has been chosen, perhaps it is his virtue which has caused the hedge to bloom—as he plunges deeper into the thicket, the castle turrets and battlements already visible to him, almost within reach, through its trembling branches.

She dreams, as she has often dreamt, of abandonment and betrayal, of lost hope, of the self gone astray from the body, the body forsaking the unlikely self. She feels like a once-proud castle whose walls have collapsed, her halls and towers invaded, not by marauding armies, but by humbler creatures, bats, birds, cats, cattle, her departed self an unkempt army marauding elsewhere in a scatter of confused intentions. Her longing for integrity is, in her spellbound innocence, all she knows of rage and lust, but this longing is itself fragmented and wayward, felt not so much as a monstrous gnawing at the core as more like the restless scurry of vermin in the rubble of her remote defenses, long since fallen and benumbed. What, if anything, can make her whole again? And what is "whole"? Her parents, as always in her dreams, have vanished, gone off to death or the continent or perhaps to one of their houses of pleasure, and she is being stabbed again and again by the treacherous spindle, impregnated with a despair from which, for all her fury, she cannot awaken.

The pale moonlit turrets of the castle, glimpsed through the brambles, rise high into the black night above like the clenched fists of an unforgiving but stonily silent father, upon whose tender terrain below he is darkly trespassing, heralded by a soft icy clatter of tinkling bones. Unlike these others who ornament the briars, he has come opportunely when the hedge is in full bloom, or perhaps (he prefers to think) the hedge has blossomed tonight because it is he who has come, its seductive caresses welcoming him even as the cold castle overhead repels, the one a promise and a lure, showing him the way, the other the test he must undertake to achieve the object of his heroic quest. Which is? Honor. Knowledge. The exercise of his magical powers. Also love of course. If the old tales be true, a sleeping princess awaits him within. He imagines her as not unlike this soft dew-bedampened wall he is plunging through, silky and fragrant and voluptuously receptive. If she is the symbolic object of his quest, her awakening is not without its promise of passing pleasures. She is said, after all, to be the most beautiful creature in the world, both fair and good, musically gifted, delicate, virtuous and graceful and with the gentle disposition of an angel, and, for all her hundred years and more, still a child, innocent and yielding. Achingly desirable. And desiring. Of course, she is also the daughter of a mother embraced by a frog, and there has been talk about ogres in the family, dominion by sorcery, and congress with witches and wizards and other powers too dark to name. If there be any truth in these century-old rumors from benighted times, this adventure could end, not in love's sweet delirium, but in its pain, its infamous cruelty. This prospect, however, does not dissuade him. On the contrary. It incites him.

There is this to be said for the stabbing pain of the spindle prick. It anchors her, locates a self when all else in sleep unbinds and scatters it. When a passing prince asks who she is, she replies simply, having no reply other to offer, I am that hurts. This prince—if prince he be, and who can truly say as he/it drifts shapeshifting past, substantial as a fog at sea?—is but one of countless princes who have visited her in her dreams, her hundred years of dreams, unceasing, without so much as day's respite. None remembered of course, no memory of her dreams at all, each forgotten in the very dreaming of them as though to dream them were to erase them. And yet, so often have her dreams revisited fragments and images of dreams dreamt before, a sort of recognizable architecture has grown up around them, such that, though each dream is, must be, intrinsically unique, there is an ambient familiarity about them all that consoles her as memory might, did she know it, and somewhat teaches her whereto to flee when terror engulfs her like a sudden wicked spell. One such refuge is what she sometimes supposes to be a kitchen or a servery, else a strange gallery with hearth and wooden tub, oft as not at ground level with a packed earthen floor and yet with grand views out an oriel's elevated bay. Sometimes there are walls, doors, ceilings, sometimes not. Sometimes she drifts in and out of this room alone, or it appears, in its drafty solitude, around her, but sometimes familiar faces greet her, if none she knows to name, like all else ever changing. Except for one perhaps: a loving old crone, hideously ugly and vaguely threatening, yet dearer to her in her dreams than any other, even courting princes.

Well, old crone. Ugly. Thank you very much. Has that smug sleeper paused to consider how she will look and smell after a hundred years, lying comatose and untended in an unchanged bed? A century of collected menses alone should stagger the lustiest of princes. The curse of the bad fairy, yes. She has reminded the forgetful creature of this in her dreams, has described the stagnant and verminous pallet whereon she idly snoozes and croned her indelible images of human decrepitude, has recounted for her the ancient legends of saints awaking from a hundred years of sleep, glimpsing with dismay the changes the world has suffered, and immediately crumbling into dust. Her little hearthside entertainments. Which are momentarily disturbing perhaps, causing her charge's inner organs to twitch and burble faintly, but nothing sticks in that wastrel's empty head, nothing except her perverse dream of love-struck princes. Or maybe she knows, instinctively, about the bewitching power of desire, knows that, in the realm first kisses, and this first kiss firstmost, she *is* beautiful, must be, the fairy herself will see to that, is obliged to, must freshen her flesh and wipe her bum, costume and coiffure her, sweep the room of all morbidity and cushion her for he who will come in lustrous opulence. Alone, the fragrances at her disposal would make a pope swoon and a saint cast off, his britches afore, eternity. No, all these moral lessons with which the fairy ornaments the century's dreaming are mere fancies invented for her own consolation while awaiting that which she herself in her ingenerate ambivalence, has ordained.

CONSTRUCTING A READING

1. Robert Coover's work has been called "experimental fiction." What's he experimenting with? And how? And why?
2. Take a passage of about 250 words and with your group members, try to work out all of the generic variations that Coover is using and why.
3. Are you disturbed by this excerpt? Why?

CHAPTER SIX

Narrative Perspectives:
How Readers Follow the Story

HOW NARRATIVE PERSPECTIVES WORK

Often, in conversation, someone asks you to assume a perspective on the topic of discussion that differs from your own. A parent asks you to imagine her worry when you stay out late. A friend expects you to share her embarrassment when she realizes that her dress is unzipped. When you agree to do that—to change the perspective from which you look at things—you don't, of course, stop being yourself. What happens, instead, is that you have a kind of double vision. You see your friend's embarrassment but you also see the humor in her predicament. You grant your mother's worry but you still think you are capable of taking care of yourself.

In this chapter, we shall look at some of the ways in which *texts* might be said to guide readers to consider other perspectives. Narrators and characters—and even generic characteristics—can be thought of as saying to the reader, "try to see things from another viewpoint. Look at the story in a different way." Such guidelines are called narrative perspectives. A *narrative perspective* is the viewpoint from which a reader, at any given moment in a reading act, raises the questions that propel his or her reading. For instance, a reader of "Babylon Revisited" might ask, "what is Marion Peters going to think about Charles Wales's drunken friends?" To raise that question, the reader needs to engage Marion Peters's perspective on the situation. But the same reader might also sympathize with Charles and hope he will get custody of his daughter while simultaneously wondering whether Honoria will suffer from yet another wrenching change.

As we discussed in Chapter Two, it is conventional to expect texts to be consistent. Therefore, if we sympathize with Charles at the beginning, we expect to continue to find him sympathetic. We also expect that a character's behavior at the end of a story will be consistent with that character's behavior in the beginning. If a character says he loves his father, for example, a reader would be surprised to discover that he had killed his father. When a character's name is Arnold Friend, a reader is likely to ask whether his actions are consistent with friendship.

Genres and plots also create perspectives: if a story starts out as realistic (as in "Young Goodman Brown"), a reader will be surprised to encounter magic midway through; when a sitcom starts out as carefree and funny, the audience expects that it will not suddenly turn tragic.

But of course, we would quickly lose interest in reading if stories met our expectations all the time. Discourse—the "how" of a story, the way in which it is told—especially in narrative texts, frustrates that impulse to build consistencies, and it does so by establishing multiple perspectives. As a reader tries to see a story from the narrator's perspective, for example, she must also encounter the perspectives of the other characters, many of which differ from the narrator's. Theodore Roethke's poem, "The Meadow Mouse," gives us an example and a place to start.

The Meadow Mouse
Theodore Roethke

1

In a shoe box stuffed in an old nylon stocking
Sleeps the baby mouse I found in the meadow,
Where he trembled and shook beneath a stick
Till I caught him up by the tail and brought him in,
Cradled in my hand,
A little quaker, the whole body of him trembling,
His absurd whiskers sticking out like a cartoon-mouse,
His feet like small leaves,
Little lizard-feet,
Whitish and spread wide when he tried to struggle away,
Wriggling like a miniscule puppy.

Now he's eaten his three kinds of cheese and drunk from his bottle-cap
        watering-trough—
So much he just lies in one corner,
His tail curled under him, his belly big
As his head; his bat-like ears
Twitching, tilting toward the least sound.

Do I imagine he no longer trembles
When I come close to him?
He seems no longer to tremble.

2

But this morning the shoe-box house on the back porch is empty.
Where has he gone, my meadow mouse,
My thumb of a child that nuzzled in my palm?—
To run under the hawk's wing,
Under the eye of the great owl watching from the elm-tree,
To live by courtesy of the shrike, the snake, the tom-cat.

I think of the nestling fallen into the deep grass,
The turtle gasping in the dusty rubble of the highway,
The paralytic stunned in the tub, and the water rising,—
All things innocent, hapless, forsaken.

Notice first that this poem tells a story—a story narrated from the perspective of one of its characters who is also the speaker. Our tendency is to identify or empathize with him. (This tendency is culturally established—readers will identify with and believe the narrator of a story until presented with good reasons not to.) In Roethke's poem, then, readers will generally accept that generic convention and understand the speaker's desire to protect the little creature from predators. From the speaker's perspective, the story is sad but inevitable: even though the speaker has carefully rescued the tiny rodent, given him three kinds of cheeses to eat, and made a watering trough from a bottle cap, still, the mouse escapes. The speaker, we might think, is basically a good person who thought his care could overpower a wild creature's instinct for freedom.

In order to form this reading, however, a reader needs also to adopt the perspective of the mouse—the tiny "hero" of an "escape-from-captivity" story. What happens, in other words, is that the narrative asks us to identify both with the narrating voice who wants to make the mouse safe by limiting its freedom and with the mouse that instinctively needs that freedom so much as to be heedless of its own safety. We sympathize with the speaker's realization that one cannot always protect everyone from danger, that creatures tend to want to be independent—even if their independence puts them in peril. With the speaker, we probably think about pets or even people who ran away from us in spite of our best efforts to make them comfortable, safe, and happy. But we also sympathize with the mouse's need for freedom from constraint.

As we engage these conflicting perspectives, we are also aware that a story is unfolding, a story that engages our generic expectations: what happens next? And then what? And why? Our sense of minimal story leads us to expect that disequilibrium will enter the story of the speaker's saving/trapping the mouse, and that the speaker's state of mind will change before the end of the story. Eventually we decide how to respond. Are we "for" the mouse or the man? Or for the man coming to understand the mouse? Or do we find ourselves engaged with both perspectives? The narrative may guide us in one direction or the other, but ultimately the reader decides.

Narrative Perspectives and Point of View

In your other courses, you may have worked with the term *point of view*. It is important in this discussion to distinguish *point of view* from *narrative perspective*. Point of view is an answer to the question "who tells the story?" The answer to that question is always "the narrator" (like the speaker in a poem), but there are many different kinds of narrators. Literary theorists discriminate kinds of narrators in terms of two criteria:

1. The amount and kind of information they are presumed to have and/or reveal about the story they tell
2. The extent to which they participate in their stories.

Robert Frost's narrator/speaker in "Home Burial" tells us what Amy and her husband say and do but offers no access to their thoughts. Hawthorne's narrator, on the other hand, tells us what goes on in the mind of Young Goodman Brown while leaving us in the dark about Faith's motivations. Neither narrator participates in the action of the story, whereas Howard Nemerov's narrator/speaker is also a character in the story of "Long Distance."

The term *narrative perspectives*, on the other hand, describes not only "who tells the story" but also the other characters, the plot, the genre, and the *narratee* (the character or characters, inside or outside the fiction, to whom the story is told). In the terms of our discussion of narrative perspectives in this book, the narrator will be understood as only one perspective among many in a given text, a fictional character in a text just like any other character. Multiple perspectives of any text can be and often are in conflict with one another. That conflict, however, is what makes reading interesting.

KINDS OF NARRATORS

Third-Person Omniscient Narrators

Third-person omniscient narrators are probably the most familiar. The word *omniscient* is derived from Latin roots meaning "to know" and "all." Thus, an *omniscient narrator* is one who knows everything about the story. Such a narrator is understood to know (and be capable of revealing) all of the characters' interiority, that is, their motivations and thoughts. Sarah Orne Jewett's "A White Heron" offers a sometimes surprising example of omniscient narration.

A White Heron
Sarah Orne Jewett

The woods were already filled with shadows one June evening, just before eight o'clock, though a bright sunset still glimmered faintly among the trunks of the trees. A little girl   The narrator begins by giving
was driving home her cow, a plodding, dilatory,   us an overview of the situation.
provoking creature in her behavior, but a valued companion for all that. They were going away from the western light, and striking deep into the dark woods, but their feet were familiar with the path, and it was no matter whether their eyes could see it or
not. There was hardly a night the summer through   The narrator knows Sylvia's
when the old cow could be found waiting at the pas-   and the cow's thoughts.
ture bars; on the contrary, it was her greatest pleasure to hide herself away among the high huckleberry bushes, and though she wore a loud bell she had made the discovery that if one stood perfectly still it would not ring. So Sylvia had to hunt for her until she
found her, and call Co'! Co'! with never an   The narrator reveals the family's
answering Moo, until her childish patience was   motives for keeping the cow in
quite spent. If the creature had not given good   spite of her annoying behavior.
milk and plenty of it, the case would have seemed
very different to her owners. Besides, Sylvia had all the time there was, and very little use to make of it. Sometimes in pleasant weather it was a consolation to look upon the cow's pranks as an intelligent attempt to play hide and seek, and as the child had no playmates she lent herself to this amusement with a good deal of zest. Though this chase had been so long that the wary animal herself had given an unusual signal of her whereabouts, Sylvia had only laughed when she came upon Mistress Moolly at the swamp-side, and urged her affectionately homeward with a twig of birch leaves. The old cow was not inclined to wander farther, she even turned in the right direction for once as they left the pasture, and stepped along the road at a good pace. She was quite ready to be milked now, and seldom stopped to browse. Sylvia wondered what her grandmother would say because they were so late. It was a great while since she had left home at half past five o'clock, but everybody knew the difficulty of making this errand a short one. Mrs. Tilley had chased the horned torment too many summer evenings herself to blame any one else for lingering, and was only thankful as she waited that she had Sylvia, nowadays, to give such valuable assistance. The good woman suspected that Sylvia loitered occasionally on her own account; there never was such a child for straying about out-of-doors since the world was made! Everybody said that it was a good change for a little maid
who had tried to grow for eight years   The narrator reveals information about Sylvia's
in a crowded manufacturing town,   past, thereby explaining why the child enjoys
but, as for Sylvia herself, it seemed as   taking care of the cow. The pastoral setting is a
if she never had been alive at all before   new experience for her.

she came to live at the farm. She thought often with wistful compassion of a wretched dry geranium that belonged to a town neighbor.

"'Afraid of folks,'" old Mrs. Tilley said to herself, with a smile, after she had made the unlikely choice of Sylvia from her daughter's houseful of children, and was returning to the farm. "'Afraid of folks,' they said! I guess she won't be troubled no great with 'em up to the old place!" When they reached the door of the lonely house and stopped to unlock it, and the cat came to purr loudly, and rub against them, a deserted pussy, indeed, but fat with young robins, Sylvia whispered that this was a beautiful place to live in, and she never should wish to go home.

The companions followed the shady wood road, the cow taking slow steps, and the child very fast ones. The cow stopped long at the brook to drink, as if the pasture were not half a swamp, and Sylvia stood still and waited, letting her bare feet cool themselves in the shoal water, while the great twilight moths struck softly against her. She waded on through the brook as the cow moved away, and listened to the thrushes with a heart that beat fast with pleasure. There was a stirring in the great boughs overhead. They were full of little birds and beasts that seemed to be wide awake, and going about their world, or else saying good-night to each other in sleepy twitters. Sylvia herself felt sleepy as she walked along. However, it was not much farther to the house, and the air was soft and sweet. She was not often in the woods so late as this, and it made her feel as if she were a part of the gray shadows and the moving leaves. She was just thinking how long it seemed since she first came to the farm a year ago, and wondering if everything went on in the noisy town just the same as when she was there; the thought of the great redfaced boy who used to chase and frighten her made her hurry along the path to escape from the shadow of the trees.

No longer limited to human and bovine consciousness, the narrator even translates birdspeak!

The narrator reveals how her past experiences affect Sylvia's current emotions and actions.

Suddenly this little woods girl is horror-stricken to hear a clear whistle not very far away. Not a bird's whistle, which would have a sort of friendliness, but a boy's whistle, determined, and somewhat aggressive. Sylvia left the cow to whatever sad fate might await her, and stepped discreetly aside into the bushes, but she was just too late. The enemy had discovered her, and called out in a very cheerful and persuasive tone, "Halloa, little girl, how far is it to the road?" and trembling Sylvia answered almost inaudibly, "A good ways."

She did not dare to look boldly at the tall young man, who carried a gun over his shoulder, but she came out of her bush and again followed the cow, while he walked alongside.

"I have been hunting for some birds," the stranger said kindly, "and I have lost my way, and need a friend very much. Don't be afraid," he added gallantly. "Speak up and tell me what your name is, and whether you think I can spend the night at your house, and go out gunning early in the morning."

Sylvia was more alarmed than before. Would not her grandmother consider her much to blame? But who could have foreseen such an accident as this? It did not appear to be her fault, and she hung her head as if the stem of it were broken, but managed to answer, "Sylvy," with much effort when her companion again asked her name.

Mrs. Tilley was standing in the doorway when the trio came into view. The cow gave a loud moo by way of explanation.

"Yes, you'd better speak up for yourself, you old trial! Where'd she tucked herself away this time, Sylvy?" Sylvia kept an awed silence; she knew by instinct that her grandmother did not comprehend the gravity of the situation. She must be mistaking the stranger for one of the farmer lads of the region.

The young man stood his gun beside the door, and dropped a heavy game bag beside it; then he bade Mrs. Tilley good evening, and repeated his wayfarer's story, and asked if he could have a night's lodging.

> The narrator reveals that Mrs. Tilley is more aware of the animal than of the fact that her granddaughter has returned with a male stranger. What do you think about Mrs. Tilley?

"Put me anywhere you like," he said. "I must be off early in the morning, before day; but I am very hungry, indeed. You can give me some milk at any rate, that's plain."

"Dear sakes, yes," responded the hostess, whose long slumbering hospitality seemed to be easily awakened. "You might fare better if you went out on the main road a mile or so, but you're welcome to what we've got. I'll milk right off, and you make yourself at home. You can sleep on husks or feathers," she proffered graciously. "I raised them all myself. There's good pasturing for geese just below here towards the ma'sh. Now step round and set a plate for the gentleman, Sylvy!" And Sylvia promptly stepped. She was glad to have something to do, and she was hungry herself.

It was a surprise to find so clean and comfortable a dwelling in this New England wilderness. The young man had known the horrors of its most primitive housekeeping, and the

> The narrator's omniscience extends to the young man's thoughts and even to his past—before this story begins.

dreary squalor of that level of society which does not rebel at the companionship of hens. This was the best thrift of an old-fashioned farmstead, though on such a small scale that it seemed like a hermitage. He listened eagerly to the old woman's quaint talk, he watched Sylvia's pale face and shining gray eyes with ever growing enthusiasm, and insisted that this was the best supper he had eaten for a month; then, afterward, the newmade friends sat down in the doorway together while the moon came up.

Soon it would be berry time, and Sylvia was a great help at picking.

The cow was a good milker, though a plaguy thing to keep track of, the hostess gossiped frankly, adding presently that she had buried four children, so that Sylvia's mother, and a son (who might be dead) in California were all the children she had left. "Dan, my boy, was a great hand to go gunning," she explained sadly. "I never wanted for pa'tridges or gray squer'ls while he was to home. He's been a great wand'rer, I expect, and he's no hand to write letters. There, I don't blame him, I'd ha' seen the world myself if it had been so I could.

"Sylvia takes after him," the grandmother continued affectionately, after a minute's pause. "There ain't a foot o'ground she don't know her way over, and the wild creatur's counts her one o'themselves. Squer'ls she'll tame to come an' feed right out o' her hands, and all sorts o' birds. Last winter she got the jay-birds to bangeing here, and I believe she'd 'a' scanted herself of her own meals to have plenty to throw out amongst 'em, if I hadn't kep' watch. Anything but crows, I tell her, I'm willin' to help support—though Dan he went an' tamed one o' them that did seem to have reason same as folks. It was round here a good spell after he went away. Dan an' his father they didn't hitch—but he never held up his head ag'in after Dan had dared him an' gone off."

The guest did not notice this hint of family sorrows in his eager interest in something else. "So Sylvy knows all about birds, does she?" he exclaimed, as he looked round at the little girl who sat, very demure but increasingly sleepy, in the moonlight. "I am making a collection of birds myself. I have been at it ever since I was a boy." (Mrs. Tilley smiled.) "There are two or three very rare ones I have been hunting for these five years. I mean to get them on my own ground if they can be found."

The narrator even knows what the young man is not thinking or noticing. But by mentioning what the ornithologist is not thinking, the narrator invites a response. How do you respond? What is your attitude toward the young man when you are told that he does not notice Mrs Tilley's sadness?

"Do you cage 'em up?" asked Mrs. Tilley doubtfully, in response to this enthusiastic announcement.

"Oh, no, they're stuffed and preserved, dozens and dozens of them," said the ornithologist, "and I have shot or snared every one myself. I caught a glimpse of a white heron three miles from here on Saturday, and I have followed it in this direction. They have never been found in this district at all. The little white heron, it is," and he turned again to look at Sylvia with the hope of discovering that the rare bird was one of her acquaintances.

But Sylvia was watching a hop-toad in the narrow footpath.

"You would know the heron if you saw it," the stranger continued eagerly. "A queer tall white bird with soft feathers and long thin legs. And it would have a nest perhaps in the top of a high tree, made of sticks, something like a hawk's nest."

Sylvia's heart gave a wild beat; she knew that strange white bird, and had once stolen softly near where it stood in some bright green swamp grass, away over at the other side of the woods. There was an open place where the sunshine always seemed strangely yellow and hot, where tall, nodding rushes grew, and her grandmother had warned her that she might sink in the soft black mud underneath and never be heard of more. Not far beyond were the salt marshes and beyond those was the sea, the sea which Sylvia wondered and dreamed about, but never had looked upon, though its great voice could often be heard above the noise of the woods on stormy nights.

Here the narrator comments on the effects of human intervention in the lives of other creatures.

"I can't think of anything I should like so much as to find that heron's nest," the handsome stranger was saying. "I would give ten dollars to anybody who could show it to me," he added desperately, "and I mean to spend my whole vacation hunting for it if need be. Perhaps it was only migrating, or had been chased out of its own region by some bird of prey."

Mrs. Tilley gave amazed attention to all this, but Sylvia still watched the toad, not divining, as she might have done at some calmer time, that the creature wished to get to its hole under the doorstep, and was much hindered by the unusual spectators at that hour of the evening. No amount of thought, that night, could decide how many wished-for-treasures the ten dollars, so lightly spoken of, would buy.

The narrator knows the toad's thoughts.

The next day the young sportsman hovered about the woods, and Sylvia kept him company, having lost her first fear of the friendly lad, who proved to be most kind and sympathetic. He told her many things about the birds and what they knew and where they lived and what they did with themselves. And he gave her a jack-knife, which she thought as great a treasure as if she were a desert-islander. All day long he did not once make her troubled or afraid except when he brought down some unsuspecting singing creature from its bough. Sylvia would have liked him vastly better without his gun; she could not understand why he killed the very birds he seemed to like so much. But as the day waned, Sylvia still watched the young man with loving admiration. She had never seen anybody so charming and delightful; the woman's heart, asleep in the child, was vaguely thrilled by a dream of love. Some premonition of that great power stirred and swayed these young foresters who traversed the solemn woodlands with soft-footed silent care. They stopped to listen to a bird's song; they pressed forward again eagerly, parting the branches—speaking to each other rarely and in whispers; the young man going first and Sylvia following, fascinated, a few steps behind, with her gray eyes dark with excitement.

She grieved because the longed-for white heron was elusive, but she did not lead the guest, she only followed, and there was no such thing as speaking first. The sound of her own unquestioned voice would have terrified her—it was hard enough to answer yes or no when there was need of that. At last evening began to fall, and they drove

The narrator characterizes Sylvia by describing her inferiority. How do you respond to her attitude toward the stranger?

the cow home together, and Sylvia smiled with pleasure when they came to the place where she heard the whistle and was afraid only the night before.

Half a mile from home, at the farther edge of the woods, where the land was highest, a great pine tree stood, the last of its generation. Whether it was left for a boundary mark, or for what reason, no one could say; the woodchoppers who had felled its mates were dead and gone long ago, and a whole forest of sturdy trees, pines and oaks and maples, had grown again. But the stately head of this old pine towered above them all and made a landmark for sea and shore miles and miles away.

On some questions, even the narrator admits ignorance. Why do you suppose the question of the tree's history is raised and then left unanswered?

Sylvia knew it well. She had always believed that whoever climbed to the top of it could see the ocean; and the little girl had often laid her hand on the great rough trunk and looked up wistfully at those dark boughs that the wind always stirred, no matter how hot and still the air might be below. Now she thought of the tree with a new excitement, for why, if one climbed it at break of day, could not one see all the world, and easily discover whence the white heron flew, and mark the place, and find the hidden nest?

What a spirit of adventure, what wild ambition! What fancied triumph and delight and glory for the later morning when she could make known the secret! It was almost too real and too great for the childish heart to bear.

All night the door of the little house stood open, and the whippoorwills came and sang upon the very step. The young sportsman and his old hostess were sound asleep, but Sylvia's great design kept her broad awake and watching. She forgot to think of sleep. The short summer night seemed as long as the winter darkness, and at last when the whippoorwills ceased, and she was afraid the morning would after all come too soon, she stole out of the house and followed the pasture path through the woods, hastening toward the open ground beyond, listening with a sense of comfort and companionship to the drowsy twitter of a halfawakened bird, whose perch she had jarred in passing. Alas, if the great wave of human interest which flooded for the first time this dull little life should sweep away the satisfactions of an existence heart to heart with nature and the dumb life of the forest!

Here, the narrator comments on the action.

There was the huge tree asleep yet in the paling moonlight, and small and hopeful Sylvia began with utmost bravery to mount to the top of it, with tingling, eager blood coursing the channels of her whole frame, with her bare feet and fingers, that pinched and held like bird's claws to the monstrous ladder reaching up, up, almost to the sky itself. First she must mount the white oak tree that grew alongside, where she was almost lost among the dark branches and the green leaves heavy and wet with dew; a bird fluttered off its nest, and a red squirrel ran to and fro and scolded pettishly at the harmless housebreaker. Sylvia felt her way easily. She had often climbed there, and knew that higher still one of the oak's upper branches chafed against the pine trunk, just where its lower boughs were set close together. There, when she made the dangerous pass from one tree to the other, the great enterprise would really begin.

She crept out along the swaying oak limb at last, and took the daring step across into the old pinetree. The way was harder than she thought; she must reach far and hold fast, the sharp dry twigs caught and held her and scratched her like angry talons, the pitch made her thin little fingers clumsy and stiff as she went round and round the tree's great stem, higher and higher upward. The sparrows and robins in the woods below were beginning to wake and twitter to the dawn, yet it seemed much lighter there aloft in the pinetree, and the child knew that she must hurry if her project were to be of any use.

The tree seemed to lengthen itself out as she went up, and to reach farther and farther upward. It was like a great main-mast to the voyaging earth; it must truly have been amazed that morning through all its ponderous frame as it felt this determined spark of human spirit creeping and climbing from higher branch to branch. Who knows how steadily the least twigs held themselves to advantage this light, weak creature on her way! The old pine must have loved his new dependent. More than all the hawks, and bats, and moths, and even the sweetvoiced thrushes, was the brave, beating heart of the solitary gray-eyed child. And the tree stood still and held away the winds that June morning while the dawn grew bright in the east.

As the narrator describes what the tree is thinking, what are you thinking? How do you react to this omniscience?

Sylvia's face was like a pale star, if one had seen it from the ground, when the last thorny bough was past, and she stood trembling and tired but wholly triumphant, high in the treetop. Yes, there was the sea with the dawning sun making a golden dazzle over it, and toward that glorious east new two hawks with slowmoving pinions. How low they looked in the air from that height when before one had only seen them far up, and dark against the blue sky. Their gray feathers were as soft as moths; they seemed only a little way from the tree, and Sylvia felt as if she too could go flying away among the clouds. Westward, the woodlands and farms reached miles and miles into the distance; here and there were church steeples, and white villages; truly it was a vast and awesome world.

The birds sang louder and louder. At last the sun came up bewilderingly bright. Sylvia could see the white sails of ships out at sea, and the clouds that were purple and rosecolored and yellow at first began to fade away. Where was the white heron's nest in the sea of green branches, and was this wonderful sight and pageant of the world the only reward for having climbed to such a giddy height? Now look down again, Sylvia, where the green marsh is set among the shining birches and dark hemlocks; there where you saw the white heron once you will see him again; look, look! a white spot of him like a single floating feather comes up from the dead hemlock and grows larger, and rises, and comes

How do you respond to the narrator's giving Sylvia a direct order about where to look for the white herons?

close at last, and goes by the landmark pine with a steady sweep of wing and outstretched slender neck and crested head. And wait! wait! do not move a foot or a finger, little girl, do not send an arrow of light and consciousness from your two eager eyes, for the heron has perched on a pine bough not far beyond yours, and cries back to his mate on the nest, and plumes his feathers for the new day!

The child gives a long sigh a minute later when a company of shouting catbirds comes also to the tree, and vexed by their fluttering and lawlessness the solemn heron goes away. She knows his secret now, the wild, light, slender bird that floats and wavers, and goes back like an arrow presently to his home in the green world beneath. Then Sylvia, well satisfied, makes her perilous way down again, not daring to look far below the branch she stands on, ready to cry sometimes because her fingers ache and her lamed feet slip. Wondering over and over again what the stranger would say to her, and what he would think when she told him how to find his way straight to the heron's nest.

"Sylvy, Sylvy!" called the busy old grandmother again and again, but nobody answered, and the small husk bed was empty, and Sylvia had disappeared.

The guest waked from a dream, and remembering his day's pleasure hurried to dress himself that it might sooner begin. He was sure from the way the shy little girl looked once or twice yesterday that she had at least seen the white heron, and now she must really be persuaded to tell. Here she comes now, paler than ever, and her worn old frock is torn and tattered, and smeared with pine pitch. The grandmother and the sportsman stand in the door together and question her, and the splendid moment has come to speak of the dead hemlock-tree by the green marsh.

But Sylvia does not speak after all, though the old grandmother fretfully rebukes her, and the young man's kind appealing eyes are looking straight in her own. He can make them rich with money; he was promised it, and they are poor now. He is so well worth making happy, and he waits to hear the story she can tell.

No, she must keep silence! What is it that suddenly forbids her and makes her dumb? Has she been nine years growing, and now, when the great world for the first time puts out a hand to her, must she thrust it aside for a bird's sake? The murmur of the pine's green branches is in her ears, she remembers how the white heron came flying through the golden air and how they watched the sea and the morning together, and Sylvia cannot speak, she cannot tell the heron's secret and give its life away.

Here, the narrator reveals Sylvia's internal conflict and then resolves it. Why? Do more recent stories give the reader these kinds of directions? Why do you suppose Jewett does?

Dear loyalty, that suffered a sharp pang as the guest went away disappointed later in the day, that could have served and followed him and loved him as a dog loves! Many a night Sylvia heard the echo of his whistle haunting the pasture path as she came home with the loitering cow. She forgot even her sorrow at the sharp report of his gun and the piteous sight of thrushes and sparrows dropping silent to the ground, their songs hushed and their pretty feathers stained and wet with blood. Were the birds better friends than their hunter might have been—who can tell? Whatever treasures were lost to her, woodlands and summer-time, remember! Bring your gifts and graces and tell your secrets to this lonely country child!

CONSTRUCTING A READING

1. With your group, discuss the ways in which the omniscient narration in this story guides a reader toward seeing a theme in the work. Ask yourselves, in other words, "what seems to be the moral of this story?" and then describe the ways in which the techniques of its narration have guided you toward making that reading.
2. This story was first published in 1886. With your group members, try to think of ways in which the narrative perspective might be changed to make it more contemporary. What would this story be like without the narrator's omniscient comments? How would it look as a film?

Limited Omniscient Narrators

A narrator with *limited omniscience* knows and tells the interiority of some but not all of a story's characters. The narrator of "Babylon Revisited" (in Chapter Five) has limited omniscience. He knows what Charlie Wales *thinks*, but can only describe what the other characters *do*. In the confrontation between Charles and the Peterses, for example, the narrator lets us in on Charlie's thoughts: he tells us that the protagonist "knew he would have to take a beating." But the narrator only reports the actions of Marion Peters; she "played with the black stars on her necklace and frowned."

Objective Narrators

An *objective narrator*, rather like a video camera panning around the text's action, describes what the characters do and say. This narrator reports what would be visible and audible to someone in the room but makes no commentary on the characters' thoughts and motives.

Ernest Hemingway's "Hills Like White Elephants" offers an example of objective narration. As you read, consider the ways in which this kind of narration calls upon you to imagine the consciousness of the characters and to speculate about their motivations and meanings.

Hills Like White Elephants

Ernest Hemingway

The hills across the valley of the Ebro were long and white. On this side there was no shade and no trees and the station was between two lines of rails in the sun. Close against the side of the station there was a warm shadow of the building and a curtain, made of strings of bamboo beads, hung across the open door into the bar, to keep out flies. The American and the girl with him sat at a table in the shade, outside the building. It was very hot and the express from Barcelona would come in forty minutes. It stopped at this junction for two minutes and went on to Madrid.

"What should we drink?" the girl asked. She had taken off her hat and put it on the table.

"It's pretty hot," the man said.

"Let's drink beer."

"Dos cervezas," the man said into the curtain.

"Big ones?" a woman asked from the doorway.

"Yes. Two big ones."

The woman brought two glasses of beer and two felt pads. She put the felt pads and the beer glasses on the table and looked at the man and the girl. The girl was looking off at the line of hills. They were white in the sun and the country was brown and dry.

"They look like white elephants," she said.

"I've never seen one," the man drank his beer.

"No, you wouldn't have."

"I might have," the man said. "Just because you say I wouldn't have doesn't prove anything."

The girl looked at the bead curtain. "They've painted something on it," she said. "What does it say?"

"Anis del Toro. It's a drink."

"Could we try it?"

The man called "Listen" through the curtain. The woman came out from the bar.

"Four reales."

"We want two Anis del Toro."

"With water?"

"Do you want it with water?"

"I don't know," the girl said. "Is it good with water?"

"It's all right."

"You want them with water?" asked the woman.

"Yes, with water."

"It tastes like licorice," the girl said and put the glass down.

"That's the way with everything."

"Yes," said the girl. "Everything tastes of licorice. Especially all the things you've waited so long for, like absinthe."

"Oh, cut it out."

"You started it," the girl said. "I was being amused. I was having a fine time."

"Well, let's try and have a fine time."

"All right. I was trying. I said the mountains looked like white elephants. Wasn't that bright?"

"That was bright."

"I wanted to try this new drink. That's all we do, isn't it—look at things and try new drinks?"

"I guess so."

The girl looked across at the hills.

"They're lovely hills," she said. "They don't really look like white elephants. I just meant the coloring of their skin through the trees."

"Should we have another drink?"

"All right."

The warm wind blew the bead curtain against the table.

"The beer's nice and cool," the man said.

"It's lovely," the girl said.

"It's really an awfully simple operation, Jig," the man said. "It's not really an operation at all."

The girl looked at the ground the table legs rested on.

"I know you wouldn't mind it, Jig. It's really not anything. It's just to let the air in."

The girl did not say anything.

"I'll go with you and I'll stay with you all the time. They just let the air in and then it's all perfectly natural."

"Then what will we do afterward?"

"We'll be fine afterward. Just like we were before."

"What makes you think so?"

"That's the only thing that bothers us. It's the only thing that's made us unhappy."

The girl looked at the bead curtain, put her hand out and took hold of two of the strings of beads.

"And you think then we'll be all right and be happy."

"I know we will. You don't have to be afraid. I've known lots of people that have done it."

"So have I," said the girl. "And afterward they were all so happy."

"Well," the man said, "if you don't want to you don't have to. 1 wouldn't have you do it if you didn't want to. But I know it's perfectly simple."

"And you really want to?"

"I think it's the best thing to do. But I don't want you to do it if you don't really want to."

"And if I do it you'll be happy and things will be like they were and you'll love me?"

"I love you now. You know I love you."

"I know. But if I do it, then it will be nice again if I say things are like white elephants, and you'll like it?"

"I'll love it. I love it now but I just can't think about it. You know how I get when I worry."

"If I do it you won't ever worry?"

"I won't worry about that because it's perfectly simple."

"Then I'll do it. Because I don't care about me."

"What do you mean?"

"I don't care about me."

"Well, I care about you."

"Oh, yes. But I don't care about me. And I'll do it and then everything will be fine."

"I don't want you to do it if you feel that way."

The girl stood up and walked to the end of the station. Across, on the other side, were fields of grain and trees along the banks of the Ebro. Far away, beyond the river, were mountains. The shadow of a cloud moved across the field of grain and she saw the river through the trees.

"And we could have all this," she said. "And we could have everything and every day we make it more impossible."

"What did you say?"

"I said we could have everything."

"We can have everything."

"No, we can't."

"We can have the whole world."

"No, we can't."

"We can go everywhere."

"No, we can't. It isn't ours any more."

"It's ours."

"No, it isn't. And once they take it away, you never get it back."

"But they haven't taken it away."

"We'll wait and see."

"Come on back in the shade," he said. "You mustn't feel that way."

"I don't feel any way," the girl said. "I just know things."

"I don't want you to do anything that you don't want to do—"

"Nor that isn't good for me," she said. "I know. Could we have another beer?"

"All right. But you've got to realize—"

"I realize," the girl said. "Can't we maybe stop talking?"

They sat down at the table and the girl looked across at the hills on the dry side of the valley and the man looked at her and at the table.

"You've got to realize," he said, "that I don't want you to do it if you don't want to. I'm perfectly willing to go through with it if it means anything to you."

"Doesn't it mean anything to you? We could get along."

"Of course it does. But I don't want anybody but you. I don't want any one else. And I know it's perfectly simple."

"Yes, you know it's perfectly simple."

"It's all right for you to say that, but I do know it."

"Would you do something for me now?"

"I'd do anything for you."

"Would you please please please please please please please stop talking?"

He did not say anything but looked at the bags against the wall of the station. There were labels on them from all the hotels where they had spent nights.

"But I don't want you to," he said, "I don't care anything about it."

"I'll scream," the girl said.

The woman came out through the curtains with two glasses of beer and put them down on the damp felt pads. "The train comes in five minutes," she said.

"What did she say?" asked the girl.

"That the train is coming in five minutes."

The girl smiled brightly at the woman, to thank her.

"I'd better take the bags over to the other side of the station," the man said. She smiled at him.

"All right. Then come back and we'll finish the beer."

He picked up the two heavy bags and carried them around the station to the other tracks. He looked up the tracks but could not see the train. Coming back, he walked through the barroom, where people waiting for the train were drinking. He drank an Anis at the bar and looked at the people. They were all waiting reasonably for the train. He went out through the bead curtain. She was sitting at the table and smiled at him.

"Do you feel better?" he asked.

"I feel fine," she said. "There's nothing wrong with me. I feel fine."

CONSTRUCTING A READING

1. Some readers are puzzled by the title of the story. The phrase *white elephant* is an instance of a trope—a metaphor. If you are unfamiliar with the metaphoric use of the term, look it up in an unabridged dictionary. Then, decide how the title is relevant to the rest of the story. Who or what is the white elephant here?

2. Objective narration generates particular kinds of gaps about continuity and context. At your teacher's direction, divide the story into segments. In groups (one per segment) write narration for the conversation between Jig and the man as though you were a limited omniscient narrator (having

access to the thoughts of one, but not the other, character). Then, write the scene as though you were an omniscient narrator.

3. With your group members, make a list of five gap questions. With the rest of your class, discuss how a different kind of narration might have changed your list.
4. The objective narrator withholds quite a bit of information here, leaving the reader to close the gaps. For example, the narrator does not tell us what kind of operation the two characters are talking about. What do you think?
5. What other pieces of information does the narrator withhold?

Indirect Narration: Filter Characters

"Town and Country Lovers," by the South African author Nadine Gordimer, illustrates yet another kind of perspective, sometimes described as that of a *filter character* or a focalized character.

Town and Country Lovers
Nadine Gordimer

One

Dr Franz-Josef von Leinsdorf is a geologist absorbed in his work; wrapped up in it, as the saying goes—year after year the experience of this work enfolds him, swaddling him away from the landscapes, the cities and the people, wherever he lives: Peru, New Zealand, the United States. He's always been like that, his mother could confirm from their native Austria. There, even as a handsome small boy he presented only his profile to her: turned away to his bits of rock and stone. His few relaxations have not changed much since then. An occasional skiing trip, listening to music, reading poetry—Rainer Maria Rilke once stayed in his grandmother's hunting lodge in the forests of Styria and the boy was introduced to Rilke's poems while very young.

Layer upon layer, country after country, wherever his work takes him—and now he has been almost seven years in Africa. First the Côte d'Ivoire, and for the past five years, South Africa. The shortage of skilled manpower brought about his recruitment here. He has no interest in the politics of the countries he works in. His private preoccupation-within-the-preoccupation of his work has been research into underground water-courses, but the mining company that employs him in a senior though not executive capacity is interested only in mineral discovery. So he is much out in the field—which is the veld, here—

seeking new gold, copper, platinum and uranium deposits. When he is at home—on this particular job, in this particular country, this city—he lives in a two-roomed flat in a suburban block with a landscaped garden, and does his shopping at a supermarket conveniently across the street. He is not married—yet. That is how his colleagues, and the typists and secretaries at the mining company's head office, would define his situation. Both men and women would describe him as a good-looking man, in a foreign way, with the lower half of the face dark and middle-aged (his mouth is thin and curving, and no matter how close-shaven his beard shows like fine shot embedded in the skin round mouth and chin) and the upper half contradictorily young, with deep-set eyes (some would say grey, some black), thick eyelashes and brows. A tangled gaze: through which concentration and gleaming thoughtfulness perhaps appear as fire and languor. It is this that the women in the office mean when they remark he's not unattractive. Although the gaze seems to promise, he has never invited any one of them to go out with him. There is the general assumption he probably has a girl who's been picked for him, he's bespoken by one of his own kind, back home in Europe where he comes from. Many of these well-educated Europeans have no intention of becoming permanent immigrants; neither the remnant of white colonial life nor idealistic involvement with Black Africa appeals to them.

One advantage, at least, of living in underdeveloped or half-developed countries is that flats are serviced. All Dr von Leinsdorf has to do for himself is buy his own supplies and cook an evening meal if he doesn't want to go to a restaurant. It is simply a matter of dropping in to the supermarket on his way from his car to his flat after work in the afternoon. He wheels a trolley up and down the shelves, and his simple needs are presented to him in the form of tins, packages, plastic-wrapped meat, cheeses, fruit and vegetables, tubes, bottles . . . At the cashiers' counters where customers must converge and queue there are racks of small items uncategorized, for last-minute purchase. Here, as the coloured girl cashier punches the adding machine, he picks up cigarettes and perhaps a packet of salted nuts or a bar of nougat. Or razor-blades, when he remembers he's running short. One evening in winter he saw that the cardboard display was empty of the brand of blades he preferred, and he drew the cashier's attention to this. These young coloured girls are usually pretty unhelpful, taking money and punching their machines in a manner that asserts with the time-serving obstinacy of the half-literate the limit of any responsibility towards customers, but this one ran an alert glance over the selection of razor-blades, apologized that she was not allowed to leave her post, and said she would see that the stock was replenished 'next time'. A day or two later she recognized him, gravely, as he took his turn before her counter—"I ahssed them, but it's out of stock. You can't get it. I did ahss about it.' He said this didn't matter. 'When it comes in, I can keep a few packets for you.' He thanked her.

He was away with the prospectors the whole of the next week. He arrived

back in town just before nightfall on Friday, and was on his way from car to flat
with his arms full of briefcase, suitcase and canvas bags when someone stopped
him by standing timidly in his path. He was about to dodge round unseeingly
on the crowded pavement but she spoke. 'We got the blades in now. I didn't see
you in the shop this week, but I kept some for when you come. So . . .'

He recognized her. He had never seen her standing before, and she was
wearing a coat. She was rather small and finely-made, for one of them. The
coat was skimpy but no big backside jutted. The cold brought an apricot-grain-
ing of warm colour to her check-bones, beneath which a very small face was
quite delicately hollowed, and the skin was smooth, the subdued satiny colour
of certain yellow wood. That crêpey hair, but worn drawn back flat and in a little knot pushed into one of the cheap wool chignons that (he recognized also)
hung in the miscellany of small goods along with the razor-blades, at the supermarket. He said thanks, he was in a hurry, he'd only just got back from a trip—
shifting the burdens he carried, to demonstrate. 'Oh shame.' She acknowledged
his load. 'But if you want I can run in and get it for you quickly. If you want.'

He saw at once it was perfectly clear that all the girl meant was that she
would go back to the supermarket, buy the blades and bring the packet to him
there where he stood, on the pavement. And it seemed that it was this certainty
that made him say, in the kindly tone of assumption used for an obliging under-
ling, 'I live just across there—*Atlantis*—that flat building. Could you drop them
by, for me—number seven-hundred-and-eighteen, seventh floor—'

She had not before been inside one of these big flat buildings near where
she worked. She lived a bus- and train-ride away to the West of the city, but
this side of the black townships, in a township for people her tint. There was a
pool with ferns, not plastic, and even a little waterfall pumped electrically over
rocks in the entrance of the building *Atlantis;* she didn't wait for the lift marked
GOODS but took the one meant for whites and a white woman with one of those
sausage-dogs on a lead got in with her but did not pay her any attention. The
corridors leading to the flats were nicely glassed-in, not draughty.

He wondered if he should give her a twenty-cent piece for her trouble—
ten cents would be right for a black; but she said, 'Oh no—please, here—'
standing outside his open door and awkwardly pushing back at his hand the
change from the money he'd given her for the razor-blades. She was smiling,
for the first time, in the dignity of refusing a tip. It was difficult to know how to
treat these people, in this country; to know what they expected. In spite of her
embarrassing refusal of the coin, she stood there, completely unassuming, fists
thrust down the pockets of her cheap coat against the cold she'd come in from,
rather pretty thin legs neatly aligned, knee to knee, ankle to ankle.

'Would you like a cup of coffee or something?'

He couldn't very well take her into his study-cum-living-room and offer
her a drink. She followed him to his kitchen, but at the sight of her pulling out
the single chair to drink her cup of coffee at the kitchen table, he said, 'No—
bring it in here—' and led the way into the big room where, among his books

and his papers, his files of scientific correspondence (and the cigar boxes of stamps from the envelopes) his racks of records, his specimens of minerals and rocks, he lived alone.

It was no trouble to her; she saved him the trips to the super-market and brought him his groceries two or three times a week. All he had to do was to leave a list and the key under the doormat, and she would come up in her lunch-hour to collect them, returning to put his supplies in the flat after work. Sometimes he was home and sometimes not. He bought a box of chocolates and left it, with a note, for her to find; and that was acceptable, apparently, as a gratuity.

Her eyes went over everything in the flat although her body tried to conceal its sense of being out of place by remaining as still as possible, holding its contours in the chair offered her as a stranger's coat is set aside and remains exactly as left until the owner takes it up to go. 'You collect?'

'Well, these are specimens—connected with my work.'

'My brother used to collect. Miniatures. With brandy and whisky and that, in them. From all over. Different countries.'

The second time she watched him grinding coffee for the cup he had offered her she said, 'You always do that? Always when you make coffee?'

'But of course. Is it no good, for you? Do I make it too strong?'

'Oh it's just I'm not used to it. We buy it ready—you know, it's in a bottle, you just add a bit to the milk or water.'

He laughed, instructive: 'That's not coffee, that's a synthetic flavouring. In my country we drink only real coffee, fresh, from the beans—you smell how good it is as it's being ground?'

She was stopped by the caretaker and asked what she wanted in the building? Heavy with the *bona fides* of groceries clutched to her body, she said she was working at number 718, on the seventh floor. The caretaker did not tell her not to use the whites' lift; after all, she was not black; her family was very light-skinned.

There was the item 'grey button for trousers' on one of his shopping lists. She said as she unpacked the supermarket carrier, 'Give me the pants, so long, then,' and sat on his sofa that was always gritty with fragments of pipe tobacco, sewing in and out through the four holes of the button with firm, fluent movements of the right hand, gestures supplying the articulacy missing from her talk. She had a little yokel's, peasant's (he thought of it) gap between her two front teeth when she smiled that he didn't much like, but, face ellipsed to three-quarter angle, eyes cast down in concentration with soft lips almost closed, this didn't matter. He said, watching her sew, 'You're a good girl'; and touched her.

She remade the bed every late afternoon when they left it and she dressed again before she went home. After a week there was a day when late afternoon became evening, and they were still in the bed.

'Can't you stay the night?'

'My mother,' she said.

'Phone her. Make an excuse.' He was a foreigner. He had been in the country five years, but he didn't understand that people don't usually have telephones in their houses, where she lived. She got up to dress. He didn't want that tender body to go out in the night cold and kept hindering her with the interruption of his hands; saying nothing. Before she put on her coat, when the body had already disappeared, he spoke. 'But you must make some arrangement.'

'Oh my mother!' Her face opened to fear and vacancy he could not read.

He was not entirely convinced the woman would think of her daughter as some pure and unsullied virgin . . . 'Why?'

The girl said, 'She'll be scared. She'll be scared we get caught.'

'Don't tell her anything. Say I'm employing you.' In this country he was working in now there were generally rooms on the roofs of flat buildings for tenants' servants.

She said: 'That's what I told the caretaker.'

She ground fresh coffee beans every time he wanted a cup while he was working at night. She never attempted to cook anything until she had watched in silence while he did it the way he liked, and she learned to reproduce exactly the simple dishes he preferred. She handled his pieces of rock and stone, at first admiring the colours—'It'd make a beautiful ring or a necklace, ay.' Then he showed her the striations, the formation of each piece, and explained what each was, and how, in the long life of the earth, it had been formed. He named the mineral it yielded, and what that was used for. He worked at his papers, writing, writing, every night, so it did not matter that they could not go out together to public places. On Sundays she got into his car in the basement garage and they drove to the country and picnicked away up in the Magaliesberg, where there was no one. He read or poked about among the rocks; they climbed together, to the mountain pools. He taught her to swim. She had never seen the sea. She squealed and shrieked in the water, showing the gap between her teeth, as—it crossed his mind—she must do when among her own people. Occasionally he had to go out to dinner at the houses of colleagues from the mining company; she sewed and listened to the radio in the flat and he found her in the bed, warm and already asleep, by the time he came in. He made his way into her body without speaking; she made him welcome without a word. Once he put on evening dress for a dinner at his country's consulate; watching him brush one or two fallen hairs from the shoulders of the dark jacket that sat so well on him, she saw a huge room, all chandeliers and people dancing some dance from a costume film—stately, hand-to-hand. She supposed he was going to fetch, in her place in the car, a partner for the evening. They never kissed when either left the flat; he said, suddenly, kindly, pausing as he picked up cigarettes and keys, 'Don't be lonely.' And added, 'Wouldn't you like to visit your family sometimes, when I have to go out?'

He had told her he was going home to his mother in the forests and mountains of his country near the Italian border (he showed her on the map) after Christmas. She had not told him how her mother, not knowing there was any other variety, assumed he was a medical doctor, so she had talked to her about the doctor's children and the doctor's wife who was a very kind lady, glad to have someone who could help out in the surgery as well as the flat.

She remarked wonderingly on his ability to work until midnight or later, after a day at work. She was so tired when she came home from her cash register at the supermarket that once dinner was eaten she could scarcely keep awake. He explained in a way she could understand that while the work she did was repetitive, undemanding of any real response from her intelligence, requiring little mental or physical effort and therefore unrewarding, his work was his greatest interest, it taxed his mental capacities to their limit, exercised all his concentration, and rewarded him constantly as much with the excitement of a problem presented as with the satisfaction of a problem solved. He said later, putting away his papers, speaking out of a silence: 'Have you done other kinds of work?' She said, 'I was in a clothing factory before. Sportbeau shirts; you know? But the pay's better in the shop.'

Of course. Being a conscientious newspaper-reader in every country he lived in, he was aware that it was only recently that the retail consumer trade in this one had been allowed to employ coloureds as shop assistants; even punching a cash register represented advancement. With the continuing shortage of semi-skilled whites a girl like this might be able to edge a little farther into the white-collar category. He began to teach her to type. He was aware that her English was poor, even though, as a foreigner, in his ears her pronunciation did not offend, nor categorize her as it would in those of someone of his education whose mother tongue was English. He corrected her grammatical mistakes but missed the less obvious ones because of his own sometimes exotic English usage—she continued to use the singular pronoun 'it' when what was required was the plural 'they'. Because he was a foreigner (although so clever, as she saw) she was less inhibited than she might have been by the words she knew she misspelled in her typing. While she sat at the typewriter she thought how one day she would type notes for him, as well as making coffee the way he liked it, and taking him inside her body without saying anything, and sitting (even if only through the empty streets of quiet Sundays) beside him in his car, like a wife.

On a summer night near Christmas—he had already bought and hidden a slightly showy but nevertheless good watch he thought she would like—there was a knocking at the door that brought her out of the bathroom and him to his feet, at his work-table. No one ever came to the flat at night; he had no friends intimate enough to drop in without warning. The summons was an imperious banging that did not pause and clearly would not stop until the door was opened.

She stood in the open bathroom doorway gazing at him across the passage into the living-room; her bare feet and shoulders were free of a big bath-towel. She said nothing, did not even whisper. The flat seemed to shake with the strong unhurried blows.

He made as if to go to the door, at last, but now she ran and clutched him by both arms. She shook her head wildly; her lips drew back but her teeth were clenched, she didn't speak. She pulled him into the bedroom, snatched some clothes from the clean laundry laid out on the bed and got into the wall-cupboard, thrusting the key at his hand. Although his arms and calves felt weakly cold he was horrified, distastefully embarrassed at the sight of her pressed back crouching there under his suits and coat; it was horrible and ridiculous. *Come out!* he whispered. *No! Come out!* She hissed: *Where? Where can I go?*

Never mind! Get out of there!

He put out his hand to grasp her. At bay, she said with all the force of her terrible whisper, baring the gap in her teeth: *I'll throw myself out the window.*

She forced the key into his hand like the handle of a knife. He closed the door on her face and drove the key home in the lock, then dropped it among coins in his trouser pocket.

He unslotted the chain that was looped across the flat door. He turned the serrated knob of the Yale lock. The three policemen, two in plain clothes, stood there without impatience although they had been banging on the door for several minutes. The big dark one with an elaborate moustache held out in a hand wearing a plaited gilt ring some sort of identity card.

Dr von Leinsdorf said quietly, the blood coming strangely back to legs and arms, 'What is it?'

The sergeant told him they knew there was a coloured girl in the flat. They had had information; 'I been watching this flat three months, I know.'

'I am alone here.' Dr von Leinsdorf did not raise his voice.

'I know, I know who is here. Come—' And the sergeant and his two assistants went into the living-room, the kitchen, the bathroom (the sergeant picked up a bottle of after-shave cologne, seemed to study the French label) and the bedroom. The assistants removed the clean laundry that was laid upon the bed and then turned back the bedding, carrying the sheets over to be examined by the sergeant under the lamp. They talked to one another in Afrikaans, which the Doctor did not understand. The sergeant himself looked under the bed, and lifted the long curtains at the window. The wall cupboard was of the kind that has no knobs; he saw that it was locked and began to ask in Afrikaans, then politely changed to English, 'Give us the key.'

Dr von Leinsdorf said, 'I'm sorry, I left it at my office—I always lock and take my keys with me in the mornings.'

'It's no good, man, you better give me the key.'

He smiled a little, reasonably. 'It's on my office desk.'

The assistants produced a screwdriver and he watched while they inserted it where the cupboard doors met, gave it quick, firm but not forceful leverage. He heard the lock give.

She had been naked, it was true, when they knocked. But now she was wearing a long-sleeved T-shirt with an appliquéd butterfly motif on one breast, and a pair of jeans. Her feet were still bare; she had managed, by feel, in the dark, to get into some of the clothing she had snatched from the bed, but she had no shoes. She had perhaps been weeping behind the cupboard door (her cheeks looked stained) but now her face was sullen and she was breathing heavily, her diaphragm contracting and expanding exaggeratedly and her breasts pushing against the cloth. It made her appear angry; it might simply have been that she was half-suffocated in the cupboard and needed oxygen. She did not look at Dr von Leinsdorf. She would not reply to the sergeant's questions.

They were taken to the police station where they were at once separated and in turn led for examination by the district surgeon. The man's underwear was taken away and examined, as the sheets had been, for signs of his seed. When the girl was undressed, it was discovered that beneath her jeans she was wearing a pair of men's briefs with his name on the neatly-sewn laundry tag; in her haste, she had taken the wrong garment to her hiding-place.

Now she cried, standing there before the district surgeon in a man's underwear.

He courteously pretended not to notice. He handed briefs, jeans and T-shirt round the door, and motioned her to lie on a white-sheeted high table where he placed her legs apart, resting in stirrups, and put into her where the other had made his way so warmly a cold hard instrument that expanded wider and wider. Her thighs and knees trembled uncontrollably while the doctor looked into her and touched her deep inside with more hard instruments, carrying wafers of gauze.

When she came out of the examining room back to the charge office, Dr von Leinsdorf was not there; they must have taken him somewhere else. She spent what was left of the night in a cell, as he must be doing; but early in the morning she was released and taken home to her mother's house in the coloured township by a white man who explained he was the clerk of the lawyer who had been engaged for her by Dr von Leinsdorf. Dr von Leinsdorf, the clerk said, had also been bailed out that morning. He did not say when, or if she would see him again.

A statement made by the girl to the police was handed in to Court when she and the man appeared to meet charges of contravening the Immorality Act in a Johannesburg flat on the night of — December, 19—. *I lived with the white man in his flat. He had intercourse with me sometimes. He gave me tablets to take to prevent me becoming pregnant.*

Interviewed by the Sunday papers, the girl said, 'I'm sorry for the sadness brought to my mother.' She said she was one of nine children of a female laundry worker. She had left school in Standard Three because there was no money at home for gym clothes or a school blazer. She had worked as a machinist in a factory and a cashier in a supermarket. Dr von Leinsdorf taught her to type his notes.

Dr Franz-Josef von Leinsdorf, described as the grandson of a baroness, a cultured man engaged in international mineralogical research, said he accepted social distinctions between people but didn't think they should be legally imposed. 'Even in my own country it's difficult for a person from a higher class to marry one from a lower class.'

The two accused gave no evidence. They did not greet or speak to each other in Court. The Defence argued that the sergeant's evidence that they had been living together as man and wife was hearsay. (The woman with the dachshund, the caretaker?) The magistrate acquitted them because the State failed to prove carnal intercourse had taken place on the night of — December, 19—.

The girl's mother was quoted, with photograph, in the Sunday papers: 'I won't let my daughter work as a servant for a white man again.'

Two

The farm children play together when they are small; but once the white children go away to school they soon don't play together any more, even in the holidays. Although most of the black children get some sort of schooling, they drop every year farther behind the grades passed by the white children; the childish vocabulary, the child's exploration of the adventurous possibilities of dam, koppies, mealie lands and veld—there comes a time when the white children have surpassed these with the vocabulary of boarding-school and the possibilities of inter-school sports matches and the kind of adventures seen at the cinema. This usefully coincides with the age of twelve or thirteen; so that by the time early adolescence is reached, the black children are making, along with the bodily changes common to all, an easy transition to adult forms of address, beginning to call their old playmates *missus* and *baasi*—little master.

The trouble was Paulus Eysendyck did not seem to realize that Thebedi was now simply one of the crowd of farm children down at the kraal, recognizable in his sisters' old clothes. The first Christmas holidays after he had gone to boarding-school he brought home for Thebedi a painted box he had made in his wood-work class. He had to give it to her secretly because he had nothing for the other children at the kraal. And she gave him, before he went back to school, a bracelet she had made of thin brass wire and the grey-and-white beans of the castor-oil crop his father cultivated. (When they used to play together, she was the one who had taught Paulus how to make clay oxen for their toy spans.) There was a craze, even in the *platteland* towns like the one where he was at school, for boys to wear elephant-hair and other bracelets beside their watch-straps; his was admired, friends asked him to get similar ones for them. He said the natives made them on his father's farm and he would try.

When he was fifteen, six feet tall, and tramping round at school dances with the girls from the 'sister' school in the same town; when he had learnt how to tease and flirt and fondle quite intimately these girls who were the daughters of prosperous farmers like his father; when he had even met one who, at a wedding he had attended with his parents on a nearby farm, had let him do with her in a locked storeroom what people did when they made love—when he was as far from his childhood as all this, he still brought home from a shop in town a red plastic belt and gilt hoop ear-rings for the black girl, Thebedi. She told her father the missus had given these to her as a reward for some work she had done—it was true she sometimes was called to help out in the farmhouse. She told the girls in the kraal that she had a sweetheart nobody knew about, far away, away on another farm, and they giggled, and teased, and admired her. There was a boy in the kraal called Njabulo who said he wished he could have bought her a belt and ear-rings.

When the farmer's son was home for the holidays she wandered far from the kraal and her companions. He went for walks alone. They had not arranged this; it was an urge each followed independently. He knew it was she, from a long way off. She knew that his dog would not bark at her. Down at the dried-up river-bed where five or six years ago the children had caught a leguaan one great day—a creature that combined ideally the size and ferocious aspect of the crocodile with the harmlessness of the lizard—they squatted side by side on the earth bank. He told her traveller's tales: about school, about the punishments at school, particularly, exaggerating both their nature and his indifference to them. He told her about the town of Middleburg, which she had never seen. She had nothing to tell but she prompted with many questions, like any good listener. While he talked he twisted and tugged at the roots of white stinkwood and Cape willow trees that looped out of the eroded earth around them. It had always been a good spot for children's games, down there hidden by the mesh of old, ant-eaten trees held in place by vigorous ones, wild asparagus bushing up between the trunks, and here and there prickly-pear cactus sunken-skinned and bristly, like an old man's face, keeping alive sapless until the next rainy season. She punctured the dry hide of a prickly-pear again and again with a sharp stick while she listened. She laughed a lot at what he told her, sometimes dropping her face on her knees, sharing amusement with the cool shady earth beneath her bare feet. She put on her pair of shoes—white sandals, thickly Blanco-ed against the farm dust—when he was on the farm, but these were taken off and laid aside, at the river-bed.

One summer afternoon when there was water flowing there and it was very hot she waded in as they used to do when they were children, her dress bunched modestly and tucked into the legs of her pants. The schoolgirls he went swimming with at dams or pools on neighbouring farms wore bikinis but the sight of their dazzling bellies and thighs in the sunlight had never made him feel what he felt now, when the girl came up the bank and sat beside him, the drops of water beading off her dark legs the only points of light in the earth-smelling, deep shade. They were not afraid of one another, they had known one another always; he did with her what he had done that time in the storeroom at the wedding, and this time it was so lovely, so lovely, he was surprised . . . and she was surprised by it, too—he could see in her dark face that was part of the shade, with her big dark eyes, shiny as soft water, watching him attentively: as she had when they used to huddle over their teams of mud oxen, as she had when he told her about detention weekends at school.

They went to the river-bed often through those summer holidays. They met just before the light went, as it does quite quickly, and each returned home with the dark—she to her mother's hut, he to the farmhouse—in time for the evening meal. He did not tell her about school or town any more. She did not ask questions any longer. He told her, each time, when they would meet again. Once or twice it was very early in the morning; the lowing of the cows being driven to graze came to them where they lay, dividing them with unspoken recognition of the sound read in their two pairs of eyes, opening so close to each other.

He was a popular boy at school. He was in the second, then the first soccer team. The head girl of the 'sister' school was said to have a crush on him; he didn't particularly like her, but there was a pretty blonde who put up her long hair into a kind of doughnut with a black ribbon round it, whom he took to see films when the schoolboys and girls had a free Saturday afternoon. He had been driving tractors and other farm vehicles since he was ten years old, and as soon as he was eighteen he got a driver's licence and in the holidays, this last year of his school life, he took neighbours' daughters to dances and to the drive-in cinema that had just opened twenty kilometres from the farm. His sisters were married, by then; his parents often left him in charge of the farm over the weekend while they visited the young wives and grandchildren.

When Thebedi saw the farmer and his wife drive away on a Saturday afternoon, the boot of their Mercedes filled with fresh-killed poultry and vegetables from the garden that it was part of her father's work to tend, she knew that she must come not to the river-bed but up to the house. The house was an old one, thick-walled, dark against the heat. The kitchen was its lively thorough-fare, with servants, food supplies, begging cats and dogs, pots boiling over, washing being damped for ironing, and the big deep-freeze the missus had ordered from town, bearing a crocheted mat and a vase of plastic irises. But the dining-room with the bulging-legged heavy table was shut up in its rich, old smell of soup and tomato sauce. The sitting-room curtains were drawn and the T.V. set silent. The door of the parents' bedroom was locked and the empty rooms where the girls had slept had sheets of plastic spread over the beds. It was in one of these that she and the farmer's son stayed together whole nights—almost: she had to get away before the house servants, who knew her, came in at dawn. There was a risk someone would discover her or traces of her presence if he took her to his own bedroom, although she had looked into it many times when she was helping out in the house and knew well, there, the row of silver cups he had won at school.

When she was eighteen and the farmer's son nineteen and working with his father on the farm before entering a veterinary college, the young man Njabulo asked her father for her. Njabulo's parents met with hers and the money he was to pay in place of the cows it is customary to give a prospective bride's parents was settled upon. He had no cows to offer; he was a labourer on the Eysendyck farm, like her father. A bright youngster; old Eysendyck had taught him brick-laying and was using him for odd jobs in construction, around the place. She did not tell the farmer's son that her parents had arranged for her to marry. She did not tell him, either, before he left for his first term at the veterinary college, that she thought she was going to have a baby. Two months after her marriage to Njabulo, she gave birth to a daughter. There was no disgrace in that; among her people it is customary for a young man to make sure, before marriage, that the chosen girl is not barren, and Njabulo had made love to her then. But the infant was very light and did not quickly grow darker as most African babies do. Already at birth there was on its head a quantity of straight, fine floss, like that which carries the seeds of certain weeds in the veld. The unfocused eyes it opened were grey flecked with yellow. Njabulo was the matt, opaque coffee-grounds colour that has always been called black; the colour of Thebedi's legs on which beaded water looked oyster-shell blue, the same colour as Thebedi's face, where the black eyes, with their interested gaze and clear whites, were so dominant.

Njabulo made no complaint. Out of his farm labourer's earnings he bought from the Indian store a cellophane-windowed pack containing a pink plastic bath, six napkins, a card of safety pins, a knitted jacket, cap and bootees, a dress, and a tin of Johnson's Baby Powder, for Thebedi's baby.

When it was two weeks old Paulus Eysendyck arrived home from the veterinary college for the holidays. He drank a glass of fresh, still-warm milk in the childhood familiarity of his mother's kitchen and heard her discussing with the old house-servant where they could get a reliable substitute to help out now that the girl Thebedi had had a baby. For the first time since he was a small boy he came right into the kraal. It was eleven o'clock in the morning. The men were at work in the lands. He looked about him, urgently; the women turned away, each not wanting to be the one approached to point out where Thebedi lived. Thebedi appeared, coming slowly from the hut Njabulo had built in white man's style, with a tin chimney, and a proper window with glass panes set in straight as walls made of unfired bricks would allow. She greeted him with hands brought together and a token movement representing the respectful bob with which she was accustomed to acknowledge she was in the presence of his father or mother. He lowered his head under the doorway of her home and went in. He said, 'I want to see. Show me.'

She had taken the bundle off her back before she came out into the light to face him. She moved between the iron bedstead made up with Njabulo's checked blankets and the small wooden table where the pink plastic bath stood among food and kitchen pots, and picked up the bundle from the snugly-blanketed grocer's box where it lay. The infant was asleep; she revealed the closed, pale, plump tiny face, with a bubble of spit at the corner of the mouth, the spidery pink hands stirring. She took off the woollen cap and the straight fine hair flew up after it in static electricity, showing gilded strands here and there. He said nothing. She was watching him as she had done when they were little, and the gang of children had trodden down a crop in their games or transgressed in some other way for which he, as the farmer's son, the white one among them, must intercede with the farmer. She disturbed the sleeping face by scratching or tickling gently at a cheek with one finger, and slowly the eyes opened, saw nothing, were still asleep, and then, awake, no longer narrowed, looked out at them, grey with yellowish flecks, his own hazel eyes.

He struggled for a moment with a grimace of tears, anger and self-pity. She could not put out her hand to him. He said, 'You haven't been near the house with it?'

She shook her head.

'Never?'

Again she shook her head.

'Don't take it out. Stay inside. Can't you take it away somewhere. You must give it to someone—'

She moved to the door with him.

He said, 'I'll see what I will do. I don't know.' And then he said: 'I feel like killing myself.'

Her eyes began to glow, to thicken with tears. For a moment there was the feeling between them that used to come when they were alone down at the river-bed.

He walked out.

Two days later, when his mother and father had left the farm for the day, he appeared again. The women were away on the lands, weeding, as they were employed to do as casual labour in summer; only the very old remained, propped up on the ground outside the huts in the flies and the sun. Thebedi did not ask him in. The child had not been well; it had diarrhoea. He asked where its food was. She said, 'The milk comes from me.' He went into Njabulo's house, where the child lay; she did not follow but stayed outside the door and watched without seeing an old crone who had lost her mind, talking to herself, talking to the fowls who ignored her.

She thought she heard small grunts from the hut, the kind of infant grunt that indicates a full stomach, a deep sleep. After a time, long or short she did not know, he came out and walked away with plodding stride (his father's gait) out of sight, towards his father's house.

The baby was not fed during the night and although she kept telling Njabulo it was sleeping, he saw for himself in the morning that it was dead. He comforted her with words and caresses. She did not cry but simply sat, staring at the door. Her hands were cold as dead chickens' feet to his touch.

Njabulo buried the little baby where farm workers were buried, in the place in the veld the farmer had given them. Some of the mounds had been left to weather away unmarked, others were covered with stones and a few had fallen wooden crosses. He was going to make a cross but before it was finished the police came and dug up the grave and took away the dead baby: someone-one of the other labourers? their women ?—had reported that the baby was almost white, that, strong and healthy, it had died suddenly after a visit by the farmer's son. Pathological tests on the infant corpse showed intestinal damage not always consistent with death by natural causes.

Thebedi went for the first time to the country town where Paulus had been to school, to give evidence at the preparatory examination into the charge of murder brought against him. She cried hysterically in the witness box, saying yes, yes (the gilt hoop ear-rings swung in her ears), she saw the accused pouring liquid into the baby's mouth. She said he had threatened to shoot her if she told anyone.

More than a year went by before, in that same town, the case was brought to trial. She came to Court with a new-born baby on her back. She wore gilt hoop ear-rings; she was calm,; she said she had not seen what the white man did in the house.

Paulus Eysendyck said he had visited the hut but had not poisoned the child.

The Defence did not contest that there had been a love relationship between the accused and the girl, or that intercourse had taken place, but submitted there was no proof that the child was the accused's.

The judge told the accused there was strong suspicion against him but not enough proof that he had committed the crime. The Court could not accept the girl's evidence because it was clear she had committed perjury either at this trial or at the preparatory examination. There was the suggestion in the mind of the Court that she might be an accomplice in the crime; but, again, insufficient proof.

The judge commended the honourable behaviour of the husband (sitting in court in a brown-and-yellow-quartered golf cap bought for Sundays) who had not rejected his wife and had 'even provided clothes for the unfortunate infant out of his slender means'.

The verdict on the accused was 'not guilty'.

The young white man refused to accept the congratulations of press and public and left the Court with his mother's raincoat shielding his face from photographers. His father said to the press, 'I will try and carry on as best I can to hold up my head in the district.'

Interviewed by the Sunday papers, who spelled her name in a variety of ways, the black girl, speaking in her own language, was quoted beneath her photograph: 'It was a thing of our childhood, we don't see each other any more.'

The narrator's omniscience is limited in this story, but the limits change as the narrator *focalizes* one or another character. Sometimes, for example, the narrator tells us, through the *filter or focus* of Professor Leinsdorf, that the girl "was rather small and finely made, for one of them. The coat was skimpy, but no big backside jutted." Professor Leinsdorf is *focalized*—that is, the narrator is focusing, and thereby guiding the reader to focus, on the fact that Professor Leinsdorf expects African women to have "big backsides," which he finds unattractive, and is pleasantly surprised to discover that the young woman who delivers his groceries has a slimmer silhouette. Later, though, when the narrator notes that "He didn't understand that people don't usually have telephones in their houses, where she lived" the young woman is the filter character—and her assumptions about the professor are focalized.

CONSTRUCTING A READING

1. Focalizing Professor Leninsdorf, the narrator reveals that he "has no interest in the politics of the countries he works in." How do you respond to this commentary when you first hear it? How do you respond later, after the couple is arrested?

2. Focalizing Professor Leinsdorf, the narrator reveals that "it was difficult to know how to treat these people, in this country; to know what they expected." How do you respond, especially in the context of the professor's lack of interest in South African politics?

3. Still focalizing Professor Leinsdorf, the narrator observes that when she first swam in the sea, the girl "squealed and shrieked in the water, showing the gap between her teeth, as—it crossed his mind—she must do when among her own people." How do you respond to this bit of information? Why does the narrator provide it?

4. The narrator gives us Thebedi's name in the "country" part of the story but does not name "the girl" in the town. Why?

5. The narrator explains the "trouble was that Paulus Eysendyck did not seem to realize that Thebedi was now simply one of the crowd of farm children down at the kraal." From the insights into Paulus's inferiority that the narrator allows, explain why this situation made for "trouble."

6. The narrator does not explain why Paulus tells Thebedi about the punishments at school. There are many things he could have emphasized instead—how difficult his classes were, how he excels at sports—but he chooses instead to tell her how well he can endure punishment. Why?

7. Is the narrator exactly the same in both parts of the story? Why do you think Gordimer arranges these two narratives as parts of a single text?

First-Person Narrators

Stories can also be told by one of their own characters. In these cases, the narration is called *first person*: the narrator is an "I" who participates in the story and tells it to someone, sometimes an anonymous reader and sometimes another character in the story—a narratee. We shall discuss the narratee later; for now let's try to keep our narrators straight. First-person narration can be reliable or unreliable: that is, the reader either believes the story just as the narrator tells it, or begins to doubt that the narrator has adequately understood the events of the story. Which is it for you in "The Lesson," by Toni Cade Bambara?

The Lesson
Toni Cade Bambara

Back in the days when everyone was old and stupid or young and foolish and me and Sugar were the only ones just right, this lady moved on our block with nappy hair and proper speech and no makeup. And quite naturally we laughed at her, laughed the way we did at the junk man who went about his business like he was some big-time president and his sorry-ass horse his secretary. And we kinda hated her too, hated the way we did the winos who cluttered up our parks and pissed on our handball walls and stank up our hallways and stairs so you couldn't halfway play hide-and-seek without a goddamn gas mask. Miss Moore was her name. The only woman on the block with no first name. And she was black as hell, cept for her feet, which were fish-white and spooky. And she was always planning these boring-ass things for us to do, us being my cousin, mostly, who lived on the block cause we all moved North the same time and to the same apartment then spread out gradual to breathe. And our parents would yank our heads into some kinda shape and crisp up our clothes so we'd be presentable for travel with Miss Moore, who always looked like she was going to church, though she never did. Which is just one of things the grown-ups talked about when they talked behind her back like a dog. But when she came calling with some sachet she'd sewed up or some gingerbread she'd made or some book, why then they'd all be too embarrassed to turn her down and we'd get handed over all spruced up. She'd been to college and said it was only right that she should take responsibility for the young ones' education, and she not even related by marriage or blood. So they'd go for it. Specially Aunt Gretchen. She was the main gofer in the family. You got some ole dumb shit foolishness you want somebody to go for, you send for Aunt Gretchen. She been screwed into the go-along for so long, it's a blood-deep natural thing with her. Which is how she got saddled with me and Sugar and Junior in the first place while our mothers were in a la-de-da apartment up the block having a good ole time.

So this one day Miss Moore rounds us all up at the mailbox and it's puredee hot and she's knockin herself out about arithmetic. And school suppose to let up in summer I heard, but she don't never let up. And the starch in my pinafore scratching the shit outta me and I'm really hating this nappy-head bitch and her goddamn college degree. I'd much rather go to the pool or to the show where it's cool. So me and Sugar leaning on the mailbox being surly, which is a Miss Moore word. And Flyboy checking out what everybody brought for lunch. And Fat Butt already wasting his peanut-butter-and-jelly sandwich like the pig he is. And Junebug punchin on Q.T.'s arm for potato chips. And Rosie Giraffe shifting from one hip to the other waiting for some-body to step on her foot or ask her if she from Georgia so she can kick ass, preferably Mercedes'. And Miss Moore asking us do we know what money is, like we a bunch of retards. I mean real money, she say, like it's only poker chips or monopoly papers we lay on the grocer. So right away I'm tired of this and say no. And would much rather snatch Sugar and go to the Sunset and terrorize the West Indian kids and take their hair ribbons and their money too. And Miss Moore files that remark away for next week's lesson on brotherhood, I can tell. And finally I say we oughta get to the subway cause it's cooler and besides we might meet some cute boys. Sugar done swiped her mama's lipstick, so we ready.

So we heading down the street and she's boring us silly about what things cost and what our parents make and how much goes for rent and how money ain't divided up right in this country. And then she gets to the part about we all poor and live in the slums, which I don't feature. And I'm ready to speak on that, but she steps out in the street and hails two cabs just like that. Then she hustles half the crew in with her and hands me a five-dollar bill and tells me to calculate 10 percent tip for the driver. And we're off. Me and Sugar and Junebug and Flyboy hangin out the window and hollering to everybody, putting lipstick on each other cause Flyboy a faggot anyway, and making farts with our sweaty armpits. But I'm mostly trying to figure how to spend this money. But they all fascinated with the meter ticking and Junebug starts laying bets as to how much it'll read when Flyboy can't hold his breath no more. Then Sugar lays bets as to how much it'll be when we get there. So I'm stuck. Don't nobody want to go for my plan, which is to jump out at the next light

and run off to the first bar-b-que we can find. Then the driver tells us to get
the hell out cause we there already. And the meter reads eighty-five cents. And
I'm stalling to figure out the tip and Sugar say give him a dime. And I decide he
don't need it bad as I do, so later for him. But then he tries to take off with
Junebug foot still in the door so we talk about his mama something ferocious.
Then we check out that we on Fifth Avenue and everybody dressed up in stockings. One lady in a fur coat, hot as it is. White folks crazy.

"This is the place," Miss Moore say, presenting it to us in the voice she
uses at the museum. "Let's look in the windows before we go in."

"Can we steal?" Sugar asks very serious like she's getting the ground rules
squared away before she plays. "I beg your pardon," says Miss Moore, and we
fall out. So she leads us around the windows of the toy store and me and Sugar
screamin, "This is mine, that's mine, I gotta have that, that was made for me, I
was born for that," till Big Butt drowns us out.

"Hey, I'm goin to buy that there."

"That there? You don't even know what it is, stupid."

"I do so." he say punchin on Rosie Giraffe. "It's a microscope."

"Watcha gonna do with a microscope, fool?"

"Look at things."

"Like what, Ronald?" ask Miss Moore. And Big Butt ain't got the first
notion. So here go Miss Moore gabbing about the thousands of bacteria in a
drop of water and the somethin or other in a speck of blood and the million
and one living things in the air around us is invisible to the naked eye. And
what she say that for? Junebug go to town on that "naked" and we rolling.
Then Miss Moore ask what it cost. So we all jam into the window smudgin it
up and the price tag say $300. So then she ask how long'd take for Big Butt and
Junebug to save up their allowances. 'Too long," I say. "Yeh," adds Sugar, "outgrown it by that time." And Miss Moore say no, you never outgrow learning
instruments. "Why, even medical students and interns and," blah, blah, blah.
And we ready to choke Big Butt for bringing it up in the first damn place.

"This here costs four hundred eighty dollars," say Rosie Giraffe. So we
pile up all over her to see what she pointin out. My eyes tell me it's a chunk of
glass cracked with something heavy, and different-color inks dripped into the
splits, then the whole thing put into a oven or something. But the $480 it don't
make sense.

"That's a paperweight made of semi-precious stones fused together under
tremendous pressure," she explains slowly, with her hands doing the mining
and all the factory work.

"So what's a paperweight?" asks Rosie Giraffe.

"To weigh paper with, dumbbell," say Flyboy, the wise man from the
East.

"Not exactly," say Miss Moore, which is what she say when you warm or
way off too. "It's to weigh paper down so it won't scatter and make your desk

untidy." So right away me and Sugar curtsy to each other and then to Mercedes who is more the tidy type.

"We don't keep paper on top of the desk in my class," say Junebug, figuring Miss Moore crazy or lyin one.

"At home, then," she say. "Don't you have a calendar and a pencil case and a blotter and a letter-opener on your desk at home where you do your homework?" And she know damn well what our homes look like cause she nosys around in them every chance she gets.

"I don't even have a desk," say Junebug. "Do we?"

"No. And I don't get no homework neither," say Big Butt.

"And I don't even have a home," say Flyboy like he do at school to keep the white folks off his back and sorry for him. Send this poor kid to camp posters, is his specialty.

"I do," says Mercedes. "I have a box of stationery on my desk and a picture of my cat. My godmother bought the stationery and the desk. There's a big rose on each sheet and the envelopes smell like roses."

"Who wants to know about your smelly-ass stationery," say Rosie Giraffe fore I can get my two cents in.

"It's important to have a work area all your own so that . . ."

"Will you look at this sailboat, please," say Flyboy, cuttin her off and pointin to the thing like it was his. So once again we tumble all over each other to gaze at this magnificent thing in the toy store which is just big enough to maybe sail two kittens across the pond if you strap them to the posts tight. We all start reciting the price tag like we in assembly. "Handcrafted sailboat of fiberglass at one thousand one hundred ninety-five dollars."

"Unbelievable," I hear myself say and am really stunned. I read it again for myself just in case the group recitation put me in a trance. Same thing. For some reason this pisses me off. We look at Miss Moore and she lookin at us, waiting for I dunno what.

Who'd pay all that when you can buy a sailboat set for a quarter at Pop's, a tube of glue for a dime, and a ball of string for eight cents? "It must have a motor and a whole lot else besides," I say. "My sailboat cost me about fifty cents."

"But will it take water?" say Mercedes with her smart ass.

"Took mine to Alley Pond Park once," say Flyboy. "String broke. Lost it. Pity."

"Sailed mine in Central Park and it keeled over and sank. Had to ask my father for another dollar."

"And you got the strap," laugh Big Butt. "The jerk didn't even have a string on it. My old man wailed on his behind."

Little Q.T. was staring hard at the sailboat and you could see he wanted it bad. But he too little and somebody'd just take it from him. So what the hell. "This boat for kids, Miss Moore?"

"Parents silly to buy something like that just to get all broke up," say Rosie Giraffe.

"That much money it should last forever," I figure.

"My father'd buy it for me if I wanted it."

"Your father, my ass," say Rosie Giraffe getting a chance to finally push Mercedes.

"Must be rich people shop here," say Q.T.

"You are a very bright boy," say Flyboy. "What was your first clue?" And he rap him on the head with the back of his knuckles, since Q.T. the only one he could get away with. Though Q.T. liable to come up behind you years later and get his licks in when you half expect it.

"What I want to know," I says to Miss Moore though I never talk to her, I wouldn't give the bitch that satisfaction, "is how much a real boat costs? I figure a thousand'd get you a yacht any day."

"Why don't you check that out," she says, "and report back to the group?" Which really pains my ass. If you gonna mess up a perfectly good swim day least you could do is have some answers. "Let's go in," she say like she got something up her sleeve. Only she don't lead the way. So me and Sugar turn the corner to where the entrance is, but when we get there I kinda hang back. Not that I'm scared, what's there to be afraid of, just a toy store. But I feel funny, shame. But what I got to be shamed about? Got as much right to go in as anybody. But somehow I can't seem to get hold of the door, so I step away for Sugar to lead. But she hangs back too. And I look at her and she looks at me and this is ridiculous. I mean, damn, I have never ever been shy about doing nothing or going nowhere. But then Mercedes steps up and then Rosie Giraffe and Big Butt crowd in behind and shove, and next thing we all stuffed into the doorway with only Mercedes squeezing past us, smoothing out her jumper and walking right down the aisle. Then the rest of us tumble in like a glued-together jigsaw done all wrong. And people lookin at us. And it's like the time me and Sugar crashed into the Catholic church on a dare. But once we got in there and everything so hushed and holy and the candles and the bowin and the handkerchiefs on all the drooping heads, I just couldn't go through with the plan. Which was for me to run up to the altar and do a tap dance while Sugar played the nose flute and messed around in the holy water. And Sugar kept givin me the elbow. Then later teased me so bad I tied her up in the shower and turned it on and locked her in. And she'd be there till this day if Aunt Gretchen hadn't finally figured I was lyin about the boarder takin a shower.

Same thing in the store. We all walkin on tiptoe and hardly touchin the games and puzzles and things. And I watched Miss Moore who is steady watchin us like she waitin for a sign. Like Mama Drewery watches the sky and sniffs the air and takes note of just how much slant is in the bird formation. Then me and Sugar bump smack into each other, so busy gazing at the toys, 'specially the sailboat. But we don't laugh and go into our fat-lady bump-stomach routine. We just stare at that price tag. Then Sugar run a finger over the whole boat. And I'm jealous and want to hit her. Maybe not her, but I sure want to punch somebody in the mouth.

"Watcha bring us here for, Miss Moore?"

"You sound angry, Sylvia. Are you mad about something?" Givin me one of them grins like she tellin a grown-up joke that never turns out to be funny. And she's lookin very closely at me like maybe she plannin to do my portrait from memory. I'm mad, but I won't give her that satisfaction. So I slouch around the store bein very bored and say, "Let's go."

Me and Sugar at the back of the train watchin the tracks whizzin by large then small then gettin gobbled up in the dark. I'm thinkin about this tricky toy I saw in the store. A clown that somersaults on a bar then does chin-ups just cause you yank lightly at his leg. Cost $35. I could see me askin my mother for a $35 birthday clown. "You wanna who that costs what?" she'd say, cocking her head to the side to get a better view of the hole in my head. Thirty-five dollars could buy new bunk beds for Junior and Gretchen's boy. Thirty-five dollars and the whole household could visit Grandaddy Nekon in the country. Thirty-five dollars would pay for the rent and the piano bill too. Who are these people that spend that much for performing clowns and $1,000 for toy sailboats? What kinda work they do and how they live and how come we ain't in on it? Where we are is who we are, Miss Moore always pointin out. But it don't necessarily have to be that way, she always adds then waits for somebody to say that poor people have to wake up and demand their share of the pie and don't none of us know what kind of pie she talkin about in the first damn place. But she ain't so smart cause I still got her four dollars from the taxi and she ain't gettin it. Messin up my day with this shit. Sugar nudges me in my pocket and winks.

Miss Moore lines us up in front of the mailbox where we started from, seem like years ago, and I got a headache for thinkin so hard. And we lean all over each other so we can hold up under the draggy-ass lecture she always finishes us off with at the end before we thank her for borin us to tears. But she just looks at us like she readin tea leaves. Finally she say, "Well, what did you think of F.A.O. Schwarz?"

Rosie Giraffe mumbles, "White folks crazy."

"I'd like to go there again when I get my birthday money," says Mercedes, and we shove her out the pack so she has to lean on the mailbox by herself.

"I'd like a shower. Tiring day," say Flyboy.

Then Sugar surprises me by sayin, "You know, Miss Moore, I don't think all of us here put together eat in a year what that sailboat costs." And Miss Moore lights up like somebody goosed her. "And?" she say, urging Sugar on. Only I'm standin on her foot so she don't continue.

"Imagine for a minute what kind of society it is in which some people can spend on a toy what it would cost to feed a family of six or seven. What do you think?"

"I think," say Sugar pushing me off her feet like she never done before, cause I whip her ass in a minute, "that this is not much of a democracy if you ask me. Equal chance to pursue happiness means an equal crack at the dough, don't it?" Miss Moore is besides herself and I am disgusted with Sugar's treachery. So I stand on her foot one more time to see if she'll shove me. She shuts up, and Miss Moore looks at me, sorrowfully I'm thinkin. And somethin weird is goin on, I can feel it in my chest.

"Anybody else learn anything today?" lookin dead at me. I walk away and Sugar has to run to catch up and don't even seem to notice when I shrug her arm off my shoulder.

"Well, we got four dollars anyway," she says.

"Uh hunh."

"We could go to Hascombs and get half a chocolate layer and then go to the Sunset and still have plenty money for potato chips and ice cream sodas."

"Uh hunh."

"Race you to Hascombs," she say.

We start down the block and she gets ahead which is O.K. by me cause I'm going to the West End and then over to the Drive to think this day through. She can run if she want to and even run faster. But ain't nobody gonna beat me at nuthin.

CONSTRUCTING A READING

1. Sylvia tells us that this story occurred "[b]ack in the days when everyone was old and stupid or young and foolish and me and Sugar were the only ones just right." When was that? How much time, in other words, has elapsed between the story and the discourse of "The Lesson"? How much and what kind of learning has occurred in that time?

2. With your group members, make a list of the times you think the narrator is not fully understanding the events of the story. Then make a list of the times when you think she is fully cognizant. On the basis of your two lists, compose a profile of Bambara's narrator as a character in the story.

3. As your teacher directs, form groups to look carefully at the discussion of the microscope, the paperweight, and the sailboat. With your group members, prepare a list of the attributes of "value" that the children in this story might have learned from the discussion of each of these objects.

4. Sylvia reveals that she feels shame when they enter the store, and then wonders "what [she has] to be shamed about? Got as much right to go in as anybody." Write in your journal for a page or two about why you think Sylvia feels ashamed, about whether you have ever felt similarly shamed, and about why you think such shame occurs in our culture—if it does— and whether Sylvia (and you) have "as much right to go in [to expensive shops] as anybody."

Unreliable Narrators

When we read, we generally assume that narrators are reliable. This is another culturally received convention—readers believe the narrator unless and until they have reason to disbelieve. To see this principle at work, look at the following story. As you read, try to monitor your responses to the narrator. Do you accept her account of the events she describes? Do you accept her assessment of the meaning and significance of the events she describes?

I Stand Here Ironing
Tillie Olsen

I stand here ironing, and what you asked me moves tormented back and forth with the iron.

"I wish you would manage the time to come in and talk with me about your daughter. I'm sure you can help me understand her. She's a youngster who needs help and whom I'm deeply interested in helping."

"Who needs help." Even if I came, what good would it do? You think because I am her mother I have a key, or that in some way you could use me as a key? She has lived for nineteen years. There is all that life that has happened outside of me, beyond me.

And when is there time to remember, to sift, to weigh, to estimate, to total? I will start and there will be an interruption and I will have to gather it all together again. Or I will become engulfed with all I did or did not do, with what should have been and what cannot be helped.

She was a beautiful baby. The first and only one of our five that was beautiful at birth. You do not guess how new and uneasy her tenancy in her now-loveliness. You did not know her all those years she was thought homely, or see her poring over her baby pictures, making me tell her over and over how beautiful she had been—and would be, I would tell her—and was now, to the seeing eye. But the seeing eyes were few or nonexistent. Including mine.

I nursed her. They feel that's important nowadays. I nursed all the children, but with her, with all the fierce rigidity of first motherhood, I did like the books then said. Though her cries battered me to trembling and my breasts ached with swollenness, I waited till the clock decreed.

Why do I put that first? I do not even know if it matters, or if it explains anything.

She was a beautiful baby. She blew shining bubbles of sound. She loved motion, loved light, loved color and music and textures. She would lie on the floor in her blue overalls patting the surface so hard in ecstasy her hands and feet would blur. She was a miracle to me, but when she was eight months old I had to leave her daytimes with the woman downstairs to whom she was no miracle at all, for I worked or looked for work and for Emily's father, who "could no longer endure" (he wrote in his good-bye note) "sharing want with us."

I was nineteen. It was the pre-relief, pre-WPA world of the depression. I would start running as soon as I got off the streetcar, running up the stairs, the place smelling sour, and awake or asleep to startle awake, when she saw me she would break into a clogged weeping that could not be comforted, a weeping I can hear yet.

After a while I found a job hashing at night so I could be with her days, and it was better. But it came to where I had to bring her to his family and leave her.

It took a long time to raise the money for her fare back. Then she got chicken pox and I had to wait longer. When she finally came, I hardly knew her, walking quick and nervous like her father, looking like her father, thin, and dressed in a shoddy red that yellowed her skin and glared at the pockmarks. All the baby loveliness gone.

She was two. Old enough for nursery school they said, and I did not know then what I know now—the fatigue of the long day, and the lacerations of group life in nurseries that are only parking places for children.

Except that it would have made no difference if I had known. It was the only place there was. It was the only way we could be together, the only way I could hold a job.

And even without knowing, I knew. I knew the teacher that was evil because all these years it has curdled into my memory, the little boy hunched in the corner, her rasp, "why aren't you outside, because Alvin hits you? that's no reason, go out, scaredy." I knew Emily hated it even if she did not clutch and implore "don't go Mommy" like the other children, mornings.

She always had a reason why we should stay home. Momma, you look sick, Momma. I feel sick. Momma, the teachers aren't there today, they're sick. Momma, we can't go, there was a fire there last night. Momma, it's a holiday today, no school, they told me.

But never a direct protest, never rebellion. I think of our others in their three-, four-year-oldness—the explosions, the tempers, the denunciations, the demands—and I feel suddenly ill. I put the iron down. What in me demanded that goodness in her? And what was the cost, the cost to her of such goodness?

The old man living in the back once said in his gentle way: "You should smile at Emily more when you look at her." What *was* in my face when I looked at her? I loved her. There were all the acts of love.

It was only with the others I remembered what he said, and it was the face of joy, and not of care or tightness or worry I turned to them—too late for Emily. She does not smile easily, let alone almost always as her brothers and sisters do. Her face is closed and sombre, but when she wants, how fluid. You must have seen it in her pantomimes, you spoke of her rare gift for comedy on the stage that rouses a laughter out of the audience so dear they applaud and applaud and do not want to let her go.

Where does it come from, that comedy? There was none of it in her when she came back to me that second time, after I had had to send her away again. She had a new daddy now to learn to love, and I think perhaps it was a better time.

Except when we left her alone nights, telling ourselves she was old enough.

"Can't you go some other time, Mommy, like tomorrow?" she would ask. "Will it be just a little while you'll be gone? Do you promise?"

The time we came back, the front door open, the clock on the floor in the hall. She rigid awake. "It wasn't just a little while. I didn't cry. Three times I called you, just three times, and then I ran downstairs to open the door so you could come faster. The clock talked loud. I threw it away, it scared me what it talked."

She said the clock talked loud again that night I went to the hospital to have Susan. She was delirious with the fever that comes before red measles, but she was fully conscious all the week I was gone and the week after we were home when she could not come near the new baby or me.

She did not get well. She stayed skeleton thin, not wanting to eat, and night after night she had nightmares. She would call for me, and I would rouse from exhaustion to sleepily call back: "You're all right, darling, go to sleep, it's just a dream," and if she still called, in a sterner voice, "now go to sleep, Emily, there's nothing to hurt you." Twice, only twice, when I had to get up for Susan anyhow, I went in to sit with her.

Now when it is too late (as if she would let me hold and comfort her like I do the others) I get up and go to her at once at her moan or restless stirring. "Are you awake, Emily? Can I get you something?" And the answer is always the same: "No, I'm all right, go back to sleep, Mother."

They persuaded me at the clinic to send her away to a convalescent home in the country where "she can have the kind of food and care you can't manage for her, and you'll be free to concentrate on the new baby." They still send children to that place. I see pictures on the society page of sleek young women planning affairs to raise money for it, or dancing at the affairs, or decorating Easter eggs or filling Christmas stockings for the children.

They never have a picture of the children so I do not know if the girls still wear those gigantic red bows and the ravaged looks on the every other Sunday when parents can come to visit "unless otherwise notified"—as we were notified the first six weeks.

Oh it is a handsome place, green lawns and tall trees and fluted flower beds. High up on the balconies of each cottage the children stand, the girls in their red bows and white dresses, the boys in white suits and giant red ties. The parents stand below shrieking up to be heard and the children shriek down to be heard, and between them the invisible wall "Not To Be Contaminated by Parental Germs or Physical Affection."

There was a tiny girl who always stood hand in hand with Emily. Her parents never came. One visit she was gone. "They moved her to Rose Cottage" Emily shouted in explanation. "They don't like you to love anybody here."

She wrote once a week, the labored writing of a seven-year-old. "I am fine. How is the baby. If I write my leter nicly I will have a star. Love." There never was a star. We wrote every other day, letters she could never hold or keep but only hear read-once. "We simply do not have room for children to keep any personal possessions," they patiently explained when we pieced one Sunday's shrieking together to plead how much it would mean to Emily, who loved so to keep things, to be allowed to keep her letters and cards.

Each visit she looked frailer. "She isn't eating," they told us.

(They had runny eggs for breakfast or mush with lumps, Emily said later, I'd hold it in my mouth and not swallow. Nothing ever tasted good, just when they had chicken.)

It took us eight months to get her released home, and only the fact that she gained back so little of her seven lost pounds convinced the social worker.

I used to try to hold and love her after she came back, but her body would stay stiff, and after a while she'd push away. She ate little. Food sickened her, and I think much of life too. Oh she had physical lightness and brightness, twinkling by on skates, bouncing like a ball up and down up and down over the jump rope, skimming over the hill; but these were momentary.

She fretted about her appearance, thin and dark and foreign-looking at a time when every little girl was supposed to look or thought she should look a chubby blonde replica of Shirley Temple. The doorbell sometimes rang for her, but no one seemed to come and play in the house or be a best friend. Maybe because we moved so much.

There was a boy she loved painfully through two school semesters. Months later she told me how she had taken pennies from my purse to buy him candy. "Licorice was his favorite and I brought him some every day, but he still liked Jennifer better'n me. Why, Mommy?" The kind of question for which there is no answer.

School was a worry to her. She was not glib or quick in a world where glibness and quickness were easily confused with ability to learn. To her over-worked and exasperated teachers she was an overconscientious "slow learner" who kept trying to catch up and was absent entirely too often.

I let her be absent, though sometimes the illness was imaginary. How different from my now-strictness about attendance with the others. I wasn't working. We had a new baby, I was home anyhow. Sometimes, after Susan grew old enough, I would keep her home from school, too, to have them all together.

Mostly Emily had asthma, and her breathing, harsh and labored, would fill the house with a curiously tranquil sound. I would bring the two old dresser mirrors and her boxes of collections to her bed. She would select beads and single earrings, bottle tops and shells, dried flowers and pebbles, old postcards and scraps, all sorts of oddments; then she and Susan would play Kingdom, setting up landscapes and furniture, peopling them with action.

Those were the only times of peaceful companionship between her and Susan. I have edged away from it, that poisonous feeling between them, that terrible balancing of hurts and needs I had to do between the two, and did so badly, those earlier years.

Oh there are conflicts between the others too, each one human, needing, demanding, hurting, taking—but only between Emily and Susan, no, Emily toward Susan that corroding resentment. It seems so obvious on the surface, yet it is not obvious. Susan, the second child, Susan, golden- and curly-haired and chubby, quick and articulate and assured, everything in appearance and manner Emily was not; Susan, not able to resist Emily's precious things, losing or sometimes clumsily breaking them; Susan telling jokes and riddles to company for applause while Emily sat silent (to say to me later: that was *my* riddle, Mother, I told it to Susan); Susan, who for all the five years' difference in age was just a year behind Emily in developing physically.

I am glad for that slow physical development that widened the difference between her and her contemporaries, though she suffered over it. She was too vulnerable for that terrible world of youthful competition, of preening and parading, of constant measuring of yourself against every other, of envy, "If I had that copper hair," "If I had that skin. . . ." She tormented herself enough about not looking like the others, there was enough of the unsureness, the having to be conscious of words before you speak, the constant caring—what are they thinking of me? without having it all magnified by the merciless physical drives.

Ronnie is calling. He is wet and I change him. It is rare there is such a cry now. That time of motherhood is almost behind me when the ear is not one's own but must always be racked and listening for the child cry, the child call. We sit for a while and I hold him, looking out over the city spread in charcoal with its soft aisles of light. "*Shoogily,*" he breathes and curls closer. I carry him back to bed, asleep. *Shoogily.* A funny word, a family word, inherited from Emily, invented by her to say: *comfort.*

In this and other ways she leaves her seal, I say aloud. And startle at my saying it. What do I mean? What did I start to gather together, to try and make coherent? I was at the terrible, growing years. War years. I do not remember them well. I was working, there were four smaller ones now, there was not time for her. She had to help be a mother, and housekeeper, and shopper. She had to set her seal. Mornings of crisis and near hysteria trying to get lunches packed, hair combed, coats and shoes found, everyone to school or Child Care on time, the baby ready for transportation. And always the paper scribbled on by a smaller one, the book looked at by Susan then mislaid, the homework not done. Running out to that huge school where she was one, she was lost, she was a drop; suffering over the unpreparedness, stammering and unsure in her classes.

There was so little time left at night after the kids were bedded down. She would struggle over books, always eating (it was in those years she developed her enormous appetite that is legendary in our family) and I would be ironing, or preparing food for the next day, or writing V-mail to Bill, or tending the baby. Sometimes, to make me laugh, or out of her despair, she would imitate happenings or types at school.

I think I said once: "Why don't you do something like this in the school amateur show?" One morning she phoned me at work, hardly understandable through the weeping: "Mother, I did it. I won, I won; they gave me first prize; they clapped and clapped and wouldn't let me go."

Now suddenly she was Somebody, and as imprisoned in her difference as she had been in anonymity.

She began to be asked to perform at other high schools, even in colleges, then at city and statewide affairs. The first one we went to, I only recognized her that first moment when thin, shy, she almost drowned herself into the curtains. Then: Was this Emily? The control, the command, the convulsing and deadly clowning, the spell, then the roaring, stamping audience, unwilling to let this rare and precious laughter out of their lives.

Afterwards: You ought to do something about her with a gift like that— but without money or knowing how, what does one do? We have left it all to her, and the gift has as often eddied inside, clogged and clotted, as been used and growing.

She is coming. She runs up the stairs two at a time with her light graceful step, and I know she is happy tonight. Whatever it was that occasioned your call did not happen today.

"Aren't you ever going to finish the ironing, Mother? Whistler painted his mother in a rocker. I'd have to paint mine standing over an ironing board." This is one of her communicative nights and she tells me everything and nothing as she fixes herself a plate of food out of the icebox.

She is so lovely. Why did you want me to come in at all? Why were you concerned? She will find her way.

She starts up the stairs to bed. "Don't get me up with the rest in the morning." "But I thought you were having midterms." "Oh, those," she comes back in, kisses me, and says quite lightly, "in a couple of years when we'll all be atom-dead they won't matter a bit."

She has said it before. She *believes* it. But because I have been dredging the past, and all that compounds a human being is so heavy and meaningful in me, I cannot endure it tonight.

I will never total it all. I will never come in to say: She was a child seldom smiled at. Her father left me before she was a year old. I had to work her first six years when there was work, or I sent her home and to his relatives. There were years she had care she hated. She was dark and thin and foreign-looking in a world where the prestige went to blondeness and curly hair and dimples, she was slow where glibness was prized. She was a child of anxious, not proud, love. We were poor and could not afford for her the soil of easy growth. I was a young mother, I was a distracted mother. There were the other children pushing up, demanding. Her younger sister seemed all that she was not. There were years she did not want me to touch her. She kept too much in herself, her life was such she had to keep too much in herself. My wisdom came too late. She has much to her and probably nothing will come of it. She is a child of her age, of depression, of war, of fear.

Let her be. So all that is in her will not bloom—but in how many does it? There is still enough left to live by. Only help her to know—help make it so there is cause for her to know—that she is more than this dress on the ironing board, helpless before the iron.

CONSTRUCTING A READING

1. The narrator describes forces outside herself and Emily—the Depression and World War II, for example, as explanations for Emily's current difficulties. On the basis of what you know about these events, do you accept her explanations as sufficient? Why or why not?
2. Do you feel sympathy for Olsen's narrator? Why or why not? Do you entirely believe her? Why or why not?
3. Do you feel sympathy for Emily? Why or why not?

ADDITIONAL PERSPECTIVES

The Narratee

The "you" whom Olsen's narrator addresses is called the *narratee*—the person to whom the story is addressed. The narratee may be actually addressed—as in this story—or merely implied—as in Toni Cade Bambara's "The Lesson." It is important to distinguish the narratee from the actual reader. In "I Stand Here Ironing," the narratee is someone who knows about the Works Project Administration instituted by President Franklin Delano Roosevelt and the kinds of instructions new mothers were given in the 1930s about nursing their babies, and about the effects of World War II on domestic life in the United States.

> "[The narrattee] must be distinguished from the real reader. . . . After all, the same real reader can read different narratives, (each having different narratees) and the same narrative (which always has the same set of narratees) can have an infinitely varying set of real readers."
>
> Gerald Prince, *A Dictionary of Narratology*. University of Nebraska Press, 1987, p. 57.

NARRATIVE PERSPECTIVES: HOW READERS FOLLOW THE STORY **501**

My guess is that you—as the actual reader of my text and Olsen's—don't know as much about these elements of the text's world as its narratee. In that case, you have gaps about world that need to be closed.

A narratee is like a mirror image of the narrator. In other words, a narratee is a fictive character who *doesn't* know precisely what the narrator *wants or needs* to tell—or at least so the narrator thinks.

To understand how narratees work, try to engage the perspective of Olsen's narratee, someone who has "asked" something important of the narrator:

> I wish you would manage the time to come in and talk to me about your daughter. I'm sure you can help me understand her. She's a youngster who needs help and whom I'm deeply interested in helping.

Try to place yourself in the position of someone who would write such a letter. Who would you be? A teacher, perhaps, or a social worker, or maybe an administrator at a community theater. You would be someone with the social power to issue an invitation to "come in." Where, you might ask yourself, is the "in" of the phrase "come in and talk." An "in" implies an "out," usually. And "out" implies exclusion. What kind of "in" are Emily and her mother excluded from? Still, when Emily's mother—the narrator—does try to explain things to the narratee, her discourse expects a certain kind of understanding— a certain shared experience. Readers are then guided toward a gap—will the "inside" narratee accept the "outsider's" explanation, or not? As reader, you too, must decide. What do you think? Do you think that the narratee believes the narrator? Is there a difference between your response and your idea of the narratee's?

CONSTRUCTING A READING

1. With your group members, continue to list the attributes of the narratee of "I Stand Here Ironing" where I have left off. About how old is the narratee? What is the narratee's gender? Social position? Ideology?
2. Do you detect a difference in tone between the discourse of the narrator as narrator and the narrator as a character in the story? If so, how do you describe and explain that difference? If not, point to the similarities that you use as evidence.
3. With your group members, list the attributes of the narratee of "The Lesson." Beginning with the narrator, try to imagine an audience to whom that narrator specifically needs to tell her story. How old is the narratee? What is his or her economic status? Race? Is the narratee male or female? What does the narratee have in common with the narrator? Are there differences?

Engaging the Perspectives of the Characters

No matter what kind of narration an author uses, readers often find themselves identifying with, or assuming the perspective of, a character in the fiction, whether that character is explicitly focalized (like Professor Leinsdorf) or not (like the mouse in Theodore Roethke's poem). As an example, reread "Home Burial" in Chapter One, noticing this time how Frost guides his readers toward engaging the visual and psychological perspectives of both husband and wife.

One way of thinking about perspectives of characters is to imagine yourself adding the phrase "but then" to the last chapter's gap questions, "what happens next?" and "why?" As we read narrative, we build consistencies for each character; then, on the basis of those consistencies, we form hypotheses about what will happen next and why. *But then* that character does something that surprises us. Or, perhaps another character intervenes and changes the course of the narrative. So, we adopt the perspective of that second character and begin another consistency for him or her. For purposes of discussion, I'll try to act like the "typical reader" and describe how I build consistency for the first few lines of "Home Burial."

I find myself sympathizing first with one character, and then with the other, as I move through the story. When Frost's narrator focalizes Amy, I build consistencies for her, consistencies that close the gaps to which her characterization gives rise. Why is she fearful, "doubtful," and sad? Is "he" making her sad? I wonder, (because my gender predisposes me to raise such a question.) *But then* that consistency is broken by "his" eagerness to help his spouse. *But then* when he says "I want to know" and "you must tell me," "Mounting until she cowered under him," I bristle at the imperative "must" and the physical threat. *But then,* when he softens the command with "dear," I engage with him as a basically sympathetic guy who is not particularly careful about his language all the time. That's OK, I think, we can't all be careful all the time. *But then,* the narrator tells me that "she refused him any help." It seems unfair not to tell a spouse what's wrong, I think, *but then* I remember times in my own life when emotions were too difficult and painful to share. Perhaps the narrator is telling me that it looks to "him" as though she refuses to "help," *but then* she might think that a spouse shouldn't need any help to understand a beloved's pain. *But then,* she is "sure that he wouldn't see"; *but then,* he does— *but then,* not immediately.

CONSTRUCTING A READING

1. Draw the scene as Frost's narrator describes it or try to sketch it as director's notes for a series of film shots. Share the results of your visualization with the rest of the class.
2. Discuss the ways in which Frost's placement of his characters in the space

of the story reflects their relations with each other. Attend specifically to the following lines but include any others that seem relevant to you.

> He saw her from the bottom of the stairs.

> She was starting down,
> Looking back over her shoulder . .

> He spoke, advancing toward her. . .

> What is it you see

> The wonder is I didn't see at once.
> I never noticed it from here before.
> I must be wonted to it . . .

> I'll come down to you . . .

> I'll follow and bring you back by force. I *will!*

3. How would you describe Frost's narrator? Limited omniscient? Objective?
4. Chart the revelations of each of the major characters' interiority. Do you learn more about one character than about the other?
5. With whom do you sympathize? What has narration to do with your sympathy?

Engaging Multiple Perspectives

Here is a story by Alice Walker that calls upon its reader to assume multiple perspectives.

Everyday Use
for your grandmama
Alice Walker

I will wait for her in the yard that Maggie and I made so clean and wavy yesterday afternoon. A yard like this is more comfortable than most people know. It is not just a yard. It is like an extended living room. When the hard clay is swept clean as a floor and the fine sand around the edges lined with tiny, irregular grooves, anyone can come and sit and look up into the elm tree and wait for the breezes that never come inside the house.

Maggie will be nervous until after her sister goes: she will stand hopelessly in corners, homely and ashamed of the burn scars down her arms and legs, eying her sister with a mixture of envy and awe. She thinks her sister has held life always in the palm of one hand, that "no" is a word the world never learned to say to her.

You've no doubt seen those TV shows where the child who has "made it" is confronted, as a surprise, by her own mother and father, tottering in weakly from backstage. (A pleasant surprise, of course: What would they do if parent and child came on the show only to curse out and insult each other?) On TV mother and child embrace and smile into each other's faces. Sometimes the mother and father weep, the child wraps them in her arms and leans across the table to tell how she would not have made it without their help. I have seen these programs.

Sometimes I dream a dream in which Dee and I are suddenly brought together on a TV program of this sort. Out of a dark and soft-seated limousine I am ushered into a bright room filled with many people. There I meet a smiling, gray, sporty man like Johnny Carson who shakes my hand and tells me what a fine girl I have. Then we are on the stage and Dee is embracing me with tears in her eyes. She pins on my dress a large orchid, even though she has told me once that she thinks orchids are tacky flowers.

In real life I am a large, big-boned woman with rough, man-working hands. In the winter I wear flannel nightgowns to bed and overalls during the day. I can kill and clean a hog as mercilessly as a man. My fat keeps me hot in zero weather. I can work outside all day, breaking ice to get water for washing; I can eat pork liver cooked over the open fire minutes after it comes steaming from the hog. One winter I knocked a bull calf straight in the brain between the eyes with a sledge hammer and had the meat hung up to chill before nightfall. But of course all this does not show on television. I am the way my daughter would want me to be: a hundred pounds lighter, my skin like an uncooked barley pancake. My hair glistens in the hot bright lights. Johnny Carson has much to do to keep up with my quick and witty tongue.

But that is a mistake. I know even before I wake up. Who ever knew a Johnson with a quick tongue? Who can even imagine me looking a strange white man in the eye? It seems to me I have talked to them always with one foot raised in flight, with my head turned in whichever way is farthest from them. Dee, though. She would always look anyone in the eye. Hesitation was no part of her nature.

"How do I look, Mama?" Maggie says, showing just enough of her thin body enveloped in pink skirt and red blouse for me to know she's there, almost hidden by the door.

"Come out into the yard," I say.

Have you ever seen a lame animal, perhaps a dog run over by some care-less person rich enough to own a car, sidle up to someone who is ignorant enough to be kind to him? That is the way my Maggie walks. She has been like this, chin on chest, eyes on ground, feet in shuffle, ever since the fire that burned the other house to the ground.

Dee is lighter than Maggie, with nicer hair and a fuller figure. She's a woman now, though sometimes I forget. How long ago was it that the other house burned? Ten, twelve years? Sometimes I can still hear the flames and feel Maggie's arms sticking to me, her hair smoking and her dress falling off her in little black papery flakes. Her eyes seemed stretched open, blazed open by the flames reflected in them. And Dee. I see her standing off under the sweet gum tree she used to dig gum out of; a look of concentration on her face as she watched the last dingy gray board of the house fall in toward the red-hot brick chimney. Why don't you do a dance around the ashes? I'd wanted to ask her. She had hated the house that much.

I used to think she hated Maggie, too. But that was before we raised the money, the church and me, to send her to Augusta to school. She used to read to us without pity; forcing words, lies, other folks' habits, whole lives upon us two, sitting trapped and ignorant underneath her voice. She washed us in a river of make-believe, burned us with a lot of knowledge we didn't necessarily need to know. Pressed us to her with the serious way she read, to shove us away at just the moment, like dimwits, we seemed about to understand.

Dee wanted nice things. A yellow organdy dress to wear to her gradua-tion from high school; black pumps to match a green suit she'd made from an old suit somebody gave me. She was determined to stare down any disaster in her efforts. Her eyelids would not flicker for minutes at a time. Often I fought off the temptation to shake her. At sixteen she had a style of her own: and knew what style was.

I never had an education myself. After second grade the school was closed down. Don't ask me why: in 1927 colored asked fewer questions than they do now. Sometimes Maggie reads to me. She stumbles along good-naturedly but can't see well. She knows she is not bright. Like good looks and money, quick-ness passed her by. She will marry John Thomas (who has mossy teeth in an earnest face) and then I'll be free to sit here and I guess just sing church songs to myself. Although I never was a good singer. Never could carry a tune. I was always better at a man's job. I used to love to milk till I was hooked in the side in '49. Cows are soothing and slow and don't bother you, unless you try to milk them the wrong way.

I have deliberately turned my back on the house. It is three rooms, just like the one that burned, except the roof is tin; they don't make shingle roofs any more. There are no real windows, just some holes cut in the sides, like the portholes in a ship, but not round and not square, with rawhide holding the shutters up on the outside. This house is in a pasture, too, like the other one. No doubt when Dee sees it she will want to tear it down. She wrote me once that no matter where we "choose" to live, she will manage to come see us. But she will never bring her friends. Maggie and I thought about this and Maggie asked me, "Mama, when did Dee ever *have* any friends?"

She had a few. Furtive boys in pink shirts hanging about on washday after school. Nervous girls who never laughed. Impressed with her they worshiped the well-turned phrase, the cute shape, the scalding humor that erupted like bubbles in lye. She read to them.

When she was courting Jimmy T she didn't have much time to pay to us, but turned all her faultfinding power on him. He *flew* to marry a cheap city girl from a family of ignorant flashy people. She hardly had time to recompose herself.

When she comes I will meet them—but there they are!

Maggie attempts to make a dash for the house, in her shuffling way, but I stay her with my hand. "Come back here," I say. And she stops and tries to dig a well in the sand with her toe.

It is hard to see them clearly through the strong sun. But even the first glimpse of leg out of the car tells me it is Dee. Her feet were always neat-looking, as if God himself had shaped them with a certain style. From the other side of the car comes a short, stocky man. Hair is all over his head a foot long and hanging from his chin like a kinky mule tail. I hear Maggie suck in her breath. "Uhnnnh," is what it sounds like. Like when you see the wriggling end of a snake just in front of your foot on the road. "Uhnnnh."

Dee next. A dress down to the ground, in this hot weather. A dress so loud it hurts my eyes. There are yellows and oranges enough to throw back the light of the sun. I feel my whole face warming from the heat waves it throws out. Earrings gold, too, and hanging down to her shoulders. Bracelets dangling and making noises when she moves her arm up to shake the folds of the dress out of her armpits. The dress is loose and flows, and as she walks closer, I like it. I hear Maggie go "Uhnnnh" again. It is her sister's hair. It stands straight up like the wool on a sheep. It is black as night and around the edges are two long pigtails that rope about like small lizards disappearing behind her ears.

"Wa-su-zo-Tean-o!" she says, coming on in that gliding way the dress makes her move. The short stocky fellow with the hair to his navel is all grinning and he follows up with "Asalamalakim,* my mother and sister!" He moves to hug Maggie but she falls back, right up against the back of my chair. I feel her trembling there and when I look up I see the perspiration falling off her chin.

---

*Arabic greeting meaning "Peace be with you" used by members of the Islamic faith.

"Don't get up," says Dee. Since I am stout it takes something of a push. You can see me trying to move a second or two before I make it. She turns, showing white heels through her sandals, and goes back to the car. Out she peeks next with a Polaroid. She stoops down quickly and lines up picture after picture of me sitting there in front of the house with Maggie cowering behind me. She never takes a shot without making sure the house is included. When a cow comes nibbling around the edge of the yard she snaps it and me and Maggie *and* the house. Then she puts the Polaroid in the back seat of the car, and comes up and kisses me on the forehead.

Meanwhile Asalamalakim is going through motions with Maggie's hand. Maggie's hand is as limp as a fish, and probably as cold, despite the sweat, and she keeps trying to pull it back. It looks like Asalamalakim wants to shake hands but wants to do it fancy. Or maybe he don't know how people shake hands. Anyhow, he soon gives up on Maggie.

"Well," I say. "Dee."

"No, Mama," she says. "Not 'Dee,' Wangero Leewanika Kemanjo!"

"What happened to 'Dee'?" I wanted to know.

"She's dead," Wangero said. "I couldn't bear it any longer, being named after the people who oppress me."

"You know as well as me you was named after your aunt Dicie," I said. Dicie is my sister. She named Dee. We called her "Big Dee" after Dee was born.

"But who was *she* named after?" asked Wangero.

"I guess after Grandma Dee," I said.

"And who was she named after?" asked Wangero.

"Her mother," I said, and saw Wangero was getting tired. "That's about as far back as I can trace it," I said. Though, in fact, I probably could have carried it back beyond the Civil War through the branches.

"Well," said Asalamalakim, "there you are."

"Uhnnnd," I heard Maggie say.

"There I was not," I said, "before 'Dicie' cropped up in our family, so why should I try to trace it that far back?"

He just stood there grinning, looking down on me like somebody inspecting a Model A car. Every once in a while he and Wangero sent eye signals over my head.

"How do you pronounce this name?" I asked.

"You don't have to call me by it if you don't want to," said Wangero.

"Why shouldn't I?" I asked. "If that's what you want us to call you, we'll call you."

"I know it might sound awkward at first," said Wangero.

"I'll get used to it," I said. "Ream it out again."

Well, soon we got the name out of the way. Asalamalakim had a name twice as long and three times as hard. After I tripped over it two or three times he told me to just call him Hakim-a-barber. I wanted to ask him was he a barber, but I didn't really think he was, so I didn't ask.

"You must belong to those beef-cattle peoples down the road," I said. They said "Asalamalakim" when they met you, too, but they didn't shake hands. Always too busy: feeding the cattle, fixing the fences, putting up salt-lick shelters, throwing down hay. When the white folks poisoned some of the herd the men stayed up all night with rifles in their hands. I walked a mile and a half just to see the sight.

Hakim-a-barber said, "I accept some of their doctrines, but farming and raising cattle is not my style." (They didn't tell me, and I didn't ask, whether Wangero (Dee) had really gone and married him.)

We sat down to eat and right away he said he didn't eat collards and pork was unclean. Wangero, though, went on through the chitlins and corn bread, the greens and everything else. She talked a blue streak over the sweet potatoes. Everything delighted her. Even the fact that we still used the benches her daddy made for the table when we couldn't afford to buy chairs.

"Oh, Mama!" she cried. Then turned to Hakim-a-barber. "I never knew how lovely these benches are. You can feel the rump prints," she said, running her hands underneath her and along the bench. Then she gave a sigh and her hand closed over Grandma Dee's butter dish. "That's it!" she said. "I knew there was something I wanted to ask you if I could have." She jumped up from the table and went over in the corner where the churn stood, the milk in it clabber by now. She looked at the churn and looked at it.

"This churn top is what I need," she said. "Didn't Uncle Buddy whittle it out of a tree you all used to have?"

"Yes," I said.

"Uh huh," she said happily. "And I want the dasher, too."

"Uncle Buddy whittle that, too?" asked the barber.

Dee (Wangero) looked up at me.

"Aunt Dee's first husband whittled the dash," said Maggie so low you almost couldn't hear her. "His name was Henry, but they called him Stash."

"Maggie's brain is like an elephant's," Wangero said, laughing. "I can use the churn top as a centerpiece for the alcove table," she said, sliding a plate over the churn, "and I'll think of something artistic to do with the dasher."

When she finished wrapping the dasher the handle stuck out. I took it for a moment in my hands. You didn't even have to look close to see where hands pushing the dasher up and down to make butter had left a kind of sink in the wood. In fact, there were a lot of small sinks; you could see where thumbs and fingers had sunk into the wood. It was beautiful light yellow wood, from a tree that grew in the yard where Big Dee and Stash had lived.

After dinner Dee (Wangero) went to the trunk at the foot of my bed and started rifling through it. Maggie hung back in the kitchen over the dishpan. Out came Wangero with two quilts. They had been pieced by Grandma Dee and then Big Dee and me had hung them on the quilt frames on the front porch and quilted them. One was in the Lone Star pattern. The other was Walk Around the Mountain. In both of them were scraps of dresses Grandma

Dee had worn fifty and more years ago. Bits and pieces of Grandpa Jarrell's Paisley shirts. And one teeny faded blue piece, about the size of a penny match-box, that was from Great Grandpa Ezra's uniform that he wore in the Civil War.

"Mama," Wangero said sweet as a bird. "Can I have these old quilts?"

I heard something fall in the kitchen, and a minute later the kitchen door slammed.

"Why don't you take one or two of the others?" I asked. "These old things was just done by me and Big Dee from some tops your grandma pieced before she died."

"No," said Wangero. "I don't want those. They are stitched around the borders by machine."

"That'll make them last better, " I said.

"That's not the point," said Wangero. "These are all pieces of dresses Grandma used to wear. She did all this stitching by hand. Imagine!" She held the quilts securely in her arms, stroking them.

"Some of the pieces, like those lavender ones, come from old clothes her mother handed down to her," I said, moving up to touch the quilts. Dee (Wangero) moved back just enough so that I couldn't reach the quilts. They already belonged to her.

"Imagine!" she breathed again, clutching them closely to her bosom.

"The truth is," I said, "I promised to give them quilts to Maggie, for when she marries John Thomas."

She gasped like a bee had stung her.

"Maggie can't appreciate these quilts!" she said. "She'd probably be back-ward enough to put them to everyday use.

"I reckon she would," I said. "God knows I been saving 'em for long enough with nobody using 'em. I hope she will!" I didn't want to bring up how I had offered Dee (Wangero) a quilt when she went away to college. Then she had told me they were old-fashioned, out of style.

"But they're *priceless!*" she was saying now, furiously; for she has a temper. "Maggie would put them on the bed and in five years they'd be in rags. Less than that!"

"She can always make some more," I said. "Maggie knows how to quilt."

Dee (Wangero) looked at me with hatred. "You just will not understand. The point is these quilts, *these* quilts!"

"Well," I said, stumped. "What would *you* do with them?"

"Hang them," she said. As if that was the only thing you *could* do with quilts.

Maggie by now was standing in the door. I could almost hear the sound her feet made as they scraped over each other.

"She can have them, Mama," she said, like somebody used to never win-ning anything, or having anything reserved for her. "I can 'member Grandma Dee without the quilts."

I looked at her hard. She had filled her bottom lip with checkerberry snuff and it gave her face a kind of dopey, hangdog look. It was Grandma Dee and Big Dee who taught her how to quilt herself. She stood there with her scarred hands hidden in the folds of her skirt. She looked at her sister with something like fear but she wasn't mad at her. This was Maggie's portion. This was the way she knew God to work.

When I looked at her like that something hit me in the top of my head and ran down to the soles of my feet. Just like when I'm in church and the spirit of God touches me and I get happy and shout. I did something I never had done before: hugged Maggie to me, then dragged her on into the room, snatched the quilts out of Miss Wangero's hands and dumped them into Maggie's lap. Maggie just sat there on my bed with her mouth open.

"Take one or two of the others," I said to Dee.

But she turned without a word and went out to Hakim-a-barber.

"You just don't understand," she said, as Maggie and I came out to the car.

"What don't I understand?" I wanted to know.

"Your heritage," she said. And then she turned to Maggie, kissed her, and said, "You ought to try to make something of yourself. too, Maggie. It's really a new day for us. But from the way you and Mama still live you'd never know it."

She put on some sunglasses that hid everything above the tip of her nose and her chin.

Maggie smiled; maybe at the sunglasses. But a real smile, not scared. After we watched the car dust settle I asked Maggie to bring me a dip of snuff. And then the two of us sat there just enjoying, until it was time to go in the house and go to bed.

CONSTRUCTING A READING

1. With your group members, make a list of the attributes of Walker's narratee on the basis of the clues you've found in the text. Decide why Alice Walker needs this narratee for her story. In your deliberations, you might consider the dedication of the story: "For Your Grandmama." Who is the "you" to whose grandmama this story is dedicated?
2. Write a sympathetic account of why Dee/Wangero wants the quilts.
3. Why does the narrator want the quilts to go to Maggie?
4. Write for a few minutes in your journal about the metaphor of quilts in this story. How, in other words, is a quilt consistent with the story and discourse of "Everyday Use"?

SHARING A READING

1. Can you engage a perspective without sympathizing with it? Can you, for example, understand why Dee/Wangero wants the quilts, without agree-

ing that she should have them? If so, make a note of the places in the text where you are guided to do so. Then, write a letter to your mother (or some other relative) in which you explain how reading this story has changed your understanding of some family dispute.

TEXTS FOR FURTHER READING

Zagrowsky Tells
Grace Paley

I was standing in the park under that tree. They call it the Hanging Elm. Once upon a time it made a big improvement on all kinds of hooligans. Nowadays if, once in a while . . . No. So this woman comes up to me, a woman minus a smile. I said to my grandson, Uh oh, Emanuel. Here comes a lady, she was once a beautiful customer of mine in the pharmacy I showed you.

Emanuel says, Grandpa, who?

She looks O.K. now, but not so hot. Well, what can you do, time takes a terrible toll off the ladies.

This is her idea of a hello: Iz, what are you doing with that black child? Then she says, Who is he? Why are you holding on to him like that? She gives me a look like God in judgment. You could see it in famous paintings. Then she says, Why are you yelling at that poor kid?

What yelling? A history lesson about the park. This is a tree in guide books. How are you by the way, Miss . . . Miss . . . I was embarrassed. I forgot her name absolutely.

Well, who is he? You got him pretty scared.

Me? Don't be ridiculous. It's my grandson. Say hello, Emanuel, don't put on an act.

Emanuel shoves his hand in my pocket to be a little more glued to me. Are you going to open your mouth sonny, yes or no?

She says, Your grandson? Really, Iz, your grandson? What do you mean, your grandson?

Emanuel closes his eyes tight. Did you ever notice children get all mixed up? They don't want to hear about something, they squinch up their eyes. Many children do this.

Now listen Emanuel, I want you to tell this lady who is the smartest boy in kindergarten.

Not a word.

Goddamnit, open your eyes. It's something new with him. Tell her who is the smartest boy—he was just five, he can already read a whole book by himself.

He stands still. He's thinking. I know his little cute mind. Then he jumps up and down yelling, Me me me. He makes a little dance. His grandma calls it his smartness dance. My other ones (three children grown up for some time already) were also very smart, but they don't hold a candle to this character. Soon as I get a chance, I'm gonna bring him to the city to Hunter for gifted children; he should get a test.

But this Miss . . . Miss . . . she's not finished with us yet. She's worried. Whose kid is he? You adopt him?

Adopt? At my age? It's Cissy's kid. You know my Cissy? I see she knows something. Why not, I had a public business. No surprise.

Of course I remember Cissy. She says this, her face is a little more ironed out.

So, my Cissy, if you remember, she was a nervous girl.

I'll *bet* she was.

Is that a nice way to answer? Cissy *was* nervous . . . The nervousness, to be truthful, ran in Mrs. Z.'s family. Ran? Galloped . . . tarum tarum tarum.

When we were young I used to go over there to visit, and while me and her brother and uncles played pinochle, in the kitchen the three aunts would sit drinking tea. Everything was Oi! Oi! Oi! What for? Nothing to oi about. They got husbands . . . Perfectly fine gentlemen. One in business, two of them real professionals. They just got in the habit somehow. So I said to Mrs. Z., one oi out of you and it's divorce.

I remember your wife very well, this lady says. *Very* well. She puts on the same face like before; her mouth gets small. Your wife *is* a beautiful woman.

So . . . would I marry a mutt?

But she was right. My Nettie when she was young, she was very fair, like some Polish Jews you see once in a while. Like for instance maybe some big blond peasant made a pogrom on her great-grandma.

So I answered her, Oh yes, very nice-looking; even now she's not so bad, but a little bit on the grouchy side.

O.K., she makes a big sigh like I'm a hopeless case. What did happen to Cissy?

Emanuel, go over there and play with those kids. No? No.

Well, I'll tell you, it's the genes. The genes are the most important. Environment is O.K. But the genes . . . that's where the whole story is written down. I think the school had something to do with it also. She's more an artist like your husband. Am I thinking of the right guy? When she was a kid you should of seen her. She's a nice-looking girl now, even when she has an attack. But then she was something. The family used to go to the mountains in the summer. We went dancing, her and me. What a dancer. People were surprised. Sometimes we danced until 2 a.m.

I don't think that was good, she says. I wouldn't dance with my son all night . . .

Naturally, you're a mother. But "good," who knows what's good? Maybe a doctor. I could have been a doctor, by the way. Her brother-in-law in business would of backed me. But then what? You don't have the time. People call you day and night. I cured more people in a day than a doctor in a week. Many an M.D. called me, said, Zagrowsky, does it work . . . that Parke-Davis medication they put out last month, or it's a fake? I got immediate experience and I'm not too stuck up to tell.

Oh, Iz, you are, she said. She says this like she means it but it makes her sad. How do I know this? Years in a store. You observe. You watch. The customer is always right, but plenty of times you know he's wrong and also a god-damn fool.

All of a sudden I put her in a certain place. Then I said to myself, Iz, why are you standing here with this woman? I looked her straight in the face and I said, Faith? Right? Listen to me. Now you listen, because I got a question. Is it true, no matter what time you called, even if I was closing up, I came to your house with the penicillin or the tetracycline later? You lived on the fourth-floor walk-up. Your friend what's-her-name, Susan, with the three girls next door? I can see it very clear. Your face is all smeared up with crying, your kid got 105°, maybe more, burning up, you didn't want to leave him in the crib screaming, you're standing in the hall, it's dark. You were living alone, am I right? So young. Also your husband, he comes to my mind, very jumpy fellow, in and out, walking around all night. He drank? I betcha. Irish? Imagine you didn't get along so you got a divorce. Very simple. You kids knew how to live.

She doesn't even answer me. She says . . . you want to know what she says? She says, Oh shit! Then she says, Of course I remember. God, my Richie was sick! Thanks, she says, thanks, god-almighty thanks.

I was already thinking something else: The mind makes its own business. When she first came up to me, I couldn't remember. I knew her well, but where? Then out of no place, a word, her bossy face maybe, exceptionally round, which is not usual, her dark apartment, the four flights, the other girls— all once lively, young . . . you could see them walking around on a sunny day, dragging a couple kids, a carriage, a bike, beautiful girls, but tired from all day, mostly divorced, going home alone? Boyfriends? Who knows how that type lives? I had a big appreciation for them. Sometimes, five o'clock I stood in the door to see them. They were mostly the way models *should* be. I mean not skinny—round, like they were made of little cushions and bigger cushions, depending where you looked; young mothers. I hollered a few words to them, they hollered back. Especially I remember her friend Ruthy—she had two little girls with long black braids, down to here. I told her, In a couple of years, Ruthy, you'll have some beauties on your hands. You better keep an eye on them. In those days the women always answered you in a pleasant way, not afraid to smile. Like this: They said, Your really think so? Thanks, Iz.

But this is all used-to-be and in that place there is not only good but bad and the main fact in regard to *this* particular lady: I did her good but to me she didn't always do so much good.

So we stood around a little. Emanuel says, grandpa, let's go to the swings. Go yourself—it's not so far, there's kids, I see them. No, he says, and stuffs his hand in my pocket again. So don't go—Ach, what a day, I said. Buds and every-thing. She says, That's a catalpa tree over there. No kidding! I say. What do you call that one, doesn't have a single leaf? Locust, she says. Two locusts, I say.

Then I take a deep breath: O.K.—you still listening? Let me ask you, if I did you so much good including I saved your baby's life, how come you did *that*? You know what I'm talking about. A perfectly nice day. I look out the window of the pharmacy and I see four customers, that I seen at least two in the bathrobes crying to me in the middle of the night, Help help! They're out there with signs. ZAGROWSKY IS A RACIST. YEARS AFTER ROSA PARKS, ZAGROWSKY REFUSES TO SERVE BLACKS. It's like an etching right *here*. I point out to her my heart. I know exactly where it is.

She's naturally very uncomfortable when I tell her. Listen, she says, we were right.

I grab on to Emanuel. You?

Yes, we wrote a letter first, did you answer it? We said, Zagrowsky, come to your senses. Ruthy wrote it. We said we would like to talk to you. We tested you. At least four times, you kept Mrs. Green and Josie, our friend Josie, who was kind of Spanish black . . . she lived on the first floor in our house . . . you kept them waiting a long time till everyone ahead of them was taken care of. Then you were very rude, I mean nasty, you can be extremely nasty, Iz. And then Josie left the store, she called you some pretty bad names. You remember?

No, I happen not to remember. There was plenty of yelling in the store. People *really* suffering; come in yelling for codeine or what to do their mother was dying. That's what I remember, not some crazy Spanish lady hollering.

But listen, she says—like all this is not in front of my eyes, like the past is only a piece of paper in the yard—you didn't finish with Cissy.

Finish? *You* almost finished my business and don't think that Cissy didn't hold it up to me. Later when she was so sick.

Then I thought Why should I talk to this woman. I see myself: how I was standing that day how many years ago?—like an idiot behind the counter waiting for customers. Everybody is peeking in past the picket line. It's the kind of neighborhood, if they see a picket line, half don't come in. The cops say they have a right. To destroy a person's business. I was disgusted but I went into the street. After all, I knew the ladies. I tried to explain, Faith, Ruthy, Mrs. Kratt—a stranger comes into the store, naturally you have to serve the old customers first. Anyone would do the same. Also, they sent in black people, brown people, all colors, and to tell the truth I didn't like the idea my pharmacy should get the reputation of being a cut-rate place for them. They move into a neighborhood . . . I did what everyone did. Not to insult people too much, but to discourage them a little, they shouldn't feel so welcome. They could just move in because it's a nice area.

All right. A person looks at my Emanuel and says, Hey! he's not altogether from the white race, what's going on? I'll tell you what: life is going on. You have an opinion. I have an opinion. Life don't have no opinion.

I moved away from this Faith lady. I didn't like to be near her. I sat down on the bench. I'm no spring chicken. Cock-a-doodle-do, I only holler once in a while. I'm tired, I'm mostly the one in charge of our Emanuel. Mrs. Z. stays home, her legs swell up. It's a shame.

In the subway once she couldn't get off at the right stop. The door opens, she can't get up. She tried (she's a little overweight). She says to a big guy with a notebook, a big colored fellow, Please help me get up. He says to her. You kept me down three hundred years, you can stay down another ten minutes. I asked her, Nettie, didn't you tell him we're raising a little boy brown like a coffee bean. But he's right, says Nettie, we done that. We kept them down.

We? We? My two sisters and my father were being fried up for Hitler's supper in 1944 and you say we?

Nettie sits down. Please bring me some tea. Yes, Iz, I say: *We.*

I can't even put up the water I'm so mad. You know, my Mrs., you are crazy like your three aunts, crazy like our Cissy. Your whole family put in the genes to make it for sure that she wouldn't have a chance. Nettie looks at me. She says, Ai ai. She doesn't say oi anymore, She got herself assimilated into ai . . . That's how come she also says "we" done it. Don't think this will make you an American, I said to her, that you included yourself in with Robert E. Lee. Naturally it was a joke, only what is there to laugh?

I'm tired right now. This Faith could even see I'm a little shaky. What should she do, she's thinking. But she decides the discussion ain't over so she sits down sideways. The bench is damp. It's only April.

What about Cissy? Is she all right?

It ain't your business how she is.

O.K. She starts to go.

Wait wait! Since I seen you in your nightgown a couple of times when you were a handsome young woman . . . She really gets up this time. I think she must be a woman's libber, they don't like remarks about nightgowns. Bathrobes, she didn't mind. Let her go! The hell with her . . . but she comes back. She says, Once and for all, cut it out, Iz. I really *want* to know. Is Cissy all right?

You want. She's fine. She lives with me and Nettie. She's in charge of the plants. It's an all-day job.

But why should I leave her off the hook. Oh boy, Faith, I got to say it, what you people put on me! And you want to know how Cissy is. *You!* Why? Sure. You remember you finished with the picket lines after a week or two. I don't know why. Tired? Summer maybe, you got to go away, make trouble at the beach. But I'm stuck there. Did I have air conditioning yet? All of a sudden I see Cissy outside. She has a sign also. She must've got the idea from you women. A big sandwich board, she walks up and down. If someone talks to her, she presses her mouth together.

I don't remember that, Faith says.

Of course, you were already on Long Island or Cape Cod or someplace—the Jersey shore.

No, she says, I was not. I was not. (I see this is a big insult to her that she should go away for the summer.)

Then I thought, Calm down, Zagrowsky. Because for a fact I didn't want her to leave, because, since I already began to tell, I have to tell the whole story. I'm not a person who keeps things in. Tell! That opens up the congestion a little—the lungs are for breathing, not secrets. My wife never tells, she coughs, coughs. All night Wakes up. Ai, Iz, open up the window, there's no air. You poor woman, if you want to breathe, you got to tell.

So I said to this Faith, I'll tell you how Cissy is but you got to hear the whole story how we suffered. I thought, O.K. Who cares! Let her get on the phone later with the other girls. They should know what they started.

How we took our own Cissy from here to there to the biggest doctor—I had good contacts from the pharmacy. Dr. Francis O'Connel, the heavy Irishman over at the hospital, sat with me and Mrs. Z. for two hours, a busy man. He explained that it was one of the most great mysteries. They were ignoramuses, the most brilliant doctors were dummies in this field. But still, in my place, I heard of this cure and that one. So we got her massaged fifty times from head to toe, whatever someone suggested. We stuffed her with vitamins and minerals—there was a real doctor in charge of this idea.

If she would take the vitamins—sometimes she shut her mouth. To her mother she said dirty words. We weren't used to it. Meanwhile, in front of my place every morning, she walks up and down. She could of got minimum wage, she was so regular. Her afternoon job is to follow my wife from corner to corner to tell what my wife done wrong to her when she was a kid. Then after a couple months, all of a sudden she starts to sing. She has a beautiful voice. She took lessons from a well-known person. On Christmas week, in front of the pharmacy she sings half the *Messiah* by Handel. You know it? So that's nice, you think. Oh, that's beautiful. But where were you you didn't notice that she don't have on a coat. You didn't see she walks up and down, her socks are falling off? Her face and hands are like she's the super in the cellar. She sings! she sings! Two songs she sings the most: one is about the Gentiles will see the light and the other is, Look! a virgin will conceive a son. My wife says, Sure, naturally, she wishes she was a married woman just like anyone. Baloney. She could of. She had plenty of dates. Plenty. She sings, the idiots applaud, some skunk yells, Go, Cissy, go. What? Go where? Some days she just hollers.

Hollers what?

Oh, I forgot about you. Hollers anything. Hollers, Racist! Hollers, He sells poison chemicals! Hollers, He's a terrible dancer, he got three left legs! (Which isn't true, just to insult me publicly, plain silly.) The people laugh. What'd she say? Some didn't hear so well; hollers, You go to whores. Also not true. She met me once with a woman actually a distant relative from Israel. Everything is in her head. It's a garbage pail.

One day her mother says to her, Ciccile, comb your hair, for godsakes, darling. For this remark, she gives her mother a sock in the face. I come home I see a woman not at all young with two black eyes and a bloody nose. The doctor said, Before it's better with your girl, it's got to be worse. That much he knew. He sent us to a beautiful place, a hospital right at the city line—I'm not sure if it's Westchester or the Bronx, but thank God, you could use the subway. That's how I found out what I was saving up my money for. I thought for retiring in Florida to walk around under the palm trees in the middle of the week. Wrong. It was for my beautiful Cissy, she should have a nice home with other crazy people.

So little by little, she calms down. We can visit her. She shows us the candy store, we give her a couple of dollars; soon our life is this way. Three times a week my wife goes, gets on the subway with delicious foods (no sugar, they're against sugar); she brings something nice, a blouse or a kerchief—a present, you understand, to show love; and once a week I go, but she don't want to look at me. So close we were, like sweethearts—you can imagine how I feel. Well, you have children so you know, little children little troubles, big children big troubles—it's a saying in Yiddish. Maybe the Chinese said it too.

Oh, Iz. How could it happen like that? All of a sudden. No signs?

What's with this Faith? Her eyes are full of tears. Sensitive I suppose. I see what she's thinking. Her kids are teenagers. So far they look O.K. but what will happen? People think of themselves. Human nature. At least she doesn't tell me it's my wife's fault or mine. I did something terrible! I loved my child. I know what's on people's minds. I know psychology *very* well. Since this happened to us, I read up on the whole business.

Oh, Iz . . .

She puts her hand on my knee. I look at her. Maybe she's just a nut. Maybe she thinks I'm plain old (I almost am). Well, I said it before. Thank God for the head. Inside the head is the only place you got to be young when the usual place gets used up. For some reason she gives me a kiss on the cheek. A peculiar person.

Faith, I still can't figure it out why you girls were so rotten to me.

But we were right.

Then this lady Queen of Right makes a small lecture. She don't remember my Cissy walking up and down screaming bad language but she remembers: After Mrs. Kendrick's big fat snotty maid walked out with Kendrick's allergy order, I made a face and said, Ho ho! the great lady! That's terrible? She says whenever I saw a couple walk past on the block, a black-and-white couple, I said, Ugh—disgusting! It shouldn't be allowed! She heard this remark from me a few times. So? It's a matter of taste. Then she tells me about this Josie, probably Puerto Rican, once more—the one I didn't serve in time. Then she says, Yeah, and really, Iz, what about Emanuel?

Don't you look at Emanuel, I said. Don't you dare. He has nothing to do with it.

She rolls her eyes around and around a couple of times. She got more to say. She also doesn't like how I talk to women. She says I called Mrs. Z. a grizzly bear a few times. It's my wife, no? That I was winking and blinking at the girls, a few pinches. A lie . . . maybe I patted, but I never pinched. Besides, I know for a fact a couple of them loved it. She says, No. None of them liked it. Not one. They only put up with it because it wasn't time yet in history to holler. (An American-born girl has some nerve to mention history.)

But, she says, Iz, forget all that. I'm sorry you have so much trouble now. She really is sorry. But in a second she changes her mind. She's not so sorry. She takes her hand back. Her mouth makes a little O.

Emanuel climbs up on my lap. He pats my face. Don't be sad, Grandpa, he says. He can't stand if he sees a tear on a person's face. Even a stranger. If his mama gets a black look, he's smart, he doesn't go to her anymore. He comes to my wife. Grandma, he says, my poor mama is very sad. My wife jumps up and runs in. Worried. Scared. Did Cissy take her pills? What's going on? Once, he went to Cissy and said, Mama, why are you crying? So this is her answer to a little boy: she stands up straight and starts to bang her head on the wall. Hard.

My mama! he screams. Lucky I was home. Since then he goes straight to his grandma for his troubles. What will happen? We're not so young. My oldest son is doing extremely well—only he lives in a very exclusive neighborhood in Rockland County. Our other boy—well, he's in his own life, he's from that generation. He went away.

She looks at me, this Faith. She can't say a word. She sits there. She opens her mouth almost. I know what she wants to know. How did Emanuel come into the story. When?

Then she says to me exactly those words. Well, where does Emanuel fit in? He fits, he fits. Like a golden present from Nasser.

Nasser?

O.K., Egypt, not Nasser—he's from Isaac's other son, get it? A close relation. I was sitting one day thinking, Why? why? The answer: To remind us. That's the purpose of most things.

It was Abraham, she interrupts me. He had two sons, Isaac and Ishmael. God promised him he would be the father of generations; he was. But you know, she says, he wasn't such a good father to those two little boys. Not so unusual, she has to add on. You see! That's what they make of the Bible, those women; because they got it in for men. Of *course* I meant Abraham. Abraham. Did I say Isaac? Once in a while I got to admit it, she says something true. You remember one son he sent out of the house altogether, the other he was ready to chop up if he only heard a noise in his head saying, Go! Chop!

But the question is, Where did Emanuel fit. I didn't mind telling. I wanted to tell, I explained that already.

So it begins. One day my wife goes to the administration of Cissy's hospital and she says, What kind of a place you're running here. I have just looked at my daughter. A blind person could almost see it. My daughter is pregnant. What goes on here at night? Who's the supervisor? Where is she this minute?

Pregnant? they say like they never heard of it. And they run around and the regular doctor comes and says, Yes, pregnant. Sure. You got more news? my wife says. And then: meetings with the weekly psychiatrist, the day-by-day psychologist, the nerve doctor, the social worker, the supervising nurse, the nurse's aide. My wife says, Cissy knows. She's not an idiot, only mixed up and depressed. She *knows* she has a child in her womb inside of her like a normal woman. She likes it, my wife said. She even said to her, Mama, I'm having a baby, and she gave my wife a kiss. The first kiss in a couple of years. How do you like that?

Meanwhile, they investigated thoroughly. It turns out the man is a colored fellow. One of the gardeners. But he left a couple months ago for the Coast. I could imagine what happened. Cissy always loved flowers. When she was a little girl she was planting seeds every minute and sitting all day in front of the flower pot to see the little flower cracking up the seed. So she must of watched him and watched him. He dug up the earth. He put in the seeds. She watches.

The office apologized. Apologized? An accident. The supervisor was on vacation that week. I could sue them for a million dollars. Don't think I didn't talk to a lawyer. That time, then, when I heard, I called a detective agency to find him. My plan was to kill him. I would tear him limb from limb. What to do next. They called them all in again. The psychiatrist, the psychologist, they only left out the nurse's aide.

The only hope she could live a half-normal life—not in the institutions: she must have this baby, she could carry it full term. No, I said, I can't stand it. I refuse. Out of my Cissy, who looked like a piece of gold, would come a black child. Then the psychologist says, Don't be so bigoted. What nerve! Little by little my wife figured out a good idea. O.K., well, we'll put it out for adoption. Cissy doesn't even have to see it in person.

You are laboring under a misapprehension, says the boss of the place. They talk like that. What he meant, he meant we got to take that child home with us and if we really loved Cissy . . . Then he gave us a big lecture on this baby: it's Cissy's connection to life; also, it happens she was crazy about this gardener, this son of a bitch, a black man with a green thumb.

You see I can crack a little joke because look at this pleasure. I got a little best friend here. Where I go, he goes, even when I go down to the Italian side of the park to play a little bocce with the old goats over there. They invite me if they see me in the supermarket: Hey, Iz! Tony's sick. You come on an' play, O.K.? My wife says, Take Emanuel, he should see how men play games. I take him, those old guys they also seen plenty in their day. They think I'm some kind of a do-gooder. Also, a lot of those people are ignorant. They think the Jews are a little bit colored anyways, so they don't look at him too long. He goes to the swings and they make believe they never even seen him.

I didn't mean to get off the subject. What is the subject? The subject is how we took the baby. My wife, Mrs. Z., Nettie, she plain forced me. She said,

We got to take this child on us. I will move out of here into the project with Cissy and be on welfare. Iz, you better make up your mind. Her brother, a top social worker, he encouraged her, I think he's a Communist also, the way he talks the last twenty, thirty years . . .

He says: You'll live, Iz. It's a baby, after all. It's got your blood in it. Unless of course you want Cissy to rot away in that place till you're so poor they don't keep her anymore. Then they'll stuff her into Bellevue or Central Islip or something. First she's a zombie, then she's a vegetable. That's what you want, Iz?

After this conversation I get sick. I can't go to work. Meanwhile, every night Nettie cries. She don't get dressed in the morning. She walks around with a broom. Doesn't sweep up. Starts to sweep, bursts into tears. Puts a pot of soup on the stove, runs into the bedroom, lies down. Soon I think I'll have to put her away too.

I give in.

My listener says to me, Right, Iz, you did the right thing. What else could you do?

I feel like smacking her. I'm not a violent person, just very excitable, but who asked her?—Right, Iz. She sits there looking at me, nodding her head from rightness. Emanuel is finally in the playground. I see him swinging and swinging. He could swing for two hours. He likes that. He's a regular swinger.

Well, the bad part of the story is over. Now is the good part. Naming the baby. What should we name him? Little brown baby. An intermediate color. A perfect stranger.

In the maternity ward, you know where the mothers lie, with the new babies, Nettie is saying, Cissy, Cissile darling, my sweetest heart (this is how my wife talked to her, like she was made of gold—or eggshells), my darling girl, what should we name this little child?

Cissy is nursing. On her white flesh is this little black curly head. Cissy says right away: Emanuel. Immediately. When I hear this, I say, Ridiculous. Ridiculous, such a long Jewish name on a little baby. I got old uncles with such names. Then they all get called Manny. Uncle Manny. Again she says— Emanuel!

David is nice, I suggest in a kind voice. It's your grandpa's, he should rest in peace. Michael is nice too, my wife says. Joshua is beautiful. Many children have these beautiful names nowadays. They're nice modern names. People like to say them.

No, she says, Emanuel. Then she starts screaming, Emanuel Emanuel. We almost had to give her extra pills. But we were careful on account of the milk. The milk could get affected.

O.K., everyone hollered. O.K. Calm yourself, Cissy. O.K. Emanuel. Bring the birth certificate. Write it down. Put it down. Let her see it. Emanuel . . . In a few days, the rabbi came. He raised up his eyebrows a couple times. Then he did his job, which is to make the bris. In other words, a circumcision. This is done so the child will be a man in Israel. That's the expression they use. He isn't the first colored child. They tell me long ago we were mostly dark. Also, now I think of it, I wouldn't mind going over there to Israel. They say there are plenty black Jews. it's not unusual over there at all. They ought to put out more publicity on it. Because I have to think where he should live. Maybe it won't be so good for him here. Because my son, his fancy ideas . . . ach, forget it.

What about the building, your neighborhood, I mean where you live now? Are there other black people in the community?

Oh yeah, but they're very snobbish. Don't ask what they got to be so snobbish.

Because, she says, he should have friends his own color, he shouldn't have the burden of being the only one in school.

Listen, it's New York, it's not Oshkosh, Wisconsin. But she gets going, you can't stop her.

After all, she says, he should eventually know his own people. It's their life he'll have to share. I know it's a problem to you, Iz, I know, but that's the way it is. A friend of mine with the same situation moved to a more integrated neighborhood.

Is that a fact? I say, Where's that?

Oh, there are . . .

I start to tell her, Wait a minute, we live thirty-five years in this apartment. But I can't talk. I sit very quietly for a while, I think and think. I say to myself, Be like a Hindu, Iz, calm like a cucumber. But it's too much. Listen, Miss, Miss Faith—do me a favor, don't teach me.

I'm not teaching you, Iz, it's just . . .

Don't answer me every time I say something. Talking talking. It's true. What for? To whom? Why? Nettie's right. It's our business. She's telling me Emanuel's life.

You don't know nothing about it, I yell at her. Go make a picket line. Don't teach me.

She gets up and looks at me kind of scared. Take it easy, Iz.

Emanuel is coming. He hears me. He got his little worried face. She sticks out a hand to pat him, his grandpa is hollering so loud.

But I can't put up with it. Hands off, I yell. It ain't your kid. Don't lay a hand on him. And I grab his shoulder and push him through the park, past the playground and the big famous arch. She runs after me a minute. Then she sees a couple friends. Now she has what to talk about. Three, four women. They make a little bunch. They talk. They turn around, they look. One waves. Hiya, Iz.

This park is full of noise. Everybody got something to say to the next guy. Playing this music, standing on their heads, juggling—someone even brought a piano, can you believe it, some job.

I sold the store four years ago. I couldn't put in the work no more. But I wanted to show Emanuel my pharmacy, what a beautiful place it was, how it sent three children to college, saved a couple lives—imagine: one store!

I tried to be quiet for the boy. You want ice cream, Emanuel? Here's a dollar, sonny. Buy yourself a Good Humor. The man's over there. Don't forget to ask for the change. I bend down to give him a kiss. I don't like that he heard me yell at a woman and my hand is still shaking. He runs a few steps, he looks back to make sure I didn't move an inch.

I got my eye on him too. He waves a chocolate popsicle. It's a little darker than him. Out of that crazy mob a young fellow comes up to me. He has a baby strapped on his back. That's the style now. He asks like it's an ordinary friendly question, points to Emanuel. Gosh what a cute kid. Whose is he? I don't answer. He says it again, Really some cute kid.

I just look in his face. What does he want? I should tell him the story of my life? I don't need to tell. I already told and told. So I said very loud—no one else should bother me—how come it's your business, mister? Who do you think he is? By the way, whose kid you got on your back? It don't look like you.

He says, Hey there buddy, be cool be cool. I didn't mean anything. (You met anyone lately who meant something when he opened his mouth?) While I'm hollering at him, he starts to back away. The women are gabbing in a little clutch by the statue. It's a considerable distance, lucky they got radar. They turn around sharp like birds and fly over to the man. They talk very soft. Why are you bothering this old man, he got enough trouble? Why don't you leave him alone?

The fellow says, I wasn't bothering him. I just asked him something.

Well, he thinks you're bothering him, Faith says.

Then her friend, a woman maybe forty, very angry, starts to holler, How come you don't take care of your own kid? She's crying. Are you deaf? Naturally the third woman makes a remark, doesn't want to be left out. She taps him on his jacket: I seen you around here before, buster, you better watch out. He walks away from them backwards. They start in shaking hands.

Then this Faith comes back to me with a big smile. She says, Honestly, some people are a pain, aren't they, Iz? We sure let him have it, didn't we? And she gives me one of her kisses. Say hello to Cissy—O.K.? She puts her arms around her pals. They say a few words back and forth, like cranking up a motor. Then they bust out laughing. They wave goodbye to Emanuel. Laughing. Laughing. So long, Iz . . . see you . . .

So I say, What is going on, Emanuel, could you explain to me what just happened? Did you notice anywhere a joke? This is the first time he doesn't answer me. He's writing his name on the sidewalk. EMANUEL. Emanuel in big capital letters.

And the women walk away from us. Talking. Talking.

CONSTRUCTING A READING

1. With your group members, make a list of the perspectives this story gives you. How many different kinds of "but thens" can you find? How do they affect your response to the characters and events that Paley describes?
2. Is Zagrowsky a reliable narrator, in your view? Why or why not?
3. When does this story seem to take place? How do you know?
4. Describe the narratee for this story. What are your clues?
5. The character Faith recurs in Grace Paley's stories. Usually she is the protagonist, and many critics regard her as semi-autobiographical. Readers are often guided toward identifying with her liberal politics. Do you identify with Faith in this story? Do you like her? Why or why not?

My Last Duchess

Robert Browning

Ferrara

That's my last Duchess painted on the wall,
Looking as if she were alive. I call
That piece a wonder, now: Frà Pandolf's hands
Worked busily a day, and there she stands.
Will't please you sit and look at her? I said
"Frà Pandolf" by design, for never read
Strangers like you that pictured countenance,
The depth and passion of its earnest glance,
But to myself they turned (since none puts by
The curtain I have drawn for you, but I)
And seemed as they would ask me, if they durst,
How much a glance came there; so, not the first
Are you to turn and ask thus. Sir, 't was not
Her husband's presence only, called that spot
Of joy into the Duchess' cheek: perhaps
Frà Pandolf chanced to say "Her mantle laps
"Over my lady's wrist too much," or "Paint
"Must never hope to reproduce the faint
"Half-flush that dies along her throat:" such stuff
Was courtesy, she thought, and cause enough
For calling up that spot of joy. She had
A heart—how shall I say?—too soon made glad,
Too easily impressed; she liked whate'er
She looked on, and her looks went everywhere.
Sir, 't was all one! My favour at her breast,
The dropping of the daylight in the West,

The bough of cherries some officious fool
Broke in the orchard for her, the white mule
She rode with round the terrace—all and each
Would draw from her alike the approving speech,
Or blush, at least. She thanked men,—good! but thanked
Somehow—I know not how—as if she ranked
My gift of a nine-hundred-years-old name
With anybody's gift. Who'd stoop to blame
This sort of trifling? Even had you skill
In speech—(which I have not)—to make your will
Quite clear to such an one, and say, "Just this
"Or that in you disgusts me; here you miss,
"Or there exceed the mark"—and if she let
Herself be lessoned so, nor plainly set
Her wits to yours, forsooth, and made excuse,
—E'en then would be some stooping; and I choose
Never to stoop. Oh sir, she smiled, no doubt,
Whene'er I passed her; but who passed without
Much the same smile? This grew; I gave commands;
Then all smiles stopped together, There she stands
As if alive. Will't please you rise? We'll meet
The company below, then. I repeat,
The Count your master's known munificence
Is ample warrant that no just pretence
Of mine for dowry will be disallowed;
Though his fair daughter's self, as I avowed
At starting, is my object. Nay, we'll go
Together down, sir. Notice Neptune, though,
Taming a sea-horse, thought a rarity,
Which Claus of Innsbruck cast in bronze for me!

CONSTRUCTING A READING

1. Who is the narratee of this poem?
2. Write the minimal story of this poem from the perspective of the narrator, of the duchess, of Frà Pandolf, of the narratee.
3. Speculate about the context for the line "nay, we'll go together down, sir."
4. What do you think the narratee should say to the Count whose daughter is about to become the Duke of Ferrara's second wife?

Dry September

William Faulkner

I

Through the bloody September twilight, aftermath of sixty-two rainless days, it had gone like a fire in dry grass—the rumor, the story, whatever it was. Something about Miss Minnie Cooper and a Negro. Attacked, insulted, frightened: none of them, gathered in the barber shop on that Saturday evening where the ceiling fan stirred, without freshening it, the vitiated air, sending back upon them, in recurrent surges of stale pomade and lotion, their own stale breath and odors, knew exactly what had happened.

"Except it wasn't Will Mayes," a barber said. He was a man of middle age; a thin, sand-colored man with a mild face, who was shaving a client. "I know Will Mayes. He's a good nigger. And I know Miss Minnie Cooper, too."

"What do you know about her?" a second barber said.

"Who is she?" the client said. "A young girl?

"No," the barber said. "She's about forty, I reckon. She aint married. That's why I dont believe—"

"Believe, hell!" a hulking youth in a sweat-stained silk shirt said. "Wont you take a white woman's word before a nigger's?"

"I dont believe Will Mayes did it" the barber said. "I know Will Mayes."

"Maybe you know who did it, then. Maybe you already got him out of town, you damn niggerlover."

"I dont believe anybody did anything. I dont believe anything happened. I leave it to you fellows if them ladies that get old without getting married dont have notions that a man cant—"

"Then you are a hell of a white man," the client said. He moved under the cloth. The youth had sprung to his feet.

"You dont?" he said. "Do you accuse a white woman of lying?"

The barber held the razor poised above the half-risen client. He did not look around.

"It's this durn weather," another said. "It's enough to make a man do anything. Even to her."

Nobody laughed. The barber said in his mild, stubborn tone: "I aint accusing nobody of nothing. I just know and you fellows know how a woman that never—"

"You damn niggerlover!" the youth said.

"Shut up, Butch," another said. "We'll get the facts in plenty of time to act."

"Who is? Who's getting them?" the youth said. "Facts, hell! I—"

"You're a fine white man," the client said. "Aint you?" In his frothy beard he looked like a desert rat in the moving pictures. "You tell them, Jack," he said to the youth. "If there aint any white men in this town, you can count on me, even if I aint only a drummer and a stranger."

"That's right, boys," the barber said. "Find out the truth first. I know Will Mayes."

"Well, by God!" the youth shouted. "To think that a white man in this town—"

"Shut up, Butch," the second speaker said. "We got plenty of time."

The client sat up. He looked at the speaker. "Do you claim that anything excuses a nigger attacking a white woman? Do you mean to tell me you are a white man and you'll stand for it? You better go back North where you came from. The South dont want your kind here."

"North what?" the second said. "I was born and raised in this town."

"Well, by God!" the youth said. He looked about with a strained, baffled gaze, as if he was trying to remember what it was he wanted to say or to do. He drew his sleeve across his sweating face. "Damn if I'm going to let a white woman—"

"You tell them, Jack," the drummer said. "By God, if they—"

The screen door crashed open. A man stood in the floor, his feet apart and his heavy-set body poised easily. His white shirt was open at the throat; he wore a felt hat. His hot, bold glance swept the group. His name was McLendon. He had commanded troops at the front in France and had been decorated for valor.

"Well," he said, "are you going to sit there and let a black son rape a white woman on the streets of Jefferson?"

Butch sprang up again. The silk of his shirt clung flat to his heavy shoulders. At each armpit was a dark halfmoon.

"That's what I been telling them! That's what I—"

"Did it really happen?" a third said. "This aint the first man scare she ever had, like Hawkshaw says. Wasn't there something about a man on the kitchen roof, watching her undress, about a year ago?"

"What?" the client said. "What's that?" The barber had been slowly forcing him back into the chair; he arrested himself reclining, his head lifted, the barber still pressing him down.

McLendon whirled on the third speaker. "Happen? What the hell difference does it make? Are you going to let the black sons get away with it until one really does it?"

"That's what I'm telling them!" Butch shouted. He cursed, long and steady, pointless.

"Here, here," a fourth said. "Not so loud. Dont talk so loud."

"Sure," McLendon said; "no talking necessary at all. I've done my talking. Who's with me? " He poised on the balls of his feet, roving his gaze.

The barber held the drummer's face down, the razor poised. "Find out the facts first, boys. I know Willy Mayes. It wasn't him. Let's get the sheriff and do this thing right."

McLendon whirled upon him his furious, rigid face. The barber did not look away. They looked like men of different races. The other barbers had ceased also above their prone clients. "You mean to tell me," McLendon said, "that you'd take a nigger's word before a white woman's? Why, you damn niggerloving—"

The third speaker rose and grasped McLendon's arm; he too had been a soldier. "Now, now. Let's figure this thing out. Who knows anything about what really happened?"

"Figure out hell!" McLendon jerked his arm free. "All that're with me get up from there. The ones that aint—" He roved his gaze, dragging his sleeve across his face.

Three men rose. The drummer in the chair sat up. "Here," he said, jerking at the cloth about his neck; "get this rag off me. I'm with him. I dont live here, but by God, if our mothers and wives and sisters—" He smeared the cloth over his face and flung it to the floor. McLendon stood in the floor and cursed the others. Another rose and moved toward him. The remainder sat uncomfortable, not looking at one another, then one by one they rose and joined him.

The barber picked the cloth from the floor. He began to fold it neatly. "Boys, dont do that. Will Mayes never done it. I know."

"Come on," McLendon said. He whirled. From his hip pocket protruded the butt of a heavy automatic pistol. They went out. The screen door crashed behind them reverberant in the dead air.

The barber wiped the razor carefully and swiftly, and put it away, and ran to the rear, and took his hat from the wall. "I'll be back as soon as I can," he said to the other barbers. "I cant let—" He went out, running. The two other barbers followed him to the door and caught it on the rebound, leaning out and looking up the street after him. The air was flat and dead. It had a metallic taste at the base of the tongue.

"What can he do?" the first said. The second one was saying "Jees Christ, Jees Christ" under his breath. "I'd just as lief be Will Mayes as Hawk, if he gets McLendon riled."

"Jees Christ, Jees Christ," the second whispered.

"You reckon he really done it to her?" the first said.

II

She was thirty-eight or thirty-nine. She lived in a small frame house with her invalid mother and a thin, sallow, unflagging aunt, where each morning between ten and eleven she would appear on the porch in a lace-trimmed boudoir cap, to sit swinging in the porch swing until noon. After dinner she lay down for a while, until the afternoon began to cool. Then, in one of the three or four new voile dresses which she had each summer, she would go downtown to spend the afternoon in the stores with the other ladies, where they would handle the goods and haggle over the prices in cold, immediate voices, without any intention of buying.

She was of comfortable people—not the best in Jefferson, but good people enough—and she was still on the slender side of ordinary looking, with a bright, faintly haggard manner and dress. When she was young she had had a slender, nervous body and a sort of hard vivacity which had enabled her for a time to ride upon the crest of the town's social life as exemplified by the high school party and church social period of her contemporaries while still children enough to be unclassconscious.

She was the last to realize that she was losing ground; that those among whom she had been a little brighter and louder flame than any other were beginning to learn the pleasure of snobbery—male—and retaliation—female. That was when her face began to wear that bright, haggard look. She still carried it to parties on shadowy porticoes and summer lawns, like a mask or a flag, with that bafflement of furious repudiation of truth in her eyes. One evening at a party she heard a boy and two girls, all schoolmates, talking. She never accepted another invitation.

She watched the girls with whom she had grown up as they married and got homes and children, but no man ever called on her steadily until the children of the other girls had been calling her "aunty" for several years, the while their mothers told them in bright voices about how popular Aunt Minnie had been as a girl. Then the town began to see her driving on Sunday afternoons with the cashier in the bank. He was a widower of about forty—a high-colored man, smelling always faintly of the barber shop or of whisky. He owned the first automobile in town, a red runabout; Minnie had the first motoring bonnet and veil the town ever saw. Then the town began to say: "Poor Minnie." "But she is old enough to take care of herself," others said. That was when she began to ask her old schoolmates that their children call her "cousin" instead of "aunty."

It was twelve years now since she had been relegated into adultery by public opinion, and eight years since the cashier had gone to a Memphis bank, returning for one day each Christmas, which he spent at an annual bachelors' party at a hunting club on the river. From behind their curtains the neighbors would see the party pass, and during the over-the-way Christmas day visiting they would tell her about him, about how well he looked, and how they heard that he was prospering in the city, watching with bright, secret eyes her haggard, bright face. Usually by that hour there would be the scent of whisky on her breath. It was supplied her by a youth, a clerk at the soda fountain: "Sure; I buy it for the old gal. I reckon she's entitled to a little fun."

Her mother kept to her room altogether now; the gaunt aunt ran the house. Against that background Minnie's bright dresses, her idle and empty days, had a quality of furious unreality. She went out in the evenings only with women now, neighbors, to the moving pictures. Each afternoon she dressed in one of the new dresses and went downtown alone, where her young "cousins" were already strolling in the late afternoons with their delicate, silken heads and thin, awkward arms and conscious hips, clinging to one another or shrieking and giggling with paired boys in the soda fountain when she passed and went on along the serried store fronts, in the doors of which the sitting and lounging men did not even follow her with their eyes any more.

III

The barber went swiftly up the street where the sparse lights, insect-swirled, glared in rigid and violent suspension in the lifeless air. The day had died in a pall of dust; above the darkened square, shrouded by the spent dust, the sky was as clear as the inside of a brass bell. Below the east was a rumor of the twice-waxed moon.

When he overtook them McLendon and three others were getting into a car parked in an alley. McLendon stooped his thick head, peering out beneath the top. "Changed your mind, did you?" he said. "Damn good thing; by God, tomorrow when this town hears about how you talked tonight—"

"Now, now," the other ex-soldier said. "Hawkshaw's all right. Come on, Hawk; jump in."

"Will Mayes never done it, boys," the barber said. "If anybody done it. Why, you all know well as I do there aint any town where they got better niggers than us. And you know how a lady will kind of think things about men when there aint any reason to, and Miss Minnie anyway—"

"Sure, sure," the soldier said. "We're just going to talk to him a little; that's all."

"Talk hell!" Butch said. "When we're through with the—"

"Shut up, for God's sake!" the soldier said. "Do you want everybody in town—"

"Tell them, by God!" McLendon said. "Tell every one of the sons that'll let a white woman—"

"Let's go; let's go: here's the other car." The second car slid squealing out of a cloud of dust at the alley mouth. McLendon started his car and took the lead. Dust lay like fog in the street. The street lights hung nimbused as in water. They drove on out of town.

A rutted lane turned at right angles. Dust hung above it too, and above all the land. The dark bulk of the ice plant, where the Negro Mayes was night watchman, rose against the sky. "Better stop here, hadn't we?" the soldier said. McLendon did not reply. He hurled the car up and slammed to a stop, the headlights glaring on the blank wall.

"Listen here, boys," the barber said; "if he's here, dont that prove he never done it? Don't it? If it was him, he would run. Dont you see he would?"

The second car came up and stopped. McLendon got down; Butch sprang down beside him. "Listen, boys," the barber said.

"Cut the lights off!" McLendon said. The breathless dark rushed down. There was no sound in it save their lungs as they sought air in the parched dust in which for two months they had lived; then the diminishing crunch of McLendon's and Butch's feet, and a moment later McLendon's voice:

"Will! . . . Will!"

Below the east the wan hemorrhage of the moon increased. It heaved above the ridge, silvering the air, the dust, so that they seemed to breathe, live, in a bowl of molten led. There was no sound of nightbird nor insect, no sound save their breathing and a faint ticking of contracting metal about the cars. Where their bodies touched one another they seemed to sweat dryly, for no more moisture came. "Christ!" a voice said; "let's get out of here."

But they didn't move until vague noises began to grow out of the darkness ahead; then they got out and waited tensely in the breathless dark. There was another sound: a blow, a hissing expulsion of breath and McLendon cursing in undertone. They stood a moment longer, then they ran forward. They ran in a stumbling clump, as though they were fleeing something. "Kill him, kill the son," a voice whispered. McLendon flung them back.

"Not here," he said. "Get him into the car." "Kill him, kill the black son!" the voice murmured. They dragged the Negro to the car. The barber had waited beside the car. He could feel himself sweating and he knew he was going to be sick at the stomach.

"What is it, captains?" the Negro said. "I aint done nothing. 'Fore God, Mr John." Someone produced handcuffs. They worked busily about the Negro as though he were a post, quiet, intent, getting in one another's way. He submitted to the handcuffs, looking swiftly and constantly from dim face to dim face. "Who's here, captains?" he said, leaning to peer into the faces until they could feel his breath and smell his sweaty reek. He spoke a name or two. "What you all say I done, Mr John?"

McLendon jerked the car door open. "Get in!" he said.

The Negro did not move. "What you all going to do with me, Mr John? I aint done nothing. White folks, captains, I aint done nothing: I swear 'fore God." He called another name.

"Get in!" McLendon said. He struck the Negro. The others expelled their breath in a dry hissing and struck him with random blows and he whirled and cursed them, and swept his manacled hands across their faces and slashed the barber upon the mouth, and the barber struck him also. "Get him in there," McLendon said. They pushed at him. He ceased struggling and got in and sat quietly as the others took their places. He sat between the barber and the soldier, drawing his limbs in so as not to touch them, his eyes going swiftly and constantly from face to face. Butch clung to the running board. The car moved on. The barber nursed his mouth with his handkerchief.

"What's the matter, Hawk?" the soldier said.

"Nothing," the barber said. They regained the highroad and turned away from town. The second car dropped back out of the dust. They went on, gaining speed; the final fringe of houses dropped behind.

"Goddamn, he stinks!" the soldier said.

"We'll fix that," the drummer in front beside McLendon said. On the running board Butch cursed into the hot rush of air. The barber leaned suddenly forward and touched McLendon's arm.

"Let me out, John," he said.

"Jump out, niggerlover," McLendon said without turning his head. He drove swiftly. Behind them the sourceless lights of the second car glared in the dust. Presently McLendon turned into a narrow road. It was rutted with disuse. It led back to an abandoned brick kiln—a series of reddish mounds and weed- and vine-choked vats without bottom. It had been used for pasture once, until one day the owner missed one of his mules. Although he prodded carefully in the vats with a long pole, he could not even find the bottom of them.

"John," the barber said.

"Jump out, then," McLendon said, hurling the car along the ruts. Beside the barber the Negro spoke:

"Mr Henry."

The barber sat forward. The narrow tunnel of the road rushed up and past. Their motion was like an extinct furnace blast: cooler, but utterly dead. The car bounded from rut to rut.

"Mr Henry," the Negro said.

The barber began to tug furiously at the door. "Look out, there!" the soldier said, but the barber had already kicked the door open and swung onto the running board. The soldier leaned across the Negro and grasped at him, but he had already jumped. The car went on without checking speed.

The impetus hurled him crashing through dust-sheathed weeds, into the ditch. Dust puffed about him, and in a thin, vicious crackling of sapless stems he lay choking and retching until the second car passed and died away. Then he rose and limped on until he reached the highroad and turned toward town, brushing at his clothes with his hands. The moon was higher, riding high and clear of the dust at last, and after a while the town began to glare beneath the dust. He went on, limping. Presently he heard cars and the glow of them grew in the dust behind him and he left the road and crouched again in the weeds until they passed. McLendon's car came last now. There were four people in it and Butch was not on the running board.

They went on; the dust swallowed them; the glare and the sound died away. The dust of them hung for a while, but soon the eternal dust absorbed it again. The barber climbed back onto the road and limped on toward town.

IV

As she dressed for supper on that Saturday evening, her own flesh felt like fever. Her hands trembled among the hooks and eyes, and her eyes had a feverish look, and her hair swirled crisp and crackling under the comb. While she was still dressing the friends called for her and sat while she donned her sheerest underthings and stockings and a new voile dress. "Do you feel strong enough to go out?" they said, their eyes bright too, with a dark glitter. "When you have had time to get over the shock, you must tell us what happened. What he said and did; everything."

In the leafed darkness, as they walked toward the square, she began to breathe deeply, something like a swimmer preparing to dive, until she ceased trembling, the four of them walking slowly because of the terrible heat and out of solicitude for her. But as they neared the square she began to tremble again, walking with her head up, her hands clenched at her sides, their voices about her murmurous, also with that feverish, glittering quality of their eyes.

They entered the square, she in the center of the group, fragile in her fresh dress. She was trembling worse. She walked slower and slower, as children eat ice cream, her head up and her eyes bright in the haggard banner of her face, passing the hotel and the coatless drummers in chairs along the curb looking around at her: "That's the one: see? The one in pink in the middle." "Is that her? What did they do with the nigger? Did they—?" "Sure. He's all right." "All right, is he?" "Sure. He went on a little trip." Then the drug store, where even the young men lounging in the doorway tipped their hats and followed with their eyes the motion of her hips and legs when she passed.

They went on, passing the lifted hats of the gentlemen, the suddenly ceased voices, deferent, protective. "Do you see?" the friends said. Their voices sounded like long, hovering sighs of hissing exultation. "There's not a Negro on the square. Not one."

They reached the picture show. It was like a miniature fairyland with its lighted lobby and colored lithographs of life caught in its terrible and beautiful mutations. Her lips began to tingle. In the dark, when the picture began, it would be all right; she could hold back the laughing so it would not waste away so fast and so soon. So she hurried on before the turning faces, the undertones of low astonishment, and they took their accustomed places where she could see the aisle against the silver glare and the young men and girls coming in two and two against it.

The lights flicked away; the screen glowed silver, and soon life began to unfold, beautiful and passionate and sad, while still the young men and girls entered, scented and sibilant in the half dark, their paired backs in silhouette delicate and sleek, their slim, quick bodies awkward, divinely young, while beyond them the silver dream accumulated, inevitably on and on. She began to laugh. In trying to suppress it, it made more noise than ever; heads began to turn. Still laughing, her friends raised her and led her out, and she stood at the curb, laughing on a high, sustained note, until the taxi came up and they helped her in.

They removed the pink voile and the sheer underthings and the stockings, and put her to bed, and cracked ice for her temples, and sent for the doctor. He was hard to locate, so they ministered to her with hushed ejaculations, renewing the ice and fanning her. While the ice was fresh and cold she stopped laughing and lay still for a time, moaning only a little. But soon the laughing welled again and her voice rose screaming.

"Shhhhhhhhhhh! Shhhhhhhhhhhhhhh!" they said, freshening the icepack, smoothing her hair, examining it for gray; "poor girl!" Then to one another: "Do you suppose anything really happened?" their eyes darkly aglitter, secret and passionate. "Shhhhhhhhhh! Poor girl! Poor Minnie!"

V

It was midnight when McLendon drove up to his neat new house. It was trim and fresh as a birdcage and almost as small, with its clean, green-and-white paint. He locked the car and mounted the porch and entered. His wife rose from a chair beside the reading lamp. McLendon stopped in the floor and stared at her until she looked down.

"Look at that clock," he said, lifting his arm, pointing. She stood before him, her face lowered, a magazine in her hands. Her face was pale, strained, and weary-looking. "Haven't I told you about sitting up like this, waiting to see when I come in?"

"John," she said. She laid the magazine down. Poised on the balls of his feet, he glared at her with his hot eyes, his sweating face.

"Didn't I tell you?" He went toward her. She looked up then. He caught her shoulder. She stood passive, looking at him.

"Don't, John. I couldn't sleep . . . The heat; something. Please, John. You're hurting me."

"Didn't I tell you?" He released her and half struck, half flung her across the chair, and she lay there and watched him quietly as he left the room.

He went on through the house, ripping off his shirt, and on the dark, screened porch at the rear he stood and mopped his head and shoulders with the shirt and flung it away. He took the pistol from his hip and laid it on the table beside the bed, and sat on the bed and removed his shoes, and rose and slipped his trousers off. He was sweating again already, and he stooped and hunted furiously for the shirt. At last he found it and wiped his body again, and, with his body pressed against the dusty screen, he stood panting. There was no movement, no sound, not even an insect. The dark world seemed to lie stricken beneath the cold moon and the lidless stars.

CONSTRUCTING A READING

1. In groups, write narratives about "what really happened" in "Dry September" from the following perspectives:
   * the narrator
   * Miss Minnie Cooper
   * Will Mayes
   * McLendon
   * Hawkshaw
2. Describe the narratee of this story. As you do so, speculate about Faulkner's intention in writing it: what do you think is the author's attitude toward the people and events his narrator describes?
3. What attitude do you suppose Faulkner wants you, his actual reader, to take? How do you know? Are you willing to take that attitude? Why or why not?
4. Trace the tropes of weather and astronomy through this story. With your group, discuss how these figures work and whether they help you to make meaning.

SHARING A READING

1. Assume that a student at your school has written a letter to the student newspaper arguing that "Dry September" should be removed from the syllabus because it is a racist story that depicts violence against blacks— violence that goes unpunished. By allowing McLendon to go unpunished, the writer continues, Faulkner appears to condone the lynching of Will Mayes. Answer this letter, using the knowledge of reading you have obtained from this book so far.

A Jury of Her Peers

Susan Glaspell

When Martha Hale opened the storm door and got a cut of the north wind, she ran back for her big woolen scarf. As she hurriedly wound that round her head her eye made a scandalized sweep of her kitchen. It was no ordinary thing that called her away—it was probably farther from ordinary than anything that had ever happened in Dickson County. But what her eye took in was that her kitchen was in no shape for leaving: her bread all ready for mixing, half the flour sifted and half unsifted.

She hated to see things half done; but she had been at that when the team from town stopped to get Mr. Hale, and then the sheriff came running in to say his wife wished Mrs. Hale would come too—adding, with a grin, that he guessed she was getting scary and wanted another woman along. So she had dropped everything right where it was.

"Martha!" now came her husband's impatient voice. "Don't keep folks waiting out here in the cold."

She again opened the storm door, and this time joined the three men and the one woman waiting for her in the big two seated buggy.

After she had the robes tucked around her she took another look at the woman who sat beside her on the back seat. She had met Mrs. Peters the year before at the county fair, and the thing she remembered about her was that she didn't seem like a sheriff's wife. She was small and thin and didn't have a strong voice. Mrs. Gorman, sheriff's wife before Gorman went out and Peters came in, had a voice that somehow seemed to be backing up the law with every word. But if Mrs. Peters didn't look like a sheriff's wife, Peters made it up in looking like a sheriff. He was to a dot the kind of man who could get himself elected sheriff—a heavy man with a big voice, who was particularly genial with the law-abiding, as if to make it plain that he knew the difference between criminals and noncriminals. And right there it came into Mrs. Hale's mind, with a stab, that this man who was so pleasant and lively with all of them was going to the Wrights' now as a sheriff.

"The country's not very pleasant this time of year," Mrs. Peters at last ventured, as if she felt they ought to be talking as well as the men.

Mrs. Hale scarcely finished her reply, for they had gone up a little hill and could see the Wright place now, and seeing it did not make her feel like talking. It looked very lonesome this cold March morning. It had always been a lonesome-looking place. It was down in a hollow, and the poplar trees around it were lonesome-looking trees. The men were looking at it and talking about what had happened. The county attorney was bending to one side of the buggy, and kept looking steadily at the place as they drew up to it.

"I'm glad you came with me," Mrs. Peters said nervously, as the two women were about to follow the men in through the kitchen door.

Even after she had her foot on the doorstep, her hand on the knob, Martha Hale had a moment of feeling she could not cross that threshold. And the reason it seemed she couldn't cross it now was simply because she hadn't crossed it before. Time and time again it had been in her mind. "I ought to go over and see Minnie Foster"—she still thought of her as Minnie Foster, though for twenty years she had been Mrs. Wright. And then there was always something to do and Minnie Foster would go from her mind. But *now* she could come.

The men went over to the stove. The women stood close together by the door. Young Henderson, the county attorney, turned around and said, "Come up to the fire, ladies."

Mrs. Peters took a step forward, then stopped. "I'm not—cold," she said.

And so the two women stood by the door, at first not even so much as looking around the kitchen.

The men talked for a minute about what a good thing it was the sheriff had sent his deputy out that morning to make a fire for them, and then Sheriff Peters stepped back from the stove, unbuttoned his outer coat, and leaned his hands on the kitchen table in a way that seemed to mark the beginning of official business. "Now, Mr. Hale," he said in a sort of semi-official voice, "before we move things about, you tell Mr. Henderson just what it was you saw when you came here yesterday morning."

The county attorney was looking around the kitchen.

"By the way," he said, "has anything been moved?" He turned to the sheriff. "Are things just as you left them yesterday?"

Peters looked from cupboard to sink; from that to a small worn rocker a little to one side of the kitchen table.

"It's just the same."

"Somebody should have been left here yesterday," said the county attorney.

"Oh—yesterday," returned the sheriff, with a little gesture as of yesterday having been more than he could bear to think of. "When I had to send Frank to Morris Center for that man who went crazy—let me tell you, I had my hands full *yesterday*. I knew you could get back from Omaha by today, George, and as long as I went over everything here myself—"

"Well, Mr. Hale," said the county attorney, in a way of letting what was past and gone go, "tell just what happened when you came here yesterday morning."

Mrs. Hale, still leaning against the door, had that sinking feeling of the mother whose child is about to speak a piece. Lewis often wandered along and got things mixed up in a story. She hoped he would tell this straight and plain, and not say unnecessary things that would just make things harder for Minnie Foster. He didn't begin at once, and she noticed that he looked queer—as if standing in that kitchen and having to tell what he had seen there yesterday morning made him almost sick.

"Yes, Mr. Hale?" the county attorney reminded.

"Harry and I had started to town with a load of potatoes," Mrs. Hale's husband began.

Harry was Mrs. Hale's oldest boy. He wasn't with them now, for the very good reason that those potatoes never got to town yesterday and he was taking them this morning, so he hadn't been home when the sheriff stopped to say he wanted Mr. Hale to come over to the Wright place and tell the county attorney his story there, where he could point it all out. With all Mrs. Hale's other emotions came the fear that maybe Harry wasn't dressed warm enough—they hadn't any of them realized how that north wind did bite.

"We come along this road," Hale was going on, with a motion of his hand to the road over which they had just come, "and as we got in sight of the house

I says to Harry, 'I'm goin' to see if I can't get John Wright to take a telephone.' You see," he explained to Henderson, "unless I can get somebody to go in with me they won't come out this branch road except for a price *I* can't pay. I'd spoke to Wright about it once before; but he put me off, saying folks talked too much anyway, and all he asked was peace and quiet—guess you know about how much he talked himself. But I thought maybe if I went to the house and talked about it before his wife, and said all the womenfolks liked the telephones, and that in this lonesome stretch of road it would be a good thing— well, I said to Harry that that was what I was going to say—though I said at the same time that I didn't know as what his wife wanted made much difference to John—"

Now, there he was!—saying things he didn't need to say. Mrs. Hale tried to catch her husband's eye, but fortunately the county attorney interrupted with:

"Let's talk about that a little later, Mr. Hale. I do want to talk about that, but I'm anxious now to get along to just what happened when you got here."

When he began this time, it was very deliberately and carefully:

"I didn't see or hear anything. I knocked at the door. And still it was all quiet inside. I knew they must be up—it was past eight o'clock. So I knocked again, louder, and I thought I heard somebody say 'Come in.' I wasn't sure— I'm not sure yet. But I opened the door—this door," jerking a hand toward the door by which the two women stood, "and there, in that rocker"—pointing to it—"sat Mrs. Wright."

Everyone in the kitchen looked at the rocker. It came into Mrs. Hale's mind that the rocker didn't look in the least like Minnie Foster—the Minnie Foster of twenty years before. It was a dingy red, with wooden rungs up the back, and the middle rung was gone, and the chair sagged to one side.

"How did she—look?" the county attorney was inquiring.

"Well," said Hale, "she looked—queer."

"How do you mean—queer?"

As he asked it he took out a notebook and pencil. Mrs. Hale did not like the sight of that pencil. She kept her eye fixed on her husband, as if to keep him from saying unnecessary things that would go into that notebook and make trouble.

Hale did speak guardedly, as if the pencil had affected him too.

"Well, as if she didn't know what she was going to do next. And kind of— done up."

"How did she seem to feel about your coming?"

"Why, I don't think she minded—one way or other. She didn't pay much attention. I said, 'Ho' do, Mrs. Wright? It's cold, ain't it!' And she said, 'Is it?'— and went on pleatin' at her apron.

"Well, I was surprised. She didn't ask me to come up to the stove, or to sit down, but just set there, not even lookin' at me. And so I said: 'I want to see John.'

"And then she—laughed. I guess you would call it a laugh.

"I thought of Harry and the team outside, so I said, a little sharp, 'Can I see John?' 'No,' says she—kind of dull like. 'Ain't he home?' says I. Then she looked at me. 'Yes,' says she, 'he's home.' 'Then why can't I see him?' I asked her, out of patience with her now. 'Cause he's dead,' says she, just as quiet and dull—and fell to pleatin' her apron. 'Dead?' says I, like you do when you can't take in what you've heard.

"She just nodded her head, not getting a bit excited, but rockin' back and forth.

"'Why—where is he?' says I, not knowing *what* to say.

"She just pointed upstairs—like this"—pointing to the room above.

"I got up, with the idea of going up there myself. By this time I—didn't know what to do. I walked from there to here; then I says: 'Why, what did he die of?'

"'He died of a rope around his neck,' says she; and just went on pleatin' at her apron."

Hale stopped speaking, and stood staring at the rocker, as if he were still seeing the woman who had sat there the morning before. Nobody spoke; it was as if everyone were seeing the woman who had sat there the morning before.

"And what did you do then?" the county attorney at last broke the silence.

"I went out and called Harry. I thought I might—need help. I got Harry in, and we went upstairs." His voice fell almost to a whisper. "There he was— lying over the—"

"I think I'd rather have you go into that upstairs," the county attorney interrupted, "where you can point it all out. Just go on now with the rest of the story."

"Well, my first thought was to get that rope off. It looked—"

He stopped, his face twitching

"But Harry, he went up to him, and he said, 'No, he's dead all right, and we'd better not touch anything.' So we went downstairs.

"She was still sitting the same way. 'Has anybody been notified?' I asked. 'No,' says she, unconcerned.

"'Who did this, Mrs. Wright?' said Harry. He said it business-like, and she stopped pleatin' at her apron. 'I don't know,' she says. 'You don't *know?*' says Harry. 'Weren't you sleepin' in the bed with him?' 'Yes,' says she, 'but I was on the inside.' 'Somebody slipped a rope round his neck and strangled him, and you didn't wake up?' says Harry. 'I didn't wake up,' she said after him.

"We may have looked as if we didn't see how that could be, for after a minute she said, 'I sleep sound.'

"Harry was going to ask her more questions, but I said maybe that weren't our business; maybe we ought to let her tell her story first to the coroner or the sheriff. So Harry went fast as he could over to High Road—the Rivers' place, where there's a telephone."

"And what did she do when she knew you had gone for the coroner?" The attorney got his pencil in his hand all ready for writing.

"She moved from that chair to this one over here"—Hale pointed to a small chair in the corner—"and just sat there with her hands held together and looking down. I got a feeling that I ought to make some conversation, so I said I had come in to see if John wanted to put in a telephone; and at that she started to laugh, and then she stopped and looked at me—scared."

At the sound of a moving pencil the man who was telling the story looked up.

"I dunno—maybe it wasn't scared," he hastened; "I wouldn't like to say it was. Soon Harry got back, and then Dr. Lloyd came, and you, Mr. Peters, and so I guess that's all I know that you don't."

He said that last with relief, and moved a little, as if relaxing. Everyone moved a little. The county attorney walked toward the stair door.

"I guess we'll go upstairs first—then out to the barn and around there."

He paused and looked around the kitchen.

"You're convinced there was nothing important here?" he asked the sheriff. "Nothing that would—point to any motive?"

The sheriff too looked all around, as if to reconvince himself.

"Nothing here but kitchen things," he said, with a little laugh for the insignificance of kitchen things.

The county attorney was looking at the cupboard—a peculiar, ungainly structure, half closet and half cupboard, the upper part of it being built in the wall, and the lower part just the old-fashioned kitchen cupboard. As if its queerness attracted him, he got a chair and opened the upper part and looked in. After a moment he drew his hand away sticky.

"Here's a nice mess," he said resentfully.

The two women had drawn nearer, and now the sheriff's wife spoke.

"Oh—her fruit," she said, looking to Mrs. Hale for sympathetic understanding. She turned back to the county attorney and explained: "She worried about that when it turned so cold last night. She said the fire would go out and her jars might burst."

Mrs. Peters' husband broke into a laugh.

"Well, can you beat the women! Held for murder, and worrying about her preserves!"

The young attorney set his lips.

"I guess before we're through with her she may have something more serious than preserves to worry about."

"Oh, well," said Mrs. Hale's husband, with good-natured superiority, "women are used to worrying over trifles."

The two women moved a little closer together. Neither of them spoke.

The county attorney seemed suddenly to remember his manners—and think of his future.

"And yet," said he, with the gallantry of a young politician, "for all their worries, what would we do without the ladies?"

The women did not speak, did not unbend. He went to the sink and began washing his hands. He turned to wipe them on the roller towel—whirled it for a cleaner place.

"Dirty towels! Not much of a housekeeper, would you say, ladies?"

He kicked his foot against some dirty pans under the sink.

"There's a great deal of work to be done on a farm," said Mrs. Hale stiffly.

"To be sure. And yet"—with a little bow to her—"I know there are some Dickson County farmhouses that do not have such roller towels." He gave it a pull to expose its full length again.

"Those towels get dirty awful quick. Men's hands aren't always as clean as they might be."

"Ah, loyal to your sex, I see," he laughed. He stopped and gave her a keen look. "But you and Mrs. Wright were neighbors. I suppose you were friends, too."

Martha Hale shook her head.

"I've seen little enough of her of late years. I've not been in this house— it's more than a year."

"And why was that? You didn't like her?"

"I liked her well enough," she replied with spirit "Farmers' wives have their hands full, Mr. Henderson. And then"—she looked around the kitchen.

"Yes?" he encouraged.

"It never seemed a very cheerful place," said she, more to herself than to him.

"No," he agreed; "I don't think anyone would call it cheerful. I shouldn't say she had the homemaking instinct."

"Well, I don't know as Wright had, either," she muttered.

"You mean they didn't get on very well?" he was quick to ask.

"No; I don't mean anything," she answered, with decision. As she turned a little away from him, she added: "But I don't think a place would be any the cheerfuler for John Wright's bein' in it."

"I'd like to talk to you about that a little later, Mrs. Hale," he said. "I'm anxious to get the lay of things upstairs now."

He moved toward the stair door, followed by the two men.

"I suppose anything Mrs. Peters does'll be all right?" the sheriff inquired. "She was to take in some clothes for her, you know—and a few little things. We left in such a hurry yesterday."

The county attorney looked at the two women whom they were leaving alone there among the kitchen things.

"Yes—Mrs. Peters," he said, his glance resting on the woman who was not Mrs. Peters, the big farmer woman who stood behind the sheriff's wife. "Of course Mrs. Peters is one of us," he said, in a manner of entrusting responsibility. "And keep your eye out, Mrs. Peters, for anything that might be of use. No telling; you women might come upon a clue to the motive—and that's the thing we need."

Mr. Hale rubbed his face after the fashion of a showman getting ready for a pleasantry.

"But would the women know a clue if they did come upon it?" he said; and, having delivered himself of this, he followed the others through the stair door.

The women stood motionless and silent, listening to the footsteps, first upon the stairs, then in the room above them.

Then, as if releasing herself from something strange, Mrs. Hale began to arrange the dirty pans under the sink, which the county attorney's disdainful push of the foot had deranged.

"I'd hate to have men comin' into my kitchen," she said testily— "snoopin' round and criticizin'."

"Of course it's no more than their duty," said the sheriff's wife, in her manner of timid acquiescence.

"Duty's all right," replied Mrs. Hale bluffly; "but I guess that deputy sheriff that come out to make the fire might have got a little of this on." She gave the roller towel a pull. "Wish I'd thought of that sooner! Seems mean to talk about her for not having things slicked up, when she had to come away in such a hurry."

She looked around the kitchen. Certainly it was not "slicked up." Her eye was held by a bucket of sugar on a low shelf. The cover was off the wooden bucket, and beside it was a paper bag—half full.

Mrs. Hale moved toward it

"She was putting this in there," she said to herself—slowly.

She thought of the flour in her kitchen at home—half sifted, half not sifted. She had been interrupted and had left things half done. What had interrupted Minnie Foster? Why had that work been left half done? She made a move as if to finish it,—unfinished things always bothered her,—and then she glanced around and saw that Mrs. Peters was watching her—and she didn't want Mrs. Peters to get that feeling she had got of work begun and then—for some reason—not finished.

"It's a shame about her fruit," she said, and walked toward the cupboard that the county attorney had opened, and got on the chair, murmuring: "I wonder if it's all gone."

It was a sorry enough looking sight, but "Here's one that's all right," she said at last. She held it toward the light. "This is cherries, too." She looked again. "I declare I believe that's the only one."

With a sigh, she got down from the chair, went to the sink, and wiped off the bottle.

"She'll feel awful bad, after all her hard work in the hot weather. I remember the afternoon I put up my cherries last summer."

She set the bottle on the table, and, with another sigh, started to sit down in the rocker. But she did not sit down. Something kept her from sitting down in that chair. She straightened—stepped back, and, half turned away, stood looking at it, seeing the woman who sat there "pleatin' at her apron."

The thin voice of the sheriff's wife broke in upon her: "I must be getting those things from the front room closet." She opened the door into the other room, started in, stepped back. "You coming with me, Mrs. Hale?" she asked nervously. "You—you could help me get them."

They were soon back—the stark coldness of that shut-up room was not a thing to linger in.

"My!" said Mrs. Peters, dropping the things on the table and hurrying to the stove.

Mrs. Hale stood examining the clothes the woman who was being detained in town had said she wanted.

"Wright was close!" she exclaimed, holding up a shabby black skirt that bore the marks of much making over. "I think maybe that's why she kept so much to herself. I s'pose she felt she couldn't do her part; and then, you don't enjoy things when you feel shabby. She used to wear pretty clothes and be lively—when she was Minnie Foster, one of the town girls, singing in the choir. But that—oh, that was twenty years ago."

With a carefulness in which there was something tender, she folded the shabby clothes and piled them at one corner of the table. She looked at Mrs. Peters, and there was something in the other woman's look that irritated her.

"She don't care," she said to herself. "Much difference it makes to her whether Minnie Foster had pretty clothes when she was a girl."

Then she looked again, and she wasn't so sure; in fact, she hadn't at any time been perfectly sure about Mrs. Peters. She had that shrinking manner, and yet her eyes looked as if they could see a long way into things.

"This all you was to take in?" asked Mrs. Hale.

"No," said the sheriff's wife; "she said she wanted an apron. Funny thing to want," she ventured in her nervous little way, "for there's not much to get you dirty in jail, goodness knows. But I suppose just to make her feel more natural. If you're used to wearing an apron—. She said they were in the bottom drawer of this cupboard. Yes—here they are. And then her little shawl that always hung on the stair door."

She took the small gray shawl from behind the door leading upstairs, and stood a minute looking at it.

Suddenly Mrs. Hale took a quick step toward the other woman.

"Mrs. Peters!"

"Yes, Mrs. Hale?"

"Do you think she—did it?"

A frightened look blurred the other things in Mrs. Peters' eyes.

"Oh, I don't know," she said, in a voice that seemed to shrink away from the subject.

"Well, I don't think she did," affirmed Mrs. Hale stoutly.

"Asking for an apron, and her little shawl. Worryin' about her friut."

"Mr. Peters says—" Footsteps were heard in the room above; she stopped, looked up, then went on in a lowered voice: "Mr. Peters says—it looks bad for her. Mr. Henderson is awful sarcastic in a speech, and he's going to make fun of her saying she didn't—wake up."

For a moment Mrs. Hale had no answer. Then, "Well, I guess John Wright didn't wake up—when they was slippin' that rope under his neck," she muttered.

"No, it's *strange*," breathed Mrs. Peters. "They think it was such a—funny way to kill a man."

She began to laugh; at sound of the laugh, abruptly stopped.

"That's just what Mr. Hale said," said Mrs. Hale, in a resolutely natural voice. "There was a gun in the house. He says that's what he can't understand."

"Mr. Henderson said, coming out, that what was needed for the case was a motive. Something to show anger—or sudden feeling."

"Well, I don't see any signs of anger around here," said Mrs. Hale. "I don't—"

She stopped. It was as if her mind tripped on something. Her eye was caught by a dish towel in the middle of the kitchen table. Slowly she moved toward the table. One half of it was wiped clean, the other half messy. Her eyes made a slow, almost unwilling turn to the bucket of sugar and the half empty bag beside it. Things begun—and not finished.

After a moment she stepped back, and said, in that manner of releasing herself:

"Wonder how they're finding things upstairs? I hope she had it a little more red-up up there. You know,"—she paused, and feeling gathered,—"it seems kind of *sneaking;* locking her up in town and coming out here to get her own house to turn against her!"

"But, Mrs. Hale," said the sheriff's wife, "the law is the law."

"I s'pose 'tis," answered Mrs. Hale shortly.

She turned to the stove, saying something about that fire not being much to brag of. She worked with it a minute, and when she straightened up she said aggressively:

"The law is the law—and a bad stove is a bad stove. How'd you like to cook on this?"—pointing with the poker to the broken lining. She opened the oven door and started to express her opinion of the oven; but she was swept into her own thoughts, thinking of what it would mean, year after year, to have that stove to wrestle with. The thought of Minnie Foster trying to bake in that oven—and the thought of her never going over to see Minnie Foster—.

She was startled by hearing Mrs. Peters say: "A person gets discouraged—and loses heart."

The sheriff's wife had looked from the stove to the sink—to the pail of water which had been carried in from outside. The two women stood there silent, above them the footsteps of the men who were looking for evidence against the woman who had worked in that kitchen. That look of seeing into things, of seeing through a thing to something else, was in the eyes of the sheriff's wife now. When Mrs. Hale next spoke to her, it was gently:

"Better loosen up your things, Mrs. Peters. We'll not feel them when we go out."

Mrs. Peters went to the back of the room to hang up the fur tippet she was wearing. A moment later she exclaimed, "Why, she was piecing a quilt," and held up a large sewing basket piled high with quilt pieces.

Mrs. Hale spread some of the blocks on the table.

"It's log-cabin pattern," she said, putting several of them together. "Pretty, isn't it?"

They were so engaged with the quilt that they did not hear the footsteps on the stairs. Just as the stair door opened Mrs. Hale was saying:

"Do you suppose she was going to quilt it or just knot it?"

The sheriff threw up his hands.

"They wonder whether she was going to quilt it or just knot it!"

There was a laugh for the ways of women, a warming of hands over the stove, and then the county attorney said briskly:

"Well, let's go right out to the barn and get that cleared up."

"I don't see as there's anything so strange," Mrs. Hale said resentfully, after the outside door had closed on the three men—"our taking up our time with little things while we're waiting for them to get the evidence. I don't see as it's anything to laugh about."

"Of course they've got awful important things on their minds," said the sheriff's wife apologetically.

They returned to an inspection of the blocks for the quilt. Mrs. Hale was looking at the fine, even sewing, and preoccupied with thoughts of the woman who had done that sewing, when she heard the sheriff's wife say, in a queer tone:

"Why, look at this one."

She turned to take the block held out to her.

"The sewing," said Mrs. Peters, in a troubled way. "All the rest of them have been so nice and even—but—this one. Why, it looks as if she didn't know what she was about!"

Their eyes met—something flashed to life, passed between them; then, as if with an effort, they seemed to pull away from each other. A moment Mrs. Hale sat there, her hands folded over that sewing which was so unlike all the rest of the sewing. Then she had pulled a knot and drawn the threads.

"Oh, what are you doing, Mrs. Hale?" asked the sheriffs wife, startled.

"Just pulling out a stitch or two that's not sewed very good," said Mrs. Hale mildly.

"I don't think we ought to touch things," Mrs. Peters said, a little help-lessly.

"I'd just finish up this end," answered Mrs. Hale, still in that mild, mat-ter-of-fact fashion.

She threaded a needle and started to replace bad sewing with good. For a little while she sewed in silence. Then, in that thin, timid voice, she heard:

"Mrs. Hale!"

"Yes, Mrs. Peters?"

'What do you suppose she was so—nervous about?"

"Oh, *I* don't know," said Mrs. Hale, as if dismissing a thing not important enough to spend much time on. "I don't know as she was—nervous. I sew awful queer sometimes when I'm just tired."

She cut a thread, and out of the corner of her eye looked up at Mrs. Peters. The small, lean face of the sheriff's wife seemed to have tightened up. Her eyes had that look of peering into something. But the next moment she moved, and said in her thin, indecisive way:

"Well, I must get those clothes wrapped. They may be through sooner than we think. I wonder where I could find a piece of paper—and string."

"In that cupboard, maybe," suggested Mrs. Hale, after a glance around.

One piece of the crazy sewing remained unripped. Mrs. Peters' back turned, Martha Hale now scrutinized that piece, compared it with the dainty, accurate sewing of the other blocks. The difference was startling. Holding this block made her feel queer, as if the distracted thoughts of the woman who had per-haps turned to it to try and quiet herself were communicating themselves to her.

Mrs. Peters' voice roused her.

"Here's a birdcage," she said. "Did she have a bird, Mrs. Hale?"

"Why, I don't know whether she did or not." She turned to look at the cage Mrs. Peters was holding up. "I've not been here in so long." She sighed. "There was a man round last year selling canaries cheap—but I don't know as she took one. Maybe she did. She used to sing real pretty herself."

Mrs. Peters looked around the kitchen.

"Seems kind of funny to think of a bird here." She half laughed—an attempt to put up a barrier. "But she must have had one—or why would she have a cage? I wonder what happened to it."

"I suppose maybe the cat got it," suggested Mrs. Hale, resuming her sewing.

"No; she didn't have a cat. She's got that feeling some people have about cats—being afraid of them. When they brought her to our house yesterday, my cat got in the room, and she was real upset and asked me to take it out."

"My sister Bessie was like that," laughed Mrs. Hale.

The sheriff's wife did not reply. The silence made Mrs. Hale turn round. Mrs. Peters was examining the bird cage.

"Look at this door," she said slowly. "It's broke. One hinge has been pulled apart."

Mrs. Hale came nearer.

"Looks as if someone must have been—rough with it."

Again their eyes met—startled, questioning, apprehensive. For a moment neither spoke nor stirred. Then Mrs. Hale, turning away, said brusquely:

"If they're going to find any evidence, I wish they'd be about it. I don't like this place."

"But I'm awful glad you came with me, Mrs. Hale." Mrs. Peters put the birdcage on the table and sat down. "It would be lonesome for me—sitting here alone."

"Yes, it would, wouldn't it?" agreed Mrs. Hale, a certain determined naturalness in her voice. She picked up the sewing, but now it dropped in her lap, and she murmured in a different voice: "But I tell you what I *do* wish, Mrs. Peters. I wish I had come over sometimes when she was here. I wish—I had."

"But of course you were awful busy, Mrs. Hale. Your house—and your children."

"I could've come," retorted Mrs. Hale shortly. "I stayed away because it weren't cheerful—and that's why I ought to have come. I"—she looked around—"I've never liked this place. Maybe because it's down in a hollow and you don't see the road. I don't know what it is, but it's a lonesome place, and always was. I wish I had come over to see Minnie Foster sometimes. I can see now—" She did not put it into words.

"Well, you mustn't reproach yourself," counseled Mrs. Peters. "Somehow, we just don't see how it is with other folks till something comes up."

"Not having children makes less work," mused Mrs. Hale, after a silence, "but it makes a quiet house—and Wright out to work all day—and no company when he did come in. Did you know John Wright, Mrs. Peters?"

"Not to know him. I've seen him in town. They say he was a good man."

"Yes—good," conceded John Wright's neighbor grimly. "He didn't drink, and kept his word as well as most, I guess, and paid his debts. But he was a hard man, Mrs. Peters. Just to pass the time of day with him—." She stopped, shivered a little. "Like a raw wind that gets to the bone." Her eye fell upon the cage on the table before her, and she added, almost bitterly: "I should think she would've wanted a bird!"

Suddenly she leaned forward, looking intently at the cage. "But what do you s'pose went wrong with it?"

"I don't know," returned Mrs. Peters; "unless it got sick and died."

But after she said it she reached over and swung the broken door. Both women watched it as if somehow held by it.

"You didn't know—her?" Mrs. Hale asked, a gentler note in her voice.

"Not till they brought her yesterday," said the sheriff's wife.

"She—come to think of it, she was kind of like a bird herself. Real sweet and pretty, but kind of timid and-fluttery. How—she—did—change."

That held her for a long time. Finally, as if struck with a happy thought and relieved to get back to everyday things, she exclaimed:

"Tell you what, Mrs. Peters, why don't you take the quilt in with you? It might take up her mind."

"Why, I think that's a real nice idea, Mrs. Hale," agreed the sheriff's wife, as if she too were glad to come into the atmosphere of a simple kindness. "There couldn't possibly be any objection to that, could there? Now, just what will I take? I wonder if her patches are in here—and her things."

They turned to the sewing basket.

"Here's some red," said Mrs. Hale, bringing out a roll of cloth. Underneath that was a box. "Here, maybe her scissors are in here—and her things." She held it up. "What a pretty box! I'll warrant that was something she had a long time ago—when she was a girl."

She held it in her hand a moment; then, with a little sigh, opened it.

Instantly her hand went to her nose.

"Why—!"

Mrs. Peters drew nearer—then turned away.

"There's something wrapped up in this piece of silk," faltered Mrs. Hale.

"This isn't her scissors," said Mrs. Peters in a shrinking voice.

Her hand not steady, Mrs. Hale raised the piece of silk. "Oh, Mrs. Peters!" she cried. "It's—"

Mrs. Peters bent closer.

"It's the bird," she whispered.

"But, Mrs. Peters!" cried Mrs. Hale. "*Look* at it! Its neck—look at its neck! It's all—other side *to*."

She held the box away from her.

The sheriff's wife again bent closer.

"Somebody wrung its neck," said she, in a voice that was slow and deep.

And then again the eyes of the two women met—this time clung together in a look of dawning comprehension, of growing horror. Mrs. Peters looked from the dead bird to the broken door of the cage. Again their eyes met. And just then there was a sound at the outside door.

Mrs. Hale slipped the box under the quilt pieces in the basket, and sank into the chair before it. Mrs. Peters stood holding to the table. The county attorney and the sheriff came in from outside.

"'Well, ladies," said the county attorney, as one turning from serious things to little pleasantries, "have you decided whether she was going to quilt it or knot it?"

"We think," began the sheriff's wife in a flurried voice, "that she was going to—knot it."

He was too preoccupied to notice the change that came in her voice on that last.

"Well, that's very interesting, I'm sure," he said tolerantly. He caught sight of the birdcage. "Has the bird flown?"

"We think the cat got it," said Mrs. Hale in a voice curiously even.

He was walking up and down, as if thinking something out.

"Is there a cat?" he asked absently.

Mrs. Hale shot a look up at the sheriff's wife.

"Well, not *now*," said Mrs. Peters. "They're superstitious, you know; they leave."

She sank into her chair.

The county attorney did not heed her. No sign at all of anyone having come in from the outside," he said to Peters, in the manner of continuing an interrupted conversation. "Their own rope. Now let's go upstairs again and go over it, piece by piece. It would have to have been someone who knew just the—"

The stair door closed behind them and their voices were lost.

The two women sat motionless, not looking at each other, but as if peering into something and at the same time holding back. When they spoke now it was as if they were afraid of what they were saying, but as if they could not help saying it.

"She liked the bird," said Martha Hale, low and slowly. "She was going to bury it in that pretty box."

"When I was a girl," said Mrs. Peters, under her breath, "my kitten— there was a boy took a hatchet, and before my eyes—before I could get there—" She covered her face an instant. "If they hadn't held me back I would have"— she caught herself, looked upstairs where footsteps were heard, and finished weakly—"hurt him."

Then they sat without speaking or moving.

"I wonder how it would seem," Mrs. Hale at last began, as if feeling her way over strange ground—"never to have had any children around?" Her eyes made a slow sweep of the kitchen, as if seeing what that kitchen had meant through all the years. "No, Wright wouldn't like the bird," she said after that—"a thing that sang. She used to sing. He killed that too." Her voice tightened.

Mrs. Peters moved uneasily.

"Of course we don't know who killed the bird."

"I knew John Wright," was Mrs. Hale's answer.

"It was an awful thing was done in this house that night, Mrs. Hale," said the sheriff's wife. "Killing a man while he slept—slipping a thing round his neck that choked the life out of him."

Mrs. Hale's hand went out to the birdcage.

"His neck. Choked the life out of him."

"'We don't *know* who killed him," whispered Mrs. Peters wildly. "'We don't *know*."

Mrs. Hale had not moved. "If there had been years and years of—nothing, then a bird to sing to you, it would be awful—still—after the bird was still."

It was as if something within her not herself had spoken, and it found in Mrs. Peters something she did not know as herself.

"I know what stillness is," she said, in a queer, monotonous voice. "When we homesteaded in Dakota, and my first baby died—after he was two years old—and me with no other then—"

Mrs. Hale stirred.

"How soon do you suppose they'll be through looking for evidence?"

"I know what stillness is," repeated Mrs. Peters, in just that same way. Then she too pulled back. "The law has got to punish crime, Mrs. Hale," she said in her tight little way.

"I wish you'd seen Minnie Foster," was the answer, "when she wore a white dress with blue ribbons, and stood up there in the choir and sang."

The picture of that girl, the fact that she had lived neighbor to that girl for twenty years, and had let her die for lack of life, was suddenly more than she could bear.

"Oh, I *wish* I'd come over here once in a while!" she cried. "That was a crime! That was a crime! Who's going to punish that?"

"'We mustn't take on," said Mrs. Peters, with a frightened look toward the stairs.

"I might 'a' *known* she needed help! I tell you, it's *queer*, Mrs. Peters. We live close together, and we live far apart. We all go through the same things—it's all just a different kind of the same thing! If it weren't—why do you and I *understand*? Why do we *know*—what we know this minute?"

She dashed her hand across her eyes. Then, seeing the jar of fruit on the table, she reached for it and choked out:

"If I was you I wouldn't *tell* her her fruit was gone! Tell her it *ain't*. Tell her it's all right—all of it. Here—take this in to prove it to her! She—she may never know whether it was broke or not."

She turned away.

Mrs. Peters reached out for the bottle of fruit as if she were glad to take it—as if touching a familiar thing, having something to do, could keep her *from* something else. She got up, looked about for something to wrap the fruit in, took a petticoat from the pile of clothes she had brought from the front room, and nervously started winding that round the bottle.

"My!" she began, in a high, false voice, "it's a good thing the men couldn't hear us! Getting all stirred up over a little thing like a—dead canary." She hurried over that. "As if that could have anything to do with—with—My, wouldn't they *laugh?*"

Footsteps were heard on the stairs.

"Maybe they would," muttered Mrs. Hale—"maybe they wouldn't."

"No, Peters," said the county attorney incisively; "it's all perfectly clear, except the reason for doing it. But you know juries when it comes to women. If there was some definite thing—something to show. Something to make a story about. A thing that would connect up with this clumsy way of doing it."

In a covert way Mrs. Hale looked at Mrs. Peters. Mrs. Peters was looking at her. Quickly they looked away from each other. The outer door opened and Mr. Hale came in.

"I've got the team round now," he said. "Pretty cold out there."

"I'm going to stay here awhile by myself," the county attorney suddenly announced. "You can send Frank out for me, can't you?" he asked the sheriff. "I want to go over everything. I'm not satisfied we can't do better."

Again, for one brief moment, the two women's eyes found one another.

The sheriff came up to the table.

"Did you want to see what Mrs. Peters was going to take in?"

The county attorney picked up the apron. He laughed.

"Oh, I guess they're not very dangerous things the ladies have picked out."

Mrs. Hale's hand was on the sewing basket in which the box was concealed. She felt that she ought to take her hand off the basket. She did not seem able to. He picked up one of the quilt blocks which she had piled on to cover the box. Her eyes felt like fire. She had a feeling that if he took up the basket she would snatch it from him.

But he did not take it up. With another little laugh, he turned away, saying:

"No; Mrs. Peters doesn't need supervising. For that matter, a sheriff's wife is married to the law. Ever think of it that way, Mrs. Peters?"

Mrs. Peters was standing beside the table. Mrs. Hale shot a look up at her; but she could not see her face. Mrs. Peters had turned away. When she spoke, her voice was muffled.

"Not—just that way," she said.

"Married to the law!" chuckled Mrs. Peters' husband. He moved toward the door into the front room, and said to the county attorney:

"I just want you to come in here a minute, George. We ought to take a look at these windows."

"Oh—windows," said the county attorney scoffingly.

"We'll be right out, Mr. Hale," said the sheriff to the farmer, who was still waiting by the door.

Hale went to look after the horses. The sheriff followed the county attorney into the other room. Again—for one moment—the two women were alone in that kitchen.

Martha Hale sprang up, her hands tight together, looking at that other woman, with whom it rested. At first she could not see her eyes, for the sheriff's wife had not turned back, since she turned away at that suggestion of being married to the law. But now Mrs. Hale made her turn back. Her eyes made her turn back. Slowly, unwillingly, Mrs. Peters turned her head until her eyes met the eyes of the other woman. There was a moment when they held each other in a steady, burning look in which there was no evasion nor flinching. Then Martha Hale's eyes pointed the way to the basket in which was hidden the thing that would make certain the conviction of the other woman—that woman who was not there and yet who had been there with them all through the hour.

For a moment Mrs. Peters did not move. And then she did it. With a rush forward, she threw back the quilt pieces, got the box, tried to put it in her handbag. It was too big. Desperately she opened it, started to take the bird out. But there she broke—she could not touch the bird. She stood helpless, foolish.

There was the sound of a knob turning in the inner door. Martha Hale snatched the box from the sheriff's wife, and got it in the pocket of her big coat just as the sheriff and the county attorney came back into the kitchen.

"Well, Henry," said the county attorney facetiously, "at least we found out that she was not going to quilt it. She was going to—what is it you call it, ladies?"

Mrs. Hale's hand was against the pocket of her coat.

"'We call it—knot it, Mr. Henderson."

CONSTRUCTING A READING

1. Both "Home Burial" and "A Jury of Her Peers" deal with gender differences in a marriage. Describe your responses to the two female characters. Do you sympathize? Distance yourself? How does the narration affect your response?
2. In " A Jury of Her Peers," the men are looking for a different kind of evidence than what Mrs. Peters and Mrs. Hale find in the kitchen. What kind of evidence are the men looking for? What are the women looking for? What, if anything, does the narration of this story imply about women's ways of knowing as opposed to men's ways of knowing?
3. Can Minnie get a fair trial with a jury of her peers in this story? Does she? How might gender influence your opinion?
4. How does the notion of "burial" function in "A Jury of Her Peers" and in "Home Burial"? Who (or what) gets buried in each story? What does each burial mean?

SHARING A READING

1. Both "My Last Duchess" and "A Jury of Her Peers" tell stories about the killing of a spouse. Narrators and narratees, however, are different. The Duke of Ferrara tells his own story to a representative of the father of his wife to be, while an unnamed narrator tells the story of Minnie Wright

and her peers to an unnamed audience. With your group, discuss the ways in which narrative perspectives affect your degree of sympathy for the characters in these stories. Then, write an essay in which you speculate about how the narration in these two literary texts affects your understanding of the problem of domestic violence in contemporary life.

Araby

James Joyce

North Richmond Street, being blind, was a quiet street except at the hour when the Christian Brothers' School set the boys free. An uninhabited house of two storeys stood at the blind end, detached from its neighbours in a square ground. The other houses of the street, conscious of decent lives within them, gazed at one another with brown imperturbable faces.

The former tenant of our house, a priest, had died in the back drawing-room. Air, musty from having been long enclosed, hung in all the rooms, and the waste room behind the kitchen was littered with old useless papers. Among these I found a few paper-covered books, the pages of which were curled and damp: *The Abbot*, by Walter Scott, *The Devout Communicant* and *The Memoirs of Vidocq*. I liked the last best because its leaves were yellow. The wild garden behind the house contained a central apple-tree and a few straggling bushes under one of which I found the late tenant's rusty bicycle-pump. He had been a very charitable priest; in his will he had left all his money to institutions and the furniture of his house to his sister.

When the short days of winter came dusk fell before we had well eaten our dinners. When we met in the street the houses had grown sombre. The space of sky above us was the colour of ever-changing violet and towards it the lamps of the street lifted their feeble lanterns. The cold air stung us and we played till our bodies glowed. Our shouts echoed in the silent street. The career of our play brought us through the dark muddy lanes behind the houses where we ran the gantlet of the rough tribes from the cottages, to the back doors of the dark dripping gardens where odours arose from the ashpits, to the dark odorous stables where a coachman smoothed and combed the horse or shook music from the buckled harness. When we returned to the street light from the kitchen windows had filled the areas. If my uncle was seen turning the corner we hid in the shadow until we had seen him safely housed. Or if Mangan's sister came out on the doorstep to call her brother in to his tea we watched her from our shadow peer up and down the street. We waited to see whether she would remain or go in and, if she remained, we left our shadow and walked up to Mangan's steps resignedly. She was waiting for us, her figure defined by the light from the half-opened door. Her brother always teased her before he obeyed and I stood by the railings looking at her. Her dress swung as she moved her body and the soft rope of her hair tossed from side to side.

Every morning I lay on the floor in the front parlour watching her door. The blind was pulled down to within an inch of the sash so that I could not be seen. When she came out on the doorstep my heart leaped. I ran to the hall, seized my books and followed her. I kept her brown figure always in my eye and, when we came near the point at which our ways diverged, I quickened my pace and passed her. This happened morning after morning. I had never spoken to her, except for a few casual words, and yet her name was like a summons to all my foolish blood.

Her image accompanied me even in places the most hostile to romance. On Saturday evenings when my aunt went marketing I had to go to carry some of the parcels. We walked through the flaring streets, jostled by drunken men and bargaining women, amid the curses of labourers, the shrill litanies of shopboys who stood on guard by the barrels of pigs' cheeks, the nasal chanting of street-singers, who sang a *come-all-you* about O'Donovan Rossa, or a ballad about the troubles in our native land. These noises converged in a single sensation of life for me: I imagined that I bore my chalice safely through a throng of foes. Her name sprang to my lips at moments in strange prayers and praises which I myself did not understand. My eyes were often full of tears (I could not tell why) and at times a flood from my heart seemed to pour itself out into my bosom. I thought little of the future. I did not know whether I would ever speak to her or not or, if I spoke to her, how I could tell her of my confused adoration. But my body was like a harp and her words and gestures were like fingers running upon the wires.

One evening I went into the back drawing-room in which the priest had died. It was a dark rainy evening and there was no sound in the house. Through one of the broken panes I heard the rain impinge upon the earth, the fine incessant needles of water playing in the sodden beds. Some distant lamp or lighted window gleamed below me. I was thankful that I could see so little. All my senses seemed to desire to veil themselves and, feeling that I was about to slip from them, I pressed the palms of my hands together until they trembled, murmuring: *O love! O love!* many times.

At last she spoke to me. When she addressed the first words to me I was so confused that I did not know what to answer. She asked me was I going to *Araby*. I forget whether I answered yes or no. It would be a splendid bazaar, she said; she would love to go.

—And why can't you? I asked.

While she spoke she turned a silver bracelet round and round her wrist. She could not go, she said, because there would be a retreat that week in her convent. Her brother and two other boys were fighting for their caps and I was alone at the railings. She held one of the spikes, bowing her head towards me. The light from the lamp opposite our door caught the white curve of her neck, lit up her hair that rested there and, falling, lit up the hand upon the railing. It fell over one side of her dress and caught the white border of a petticoat, just visible as she stood at ease.

—It's well for you, she said.

—If I go, I said, I will bring you something.

What innumerable follies laid waste my waking and sleeping thoughts after that evening! I wished to annihilate the tedious intervening days. I chafed against the work of school. At night in my bedroom and by day in the class-room her image came between me and the page I strove to read. The syllables of the word *Araby* were called to me through the silence in which my soul luxu-riated and cast an Eastern enchantment over me. I asked for leave to go to the bazaar on Saturday night. My aunt was surprised and hoped it was not some Freemason affair. I answered few questions in class. I watched my master's face pass from amiability to sternness; he hoped I was not beginning to idle. I could not call my wandering thoughts together. I had hardly any patience with the serious work of life which, now that it stood between me and my desire, seemed to me child's play, ugly monotonous child's play.

On Saturday morning I reminded my uncle that I wished go to the bazaar in the evening. He was fussing at the hallstand, looking for the hat-brush, and answered me curtly:

—Yes, boy, I know.

As he was in the hall I could not go into the front parlour and lie at the window. I left the house in bad humour and walked slowly towards the school. The air was pitilessly raw and already my heart misgave me.

When I came home to dinner my uncle had not yet been home. Still it was early. I sat staring at the clock for some time and, when its ticking began to irritate me, I left the room. I mounted the staircase and gained the upper part of the house. The high cold empty gloomy rooms liberated me and I went from room to room singing. From the front window I saw my companions playing below in the street. Their cries reached me weakened and indistinct and, leaning my forehead against the cool glass, I looked over at the dark house where she lived. I may have stood there for an hour, seeing nothing but the brown-clad figure cast by my imagination, touched discreetly by the lamp-light at the curved neck, at the hand upon the railings and at the border below the dress.

When I came downstairs again I found Mrs Mercer sitting at the fire. She was an old garrulous woman, a pawnbroker's widow, who collected used stamps for some pious purpose. I had to endure the gossip of the tea-table. The meal was prolonged beyond an hour and still my uncle did not come. Mrs Mercer stood up to go: she was sorry she couldn't wait any longer, but it was after eight o'clock and she did not like to be out late, as the night air was bad for her. When she had gone I began to walk up and down the room, clenching my fists. My aunt said:

—I'm afraid you may put off your bazaar for this night of Our Lord.

At nine o'clock I heard my uncle's latchkey in the halldoor. I heard him talking to himself and heard the hallstand rocking when it had received the weight of his overcoat. I could interpret these signs. When he was midway through his dinner I asked him to give me the money to go to the bazaar. He had forgotten.

—The people are in bed and after their first sleep now, he said.

I did not smile. My aunt said to him energetically:

—Can't you give him the money and let him go? You've kept him late enough as it is.

My uncle said he was very sorry he had forgotten. He said he believed in the old saying: *All work and no play makes Jack a dull boy.* He asked me where I was going and, when I had told him a second time he asked me did I know *The Arab's Farewell to his Steed.* When I left the kitchen he was about to recite the opening lines of the piece to my aunt.

I held a florin tightly in my hand as I strode down Buckingham Street towards the station. The sight of the streets thronged with buyers and glaring with gas recalled to me the purpose of my journey. I took my seat in a third-class carriage of a deserted train. After an intolerable delay the train moved out of the station slowly. It crept onward among ruinous houses and over the twinkling river. At Westland Row Station a crowd of people pressed to the carriage doors; but the porters moved them back, saying that it was a special train for the bazaar. I remained alone in the bare carriage. In a few minutes the train drew up beside an improvised wooden platform. I passed out on to the road and saw by the lighted dial of a clock that it was ten minutes to ten. In front of me was a large building which displayed the magical name.

I could not find any sixpenny entrance and, fearing that the bazaar would be closed, I passed in quickly through a turnstile, handing a shilling to a weary-looking man. I found myself in a big hall girdled at half its height by a gallery. Nearly all the stalls were closed and the greater part of the hall was in darkness. I recognised a silence like that which pervades a church after a service. I walked into the centre of the bazaar timidly. A few people were gathered about the stalls which were still open. Before a curtain, over which the words *Café Chantant* were written in coloured lamps, two men were counting money on a salver. I listened to the fall of the coins.

Remembering with difficulty why I had come I went over to one of the stalls and examined porcelain vases and flowered tea-sets. At the door of the stall a young lady was talking and laughing with two young gentlemen. I remarked their English accents and listened vaguely to their conversation.

—O, I never said such a thing!

—O, but you did!

—O, but I didn't!

—Didn't she say that?

—Yes. I heard her.

—O, there's a . . . fib!

Observing me the young lady came over and asked me did I wish to buy anything. The tone of her voice was not encouraging; she seemed to have spoken to me out of a sense of duty. I looked humbly at the great jars that stood like eastern guards at either side of the dark entrance to the stall and murmured:

—No, thank you.

The young lady changed the position of one of the vases and went back to the two young men. They began to talk of the same subject. Once or twice the young lady glanced at me over her shoulder.

I lingered before her stall, though I knew my stay was useless, to make my interest in her wares seem the more real. Then I turned away slowly and walked down the middle of the bazaar. I allowed the two pennies to fall against the sixpence in my pocket. I heard a voice call from one end of the gallery that the light was out. The upper part of the hall was now completely dark.

Gazing up into the darkness I saw myself as a creature driven and derided by vanity; and my eyes burned with anguish and anger.

CONSTRUCTING A READING

1. Compare the shame of the narrator of "The Lesson" with the "Araby" narrator's realization that he has been "driven and derided by vanity." What does each learn? How? Why?

2. What differences do you perceive between the two narrators? How do you account for them?

3. Two distinct locations are present in "Araby." One, North Richmond Street, is "personified" in the beginning—the street itself is described as "blind," and its houses are "conscious of decent life within them." At the end of the story, the hall is "absent of life." What do you make of this contrast? Does it hold up? That is, are there ways in which the setting of the beginning of the story is "dead," whereas the hall at the end has potential for living?

4. How might this story differ if Mangan's sister told it?

5. What would happen if an omniscient narrator, rather than Joyce's first-person narrator, told the story?

CHAPTER SEVEN

Intertextuality:
How Texts Keep Going
and Going and Going

Throughout the 1990s, the Eveready Battery Company, manufacturer of Energizer batteries, aired a series of TV commercials featuring a fuzzy pink battery-powered toy rabbit with black sunglasses, blue flip-flops, and a bright white drum. In each of several versions of this advertisement, the Energizer Bunny breaks through the frame of one "text"—apparently a commercial for a household product—and into another—his "own" commercial, delivering the message that Energizer Batteries "keep going and going and going." When the Energizer Bunny first appeared, most viewers were surprised to discover that what they had at first perceived to be a story about shampoo or snack crackers or air freshening spray had turned into a story about batteries. One text had entered another. Both texts changed as a result.

After a while, the Energizer Bunny's sphere of influence expanded. He began to appear in narratives that looked like episodes of *Star Wars* or James Bond. In these stories, however, the Energizer Bunny, no longer content merely to interrupt an announcer proclaiming the virtues of a new shampoo, actually entered the adventure plot and changed it. The Energizer Bunny's ability to keep going and going and going became part of the story. Again, one text entered another. Again, both texts changed as a result.

Later still, as the Energizer Bunny passed into ordinary language to become a metaphor for unflagging energy, he began to enter other kinds of texts: late show monologues, riddles and jokes, political cartoons, magazine articles. Now, the Energizer Bunny has become a commodity; there are Energizer Bunny T-shirts, Energizer Bunny flashlights, and even Energizer Bunny calendars (from which I clipped the photo on page 560). The indefatigable Energizer Bunny has entered the "text" of world commerce and changed it, too. What do these new Energizer Bunny texts mean? What does it "say" when you wear an Energizer Bunny T-shirt or place an Energizer Bunny flashlight on the shelf of your room? What does it mean when people (like me) use them for purposes the advertizers did not intend? What does it mean—what does it do to our sense of meaning—and, how do we read a situations in which one text enters another and both texts change as a result?

"Dance With Your Feet" Commercial First Aired: December 30, 1990

WHAT IS INTERTEXTUALITY?

In this chapter, to offer some answers to these questions, I use the Energizer Bunny as a trope for the theoretical conception of intertextuality. The term "intertextuality" describes the many ways in which texts enter other texts and change them: texts can refer or allude to other texts, play with them, parody them, satirize them, argue with them, answer their questions, and raise other ones. Intertextuality occurs whenever one text makes its audience think of another text. When we choose, as readers, to focus on intertextuality, the text that we read, what we interpret, is no longer a single object, but rather a set of relations between and among texts.

For example, in 1995 and 1996, two motion pictures—*Emma* and *Clueless*—were made "from" Jane Austen's novel, *Emma*. One film was set in early nineteenth-century England; one in late twentieth-century California, but the plots of both films resembled that of Jane Austen's novel, to some extent. A member of the film audience who is alert to this intertextuality will read relations between and among these three texts. Even if the reader/viewer of *Clueless* has never heard of Jane Austen or *Emma*, the relations are there to be read. If a

> Michael Riffiaterre writes that "a sign is only a relationship to something else." In other words, meaning can only come from relations between texts that exist in a "continuous translatability."
>
> ———
>
> Michael Riffiaterre, *Semiotics of Poetry*. Indiana University Press, 1978.

reader who has viewed one or both films then turns to the novel, his or her reading of that novel will inevitably reflect his viewing of the film(s). The three texts have varying degrees of similarity, but each one has the potential to make us think of the other(s), so that part of the meaning the audience makes from each text depends on the meaning that audience (or someone else, such as the author, director, producer, costumer, etc.) has made from the other.

When students say, "party-on!" or "why ask why?", when the lyrics of a song make you think about your own love life, when a flower shop calls itself "This Bud's for You," when you "click" in a website to go somewhere else, intertextuality is working. At every moment, as we watch TV, notice bumper stickers, read poems and stories, and view films and videos, we are bombarded with instances of intertextuality.

Many theorists say that these instances of intertextuality remind us that language, as our most important (and, some say, only) way of knowing and communicating in the world, is not entirely under our control. Language is not just a simple instrument that we can use for identifying and indicating things like tables and chairs and cats; instead, while it seems to be pointing to tables and chairs and cats and bunnies, language can always say and do things that we don't intend and can't predict. Like the Energizer Bunny bursting into a soap commercial and turning it into a battery commercial, language can enter our speech and writing and make them mean something else, something that we did not intend. Language "plays" with us by constantly calling attention to itself as language—a(n imperfect) way of communicating and a(n imperfect) way of naming or knowing. Language refers, not only to things in the world, but also to other language, endlessly. Language, and our cultural need to use it both playfully and seriously, has its own energy as indefatigable as that of the Energizer Bunny.

What does this arcane discussion have to do with our concerns in this textbook? My answer is that intertextuality has everything to do with making meaning. A culture is made up of its texts, and those texts constantly call upon us to think and act and be and believe: how to be patriotic or in love, how to know what we know. What we read, what we interpret—or make meaning from—is not just one text with definite limits, but rather an infinite number of relations between the text we happen to be looking at and all the other texts we have ever known, or even all the other texts that have ever existed, whether we know about them or not. Intertextuality shows us that cultures carry on elaborate conversations about identity and knowledge and values through the relations of texts.

AUTHORIAL INTENTIONS AND INTERTEXTUALITY

When one text reminds us of another, it can be because the author intends for us to make the connection (as in the Energizer Bunny commercials) or it can be a matter of our own personal affections and associations (like the ones we discussed in Chapter One.) Here, for example, is a set of texts in which the second author (Ogden Nash) obviously intended to refer to the first (Lord Byron).

The Destruction of Sennacherib

George Noel Gordon, Lord Byron

I
The Assyrian came down like the wolf on the fold,
And his cohorts were gleaming in purple and gold;
And the sheen of their spears was like stars on the sea,
When the blue wave rolls nightly on deep Galilee.

II
Like the leaves of the forest when Summer is green,
That host with their banners at sunset were seen:
Like the leaves of the forest when Autumn hath blown,
That host on the morrow lay wither'd and strown.

III
For the Angel of Death spread his wings on the blast,
And breathed in the face of the foe as he pass'd;
And the eyes of the sleepers wax'd deadly and chill,
And their hearts but once heaved, and for ever grew still!

IV
And there lay the steed with his nostril all wide,
But through it there roll'd not the breath of his pride;
And the foam of his gasping lay white on the turf,
And cold as the spray of the rock-beating surf.

V
And there lay the rider distorted and pale,
With the dew on his brow, and the rust on his mail:
And the tents were all silent, the banners alone,
The lances unlifted, the trumpet unblown.

VI
And the widows of Ashur are loud in their wail,
And the idols are broke in the temple of Baal;
And the might of the Gentile, unsmote by the sword,
Hath melted like snow in the glance of the Lord!

CONSTRUCTING A READING

1. As you read this poem aloud (or listen to your teacher read it), be attentive to its rhythm, one of the consistencies that help us make meaning. How does the repetition of beats and sounds make you feel? Does it evoke any memories or associations?
2. Make a list, with your group members, of Byron's tropes. In groups, discuss the aptness of these tropes. How is an Assyrian warrior like a wolf? How are spears like stars? How are soldiers like leaves?
3. Do you like this poem? Briefly, write in your journal about why or why not and discuss your answer with your group members.

Very Like a Whale
Ogden Nash

One thing that literature would be greatly the better
    for
Would be a more restricted employment by authors
    of simile and metaphor.
Authors of all races, be they Greeks, Romans, Teutons
    or Celts,
Can't seem just to say that anything is the thing it is
    but have to go out of their way to say that it is like
    something else.
What does it mean when we are told
That the Assyrian came down like a wolf on the fold?
In the first place, George Gordon Byron had had
    enough experience
To know that it probably wasn't just one Assyrian, it
    was a lot of Assyrians.
However, as too many agruments are apt to induce
    apoplexy and thus hinder longevity,
We'll let it pass as one Assyrian for the sake of brevity.
Now then, this particular Assyrian, the one whose
    cohorts were gleaming in purple and gold,
Just what does the poet mean when he says he came
    down like a wolf on the fold?
In heaven and earth more than is dreamed of in our
    philosophy there are a great many things,
But I don't imagine that among them there is a wolf
    with purple and gold cohorts or purple and gold
    anythings.
No, no, Lord Byron, before I'll believe that this
    Assyrian was actually like a wolf I must have some
    kind of proof;

Did he run on all fours and did he have a hairy tail
and a big red mouth and big white teeth and did
he say Woof woof woof?
Frankly I think it very unlikely, and all you were entitled to say, at the very most,
Was that the Assyrian cohorts came down like a lot of
Assyrian cohorts about to destroy the Hebrew
host.
But that wasn't fancy enough for Lord Byron, oh dear
me no, he had to invent a lot of figures of speech
and then interpolate them,
With the result that whenever you mention Old Tes-
tament soldiers to people they say Oh yes, they're
the ones that a lot of wolves dressed up in gold and
purple ate them.
That's the kind of thing that's being done all the time
by poets, from Homer to Tennyson;
They're always comparing ladies to lilies and veal to
venison,
And they always say things like that the snow is a
white blanket after a winter storm.
Oh it is, is it, all right then, you sleep under a six-inch
blanket of snow and I'll sleep under a half-inch
blanket of unpoetical blanket material and we'll
see which one keeps warm,
And after that maybe you'll begin to comprehend
dimly
What I mean by too much metaphor and simile.

Ogden Nash's poem, which refers both to Shakespeare's play *Hamlet: Prince of Denmark* and to Byron's "The Destruction of Sennacherib," is a *parody*, an instance of intertextuality in which one text makes a humorous reference to its precursor in such a way as to call the earlier text into question somehow. In this case, Ogden Nash comments on Byron's poetic language, especially the metaphors wherein he compares soldiers to leaves, stars, and a wolf. But Nash's title, "Very Like a Whale" adds another dimension to the parody. The phrase is taken from a scene in which Hamlet, who is pretending to be insane, claims to see various shapes in the clouds.

from *Hamlet*

William Shakespeare

HAMLET. Do you see yonder cloud that's almost in shape of a camel?
POLONIUS. By th' mass and 'tis, like a camel indeed.
HAMLET. Methinks it is like a weasel.
POLONIUS. It is backed like a weasel.

HAMLET. Or like a whale.
POLONIUS. Very like a whale.

Believing that the prince is hallucinating, the courtier Polonius humors him by agreeing that the cloud looks "very like a whale." Most interpreters of Shakespeare believe that Hamlet is not really mad; instead he is very shrewdly laying a trap for the murderer of his father. There is, in other words, "method" in the prince's "madness," a kind of genius for saying one thing and meaning another—or, in other words, for intertextuality.

Nash again alludes to Hamlet in the line

> In heaven and earth more than is dreamed of in our
> philosophy there are a great many things,

Here, the reference is to a conversation in which Hamlet, having seen his father's ghost, assures his frightened and somewhat skeptical friend Horatio that

> There are more things in heaven and earth, Horatio,
> Than are dreamt of in your philosophy. (*Hamlet* I, v, 67–68)

Nash's rhythm also parodies Byron's. The striking rhythm of "The Destruction of Sennacherib" suggests to some readers a heartbeat, or a war drum. By contrast, Nash's crazy rhythm reminds readers of Byron's very carefully measured one and points both to the artificiality of the earlier poem—and to the striking effect of that artifice.

CONSTRUCTING A READING

1. What do you perceive as Nash's attitude toward Byron?
2. What do you perceive as Nash's attitude toward figural language itself?
3. What do you perceive as Nash's attitude toward people who don't like figural language?
4. With your group members, discuss how reading these two poems together might change your reading of either or both. For example, you might make a list of the things that "Very Like a Whale" makes you notice in "The Destruction of Sennacherib."
5. Does reading Nash make you like Byron more or less?

In Nash's parody of Byron we see *intentional* intertextuality, in which the later author seeks deliberately to comment humorously upon the work of an earlier one. In the case of the three texts that follow, however, the authors' intentions are not so clear.

A Drumlin Woodchuck

Robert Frost

One thing has a shelving bank,
Another a rotting plank,
To give it cozier skies
And make up for its lack of size.

My own strategic retreat
Is where two rocks almost meet,
And still more secure and snug,
A two-door burrow I dug.

With those in mind at my back
I can sit forth exposed to attack
As one who shrewdly pretends
That he and the world are friends.

All we who prefer to live
Have a little whistle we give,
And flash, at the least alarm
We dive down under the farm.

We allow some time for guile
And don't come out for a while
Either to eat or drink
We take occasion to think.

And if after the hunt goes past
And the double-barrelled blast
(Like war and pestilence
And the loss of common sense),

If I can with confidence say
That still for another day,
Or even another year,
I will be there for you, my dear,

It will be because, though small
As measured against the All,
I have been so instinctively thorough
About my crevice and burrow.

CONSTRUCTING A READING

1. Who is the speaker in this poem?
2. In terms of narrative genres, what kind of a story is this?
3. Many of Frost's critics think that his poems about animals and insects are also commentaries on humankind. If so, what is the commentary that this poem makes?
4. Draw the Drumlin Woodchuck's habitat. Make, that is, a visual text of this poem. What does your drawing tell you about the woodchuck's ability to be so "instinctively thorough"?

Now, look at this text:

Woodchucks

Maxine Kumin

Gassing the woodchucks didn't turn out right.
The knockout bomb from the Feed and Grain Exchange
was featured as merciful, quick at the bone
and the case we had against them was airtight,
both exits shoehorned shut with puddingstone,
but they had a sub-sub-basement out of range.

Next morning they turned up again, no worse
for the cyanide than we for our cigarettes
and state-store Scotch, all of us up to scratch.
They brought down the marigolds as a matter of course
and then took over the vegetable patch
nipping the broccoli shoots, beheading the carrots.

The food from our mouths, I said, righteously thrilling
to the feel of the .22, the bullets' neat noses.
I, a lapsed pacifist fallen from grace
puffed with Darwinian pieties for killing,
now drew a bead on the littlest woodchuck's face.
He died down in the everbearing roses.

Ten minutes later I dropped the mother. She
flipflopped in the air and fell, her needle teeth
still hooked in a leaf of early swiss chard.
Another baby next. O one-two-three
the murderer inside me rose up hard,
the hawkeye killer came on stage forthwith.

There's one chuck left. Old wily fellow, he keeps
me cocked and ready day after day after day.
All night I hunt his humped-up form. I dream
I sight along the barrel in my sleep.
If only they'd all consented to die unseen
gassed underground the quiet Nazi way.

Perhaps Maxine Kumin intended us to think of Robert Frost's poem; perhaps not. Regardless of her intention, though, I always do think of Frost. In
fact, I've often thought that the one wily old woodchuck who survives Kumin's
speaker's efforts to exterminate him is Frost's speaker.

CONSTRUCTING A READING

1. What do you make of the phrase "quick at the bone"?
2. Write in your journal for a few minutes about possible interpretations of
   the phrase "everbearing roses."
3. Speculate about the gender of Kumin's speaker, supporting your speculations with quotations from the poem.
4. If you're not familiar with the other explicit intertextual references, for
   example, to Darwin's *On the Origin of Species*, as well as references to historical events such as the holocaust, look them up (in an encyclopedia or
   unabridged dictionary) and explain how they work in the poem.
5. With your group members, compare these two poems in terms of the
   characterization of the woodchuck and the narrative perspective from
   which the story is told. What did Frost accomplish by his narrative focus?
   What did Kumin accomplish?
6. Talk with your group members or write in your journal about how the
   two poems work in dialogue with each other through their readers. If,
   that is, a reader of Kumin's poem thinks of Frost's, how does the meaning
   of each poem change? If a reader of Frost's poem thinks of Kumin's, what
   happens?

Here is still another text that I experience intertextually with both Frost and Kumin.

"Not your typical burrowing rodents, that's for sure."

Whether or not Charles Addams had Robert Frost or Maxine Kumin in mind when he drew this cartoon, I always think of the two poems when I see the cartoon. I see it, in fact, as sharing one of the poems' themes: the tendency to perceive other forms of life as though they were human. If we project our own feelings of care or thoroughness or determination or "family values" onto a woodchuck, then it's just a short step to imagining garden rodents building a little subway station. Therefore, this Charles Addams cartoon becomes an instance of intertextuality for me.

There is yet another way of thinking about intertextuality that this cartoon brings to mind. It is that all three texts might be said to refer to the same intertext: that animals are "almost human," that we understand animal behavior as though it were human, by projecting our thoughts and values and fears onto animals. In other words, the *intertext* to which these texts refer is not a published text at all but rather just a *notion that tends to float around in a culture.*

MYTH AND INTERTEXTUALITY

Sometimes, intertextuality is broader in scope. Entire narratives, for example, might be passed down from generation to generation. At times, these stories become master narratives, sacred to the culture from which they emerge. Such master narratives are called *myths*. A *myth* is a narrative that helps a culture understand itself or that resolves a cultural contradiction or anomaly. For example, the myth of Demeter and Kore (or Persephone) explains the cyclical disappearance and return of crops. Each "autumn," Kore's father, Pluto, abducted her into his kingdom under the sea. All during the winter, Demeter would search for her daughter, neglecting the earth's vegetation, and allowing it to die. Each spring, Demeter would find her daughter and bring her back to earth, causing a rebirth of vegetation. In very specific terms, then, the myth of Demeter and Kore answered the questions "why does the vegetation go away and is it coming back?"

Some theorists believe that myths have their origin in the collective unconscious of humankind, and that some of them, such as redemption myths, death and rebirth narratives, and journey stories, have a kind of structural universality—that they crop up on all cultures, even though their character names and settings change from culture to culture. Other theorists stop short of arguing for universality but they still grant that stories can be widespread and cross-cultural.

Often, people use the term *myth* colloquially to mean "false stories." From the perspective of modern science and philosophy, certainly, the story of Demeter and Kore would seem to be an unsatisfactory way to understand seasonal change. Today, most people believe that science's story about the earth's revolution around the sun helps us to cope better with problems of agriculture and meteorology than a story about the annual kidnapping of a young goddess. But from another perspective, science might be thought of as a myth that helps late twentieth-century culture explain the world.

It would probably be most helpful to think of myth in terms of models for living, exemplary stories, rather than in terms of truth or falsehood. The "myth of the American dream," in that context, is a text exemplifying the belief that success comes from working hard. That belief explains why some people have more goods than others do, motivates people to work, and helps them to cope with economic problems and setbacks. It stands behind their thinking and

---

Mircea Eliade writes that myth is a story that is a most precious possession because it is sacred, exemplary, significant.

The Sacred and the Profane: The Nature of Religion. Trans. Willard R. Trask. Harper & Row, 1961.

directs their actions. It's not always true (and it's not always false either) but it is a set of instructions for living in capitalism—an *exemplary narrative*.

An Example: The Oedipus Myth

Let's look at one of the most widespread stories in Western culture, the Oedipus narrative, to get a sense of how one myth has functioned in Western thought. Specifically, we shall look at several ways in which "the Oedipus story" has been told and retold in Western culture and at some relations between and among those tellings.

The "story" is as follows: Jocasta and Laius were the monarchs of Thebes. An oracle predicted that their son would grow up to kill his father and marry his mother. Frightened, Jocasta and Laius gave orders that the child should be killed. The servant who was charged with the job of doing away with the infant decided instead merely to leave him on a mountainside to die of exposure. The servant bound the baby's feet together and to the ground to prevent him from escaping. But a shepherd found the baby and gave him to a Corinthian who in turn gave him to the childless king and queen of Corinth, Polybus and Merope. They called him Oedipus, which means "swollen-footed," a reference to his wounded feet. When Oedipus grew to manhood, an oracle again predicted that he would kill his father and marry his mother. Thinking that Polybus and Merope were his parents, Oedipus decided to leave Corinth in order to escape this fate. On the road, he met an older man and his servant at a place where three roads meet. They quarreled about right of way and Oedipus killed the older man. He also encountered the Sphinx (a being with the head of a woman and the body of a lion) and solved her riddle: "what creature goes on two, three, and four feet?" Oedipus correctly answered "man": a human being crawls on four feet as a baby, walks on two feet in adulthood, and on three feet (with a cane) in old age. Then, he went to Thebes where he met and married that city's recently widowed queen Jocasta, whose husband had been killed at a place where three roads meet. They had four children together: Eteocles, Polyneices, Antigone, and Iphegenia. After many prosperous and happy years, Thebes was struck by a plague. Oedipus again consulted an oracle to find the cause and cure of this misfortune. The oracle revealed that the plague would continue until the murderer of Laius was brought to justice. Ultimately, Oedipus and Jocasta came to know the reality of their situation. Jocasta hanged herself, and Oedipus, after blinding himself with Jocasta's brooch, left Thebes in voluntary exile. All Greeks knew this story just as virtually every American knows the story of the Declaration of Independence and the Revolutionary War.

When Sophocles wrote his *Oedipus the King* in the fifth century B.C.E., then, the task he faced was not the narrative problem of telling his readers what happened next and why. They already knew the story. Instead, Sophocles faced a problem with discourse, the "how" of his narrative: What genre would he use to tell this story to his audience in Athens? For which perspective would he seek his audience's sympathy? Would he solicit sympathy for Oedipus? Or, would he show us his pride? Or both? How would he present the events that led up to the action of the play? Would he evoke sympathy for Jocasta? For the children? For the Thebans? Sophocles used many such devices in response to these challenges. As you read this important play, be particularly attentive to narrative perspectives. Mark where your sympathy is engaged with Oedipus, with Jocasta, with Creon, with Tiresias.

Oedipus the King

Sophocles

(A crowd of Theban citizens—priests, young men and children—kneel in supplication before the palace, wearing wreaths and carrying branches. Enter OEDIPUS from the palace to address them.]

OEDIPUS. My children, in whom old Cadmus is reborn,
  Why have you come with wreathed boughs in your hands
  To sit before me as petitioners?
  The town is full of smoke from altar-fires
  And voices crying, and appeals to heaven.
  I thought it, children, less than just to hear
  Your cause at second-hand, but come in person—
  I, Oedipus, a name that all men know.
  Speak up, old man; for you are qualified
  To be their spokesman. What is in your minds?   10
  Are you afraid? In need? Be sure I am ready
  To do all I can. I should truly be hard-hearted
  To have no pity on such prayers as these.
PRIEST. Why, Oedipus, my country's lord and master,
  You see us, of all ages, sitting here
  Before your altars—some too young to fly
  Far from the nest, and others bent with age,

---

1 *Cadmus* legendary founder of Thebes. He killed the dragon guarding the site and sowed its teeth in the ground. From them sprang up armed men who fought each other. All were killed except five, who became the ancestors of the Thebans. 2 *wreathed boughs* branches entwined with wool, the customary symbol of supplication 18 *Zeus* king of the gods

Priests—I of Zeus—and these, who represent
Our youth. The rest sit with their boughs
In the city squares, at both of Pallas' shrines,   20
And where Ismenus' ashes tell the future.
The storm, as you can see, has hit our land
Too hard; she can no longer raise her head
Above the waves of this new sea of blood.
A blight is on the blossoms of the field,
A blight is on the pastured herds, on wives
In childbed; and the curse of heaven, plague,
Has struck, and runs like wildfire through the city,
Emptying Cadmus' house, while black Death reaps
The harvest of our tears and lamentations.   30
Not that we see you as a god, these boys
And I, who sit here at your feet for favors,
But as one pre-eminent in life's affairs
And in man's dealings with the powers above.
For it was you who came to Cadmus' town
And freed us from the monster who enslaved us
With her song, relying on your wits, and knowing
No more than we. Some god was at your side,
As men believe, when you delivered us.
So now, great Oedipus, giant among men,   40
We beg you, all of us who come in prayer,
Find us some remedy—a whisper heard
From heaven, or any human way you know.
In men proved by experience we see
A living promise, both in word and deed,
Greatest of men, give our city back its pride!
Look to your name! This country now remembers
Your former zeal, and hails you as her savior.
Never leave us with a memory of your reign
As one that raised and let us fail again,   50
But lift our city up, and keep it safe.
You came to make us happy years ago,
Good omens; show you are the same man still.
If you continue in your present power
Better a land with citizens than empty.
For city walls without their men are nothing,
Or empty ships, when once the crew has gone.

---

20 *Pallas* Athena, goddess of wisdom   21 *Ismenus* river near Thebes. Here the reference is to the prophetic shrine of Apollo by the river, where divination by burnt offerings was practised   36 *the monster . . . her song* the Sphinx and the riddle.

OED. Poor children, I already know too well
 The desires that bring you here. Yes, I have seen
 Your sufferings; but suffer as you may,   60
 There is not one of you who knows my pain.
 Your griefs are private, every man here mourns
 For himself, and for no other; but my heart grieves
 At once for the state, and for myself, and you.
 So do not think you rouse me from my sleep.
 Let me tell you, I have wept, yes, many tears,
 And sent my mind exploring every path.
 My anxious thought found but one hope of cure
 On which I acted—sent Creon, Menoeceus' son,
 My own wife's brother, to Apollo's shrine   70
 At Delphi, with commission to enquire
 What I could say or do to save this town,
 Now I am counting the days, and growing anxious
 To know what he is doing. It is strange
 He should delay so long beyond his time.
 But when he comes, I shall be no true man
 If I fail to take the course the god has shown us.
PRIEST. Well said, and timely! My friends are signaling.
 This very moment that Creon is in sight.
OED. O Lord Apollo, let him bring us news   80
 Glad as his face, to give our town good fortune.
PRIEST. I think he brings us comfort; otherwise
 He would not wear so thick a crown of laurel.

   [*Enter* CREON]

OED. We shall soon know, he is close enough to hear us.
 Prince, brother of my house, Menoeceus' son
 What is the news you bring us from the god?
CREON. Good news! Our Sorrows, heavy as they are,
 With proper care may yet end happily.
OED. What is the oracle? So far you have said nothing
 To raise my spirits or to dampen them.   90
CREON. If you wish to have it here and now, in public,
 I am ready to speak; if not, to go inside.

---

70 *Apollo's shrine at Delphi* most famous and prosperous of Greek oracular shrines,
believed to stand at the geographical center of the earth 83 *crown of laurel* leaves from
Apollo's sacred tree 96 *Phoebus* Apollo

OED. Speak before all. The sorrows of my people
  I count of greater weight than life itself.
CREON. Then, by your leave, I speak as I was told.
  Phoebus commands us, in plain terms, to rid
  Our land of some pollution, nourished here,
  He says, and not to keep a thing past cure.
OED. How shall we purge ourselves? What stain is this?
CREON. By banishing a man, or taking life   100
  For life, since murder brought this storm on us.
OED. Who is the man whose fate the god reveals?
CREON. Our country once had Laius for its king,
  My lord, before you came to guide this city.
Oed. I have been told as much; I never saw him.
CREON. Laius was murdered. Phoebus tells us plainly
  To find his murderers and punish them.
Oed. Where on earth are they? An ancient crime,
  A scent grown cold; where shall we find it now?
CREON. Here, in this land, he said; seek it, and we   110
  Shall find; seek not, and it shall be hidden.
OED. And where did Laius meet his bloody end?
  In the country? The palace? Traveling abroad?
CREON. He left us on a visit, as he said,
  To Delphi, and he never came back home.
OED. Could no-one tell you? Had he no companion,
  No witness, who could give you facts to work on?
CREON. All were killed but one, who ran away in fright,
  And will swear to only one thing that he saw.
OED. What was that? One thing might give the clue to more   120
  If we had some encouragement, some small beginning.
CREON. He said they met with bandits; it was not
  By one man's hands that Lains died, but many.
OED. What bandit would have taken such a risk
  Unless he were bribed—by someone here, in Thebes?
CREON. It was suspected; but then our troubles came
  And there was no-one to avenge dead Laius.
OED. It must have been great trouble, that could make you
  Leave the death of royalty unsolved!
CREON. The Sphinx, whose riddles made us turn our minds   130
  To things at home, and abandon mysteries.
OED. Then I shall start afresh, and once again
  Find secrets out. Apollo and you too

Have rightly taken up the dead man's cause.
You will see me working with you, as is just,
To avenge the land, and give the god his due.
It is not on some far-distant friend's behalf
But on my own, that I shall purge this stain.
The man whose hand killed Laius might some time
Feel a desire to do the same to me,   140
And so by avenging him I protect myself.
Waste no more time, my children, take away
Your branches and your wreaths, and leave my steps.
Have Cadmus' people summoned here and tell them
I will see to everything. We shall be happy now,
God helping us, or be forever damned.

        [*Exeunt* OEDIPUS *and* CREON]

PRIEST. Let us arise, my sons. He promises
    The favors that we first came here to ask.
    May Phoebus who has sent this oracle
    Come to save Thebes, and cure us of the plague!   150

        [*Exeunt. Enter* CHORUS *of Theban elders*]

CHORUS. Sweet voice of Zeus, what word do you bring
    From golden Pytho to glorious Thebes?
    I am heart-shaken, torn on the rack of fear.
    Apollo, Healer, to whom men cry,
    I tremble before you; what will it please you
    To send us? Some new visitation?
    Or something out of the past, come due
    In fullness of time? Tell me, Voice undying,
    The child of golden Hope.

    Daughter of Zeus, to you first I cry,   160
    Immortal Athena; and then her sister
    Artemis, guardian of our land, enthroned
    In honor in our assemblies; Apollo,
    Heavenly archer; now shine on us all three,
    Champions strong against death; if ever
    In time gone by you stood between Thebes
    And threatened disaster, turning the fire
    Of pestilence from us, come now!

---

152 *Pytho* Delphi   162 *Artemis* goddess of childbirth and of wild things

For my sorrows have grown past counting.
The plague is on all our people, and wit   170
Can devise no armor. No more the good earth
Brings forth its crops; women groan in their barren labors,
And you may see, like flying birds,
Souls speeding, one by one,
To join the sunset god; their flight
Is faster than the racing flame.

Thebes dies a new death each moment; her children
Lie in the dust, death's agents, and no-one
Spares them a tear; their wives and gray-haired mothers
Flock screaming to the altars, and pray for their own lives.   180
Above the counterpoint of tears
There rings out clear the healing chant.
Show us, golden child of Zeus,
The smiling face of comfort!

Grim Death is marching on us, not now with clashing shields
But blasts of fiery breath, and the cry goes up around him.
Turn him away from us, drive him from our land!
Come, fair wind, and blow him away
To the vasty halls of the western ocean
Or the Thracian seas, where sailors fear to go.   190
For if night has left any harm undone
Day treads on its heels to finish the work.
Zeus our Father, lord of the bright lightning,
Come with your thunder and destroy!

And we pray Apollo the archer to string his golden bow
And send invincible arrows to fight for us in the field,
And Artemis' blazing torches, that she carries
To light her way through the Lycian mountains.
On the god with gold-bound hair I call,
Bacchus, whose name we have made our own,   200
Who comes with a cry of maidens dancing.
Bright comforter, bring the joyous light
Of your torch, stand with us against our foe,
The rogue-god, whom his brothers shun!

---

190 *Thracian seas* off the north-east coast of Greece, notoriously treacherous. Ares, god of war, was regarded as having his home in this wild region   198 *Lycian mountains* in Asia Minor   200 *Bacchus* Dionysus, god of wine, traditionally born in Thebes from the union of Zeus and a mortal woman, Semek.

[Enter OEDIPUS]

OED. You pray; now for answer. If you are prepared
　To accept what I say, and be your own physician,
　Cure may be yours, and respite from your pain.
　I must speak as a stranger to your story, one
　Unacquainted with the facts; I could not press
　My enquiries far alone, without some clue.   210
　But now I am a Theban among Thebans
　And make this proclamation to the sons
　Of Cadmus: if anyone among you knows
　Who murdered Laius, son of Labdacus,
　I order him to make a full disclosure.
　If he should fear to implicate himself
　By confessing, why, nothing unpleasant will happen;
　He will leave the land unharmed, and that is all.
　If anybody knows another guilty—
　An alien perhaps—then let him not keep silent.   220
　He will earn a reward and my gratitude besides.
　But if you refuse to talk; if anyone
　Is frightened into shielding self or friend,
　Pay good attention to the consequences.
　As lord and master of this land of Thebes
　I declare this man, whoever he may be
　An outlaw; order you to break off speech
　With him, to excommunicate him from your prayers
　And sacrifices, to deny him holy water,
　To drive him from your doors, remembering   230
　That this is our pollution, which the god
　This day revealed to me in oracles.
　In this I show myself on heaven's side,
　One with the murdered man. My solemn curse
　Is on the killer, whether he is hiding
　In lonely guilt or has accomplices.
　May he reap the harm he sowed, and die unblest
　And what is more, I pray that if this man
　Should live among my household with my knowledge,
　The curse I swore just now should fall on me.   240
　I lay the responsibility on you,
　For my sake, and the gods', and for our country
　Turned to a stricken, god-forsaken waste.
　For even if heaven had not shown its hand
　Fitness alone forbade such negligence

When one so noble, and your king, had died.
You should have held enquiries. Now since I
Have fallen heir to the power which once was his,
Sleep in his bed, and take his bride to wife,
And since, if he had not been disappointed   250
In his succession, we two would have had
A bond between us, children of one mother,
But as it was, his fortune struck him down,
For all these reasons, I shall fight for him
As I would for my own father, leave no stone
Unturned to find the man who shed his blood
In honor of the son of Labdacus,
Of Polydorus, Cadmus, and Agenor.
For those who disobey my words I pray
The gods to send no harvest to their fields,   260
Their wives no children, but to let them die
In present misery, or worse to come.
But as for you, the rest of Cadmus' children,
Who think as I do, may our ally, Right,
And all the gods be with you evermore.
CHORUS. You put me on my oath and I must speak.
I did not kill him, nor can I point to the man
Who did. It was for Phoebus, who sent the question,
To answer it, and find the murderer.
OED. What you say is fair enough, but no man living   270
Can force the gods to speak when they do not want to.
CHORUS. By your leave, a second best occurs to me. . . .
OED. Second or third best, do not keep it from us!
CHORUS. I know Teiresias has powers of vision
Second only to Phoebus. A man who asked of him,
My lord, might find his questions answered.
OED. Another thing that I have not neglected.
On Creon's bidding I have sent men twice
To bring him; it is strange he is not yet come.
CHORUS. We have nothing else but vague and ancient rumors.   280
OED. What are they? I must examine every story.
CHORUS. He is said to have been killed by men on the road.
OED. Yes, so I hear; but no-one knows who did it.
CHORUS. If he has any fear in him, a curse
Such as you swore will bring him out of hiding.
OED. Words will not scare a man when actions do not.

CHORUS. But here is one to convict him. They are bringing
The prophet here at last, the man of god,
The only one who has the truth born in him.

[*Enter* TEIRESIAS, *led by a boy*]

OED. Teiresias, all things are known to you,   290
Open and secret, things of heaven and earth.
Blind though you are, you sense how terrible
A plague is on us; and in you, great prophet,
We find our only means of self-defence.
We sent—perhaps my messengers have told you—
To Phoebus; he replied, by one way only
Could Thebes secure deliverance from the plague,
By hunting down the murderers of Laius
And killing them or driving them abroad.
So grudge us nothing of your bird-cry lore   300
Or any means of prophecy you know.
Come, save the city; save yourself and me,
And heal the foulness spread by Laius' blood.
We are in your hands. Man knows no finer task
Than helping friends with all his might and means.

TEIRESIAS. How terrible is wisdom when it turns
Against you! All of this I know, but let it
Slip from my mind, or I should not have come here.

OED. What is it? Why have you come in so black a mood?

TEIR. Send me home. It will be easiest for each of us   310
To bear his own burden to the end, believe me.

OED. A fine way to talk! You do your motherland
No kindness by witholding information.

TEIR. When I see you opening your mouth at the wrong moment
I take care to avoid a like mistake.

OED. By heaven, if you know something, do not turn away!
You see us all on our knees imploring you.

TEIR. Yes, for you all know nothing. I shall never
Reveal my sorrows—not to call them yours.

OED. What do you say? You know and will not talk?   320
Do you mean to turn traitor and betray the state?

TEIR. I wish to cause no pain—to either of us.
So why ask useless questions? My lips are sealed.

---

300 *bird-cry lore* omens were commonly deduced from the flight of birds

OED. Why, you old reprobate, you could provoke
   A stone to anger! Will you never speak?
   Can nothing touch you? Is there no end to this?

TEIR. You blame my temper, but you fail to recognize
   Your own working in you; no, you criticize me!

OED. And who would not be angry when he hears you
   Talking like this, and holding Thebes in contempt?   330

TEIR. These things will happen, if I speak or not.

OED. Then if they must, it is your duty to tell me.

TEIR. This discussion is at an end. Now, if you like,
   You may be as angry as your heart knows how.

OED. Then in my anger I will spare you none
   Of my suspicions. This is what I think;
   You helped contrive the plot—no, did it all
   Except the actual killing. If you had
   Your eye sight I should say you did that too.

TEIR. Indeed? Then listen to what I say. Obey   340
   Your own pronouncement, and from this day on
   Speak not to me or any man here present.
   You are the curse, the defiler of this land.

OED. You dare fling this at me? Have you no fear?
   Where can you hope for safety after this?

TEIR. I am safe enough. My strength is in my truth.

OED. Who put you up to this? No skill of yours!

TEIR. You did—by forcing me to speak against my will.

OED. What was it? Say it again, I must be sure.

TEIR. Did you not understand? Or are you tempting me?   350

OED. I have not quite grasped it. Tell it me again.

TEIR. You hunt a murderer, it is yourself.

OED. You will pay for uttering such slanders twice.

TEIR. Shall I say something else, to make you angrier still?

OED. Say what you like, it is a waste of breath.

TEIR. You have been living in unimagined shame
   With your nearest, blind to your own degradation.

OED. How long do you think such taunts will go unpunished?

TEIR. For ever, if there is any strength in truth.

OED. In truth, but not in you. You have no strength,   360
   Failing in sight, in hearing, and in mind.

TEIR. And you are a fool to say such things to me,
   Things that the world will soon hurl back at you!

OED. You live in the dark; you are incapable
　Of hurting me or any man with eyes.
TEIR. Your destiny is not to fall by me.
　That is Apollo's task, and he is capable.
OED. Who is behind this? You? Or is it Creon?
TEIR. Your ruin comes not from Creon, but yourself.
OED . Oh wealth! Oh monarchy! Talent which outruns　　　　　370
　Its rivals in the cutthroat game of life,
　How envy dogs your steps, and with what strength,
　When tempted by the power the city gave
　Into my hands, a gift, and never asked for,
　The man I trusted, Creon, my earliest friend,
　Yearns to depose me, plots behind my back,
　Makes accomplices of conjurers like this
　Who sells his tricks to the highest bidder, who looks
　Only for profits, and in his art is blind.
　Let us hear where you have proved yourself a seer!　　　　　380
　Why did you not, when the Singing Bitch was here,
　Utter one word to set your people free?
　For this was not a riddle to be solved
　By the first-comer; it cried out for divination.
　You were tried and found wanting; neither birds
　Nor voices from heaven could help you. Then I came,
　I, ignorant Oedipus, and put a stop to her
　By using my wits, no lessons from the birds!
　And it is I you try to depose, assuming
　That you will have a place by Creon's throne.　　　　　390
　You and your mastermind will repent your zeal
　To purge this land. You are old, by the look of you;
　If not, you would have learnt the price of boldness.
CHORUS. It seems to me that this man's words were spoken
　In anger, Oedipus, and so were yours.
　This is not what we need; we ask to know
　How we can best obey the oracle.
TEIR. King though you are, the right of speech must be
　The same for all. Here, I am my own master.
　I live in Apollo's service, not in yours,　　　　　400
　And have no need of Creon to endorse me.
　Listen to me; you taunt me with my blindness,
　But you have eyes, and do not see your sorrows,
　Or where you live, or what is in your house.

---

381 *Singing Bitch* the Sphinx

Do you know whose son you are? You are abhorrent
To your kin on earth and under it, and do not know.
One day your mother's and your father's curse,
A two-tongued lash, will run you out of Thebes,
And you who see so well will then be blind.
What place will not give shelter to your cries?   410
What corner of Cithairon will not ring with them,
When you have understood the marriage song which brought you
From prosperous voyage to uneasy harbor?
And a throng of sorrows that you cannot guess
Will drag you down and level you with those
You have begotten, and your proper self.
So go your way; heap mockery and insult
On Creon and my message; you will be crushed
More miserably than any man on earth.

OED. Am I to listen to such things from him   420
    Without protest? Out of my sight this instant! Leave my house !
    Go back where you came from, and be damned!

TEIR. I would never have come here, if you had not called me.

OED. If I had known you would rave like this, it would have been
    A long time before I asked you to my house.

TEIR. I am what I am. I pass for a fool to you,
    But as sane enough for the parents who begot you.

OED. Who were they? Wait! What is my father's name?

TEIR. This day will give you parents and destroy you.

OED. All the time you talk in riddles, mysteries.   430

TEIR. And who can decipher riddles better than you?

OED. Yes, laugh at that! There you will find my greatness!

TEIR. And it is just this luck that has destroyed you.

OED. I saved the city; nothing else can matter.

TEIR. Very well then, I shall go. Boy, take me home.

OED. Yes, let him take you. Here you are in the way,
    A hindrance; out of sight is out of mind.

TEIR. I will go when my errand is done. I do not fear
    Your frown. There is no way that you can harm me.
    Listen to me: the man you have sought so long,   440
    Threatening, issuing your proclamations
    About the death of Laius—he is here,
    Passing for an alien, but soon to be revealed
    A Theban born; and he will find no pleasure

---

411 *Cithairon* mountain near Thebes where Oedipus was exposed

In this turn of fortune. He who now has eyes
Will be blind, who now is rich, a beggar,
And wander abroad with a stick to find his way.
He will be revealed as father and as brother
Of the children in his home, as son and husband
Of the woman who bore him, his father's murderer   450
And successor to his bed. Now go away
And think about these things; and if you find I lie
Then you can say that I am no true prophet.

    [Exeunt TEIRESIAS *and* OEDIPUS]

CHORUS. Who is the man denounced
    By the voice of god from the Delphian rock?
    Who is the man with bloody hands
    Guilty of horrors the tongue cannot name?
    It is time for him to run
    Faster of foot than the horses of the storm,
    For the Son of Zeus is leaping upon him   460
    With fire and lightning, and at his side
    The Fates, remorseless avengers.

    Fresh from Parnassus' snows
    The call blazes forth: the hunt is up!
    Search every place for the unknown man!
    He doubles among the wild woods for cover,
    From hole to hole in the hills,
    A rogue bull running a lost race, trying
    To shake off the sentence ringing in his ears
    Pronounced by the shrine at earth's center, forever   470
    Haunting him, goading him on.

    The wise man with his birds and omens
    Leaves me troubled and afraid,
    Unable to believe or disbelieve.
    What can I say? I fly from hope to fear.
    Dark is the present, dark the days to come.
    There is no quarrel that I know of
    Now or in the past between
    Labdacus' house and the son of Polybus,
    Nothing that I could use as proof   480

---

463 *Parnassus* mountain near Delphi celebrated as the home of Apollo and the Muses,
and also as the haunt of Dionysus

Against Oedipus' reputation
In avenging Labdacus' line, and solving
The riddle of Laius' death.

To Zeus and Apollo all things are known,
They see the doings of mankind.
But who is to say that a human prophet
Knows any more of the future than I?
Though some men, I know, are wiser than others.
But I shall never join with his accusers
Until they have made good their charge.   490
We saw his wisdom tried and tested
When he fought the girl with wings.
Thebes took him then to her heart, and I
Will never name him guilty.

    [*Enter* CREON]

CREON. Citizens, I hear that Oedipus our king
    Lays monstrous charges against me, and am here
    In indignation. If in the present crisis
    He thinks I have injured him in any way
    By word or action calculated to harm him,
    I would rather die before my time is up   500
    Than bear this stigma. Such malicious slander
    Touches me on more than one tender spot.
    What hurts me most is this—to have my friends
    And you and my city brand me as a traitor.
CHORUS. This insult was probably spoken under stress,
    In anger, not with deliberate intent.
CREON. And what about the taunt that the seer was coerced
    Into lying by my design? Who started it?
CHORUS. It was said—I do not know how seriously.
CREON. Did he lay this charge against me steady eyed?   510
    Did he sound as if he knew what he was saying?
CHORUS. I know nothing about it. I do not look at what
    My masters do. Here he comes himself, from the palace.

    [*Enter* OEDIPUS]

OED. You! And what brings you here? Can you put on

---

492 *the girl with wings* the Sphinx

So bold a face, to visit your victim's house,
Shown up for what you are, a murderer
Openly plotting to rob me of my crown?
In heaven's name, what did you take me for?
A fool? A coward? to entertain such schemes?
Do you think I would let you work behind my back   520
Unnoticed, or not take precautions once I knew?
Then is it not senseless, this attempt of yours
To bid for the throne alone and unsupported?
It takes men and money to make a revolution.

CREON. Wait! You have said your say; it is now your turn
To listen. Learn the facts and then pass judgment.

OED. Smooth talker! But I have no inclination
To learn from you, my bitter enemy.

CREON. One thing let me say, before we go any further.

OED. One thing you must never say—that you are honest!   530

CREON. If you think there is any virtue in stubbornness
Devoid of reason, you have little sense.

OED. If you think you can wrong one of your family
And get away unpunished, you are mad.

CREON. Justly said, I grant you. But give me some idea,
What injury do you say that I have done you?

OED. Did you suggest it would he advisable
To bring the prophet here, or did you not?

CREON. I did; and I am still of the same opinion.

OED. And how many years ago was it that Laius. . . .   540

CREON. That Laius what? I cannot follow you.

OED. Was lost to his people by an act of violence.

CREON. That would take us a long way back into the past.

OED. And was the prophet practicing in those days?

CREON. As skillfully as today, with equal honor.

OED. And did he then make any mention of me?

CREON. Not at any time when I was there to hear him.

OED. But did you not investigate the murder?

CREON. We were bound to, of course, but discovered nothing.

OED. And why did this know-all not tell his story then?   550

CREON. I prefer not to talk about things I do not know.

OED. You know one thing well enough that you could tell me.

CREON. What is it? If I know, I shall keep nothing back.

OED. This: if you had not put your heads together
  We should never have heard about my killing Laius.
CREON. If he says so, you know best. Now let me ask
  And you must answer as I answered you.
OED. Ask what you like. I am innocent of murder.
CREON. Come now; are not you married to my sister?
OED. A question to which I can hardly answer no.   560
CREON. And you rule the country with her, equally?
OED. I give her everything that she could wish for.
CREON. Do I, the third, not rank with both of you?
OED. You do; which makes your treachery the worse.
CREON. Not if you reason with yourself as I do.
  First ask yourself this question: would any man
  Be king in constant fear, when he could live
  In peace and quiet, and have no less power?
  I want to be a king in everything
  But name—and I have no desire for that,   570
  Nor has any man who knows what is good for him.
  As it is, I am carefree. You give me all I want,
  But as king I should have many tiresome obligations.
  Then why should I find monarchy more desirable
  Than power and influence without the trouble?
  So far I have not been misguided enough
  To hanker after dishonorable gains.
  As it is, all wish me well and greet me kindly,
  And people with suits to you call first on me
  For there are all their chances of success.   580
  So why should I give up one life for the other?
  No man with any sense would stoop to treason.
  I have no love for such ideas, nor would I
  Associate with any man who did.
  Do you look for proof of this? Then go to Delphi
  And ask if I quoted the oracle correctly.
  And another thing; if you find that I have made
  A plot with the prophet, there will be two voices
  To sentence me to death—yours and my own.
  But do not convict me out of mere suspicion!   590
  It is hardly just to label good men bad
  Or bad men good, according to your whim.
  Mark my words: the man who drops an honest friend
  Cuts out his heart, the thing he loves the best.
  But you will learn this sure enough in time,

For time alone can tell an honest man
While one day is enough to show a villain.

CHORUS. Good advice, my lord, for one who keeps a watch
For pitfalls. Hasty thoughts are dangerous.

OED. When conspirators make haste to set plots moving   600
I must make haste myself to counteract them.
If I waited and did nothing it would mean
Success for him and ruin for myself.

CREON. Then what do you want? My banishment from Thebes?

OED. No, not your banishment. I want your death!

CREON. There speaks a man who will not listen to reason.

OED. No, you must show the world what comes of envy!

CREON. I think you must be mad.

OED.   And I think sane.

CREON. Then hear me sensibly.

OED.   Hear you, a traitor?

CREON. Suppose you are wrong?

OED.   Kings must still be obeyed.

CREON. Kings, but not tyrants.

OED.   City, oh my city!   610

CREON. My city also. I have rights here too.

CHORUS. Stop this, my lords. I can see Jocasta coming
From the palace just in time. Let her advise you,
Put your quarrel aside and be friends again.

[*Enter* JOCASTA]

JOCASTA. Have you both gone out of your minds? What is the sense
Of bandying insults? Are you not ashamed
To start a private feud, when Thebes is ailing?
Come inside. And Creon, you must go back home.
Do not make a mortal grievance out of nothing.

CREON. Sister, your husband Oedipus thinks fit   620
To make me suffer one way or the other—
To drive me into banishment or kill me.

OED. Exactly. I have caught him plotting mischief—
A criminal attempt on the royal person.

CREON. May heaven's anger strike me dead this minute
If I have done anything to deserve this charge!

JOC. In the gods' name, Oedipus, believe what he says!

If not from respect of the oath he has sworn,
For the sake of your wife and everyone here!
CHORUS. Listen to reason, my lord;   630
  I beg you, be guided by us.
OED. You ask for a favor; what is it?
CHORUS. He has been no fool in the past;
  He is strong in his oath; respect him.
OED. Do you know what it is you ask?
CHORUS. I do.
OED.   Then explain yourselves; what do you mean?
CHORUS. Your friend has invoked a curse on his head.
  Do not brand him traitor on rumor alone.
OED. You must know, by asking this
  You are asking my exile or death.   640
CHORUS. No, by the Sun, the first among gods!
  May I die the death that men fear most,
  Shunned, unclean in the sight of heaven,
  If I have such thoughts in my mind.
  But my heart is heavy at our country's dying
  If you add new troubles to her present load.
OED. Let him go then; but I am signing my own death warrant
  Or condemning myself to exile and disgrace.
  Your voice has moved me where his oath could not.
  As for him, wherever he may go, I hate him.   650
CREON. Now we have seen you—wild when you lose your temper,
  And yielding with bad grace. Such a nature as yours
  Is its own worst enemy, and so it should be.
OED. Get out, and leave me in peace.
CREON.   I am going.
  They know I am honest, though you will not see it.

    [Exit]

CHORUS. Now quickly, my lady, take him inside.
JOC. Not before I know what has happened.
CHORUS. There were words, a vague suspicion,
  False, but injustice stings.
JOC. On both sides?
CHORUS.   Yes.
JOC.   What was said?   660

CHORUS. Our country has troubles enough.
  Better let sleeping dogs lie.
OED. You meant well enough, but see where it leads you,
  Checking me, blunting the edge of my anger.
CHORUS. I have said it before and say it again:
  Men would think that my wits had wandered,
  Would think me insane, to abandon you.
  Our beloved country was sinking fast
  Till you took the helm; and now you may prove
  Our guide and salvation again.   670
JOC. Tell me as well, my lord, in heaven's name,
  What can have set such fury working in you?
OED. I will tell you; you are more to me than they are.
  It is Creon, and the way he is plotting against me.
JOC. Go on, and tell me how this quarrel started.
OED. He says that I am Laius' murderer.
JOC. Does he speak from knowledge or from hearsay only?
OED. Neither; he sent a mischief-making prophet.
  He is taking care to keep his own mouth clean.
JOC. You can relieve your mind of all such fears.   680
  Listen, and learn from me: no human being
  Is gifted with the art of prophecy.
  Once an oracle came to Laius—I will not say
  From Apollo himself, but from his ministers—
  To say a child would be born to him and me
  By whose hand it was fated he should die.
  And Laius, as rumor goes, was killed by bandits,
  From another land, at a place where three roads meet.
  And as for our son, before he was in this world
  Three days, Laius pinned his ankles together   690
  And had him abandoned on the trackless mountain.
  So in this case Apollo's purpose failed—
  That the child should kill his father, or that Laius
  Should be murdered by his son, the fear that haunted him.
  So much for oracles which map our future!
  Then take no notice of such things; whatever the god
  Finds needful, he will show without assistance.
OED. Oh wife, the confusion that is in my heart,
  The fearful apprehension, since I heard you speak!
JOC. What is it? What have I said to startle you?   700
OED. I thought I heard you telling me that Laius
  Was murdered at a place where three roads meet.

JOC. Such was the story. People tell it still.

OED. What country was it where the thing was done?

JOC. In the land called Phocis, at the meeting-point
   Of the roads from Delphi and from Daulia.

OED. And how many years have gone by since it happened?

JOC. It was just before you first appeared in Thebes
   To rule us; that is when we heard of it.

OED. Oh Zeus, what have you planned to do with me?   710

JOC. Oedipus, what is it? Why has this upset you?

OED. Do not ask me yet; but tell me about Laius.
   What did he look like? How far gone in years?

JOC. A tall man, with his hair just turning gray,
   To look at, not so different from you.

OED. Oh, what have I done? I think that I have laid
   A dreadful curse on myself and never knew it!

JOC. What are you saying? It frightens me to look at you.

OED. I am terrified the prophet sees too well.
   I shall know better if you tell me one thing more.   720

JOC. You frighten me; but ask and I will tell you.

OED. Did he ride with a handful of men, or with a band
   Of armed retainers, as a chieftain should?

JOC. There were five in all—a herald one of them,
   And a single carriage in which Laius rode.

OED. Oh, now I see it all. Jocasta, answer me,
   Who was the man who told you what had happened?

JOC. A servant—the only one who returned alive.

OED. Is he with us? Is he in our household now?

JOC. No, he is not. When he came back and found   730
   You ruling here in Thebes and Laius dead
   He wrung me by the hand and begged me send him
   Into the country where we graze our sheep
   As far as possible from the sight of Thebes.
   I let him go away; slave though he was
   He could have asked far more and had it granted.

OED. I want him here, as fast as he can come.

JOC. That can be seen to. What is in your mind?

OED. I fear I have already said
   More than I should; that is why I want to see him.   740

Joc. He shall come then; but I too have a right
   To know what lies heavy on your heart, my lord.

OED. I shall keep nothing from you, now my apprehension
   Has gone so far. Who else should I confide in
   Unless in you, when this crisis is upon me?
   My father's name was Polybus of Corinth,
   My mother a Dorian, Merope. In that city
   I lived as first in honor, till one day
   There happened something—worth surprise perhaps,
   But not such anger as it roused in me.   750
   A man at dinner, too far gone in wine,
   Jeered in his cups, I was my father's bastard.
   It preyed on my mind; and I restrained myself
   That day as best I could, but in the morning
   Went questioning my parents. They were angry
   At such a taunt, and the man who let it fly,
   So on their part I was satisfied; but still
   The slander rankled as it spread and grew.
   And so I went, without my parents' knowledge,
   On a journey to Delphi. Phoebus sent me away   760
   No wiser than I came, but something else
   He showed me, sad and strange and terrible:
   That I was doomed to mate with my own mother,
   Bring an abhorrent brood into the world;
   That I should kill the father who begat me.
   When I heard, I fled from Corinth, ever since
   Marking its whereabouts only by the stars,
   To find some place where I should never see
   This evil oracle's calamities fulfilled,
   And in my travels reached that very place   770
   Where, as you tell me, Laius met his death.
   Wife, I shall tell the truth: I was on my way
   And had nearly come to the joining of the roads
   When there met me, from the opposite direction,
   A herald, and a man in a horse-drawn carriage
   Exactly as you described. The fellow in front
   And the old man tried to push me out of the way.
   I lost my temper, hit out at the one
   Who jostled me, the driver; when the old man saw it,
   He watched me, from the carriage, coming past   780
   And brought his double goad down on my head—
   But took it back with interest! One swift blow
   From the good staff in my hand, and over he went

---

747 *Dorian* one of the oldest Greek tribes; Oedipus says this with some pride

Clean out of the chariot, sprawling on his back,
And I killed every man in sight. If this stranger
Should turn out to have anything to do with Laius,
Who is more wretched than this man before you,
And who could be more hateful to the gods,
A man no citizen, no stranger even,
May take into his house or speak with him   790
But drive him from their doors; and this, this curse
Was laid on me by no-one but myself.
And now my hands, by which he met his death,
Defile his bed. Am I not evil? Am I not
Foul through and through, when I must go to exile
And in that exile never see my people,
Or set foot in my homeland—for if I do
I must marry my mother, murder Polybus,
The father who gave me life and livelihood.
Then if you saw in Oedipus the prey   800
Of some tormenting power, would you be wrong?
Never, oh never, pure and awful gods,
Let me see that day; no, let me rather vanish
Out of the sight of men, before I see
This dreadful visitation come upon me.
CHORUS. This is fearful, my lord; but do not give up hope
    Until you have questioned the man who saw it done.
OED. Yes, that is all the hope I have left me now,
    To wait the coming of this man, our shepherd.
JOC. And when he comes, what would you have from him?   810
OED. I will tell you. If I find his story tallies
    With yours, then it will mean that I am safe.
JOC. And what is so important in my story?
OED. You said that Laius, as he told the tale,
    Was killed by robbers. If he stands by this,
    That there were more than one, I did not kill him;
    You could not make one man a company.
    But if he names one solitary traveler
    There is no more doubt; the deed swings back to me.
JOC. You can be sure that this is what he said.   820
    He cannot go back on it, all the city heard him.
    I was not the only one. But even supposing
    We find he tells a different tale today,
    My lord, he can never show that Laius' death
    Ran true to prophecy. Phoebus expressly said
    That he was doomed to die at my child's hands;

But that unhappy babe went to his death
Before he did; then how could he have killed him?
So when it comes to oracles, after this
I shall keep both eyes fixed firmly on the front.   830
OED. You speak good sense. But all the same, send someone
    To bring the peasant here; do as I say.
JOC. I will send at once. Come now, let us go home.
    Would I ever fail to do anything you wanted?

    [*Exeunt*]

CHORUS. I pray that this may crown my every day,
    In all my words and deeds to walk
    Pure-hearted, in proper fear;
    For thus we are commanded from on high
    By laws created in the shining heavens,
    Who know no other father but Olympus,   840
    In their birth owing nothing to mortals
    Nor sleeping though forgotten; great the god
    Within them, and he grows not old.

    Out of insolence is born the tyrant,
    Insolence grown fat in vain
    On things immoderate, unfit.
    For a man who has mounted to the highest places
    Must fall to meet his destiny below
    Where there can be no help, no footing.
    But honest ambition let us keep,   850
    For thus the state is served; O Lord Apollo
    Guide and strengthen me all my days.

    But I pray that the man whose hands and tongue
    Are arrogant, careless of retribution,
    Who blasphemes in the holy places,
    May fall upon evil days, the reward
    Of the sin of self-conceit.
    If he goes the wrong way to gain his ends,
    And follows unholy courses, laying
    Profaning hands on things he should not touch,   860
    Could any man boast his life was safe
    From the arrows of angry heaven?

---

840 *Olympus* mountain home of the gods

But when such things as these are held in honor
Why should I sing the praises of the gods?

No longer shall I visit with my prayers
The inviolate shrine at the center of the world,
Or Abae's temple, or Olympia,
If the prophecy should fail to come to pass
As spoken, for all the world to see.
O Zeus, if you are rightly called   870
The Almighty, the ruler of mankind,
Look to these things; and let them not escape
Your power eternal; for the oracles
Once told of Laius are forgotten, slighted;
Apollo is divested of his glory
And man turns his face away from heaven.

      [Enter Jocasta]

Joc. Elders of Thebes, I have a mind to pay
A visit to the holy shrines, with gifts
Of incense and wreathed branches in my hands.
For Oedipus has let his mind succumb   880
To all manner of fears, and will not judge the present
By what has gone before, like a sensible man,
But is the prey of every fearful rumor.
There is nothing more that I can say to help him,
And so I bring offerings to you, Apollo—
The nearest to us—and request this favor:
Show us how we can find a clean way out,
For now we are afraid to see him frightened,
Like sailors who see panic in their steersman.

      [Enter MESSENGER]

MESSENGER. Could you tell me, my friends, where a man might find   890
The palace of King Oedipus—better still,
Where the king himself is, if you happen to know?
CHORUS. This is his house, and the king is indoors.

---

866 *the inviolate . . . world* De]phi; see n. on v.70   867 *Abae* near Thebes, site of temple and oracle of Apollo   *Olympia* home of the temple of Zeus and the famous Olympic Games   876 *and man . . . heaven* a fair description of the growing agnosticism of Sophocles' own time

This lady is the mother of his children.

MESS. May heaven bless Oedipus' honored queen
Her whole life long with every happiness!

JOC. Stranger, I wish you the same; so fair a greeting
Deserves no less. But tell us why you come.
What have you to ask of us, or tell us?

MESS. Good news for your house, my lady, and your husband!   900

JOC. What news is this? Who sent you here to us?

MESS. I come from Corinth; what I have to tell
Will please you, no doubt; but there is sadness too.

JOC. Pleasure and pain at once? What is this message?

MESS. The people living in the Isthmian land
Will have him for their king; so goes the story.

JOC. Why? Is old Polybus no longer king?

MESS. No, death has claimed him. He is in his grave.

JOC. What are you saying? Oedipus' father dead?

MESS. If I am lying, may I die myself!   910

JOC. Maid, run away and tell this to your master
As fast as you can. Oh gods, where are
Your oracles now? This is the man that Oedipus
Has shunned for years, for fear of killing him,
And now he is dead, and Oedipus never touched him!

[*Enter* OEDIPUS]

OED. Jocasta, dearest wife, why have you sent
For me, and called me from the palace?

JOC. Listen to this man here, and learn from his words
To what these holy oracles have come!

OED. This man? Who is he? What has he to say?   920

JOC. From Corinth; his message is that Polybus,
Your father, lives no longer—he is dead!

OED. What? Stranger, let me have it from your mouth.

MESS. If this is where I must begin my message,
I assure you, Polybus is dead and gone.

OED. Did it happen by foul play? Or was be sick?

MESS. When a man is old his life hangs by a thread.

OED. Poor Polybus. He died of illness, then?

---

905 *Isthmian land* Corinth, situated on the narrow neck of land which joins the two
parts of Greece

MESS. That and old age. He had lived a long life.

OED. Oh, wife, why should we ever spare a glance 930
    For the shrine of Delphi, or the birds that scream
    Above our heads? On their showing, I was doomed
    To be my father's murderer; but he
    Is dead and buried, and here am I, who never
    Laid hand on sword. Unless perhaps he died
    Through pining for me; thus I could have killed him.
    But as they stand, the oracles have gone
    To join him underground, and they are worthless!

JOC. Did I not tell you so a long while since?

OED. You did, but I was led astray through fear. 940

JOC. Then do not take them any more to heart.

OED. But my mother's bed . . . how should I not fear that?

JOC. What has a man to fear, when life is ruled
    By chance, and the future is unknowable?
    The best way is to take life as it comes.
    So have no fear of marriage with your mother.
    Many men before this time have dreamt that they
    Have shared their mother's bed. The man to whom
    These things are nothing lives the easiest life.

OED. It would be well enough to talk in such a way 950
    If my mother were not living. As she is,
    Though your words make sense, I have good cause to fear.

JOC. But your father's death is a ray of light in darkness.

OED. A bright one; but I fear the living woman.

MESS. Who is this woman that you are afraid of?

OED. Merope, old man, the wife of Polybus.

MESS. And what is there in her to make you afraid?

OED. A terrifying oracle from heaven.

MESS. May it be told? Or are you sworn to silence?

OED. Why should it not? Apollo told me once 960
    That I was doomed to marry with my mother
    And shed my father's blood with these my hands.
    And that is why I put my home in Corinth
    Behind me—for the best, but all the same
    There is nothing so sweet as the sight of parents' faces.

MESS. Was it for fear of this you left our city?

OED. It was; and to avoid my father's murder.

MESS. Then had I better not remove your fear,
    My lord, since I am here with friendly purpose? 970

OED. If so you would deserve reward, and have it.

MESS. Indeed, this was my principal reason for coming,
  To do myself some good when you came home.

OED. I shall never come. I must not see my parents.

MESS. My son, I see you are making a mistake—

OED. What do you mean, old man? In god's name tell me.

MESS. —if you shrink from going home because of this.

OED. I am terrified of proving Phoebus true.

MESS. Of the guilt and shame that will come to you through your parents?

OED. You have it, old man; that fear is always with me.   980

MESS. Then let me tell you that these fears are groundless!

OED. How can they be, if I were born their son?

MESS. Because there is none of Polybus' blood in you.

OED. Are you telling me that he was not my father?

MESS. No more than I—one thing we had in common.

OED. What could he have in common with a nobody?

MESS. Why, I am not your father, and neither was he.

OED. But then . . . he called me son . . . what made him do it?

MESS. He took you as a present from my hands.

OED. He had such love . . . for an adopted son?

MESS. He had no sons of his own; this moved his heart.   990

OED. You gave me to him—had you bought me? Found me?

MESS. I found you, in the wild woods of Cithairon.

OED. What led your wanderings to such a place?

MESS. I was in charge of sheep there, on the mountain.

OED. A shepherd, going from place to place for hire?

MESS. But your preserver at that time, my son.

OED. Why? What was matter with me when you found me?

MESS. Your ankles are best witnesses of that.

OED. Oh, why do you have to talk of that old trouble?

MESS. They were pinned together, and I cut you loose.   1000

OED. A shameful mark I carried from my cradle.

MESS. And from this chance you took the name you bear.

OED. Who did this to me? My father or my mother?

MESS. The man who gave you me knows; I do not.

OED. You took me from someone else? You did not find me?

MESS. No, another shepherd passed you on to me.

OED. Who was this man? Can you identify him?

MESS. We knew him, I think, as one of Laius' people.

OED. You mean the king who used to rule this country?

MESS. The very same. This man was Laius' herdsman.   1010

OED. And is he still alive for me to see him?

MESS. You in this country would best know of that.

OED. My people, is there anyone here present
    Who knows the herdsman he is talking of,
    Who has seen him in the country or the town?
    Come, tell me; it is time to solve this riddle.

CHORUS. I think he means no other than the man
    You already want to see. Jocasta here
    Would be best qualified to tell you that.

OED. My lady, do you know the man we mean—   1020
    The man we just sent for; is he speaking of him?

JOC. Why ask who he means? Do not bother with it.
    This story is not worth thinking of; it is nothing.

OED. No, that can never be. I have the clues
    Here in my hand. I must find out my birth.

JOC. No, by the gods! If you care for your own safety
    Ask no more questions. I have suffered enough.

OED. Take courage. If my mother was a slave, and hers,
    And hers before her, you are still pure-born.

JOC. Listen, please listen to me! Do not do this!   1030

OED. No-one could stop me finding out the truth.

JOC. It is for your sake; I advise you for the best.

OED. If this is your best, I have no patience with it

JOC. I pray you may never find out who you are.

OED. Go, somebody, and fetch the herdsman here.
    Leave her to glory in her wealthy birth!

JOC. Accursed! Accursed! I have no other name
    To call you; you will never hear me again.

    [Exit]

CHORUS. What can have made her leave you, Oedipus,
    In this burst of frantic grief? I have a fear   1040
    That from her silence there will break a storm.

OED. Let break what will! As for my parentage,
    Humble though it may be, I want to know it.
    She is a woman, with a woman's pride,
    And is ashamed, no doubt, of my low birth.

But I proclaim myself the child of Luck,
My benefactress; this is no dishonor.
Yes, Luck is my mother, and the months, my cousins,
Saw me first humble and then saw me great.
With such a parentage I could not be false   1050
To myself again, or let this secret rest.
CHORUS. If I am any judge of the future,
   If my mind does not play me false,
   Cithairon, tomorrow at the full moon's rising,
   By Olympus, you will need no second telling
   That Oedipus boasts of your kinship, hailing you
   As nurse and mother.
   And we shall be there with dances in your honor
   Because you have found favor in our king's sight.
   Apollo, hear us when we pray,
   And bless our good intentions!   1060

   Which of the nymphs, the long-lived ones,
   Lay with the mountain-wanderer Pan
   To bring you to birth? Or was it Loxias?
   He is a god who loves the upland pastures.
   Or was it Cyllene's lord, or the god
   Of the Bacchanals, dwelling
   High in the hilltops, who received you,
   A new-born treasure, from the arms of a nymph
   Of Helicon, the favorite   1070
   Companions of his pleasure?

      [Enter attendants with HERDSMAN]

OED. Elders, if I, who never saw the man,
   May make a guess, I think I see the herdsman
   We have sought so long; he is well advanced in years—
   This answers the description—and besides
   I recognize the men escorting him
   As servants of my own. But you may well
   Have the advantage of me, if you have seen him before;
CHORUS. I know him, no mistake. He worked for Laius,

1063 *Pan* primitive nature deity, half man, half goat   1064 *Loxias* Apollo   1066 *Cyllene's lord* Hermes, the messenger god, born on Mount Cyllene   1067 *Bacchanals* frenzied women who worshipped Dionysus   1070 *Helicon* mountain sacred to Apollo and the Muses

As honest a shepherd as you could hope to find.   1080
OED. First let me hear from you, my Corinthian friend.
   Is this your man?
MESS. The one you see before you.
OED. Come here, old man, and look me in the face.
   Answer my questions. You once worked for Laius?
HERDSMAN. I did; and I was palace-bred, not bought.
OED. In what employment? How did you spend your time?
HERDS. For the best part of my life I watched the flocks.
OED. What part of the country did you mostly work in?
HERDS. Sometimes Cithairon, sometimes round about.
OED. Have you seen this man in those parts, to your knowledge?   1090
HERDS. Who? Doing what? What man are you talking about?
OED. This man in front of you. Have you ever met him?
HERDS. Not to remember off-hand. I cannot say.
MESS. Small wonder, master. But let me refresh
   His failing memory. I have no doubt
   That he recalls the time we spent together
   In the country round Cithairon. He had two flocks,
   And I, his mate, had one. Three years we did this,
   For six months at a time, from spring to fall.
   Then, for the winter, I used to drive my flocks   1100
   Home to my fold, he his to that of Laius.
   Did it happen as I say, or did it not?
HERDS. Yes, true; but it was many years ago.
MESS. Now tell me: do you remember giving me
   A boy for me to bring up as my own?
HERDS. What now? What has put that question in your head?
MESS. That child, my friend, is the man you see before you.
HERDS. Curse you! Do not say another word!
OED. Old man, do not reprove him. Your words stand
   In greater need of admonition than his.   1110
HERDS. And where do I offend, most noble master?
OED. In not telling of the boy he asks about.
HERDS. This meddler does not know what he is saying.
OED. If you will not speak to oblige me I must make you.
HERDS. No, no, for god's sake; you would not hurt an old man?
OED. Quickly, somebody, tie his arms behind him.
HERDS. Unhappy man, what more do you want to know?

OED. This child he talks of; did you give it him?

HERDS. I did; and I wish that day had been my last.

OED. It will come to that, unless you tell the truth. 1120

HERDS. I shall do myself more harm by telling you.

OED. It seems he is determined to waste our time.

HERDS. No, no! I told you once, I gave it him.

OED. Where did you get it? Your home or another's?

HERDS. It was not mine. Somebody gave it me.

OED. Who? Which one of my people? Where does he live?

HERDS. No, master, in heaven's name, ask no more questions.

OED. You are a dead man if I have to ask again.

HERDS. It was a child of the house of Laius.

OED. A slave? Or one of his own family? 1130

HERDS. I am near to saying what should not be said.

OED. And I to hearing; but it must he heard.

HERDS. They said it was Laius' son. But go inside
And ask your wife; for she could tell you all.

OED. You mean she gave it you?

HERDS.   She did, my lord.

OED. But why?

HERDS.   For me to make away with it.

OED. Her child!

HERDS.   She feared an evil prophecy.

OED. What was it?

HERDS.   That the son should kill his father.

OED. Then why did you give him up to this old man?

HERDS. For pity, master, thinking he would take 1140
The child home, out of Thebes; but he preserved him
For a fate worse than any other. If you are truly
The man he says, then know you were born accursed.

    [*Exit*]

OED. Oh, oh, then everything has come out true.
Light, I shall not look on you again.
I have been born where I should not be born,
I have married where I should not marry,
I have killed whom I should not kill; now all is clear.

    [*Exit*]

Chorus. You that are born into this world,
    I count you in your lives as nothing worth.   1150
    What man has ever won for himself
    More of happiness than this,
    To seem, and having seemed, to pass?
    For Oedipus, when I look at you
    And the fate which fell upon you, can I
    Call any human being happy?

    Zeus knows, his arrow went straight to its mark
    And all of life's blessings became his prize.
    He killed the girl with the crooked claws,
    The riddle-monger, and stood up among us   1160
    A tower of strength to drive death from our land,
    For which we called you our king, paid you honors
    The greatest we knew; in the proud land
    Of Thebes you were lord and master.

    Now who has a sadder tale to tell?
    A life turned upside down,
    The door flung wide to misfortune,
    The hounds of fate let loose.
    Oh Oedipus, famous Oedipus,
    The same ample shelter sufficed   1170
    For father and son, a bed for the mating.
    How could the furrows your father sowed
    Have endured you so long in silence?

    Time sees all, and has found you out
    Despite yourself, passing sentence
    On the marriage that is no marriage,
    Where begetter is one with begotten.
    Laius' child, oh Laius' child,
    Better if I had not seen you,
    For when all is said, he that gave me new life   1180
    Has taken all my joy in living.

        [*Enter* SECOND MESSENGER]

MESS. Ancestral and most honorable lords,
    Such things you will see and hear of; such a weight
    Of grief is yours, if like true sons of Thebes
    You still care for the sons of Labdacus.
    I think there is no river wide enough

To wash this palace clean, so many are
The horrors it hides, or soon will bring to light,
Done willfully, from choice; no sufferengs
Hurt more than those we bring upon ourselves.   1190
CHORUS. Those that we know already claim their weight
Of tears. What more have you to add to these?
MESS. A tale which can be very briefly told
And heard: our royal lady Jocasta is dead.
CHORUS. Oh miserable queen; what was the cause?
MESS. By her own hand. The worst of what has happened
You shall be spared, you were not there to see it
But you shall hear as much as I recall
About the sufferings of the wretched queen.
Past caring what she did, she rushed inside   1200
The hall, and made straight for her marriage bed,
Head in hands, and fingers tearing at her hair.
Once in the room she slammed the doors behind her
And called on Laius rotting in his grave,
Remembering a once begotten child
By whom the father should die, and leave the mother
To bear his son's cursed children; she bewailed
The bed where she had borne a double brood,
Husband by husband, children by her child
And then she died—I cannot tell you how,   1210
For Oedipus burst on us with a cry
And we had no chance to watch her agonies.
We had eyes for none but him, as he ran from one
To another, demanding a sword, and where
He might find his wife—his mother, not his wife,
The womb that gave him and his children birth.
In his frenzy he was guided by some power
More than human—not by any of us who stood there.
With a dreadful cry, as though a hand had pointed,
He sprang at the double doors, forced back the bolts   1220
Till the sockets gave, and ran into the room.
And there inside we saw the woman hanging,
Her body swinging in a twist of rope.
When he saw, a shuddering cry welled up inside him;
He cut the noose that held her; when she lay
Cold on the ground, we saw a ghastly sight.
He tore away the golden brooches from
Her dress, that she had used as ornaments,
And lifted them, and plunged them in his eyes   1230

With words like these: "You shall not see again
Such horrors as I did, saw done to me,
But stare in darkness on forbidden faces,
Meet those I longed to find, and pass them by."
And to this tune he raised his hands and struck
His eyes again and again; with every blow
Blood spurted down his cheeks. It did not fall
In slow and sluggish drops, but all at once
Black blood came pouring like a shower of hail.
This storm has broken on two people's heads,
Not one alone; both man and wife have suffered.   1240
Till now, the happiness they inherited
Was happiness indeed; and now, today,
Tears, ruin, death, disgrace, as many ills
As there are names for them; not one is lacking.

CHORUS. How is he now? Is he in peace from pain?

MESS. He shouts for the doors to be opened, for every man
In Thebes to see his father's murderer,
His mother's—heaven forbid I speak that word.
He means to cast himself from Thebes, to stay
In this house no more, a self-inflicted curse.   1250
But his strength is gone; he needs someone to guide
His steps, the pain is more than he can bear.
And this too he will show you. See, the doors
Are opening, and soon you will see a sight
To move your tears, though you recoil from it.

[*Enter* OEDIPUS, *blind*]

CHORUS. Oh sufferings dreadful to see,
    Most dreadful of all that ever
    Greeted my eyes. Wretched king,
    What insanity possessed you?
    What demon, in one colossal spring   1260
    Pounced on your ill-fated life?
    Unhappy king,
    I cannot even look you in the face,
    Though there are still many questions to be asked,
    Many things left unsaid, much remaining to be seen,
    You fill me with such shuddering.

OED. Oh, oh, the pain, the pain!
    Where do my poor legs take me?
    Where do the wild winds scatter my words?

Oh, my fate, where have you leapt with me?   1270

CHORUS. To a dreadful place that must not be named,
To a place unfit for the eyes of man.

OED. Oh, this fog,
This horrible darkness all around me,
Unspeakable visitation
Blown by an evil wind; I am powerless.
Oh, when I remember my sorrows
I feel again the points in my eyes.

CHORUS. No wonder; in such sorrows you must have
Evils redoubled to endure and mourn.   1280

OED. Oh, my friend,
You are my faithful servant still,
Blind Oedipus' patient nurse.
I know you are here, I can feel your presence.
Although I am in the darkness
I can recognize your voice.

CHORUS. Oh man of wrath, how could you bring yourself
To blind your eyes? What demon drove you on?

OED. It was Apollo, my friends, Apollo
Who contrived my ruin, who worked my fall,   1290
But no-one blinded my eyes
But myself, in my own grief.
What use are eyes to me, who could never
See anything pleasant again?

CHORUS. Yes, it was as you say.

OED. What is there left for me to see,
To love? Who still has a kindly word
My friends, for me?
Take me away from this land, my friends,
Take me with all the speed you may,   1300
For Oedipus is no more,
Contaminated, cursed,
Unclean in heaven's sight.

CHORUS. Knowledge and pain; they hurt you equally.
I wish your path and mine had never crossed.

OED. Cursed be the man who struck the cruel chains
From my feet as I lay abandoned,
And saved me from death, gave me back
To the world of the living—why?
If I had died then, I should never   1310
Have grieved myself or my loved ones so.

CHORUS. I too would have had it so.

OED. I would not have shed my father's blood
Or heard men call me my mother's husband.
And now I am
God-shunned, the son of a mother defiled,
Have taken my turn in my mother's bed.
If there is any sorrow
Greater than all others
It belongs to Oedipus.   1320

CHORUS. I cannot praise your judgment. You would be
Far better dead than living still and blind.

OED. Do not tell me I am wrong. What I have done
Is best as it is. Give me no more advice.
If I had sight, I know not with what eyes
I would have looked upon my father, when
I walked among the dead, or my sad mother,
For sins so great cannot be paid by hanging.
Or do you think the sight of children born
As mine were born could give me any joy?   1330
No, never to these eyes of mine again,
Nor the proud wall of our city, nor the holy
Statues of our gods; these I, ten times accursed,
I, who was noblest of the sons of Thebes,
Have set behind me by my own command
That all cast out the sinner, the man revealed
By heaven as unclean, as Laius' son.
And tainted thus for all the world to see
How could I look my people in the face?
I could not. If I could have stopped my ears,   1340
My fount of hearing, I would not have rested
Till I had made a prison of this body
Barred against sight and sound. How happy the mind
That can so live, beyond the reach of suffering.
Cithairon, why did you shelter me? Why did you not
Kill me there, where you found me, so that I might never
Show to mankind the secret of my birth?
Oh Polybus, Corinth, the ancestral home
Men called my father's; oh, how fair of face
Was I, your child, and how corrupt beneath!   1350
For now I am found evil, evil born.
Those three roads, and the hidden clump of trees,
The wood, the narrow place where three paths met,
Who drank from my own hands the father's blood,
And so, my own blood; do you still remember

The things you saw me do? Then I came here
To do other things besides. Oh marriage, marriage,
You gave me birth, and after I was born
Bore children to your child, and brought to light
Sons, fathers, brothers in a web of incest,   1360
Than which men know nothing more abominable.
But what is sin to do is sin to speak of.
For heaven's love, hide me in some wilderness,
Or strike me dead, or throw me in the sea,
Where you will never set eyes on me again.
Come, do not shrink from touching my poor body.
Please; do not be afraid. My sufferings
Are all my own, no-one will be infected.

CHORUS. No. Here is Creon, in time to listen to you,
Ready to act or advise. Now you are gone   1370
He is the only one we have to turn to

OED. Oh, what words can I find to say to him?
What proof of my good faith? I have been found
An arrant traitor to him in the past.

[*Enter* CREON *with attendants*]

CREON. Oedipus, I have not come to jeer at you
Or throw your past misconduct in your face.

[*To the* CHORUS]

As for you, if you have no sense of decency
To a fellow man, at least have some respect
For holy sunlight, giver of warmth and life.
Do not leave this pollution uncovered, an offence   1380
To earth, to light, to the pure rain from heaven.
Take him indoors as quickly as you can.
Propriety forbids he should be made
A public spectacle. These things are for his family.

OED. Listen: since you have removed my apprehension
And behave so nobly to a man so low
Grant me this favor—for your good, not for mine.

CREON. What is it you are so anxious to have me do?

OED. Lose no more time; drive me away from Thebes
To some place where nobody will know my name.   1390

CREON. Believe me, I would have done so; but first I wanted
To find out from the god what I should do.

OED. The will of god is clear enough already.
  Kill the parricide, the sinner; and that am I.
CREON. So he said. But all the same, now things have gone
  So far, it is better that we seek clear guidance.
OED. You will go to the god? For a poor wretch like myself?
CREON. I will. Perhaps you will believe him this time.
OED. I do. And I will urge your duties on you.
  The woman inside—bury her as you would wish   1400
  To be buried yourself. It is right, she is your sister.
  But as for me, never sentence my father's city
  To have me within its walls, as long as I live,
  But leave me to the hills, to my Cithairon
  As men now call it—destined for my grave
  By my father and mother when they were alive.
  They tried to kill me; let me die the way they wanted.
  But I am sure of one thing; no disease,
  Nothing can kill me now. I would not have been saved
  From death, unless it were for some strange destiny.   1410
  But let my destiny go where it will.
  As for my children—Creon, do not trouble yourself
  About my sons. They are men, they can never lack
  A livelihood, wherever they may be.
  But my two girls, my poor unhappy daughters,
  Who never knew what it was to eat a meal
  Away from their father's side, but had their share
  Of every little thing I had myself. . . .
  Please look after them. And I beg this favor now,   1420
  Let me lay my hands on them and weep with them.
  Please, my lord,
  Please, noble heart. If I could touch them now
  I should think they were with me, as if I could see them.

    [*Enter* ANTIGONE *and* ISMENE]

  What is that?
  Oh you gods; is it my darlings that I hear
  Sobbing? Has Creon taken pity on me
  And sent my darlings, sent my children to me?
  Am I right?
CREON. Yes, I had them brought to you; I knew
  They would delight you as they always have done.   1430
OED. Bless you for your trouble. May you find
  A kinder fate than what has come to me.

Where are you now, my children? Over here:
Come to these hands of mine, your brother's hands,
Whose offices have made your father's eyes
That were once so bright, to see as they see now.
For the truth is out; your father, stupid, blind,
Begot you in the womb where he was born.
Sight have I none, but tears I have for you
When I think of how you will be forced to live   1440
At men's hands in the bitter days to come.
What gathering of the folk will you attend,
What festival that will not send you home
In tears, instead of making holiday?
And when the time has come for you to marry,
Show me the man, my children, bold enough
To take upon his own head such disgrace,
The stain that you and your brothers will inherit.
What sorrow is not ours? Your father killed
His father, sowed his seed in her   1450
Where he was sown as seed, and did beget you
In the selfsame place where he was once begotten.
That is how men will talk. Then who will marry you?
No-one, my children. Marriage is not for you.
You must be barren till your lives are done.
Son of Menoeceus, you are the only father
These girls have left, for we, their parents,
Are both of us gone. So do not let them wander
Beggared and husbandless. They are your kin.
And do not level them with my misfortunes   1460
But pity them. You see how young they are.
You are the only friend they have in the world.
Touch me, kind heart, in token of your promise.
Children, if you were old enough to understand,
There is much I could say to help you. As it is,
Pray after me—to live with moderation
And better fortune than your father did.

CREON. Your time is up. Dry your tears and go in-doors.

OED. It is hard, but I must obey.

CREON.   There must be moderation in all things.

OED. I shall go on one condition.

Creon.   Tell me what it is.   1470

OED. Send me away from Thebes to live.

CREON.   That is for the gods to say.

OED. They will be glad to see me gone.

CREON.   Then your wish will soon be granted.

OED. You agree then?

CREON.   When I do not know, I do not speak.

OED. Take me away, it is time.

CREON.   Come along. Leave your children here.

OED. Never part us!

CREON.   Do not ask to have everything your way.
   Your time for giving orders is over.

   [*Exeunt*]

CHORUS. People of this city, look, this man is Oedipus,
   Who guessed the famous riddle, who rose to greatness,
   Envy of all in the city who saw his good fortune.
   And now what a fearful storm of disaster has struck him.   1480
   That is why we wait until we see the final day,
   Not calling anybody happy who is mortal
   Until he has passed the last milestone without calamity.

CONSTRUCTING A READING

1. If a myth is a story through which a culture understands itself, what do
    you suppose the Greeks understood about themselves through the basic
    story of Oedipus prior to Sophocles's play? Discuss this question with
    your group.

2. In groups or individually, as your teacher directs, do some research on
    ancient Greek culture and theatre and present your results to the class.
    Your research should include, for example:

    Religious origins of the Greek Theatre
    Prize competitions
    The method of funding for Greek Theatre
    The function of the chorus
    A definition of dramatic (Sophoclean) irony
    An account of oracles and their function in ancient Greek belief

3. One of Sophocles's problems was making his story and characters seem
    true to life. What dramatic techniques does he use to make his audience
    believe that Oedipus could possibly marry his mother and kill his father?

4. Another challenge is the characterization of Jocasta as both wife and
    mother to Oedipus. Does she seem both motherly and wifely to you?
    Point to places in Jocasta's characterization that lead you to one or the
    other conclusion, or both.

5. View the Woody Allen film *Mighty Aphrodite* and, with your group, discuss the effects of its use of the chorus. Do you perceive Allen's text intertextually with *Oedipus the King*?
6. If, as Eliade maintains, myth functions to offer exemplary ways of living, what is exemplary about Oedipus as Sophocles presents him?
7. If myth is a story by which a culture understands itself, what do you think the Greek culture understood from Sophocles' play?

In the nearly two thousand years since Sophocles wrote his version of the Oedipus myth, the story has served a number of functions in Western culture. The Greek philosopher Aristotle used Sophocles's play as a paradigmatic example of *tragedy*, a kind of play that allows its audience to rid itself of pity and fear by providing *catharsis*, or purgation for those feelings. Aristotle held that tragic stories first arouse the emotions by representing the pitiful and fearful fall of a person who is basically good, but flawed in some way. As a result of his tragic flaw, the great man falls, and the audience receives an exemplary lesson. Sigmund Freud used the Oedipus story to describe and explain certain aspects of his theory of the psychosexual development of young males. According to Freud, the development of sexuality in children occurs in part as a process of identification and separation from the parent. In infancy and early childhood, a boy first identifies with his mother, often saying that he wants to marry her. Later, he realizes that his desire for his mother could potentially cause his father to become angry and harm him. The "Oedipus complex" is resolved, according to Freud, when the young male child finds a more appropriate object for his sexual feelings, begins to identify with and imitate his father, and begins to develop a heterosexual orientation.

In positing his theories of sexuality, Freud construes the myth of Oedipus as an exemplary story that helps people to understand otherwise inexplicable aspects of their sexual lives. When we read Freud's version of the Oedipus story, the meaning we make comes from intertextuality, our sense of the relations between the Sophoclean story and the Freudian one. Freud uses Sophocles's plotting of the ancient Greek myth to explain his theories of sexuality; at the same time, a Freudian could use the psychoanalyst's theories to re-understand the meaning and function of the Greek myth and the Sophoclean play. Similarly, the French anthropologist Claude Levi-Strauss, working intertextually with Sophocles, Aristotle, and Freud, used the story to develop his own theory of myth as a story in which contradictions are resolved.

Here is a cartoon by Garry Trudeau.

CONSTRUCTING A READING

1. If myth is a story by which a culture understands itself, how does Garry Trudeau ask us to understand this culture?
2. If a myth is a story that resolves a contradiction, what contradiction does Trudeau see and how does he (ask us to) understand it?

Myth

Muriel Rukeyser

Long afterward, Oedipus, old and blinded, walked the
roads.   He smelled a familiar smell.   It was
the Sphinx.   Oedipus said, "I want to ask one question.
Why didn't I recognize my mother?"   "You gave the
wrong answer," said the Sphinx.   "But that was what
made everything possible," said Oedipus.   "No," she said.
"When I asked, What walks on four legs in the morning,

two at noon, and three in the evening, you answered,
Man.   You didn't say anything about woman."
"When you say Man," said Oedipus, "you include women
too. Everyone knows that."   She said, "That's what
you think."

CONSTRUCTING A READING

1. With your group members, discuss some possible meanings for the word, *myth* in Rukeyser's title. How do they work, and how do they change the meaning of this poem and of Sophocles's play?
2. If a myth is a story that resolves a contradiction, what contradiction does Rukeyser's poem describe?
3. If a myth is a story that explains things, what does this poem explain?

from *Power Dreamers*
The Jocasta Complex

Ursule Molinaro

Chapter 4

On this, the 24th day of Pyanepsion, I gave birth to a splendidly healthy, perfectly formed little boy, with intelligent eyes. He looks very much like me.
    . . .
    I'm ridiculously happy. & surprised. I didn't expect to find such joy in motherhood. I used to think breeding was the fulfillment of less intelligent women. Now I think that the body has an intelligence all its own.

Chapter 5

What kind of beings are these wizened virgins Apollo appoints to sit astride tripods, & predict human misery from the mists of sulphur fumes? Do they envy motherhood for which they are too old, even if they were to break their vows of chastity? Do they hate children? Do they hate humanity?
    Is this yellow-eyed hyena aware that she is murdering a beautiful, now forever nameless baby with the venom of her words? Does she remember what she said when she comes out of her trance? & asks for water to relieve her throat? & perfumed lotions, to relieve the sulphur stench. & combs to comb her spastic hair?
    I feel like confronting her myself. Not in consultation. I want her to see

my empty arms, from which a bright new life was torn, & handed to a messenger of death, because of her drug-induced mutterings. To be murdered, instead of growing up to be a murderer. A parricide.

Allegedly, infants don't suffer death as keenly as adults. They haven't been in life long enough to have learned fear. That is Laius' miserable consolation to me. I shouldn't give the child a name, in my thoughts of him. I'm only personalizing my grief.

Chapter 7

Decidedly: the gods are at it again: I was awakened in the middle of the night by our chief runner, who brought me the news that Laius had met with an accident on his drive to the oracle. On the rocky, winding road half a day's distance from Delphi. The breathless man said the King had been dragged to his death by the suddenly shying horses of his own chariot.

I'm having my brother Creon organize mourning ceremonies throughout the city. Every household will be issued white fabric for robes, & ashes. Which he assures me   purge the surviving of resentment.

It hasn't worked for me during all these years. I've dressed in white without the ashes, but discarding all jewelry   mourning the murder of my son. But my resentment has grown deeper with every day. Against his murderous father. Against the oracle. Against the gods, playing games with our mousetrap lives to alleviate their immortal boredom. Taking bets on if & how we'll chew our way out.

I look beautiful in white: my attending women tell me every morning, with the sincere flattery that qualifies them for their office. White sets off the darkness of my hair & eyes. & every morning they look sincerely shocked when I reply that it sets off mainly the darkness in my heart.

. . .

& suddenly I knew! The oracle was fulfilling itself.

Chapter 9

I've been sitting before my polished silver panel all morning, studying my face. Not out of vanity, or sudden self-doubt, like an actor's dread at the opening of a new play. —The tension allegedly heightens his performance. —I don't distrust my desirability at this point in my life. I'm of that certain age intelligent young men are often drawn to. & find alluring. Feeling better understood than by girls of their own selfish youth, that is still blunt like the horns of young deer.

I'm convinced that a woman close to 40 & a man soon to be 20 make an ideal couple. —Their difference in age compensating for the greater importance our society has begun to accord to men.—

At least the ideal couple is the image I wish to project to my people. I want them to think of my new husband as: a brilliant, beautiful stranger, who freed us from the Sphinx. A perfect new mate for their widowed queen, whose happiness will leak down to them.

But I worry that the more observant among my people might begin to notice an uncanny resemblance between their queen & the stranger, as they watch them drive   or walk   side by side through our city streets. On display during the wedding ceremonies, that will follow the mourning ceremonies almost without intermission. A sameness of look in the eyes, for instance, that cannot be smiled away as the body gratitude of newlyweds.

Which may prompt the older among my citizens to count the years since the alleged crib death of the royal baby. Whose arrival they'd all so anxiously awaited. Whose natural death they'd never quite believed, right after the old king's return from consulting the oracle. & figure that their new king & heralded liberator must be about the age that mysteriously dead royal baby would be by now. & revive dark ugly rumors. Prompting the jokers among them to start snickering about: a marriage made on Olympus . . .

I am an intelligent woman. & I intend to use my intelligence not only to embrace my fate with my eyes wide open, but to seduce it. I want my second marriage to become a model of harmony & enlightened co-rulership. The secret desire of future generations. I will add to Creon's mating rites of fashion by changing the look of my eyes, in case the eyes of the bright, beautiful stranger still look very much like mine.

—After looking at a totally different life, for 18 years. At different sceneries, & people. Which may have influenced his looks. Perhaps environment moulds our features more than kinship. But I can't count on that.

I keep wondering where he grew up, & how. In another city, or among shepherds, or peasants somewhere in the countryside? Was he raised by fishermen near the ocean? What may be his social class? His education? His manners?

So many questions. Some of which will answer themselves, by the way he'll enter our gates, & greet us. & tell us how he did away with the dreaded Sphinx.

The other questions I plan to ask sparingly, through long years of happy cohabitation. Never letting on that I may know the answers more truthfully than he does. Which he must never know, in case he is conservative, like most daring young men. Who believe in the moral justification of our various social taboos.

Marriage taboos the strictest among them. —Which seem moral even to my amoral outlook when they restrain an impetuous father from forcing himself upon an adolescent daughter. Who is ill placed to withhold her consent. As is the younger sister of a lustful brother. A mother   or a sister; any female   is less empowered to force her desires upon a son, or a brother. On any man, whose flesh would have to be somewhat willing it seems to me to achieve inbreeding. The subject of the taboo.

Which allegedly produces deformed or feeble-minded children. Although the gods seem to do it with impunity. No taboo was invoked when Zeus married his sister Hera. & brothers are traditionally marrying their sisters, in the royal families of Egypt. Without any evidence of deficient offspring. —Perhaps because the marrying siblings are all superior specimens.

As I am. My father Menoeceus is one of the few surviving men who sprouted   in full armor   from the dragon's teeth our City's founder Cadmus sowed in Boetia, the Heiferland. Sometimes I feel a streak of dragon deep inside me giving me the strength to continue to be. & my son was a perfect baby for 2 happy months of my life.

& we purposely inbreed our dogs & horses   our sheep   when we wish to emphasize a mother's particularly valued trait. Mating an exceptionally intelligent bitch with the strongest male in her litter. A swift mare with her colt. A golden-fleeced ewe with her lamb.

I shan't have recourse to the luckless parsley to abort a child that may grow inside me after fate mates me with my son. Certainly not the first child, the test child, whose mind & body will reflect the further intentions of the gods. If he   or she   is beautiful & bright, & of a smiling disposition, I will know that Hera lifted the curse the oracle intended. & I will sacrifice to her every day of my remaining life.

Meanwhile I have destroyed the potential detection of the curse, by changing my appearance.

There's an Egyptian among my attending women, who paints her eye lashes the color of her river at home: Nile green. I've had her paint mine, but blue, which I consider more in keeping with mourning. The result is quite startling; slightly Sphinx-like. A total transformation.

Creon squinted at me for the longest time, then asked: What it was that made me look so different?

I told him I was wearing my widow face. It was my elaboration on his ritual of mourning. Which I thought ought to begin with the eyes.

He approved enthusiastically. A splendid addition. It defined the eyes, yet made them look mysterious. Like held-back tears. He hoped other women would follow my example.

I hope they will. —& that my son will defer his hero's welcome long enough for our people to get used to my new face. I wish I'd believed in the oracle as soon as Laius told me what Tiresias' daughter had said. It would have given me 18 years to work on developing a lack of family resemblance.

Chapter 11

Our treasurer is trying to argue Creon out of giving a city-wide week of banquets —each day to be centered at 1 of our gates— to celebrate my wedding to our liberator & new King-to-be.

Who walks in on the discussion, unannounced. Scrubbed, & smelling like a cloud of musk blended with roses. Looking very regal, in that ornate Corinthian style our men here may find a trifle too decadent to imitate.

He slightly surprises us all, when he instantly sides with the treasurer. Declaring that: A whole week of free roasts   & especially of free wine   will debilitate the citizenry. Who'll need twice as long to recover from such unaccustomed high living. Creon's generosity is not only a waste of existing funds, it also jeopardizes future work energy.

Our treasurer beams & nods. & complains about the further outlay for fabric for festive gowns to be issued citywide, just after the recent issue of fabric for robes of mourning.

Our liberator & King-to-be instantly questions that need: Why new fabric? Why whole new robes? Why not simply give them colorful ribbons, which the citizens can affix inventively to their mourning dress? It will be an incentive to their inventive spirit. To the artist that dwells inside all of us . . .

Our treasurer praises the idea. I can see nothing wrong with it myself. Creon shrugs: All right. But his eyes are pleading with me for arbitration.

So I say: Our liberator's modesty is admirable. Most auspicious for his & my co-rulership. —At the word: co-rulership, his eyebrows rise, & his eyes harden.— But surely, having been raised with the principles of government in his mother's milk, so to speak, as a royal child in Corinth, he must understand that rituals & ceremonies   food & entertainment   are essential to keep contentment among the people. Rituals & ceremonies not only disperse pent-up emotions which otherwise risk to crystallize into acts of rebellion, into riots, they're also an incentive to work better afterwards.

Our people had just experienced the loss of their beloved king . . .

He interrupts me: He noticed quite a bit of revelry, upon entering Thebes. If the bereft people were drowning their grief, that grief must have been thoroughly drowned by the time he arrived   as drowned as the Sphinx to judge by their high spirits.

Our people are in high spirits, because they're at last free of the Sphinx: I retort: It would be a political mistake to dampen their spirits with a shabby wedding ceremony.

The stern finality in my voice surprises everyone, including myself I sound more like an exasperated mother, than like a bride-to-be. & just like a mother, who feels that she has scolded enough, I switch to endearment.

We're all eager to hear how he managed to do away with the man-eating monster from Ethiopia: I smile sweetly: Won't he tell us how he was able to solve a riddle that had stumped every young man before him. Including my unfortunate nephew Haemon.

He isn't fooled. He knows I'm telling him to change the subject. To keep his nose out of the affairs of our city, at least until after he has officially been appointed my co-ruler.

During all my speculations & anticipatory fantasies it never occurred to me that my second husband might disagree with my   or my brother's   decisions. That he might have political ambitions & ideas of his own. A worrisome thought.

It makes me wonder about the relationship he had with his 'parents'. Of whom he spoke at his arrival; with enviable fondness. Had he perhaps been a little too opinionated for them? & was that why he had left Corinth or perhaps been made to leave?

—Renouncing the throne that would have been his at the death of King Polybus, according to the 'progressive' laws of succession that prevail in Corinth, that pass power & property on to the son, bypassing the line of the mother.

After my airless marriage to a hypochondriachal child murderer, am I about to marry a neo-patriarch? Or is his butting in just the insecurity of youth, trying to make an impression on a new environment?

He obligingly begins telling us about his encounter with the Sphinx. How she loomed before him after the last bend in the road, with the walls of Thebes almost close enough to vault over. But soon he is belittling his undeniable feat, in a way I consider most unflattering to my sex. Intentionally unflattering, to get even with my reprimand, & put me back in my place? Wherever he thinks my place may be.

We're giving him too much credit, he begins. Fixing each of us in turn with a disarming smile. —He has the same white, even teeth Laius used to admire about Chrysippus. They must have impressed me, too, at the very instant I conceived my son.—   We might change our opinion, we might even think him a cheat, after he tells us that he has a certain knack that sometimes permits him to guess another's thoughts. Usually under circumstances of extreme concentration, when he's alone with that other person. His tutor discovered that he had this ability   this gift from the gods   when he was 11. When he answered questions about subjects they had as yet not studied. When he was able to read the answers in his tutor's mind.

& then there was another fact to be borne in mind. The riddle the Sphinx had asked   —What being with only 1 voice has sometimes 2 feet, sometimes 3, & sometimes 4, & is weakest when it has the most?— was not all that difficult when you took into account that it was being asked by a woman. What was foremost on a woman's mind? The obvious answer was: Man. The rest   the crawling baby / the upright adult / the old man with his cane   had inserted themselves later, as he thought about the other predominant preoccupation of women: Age . . . aging.

I squint at him. I probably look annoyed. He smiles disarmingly, & tells me that: My eyes look very much like the eyes of the Sphinx before she leapt from the rock.

Do they really? & can he read in my mind whether I'm flattered or offended by being likened to a monster?

The Sphinx had the most mysterious eyes he'd seen on any female face, until he saw me. & he's looking forward to reading my mind as soon as we're alone together. When he hopes to read the same thing that has been on his own mind since the moment he walked into the throne room.

Creon clears his throat: He'll see to it then that the arrangements get under way for the wedding ceremonies. Minus new gowns . . . This wedding marks a new era for our city, & since the outcome is contained in the seed, he promises me that my wedding will be magnificent. An event all of Greece will talk about & envy.

Our liberator turns his hands, palms up, toward the treasurer. Who promptly imitates the gesture.

I ask: If he would like me to dispatch a runner to Corinth, to invite his parents to the festivities.

He hastily refuses: Even a whole week of celebrations would be over, before his parents could reach Thebes. They aren't the youngest any more. His mother was close to 40 when she gave birth to him.

I don't suggest horses, or litter bearers. His face has become a mask of anguish. I shall definitely ask about his relationship with his parents as soon as we're alone.

It will provide a pretext for not allowing him to lie with me just yet. I want to build his desire for me, & prolong it. It will be a typical 'woman's' revenge for belittling her sex, when he belittled the intelligence of the Sphinx.

I must discipline my mind not to think anything I don't want him to know. That should be quite a lesson in self-awareness.

Chapter 14

Oedipus has been writing letters all night, instead of making love to me.

I was going to let him in at last, after 6 long nights of lying side by side. Desire lying between us like an obstacle, across which we seduced each other with our eyes   our hands   our lips & tongues   our toes   groping and grasping   doing everything but the final, total thing. Which   I said   had to be saved for the 7th night, until the ceremonies were over, & all of Thebes had gone to bed, after he had officially become my husband.

I didn't even laugh when he chided me   paradoxically respecting me for: being very religious; very conventional.

Now he's writing endless letters to Corinth, about me, I imagine, to keep me waiting in turn. To get back at me. The obviousness of his strategy is touchingly juvenile. & effective.

In a way, though, I'm grateful for the reprieve. Despite my sincere contempt for man-made taboos & religious scare tactics, something dark inside me balks at the prospect of letting Oedipus reenter whence he came forth into the world.

Many times, during these exhausting nights of stayed seduction, I felt on the brink of hinting that I know who he 'really' is. But he doesn't doubt that he really is Oedipus of Corinth. Oedipus of Thebes only as of tonight. & can I be sure that he always was Oedipus of Thebes?

That he is indeed the unlikely survivor of my dead husband's precautionary measures? That he already fulfilled the first half of the predicted abomination he thinks he's running away from by not returning to Corinth —If that is why he did not return to Corinth after consulting Tiresias' daughter?— & is now about to consumate the second half, whenever he finishes writing his letters.

Why would he believe me, if I told him that after being hailed as the liberator of Thebes, he should now stand trial for the murder of her king? Do I know for sure that he met & killed Laius before he met & killed the Sphinx?

Whom he actually did not kill. Who killed herself when he solved her riddle.

Ironically, I find myself mourning for her. I grieve that female intelligence is currently being perceived as a monster that must be slain.

The Sphinx was not mentioned by the oracle 18 years ago. She wasn't part of my son's scenario. Could that mean that Oedipus is *not* my son, after all?

During those 6 long nights of stayed seduction I asked him about his journey. Guardedly: Had the road been much traveled, this pretty spring season? Had he met anyone interesting . . . other than the Sphinx?

He smiled into my eyes, telling me nothing. He didn't wish to be distracted from our desire games.

I asked: Why had he left Corinth? Had he not felt happy there? Had he perhaps quarreled with his parents? About the succession, perhaps?

I had offended him. Only a matrilinear-thinking mind could come up with such a ludicrous notion. His parents are & always will be what he holds dearest in his life. —A little stab in my direction: I am not what he holds dearest.

Then why did he not wish them to be present at our wedding? I stabbed back.

My questions have spoiled his mood. Moreover, they're gratuitous. As Tiresias told me: Why do I keep asking what was answered 18 years ago? But once again I'm no longer sure of anything. The sudden belief that flooded me at Laius' death ebbs & crests, & ebbs again.

When I first heard his name: Oedipus: I was sure my horror fantasy of the thorn-pierced baby feet had been the gruesome reality. That Laius' torture tactic had left him swollen-footed. The first time we were alone together, I inspected his feet the soles, the insteps under the pretext of a love massage. I found no scar, not even a healed, closed-up puncture point.

I asked how he got his name, & he told me: His mother was close to 40 when she was pregnant with him. He was her first & only child, & was giving her intolerable labor pains. Finally, her attending women carried her to the ocean, & seated her with her back to the waves. The first incoming wave brought him forth. He was the son of the Cresting Wave.

It sounds possible. More plausible than the ruse of a childless royal couple happening upon a 2-month-old baby on a beach, after it survived being thrown into the sea. —Perhaps at the same spot where the Sphinx drowned herself— A baby that floated the distance from Thebes to Corinth unharmed. & now, 18 years later, the survivor, the adolescent hero, walks back the distance from Corinth to Thebes, to fulfill his fate in my bed.

If that is the implausible truth, I still have time to stop it. At least the second act of it. I can wait up for him, & tell him that we need to talk.

Chapter 19

Our little Antigone is 6 months old today. She slipped out of me   causing me barely the slightest discomfort during the night of the winter solstice. Heralding the Return of the Light: Oedipus says. She's an undeniable stamp of divine approval. I'd be an ungrateful wretch, if I still doubted that my second marriage is pleasing to the gods. Anyone who looks at our little daughter feels joy.

Even the twins stop their war cries in her presence. They waddle toward her on their still bowed, unsteady legs, unclenching their little boxers' fists to touch her cheek with the gentlest care. Beaming as though caught in a ray of sun.

—Their resemblance grows uncannier every day. They really look interchangeable. Oedipus had 2 arm clasps made for them: a golden lion's head for Eteocles, & a silver serpent for Polyneices, to help us tell them apart. I suspect them of switching their clasps when no one is looking, to confuse their nurses. Oedipus says: Perhaps they think they're switching each other. That Eteocles wants to be Polyneices, & Polyneices wants to be Eteocles, at least for a day. Their precocious cleverness never ceases to amuse him. His love for me, & those who come out of me, is Hera's most precious gift.

I've created a miracle: he says: Antigone is so beautiful & sweet. Exactly how he imagines me to have been, when I was 6 months old. I have miraculously recreated myself

I don't quote what I've read about breeding a mare with her colt, or a bitch with the sturdiest pup in her litter. Nor do I point out that I was a defiant child   a cynical adolescent   a jaded, disappointed adult. That I was far from sweet, until he came   back   into my life. I kiss his mouth shut, & hurry him off to Hera's temple, for another thank-you sacrifice.

We're offering the wide golden armband Oedipus gave me for the birth of Antigone. From Antigone with love: it says on the inside. It looks beautiful on my arm, just above the elbow, but we agreed that Hera must have it. Even if it gets stolen during the night, as all our valuable sacrifices do. Thebes has her network of irreverent thieves, who hide behind the official explanation that: the goddess has come down from Olympus to collect her pickings. They sneer at the curse I placed on anyone robbing the gods. They sell their loot to invisible middlemen, who conduct an underground export trade with equally invisible middlemen in other Greek cities. All of it cloaked in pious respectability.

My awareness of this practice used to keep me from offering valuable sacrifices during my first marriage. When I had only my awareness to be thankful for. Now I feel that, what matters is to give up something you value.

Oedipus agrees with me. He rarely worshipped, in Corinth, but at that time the gods had as yet not intervened in his life. When they placed him on the road to Thebes   on the road that led to me, to my secret door   they changed his life: he says enthusiastically: He became aware of their guidance. Every day they give him new reasons to offer his thanks. Especially to Hera, whose favorite highpriestess I am. Who favors him also, by association with me.

My heart shudders at what he is saying.   —He really doesn't know, then. He doesn't even suspect!— Then shudders again at my lack of faith. Hera's pleasure about the armband   or at least about our readiness to part with it   becomes evident as soon as we return from the temple. When my brother Creon emerges from his 2-year-long seclusion, with Antigone asleep in his arms. He is smiling. He has a suggestion for Oedipus.

I anticipate a hint about spacing my pregnancies, but no. Not at all. He wants to show us drawings of armbands, clasps, & brooches he has been designing. Bold, harmonious shapes, which he proposes to combine with Oedipus' perfumes. He thinks that, together, they might launch an innovative beauty trade. Build Thebes into an export center for luxury items.

Luxury: my brother declares: is an underrated basic need. It is a child of beauty, as important to our senses as food, clothing, & shelter are to the body. Which is the scaffolding for the senses. A useless structure, when deprived of the senses. Whose refinement   through the cultivation of beauty, in art as well as in artifact precludes the uglifying impulses. Such as apoplectic anger   thin-lipped miserliness   bulbous gluttony. Steeping the senses in beauty inhibits ugly thoughts & emotions. Therefore, selling the ingredients of beauty   the tools of beauty   to the largest possible number of people will not only promote prosperity within the 7 gates of our city, it will spread beauty's message of harmony & peace throughout Greece.

My brother is beaming. Oedipus looks happy, too. They shake hands on their project. Antigone wakes up with a tiny burp of joy.

I don't say that: Wearing beautiful arm clasps hasn't pacified the twins.

As soon as my brother leaves, Oedipus starts looking through his collection of costumes. He plans to go into town tonight, to check on our people's reaction to the manufacture & export of luxury items. —He, for one, likes the idea very much. What a prompt response to our sacrifice. Hera must have been pleased with her armband. Antigone liked the idea, too. He thinks that little girl is our good-luck charm.

—Once a week, always on a different day, Oedipus goes into the city in disguise. Sometimes he's a bellied grain merchant from the surrounding countryside. Sometimes a pretty young washerwoman. A water carrier. A midwife from Crete. A stone cutter. Every detail of his costume is carefully studied, including the accent & vocabulary that are typical of each trade. When needed, he chips & blackens his fingernails & roughens the skin of his hands. Tonight he's planning to go as a jeweller's apprentice from Athens. What do I think?

I think he should let me go with him. I could be his pompous master. I do a very convincing Athenian accent.

He laughs. He'd love it. But it wouldn't work. We'd give each other away, acting off each other. He, at any rate, would not be able to keep a straight face. He'd be embarrassed, acting in front of me. It would make him feel insecure. After all, he isn't doing this just for the fun of it.

I stare at him. I don't know if it's the way I see him, or his face, that has changed. Suddenly he looks & even sounds shockingly like his father Laius, extolling the philosophical superiority of a man's love for another man, or the significance of his regiment of lover-charioteers, which I a mere woman can neither share nor understand.

Good! I say in a voice honed with rage. The voice of an indignant mother, whose son is disputing her authority in household matters. Good! Perhaps he'd do well to feel a little insecure. Even without my embarrassing presence. Does he really believe that our people suspect nothing! For 2 years they've been running into midwives from Crete, or stone cutters from Sparta, or grain merchants from Egypt, once a week, who draw them into political conversations over cups of wine. Who draw them out, listening to a problem they happen to have, a complaint. Which miraculously, mysteriously solves itself soon after. Does he not think our people are smart enough to make the connection? I'm not saying that they know they're talking to their king, when they're flirting with a pretty young washerwoman they never saw around before, who disappears into the night, never to be seen again, but I *am* saying that they're pretty sure they're flirting with someone connected to the royal court a spy from & for the palace & that they're slanting their conversations accordingly. One should never overestimate the gullibility of the people.

& just like a son trying to reason with an unreasonable mother, Oedipus invokes the higher authority of his father. Who has been mingling with the people of Corinth once a week for over 40 years. In varying disguises. With excellent results. His father calls that: Feeling the public pulse.

How does he know the people of Corinth haven't been humoring their king for over 40 years? The same way the people of Thebes have been humoring their new king for 2?

He shakes his head. He doesn't know, but he seriously doubts that anyone suspects him. His disguise is always authentic. He really becomes the characters he impersonates. —Even the female characters. Whom he finds particularly enjoyable. There are more advantages to my sex than most women realize, or are willing to acknowledge. He's smiling. Displaying patience, while I'm being difficult.

Like being pregnant all the time: I say. Being difficult.

At least I've wiped the smugness off his face. What do I mean: All the time? I've been pregnant only twice.

I don't correct him. I don't say that: I've been pregnant 3 times. That the first time was 20 years ago, with him. I simply say: Twice in 2 years *is* all the time.

But . . . he thought I'd enjoyed bearing our beautiful children. He hoped we'd have many more.

I was hoping just the opposite. I was hoping that he'd use his cleverness with potions & perfumes to concoct something   a salve, maybe   that would render sperm infertile. Something to prevent conception. He could market it along with Thebes' new line of luxury items. It would be a huge success. Every moneyed woman in Greece would want to buy it. The midwives could stock it at reduced prices.

We've never quarrelled before, & we're not quarrelling now. Oedipus won't allow it. What a brilliant idea! he exclaims, beaming again. I'm his shrewd economist of fear, suggesting to exploit the fear of giving life. If that really is a general fear among women. He'd always thought people considered their children assets. He certainly thinks of *our* children as glorious little assets. But that is, of course, his male point of view. He promises to work on something... maybe with a citrus base. As long as I promise him at least one more little daughter. One more lovely little Antigone.

I burst out sobbing. I feel totally cut off from this smiling man, who lives his life with blinders on. For which I suddenly respect him less. I envy his blindness, which I don't respect. He takes me in his arms. He asks: If I'm having my period?

No! I'm not. Not everything a woman thinks   & says & does is dictated by her menstrual cycle. My brain isn't located between my legs.

He's soothing me. Stroking me like a child who didn't mean to be naughty. Or perhaps like a nagging mother, who needs to be told that she's still loved. He won't go out as an Athenian jeweler's apprentice. At least not tonight.

Predictably, our first quarrel that was no quarrel ends on the couch. But I'm still angry. Brusquely awakened from my dream of us as the ideal couple. My body refuses to participate in his desire, which suddenly feels proprietary to me. My orgasm is purely mechanical. I wonder if this is how most married women feel, after 2 years of conjugal exertion. If they feel used, as I feel used tonight. All the more since I'm sure   absolutely certain   that I conceived yet another child.

The next morning I tell him: I'm pregnant again.

My tone is far from joyful, but he beams at me. He takes my hands. He kisses my palms. I've made him the happiest man in the world. Do I think it will be another adorable little girl? Another Antigone? Another me?

I shrug. He seems to be getting all his wishes. Meanwhile, I have a wish of my own: From this night on I need to sleep alone.

His joy collapses. His face turns grey. But why? Our nights have been the best parts of our days.

A mother-body needs more space. It needs the whole couch to itself.

But I'm as slender as I was 2½ years ago. My hips are still as narrow as when he met me. & my breasts have remained the same also, since we bound them so tightly to prevent lactation. & I won't get big with the new child for another 5 months at least. & we always made love through all the other pregnancies. So why not through this one, when we'll be able to do anything we want to, since it has already happened anyway.

Do anything *he* wants to, is what he is saying. But I am saying that I don't want to make love anymore. At least not for a while.

Don't I feel well?

I feel invaded. Too much motherhood turns a lover into a parent.

But . . . what about HIM? he says, smiling sheepishly, pointing to a little tent his tunic is forming in his crotch.

I'm sure any one of my women will be glad to take care of that end of the problem.

I wouldn't really want that, would I?

I shrug, wondering how I will feel if he starts lying with other women. All I want for now is to sleep alone.

All through the day, Oedipus looks crestfallen   —in blatant denial of his name—   every time he looks at me. He has been drinking when he arrives late   for dinner. Red wine has tainted his shiny teeth a dirty blue. He continues to drink heavily all through the meal. He's boisterous, quite obnoxious, telling unfunny jokes that remind me once again of his father Laius.

Creon shows us several arm clasps the jeweler made after his designs. Among them a golden dragon I particularly admire. He offers it to me, fastening it around my upper left arm, slightly above the elbow. It is a beautiful thing; I make a silent vow that Hera shall not have it.

Oedipus spouts obscenities about the mating rituals of dragons & dragonesses, which Creon & I try to ignore. But which rouse my father Menoeceus from his usual peaceful old-age dinner stupor. Dragons: he admonishes sternly: are chaste androgynes, who do not mate at all. Twice in their lifetime they spew a trail of fire, which condenses into a baby dragon, whom they nurse for as many years as they have teeth in their mouths.

Oedipus laughs. & when my father offers to fight him, he tells him that: He'll have to find himself another midwife to deliver him from life.

Let's go: he says to me: We've eaten enough.

On the walk back to our wing of the palace he weaves alongside me, bumping into me. Outside my chamber I bid him good night.

I can't do that to him! he protests, grabbing my left arm. So hard, the golden dragon cuts into my flesh. I scream, & in a reflex I slap his face. His arm rises in reflex also. I wonder if he gets brutal when he's drunk, like his father used to. My body is not his property: I say angrily: I'm not his chattel. I'm still the Queen of Thebes.

He looks surprised & hurt. His hand has fallen back to his side. Good night, Your Majesty: he sneers, & stumbles off.

Chapter 24

The peasants started the harvest at sunrise this morning. It promises to be the most plentiful Thebes has reaped, due to irrigation ditches Oe had them dig through the fields last spring.

This year we'll be able to export grain, instead of importing it: he's telling our treasurer. Who beams at him with such adoration, I fleetingly wonder if they're lovers. If that explains the fixed tautness in Oe's face. But he's listening to the faint rumbling I also begin to hear coming towards us, culminating in a deafening thunderclap. Followed by heavy pelting of hailstones.

Oe rushes from the throne room, to recruit every able-bodied man & woman in the palace to help the peasants bring in the crops. Several of my women rush out after him, the niece Neirete among them.

Creon & I look at each other, shaking our heads. Oe is making a mistake: my brother says: He'll lose the peasants' respect, working alongside them with his royal hands. They'll see his help as interference, & feel criticized. Besides, it's useless anyway, & they know it. The hail must have flattened every remaining stalk by now, & knocked out the grains. They're harvesting wet straw. What's left of grains will ferment, & rot.

Maybe Oe will find a way to make liquor out of the fermenting grain: I half-joke.

My brother laughs: He just might. —I don't have much luck with my husbands, do I? The first one was an egomaniacal hypochondriac, & the second one is a maniacal humanitarian. It's odd, despite the diametrical differences of their goals, there's a lot of similarity between the two.

I stare at him. Is he subtly telling me that he knows who Oe really is. He's staring back at me. Suddenly I see desire in his eyes. I look away.

He's sorry he foisted this juvenile hero upon me: he says. Obviously I've grown disenchanted with him, after an initial flurry of enthusiasm about a youthful lover. It's amazing how fast that boyish face has aged. Those lines down his cheeks. Real maniac lines. Laius had them, too. Too bad we're brother & sister. & not living in Egypt. We'd make a much better royal couple, he & I.

In the evening, the skies are serene again, with an innocent slice of moon grinning down on the wasted fields. We're gloomy company at dinner. Oe praises the girls, whose hands are raw from breaking off stalks. He praises the twins, who cut & baled like demons. He praises our treasurer, who hurt his clerical back. He praises my dishevelled women. But their combined efforts saved very little, hampered as they were by the uncooperative sullenness of the peasants, men & women alike. The peasants feel that he interfered with nature, with his irrigation system. It provoked the gods, & they were showing him what they could do, & sent the hailstorm.

Maybe we can barter our luxury items for staples, then we wouldn't have to deplete the just refilled treasury. He wishes he knew of a way to dry the stuff. At least to feed the cattle.

He should get a dragon to breathe on it: my father Menoeceus cuts in: Dragon breath is made of wind & sunshine. Those crops will dry in no time.

My father should get us a dragon then: Oe says in a tone of exasperation: This is not the time for hero tales.

I expect an invitation to a fight, but my father has sunk back into his peaceful stupor.

Oe's face is white & drawn. I feel sorry for him.

He shouldn't take the peasant's attitude so personally: I say to him: They're a superstitious lot. Always looking for a scapegoat when something goes wrong.

But what if they're right! Maybe the gods *are* angered by human inventiveness. One of us should go to Delphi, & find out.

He's looking from me to Creon, & back to me. He'd go himself but he doesn't want to give the impression that he's backing out. Besides, he needs to think up some use for those fermenting grains.

Creon says that: He hasn't much faith in oracles. They're usually ambiguous, & get you into deeper trouble, as you try to prevent the bad ones from coming true.

. . .

Too many questions beget unwanted answers: I say: We've had hailstorms before.

What if the peasants act up?

Then we'll have to put them down: my brother says: That, too, has happened before. Nothing is new under the sun. Everything is repetition, with slight variations. Like waves cresting on the shore.

Oe hears the reference to cresting waves as a swipe at his name, as perhaps it was. He's had enough hostility in one day: he declares sullenly: He's going to sleep.

The rest of us finish our meal, then we, too, drag ourselves off to our respective quarters.

I lie awake on my couch, wondering if the hailstorm is the opening scene of the last act in this farce the gods started playing with us 34 years ago. Again I feel the bottomless grief I felt looking one last time into my nameless son's baby face, pink & blunt with sleep, as he is lifted from his bed by hands intent on murder. I felt a similar hopelessness, looking at the drawn face of the grown man at dinner. The hopelessness of a situation does not diminish our responsibility to change it: I think: We must stand united against the gods. Who may yet amend their script, swayed by the truth & strength of our love. My heart floods with long-forgotten tenderness for this hopelessly struggling man. I imagine that he, too, is lying awake, torturing his brain about the crops.

Quietly I get up, & glide to his rooms. He's lying in the arms of the niece Neirete. Who notices me first, & nudges him repeatedly before he looks up. His eyes are like holes in Hades. The niece hides her face in her hennaed hair.

. . .

Then I quickly state my reason for interrupting their coitus. I'd come to suggest that we send our treasurer to Delphi, if Oe still feels that we need oracular advice to solve our harvest problem. & retrieve my steps

Good night, Queen Jocasta! the niece calls after me.

Back on my couch, I don't know if I should laugh or cry. I opt for laughing.

Chapter 28

The number of plague victims has passed the 200 mark. Madame Tiresias comes to me before the morning audience, to request release from her vow of silence. The time has come to tell the king. Enough innocent people have died to keep my guilty secret.

I don't challenge her to name just one person who died on my account. I shrug. Which she can't see, & would interpret as arrogance, if she could see it. I know she doesn't like me. Especially not when she's a woman. She dislikes me, along with the female phases of her life. She knows I kept silent only in the hope of improving my son's hopeless fate.

Which unlike mine seems to touch her old seer's heart. Can she not foresee the consequences of her revelation? How does she think Oedipus will react to what she feels she has to tell him? Will he believe her, even? Will anyone believe her?

But that is her concern, not mine. I will be no part of it any longer. The moment she opens her mouth I shall walk from the throne room under the pretext of an overdue sacrifice. I shall bow out with dignity, the way the shining moon slips behind a cloud.

I make Madame Tiresias sit on my couch & wait, while I put on my ceremonial robes perfume my hair fasten Oedipus' radiant sun brooch on my right shoulder the silver moon brooch on the left my brother's dragon clasp around my left arm. When I have finished, the silver panel obligingly reflects a regal highpriestess, ready to meet the gods.

I overcome the slight revulsion I always feel for Tiresias, whether male or female, & take her elbow to steer her down the hall. She stiffens, equally repulsed by my touch.

Go ahead: I say to her: Tell him if you must.

But the time to tell has not yet come. A special messenger has arrived from Corinth. King Polybus has died   in his sleep; with a smile on his face. Queen Periboea wants Oedipus to come back & take the vacant seat on the throne. Could he not be a king to both cities? Divide the year between 2 worlds, like the godly daughter Core, & rule 3 months over Corinth, & 9 over Thebes, or the other way round?

I study Oedipus' intense face, & see relief replace grief for the man he thinks was his father. Whom he loved, & lived in the fear of killing, as the oracle had told him he would. Who has now relieved him of that 17-year-long fear by dying of his own accord. Must that not also relieve him of his dread of bedding down with the by-now-ancient Queen Periboea?

I urge him to fulfill the Queen's request. She is bereft, & very old. He should go to her at once.

But what about the murder investigation?

It can be continued during his absence.

Of course. He didn't mean to imply that he's irreplaceable.

Creon smiles a thin-lipped smile in my direction. He has been staring at my ceremonial dress. I wish I could spare him the grief I am about to cause him.

Madame Tiresias is fidgeting, clearing her throat.

The special messenger hands Oedipus a letter from Queen Periboea. A long letter, in her minute, convoluted writing. Which he begs Oedipus not to read until he has heard what else he has to say. Which   he must think   are glad tidings, to judge by his radiant face. His eyes are clear & brilliant, like fountain water in sunlight.

He is an old shepherd, possibly in his sixties, with the landscape-like beauty nature sometimes bestows on those living close to her. He looks like a noble ram, with grey curls in the place of horns.

Queen Periboea chose him to bring the news, because he has a special relationship to King Oedipus: he begins slowly, as though about to tell a story around a fire in the pastures at night: He is, you might say, a kind of midwife to the king.

I hear a smile behind his voice, & know the story. A story that would have fulfilled my most desperate wish, had I heard it 35 years ago. Yet, I want to hear it even now. I'll finally know how my little son was saved.

—For his doom.— & I shall reward the savior. Who expects to be rewarded. Not out of greed, but out of joy in his good deed. A joy in which he expects us all to share at the end of his story.

He starts telling us how it all happened: On a clear fall night, filled with shooting stars. He'd still been young then. His first summer out alone with the herd. Which he was getting ready to drive back to Corinth.

Suddenly old Picus is standing before him. Picus the Woodpecker, a shepherd from Thebes who'd been grazing his flocks alongside him all summer. He's breathless, & in a panic. He's too old to be running like that. He can barely speak. He hands him a bundle, wrapped in a blanket, which he asks him to take away with him to Corinth.

The blanket is of the finest quality. He can tell, he knows wool. & inside is a little boy, also of the finest quality. Whom a powerful Theban has ordered old Picus to put to death. But old Picus can't do it. He's a shepherd. He recognizes good livestock when he sees it. & he figures: As long as the child is out of Thebes, it's like dead to the powerful man who lives there.

The then-still-young shepherd takes the little boy in the blanket, & carries him all the way to Corinth. Making him drink ewes' milk directly from the teat.

While they walk, he's thinking: The king & queen of Corinth have no children . . . The palace would be a good home for a well-born little boy from Thebes . . .

Whom the king & queen want to adopt as soon as they see him, rosy-cheeked, with alert little eyes. But the news of a royal adoption might travel to Thebes, & put the child in danger. Not to mention old Picus. They decide that Queen Periboea will pretend to give birth to the little boy. Surrounded by her women she walks to the seashore, with the child hidden under her tunic, making her look very pregnant. She squats down, cries out in pain for a while, then pulls him from between her legs. They name him the child of the Cresting Wave.

But now that King Polybus has died, & the man who ordered the baby killed probably also died, or is at least peacefully old, the Queen feels that Oedipus needs to know where he came from. & that he's welcome back in Corinth nonetheless.

The relief I saw on Oedipus' face at the news of King Polybus' natural death has changed back to anguish. That old shepherd   Picus   is he still alive? he asks.

No. He died abruptly, some 15 maybe 18 years ago. His son took over for him.

My brother Creon remembers Picus. He was one of King Laius' most trusted shepherds. & so devoted to the king, he hanged himself a month or so after the king died.

Oedipus looks at him: Could that old shepherd be the murderer we're looking for?

Creon protests: Absolutely not!

The messenger's radiance turns to shock.

Madame Tiresias clears her throat again.

I rise. I walk over to the beautiful old man & give him the moon brooch from my left shoulder. He did a noble deed: I say: & old Picus acted nobly, too. More nobly than many a wellborn person might have acted in the situation.

I look around the room, & excuse myself to all assembled: I need to offer a long-due sacrifice.

I feel a hundred eyes boring into my back on my way out. I'm passing through the East Gate, when I hear a roar behind me. Perhaps not a roar so much, as a bellow. Boundless pain, condensed into sound. Oedipus' reply to Madame Tiresias' revelation: It whips me forward to the rock on which the Sphinx crouched, 17 years ago.

An inaccessible rock, to a woman without wings. But there are cracks in the stone, where the wingless woman can fit her toes. My father Menoeceus jumped to his sacrificial death, a warrior in houseshoes. I shall jump to mine, a barefoot queen, a highpriestess of Hera, with a drop of dragon blood boiling in my veins.

My knees & hands are bloody when I reach the top. My ceremonial robe tears along the left side as I go into a crouch. I apologize for my imperfections to the immortal intelligence of the Sphinx, whom I invoke to propel my leap. After all, we were defeated by the same man.

CONSTRUCTING A READING

1. Arguably the most significant difference between Molinaro's and Sophocles's telling of the Oedipus story has to do with the extent of Jocasta's knowledge of the "truth." With your group members, discuss some of the effects of this change: if Jocasta knows that Oedipus is her son, for example, why does she proceed with the marriage? What does her motivation suggest about a feminist reading of the myth?
2. Another important difference is Molinaro's focus on Jocasta's emotions. Does Jocasta's account of her emotions seem "mythic" to you? If this is a myth about how women experience marriage and motherhood, what does it explain?
3. Why does Jocasta not tell Oedipus?
4. Why does Jocasta refuse to have sex withOedipus?
5. Why does Jocasta kill herself?

SHARING A READING

1. Write your own adaptation of the Oedipus story from the perspective of Eteocles or Antigone or Creon or Tiresias or a Theban peasant. What contradiction does your story explain?
2. With your class members, collect an assortment of instances of intertextuality—in song lyrics, TV commercials, poetry and stories, films, TV shows, and so on. Exhibit them to the rest of your class or even to other classes if possible. Explain the uses of intertextuality in the examples that interest you. What do the intertextual references do in the texts you've chosen? Does the later text comment on the earlier one in some way? Does it reinforce or contradict the earlier text?

3. Sophocles's *Oedipus the King* is commonly regarded as one of the greatest texts of Western literature; I found Ursule Molinaro's book in a remainder bin at a bookstore. In a letter to Ms. Molinaro, explain how you understand the relative positions of the two texts.

TEXTS FOR FURTHER READING

The Gold Key
Anne Sexton

The speaker in this case
is a middle-aged witch, me—
tangled on my two great arms,
my face in a book
and my mouth wide,
ready to tell you a story or two.
I have come to remind you,
all of you:
Alice, Samuel, Kurt, Eleanor,
Jane, Brian, Maryel,
all of you draw near.
Alice,
at fifty-six do you remember?
Do you remember when you
were read to as a child?
Samuel,
at twenty-two have you forgotten?
Forgotten the ten P.M. dreams
where the wicked king
went up in smoke?
Are you comatose?
Are you undersea?

Attention,
my dears,
let me present to you this boy.
He is sixteen and he wants some answers.
He is each of us.
I mean you.
I mean me.
It is not enough to read Hesse
and drink clam chowder,
we must have the answers.
The boy has found a gold key
and he is looking for what it will open.
This boy!
Upon finding a nickel
he would look for a wallet.
This boy!
Upon finding a string
he would look for a harp.
Therefore he holds the key tightly.

Its secrets whimper
like a dog in heat.
He turns the key.
Presto!
It opens this book of odd tales
which transform the Brothers Grimm.
Transform?
As if an enlarged paper clip
could be a piece of sculpture.
(And it could.)

Briar Rose (Sleeping Beauty)

Anne Sexton

Consider
a girl who keeps slipping off,
arms limp as old carrots,
into the hypnotist's trance,
into a spirit world
speaking with the gift of tongues.
She is stuck in the time machine,
suddenly two years old sucking her thumb,
as inward as a snail,
learning to talk again.
She's on a voyage.
She is swimming further and further back,
up like a salmon,
struggling into her mother's pocketbook.
Little doll child,
come here to Papa.
Sit on my knee.
I have kisses for the back of your neck.
A penny for your thoughts, Princess.
I will hunt them like an emerald.
Come be my snooky
and I will give you a root.
That kind of voyage,
rank as honeysuckle.

Once
a king had a christening
for his daughter Briar Rose
and because he had only twelve gold plates
he asked only twelve fairies
to the grand event.
The thirteenth fairy,

her fingers as long and thin as straws,
her eyes burnt by cigarettes,
her uterus an empty teacup,
arrived with an evil gift.
She made this prophecy:
The princess shall prick herself
on a spinning wheel in her fifteenth year
and then fall down dead.
Kaputt!
The court fell silent.
The king looked like Munch's *Scream*.
Fairies' prophecies,
in times like those,
held water.
However the twelfth fairy
had a certain kind of eraser
and thus she mitigated the curse
changing that death
into a hundred-year sleep.

The king ordered every spinning wheel
exterminated and exorcized.
Briar Rose grew to be a goddess
and each night the king
bit the hem of her gown
to keep her safe.
He fastened the moon up
with a safety pin
to give her perpetual light
He forced every male in the court
to scour his tongue with Babo
lest they poison the air she dwelt in.
Thus she dwelt in his odor.
Rank as honeysuckle.

On her fifteenth birthday
she pricked her finger
on a charred spinning wheel
and the clocks stopped.
Yes indeed. She went to sleep.
The king and queen went to sleep,
the courtiers, the flies on the wall.
The fire in the hearth grew still
and the roast meat stopped crackling.
The trees turned into metal
and the dog became china.
They all lay in a trance,
each a catatonic

stuck in the time machine.
Even the frogs were zombies.
Only a bunch of briar roses grew
forming a great wall of tacks
around the castle.
Many princes
tried to get through the brambles
for they had heard much of Briar Rose
but they had not scoured their tongues
so they were held by the thorns
and thus were crucified.
In due time
a hundred years passed
and a prince got through.
The briars parted as if for Moses
and the prince found the tableau intact.
He kissed Briar Rose
and she woke up crying:
Daddy! Daddy!
Presto! She's out of prison!
She married the prince
and all went well
except for the fear—
the fear of sleep.

Briar Rose
was an insomniac . . .
She could not nap
or lie in sleep
without the court chemist
mixing her some knockout drops
and never in the prince's presence.
If it is to come, she said,
sleep must take me unawares
while I am laughing or dancing
so that I do not know that brutal place
where I lie down with cattle prods,
the hole in my cheek open.
Further, I must not dream
for when I do I see the table set
and a faltering crone at my place,
her eyes burnt by cigarettes
as she eats betrayal like a slice of meat.

I must not sleep
for while asleep I'm ninety
and think I'm dying.
Death rattles in my throat

like a marble.
I wear tubes like earrings.
I lie as still as a bar of iron.
You can stick a needle
through my kneecap and I won't flinch.
I'm all shot up with Novocain.
This trance girl
is yours to do with.
You could lay her in a grave,
an awful package,
and shovel dirt on her face
and she'd never call back: Hello there!
But if you kissed her on the mouth
her eyes would spring open
and she'd call out: Daddy! Daddy!
Presto!
She's out of prison.

There was a theft.
That much I am told.
I was abandoned.
That much I know.
I was forced backward.
I was forced forward.
I was passed hand to hand
like a bowl of fruit.
Each night I am nailed into place
and I forget who I am.
Daddy?
That's another kind of prison.
It's not the prince at all,
but my father
drunkenly bent over my bed,
circling the abyss like a shark,
my father thick upon me
like some sleeping jellyfish.

What voyage this, little girl?
This coming out of prison?
God help—
this life after death?

CONSTRUCTING A READING

1. In your journal, speculate about the gold key in the first of these two poems. How does Sexton use this common element of fairy tales in her "transformation?" What does this key transform? To what?

2. With your group members, piece together what happens in this "Briar Rose" (Sleeping Beauty) by attending to minimal stories and narrative perspectives.
3. Why could Briar Rose not sleep (without drugs) after the prince awakened her? Why is she afraid of sleep?
4. With your group members, thematize sleep, sex, and death in this poem. What does the poem say about these three phenomena?
5. In your journal, write for a page or two about how the following trope works:

She is swimming further and further back,
up like a salmon
struggling into her mother's pocketbook.

6. Do you consider this a "feminist" reading of the fairy tale? Why or why not?

Sleeping Beauty

Chuck Wachtel

1

Larry watches the blood in the thin plastic tube that tapers into the boot of the metal needle that cuts into his wife's forearm. He then checks the plastic bag that hangs from the aluminum rack beside the bed to see if the level has gone down any. If the space on top has grown, the part he can see light through, time has passed. He rubs the stiffness out of the back of his neck. He has just woken up, and in this last period of sleep his head had drifted over the cool back of the aluminum chair until it rested against the wall.

Four days ago, when she came out of surgery and he first saw her, he thought the blood in the tube wasn't moving. He knows gravity will impel its downward motion, but he also knows it can't flow unless her body allows it to enter. One of the nurses told him it looks that way because it never changes color. But it moves, she told him, slowly, like the hands of a clock. That's when he stopped trying to discern the blood's passage from the elevated plastic bag to Marlene's motionless body, and started measuring the empty space on top.

There are also tubes running into her leg and through the bandage that enwraps her midsection. An electrode plate, attached to two thin wires, is taped to her chest. Her entire body, where she is not covered with the bedsheet, or the bandage, is black and blue. When he first saw her, he was sure she was already dead. Since the blood wasn't moving, he couldn't believe the electronic life signs were messages sent from within Marlene's body; he thought they were manufactured by the machines.

He has since come to believe she is alive but not, yet, fully. It's as if four days ago, when she had the accident, she went somewhere else, and since then only a small part of her has come back: the part that can cause the lights to throb and the hands of the dials to move back and forth.

Larry has gone home only twice in the last four days. Not to sleep—he's been sleeping in the chair in the hospital room. He's gone home to change, and then gone to see the children, who are staying with Ruby, Marlene's mother.

Ruby has come every day but has only stayed briefly. She's so angry at Larry, and he at her, that she's too uncomfortable to stay very long. Larry gets uncomfortable as well, but he won't budge. They haven't spoken since the day after the accident, when she told him she'd given permission for the local newspaper to use the picture of Marlene from their high school yearbook.

2

Marlene and Larry began dating twenty years ago, less than a month after he got out of the service. They were soon spending all their free time together, and within a year they were married. Neither Ruby nor any of Marlene's friends could understand it. And none of them made any secret of this. Ruby said Marlene was twice as good-looking as Larry. Marlene had a high school diploma and had just finished the courses for her certificate in dental hygiene. All Larry had was an honorable discharge. He had just begun working as a projectionist in the Florence Theater.

Before that, they'd hardly known each other. That was also part of everyone's surprise. He'd always been in the slower classes and, out of school, kept mostly to himself. The only times they were in the same classroom were when Marlene's class was seeing a film. Larry would set up the screen and operate the projector. He was already good at that.

Marlene was petite and wore her thick brown hair short and cut straight at the sides. She was articulate and pretty. During her high school years, everyone who knew her envied the life they were certain she would have.

Larry was tall and slouched into himself when he stood still. And there was this odd change in his voice. When he came back from Vietnam, he spoke with a Southern accent, like someone from Georgia or Alabama. He was the only one in Florence, New Hampshire, to speak that way. He'd lost a lot of hair in the two years he was in the army, and in their wedding portrait he looks ten years older than Marlene.

They didn't have a child until the fourth year of their marriage. When Ruby pressed her on this, Marlene told her she was still too young and that she liked it being just the two of them. Women wait these days, she told her mother. Where have you been? Then, after the first—Asa, named for Marlene's father, who died when she was in the fifth grade—she had the other two, Darla and Melanie, barely more than a year apart. This week—the week of Marlene's accident—falls in the one month of the year when their ages follow one after the other: twelve, thirteen, fourteen—Melanie, Darla, Asa—like three steps on a flight of stairs as long as their marriage.

After the births of her three children, Marlene never got her looks back. She'd gotten heavier. Her eyes grew tired, and softer, and sometimes gave the impression that she was farther away than she actually was from the person she was looking at.

Ruby had told everyone that Marlene had done this—let herself go—on purpose. She knew what she was doing. She wanted to equalize their value in the economy of beauty. Ruby never forgave Larry for this.

3

No one knows how Marlene could have fallen from the catwalk that encircles the upper level of the Florence Lumber yard. The railings that surround the walkway are three feet high. One of the men on the floor below caught a glimpse of her just before she landed on the ten-inch platform saw. He said her body, as she was falling, was stretched out, almost relaxed, as if she were lying on a mattress.

Ruby works as a shipping clerk in the yard. Marlene had come to meet her for lunch, as she often does, and afterwards had walked her back to her desk. The shipping office, like the other offices, opens out onto the catwalk. Often, while waiting for Ruby, or after they'd had lunch, Marlene would lean against the railing and watch the sawyers below cut the rough lumber into boards, stack them onto pallets, then wrap the heavy neat piles in tight bands of aluminum.

The elevated, insular walkways always reminded Marlene of a prison cell block. She had never been in a real prison but had built a strong, clear image of one from the memory of two different movies, one starring Sissy Spacek, the other starring Robert Redford. She doesn't remember their titles—she never remembers the titles of movies—but she imagines they were filmed in the same prison because the concrete catwalks and the metal railings were the same. They are also the same as the ones in the Florence Lumber yard.

What Marlene likes most about movies is how they grow to be a part of her after she's watched them. Sometimes, when she sees them again years later, she is disappointed to find how different they are, or have become, from the movie she remembers. There is always more silence, and the people seem less connected to each other. In her memory, the characters understand each other's inner thoughts with an easy fluency, and they keep talking during all the times the audience can t hear or see them.

Each year on midsummer night, the Florence Drive-in would have a dusk-till-dawn special. For the same price they'd run as many movies as they could before the sun came up. The year before her father died, he and Ruby brought Marlene along, and all the movies they showed that night were about people running for their lives. Dean Martin and Jerry Lewis were running from gangsters, so Jerry Lewis, who looked really young anyway, got dressed up like a teenager. Dean Martin pretended he was a teacher, and they both hid out in a school. Tony Curtis had escaped from prison with Sidney Poitier. No place they hid was safe for long, so they had to keep moving. Their arms were shackled together, which made it hard to run, and besides that, they didn't like each other, so they decided to go their separate ways when they got a chance to cut the chains. However, when they finally did, near the end of the movie, they stayed together. Then Tony Curtis and Jack Lemmon were musicians who had to get out of town because some gangsters wanted to kill them. They got dressed up like women and joined an all-women band that had Marilyn Monroe in it, too. She played the ukulele. No one knew who they were, though everyone in the audience could tell they were men.

Once, at lunch, Marlene asked her mother if she remembered that summer night. She wanted to tell her about how the films keep changing and getting all mixed up together. She sometimes remembers Sidney Poitier running down a hillside, shackled to Jerry Lewis. They are both frightened because men and dogs are chasing them, and Jerry Lewis keeps crying in fear. At first Sidney Poitier gets angry with him because the noises he makes are so silly, but then he becomes tender, like a father, and tells him not to worry, they will get safely away and then everything will be all right.

"Films never remain the same," she told Ruby.

"I forget them, if that's what you mean. The only one I remember from that summer is *Some Like It Hot*. That's the one with Marilyn Monroe. And you know why, don't you?"

Marlene shook her head.

"Because Marilyn and Marlene are really the same name."

"But what I mean is the stories keep changing. The stories don't hold still."

"Of course," her mother said. "That's why they call them moving pictures."

4

Papers from Boston and New York have already called the hospital, and Larry is imagining the newspaper accounts as the knowledge of his wife's accident is carried farther and farther away from them, out into a world where no one knows who they are.

He and Marlene had once seen a documentary on TV about how humans have changed over the years. We used to have longer arms, the narrator had said, and our memories have been getting worse and worse since the invention of the written word. These changes took a very long time. But somehow—

maybe just in the years since Larry was a teenager—people have changed in another way. They no longer have any way of understanding the things that happen at a distance, to absolute strangers, other than to imagine seeing them lit up on a screen. This scares him. No matter how many times he's seen them, the people Larry sees in the films he shows every day are as unlike him as trees are unlike him, as cars are unlike him.

A reporter from Texas has left three messages on their answering machine at home. He wants permission to reprint the picture Ruby had given to the Florence Courier, which has already used it two days running. It's the one from their high school yearbook. Ruby cannot understand why this has made Larry so angry.

Didn't he agree, she asked him, that she had protected Marlene by refusing to give them a more recent photo? Larry has not said a word to her since. The Texas reporter said they've already got permission to use some of the other photos the local paper has run: the one of the surgeon who'd flown in from Minnesota, and the one of the platform saw, already back in operation at the lumber mill.

They will hold his wife captive in their vocabulary, use the same words as the tabloid headlines that hover in front of you while you're waiting on the checkout line at the supermarket:

WOMAN SAWED IN HALF
IS SEWN TOGETHER BY DOCTORS

He imagines a line of strangers staring through these words as if through a window, into their lives, into this hospital room. But he can't imagine what they'll think, reading such a thing and looking at the picture of his beautiful wife when she was seventeen years old.

Everyone in Florence is wondering how it happened. Larry doesn't care *how* it happened. What people should realize at times like this is that we don't know how most things happen. What he's doing is waiting.

Ruby told him that Marlene probably fainted. She'd done it at least a half-dozen times when she was growing up. And she didn't care where, either. In the car, at school, it didn't matter. Once she just swooned and slipped off a stool at the Florence Diner. The woman working the counter said she never made a sound.

Marlene had just walked her back to her office after lunch, then stood outside, leaning against the railing, looking down onto the work floor. Ruby's desk faces the side wall, not the window, so she only saw her out of the corner of her eye. It was the sudden movement that caught her attention. She said it was as if the top half of her daughter's body had suddenly become heavier than the bottom half. The weight just lifted her feet off the walkway and she toppled over. Fainting is the only possible explanation, Ruby said.

She was in surgery sixteen hours. Everyone said it was a miracle that she hadn't died instantly and that her spinal cord had not been severed. They put pins into her bones, they reunited the walls and inner tissues of damaged organs. With microsurgery they reconnected arteries and veins.

For Larry, it's not a time to understand anything as being a miracle. They are in this moment, in their lives, and this is what has happened. It's not a time to understand things; it's a time to wait.

5

Marlene says hello to Larry. She's awake.

He's been standing beside the bed since her eyes opened ten minutes ago. Her eyes were dark and completely still until this moment, when she focused on him.

Larry's in tears and cannot, yet, go any nearer to her. Ruby and the doctor are standing beside him.

"I had a dream," Marlene says to Larry. She then falls silent.

A moment passes.

Then she notices Ruby and says, "We're having lunch today."

The doctor leans over Marlene. For a moment she glances toward him, but she does not see him. Larry, slowly, pushes him aside.

He then kneels beside the bed and takes her hand in both of his. She seems unaware of anything else in the moment but this.

"What did you dream?" Larry asks her.

"My body is getting older," she says.

"Whose isn't?" Ruby says softly, then smiles.

"No. In the dream my body is getting older. That's how it talks to me. The wrinkles . . . it gets heavier . . . other things. And it's getting tired. I didn't understand at first."

The doctor begins to approach Marlene, and again Larry motions for him to stop.

"I was afraid to understand," she says. "It all meant the opposite of what I thought it meant. My body told me that getting older, it was really getting younger. More like a child each day. And *I* would have to grow up again. I'd have to start taking care of it, more and more. It would be like Asa and the girls,

and that scared me. . . ." Her fingers move slightly in Larry's hand. "Because it will never grow up. Only get younger and younger . . .

She takes in a short breath, falls silent for a second, and looks back at her husband.

"Larry," she then says. She slowly draws in another small breath. "Larry, I've been so afraid."

CONSTRUCTING A READING

1. Consider this story in relation to the traditional fairy tale "Sleeping Beauty." Describe the intertextual relation as carefully as you can. What comment is Wachtel making on the earlier text?
2. Consider the newspaper headline, "Woman sawed in half is sewn together by doctors" as a trope. How does the figure work? What do doctors have to do with it?
3. Consider Larry's and Ruby's jobs as tropes. How do those figures work?
4. Why does Ruby provide Marlene's high school picture to the newspapers?
5. Why is Larry angered by Ruby's gesture?
6. Do you agree with Ruby that Marlene let herself go because she wanted to equalize [her value with Larry's] . . . in the economy of beauty?
7. Does Chuck Wachtel's story remind you of "Carried Away" from Chapter Five? If so, how, and what do you make of the resemblance?

SHARING A READING

1. What do you think a story in which a woman sleeps until she is awakened by a man means in Western culture? Discuss this question with your class members. Can you arrive at consensus?
2. Compare the Disney film, the Grimm story, the Sexton poem, the Wachtel story, and the excerpt from Robert Coover's "Briar Rose" from Chapter Five. With your classmates, make a chart or computer graphic that represents the similarities and differences to serve as a basis for discussion. How do the various authors play with the meaning you (and/or your class) made? To what effect? Do the several stories comment on one another? Reverse one another? Parody one another?

A Failure of Apology

Jamie Barlowe

On perfectly reasonable days
I glide between knowing
and believing,
with perfect equanimity,
swallowing the hemlock
slowly enough
to make sure all those seated
cross-legged around me

aren't suffering.
On other days
I violently spill the poison,
striking the hand
that offers the chalice,
And reach instead for Crito's
outstretched hand.

CONSTRUCTING A READING

1. The fifth-century B.C.E. Greek philosopher Socrates was tried and condemned to death for impiety. The method of execution was for the condemned person to commit suicide by drinking hemlock. The most
famous image of Socrates' death comes from a painting by Jacques Louis
David, *The Death of Socrates*, which shows the philosopher reaching for a
chalice of hemlock with one hand and gesturing with his other hand during a final speech to his grief-stricken friends gathered around him. How
do various parts of "A Failure of Apology" re-create this scene? What
things do you read as references to Socrates or, specifically, the image of
the David painting?

2. The author, and therefore perhaps the speaker, of this poem is a woman.
In what ways does the speaker compare herself to Socrates? Does it matter to you whether the speaker is a woman or a man? How or how not?

3. What does "swallowing the hemlock" seem to mean to the speaker?

4. How does the speaker relate to the gathered witnesses? How is that relation different from the more traditional rendering of the scene in the
David painting?

5. Why does the speaker contrast the "violent" actions of spilling the poison
and reaching for Crito to displaying "perfect equanimity" . . . "on perfectly reasonable days"?

Dover Beach

Matthew Arnold

The sea is calm tonight.
The tide is full, the moon lies fair
Upon the straits;—on the French coast the light
Gleams and is gone; the cliffs of England stand,
Glimmering and vast, out in the tranquil bay.
Come to the window, sweet is the night-air!
Only, from the long line of spray
Where the sea meets the moon-blanched land,
Listen! you hear the grating roar
Of pebbles which the waves draw back, and fling,
At their return, up the high strand,
Begin, and cease, and then again begin,
With tremulous cadence slow, and bring
The eternal note of sadness in.

Sophocles long ago
Heard it on the Aegean, and it brought
Into his mind the turbid ebb and flow
Of human misery; we
Find also in the sound a thought,
Hearing it by this distant northern sea.

The Sea of Faith
Was once, too, at the full, and round earth's shore
Lay like the folds of a bright girdle furled.
But now I only hear
Its melancholy, long, withdrawing roar,
Retreating, to the breath
Of the nigh-wind, down the vast edges drear
And naked shingles of the world.

Ah, love, let us be true
To one another! for the world, which seems
To lie before us like a land of dreams,
So various, so beautiful, so new,
Hath really neither joy, nor love, nor light,
Nor certitude, nor peace, nor help for pain;
And we are here as on a darkling plain
Swept with confused alarms of struggle and flight,
Where ignorant armies clash by night.

CONSTRUCTING A READING

1. Who is the narratee of this poem?
2. Whom does the speaker address as "love"?
3. Write a paraphrase of Arnold's speaker's perceptions of the world.
4. What do you think the speaker means by being "true to one another"? How and what would it help? What, in other words, is the problem?
5. What did Sophocles hear on the Aegean?

The Dover Bitch
A Criticism of Life

Anthony Hecht

So there stood Matthew Arnold and this girl
With the cliffs of England crumbling away behind them,
And he said to her, "Try to be true to me,
And I'll do the same for you, for things are bad
All over, etc., etc."
Well now, I knew this girl. It's true she had read
Sophocles in a fairly good translation
And caught that bitter allusion to the sea,
But all the time he was talking she had in mind
The notion of what his whiskers would feel like
On the back of her neck. She told me later on
That after a while she got to looking out
At the lights across the channel, and really felt sad,
Thinking of all the wine and enormous beds
And blandishments in French and the perfumes.
And then she got really angry. To have been brought
All the way down from London, and then be addressed
As a sort of mournful cosmic last resort
Is really tough on a girl, and she was pretty.
Anyway, she watched him pace the room
And finger his watch-chain and seem to sweat a bit,
And then she said one or two unprintable things,
But you mustn't judge her by that. What I mean to say is,
She's really all right. I still see her once in a while
And she always treats me right. We have a drink
And I give her a good time, and perhaps it's a year
Before I see her again, but there she is,
Running to fat, but dependable as they come.
And sometimes I bring her a bottle of *Nuit d'Amour*.

CONSTRUCTING A READING

1. Who is the narratee of this poem?
2. What does France mean to the Dover Bitch? What does France mean to the speaker of "Dover Beach"? What does France mean to you? How do these meanings work together?
3. Would you describe either or both speakers as sexist? Why or why not?

The Tyger

William Blake

Tyger Tyger, burning bright,
In the forests of the night;
What immortal hand or eye,
Could frame thy fearful symmetry?

In what distant deeps or skies
Burnt the fire of thine eyes!
On what wings dare he aspire?
What the hand, dare sieze the fire?

And what shoulder, & what art,
Could twist the sinews of thy heart?
And when thy heart began to beat,
What dread hand? & what dread feet?

What the hammer? what the chain,
In what furnace was thy brain?
What the anvil? what dread grasp,
Dare its deadly terrors clasp?

When the stars threw down their spears
And water'd heaven with their tears:
Did he smile his work to see?
Did he who made the Lamb make thee?

Tyger, Tyger burning bright,
In the forests of the night:
What immortal hand or eye,
Dare frame thy fearful symmetry?

The Beggar
(After William Blake)
Ogden Nash

Beggar, beggar, buring low
In the city's trodden snow,
What immortal hand or eye
Could frame thy dread asymmetry?

In what distant deep of lies
Died the fire of thine eyes?
What the mind that planned the shame?
What the hand dare quench the flame?

And what shoulder and what art
Could rend the sinews of thy heart?
And when thy heart began to fail,
What soft excuse, what easy tale?

What the hammer? What the chain?
What the furnace dulled thy brain?
What the anvil? What the blow
Dare to forge this deadly woe?

When the business cycle ends
In flaming extra dividends,
Will He smile his work to see?
Did He who made the Ford make thee?

CONSTRUCTING A READING

1. What do you think is Nash's attitude toward his topic and toward Blake's poem?
2. What does the Ford trope mean to you? How is the trope apt for this poem?
3. Think of a contemporary trope that would do the work of "Ford" in Nash's poem.

Capitalist Poem #7

Campbell McGrath

I stole the UNICEF box.
I didn't mean to.
It was an accident.
I didn't turn it in at school.
I wanted it.
I kept it.
I hid it in my closet.

The box grew on my mind every day.
I thought of what it would buy for the Africans.
Four schoolbooks.
A dozen meals.
Eighty-five polio vaccinations.
Nine hundred million vitamin tablets.

Eventually I think I blew all the money at 7-11.
Some friends came with me and we splurged.

We bought: Chunkies, Big Buddies, baseball cards,
M&M's, Charleston Chews, fire balls, rootbeer barrels,
Clark Bars, Snickers, Milky Ways, bubble gum,
Sweet 'n' Sours, Red Hots, Marathon Bars, and Pixie Stix.

To be perfectly honest, I might have gotten that money
one year at Christmas when my best friend Bobby Wixam
broke both his legs sledding. I was OK, even though I
was on the sled too when we ran into the light pole. But it
was Bobby's birthday, either that day or the next, and the
party favors were sets of little blue dinosaurs which I
really wanted. They actually looked more like a pack of
prehistoric dogs, or wolves. And on Sunday his dad was
going to take us to the Redskins game. But when Bobby
broke his legs we couldn't go. Everything was cancelled. I
was so disappointed that my mother gave me five dollars.

I don't really remember what happened to the UNICEF box.
I might have lost it.

CONSTRUCTING A READING

1. With your group members, talk about the ambiguity in Campbell
   McGrath's "Capitalist Poem #7." Why do you think he can't remember
   what happened to the UNICEF box or where he got the money?

2. In your journal, write for a few minutes about your earliest memories of money. How especially, did you learn about the use and value of money? Do your memories connect with the speaker's in any way?

3. Write for a few minutes in your journal about the story of Bobby Wixam's broken legs, the speaker's response, and the speaker's mother's response. What is your response?

Socialist Poem #1
England, The Winter of Discontent, 1979–
(After Campbell McGrath)
Martin Walls

I am seven & see things simply, as a fish does. I can see the flat colors of the 1970s: greens, browns, cold grays like fading Kodachrome. I see the unburied of the gravedigger's strike, batblack mortuaries crawling with terror. Monsterish heaps of uncollected trash bags, evil smelling, pulling snow into their black folds as if they're pantomime villains making off with the hero.

All day scavenging seagulls squark in a festering sky. Evenings, the sounds of crisis mix with smell of frying fat, pungent Polish coal. I watch Mr. Callaghan sing *I'm the Man Who Waters the Workers' Beer* at the Labour Party conference. Later, he's beetling from Number 10 in his shiny black Bentley.

Socialists. Their winter's as cold & harsh as nylon sheets. At six thirty electricity's cut off, the union on a three day week. So we sit in the kitchen while mum smokes her thin cigarettes & grandma's reminded of the war. A hazy blue light from the gas stove throws crazy shadows against the wall. Doom-dark drifts against the house, an awful reverse snow. Above the rattle of boiling spuds my transistor radio speaks a strange tongue: *tripartite bargaining, arbitration*, it trills.

Seven o'clock: soon dad'll be home, hair slick from snow-drizzle, no shower till the heater growls awake. Nine thirty: I fold icy sheets around me, keeping the curtains open. The moon's glowing like a pilot light. All winter, I've watched filaments of ice lay down shapes in the corner of the window: a spaceship, a fabulous continent, a rose. Tonight, a hand sets out. It grows into one of grandpa's big, bony hands. Only it grows bigger than that, more scary. Pane after pane in its clutch.

CONSTRUCTING A READING

1. With your group members, and consulting dictionaries or other resources, discuss what you know and think about the words "capitalism"

and "socialism" and the systems they represent. Are the terms (and systems) marked as "good" or "bad" for you? How so?

2. Write in your journal for a few minutes about Walls's opening trope: "I . . . see things simply, as a fish does." How does a fish see things? What does the trope tell you about the speaker's relations to socialism? What does it tell you about the poet's relation to Campbell McGrath? Does McGrath's speaker see things simply, as a fish does?

3. Write in your journal for a few minutes about the final trope: "It grows into one of grandpa's big, bony hands. Only it grows bigger than that, more scary. Pane after pane in its clutch." What does the trope mean to you? How does it work and what does it tell you about the speaker's vision?

4. Walls has written his poem "after Campbell McGrath." What relations do you see between the two poems and poets?

CHAPTER EIGHT

Conventions
of Shared Readings:
How Readers Talk
with One Another about Texts

This book began with a story about a young woman who asks a man for help with a school assignment. The last chapter begins with another such story: David Mamet's play *Oleanna*.

In the intervening chapters, you have thought about and practiced some of the many ways in which readers respond to texts, close gaps, analyze tropes, investigate world, recognize genres, follow differing perspectives, and perceive intertextuality. You have also seen that there are infinite possibilities for difference in the meanings that individual readers make. Your experience of a text, for example, may differ from that of another reader because you have different affections or associations that emerge from differing racial, gendered, or social experience. Your familiarity (or lack of it) with a text's world might cause you to perceive different gaps, interpret tropes differently, find different themes, sympathize with different characters, and experience differing kinds of intertextuality than other readers do. All these differences are confusing and troublesome at times, but they can also occasion rich and full discussions. In this chapter, I'll ask you to think of these differences as elements of an ongoing conversation in which you are taking part.

In *Philosophy of Literary Form*, Kenneth Burke describes a group of people gathered in a parlor, talking animatedly. Someone enters, approaches the group, and listens, but can't quite grasp what they are talking about. Later, the newcomer gets the topic of the conversation, and wants to contribute, but doesn't know what has already been said, and, unsure how to intervene, remains silent. Finally, the newcomer works up the courage to make a point. Some people listen; others don't. Still, the direction of the conversation changes ever so slightly as a result of the new contribution. New people join the conversation; others leave. Finally, the newcomer leaves, but the conversation goes on.

Critical reading of literary and cultural texts is like that conversation. When you speak and write about the texts you read, you "go public" with your ideas—sharing them with others even when you feel uncertain, taking the risk of entering a new and unfamiliar conversation rather than keeping your ideas to yourself. When you join a conversation, you change it ever so slightly. When you change the ongoing conversation of humankind, however slightly, you exercise power over the ways in which your culture represents itself.

JOINING THE CONVERSATION: LEARNING THE CONVENTIONS

Just as our ways of reading texts are conventional, so are our conversations about them. When you enter a conversation about literary and cultural texts, you'll find that your audience expects you to follow certain conventions—the conventions of *literary criticism*. When you discuss a film or book informally among your friends, it's probably enough simply to register your opinion. They might in fact find it strange if you engage in a detailed description of your reading. But when you participate in an academic conversation about a text, in the form of a scholarly essay for example, it is important to describe your position clearly, to support it with evidence of some kind, and to indicate that you know about and have tried to understand other positions. Reviews of texts in newspapers, magazines, and the visual media take a kind of middle ground: less formally demanding than the scholarly paper but not so loose as a casual comment to a friend. Because reviews are oriented toward the specific audience of the venue in which they appear, they say as much or as little as that audience expects. This chapter will illustrate some of the conventions of conversations about texts and offer you an opportunity to practice them.

A Sample Conversation among Readers: On *Oleanna*

Oleanna has occasioned quite a bit of conversation—some of which you are about to read. The play is about difference in gender and social class, and it evokes different readings, in part, because of that subject matter. In that sense, the play illustrates what we have been talking about for the last seven chapters. Before you begin to participate in the "*Oleanna* conversation," you'll probably want to arrive at your own preliminary reading—to decide what you think now and what you need to find out in order read this text as fully as you can. As you read *Oleanna* for the first time, please record your own feelings and associations. Mark the places in the text where you find yourself feeling angry—or sympathetic—toward one or the other character. (*Oleanna* is, by the way, also available as a videotape, so you can see the play performed as well as read the text.) The extensive exercise that follows the play will help you explore your reaction in more detail.

Oleanna
David Mamet

The want of fresh air does not seem much to affect the happiness of children in a London alley: the greater part of them sing and play as though they were on a moor in Scotland. So the absence of a genial mental atmosphere is not commonly recognized by children who have never known it. Young people have a marvelous faculty of either dying or adapting themselves to circumstances. Even if they are unhappy—very unhappy—it is astonishing how easily they can be prevented from finding it out, or at any rate from attributing it to any other cause than their own sinfulness.

—Samuel Butler, *The Way of All Flesh*

"Oh, to be in *Oleanna*,
That's where I would rather be.
Than be bound in Norway
And drag the chains of slavery."
—folk song

Characters

CAROL A woman of twenty
JOHN A man in his forties

The play takes place in John's office.

One

JOHN *is talking on the phone.* CAROL *is seated across the desk from him.*

JOHN *(on phone):* And what about the land. *(Pause)* The land. And what about the land? *(Pause)* What about it? *(Pause)* No. I don't understand.

Well, yes, I'm I'm . . . no, I'm *sure* it's signif . . . I'm sure it's significant. *(Pause)* Because it's significant to mmmmmm . . . . did you call Jerry? *(Pause)* Because . . . no, no, no, no, no. What did they say . . . ? Did you speak to the *real* estate . . . where *is* she . . . ? Well, well, all right. Where are her notes? Where are the notes we took with her. *(Pause)* I thought you were? No. No, I'm sorry, I didn't mean that, I just thought that I saw you, when we were there . . . what . . . ? I thought I saw you with a *pencil*. WHY NOW? is what I'm say . . . well, that's why I say "call Jerry." Well,

I can't right now, be . . . no, I *didn't* schedule any . . . Grace: I *didn't* . . . I'm well aware . . . Look: Look. Did you call Jerry? Will you call Jerry . . . ? Because I can't now. I'll be there, I'm sure I'll be there in fifteen, in twenty. I intend to. No, we aren't *going* to lose the, we aren't *going* to lose the house. Look: Look, I'm not minimizing it. The "easement." Did she say "easement"? *(Pause)* What did she *say; is* it a "term of art," are we *bound* by it . . . I'm sorry . . . *(Pause)* are: we: yes. *Bound* by . . . Look: *(He checks his watch)* before the other side *goes home,* all right? "a term of art." Because: that's right *(Pause)* The yard for the boy. Well, that's the whole . . . Look: I'm going to meet you there . . . *(He checks his watch.)* Is the realtor there? All right, tell her to show you the basement again. Look at the *this* because. . . Bec . . . I'm leaving in, I'm leaving in ten or fifteen . . . Yes. No, no, I'll meet you at the new . . . That's a good. If he thinks it's necc . . . you tell Jerry to meet. . . All right? We *aren't* going to lose the deposit. All right? I'm sure it's going to be . . . *(Pause)* I hope so. *(Pause)* I love you, too. *(Pause)* I love you, too. As soon as . . . I will.

(He hangs up.) (He bends over the desk and makes a note.) (He looks up.) (To CAROL:*)* I'm sorry . . .

CAROL: *(Pause)* What is a "term of art"?

JOHN : *(Pause)* I'm sorry . . . ?

CAROL: *(Pause)* What is a "term of art"?

JOHN : Is that what you want to talk about?

CAROL: . . . to talk about . . .

JOHN : Let's take the mysticism out of it, shall we? Carol? *(Pause)* Don't you think? I'll tell you: when you have some "thing." Which must be broached. *(Pause)* Don't you think . . . ? *(Pause)*

CAROL: . . . don't I think . . . ?

JOHN : Mmm?

CAROL: . . . did I . . . ?

JOHN : . . . what?

CAROL: Did . . . did I . . . did I say something wr . . .

JOHN : *(Pause)* No. I'm sorry. No. You're right. I'm very sorry. I'm somewhat rushed. As you see. I'm sorry. You're right. *(Pause)* What is a "term of art"? It seems to mean a *term,* which has come, through its use, to mean something *more specific* than the words would, to someone *not acquainted* with them . . . indicate. That, I believe, is what a "term of art," would mean. *(Pause)*

CAROL: You don't know what it means . . . ?

JOHN : I'm not sure that I know what it means. It's one of those things, perhaps you've had them, that, you look them up, or have someone explain them to you, and you say "aha," and, you immediately *forget* what . . .

CAROL: You don't do that.

JOHN : . . . I . . . ?

CAROL: You don't do . . .

JOHN : . . . I don't, what . . . ?

CAROL: . . . for . . .

JOHN : . .I don't for . . .

CAROL: . . . no . . .

JOHN : . . . forget things? Everybody does that.

CAROL: No, they don't.

JOHN : They don't . . .

CAROL: No.

JOHN : *(Pause)* No. Everybody does that.

CAROL: Why would they do that . . . ?

JOHN : Because. I don't know. Because it doesn't interest them.

CAROL: No.

JOHN : I think so, though. *(Pause)* I'm sorry that I was distracted.

CAROL: You don't have to say that to me.

JOHN : You paid me the compliment, or the "obeisance"—all right—of coming in here . . . All right. *Carol.* I find that I am at a *standstill.* I find that I . . .

CAROL: . . . what . . .

JOHN : . . . one moment. In regard to your . . . to your . . .

CAROL: Oh, oh. You're buying a new house!

JOHN : No, let's get on with it.

CAROL: "get on"? *(Pause)*

JOHN : I know how . . . *believe* me. I know how . . . potentially *humiliating* these . . . I have no desire to . . . I have no desire other than to help you. But: *(He picks up some papers on his desk.)* I won't even say "but." I'll say that as I go back over the . . .

CAROL: I'm just, I'm just trying to . . .

JOHN : . . . no, it will not do.

CAROL: . . . what? What will . . . ?

JOHN : No. I see, I see what you, it . . . *(He gestures to the papers.)* but your work . . .

CAROL: I'm just: I sit in class I . . . *(She holds up her notebook.)* I take notes . . .

JOHN *(simultaneously with* "notes"*)*: Yes. I understand. What I am trying to *tell* you is that some, some basic . . .

CAROL: . . .I . . .

JOHN : . . . one moment: some basic missed communi . . .

CAROL: I'm doing what I'm told. I bought your book, I read your . . .

JOHN : No, I'm sure you . . .

CAROL: No, no, no. I'm doing what I'm told. It's *difficult* for me. It's *difficult* . . .

JOHN : . . . but . . .

CAROL: I don't . . . lots of the *language* . . .

JOHN : . . . please . . .

CAROL: The *language*, the "things" that you say . . .

JOHN : I'm sorry. No. I don't think that that's true.

CAROL: It *is* true. I . . .

JOHN : I think . . .

CAROL: It *is* true.

JOHN : . . . I . . .

CAROL: Why would I . . . ?

JOHN : I'll tell you why: you're an incredibly bright girl.

CAROL: . . . I . . .

JOHN : You're an incredibly . . . you have no problem with the . . . Who's kidding who?

CAROL: . . . I . . .

JOHN : No. No. I'll tell you why. I'll tell . . . . I think you're *angry*, I . . .

CAROL: . . . why would I . . .

JOHN : . . . wait one moment. I . . .

CAROL: It *is* true. I have *problems* . . .

JOHN : . . . every . . .

CAROL: . . . I come from a different *social* . . .

JOHN : . . . ev . . .

CAROL: a different economic . . .

JOHN : . . . Look:

CAROL: No. I: when I *came* to this school:

JOHN : Yes. Quite . . . *(Pause)*

CAROL: . . . does that mean nothing . . . ?

JOHN : . . . but look: look. . .

CAROL: . . . I . . .

JOHN : *(Picks up paper.)* Here: Please: Sit down. *(Pause)* Sit down. *(Reads from her paper.)* "I think that the ideas contained in this work express the author's feelings in a way that he intended, based on his results." What can that mean? Do you see? What . . .

CAROL: I, the best that I . . .

JOHN : I'm saying, that perhaps this course . . .

CAROL: No, no, no, you can't, you can't . . . I have to . . .

JOHN : . . . how . . .

CAROL: . . . I have to pass it . . .

JOHN : Carol, I . . .

CAROL: I *have* to pass this course, I . . .

JOHN : Well.

CAROL: . . . don't you . . .

JOHN : Either the . . .

CAROL: . . . I . . .

JOHN : . . . either the, I . . . either the *criteria* for judging progress in the class are . . .

CAROL: No, no, no, no, I have to pass it.

JOHN : Now, look: I'm a human being, I . . .

CAROL: I did what you told me. I did, I did everything that, I read your *book*, you told me to buy your book and read it. Everything you *say* I . . . *(She gestures to her notebook.) (The phone rings.)* I do. . . . Ev . . .

JOHN : . . . look:

CAROL: . . . everything I'm told . . .

JOHN : Look. Look. I'm not your *father. (Pause)*

CAROL: What?

JOHN: I'm.

CAROL: Did I say you were my father?

JOHN: . . . no . . .

CAROL: Why did you say that . . . ?

JOHN: I . . .

CAROL: . . . why . . . ?

JOHN: . . . in class I . . . *(He picks up the phone.) (In to phone:)* Hello. I can't talk now. Jerry? Yes? I underst . . . I can't talk now. I know. . . I know . . . Jerry. I can't *talk* now. Yes, I. Call me back in . . . Thank you. *(He hangs up.) (To* CAROL:) What do you want me to do? We are two people, all right? Both of whom have subscribed to . . .

CAROL: No, no . . .

JOHN: . . . certain arbitrary . . .

CAROL: No. You have to help me.

JOHN: Certain institutional . . . you tell me what you want me to do. . . . You tell me what you want me to . . .

CAROL: How can I go back and tell them the *grades* that I . . .

JOHN: . . . what can I do . . . ?

CAROL: *Teach* me. *Teach* me.

JOHN: . . . I'm trying to teach you.

CAROL: I read your book. I read it. I don't under . . .

JOHN: . . . you don't understand it.

CAROL: No.

JOHN: Well, perhaps it's not well *written* . . .

CAROL (*simultaneously with* "written"): No. No. No. I want to understand it.

JOHN: What don't you understand? (*Pause*)

CAROL: Any of It. What you're trying to say. When you talk about . . .

JOHN: . . . yes . . . ? (*She consults her notes.*)

CAROL: "Virtual warehousing of the young" . . .

JOHN: "Virtual warehousing of the young." If we artificially prolong adolescence . . .

CAROL: . . . and about "The Curse of Modern Education."

JOHN: . . . well . . .

CAROL: I don't . . .

JOHN: Look. It's just a *course*, it's just a *book*, it's just a . . .

CAROL: No. No. There are *people* out there. People who came *here*. To know something they didn't *know*. Who *came* here. To be *helped*. To be *helped*. So someone would *help* them. To *do* something. To *know* something. To get, what do they say? "To get on in the world." How can I do that if I don't, if I fail? But I don't *understand*. I don't *understand*. I don't understand what anything means . . . and I walk around. From morning 'til night: with this one thought in my head. I'm *stupid*.

JOHN: No one thinks you're stupid.

CAROL: No? What am I . . . ?

JOHN: I . . .

CAROL: . . . what am I, then?

JOHN: I think you're angry. Many people are. I have a *telephone* call that I have to make. And an *appointment*, which is rather *pressing*; though I sympathize with your concerns, and though I wish I had the time, this was not a previously scheduled meeting and I . . .

CAROL: . . . you think I'm nothing . . .

JOHN: . . . have an appointment with a *realtor*, and with my wife and . . .

CAROL: You think that I'm stupid.

JOHN: No. I certainly don't.

CAROL: You said it.

JOHN: No. I did not.

CAROL: You did.

JOHN: When?

CAROL: . . . you . . .

JOHN: No. I never did, or never would say that to a student, and . . .

CAROL: You said, "What can that mean?" (*Pause*) "What can that mean?" . . . (*Pause*)

JOHN: . . . and what did that mean to you . . . ?

CAROL: That meant I'm stupid. And I'll never learn. That's what that meant. And you're right.

JOHN: . . . I . . .

CAROL: But then. But then, what am I doing here . . . ?

JOHN: . . . if you thought that I . . .

CAROL: . . . when nobody wants me, and . . .

JOHN: . . . if you interpreted . . .

CAROL: Nobody *tells* me anything. And I *sit* there . . . in the *corner*. In the *back*. And everybody's talking about "this" all the time. And "concepts," and "precepts" and, and, and, and, and, WHAT IN THE WORLD ARE YOU *TALKING* ABOUT? And I read your book. And they said, "Fine, go in that class." Because you talked about responsibility to the young. I DON'T KNOW WHAT IT MEANS AND I'M *FAILING* . . .

JOHN: May . . .

CAROL: No, you're right. "Oh, hell." I failed. Flunk me out of it. It's garbage. Everything I do. "The ideas contained in this work express the author's feelings." That's right. That's right. I know I'm stupid. I know what I am. (*Pause*) I know what I am, Professor. You don't have to tell me. (*Pause*) It's pathetic. Isn't it?

JOHN: . . . Aha . . . (*Pause*) Sit down. Sit down. Please. (*Pause*) Please sit down.

CAROL: Why?

JOHN: I want to talk to you.

CAROL: Why?

JOHN: Just sit down. (*Pause*) Please. Sit down. Will you, please . . . ? (*Pause. She does so.*) Thank you.

CAROL: What?

JOHN: I want to tell you something.

CAROL: (*Pause*) What?

JOHN: Well, I know what you're talking about.

CAROL: No. You don't.

JOHN: I think I do. (*Pause*)

CAROL: How can you?

JOHN: I'll tell you a story about myself. (*Pause*) Do you mind? (*Pause*) I was raised to think myself stupid. That's what I want to tell you. (*Pause*)

CAROL: What do you mean?

JOHN: Just what I said. I was brought up, and my earliest, and most persistent memories are of being told that I was stupid. "You have such *intelligence*.

Why must you behave so *stupidly?*" Or, "Can't you *understand?* Can't you *understand?*" And I could *not* understand. I could *not* understand.

CAROL: What?

JOHN: The simplest problem. Was beyond me. It was a mystery.

CAROL: What was a mystery?

JOHN: How people learn. How *I* could learn. Which is what I've been speaking of in class. And of course you can't hear it. Carol. Of *course* you can't. (*Pause*) I used to speak of "real people," and wonder what the *real* people did. The *real* people. Who were they? *They* were the people other than myself. The *good* people. The *capable* people. The people who could do the things, I could not do: learn, study, retain . . . all that *garbage*—which is what I have been talking of in class, and that's exactly what I have been talking of—If you are told . . . . Listen to this. If the young child is told he cannot understand. Then he takes it as a *description* of himself What am I? I am *that which can not understand.* And I saw you out there, when we were speaking of the concepts of . . .

CAROL: I can't understand any of them.

JOHN: Well, then, that's *my* fault. That's not your fault. And that is not ver- biage. That's what I firmly hold to be the truth. And I am sorry, and I owe you an apology.

CAROL: Why?

JOHN: And I suppose that I have had some *things* on my mind. . . . We're buy- ing a *house*, and . . .

CAROL: People said that you were stupid . . . ?

JOHN: Yes.

CAROL: When?

JOHN: I'll tell you when. Through my life. In my childhood; and, perhaps, they stopped. But I heard them continue.

CAROL: And what did they say?

JOHN: They said I was incompetent. Do you see? And when I'm tested the, the, the *feelings* of my youth about the *very subject of learning* come up. And I . . . I become, I feel "unworthy," and "unprepared." . . .

CAROL: . . . yes.

JOHN: . . . eh?

CAROL: . . . yes.

JOHN: And I feel that I must fail. (*Pause*)

CAROL: . . . but then you *do* fail. (*Pause*) You have to. (*Pause*) Don't you?

JOHN: A *pilot.* Flying a plane. The pilot is flying the plane. He thinks: Oh, my *God*, my mind's been drifting! Oh, my God! What kind of a cursed imbe- cile am I, that I, with this so precious cargo of *Life* in my charge, would allow my attention to wander. Why was I born? How deluded are those who put their trust in me, . . . et cetera, so on, and he crashes the plane.

CAROL: (*Pause*) He could just . . .

JOHN: That's right.

CAROL: He could say:

JOHN: My attention *wandered* for a moment . . .

CAROL: . . . uh huh . . .

JOHN: I had a *thought* I did not like . . . but now:

CAROL: . . . but now it's . . .

JOHN: That's what I'm telling you. It's time to put my attention . . . see: it is not: this is what I learned. It is Not Magic. Yes. Yes. *You.* You are going to be frightened. When faced with what may or may not be but which you are going to perceive as a test. You will become frightened. And you will say: "I am incapable of . . ." and everything *in* you will think these two things. "I must. But I can't." And you will think: Why was I born to be the laughingstock of a world in which everyone is better than I? In which I am entitled to nothing. Where I can not learn.

(*Pause*)

CAROL: Is that . . . (*Pause*) Is that what I have . . . ?

JOHN: Well. I don't know if I'd put it that way. Listen: I'm talking to you as I'd talk to my son. Because that's what I'd like him to have that I never had. I'm talking to you the way I wish that someone had talked to me. I don't know how to do it, other than to be *personal*, . . . but . . .

CAROL: Why would you want to be personal with me?

JOHN: Well, you see? That's what I'm saying. We can only interpret the behavior of others through the screen we . . . (*The phone rings.*) Through . . . (*To phone:*) Hello . . . ? (*To* CAROL:) Through the screen we create. (*To phone:*) Hello. (*To* CAROL:) Excuse me a moment. (*To phone:*) Hello? No, I can't talk nnn . . . I know I did. In a few . . . I'm . . . is he coming to the . . . yes. I talked to him. We'll meet you at the No, because I'm with a *student.* It's going to be fff . . . This is important, too. I'm with a *student,* Jerry's going to . . . Listen: the sooner I get off, the sooner I'll be down, all right. I love you. Listen, listen, I said "I love you," it's going to work *out* with the, because I feel that it is, I'll be right down. All right? Well, then it's going to take as long as it takes. (*He hangs up.*) (*To* CAROL:) I'm sorry.

CAROL: What was that?

JOHN: There are some problems, as there usually are, about the final agreements for the new house.

CAROL: You're buying a new house.

JOHN: That's right.

CAROL: Because of your promotion.

JOHN: Well, I suppose that that's right.

CAROL: Why did you stay here with me?

JOHN: Stay here.

CAROL: Yes. When you should have gone.

JOHN: Because I like you.

CAROL: You like me.

JOHN: Yes.

CAROL: Why?

JOHN: Why? Well? Perhaps we're similar. (*Pause*) Yes. (*Pause*)

CAROL: You said "everyone has problems."

JOHN: Everyone has problems.

CAROL: Do they?

JOHN: Certainly.

CAROL: You do?

JOHN: Yes.

CAROL: What are they?

JOHN: Well. (*Pause*) Well, you're perfectly right. (*Pause*) If we're going to take off the Artificial *Stricture*, of "Teacher," and "Student," why should *my* problems be any more a mystery than your own? Of *course* I have problems. As you saw.

CAROL: . . . with what?

JOHN: With my *wife* . . . with work . . .

CAROL: With work?

JOHN: Yes. And, and, perhaps my problems are, do you see? *Similar* to yours.

CAROL: Would you tell me?

JOHN: All right. (*Pause*) I came *late* to teaching. And I found it Artificial. The notion of "I know and you do not"; and I saw an *exploitation* in the education process. I told you. I hated school, I hated teachers. I hated everyone who was in the position of a "boss" because I *knew*—I didn't *think*, mind you, I *knew* I was going to fail. Because I was a fuckup. I was just no goddamned good. When I . . . late in life . . . (*Pause*) When I *got out from under*. . . when I worked my way out of the need to fail. When I . . .

CAROL: How do you do that? (*Pause*)

JOHN: You have to look at what you are, and what you feel, and how you act. And, finally, you have to look at how you act. And say: If that's what I *did*, that must be how I think of myself.

CAROL: I don't understand.

JOHN: If I fail all the time, it must be that I think of myself as a failure. If I do not want to think of myself as a failure, perhaps I should begin by *succeeding* now and again. Look. The tests, you see, which you encounter, in school, in college, in life, were designed, in the most part, for idiots. *By* idiots. There is no need to fail at them. They are not a test of your worth. They are a test of your ability to retain and spout back misinformation. Of *course* you fail them. They're *nonsense*. And I . . .

CAROL: . . . no . . .

JOHN: Yes. They're *garbage*. They're a *joke*. Look at me. Look at me. The Tenure Committee. The Tenure Committee. Come to judge me. The Bad Tenure Committee.

The "Test." Do you see? They put me to the test. Why, they had people voting on me I wouldn't employ to wax my car. And yet, I go before the Great Tenure Committee, and I have an urge, to *vomit*, to, to, to puke my *badness* on the table, to show them: "I'm no good. Why would you pick *me*?"

CAROL: They granted you tenure.

JOHN: Oh no, they announced it, but they haven't *signed*. Do you see? "At any moment . . ."

CAROL: . . . mmm . . .

JOHN: "They might not *sign*" . . . I might not . . . the *house* might not go through . . . Eh? Eh? They'll find out my "dark secret." (*Pause*)

CAROL: . . . what is it . . . ?

JOHN: There *isn't* one. But *they* will find an index of my badness . . .

CAROL: Index?

JOHN: A ". . . pointer." A "Pointer." You see? Do you see? I *understand* you. I. Know. That. Feeling. Am I entitled to my job, and my nice *home*, and my *wife*, and my *family*, and so on. This is what I'm saying: That theory of education which, that *theory*:

CAROL: I . . . I . . . (*Pause*)

JOHN: What?

CAROL: I . . .

JOHN: What?

CAROL: I want to know about my grade. (*Long pause*)

JOHN: Of course you do.

CAROL: Is that bad?

JOHN: No.

CAROL: Is it bad that I asked you that?

JOHN: No.

CAROL: Did I upset you?

JOHN: No. And I apologize. Of *course* you want to know about your grade. And, of course, you can't concentrate on anyth . . . (*The telephone starts to ring.*) Wait a moment.

CAROL: I should go.

JOHN: I'll make you a deal.

CAROL: No, you have to . . .

JOHN: Let it ring. I'll make you a deal. You stay here. We'll start the whole course over. I'm going to say it was not you, it was I who was not paying attention. We'll start the whole course over. Your grade is an "A." Your final grade is an "A." (*The phone stops ringing.*)

CAROL: But the class is only half over . . .

JOHN (*simultaneously with* "over"): Your grade for the whole term is an "A." If you will come back and meet with me. A few more times. Your grade's an "A." Forget about the paper. You didn't like it, you didn't like writing it. It's not important. What's important is that I awake your interest, if I can, and that I answer your questions. Let's start over. (*Pause*)

CAROL: Over. With what?

JOHN: Say this is the beginning.

CAROL: The beginning.

JOHN: Yes.

CAROL: Of what?

JOHN: Of the class.

CAROL: But we can't start over.

JOHN: I say we can. (*Pause*) I say we can.

CAROL: But I don't believe it.

JOHN: Yes, I know that. But it's true. What is The Class but you and me? (*Pause*)

CAROL: There are rules.

JOHN: Well. We'll break them.

CAROL: How can we?

JOHN: We won't tell anybody.

CAROL: Is that all right?

JOHN: I say that it's fine.

CAROL: Why would you do this for me?

JOHN: I like you. Is that so difficult for you to . . .

CAROL: Um . . .

JOHN: There's no one here but you and me. (*Pause*)

CAROL: All right. I did not understand. When you referred . . .

JOHN: All right, yes?

CAROL: When you referred to hazing.

JOHN: Hazing.

CAROL: You wrote, in your book. About the comparative . . . the comparative . . . *(She checks her notes.)*

JOHN: Are you checking your notes . . .

CAROL: Yes.

JOHN: Tell me in your own . . .

CAROL: I want to make sure that I have it right.

JOHN: No. Of course. You want to be exact.

CAROL: I want to know everything that went on.

JOHN: . . . that's good.

CAROL: . . . so I . . .

JOHN: That's very good. But I was suggesting, many times, that that which we wish to retain is retained oftentimes, I think, better with less expenditure of effort.

CAROL: *(Of notes)* Here it is: you wrote of *hazing.*

JOHN: . . . that's correct. Now: I said "hazing." It means ritualized annoyance. We shove this book at you, we say read it. Now, you say you've read it? I think that you're *lying.* I'll *grill* you, and when I find you've lied, you'll be disgraced, and your life will be ruined. It's a sick game. Why do we do it? Does it educate? In no sense. Well, then, what is higher education? It is something-other-than-useful.

CAROL: What is "something-other-than-useful?"

JOHN: It has become a ritual, it has become an article of faith. That all must be subjected to, or to put it differently, that all are entitled to Higher Education. And my point . . .

CAROL: You disagree with that?

JOHN: Well, let's address that. What do you think?

CAROL: I don't know.

JOHN: What do you think, though? *(Pause)*

CAROL: I don't know.

JOHN: I spoke of it in class. Do you remember my example?

CAROL: Justice.

JOHN: Yes. Can you repeat it to me? *(She looks down at her notebook.)* Without your notes? I ask you as a favor to me, so that I can see if my idea was interesting.

CAROL: You said "justice" . . .

JOHN: Yes?

CAROL: . . . that all are entitled . . . *(Pause)* I . . . I . . . I . . .

JOHN: Yes. To a speedy trial. To a fair trial. But they needn't be given a trial *at all* unless they stand accused. Eh? Justice is their right, should they choose to avail themselves of it, they should have a fair trial. It does not follow, of necessity, a person's life is incomplete without a trial in it. Do you see?

My point is a confusion between equity and *utility* arose. So we confound the *usefulness* of higher education with our, granted, right to equal access to the same. We, in effect, create a *prejudice* toward it, completely independent of . . .

CAROL: . . . that it is prejudice that we should go to school?

JOHN: Exactly. (*Pause*)

CAROL: How can you say that? How . . .

JOHN: Good. Good. *Good.* That's right! Speak up! What is a prejudice? An unreasoned belief. We are all subject to it. None of us is not. When it is threatened, or opposed, we feel anger, and feel, do we not? As you do now. Do you not? Good.

CAROL: . . . but how can you . . .

JOHN: . . . let us examine. Good.

CAROL: How . . .

JOHN: Good. Good. When . . .

CAROL: I'M SPEAKING . . . (*Pause*)

JOHN: I'm sorry.

CAROL: How can you . . .

JOHN: . . . I beg your pardon.

CAROL: That's all right.

JOHN: I beg your pardon.

CAROL: That's all right.

JOHN: I'm sorry I interrupted you.

CAROL: That's all right.

JOHN: You were saying?

CAROL: I was saying . . . I was saying . . . (*She checks her notes.*) How can you say in a class. Say in a college class, that college education is prejudice?

JOHN: I said that our predilection for it . . .

CAROL: Predilection . . .

JOHN: . . . you know what that means.

CAROL: Does it mean "liking"?

JOHN: Yes.

CAROL: But how can you say that? That College . . .

JOHN: . . . that's my *job*, don't you know.

CAROL: What is?

JOHN: To provoke you.

CAROL: No.

JOHN: Oh. Yes, though.

CAROL: To provoke me?

JOHN: That's right.

CAROL: To make me mad?

JOHN: That's right. To force you . . .

CAROL: . . . to make me mad is your job?

JOHN: To force you to . . . listen: (*Pause*) Ah. (*Pause*) When I was young somebody told me, are you ready, the rich copulate less often than the poor. But when they do, they take more of their clothes off. Years. Years, mind you, I would compare experiences of my own to this dictum, saying, aha, this fits the norm, or ah, this is a variation from it. What did it mean? Nothing. It was some jerk thing, some school kid told me that took up room inside my head. (*Pause*)

Somebody told *you*, and you hold it as an article of faith, that higher education is an unassailable good. This notion is so dear to you that when I question it you become angry. Good. Good, I say. Are not those the very things which we should question? I say college education, since the war, has become so a matter of course, and such a fashionable necessity, for those either of or aspiring *to* to the new vast middle class, that we *espouse* it, as a matter of right, and have ceased to ask, "What is it good for?" (*Pause*)

What might be some reasons for pursuit of higher education?

One: A love of learning.

Two: The wish for mastery of a skill.

Three: For economic betterment.

(Stops. Makes a note.)

CAROL: I'm keeping you.

JOHN: One moment. I have to make a note . . .

CAROL: It's something that I said?

JOHN: No, we're buying a house.

CAROL: You're buying the new house.

JOHN: To go with the tenure. That's right. Nice *house*, close to the *private school* . . . (*He continues making his note.*) . . . We were talking of economic *betterment* (CAROL *writes in her notebook.*) . . . I was thinking of the School Tax. (*He continues writing.*) (*To himself:*) . . . *where is it written* that I have to send my child to public school. . . . Is it a law that I have to improve the City Schools at the expense of my own interest? And, is this not simply *The*

White Man's Burden? Good. And (Looks up to CAROL) . . . does this interest you?

CAROL: No. I'm taking notes . . .

JOHN: You don't have to take notes, you know, you can just listen.

CAROL: I want to make sure I remember it. (*Pause*)

JOHN: I'm not lecturing you, I'm just trying to tell you some things I think.

CAROL: What do you think?

JOHN: Should all kids go to college? *Why* . . .

CAROL: (*Pause*) To learn.

JOHN: But if he does not learn.

CAROL: If the child does not learn?

JOHN: Then why is he in college? Because he was told it was his "right"?

CAROL: Some might find college instructive.

JOHN: I would hope so.

CAROL: But how do they feel? Being told they are wasting their time?

JOHN: I don't think I'm telling them that.

CAROL: You said that education was "prolonged and systematic hazing."

JOHN: Yes. It can be so.

CAROL: . . . if education is so *bad*, why do you do it?

JOHN: I do it because I love it. (*Pause*) Let's . . . . I suggest you look at the
demographics, wage-earning capacity, college- and non-college educated
men and women, 1855 to 1980, and let's see if we can wring some worth
from the statistics. Eh? And . . .

CAROL: No.

JOHN: What?

CAROL: I can't understand them.

JOHN: . . . you . . . ?

CAROL: . . . the "charts." The *Concepts*, the . . .

JOHN: "Charts" are simply . . .

CAROL: When I leave here . . .

JOHN: Charts, do you see . . .

CAROL: No, I can't . . .

JOHN: You can, though.

CAROL: NO, NO—I DON'T UNDERSTAND. DO YOU SEE??? I DON'T
UNDERSTAND . . .

JOHN: What?

CAROL: *Any* of it. *Any* of it. I'm *smiling* in class, I'm *smiling*, the whole time.
What are you *talking* about? What is everyone *talking* about? I don't
understand. I don't know what it *means*. I don't know what it means to *be*

here . . . you tell me I'm intelligent, and then you tell me I should not be *here*, what do you *want* with me? What does it *mean*? Who should I *listen to* . . I . . .

(*He goes over to her and puts his arm around her shoulder.*)
NO! (*She walks away from him.*)

JOHN: Sshhhh.

CAROL: No, I don't under . . .

JOHN: Sshhhhh.

CAROL: I don't know what you're *saying* . . .

JOHN: Sshhhhh. It's all right.

CAROL: . . . I have no . . .

JOHN: Sshhhhh. Sshhhhh. Let it go a moment. (*Pause*) Sshhhhh . . . let it go. (*Pause*) Just let it go. (*Pause*) Just let it go. It's all right. (*Pause*) Sshhhhh. (*Pause*) I understand . . . (*Pause*) What do you feel?

CAROL: I feel bad.

JOHN: I know. It's all right.

CAROL: I . . . (*Pause*)

JOHN: What?

CAROL: I . . .

JOHN: What? Tell me.

CAROL: I don't understand you.

JOHN: I know. It's all right.

CAROL: I . . .

JOHN: What? (*Pause*) What? *Tell* me.

CAROL: I can't tell you.

JOHN: No, you must.

CAROL: I can't.

JOHN: No. Tell me. (*Pause*)

CAROL: I'm bad. (*Pause*) Oh, God. (*Pause*)

JOHN: It's all right.

CAROL: I'm . . .

JOHN: It's all right.

CAROL: I can't talk about this.

JOHN: It's all right. Tell me.

CAROL: Why do you want to know this?

JOHN: I don't want to know. I want to know whatever you . . .

CAROL: I always . . .

JOHN: . . . good . . .

CAROL: I always . . . all my life . . . I have never told anyone this . . .

JOHN: Yes. Go on. *(Pause)* Go on.

CAROL: All of my life . . . *(The phone rings.) (Pause.* JOHN *goes to the phone and picks it up.)*

JOHN *(into phone)*: I can't talk now. *(Pause)* What? *(Pause)* Hmm. *(Pause)* All right, I . . . I. Can't. Talk. Now. No, no, no, I *Know* I did, but . . . What? Hello. What? She *what*? She *can't*, she said the agreement is void? How, how is the agreement *void*? *That's Our House.*

I have the *paper*; when we come down, next week, with the payment, and the paper, that house is . . . wait, wait, wait, wait, wait, wait, wait: Did Jerry . . . is Jerry there? *(Pause)* is *she* there . . . ? Does she have a *lawyer* . . . ? How the *hell*, how the *Hell*. That is . . . it's a question, you said, of the *easement*. I don't underst . . . it's not the *whole agreement*. It's just the *easement*, why would she? Put, put, put, *Jerry* on. *(Pause)* Jer, *Jerry*: What the *Hell* . . . that's my *house*. That's . . . Well, I'm, no, no, no, I'm *not* coming ddd . . . List, *Listen, screw* her. You *tell* her. You, listen: I want you to take *Grace*, you take Grace, and get out of that house. You *leave* her there. Her and her lawyer, and you *tell* them, we'll see them in court next . . . no. No. Leave her there, leave her to *stew* in it: You tell her, we're *getting* that house, and we are going to . . . No. I'm *not* coming down. I'll be damned if I'll sit in the same rrr . . . the next, you tell her the next time I *see* her is in court . . . I . . . *(Pause)* What? *(Pause)* What? I don't understand. *(Pause)* Well, what about the house? *(Pause)* There isn't any problem with the hhh . . . *(Pause)* No, no, no, that's all right. All ri . . . All right . . . *(Pause)* Of course. Tha . . . Thank you. No, I will. Right away. *(He hangs up.) (Pause)*

CAROL: What is it? *(Pause)*

JOHN: It's a surprise party.

CAROL: It is.

JOHN: Yes.

CAROL: A party for you.

JOHN: Yes.

CAROL: Is it your birthday?

JOHN: No.

CAROL: What is it?

JOHN: The tenure announcement.

CAROL: The tenure announcement.

JOHN: They're throwing a party for us in our new house.

CAROL: Your new house.

JOHN: The house that we're buying.

CAROL: You have to go.

JOHN: It seems that I do.

CAROL: *(Pause)* They're proud of you.
JOHN: Well, there are those who would say it's a form of aggression.
CAROL: What is?
JOHN: A surprise.

Two

JOHN *and* CAROL *seated across the desk from each other.*

JOHN: You see, *(pause)* I love to teach. And flatter myself I am *skilled* at it. And I love the, the aspect of *performance.* I think I must confess that.

When I found I loved to teach I swore that I would not become that cold, rigid automaton of an instructor which I had encountered as a child.

Now, I was not unconscious that it was given me to err upon the other side. And, so, I asked and *ask* myself if I engaged in heterodoxy, I will not say "gratuitously" for I do not care to posit orthodoxy as a given good— but, "to the detriment of, of my students." *(Pause)*

As I said. When the possibility of tenure opened, and, of course, I'd long pursued it, I was, of course *happy,* and *covetous* of it.

I asked myself if I was wrong to covet it. And thought about it long, and, I hope, truthfully, and saw in myself several things in, I think, no particular order. *(Pause)*

That I *would* pursue it. That I *desired* it, that I was not pure of longing for security, and that that, perhaps, was not reprehensible in me. That I had duties *beyond* the school, and that my duty to my home, for instance, was, or should be, if it were not, of an equal weight. That tenure, and security, and yes, and *comfort,* were not, of themselves, to be scorned; and were even worthy of honorable pursuit. And that it was given me. Here, in this place, which I enjoy, and in which I find comfort, to assure myself of—as far as it rests in The Material—a continuation of that joy and comfort. In exchange for what? Teaching. Which I love.

What was the price of this security? To obtain *tenure.* Which tenure the committee is in the process of granting me. And on the basis of which I contracted to purchase a house. Now, as you don't have your own family, at this point, you may not know what that means. But to me it is important. A home. A Good Home. To raise my family. Now: The Tenure Committee will meet. This is the process, and a *good* process. Under which the school has functioned for quite a long time. They will meet, and hear your complaint—which you have the right to make; and they will dismiss it. They will *dismiss* your complaint; and, in the intervening period, I will lose my house. I will not be able to close on my house. I will lose my *deposit,* and the home I'd picked out for my wife and son will go by the boards. Now: I see I have angered you. I understand your anger at teachers. I was angry with mine. I felt hurt and humiliated by them. Which is one of the reasons that I went into education.

CAROL: What do you want of me?

JOHN: *(Pause)* I was hurt. When I received the report. Of the tenure committee. I was shocked. And I was hurt. No, I don't mean to subject you to my weak sensibilities. All right. Finally, I didn't understand. Then I thought: is it not always at those points at which we reckon ourselves unassailable that we are most vulnerable and . . . *(Pause)* Yes. All right. You find me pedantic. Yes. I am. By nature, by *birth*, by profession, I don't know . . . I'm always looking for a paradigm for . . .

CAROL: I don't know what a paradigm is.

JOHN: It's a model.

CAROL: Then why can't you use that word? *(Pause)*

JOHN: If it is important to you. Yes, all right. I was looking for a model. To continue: I feel that one point . . .

CAROL: I . . .

JOHN: One second. . . . upon which I am unassailable is my unflinching concern for my students' dignity. I asked you here to . . . in the spirit of *investigation*, to ask you . . . to ask . . . *(Pause)* What have I done to you? *(Pause)* And, and, I suppose, how I can make amends. Can we not settle this now? It's pointless, really, and I want to know.

CAROL: What you can do to force me to retract?

JOHN: That is not what I meant at all.

CAROL: To bribe me, to convince me . . .

JOHN: . . . No.

CAROL: To retract . . .

JOHN: That is not what I meant at all. I think that you know it is not.

CAROL: That is not what I know. I *wish* I . . .

JOHN: I do not want to . . . you wish what?

CAROL: No, you said what amends can you make. To force me to retract.

JOHN: That is not what I said.

CAROL: I have my notes.

JOHN: Look. Look. The Stoics say . . .

CAROL: The Stoics?

JOHN: The Stoical Philosophers say if you remove the phrase "I have been injured," you have removed the injury. Now: Think: I know that you're upset. Just tell me. Literally. Literally: what wrong have I done you?

CAROL: Whatever you have done to me—to the extent that you've done it to *me*, do you know, rather than to me as a *student*, and, so, to the student body, is contained in my report. To the tenure committee.

JOHN: Well, all right. *(Pause)* Let's see. *(He reads.)* I find that I am sexist. That I am *elitist*. I'm not sure I know what that means, other than it's a derogatory word, meaning "bad." That I . . . That I insist on wasting time, in nonprescribed, in self-aggrandizing and theatrical *diversions* from the prescribed *text* . . . that these have taken both sexist and pornographic forms . . . here we find listed . . . *(Pause)* Here we find listed . . . instances ". . . closeted with a student" . . . "Told a rambling, sexually explicit story, in which the frequency and attitudes of fornication of the poor and rich are, it would seem, the central point . . . moved to *embrace* said student and . . . all part of a pattern . . . ." *(Pause)*

    (He reads.) That I used the phrase "The White Man's Burden" . . . that I told you how I'd asked you to my room because I quote like you. *(Pause)*

    (He reads.) "He said he 'liked' me. That he 'liked being with me.' He'd let me write my examination paper over, if I could come back oftener to see him in his office." *(Pause)* *(To* CAROL:) It's *ludicrous*. Don't you know that? It's not *necessary*. It's going to *humiliate* you, and it's going to cost me my *house*, and . . .

CAROL: It's *"ludicrous . . ."*?

*(*JOHN *picks up the report and reads again.)*

JOHN: "He told me he had problems with his wife; and that he wanted to take off the artificial stricture of Teacher and Student. He put his arm around me . . ."

CAROL: Do you deny it? Can you deny it . . . ? Do you see? *(Pause)* Don't you see? You don't see, do you?

JOHN: I don't see . . .

CAROL: You think, you think you can deny that these things happened; or, if they *did*, if they *did*, that they meant what you *said* they meant. Don't you see? You drag me in here, you drag us, to listen to you "go on"; and "go on" about this, or that, or we don't "express" ourselves very well. We don't say what we mean. Don't we? Don't we? We *do* say what we mean. And you say that "I don't understand you . . .": Then *you* . . . *(Points.)*

JOHN: "Consult the Report"?

CAROL: . . . that's right.

JOHN: You see. You see. Can't you . . . . You see what I'm saying? Can't you tell me in your own words?

CAROL: Those are my own words. *(Pause)*

JOHN: *(He reads.)* "He told me that if I would stay alone with him in his office, he would change my grade to an A." *(To* CAROL:) What have I done to you? Oh. My God, are you so hurt?

CAROL: What I "feel" is irrelevant. *(Pause)*

JOHN: Do you know that I tried to help you?

CAROL: What I know I have reported.

JOHN: I would like to help you now. I would. Before this escalates.

CAROL *(simultaneously with* "escalates"): You see. I don't think that I need your help. I don't think I need anything you have.

JOHN: I feel . . .

CAROL: I don't *care* what you feel. Do you see? DO YOU SEE? You can't *do* that anymore. You. Do. Not. Have. The. Power. Did you misuse it? *Someone* did. Are you part of that group? *Yes. Yes.* You Are. You've *done* these things. And to say, and to say, "Oh. Let me help you with your problem . . ."

JOHN: Yes. I understand. I understand. You're *hurt.* You're *angry.* Yes. I think your *anger* is *betraying* you. Down a path which helps no one.

CAROL: I don't *care* what you think.

JOHN: You don't? *(Pause)* But you talk of *rights.* Don't you see? *I* have rights too. Do you see? I have a *house* . . . part of the *real* world; and The Tenure Committee, Good Men and True . . .

CAROL: . . . Professor . . .

JOHN: . . . Please: *Also* part of that world: you understand? This is my *life.* I'm not a *bogeyman.* I don't "stand" for something, I . . .

CAROL: . . . Professor . . .

JOHN: . . . I . . .

CAROL: Professor. I came here as *a favor.* At your personal request. Perhaps I should not have done so. But I did. On my behalf, and on behalf of my group. And you speak of the tenure committee, one of whose members is a woman, as you know. And though you might call it Good Fun, or An Historical Phrase, or An Oversight, or, All of the Above, to refer to the committee as Good Men and True, it is a demeaning remark. It is a sexist remark, and to overlook it is to countenance continuation of that method of thought. It's a remark . . .

JOHN: OH COME ON. Come on. . . . Sufficient to deprive a family of . . .

CAROL: Sufficient? Sufficient? Sufficient? Yes. It is a *fact* . . . and that story, which I quote, is *vile* and *classist,* and *manipulative* and *pornographic.* It . . .

JOHN: . . . it's pornographic . . . ?

CAROL: What gives you the *right.* Yes. To speak to a *woman* in your private . . . Yes. Yes. I'm sorry. I'm sorry. You feel yourself empowered . . . you say so yourself. To *strut.* To *posture.* To "perform." To "Call me in here . . ." Eh? You say that higher education is a joke. And treat it as such, you *treat* it as such. And *confess* to a taste to play the *Patriarch* in your class. To grant *this.* To deny *that.* To embrace your students.

JOHN: How can you assert. How can you stand there and . . .

CAROL: How can you *deny* it. You did it to me. *Here.* You *did* . . . . You *confess.* You love the Power. To *deviate.* To *invent,* to transgress . . . to *transgress* whatever norms have been established for us. And you think it's charming to "question" in yourself this taste to mock and destroy. But you should question it. Professor. And you pick those things which you feel *advance* you: publication, *tenure,* and the steps to get them you call "harmless rituals." And you perform those steps. Although you say it is hypocrisy. But to the aspirations of your students. Of *hardworking students,* who come here, who slave to come here—you have no idea what it cost me to come to this school—you *mock* us. You call education "hazing," and from your so-protected, so-elitist seat you hold our confusion as a *joke,* and our hopes and efforts with it. Then you sit there and say "what have I done?" And ask me to understand that *you* have aspirations too. But I tell you. I tell you. That you are vile. And that you are exploitative. And if you possess one ounce of that inner honesty you describe in your book, you can look in yourself and see those things that I see. And you can find revulsion equal to my own. Good day. *(She prepares to leave the room.)*

JOHN: Wait a second, will you, just one moment. *(Pause)* Nice day today.

CAROL: What?

JOHN: You said "Good day." I think that it is a nice day today.

CAROL: *Is* it?

JOHN: Yes, I think it is.

CAROL: And why is that important?

JOHN: Because it is the essence of all human communication. I say something conventional, you respond, and the information we exchange is not about the "weather," but that we both agree to converse. In effect, we agree that we are both human. *(Pause)*

I'm not a . . . "exploiter," and you're not a . . . "deranged," what? *Revolutionary* . . . that we may, that we may have . . . positions, and that we may have . . . desires, which are in *conflict,* but that we're just human. *(Pause)* That means that sometimes we're *imperfect.* *(Pause)* Often we're in conflict . . . *(Pause) Much* of what we do, you're right, in the name of "principles" is *self-serving* . . . much of what we do is *conventional.* *(Pause)* You're right. *(Pause)* You said you came in the class because you wanted to learn about *education.* I don't know that I can teach you about education. But I know that I can tell you what I *think* about education, and then *you* decide. And you don't have to fight with me. *I'm* not the subject. *(Pause)* And where I'm *wrong* . . . perhaps it's not your job to "fix" me. I don't want to fix *you.* I would like to tell you what I *think,* because that *is* my job, conventional as it is, and flawed as I may be. And then, if you can show me some better *form,* then we can proceed from there. But, just like "nice day, isn't it . . . ?" I don't think we can proceed until we accept that each of us is human. (*Pause*) And we still can have difficulties. We *will* have them . . . that's all right too. (*Pause*) Now:

CAROL: . . . wait . . .

JOHN: Yes. I want to hear it.

CAROL: . . . the . . .

JOHN: Yes. Tell me frankly.

CAROL: . . . my position . . .

JOHN: I want to hear it. In your own words. What you want. And what you feel.

CAROL: . . . I . . .

JOHN: . . . yes . . .

CAROL: My Group.

JOHN: Your "Group" . . . ? (*Pause*)

CAROL: The people I've been talking to . . .

JOHN: There's no shame in that. Everybody needs advisers. Everyone needs to expose themselves. To various points of view. It's not wrong. It's essential. Good. Good. Now: You and I . . . (*The phone rings.*)

You and I . . .

(*He hesitates for a moment, and then picks it up.*) (*Into phone*) Hello. (*Pause*) Um . . . no, I know they do. (*Pause*) I know she does. Tell her that I . . . can I call you back? . . . Then tell her that I think it's going to be fine. (*Pause*) Tell her just, just hold on, I'll . . . can I get back to you? . . . Well . . . no, no, no, we're taking the house . . . we're . . . no, no, nn . . . no, she will nnn, it's not a *question* of refunding the dep . . . no . . . it's not a *question* of the deposit . . . will you call Jerry? Babe, baby, will you just call Jerry? Tell him, nnn . . . tell him they, well, they're to keep the deposit, because the deal, be . . . because the deal is going to go *through* . . . because I know . . . be . . . will you please? Just *trust* me. Be . . . well, I'm dealing with the complaint. Yes. Right *Now*. Which is why I . . . yes, no, no, it's really, I can't *talk* about it now. Call Jerry, and I can't talk now. Ff . . . fine. Gg . . . good-bye. (*Hangs up.*) (*Pause*) I'm sorry we were interrupted.

CAROL: No . . .

JOHN: I . . . I was saying:

CAROL: You said that we should agree to talk about my complaint.

JOHN: That's correct.

CAROL: But we *are* talking about it.

JOHN: Well, that's correct too. You see? This is the *gist* of education.

CAROL: No, no. I mean, we're talking about it at the Tenure Committee Hearing. (*Pause*)

JOHN: Yes, but I'm saying: we can talk about it *now*, as easily as . . .

CAROL: No. I think that we should stick to the process . . .

JOHN: . . . wait a . . .

CAROL: . . . the "conventional" process. As you said. *(She gets up.)* And you're right, I'm sorry if I was, um, if I was "discourteous" to you. You're right.

JOHN: Wait, wait a . . .

CAROL: I really should go.

JOHN: Now, look, granted. I have an interest. In the status quo. All right? Everyone does. But what I'm saying is that the *committee* . . .

CAROL: Professor, you're right. Just don't impinge on me. We'll take our differences, and . . .

JOHN: You're going to make a . . . look, look, look, you're going to . . .

CAROL: I shouldn't have come here. They told me . . .

JOHN: One moment. No. No. There are *norms*, here, and there's no reason. Look: I'm trying to *save* you . . .

CAROL: No one *asked* you to . . . you're trying to save *me?* Do me the courtesy to . . .

JOHN: I *am* doing you the courtesy. I'm talking *straight* to you. We can settle this *now*. And I want you to sit *down* and . . .

CAROL: You must excuse me . . . *(She starts to leave the room.)*

JOHN: Sit down, it seems we each have a . . . . . Wait one moment. Wait one moment . . . just do me the courtesy to . . .

(He restrains her from leaving.)

CAROL: LET ME GO.

JOHN: I have no desire to *hold* you, I just want to *talk* to you . . .

CAROL: LET ME GO. LET ME GO. WOULD SOMEBODY *HELP* ME? WOULD SOMEBODY *HELP* ME PLEASE . . . ?

Three

(At rise, CAROL and JOHN are seated.)

JOHN: I have asked you here. *(Pause)* I have asked you here against, against my . . .

CAROL: I was most surprised you asked me.

JOHN: . . . against my better *judgment*, against . . .

CAROL: I was most surprised . . .

JOHN: . . . against the . . . yes. I'm sure.

CAROL: . . . If you would like me to leave, I'll leave. I'll go right now . . . *(She rises.)*

JOHN: Let us begin *correctly*, may we? I feel . . .

CAROL: That is what I wished to do. That's why I came here, but now . . .

JOHN: . . . I feel . . .

CAROL: But now perhaps you'd like me to leave . . .

JOHN: I don't want you to leave. I asked you to come . . .

CAROL: I didn't have to come here.

JOHN: No. *(Pause)* Thank you.

CAROL: All right. *(Pause) (She sits down.)*

JOHN: Although I feel that it *profits*, it would *profit* you something, to . . .

CAROL: . . . what I . . .

JOHN: If you would hear me out, if you would hear me out.

CAROL: I came here to, the court officers told me not to come.

JOHN: . . . the "court" officers . . . ?

CAROL: I was shocked that you asked.

JOHN: . . . wait . . .

CAROL: Yes. But I did *not* come here to hear what it "profits" me.

JOHN: The "court" officers . . .

CAROL: . . . no, no, perhaps I should leave . . . *(She gets up.)*

JOHN: Wait.

CAROL: No. I shouldn't have . . .

JOHN: . . . wait. Wait. Wait a moment.

CAROL: Yes? What is it you want? *(Pause)* What is it you want?

JOHN: I'd like you to stay.

CAROL: You want me to stay.

JOHN: Yes.

CAROL: You do.

JOHN: Yes. *(Pause)* Yes. I would like to have you hear me out. If you would. *(Pause)* Would you please? If you would do that I would be in your debt. *(Pause) (She sits.)* Thank You. *(Pause)*

CAROL: What is it you wish to tell me?

JOHN: All right. I cannot . . . *(Pause)* I cannot help but feel you are owed an apology. *(Pause) (Of papers in his hands)* I have read. *(Pause)* And reread these accusations.

CAROL: What "accusations"?

JOHN: The, the tenure comm . . . what other accusations . . . ?

CAROL: The tenure committee . . . ?

JOHN: Yes.

CAROL: Excuse me, but those are not accusations. They have been *proved*. They are facts.

JOHN: . . . I . . .

CAROL: No. Those are not "accusations."

JOHN: . . . those?

CAROL: . . . the committee (*The phone starts to ring.*) the committee has . . .

JOHN: . . . All right . . .

CAROL: . . . those are not accusations. The Tenure Committee.

JOHN: ALL RIGHT. ALL RIGHT. ALL RIGHT. (*He picks up the phone.*) Hello. Yes. No. I'm here. Tell Mister . . . No, I can't talk to him now . . . I'm sure he has, but I'm fff . . . I know . . . No, I have no time t . . . tell Mister . . . tell Mist . . . tell Jerry that I'm fine and that I'll call him right aw. . . . (*Pause*) My wife . . . Yes. I'm sure she has. Yes, thank you. Yes, I'll call her too. I cannot talk to you now. (*He hangs up.*) (*Pause*) All right. It was good of you to come. Thank you. I have studied. I have spent some time studying the indictment.

CAROL: You will have to explain that word to me.

JOHN: An "indictment" . . .

CAROL: Yes.

JOHN: Is a "bill of particulars." A . . .

CAROL: All right. Yes.

JOHN: In which is alleged . . .

CAROL: No. I cannot allow that. I cannot allow that. Nothing is alleged. Everything is proved . . .

JOHN: Please, wait a sec . . .

CAROL: I cannot *come* to allow . . .

JOHN: If I may . . . If I may, from whatever you feel is "established," by . . .

CAROL: The issue here is not what I "feel." It is not my "feelings," but the feelings of women. And men. Your superiors, who've been "polled," do you see? To whom *evidence* has been presented, who have *ruled*, do you see? Who have weighed the testimony and the evidence, and have *ruled*, do you see? That you are *negligent*. That you are *guilty*, that you are found *wanting*, and in *error*; and are *not*, for the reasons so-told, to be given tenure. That you are to be disciplined. For facts. For *facts*. Not "alleged," what is the word? But *proved*. Do you see? *By your own actions.*

   That is what the tenure committee has said. That is what my lawyer said. For what you did in class. For what you did *in this office.*

JOHN: They're going to discharge me.

CAROL: As full well they should. You don't understand? You're angry? What has *led* you to this place? Not your sex. Not your race. Not your class. YOUR OWN ACTIONS. And you're *angry*. You *ask* me here. What *do* you want? You want to "charm" me. You want to "convince" me. You want me to recant. I will *not* recant. Why should I . . . ? What I say is right. You tell me, you are going to tell me that you have a wife and child. You are going to say that you have a career and that you've worked for twenty years for this. Do you know what you've *worked* for? *Power.* For *power.* Do you understand? And you sit there, and you tell me *stories.* About your *house,* about all the private *schools,* and about *privilege,* and how you are entitled. To *buy,* to *spend,* to *mock,* to *summon.* All your stories. All your silly weak *guilt,* it's all about *privilege;* and you won't know it. Don't you see? You worked twenty years for the right to *insult* me. And you feel entitled to be *paid* for it. Your Home. Your Wife . . . Your sweet "deposit" on your house . . .

JOHN: Don't you have feelings?

CAROL: That's my point. You see? Don't you have feelings? Your final argument. What is it that has no feelings. *Animals.* I don't take your side, you question if I'm Human.

JOHN: Don't you have feelings?

CAROL: I have a responsibility. I . . .

JOHN: . . . to . . . ?

CAROL: To? This institution. To the *students.* To my *group.*

JOHN: . . . your "group." . . .

CAROL: Because I speak, yes, not for myself But for the group; for those who suffer what I suffer. On behalf of whom, even if I, were, inclined, to what, forgive? Forget? What? Overlook your . . .

JOHN: . . . my behavior?

CAROL: . . . it would be wrong.

JOHN: Even if you were inclined to "forgive" me.

CAROL: It would be wrong.

JOHN: And what would transpire.

CAROL: Transpire?

JOHN: Yes.

CAROL: "Happen?"

JOHN: Yes.

CAROL: Then *say* it. For Christ's sake. Who the *hell* do you think that you are? You want a post. You want unlimited power. To do and to say what you want. As it pleases you—Testing, Questioning, Flirting.

JOHN: I never . . .

CAROL: Excuse me, one moment, will you?

(She reads from her notes.)

The twelfth: "Have a good day, dear."
The fifteenth: "Now, don't *you* look fetching . . .
April seventeenth: "If you girls would come over here . . . ." I saw you.
I saw you, Professor. For two semesters sit there, stand there and exploit
our, as you thought, "paternal prerogative," and what is that but rape; I
swear to God. You asked me in here to explain something to me, as a
child, that I did not understand. But I came to explain something to you.
You Are Not God. You ask me why I came? I came here to instruct you.

(She produces his book.)

And your book? You think you're going to show me some "light"? You
"maverick." Outside of tradition. No, no, *(She reads from the book's liner
notes.)* "of that fine tradition of *inquiry*. Of Polite *skepticism"*. . . and you
say you believe in free intellectual discourse. YOU BELIEVE IN
NOTHING. YOU BELIEVE IN NOTHING AT ALL.

JOHN: I believe in freedom of thought.

CAROL: Isn't that fine. *Do* you?

JOHN: Yes. I do.

CAROL: Then why do you question, for one moment, the committee's decision
refusing your tenure? Why do you question your suspension? You believe
in what *you call* freedom of thought. Then, fine. You believe in freedom-
of-thought *and* a home, and, *and* prerogatives for your kid, *and* tenure.
And I'm going to tell you. You believe *not* in "freedom of thought," but in
an elitist, in, in a protected hierarchy which rewards you. And for whom
you are the clown. And you mock and exploit the system which pays your
rent. You're wrong. I'm not wrong. You're wrong. You think that I'm full
of hatred. I know what you think I am.

JOHN: Do you?

CAROL: You think I'm a, of course I do. You think I am a frightened, repressed,
confused, I don't know, abandoned young thing of some doubtful sexuality, who wants, power and revenge. *(Pause) Don't* you? *(Pause)*

JOHN: Yes. I do. *(Pause)*

CAROL: Isn't that better? And I feel that that is the first moment which you've
treated me with respect. For you told me the truth. *(Pause)* I did not come
here, as you are assured, to gloat. Why would I want to gloat? I've profited
nothing from your, your, as you say, your "misfortune." I came here, as
you did me the honor to *ask* me here, I came here to *tell* you something.

(Pause) That I think . . . that I think you've been wrong. That I think
you've been terribly wrong. Do you hate me now? *(Pause)*

JOHN: Yes.

CAROL: Why do you hate me? Because you think me wrong? No. Because I have, you think, *power* over you. Listen to me. Listen to me, Professor. *(Pause)* It is the power that you hate. So deeply that, that any atmosphere of free discussion is impossible. It's not "unlikely." It's *impossible*. Isn't it?

JOHN: Yes.

CAROL: *Isn't it* . . . ?

JOHN: Yes. I suppose.

CAROL: Now. The thing which you find so cruel is the selfsame process of selection I, and my group, go through *every day of our lives.* In admittance to school. In our tests, in our class rankings. . . . Is it unfair? I can't tell you. But, if it is fair. Or even if it is "unfortunate but necessary" for us, then, by God, so must it be for you. *(Pause)* You write of your "responsibility to the young." Treat us with respect, and that will show you your responsibility. You write that education is just hazing. *(Pause)* But we worked to get to this school. *(Pause)* And some of us. *(Pause)* Overcame prejudices. Economic, sexual, you cannot begin to imagine. And endured humiliations I *pray* that you and those you love never will encounter. *(Pause)* To gain admittance here. To pursue that same dream of security *you* pursue. We, who, who are, at any moment, in danger of being deprived of it. By . . .

JOHN: . . . by . . . ?

CAROL: By the administration. By the teachers. By *you.* By, say, one low grade, that keeps us out of graduate school; by one, say, one capricious or inventive answer on our parts, which, perhaps, you don't find amusing. Now you *know*, do you see? What it is to be subject to that power. *(Pause)*

JOHN: I don't understand. *(Pause)*

CAROL: My charges are not trivial. You see that in the haste, I think, with which they were accepted. A *joke* you have told, with a sexist tinge. The language you use, a verbal or physical caress, yes, yes, I know, you say that it is meaningless. I understand. I differ from you. To lay a hand on someone's shoulder.

JOHN: It was devoid of sexual content.

CAROL: I say it was not. I SAY IT WAS NOT. Don't you begin to *see* . . . ? Don't you begin to understand? IT'S NOT FOR YOU TO SAY.

JOHN: I take your point, and I see there is much good in what you refer to.

CAROL: . . . do you think so . . . ?

JOHN: . . . but, and this is not to say that I cannot change, in those things in which I am deficient . . . But, the . . .

CAROL: Do you hold yourself harmless from the charge of sexual exploitativeness . . . ? *(Pause)*

JOHN: Well, I . . . I . . . I . . . You know I, as I said. I . . . think I am not too old to *learn*, and I *can* learn, I . . .

CAROL: Do you hold yourself innocent of the charge of . . .

JOHN: . . . wait, wait, wait . . . All right, let's go back to . . .

CAROL: YOU FOOL. Who do you think I am? To come here and be taken in by a *smile*. You little yapping fool. You think I want "revenge." I don't want revenge. I WANT UNDERSTANDING.

JOHN: . . . *do* you?

CAROL: I do. *(Pause)*

JOHN: What's the use. It's over.

CAROL: Is it? What is?

JOHN: My job.

CAROL: Oh. Your job. That's what you want to talk about. *(Pause)* *(She starts to leave the room. She steps and turns back to him.)* All right. *(Pause)* What if it were possible that my Group withdraws its complaint. *(Pause)*

JOHN: What?

CAROL: That's right. *(Pause)*

JOHN: Why.

CAROL: Well, let's say as an act of friendship.

JOHN: An act of friendship.

CAROL: Yes. *(Pause)*

JOHN: In exchange for what.

CAROL: Yes. But I don't think, "exchange." Not "in exchange." For what do we derive from it? *(Pause)*

JOHN: "Derive."

CAROL: Yes.

JOHN: *(Pause)* Nothing. *(Pause)*

CAROL: That's right. We derive nothing. *(Pause)* Do you see that?

JOHN: Yes.

CAROL: That is a little word, Professor. "Yes." "I see that." But you will.

JOHN: And you might speak to the committee . . . ?

CAROL: To the committee?

JOHN: Yes.

CAROL: Well. Of course. That's on your mind. We might.

JOHN: "If" what?

CAROL: "Given" what. Perhaps. I think that that is more friendly.

JOHN: GIVEN WHAT?

CAROL: And, believe me, I understand your rage. It is not that I don't feel it.

But I do not see that it is deserved, so I do not resent it . . . . . All right. I have a list.

JOHN: . . . a list.

CAROL: Here is a list of books, which we . . .

JOHN: . . . a list of books . . . ?

CAROL: That's right. Which we find questionable.

JOHN: What?

CAROL: Is this so bizarre . . . ?

JOHN: I can't believe . . .

CAROL: It's not necessary you believe it.

JOHN: Academic freedom . . .

CAROL: Someone chooses the books. If you can choose them, others can. What are you, "God"?

JOHN: . . . no, no, the "dangerous." . . .

CAROL: You have an agenda, we have an agenda. I am not interested in your feelings or your motivation, but your actions. If you would like me to speak to the Tenure Committee, here is my list. You are a Free Person, you decide. (*Pause*)

JOHN: Give me the list. (*She does so. He reads.*)

CAROL: I think you'll find . . .

JOHN: I'm capable of reading it. Thank you.

CAROL: We have a number of *texts* we need re . . .

JOHN: I see that.

CAROL: We're amenable to . . .

JOHN: Aha. Well, let me look over the . . . (He reads.)

CAROL: I think that . . .

JOHN: LOOK. I'm reading your demands. All right?! *(He reads) (Pause)* You want to ban my book?

CAROL: We do not . . .

JOHN *(Of list)*: It says here . . .

CAROL: . . . We want it removed from inclusion as a representative example of the university.

JOHN: Get out of here.

CAROL: If you put aside the issues of personalities.

JOHN: Get the fuck out of my office.

CAROL: No, I think I would reconsider.

JOHN: . . . you think you can.

CAROL: We can and we *will*. Do you want our support? That is the only quest . . .

JOHN: . . . to ban my *book* . . .

CAROL: . . . that is correct . . .

JOHN: . . . this . . . this is a university . . . we . . .

CAROL: . . . and we have a statement. . . . which we need you to . . . *(She hands him a sheet of paper.)*

JOHN: No, no. It's out of the question. I'm sorry. I don't know what I was thinking of. I want to tell you something. I'm a teacher. I am a teacher. Eh? It's my *name* on the door, and *I* teach the class, and that's what I do. I've got a book with my name on it. And my son will *see* that *book* someday. And I have a respon . . . No, I'm sorry I have a *responsibility* . . . to *myself*, to my *son*, to my *profession* . . . I haven't been *home* for two days, do you know that? Thinking this out.

CAROL: . . . you haven't?

JOHN: I've been, no. If it's of interest to you. I've been in a *hotel. Thinking. (The phone starts ringing.) Thinking* . . .

CAROL: . . . you haven't been home?

JOHN: . . . *thinking*, do you see.

CAROL: Oh.

JOHN: And, and, I owe you a debt, I see that now. *(Pause)* You're *dangerous*, you're *wrong* and it's my *job* . . . to say no to you. That's my job. You are absolutely right. You want to ban my book? Go to *hell*, and they can do whatever they want to me.

CAROL: . . . you haven't been home in two days . . .

JOHN: I think I told you that.

CAROL: . . . you'd better get that phone. *(Pause)* I think that you should pick up the phone. *(Pause)*

*(*JOHN *picks up the phone.)*

JOHN (on *phone)*: Yes. *(Pause)* Yes. Wh . . . I. I. I had to be away. All ri . . . did they wor . . . did they worry ab . . . No. I'm all right, now, Jerry. I'm f . . . I got a little turned *around*, but I'm *sitting* here and . . . I've got it figured out. I'm fine. I'm fine don't worry about me. I got a little bit mixed up. But I am not sure that it's not a blessing. It cost me my job? Fine. Then the job was not worth having. Tell Grace that I'm coming home and everything is fff . . . *(Pause)* What? *(Pause)* *What? (Pause)* What do you *mean?* WHAT? Jerry . . . Jerry. They . . . Who, who, what can they do . . . ? *(Pause)* NO. *(Pause)* NO. They can't do th . . . What do you mean? *(Pause)* But how . . . *(Pause)* She's, she's, she's *here* with me. To . . . Jerry. I don't underst . . . *(Pause) (He hangs up.) (To* CAROL:) What does this mean?

CAROL: I thought you knew.

JOHN: What. (*Pause*) What does it mean. (*Pause*)

CAROL: You tried to rape me. (*Pause*) According to the law. (*Pause*)

JOHN: . . . what . . . ?

CAROL: You tried to rape me. I was leaving this office, you "pressed" yourself into me. You "pressed" your body into me.

JOHN: . . . I . . .

CAROL: My Group has told your lawyer that we may pursue criminal charges.

JOHN: . . . no . . .

CAROL: . . . under the statute. I am told. It was battery.

JOHN: . . . no . . .

CAROL: Yes. And attempted rape. That's right. (*Pause*)

JOHN: I think that you should go.

CAROL: Of course. I thought you knew.

JOHN: I have to talk to my lawyer.

CAROL: Yes. Perhaps you should.

(*The phone rings again.*) (*Pause*)

JOHN: (*Picks up phone. Into phone:*) Hello? I . . . Hello . . .? I . . . Yes, he just called. No . . . I. I can't talk to you now, Baby. (*To* CAROL:) Get out.

CAROL: . . . your wife . . . ?

JOHN: . . . who it is is no concern of yours. Get out. (*To phone:*) No, no, it's going to be all right. I. I can't talk now, Baby. (*To* CAROL:) Get out of here.

CAROL: I'm going.

JOHN: Good.

CAROL (*exiting*): . . . and don't call your wife "baby."

JOHN: What?

CAROL: Don't call your wife baby. You heard what I said.

(CAROL *starts to leave the room.* JOHN *grabs her and begins to beat her.*)

JOHN: You vicious little bitch. You think you can come in here with your political correctness and destroy my life?

(*He knocks her to the floor.*)

After how I treated you . . . ? You should be . . . *Rape you . . . ?* Are you kidding me . . . ?

(He picks up a chair, raises it above his head, and advances on her.)

I wouldn't touch you with a ten-foot pole. You little *cunt* . . .

(She cowers on the floor below him. Pause. He looks down at her. He lowers the chair. He moves to his desk, and arranges the papers on it. Pause. He looks over at her.)

. . . well . . .

(Pause. She looks at him.)

CAROL: Yes. That's right.
    (She looks away from him, and lowers her head. To herself:) . . . yes. That's right.

END

CONSTRUCTING A READING

Readings and Feelings
1. In your journal, describe at least one place in the text when you sympathize with each character. Then, try to explain the reasons for your sympathy. Your reason might be broad and general (like gender, age, or student status) or as specific as a childhood memory—try to give as full and clear an account of it as you can.
2. How do you respond to the rapid dialogue? Can you follow it? Does it seem to you like the conversations you have with your teachers? Does it remind you of a TV talk show? Conversations with your family? A Woody Allen film? *Oedipus the King?* What effect do you think Mamet intended to achieve with this dialogue?
3. Write in your journal about your response to one of the phrases that follows. Have you ever felt this way? When and why?
   • I don't understand.
   • I did what you told me.
   • We confuse the *usefulness* of higher education with our, granted, right to equal access to the same.
   • Education is prolonged and systematic hazing.
   • What does it profit me?
   • Did you come to college to learn something that you did not know?
   • I think you're angry.
   • I have to pass it.
   • How can I go back and tell them the *grades?*

- . . . and I walk around. From morning to night: with this one thought in my head. I'm *stupid*.

Gaps
1. Why does John
   - say, "I'm not your father"?
   - stop talking and begin to write when he comes to the idea of economic betterment?
   - say that surprise can be a form of aggression?
2. Why does Carol
   - repeat John's use of "profit" in Act 3?
   - demand that John define the terms he uses?
   - join her group?
3. Make your own list of the gaps you experience in this text.

World
1. With your group, discuss the information that a reader who has never been to college might need to understand this play.
2. This play originally opened within a year of the Clarence Thomas/Anita Hill hearings. Look up the coverage of these hearings (which occurred in October 1991) in a big-city newspaper or national newsmagazine and familiarize yourself with what went on. With your group, discuss the connections you perceive between the hearings and the play.
3. "Oleanna" is the name of a folk song written by Pete Seeger and Alan Lomax. Mamet provides the lyrics of one stanza of this song at the beginning of his script. Thinking of these lyrics as world for Mamet's play, describe how they affect your reading.
4. With your group members, talk about why you have come to college. Note differences in people's answers and try to find reasons for them. Consider as well what college means to other people who are important to you—parents, siblings, friends, significant others.

Thematizing
1. John defines *term of art* as "a *term*, which has come, through its use, to mean something *more specific* than the words would, to someone not acquainted with them, indicate." Think about this definition in terms of some of the conflicts in the play. Then try, with your group members, to construct "term of art" as a theme in this text.
2. Look up the phrase *white man's burden* in an unabridged dictionary. Try, with your group members, to construct a reading in which "white man's burden" is a theme in this play.
3. Look up the term *easement* in an unabridged dictionary. Try, with your group members, to construct a reading in which "easement" is a theme in this play.

4. John speaks of testing and grading as conventional processes to which both parties agree. Later, Carol compares the Tenure Committee's decision to the conventional processes of grading and testing. Do you think her analogy is apt? Try, with your group members, to construct a reading in which "consensual conventional judgment" is a theme in the play.

Narrative

1. John says to Carol: "I'll tell you a story about myself. Do you mind? I was raised to think myself stupid. That's what I want to tell you." Apply the definition of "minimal story" to John's narrative about thinking himself stupid. What point is he trying to make? What does he want Carol to learn from his story?
2. "When I was young somebody told me, are you ready, the rich copulate less often than the poor. But when they do, they take more of their clothes off." Think about this story of John's as the expression of an ideology. What might the story have meant to the person who told it to John? What do you think it means to John? to Carol?
3. In Act 3, Carol says: "and you sit there, and you tell me *stories*. About your house, about all the private schools, and about *privilege*, and how you are entitled . . ." What do his stories say to you about John? What does her response to them say about Carol?

Narrative Perspectives

1. How does Mamet make Carol sympathetic? Unsympathetic? Make a list of lines that make you like or dislike her.
2. How does Mamet make John sympathetic? Unsympathetic? Again, make a list of the lines that evoke your response.
3. Are there times in your reading when you sympathize with both of the characters at once, or with neither? Point to them and explain your response.

Now, view the film, *Oleanna*, written and directed by David Mamet.

CONSTRUCTING A READING

1. Write in your journal for a few minutes about how this visual reading affects your emotions. Specifically, consider whether your visual reading is different from your reading of the printed text. That is, do you sympathize more with one or the other character in the film than you did on your first (print) reading?
2. Think about the visual version of *Oleanna* as a "re-reading" of the printed text by its author. When David Mamet directed the film, in other words, he interpreted the play he had written a few years earlier. What differences do you find?

3. Can you determine, from the film, whose "side" the author wants you to take? Compare your answers with those of your classmates.

4. Consider the costumes of John and Carol. How does costuming affect your responses to them?

5. Is the procedure for distributing grades at your school like the one at Carol and John's? If not, how do you account for the difference? In other words, what does Mamet achieve by setting up a scene in which students line up to get their mid-term grades from a secretary? Does he lose anything?

6. Listen carefully to the lyrics of the song that is heard during the opening and closing credits. How do you respond to the song lyrics?

7. How do you respond to the visual beginning of the film? Does the red brick building look like the buildings at your school? What kind of mood is it designed to evoke?

8. The play opens with Carol already in John's office, whereas the film begins with Carol picking up her grades. Does the difference affect your sympathy in any way? How or why not?

Conventions of the Review

When *Oleanna* was presented on the New York stage in 1992, it created quite a stir. *The New Yorker* for November 16, 1992 included a review by John Lahr, one of the magazine's drama critics. I ask you to look at it for two reasons: first to familiarize yourself with some of the conventions of the genre called "review," and next, to perceive the review itself as a text to be interpreted. As you read, ask yourself *what* Lahr says in his review as well as *how* he says it. *What he says* will (I hope) prompt you to enter the conversation; *how he says it* will give you a sense of the review's conventions.

For example, Lahr begins by stating that the play is about envy. A statement of the work's theme is a generic convention—part of the "how"—of a review of that work. The assertion that the theme is *envy* is part of the "what" of Lahr's review. If you disagree with Lahr's thematization of envy, or with how he supports it, you might be interested in presenting your own view. Or, you might agree with it, but for other reasons than the ones he presents. In either case, the manner in which he makes his reading of the play will have drawn you into conversation with him about it. As you read the review, mark passages with which you agree, with which you disagree, or that you do not understand.

Dogma Days

John Lahr

David Mamet understands that envy is the gasoline on which a competitive society runs, and no modern American playwright has been bolder or more brilliant in analyzing its corrosive social effects. In his most recent play, "Oleanna," at the Orpheum, Mamet returns to this theme but stages it in the upwardly mobile arena of university life. Here a sense of shaming humiliation at ignorance becomes the subtext of Mamet's powerful dissection of political correctness. John, a teacher with bona-fide intellectual credentials, tries to help Carol, a student who is paralyzed by her sense of inadequacy. "I don't *understand.* I don't *understand.* I don't understand what anything means. . . . I'm stupid," she says. Mamet is shrewdly setting the stage for the bracingly unfashionable notion of a woman harassing a man. What finally humiliates Carol is not so much her ignorance as his prowess. The battle that ensues brings the audience up against the awful spoiling power of envy disguised as political ideology. Carol ends up trashing the professor's life. To offer a story that risks the hue and cry of underclass ideologues is typical of Mamet's curmudgeonly brilliance. It's the theatrical equivalent of pulling to an inside straight, and Mamet, with his great narrative gifts, accomplishes it deftly, with a competent assist from two of his ever-expanding family of performers, William H. Macy and his new wife, the British-born Rebecca Pidgeon.

Mamet likes to jump the audience into the middle of a dramatic situation, and let it piece together the jigsaw of the story from the tantalizing chunks of speech his characters scatter around the stage. Here we encounter the professor on the phone, trying to close on the new house that is the first fruit of his tenure (newly granted but not yet confirmed). Across the stage, Carol, turned away from him, sits morosely on a bench. John is all orders and authority; Carol is subservience in a schmatte. Carol has arrived for an unscheduled appointment, and her professor is obviously in a rush. "Words are acts," Mamet has written, and when John and Carol finally talk to each other the authority both of John's position and of his knowledge makes the gap between them almost unbridgeable. John brusquely cuts through Carol's tentative opening questions. "Let's take the mysticism out of it," he says, sternly trying to teach Carol how to negotiate and to think like an adult. The line haunts the evening. Mystification of power is precisely the point on which John will be shafted. Carol has no apparent powers of analysis—something John demonstrates by reading a snatch of her failing essay. "'I think that the ideas contained in this work express the author's feelings in away that he intended, based on his results,'" he says, and breaks off in understandable professorial frustration. "What can that mean?" Carol asks the same question, not just about his lectures but about his language. Carol continually interrupts the discourse for definitions of John's educated vocabulary. Words like "predilection," "paradigm," "transpire" throw her. She demands meaning but hasn't the language to define her feelings to herself or to the world. Her adamant dimness is rightly interpreted by John as anger. In their stutter-speech, which Mamet orchestrates with overlapping rhythms, interjected phrases, emotional retreats, and attempted advances, the drama of their missed communication is made transparent and startling. No American playwright is more expert than Mamet at externalizing the sludge of consciousness and dramatizing both the meaning and the music in our stammerings:

> CAROL: I'm just: I sit in class I . . . I take notes . . .
> JOHN (*simultaneously with "notes"*): Yes. I understand. What I am trying to *tell* you is that some, some basic . . .
> CAROL: . . . I . . .
> JOHN: . . .one moment: some basic missed communi . . .
> CAROL: No, no, no. I'm doing what I'm told. It's *difficult* . . .
> JOHN: . . . but . . .
> CAROL: I don't . . . lots of the *language* . . .
> JOHN: . . . please . . .
> CAROL: The *language*, the "things" that you say . . .
> JOHN: I'm sorry. No. I don't think that that's true.
> CAROL: It *is* true. I . . .
> JOHN: I think . . .
> CAROL: It *is* true.

By making Carol's situation so immediately poignant, Mamet sets a cunning trap for the sympathies of the audience. "*Teach* me. *Teach* me," she pleads, with that combination of fierce vacancy and ambition which distinguishes the American undergraduate. "I'm not your *father,*" says John, who is nonetheless put in a parental role by her show of powerlessness. Carol literally calls out John's power. She has no command of language, no knowledge, no psychological understanding. But she has the pedigree of the underprivileged:

> CAROL: It *is* true. I have problems.
> JOHN: . . . every . . .
> CAROL: . . . I come from a different social . . .
> JOHN: . . . ev . . .
> CAROL: a different . . .
> JOHN: . . . Look:
> CAROL: No. I: when I *came* to this school:
> JOHN: Yes. quite . . .
> CAROL: . . . does that mean nothing . . . ?

The issue of class does mean something to John. From their different positions in the pecking order, he has arrived at the secure place Carol wants a university education to get her to. After twenty years on the tenure track, John is now set to move into the upper middle class and to shift his son from public to private school. He interrupts their talk to make a note to himself about the school tax. "Is it a law that I have to improve the city schools at the expense of my own interest?" says John, whose liberality is confined to the classroom, and doesn't extend to society. "Is this not simply 'The White Man's Burden'?" John recognizes in Carol not only the same class struggle he underwent but the same educational struggle. His career in academe and his iconoclastic views on education are his revenge on early learning difficulties, which he spells out to Carol to assuage her panic. He immediately names her feeling of humiliation, and later shows her the dynamic of her terror, saying, "Why was I born to be the laughingstock of a world in which everyone is better than I? In which I am entitled to nothing. Where I can not learn." He is pedantic but decent. "Men are the puppydogs of the universe," Mamet wrote in his essay collection, "Some Freaks." And so John seems. He takes Carol's failure as his own, and in a rush of pedagogic vainglory he throws away the offending essay, takes up her educational challenge, and gives her a comradely hug. John becomes a latter-day Professor Higgins, offering to recap the course for her in private tutorials, and easing her anxiety about grades by promising her an A. When Carol asks why he's doing this for her, he replies, "I like you."

John, like Mamet, is a self-styled provocateur; he holds to the antique notion that education should encourage thought, and argues that the job of a teacher is to provoke. "To make me mad is your job?" says his incredulous, pragmatic pupil. John is a bit of a wag. He swaggers in speech, and the idioms that Carol finds impenetrable are metaphoric turns of phrase that intelligently tease received opinion about higher education. He talks of college as "warehousing of the young," as something that prolongs adolescence; refers to tests as "hazing"; and, like the American sociologist Thorstein Veblen, whose argument about higher learning Mamet cunningly glosses, characterizes university education as a "ritual" of "something-other-than-useful"—what Veblen called "a by-product of the priestly vicarious leisure class." Carol is a zealot who, having got educational religion, can't comprehend backsliders. As the audience soon discovers, John's skepticism about education marks him as a heretic.

When John and Carol square off in Act II, John is no longer the master, although at first he fondly thinks he is. His power and his blocking have changed. He sits face to face with Carol, who is now dressed in greens and blacks that hint at the paramilitary, and tries to shortcut procedure by reasoning her out of her accusations of sexism, racism, and elitism before the Tenure Committee reconvenes, by which time he will have lost his new house and his deposit. "You think, you think you can deny that these things happened; or, if they *did*, if they *did*, that they meant what you *said* they meant," Carol says. Every gesture in Act I, every exchange, every idea has been taken out of context and turned into an indictment. "What gives you the *right*," she says, in highest dudgeon, "to speak to a woman in your private, yes. Yes. I'm sorry. I'm sorry. You feel yourself empowered. . . . To *strut*. To *posture*. . . . And *confess* to a taste to play the *Patriarch* in your class. To grant *this*. To deny *that*. To embrace—your students." Mamet puts the audience exactly where John sits: up against it. Such is the power of Mamet's storytelling that the audience receives each willful misinterpretation like a body blow, audibly catching its breath at Carol's argument. Carol, who lacked words before, has got educated in a hurry by what she refers to as her Group, and she speaks now with the righteous fervor of a woman whose day has come. This transition is jarring but intentional. She has acquired a new voice and a new vocabulary, whose authority precludes ambiguity. She adopts political correctness as an intellectual carapace that substitutes dogma for thought, mission for mastery. Naming is claiming, and since Carol won't work to master a world she can't comprehend, she changes the frame of reference to a world she can. She advocates a kind of linguistic affirmative action, forcing John to define "paradigm," for example. "It's a model," he says. Carol counters, sharpish, "Then why can't you use that word?" And later, when she requires a simpler definition for the word "transpire," she rounds on John with the full malice of her envy, offering "happen" as an alternative. "Then *say* it. For Christ's sake. Who the *hell* do you think that you are? You want a post. You want unlimited power. To do and to say what you want. As it pleases you—Testing, Questioning, Flirting." This policing of language leads inevitably to a policing of the curriculum. Carol holds out the possibility of reprieve from the Tenure Committee if he'll agree to a new reading list, from which his book, among many, has been banned. "If you can choose them, others can," Carol tells him. "What are you, God?" Here, in a series of exchanges, Mamet exposes the central paradox of political correctness, which demands diversity in everything but thought.

Carol remains staunch. She is the embodiment of Mamet's mischievous assertion that "women don't give a tinker's damn about being well-liked, which means they don't know how to compromise." Carol's rigidity is a sign of her insecurity. Her ruthless orthodoxy is skillfully shown as her means of controlling her enormous anxiety of ignorance. In this production, the intelligence of Rebecca Pidgeon, who plays Carol, makes it hard to suspend disbelief in her academic ineptness but also makes her puritan willfulness powerfully credible. Dressed now, in the last of their three encounters, in a loose-fitting black jacket, green chinos, and sensible black shoes, and peering out from behind wire-rimmed glasses, Carol stands above John like some Maoist enforcer. By this last scene, it is the student who is dishing out the humiliation to the professor, calling him a "little yapping fool." William H. Macy plays John with droll liberal long-suffering. He's slow to kindle, but when Carol interprets as rape his attempt to keep her in the room to settle their disagreement ("I was leaving this office, you 'pressed' yourself into me. You 'pressed' your body into me") he finally ignites. A telephone call from his wife interrupts the final argument. "I can't talk now, baby," John says, and then orders Carol out of the office. "Don't call your wife 'baby,'" she says. It is Mamet's shrewdly placed parting shot. The throw-away line turns out to be the last straw. John belts Carol around the room. The explosion of violence sends both Carol and John's academic career crashing.

Because of the limits of the scope and intention in this short polemical play, "Oleanna" may not belong to the major part of Mamet's canon, but it's a powerful, exciting play that shows off his enormous skills as a writer. The production, however, reveals his limitations as a director. The actors' job, according to Mamet, "is to accomplish *beat by beat,* as simply as possible, the specific action set out for them by the script and the director." Both Mr. Macy and Ms. Pidgeon are a bit under wraps here, at once awed and cowed by Mamet's authority, which takes some of the acting oxygen out of the air. In this, Mamet joins the likes of Samuel Beckett and Harold Pinter, whose literary touch was always much surer than their directorial hand. Mamet keeps his show clean and crisp, but leaves a lot of production values still to be explored in the many other versions that "Oleanna" will certainly have.

On the night I saw it, the play was already doing its work in the world as the audience filed out of the theatre; it was a drizzly evening, and people clustered under the Orpheum Theatre marquee to keep talking.

"Too bad he had to have a woman be the heavy," one matron said.

"He's a bit of a misogynist," her friend said, and then turned to a stooped man who was obviously her husband. "what do you think?"

"No one escaped sin in the Garden of Eden," the man said—an acid thought, in keeping with the evenhanded skepticism of the play, and one that echoed something Mamet had written elsewhere about corruption. "The corrupted person, politician, parent, doctor, and artist offer us two choices," he said in "Some Freaks." "To accept them and their presumption of power *totally,* or to reject them *totally* and, so, realize that we have been cruelly duped and accept the humiliation, anger, and despair that realization entails." "Oleanna" bravely makes the audience own the ambiguity of its idealism.

My friend Liz and I walked away talking about the play's title, which is never mentioned. Liz remembered the old Pete Seeger/Alan Lomax song about a world turned upside down—song as oblique, and as knowing, as the play. The last stanza goes:

> So if you'd like a happy life,
> To Oleana you must go,
> The poorest man from the old country
> Becomes a king in a year or so.

After asserting that "envy" is the theme of the play, Lahr recounts the narrative.

> John, a teacher with bona-fide intellectual credentials, tries to help Carol, a student who is paralyzed by her sense of inadequacy . . . Mamet is . . .setting the stage for the bracingly unfashionable notion of a woman harassing a man. . . . Carol ends up trashing the professor's life. . . .

Recounting the narrative, then, is another part of the *how* of a review. And, in that recounting, the reviewer inevitably reveals his or her interpretation of the story. Lahr would seem to side with John: (he has "bona-fide intellectual credentials," whereas Carol "is paralyzed by her sense of inadequacy.") Much of the rest of Lahr's review is devoted to presenting support for his reading and elaborating his responses to the story.

Next, Lahr infers, from his account of and response to the story, what Mamet intended to do, the effect he must have intended to create.

> To offer a story that risks the hue and cry of underclass ideologues is typical of Mamet's curmudgeonly brilliance.

On the basis of his "reading" of Mamet's intention, Lahr then evaluates the text. He makes a judgment, in other words, about whether Mamet succeeded in realizing the intention that Lahr has ascribed to him.

> *Oleanna* may not belong to the major part of Mamet's canon, but it's a powerful, exciting play that shows off his enormous skills as a writer.

In order to arrive at his statement of theme, to retell the narrative, and to evaluate the play, John Lahr engaged in the same acts of reading that we have been discussing in the last seven chapters: he experienced an emotional response to John and Carol, he identified gaps about their motivation, he constructed a world in contemporary culture, he followed differing narrative perspectives, he constructed a theme, and he perceived intertextuality. Lahr sympathizes with John, finding him "pedantic but decent," and finding Carol guilty of harassing her teacher and of lacking "the language to define her feelings to herself and to the world." Lahr finds world for this text in the writings of the sociologist Thorstein Veblen, in the folk song, "Oleanna," and in the public discussions of what he calls "political correctness." As support for his assertions, Lahr quotes from the script.

Notice that, in assuming that what he reads is the author's intention, Lahr makes a move that I have cautioned you against. Let's unpack the logic here: Lahr seems to be saying, "I'm a good reader (or audience member), and I define good reading as grasping the author's intention. What I perceive as the meaning of this play (what it means to me), therefore, is what Mamet intended." In this book, we have used a contradictory assumption: that readers construct meaning that may or may not be identical to the author's intention. It is, I think, worth noting that Lahr's process is the same as the one Carol uses in her paper; she writes, "I think that the ideas contained in this work express the author's feelings in a way that he intended, based on his results." For this, Carol receives a failing grade from John. For his speculation, John Lahr is published in a national magazine. With your teacher and your group, talk about this situation. Can you perceive differences between John Lahr and Carol? If so, what are they? If not, how does that circumstance affect your reading of the play and the review?

CONSTRUCTING A READING OF A READING

1. Lahr asserts that Carol speaks with "that combination of fierce vacancy and ambition which distinguishes the American undergraduate." Do you agree with this description of Carol? Do you think it an accurate description of you? Why or why not?
2. What does the word "mystification" mean in this context? Do you agree with Lahr that the "mystification of power is precisely the point on which John will be shafted"?
3. Lahr's comparison between John and Professor Higgins is an allusion to George Bernard Shaw's *Pygmalion* and/or Loerner and Loewe's *My Fair Lady*. In both plays, Professor Higgins tries (successfully) to make the speech patterns of a Cockney flower seller named Eliza Doolittle sound like those of an upper class English woman. Higgins then falls in love with the "Eliza" whom he has created. Is Lahr's comparison apt, in your view?
4. Explain in your own words Lahr's contention that

   John . . . swaggers in speech, and the idioms that Carol finds impenetrable are the metaphoric turns of phrase that intelligently tease received opinion about higher education. He talks of college as "warehousing of the young," as something that prolongs adolescence; refers to tests as "hazing"; and . . . characterizes university education as a "ritual of "something-other-than-useful"–what [sociologist Thorstein] Veblin called "a by-product of the priestly vicarious leisure class."

5. Do you agree that Carol's "ruthless orthodoxy is skillfully shown as her means of controlling her enormous anxiety of ignorance"? Why or why not?

The following reading of *Oleanna* differs substantially from Lahr's. Elaine Showalter's review of the play appeared in *The London Times Literary Supplement* on November 6, 1992 as part of a longer essay in which she also reviewed Mamet's film *Glengarry Glen Ross*. Look for differences between Showalter's and Lahr's contributions to the conversation. Then, with your group members, try to explain why Showalter, a university professor in the field of women's studies who has written extensively about feminism, sees what she sees.

Acts of Violence
David Mamet and the Language of Men

Elaine Showalter

It's in *Oleanna* (subtitled "A Power Play"), where the Mamet techniques are stretched to cover larger and more complex social issues, that the limitations of his talent become clear. There are two programme graphics for *Oleanna;* one shows a seated man with a target on his chest, the other a targeted woman. He is John (William H. Macy), a middle-aged professor who has just been recommended for tenure, and is in the process of buying a house, a premise which allows Mamet to make more real-estate gags and to interject some amusing one-sided phone conversations. She is Carol (Rebecca Pidgeon), a failing student who comes to his office, ostensibly to argue about her grade on a paper. Sexless and childlike in a baggy dress worn over two pairs of long underwear, Carol anxiously protests that she has not understood anything of John's lectures, and not a word of his book. At first preoccupied, self-centred and harsh, John gradually is moved by (and identifies with) her desperation, her hopeless incomprehension, her slavish note-taking, her sense of being stupid and out-of-place; he offers to wipe her failing grades from the slate, and to tutor her in his office. Recklessly, he promises her an A in the course, and in answer to her persistent, wide-eyed questions, confides that he too had difficulties in school, that he too has problems—with his wife, with his job—and that he does not feel contempt for her ignorance, but likes her. When she seems to break down in despair, he attempts to comfort her with a hug, from which she springs away with a start. Carol's attempts to express herself and, at one point, to confide in John, are interrupted, either by the telephone, or by his educational theorizing. At another point, he uses a tasteless sexual metaphor: "The rich copulate less than the poor but they take off more of their clothes."

But by Act II, it appears that the scene we have witnessed, in which the professor is vain and foolish, but basically well-intentioned, and the student is more worried about grades than about learning, but basically grateful for the professor's effort to help, was not at all what we had supposed. Carol has made charges to John's tenure committee that she has been the victim of sexual harassment. She has rewritten the narrative of Act I in the most sinister terms—a man having problems with his wife has made sexual overtures, and promised her an A in his course if she will meet privately with him in his office. She now reappears alone, at his extremely unwise and unrealistic request, to listen with unshakable self-righteousness to his efforts to sort things out.

While in Act I she could barely understand words like "paradigm" and "transpire," Carol is now given to solemn polysyllabic oratory on questions of legal propriety, class exploitation and academic morality. Boyishly dressed in a little vest and trousers, she sits primly in a straight-backed chair, writing John's remarks in a blue ledger like a recording angel. And where before she seemed isolated and waif-like, in contrast to John, who has a wife and son, now she is the representative of an unidentified "group," in whose name she makes her accusations. When she insists on leaving, John, who seems not to have figured out what he is up against, attempts to hold her back.

By Act III, she has called this gesture an act of attempted rape; his tenure has been revoked; and he is about to lose his job. Their roles are reversed; he is dishevelled, in his shirtsleeves, and distraught; she is calm and neatly garbed in a man's suit. His pleas for human sympathy are met first with her sermons about his cynicism and elitism, and then with a proposal: if he will accept her group's list of books to be removed from the reading list, including his own, she will withdraw her charges. On a realistic level, it's an absurd situation; even in the dire terms of the play, such a demand could immediately backfire on the accuser, while the withdrawal of criminal charges would not bring instant rein-statement. But instead of handing the blacklist to his lawyer, his supporters, the press and the union, John makes an impassioned speech in favour of freedom of thought, and, after a final taunt from Carol, the play ends with a long-antici-pated act of violence (the programme credits a Fight Director), which, though not calculated to help John's legal position, certainly provides a much-desired catharsis for the audience. As the man sitting next to me commented, "I nearly climbed up on the stage to kick the shit out of the little bitch myself," and while various New York reviewers remarked on the unusual phenomenon of audience members shouting one-liners back to the actors, "Right on, sister!" was not among them.

It may safely be said that *Oleanna* is an involving theatrical experience, although the nature of that involvement is highly questionable. Frank Rich in the *New York Times* described *Oleanna* as Mamet's "impassioned response to the Thomas hearings," and told his readers to "imagine eavesdropping on a hypo-thetical, private Anita Hill–Clarence Thomas confrontation in an empty room," to get an idea of "what the playwright is aiming for and sometimes achieves." This is nonsense: the Hill–Thomas hearings, which continue to have unforeseen repercussions in American political life, constituted a social drama, played out before an audience of millions, in which the original conversations, a decade past, played a minor role. What the hearings displayed were the mas-sive inequalities of gender and race within American democracy, not the com-munication problems of two conservative, upwardly-mobile African-American lawyers. And, of course, Thomas was confirmed and took his seat, for life, on the Supreme Court.

Mamet himself has explained that he drafted the play eight months before the Hill–Thomas hearings, drawing on the experience of a college teacher friend who had been "the target of a sexual harassment charge," but pulled it out of the drawer while they were going on. Asked by the *New York Times* what had drawn him to the subject to begin with, Mamet replied, "That's like asking Capa why he took pictures of war."

These combative metaphors make clear why *Oleanna* does indeed exploit the audience's reservoir of emotion from the Hill–Thomas hearings, or from other widely publicized cases of sexual harassment. Like Strindberg's dramas of sexual combat, or Patrick Buchanan's anti-feminist rantings ("a socialist, anti-family political movement that encourages women to leave their husbands, kill their children, practice witchcraft, destroy capitalism and become lesbians"), hyped-up charges of female vengeance and sexual warfare will readily tap a latent male rage, especially in *fin-de-siècle* periods of political confusion and economic decline. On the whole, critics have been too soft on Mamet's failure to distance himself from his characters' violence. An exception is David Van Leer, who noted in a prophetic essay in the *New Republic* in 1990 that "the racism, the sexism and the homophobia of his characters is not effectively defused by their author, and Mamet may seriously misjudge the psychological effect of so regularly venting those emotions in his work. . . The venom of Mamet's plays permits audiences to credit their own worst biases under the cover of moral distance."

Mamet expresses his own biases at some length in his essays as well as his plays; he believes, for example, that "women do not, on the whole, get *along* with women"; that "the true nature of the world, as between men and women, is sex, and any other relationship between us is either an elaboration, or an avoidance"; and that "the joy of male companionship is a quest for and can be an experience of *true* grace, and transcendent of the rational, and so, more approximate to the real nature of the world".

In the all-male plays, like *Glengarry Glen Ross*, even a feminist spectator can take pleasure in the dramatic conventions Mamet has developed to express this grace. But *Oleanna* gives Mamet little scope for his usual gifts. There's very little humour, and little of the staccato, aphasic obscenity which gives his dialogue its driving rhythms. Only in the ultimate confrontation ("Rape you? I wouldn't touch you with a ten-foot pole, you little cunt"), does he get to use the magic words. Moreover, his usual stylistic tricks—rhetorical questions, unfinished sentences, italics, pauses—fall flat because these characters do not speak the same language; they simply declaim to each other. Bill Macy, a long term associate of Mamet's who was in the original Chicago cast of *American Buffalo*, seems more at ease with the dialogue than Rebecca Pidgeon, Mamet's wife, although her failure to elicit any sympathy is more the playwright's problem than her own.

In making his female protagonist a dishonest, androgynous zealot, and his male protagonist a devoted husband and father who defends freedom of thought, Mamet does not exactly wrestle with the moral complexities of sexual harassment. What he has written is a polarizing play about a false accusation of sexual harassment, and that would be fair enough—false accusations of harassment, rape and child abuse indeed occur—if he were not claiming to present a balanced, Rashomon-like case. The disturbing questions about power, gender and paranoia raised in *Oleanna* cannot be resolved with an irrational act of violence.

CONSTRUCTING A READING OF ANOTHER READING

1. Like Lahr, Elaine Showalter recounts the story of the play. Even though both writers describe the same events, their narratives are markedly different. With your group members, apply the minimal story structure to both tellings. What differences do you turn up?
2. What do you think is Elaine Showalter's purpose in writing her review?
3. Showalter calls John's second act request for a meeting with Carol "extremely unwise and unrealistic," and asserts that the scene in which Carol presents John with a list of "suspect" books is "[o]n a realistic level . . . absurd. Even in the dire terms of the play, such a demand could immediately backfire on the accuser, while the withdrawal of criminal charges would not bring instant reinstatement." Do you agree? Why or why not? If the scene is unrealistic, why do you suppose Mamet used it?
4. Showalter concludes "in making his female protagonist a dishonest, androgynous zealot, and his male protagonist a devoted husband and father who defends freedom of thought, Mamet does not exactly wrestle with the moral complexities of sexual harassment." Does this judgment count as an evaluation of the play? If so, how? Trace Showalter's logic as I have traced Lahr's.

Generic Characteristics of Reviews

It's fair to assume (even from our very small sample) that a "review" of a play, film, or novel will usually contain a statement of theme, a recapitulation of the plot or content, and an evaluation. Reviews of texts (like some poems) that can't be said to have plots usually entail at least some description of the contents. When someone like Lahr publishes this review in a national publication like *The New Yorker*, he or she expects to be read by people who

1. are deciding whether to see the play;
2. have already seen it and wonder what he thought because
    they usually like what he likes
    they usually don't like what he likes
    they usually like what he doesn't like;
3. will probably never see the play but wonder what it's about.

Reviewers need to meet the needs of all three audiences by explaining as far as possible, within space constraints, how they arrived at their conclusions. We can "read" the reviewer's audience, then, by attending carefully to the review.

CONSTRUCTING A READING OF A READING

1. From what you've seen here, and/or what you may already know about *The New Yorker*, describe the economic and educational level of the audience Lahr addresses.
2. How would you describe the ways in which Lahr attends to his audience's needs and purposes? For example, do you see him as trying to help his readers decide whether to attend the play? (Where? How?) To interpret the play for those of his readers who have already seen it? (Where? How?) To enter a conversation with Mamet's many audiences? To show us how smart he is?
3. From what you've seen here, and what you may already know about readers of *The Times Literary Supplement*, describe the audience to whom Showalter is writing with respect to economic and educational level and politics with respect to feminism.

Other Voices: Less Formal Readings of *Oleanna*

In November 1992, *The New York Times* invited several authors to respond to *Oleanna*. Notice that these brief responses do not contain all of the generic conventions of review. They are more like the "constructing a reading" exercises throughout this book that have asked you to get your thoughts in order and (I hope) helped you to do so. These brief responses do not contain elaborate references to the text, and they often deal with only one or two acts of reading. They resemble such informal readings as letters and postings to listservs or websites.

Responses to *Oleanna*

Deborah Tannen

Author of *You Just Don't Understand; Women and Men in Conversation*

"Oleanna" isn't about sexual harassment. It is about the fear of witches: a woman lures a man by seeming helpless and feminine, then, after he becomes vulnerable by trying to help her, she destroys him.

There is no other way to understand the student Carol's unexplained transformation from the first half of "Oleanna" to the second. A soldier in a 17th-century play by Walter Charleton, "Ephesian Matron," addresses witches who "allure us with the fairness of your skins; and when folly hath brought us within your reach, you leap upon us and devour us."

There you have it: in the first act Carol is a shy, almost speechless young woman in a shapeless dress who wails that she sits smiling in a back corner in class but cannot understand anything because she's stupid. In the second she is an aggressively articulate, self-satisfied, theory-spouting caricature of a "feminist," dressed in man-styled trousers and vest. This witch turns the university into a dystopia where power relations are reversed and a woman student destroys an innocent man's life in the name of political correctness. *Vagina dentata* goes to college.

"Oleanna" would have us believe that Carol manipulated the professor by pretending to be vulnerable when she was really lying in wait to assault him. In fact, it is "Oleanna" that manipulates, pretending to be an honest play about the indeterminacy of language and abuse of power, then assaulting us with its simplistic and dehumanizing denouement.

Act I is Pinteresque, seemingly about the failure of communication, with endless repetitions of phrases like "I don't understand," unfinished sentences and broken-off words. Act II is Kafkaesque: the woman's unnamed "group," like a witches' coven, is out to get the lone professor, to pillory him for offenses he didn't know he committed, offenses the audience saw were minor.

Many men worry, "What would I do if someone brought a false charge against me? What remark have I made, in innocence, that could be misconstrued?" This tension could make a fascinating play—even a paranoid fantasy, for part of what art does is let us play out our nightmares, think through what we would do. But David Mamet doesn't touch these ambiguities. Carol is all surface: just a stereotype that audiences can join in hating.

The most dangerous aspect of the play is its ending: the professor beats the young woman, punching her, hurling her to the floor, cursing at her and lifting a chair to break over her head as she crawls under a bench and huddles in fetal position. The evening I saw the play, the audience cheered and urged him on. All over the country, battered women's shelters fill up as quickly as they're opened. Yet many people feel, "She probably provoked it; she probably was asking for it." In "Oleannna," these cruel misconceptions are given weight: a woman is beaten because she provoked it, she deserved it. Right now, we don't need a play that helps anyone feel good about a man beating a woman.

Mark Alan Stamaty

Creator of the comic strip "Washingtoon"

In this era of political correctness, "Oleanna" is "'Rambo' Meets P.C." And "Rambo" wins for both sensitivity and humanity. On one level, the play can appear to be a kind of Lady-or-Tiger Rorschach test, intended to stir equal empathy and argument from "both sides." If so, maybe I'm about to take the bait and expose myself as an unconscious sexist. But I think not.

Despite the possibly equal justification that Carol and John are given for their individual behaviors, this play *does* take sides. With John, the man. Carol and John both struggle and suffer. But John suffers more, and his suffering is far more palpably articulated. Like "Rambo" or "Rocky," John is abused to a breaking point and finally explodes. When he does—like "Rambo" or "Rocky"—the audience is with him emotionally.

"Well," says John, who has just hit, kicked and thrown Carol around his office in the climax of "Oleanna." John appears sheepish and possibly shocked by his brief explosion of violent rage.

"Yes, that's right! . . ." says Carol twice in the last line of the play, seeming to imply: "Yes, you *are* a monster!"

Men should not be physically violent to women. And vice versa. If a man is violent toward a woman on stage without it being declared evil, is that a recommendation to society? Or can it simply be viewed as theater, as thought, but not suggested action?

John certainly is pompous, arrogant and self-absorbed. And he has power over the academic lives and destinies of students like Carol, which he somewhat unconsciously abuses. But John attempts always to see his flaws and change. He has tried to find truth and humanness beyond false structures, but finally decided on survival in a world of hollow rituals and institutions that he sees through but seems unable to change.

Carol's flaw is her fanaticism. Faced with John's power and privilege, which she covets, and viewing his vulnerabilities simply as means by which to conquer, control and even destroy him, Carol increasingly exposes herself as single-mindedly obsessed with power. John's attitude toward power is more ambivalent. She becomes the villain, the automaton they both despise.

Despite Carol's effort in the play's last line to condemn John's final eruption, as if it were proof of his evil, John's attack against the automaton Carol has become is cathartic, an explosion of the humanness suffocating inside both of them.

Ellen Schwartzman

Vice president of the Student Government Association at Barnard College

"No—I don't understand. Do you see? I don't understand," says the student in "Oleanna," as she proclaims her view of academia. These words aptly describe my own amazement at David Mamet's new play.

As a woman in college, I'm concerned and disturbed by Mr. Mamet's Carol. Her sheer stupidity, marked in part by her inability to grasp basic ideas and vocabulary, such as "paradigm," or her constant whining reply, "I don't understand," combined with her ability to be swept away on a crusade for the destruction of a man's life (using twisted facts as evidence), provide a totally negative portrayal of women.

Carol is rapidly transformed from the imbecilic automaton of Act I to the vengeful calculating champion of female rights of Act II, as the audience witnesses a new McCarthyism—that of sexual harassment.

In some quarters, "Oleanna" has been called the consummate rejoinder to the controversy surrounding the Thomas–Hill hearings. But it is not. Rather, Mr. Mamet's treatment of sexual harassment does a disservice to the subject's seriousness.

The audience's focus is shifted from the supposed ambiguity surrounding some cases of sexual harassment at the same time that the author funnels blame onto the alleged victim for her hateful actions. Furthermore, Mr. Mamet does nothing to create sympathy for this militant flat female character, leaving viewers to side with no other than the alleged harasser, John.

In his version of the Thomas–Hill hearings, Mr. Mamet presents a plot devoid of ambiguity, while perpetuating a myth prevalent in American culture: harassment exists in the mind of the victim alone.

Lionel Tiger

Charles Darwin Professor of Anthropology at Rutgers University and author of *Men in Groups* and *The Pursuit of Pleasure*

"Oleanna" confronts two principal features of The New Improved American Puritanism. The Scarlet Letter is now affixed to men *and* women. And the university, not the church, is the arena for the most dogmatic assertions about how to live and think.

The play also explores the transformation of even personal behavior into symptoms of contemporary political currents. Touching a person's shoulder, calling a spouse "baby," as in the play, cause mighty accusations of fiery guilt. Eternal vigilance and self-censorship are the price of moral purity.

University women and men in particular perch on platforms paved with eggshells. The situation can be forbidding. While good institutions may cope sensibly and fairly with this rectitudinous zeal, there is clearly a broad deadening of controversy and variety about hot-button issues, such as sex and race. One result is that ludicrous, flat-earther assertions—Andrea Dworkin's, for example, that all heterosexual sex is rape—are taken with undue seriousness because they fit into a larger picture of a world alive with chronic exploitation and harassment.

Of course exploitation and harassment exist. "Oleanna" describes one extreme of the response to advantage taken unfairly. A female student, coached by her "group," secures the dismissal of a male instructor for acts, attitudes and sentences about which many audience members appeared to have more than reasonable doubts. But the audience vote is not the point. The case made against the male is internally consistent and sturdy, given the assumptions of current discussion. The main one is that men are predatory and women potential victims. The scarlet letter is ready and waiting.

The problem is that the main assumption is broadly correct. Presumably both women and men display lively enthusiasm for sexual congress (and even reproduction—after all, those pleasure centers had to evolve for a reason). Nevertheless, it is characteristic that males will press their sexual case and females determine their own responses. As biologists know now, females are the evolutionary gatekeepers of any species. So there is a difference of sexual strategy that is rather hard-wired and affects not only sexual behavior directly but also how people talk.

This angular strategic difference is in part what animates the current legal turmoil. To solve the problem compassionately, the underlying biology has to be appreciated. Otherwise the dialogue will continue in two separate languages, translated by yet more lawyers who speak a common language, which they adore to operate for a fee.

Only one moment in "Oleanna"—the very last—suggests this central force field, perhaps inadvertently. The stage direction is not in the script; the dramatic impact is unexpected. The male has struck the female. She is huddled under a bench. She peers at him across the turmoiled air. Foul aggression has occurred. Her case about his malevolence appears to have been proved. Then she slowly removes her granny glasses and *looks* at him. The first sexuality in the play, after the first knockdown. Grim. One mean play ends and a harsher one begins.

CONSTRUCTING A READING

1. Develop a chart or a computer graphic that details the differences among all these writings on *Oleanna* in terms of the acts of reading we've described in this book. For example, you might have a column labeled "theme," in which Lahr's "envy," Showalter's "false accusation of sexual harassment," Deborah Tannen's "fear of witches," and so on are juxtaposed. Perhaps another column, on narrative perspectives, could be labeled "descriptions of John," "descriptions of Carol." That column might feature Showalter's description of John as "preoccupied, self-centered, and harsh" while Lahr sees him as "pedantic but decent."

2. Ellen Schwartzman, who in 1992 was vice-president of the student government at Barnard College, is the only student author among these respondents. Ms. Schwartzman describes herself as disturbed by Carol's "stupidity." Do you find Carol stupid? If so, do you find her stupidity disturbing? If not, point to the evidence that prompts a different conclusion.

3. What do you think Mark Alan Stamaty means when he writes that "*Oleanna* is *Rambo* meets P.C."?

4. Do you agree with Lionel Tiger that "the university, not the church, is

the arena for the most dogmatic assertions about how to live and think"?
Do you think the play/film supports Tiger's assertion?

SHARING A READING

1. Using the generic characteristics that we have just established, write a
   review of the film *Oleanna* for one of the following audiences:
   • your school newspaper
   • your local paper at school
   • your local paper at home
   • the magazine of an organization to which you belong
2. Write a letter to the editor of *The London Times Literary Supplement, The
   New York Times,* or *The New Yorker,* responding to one or more of the
   reviews or responses to the play.
3. Write a letter to
   • a friend
   • your mother
   • an older friend or relative of the opposite sex
   in which you advise for or against seeing the film and explain your reasons.
4. Compose a reading of *Oleanna* (the film or the play) to be posted to a real
   or imaginary listserv subscribed to (or a website likely to be searched for)
   by
   • film buffs
   • Mamet fans
   • listeners to conservative radio talk shows
   • university professors
   • members of NOW
   • members of the ACLU.
5. Assume that you encounter any one of *The New York Times* responses on a
   listserv and write an answer to it.

THE ACADEMIC READING: ARTICLES
AND RESEARCH PAPERS

The academic article and its cousin, the research paper, are among the most
conventional genres in our culture. In the academic essay, as in the review, it is
important to explain how and why you arrive at your readings, and to argue for
them in such a way that your reader can, if he or she wishes, follow your reading
procedures. Like the review, a contribution to an academic conversation usually
interprets a text and renders a judgment of some kind about it. But unlike

reviews, academic papers are themselves subject to institutional judgment by one or more authoritative readers. Academic journals have a system called *peer review* in which other scholars in the author's field read a submitted article and decide whether it should be published. Often, these readers' criteria concern such issues as whether the article contains an "original" contribution to scholarship, whether and how it supports its position(s) and whether it is "readable." College research papers are submitted to teachers, many of whom look for analogous characteristics: Does the author support his or her conclusions with reference to the text? Is the paper well written in terms of the conventions of writing that this class has been using? One of the most important generic characteristics of academic conversations, however, is their requirement that their authors *take account* of other readers and readings. Consequently teachers and peer reviewers almost always ask whether the paper shows evidence that its author knows the scholarship in her subject area and cites it appropriately.

Just as you and your peers have often arrived at different readings of the texts in this book, so the authoritative readers of academic articles often disagree about the scholarly value of the submissions they read. Like you and your group members, and like the peer reviewers for scholarly journals, teachers, too, can differ in the criteria they use to make their judgments and in their applications of these criteria. Different kinds of conversations call for different kinds of writing, different kinds of evidence, different word choices. Sometimes you'll need to follow academic conventions quite closely, while at other times you'll want to—and be encouraged to—respond precisely as you wish. Most teachers are willing to describe their criteria and explain why they invoke them for a specific situation. It is very much in your interest as a writer to ask your authoritative readers about the situation for your writing and about the criteria they will use to judge your work—because the stakes are high—for everyone. In the case of academic professionals (like John) negative readings by peer reviewers can result in the denial of tenure. In the case of students (like Carol and you) the results of a negative reading are all too familiar. It's obviously wise to discover as much as you can about the situation in which you write and, insofar as you can, to negotiate the standards by which you will be judged.

A Sample Conversation between Academic Readers on "Leda and the Swan"

The following conversations about William Butler Yeats's poem, "Leda and the Swan," provide an opportunity to look at the conventions of academic research writing in practice. Like *Oedipus the King*, Yeats's story of the encounter between the Greek god Zeus and the mortal Leda retells one of western culture's most familiar myths and raises questions about the meaning of that myth. Like many of the stories and poems and plays we've read, this one concerns gender and power, love and war, and individual difference. Here is some information about the world of the poem that might help you to place it in context.

Leda and the Swan. Helen, the young beauty who is better known as Helen of Troy, came from a family that could trace its descent back to Aeolus. When Tyndareus, king of Sparta, had to seek political asylum among the Aetolians, he met Leda, the daughter of King Thestius. She was given to him in marriage and he took her back to Sparta when his kingdom was restored. The two had a number of children. Up to this point the married life of Tyndareus and his spouse had nothing unusual about it. But one night Zeus appeared to Leda in the form of a swan and made love to her; and later that very night Tyndareus also made love to her. The result of this double union was most unusual and hardly two accounts give the same versions. Common tradition has it that Leda bore Helen and Polydeuces (latinized to Pollux) to Zeus, Clytemnestra (or Clytaemnestra) and Castor to Tyndareus.

Another version reports that Helen was a daughter of Nemesis and Zeus and that her birth came about in this fashion: Nemesis, attempting to escape from the passionate embraces of Zeus, changed herself into a goose. Undaunted by this transformation, Zeus turned himself into a swan and so had his way with her. As a consequence of this love affair, Nemesis laid an egg which a shepherd found and brought to Tyndareus's wife. Leda put the egg in a chest and kept it there until it hatched. Out came Helen whom Leda brought up as her own daughter. In some versions, Leda herself is represented as having brought forth two eggs: Castor and Polydeuces are born from one, Helen from the other. In yet another account, Zeus is called the father of Helen and Polydeuces, and Tyndareus the father of Clytemnestra and Castor. Our earliest source, Homer, considers only Helen to be the daughter of Zeus by Leda; Castor, Polydeuces and Clytemnestra are said to be children of Tyndareus and Leda. The egg which Leda brought forth after her encounter with Zeus became a sacred relic; Pausanias, that indefatigable traveler of the second century A.D., reported that he saw it hanging by ribbons from the ceiling of a temple at Sparta.

The story of how Leda conceived her children was represented by one of the finest artists of the Renaissance, Leonardo da Vinci. *Leda and the Swan*, now in the Spiridon Collection at Rome, depicts the version of the two eggs out of which were hatched Helen and Polydeuces, Clytemnestra and Castor. Other artists of the period who put Leda on canvas were Correggio, Veronese, and Tintoretto. A modern approach to the ancient story was painted by the surrealist Salvador Dali, his *Leda atomica* (1945). In literature Spenser used the tale in the *Faerie Queene* when describing the mythological tapestries which hung in the house of Busyrane, the "vile Enchaunter," Spenser's symbol of unlawful love. But Spenser's description of Leda's encounter with Zeus hardly makes profane love seem evil and gross.

> Then he was turned into a snowy Swan,
> To win faire Leda to his lovely trade:
> O wondrous skill, and sweet wit of the man,
> That her in daffadillies sleeping made,
> From scorching heat her daintie limbes to shade:
> Whiles the proud Bird ruffing his fethers wyde,
> And brushing his faire brest, did her invade;
> She slept, yet twixt her eyelids closely spyde,
> How towards her he rusht, and smiled at his pryde.

No painter and no poet was to find in Leda—and in her fateful children as well—a symbol more complex and more involuted than W. B. Yeats, a symbol that embraced the philosophical and esthetic, the mystical and occult views of the poet. To Yeats the union of Leda and the swan symbolized, as he tells us in *A Vision* (1925), the opening of a two-thousand-year cycle which came to an end with the birth of Christ and which in turn marked the beginning of another cycle; it was "the annunciation that founded Greece as made to Leda, remembering that they showed in a Spartan temple, strung up to the roof as a holy relic, an unhatched egg of hers; and from one of her eggs came Love (Helen and Clytemnestra) and from the other War (Castor and Polydeuces)." Yeats' finest lyrical statement on the ancient story of the primal embrace of god and mortal appears in *Leda and the Swan* (1924), a fusion of mythology, sexuality and prophecy (from *Classical Mythology in Literature, Art, and Music*).

Now, here is the poem:

Leda and the Swan
William Butler Yeats

A sudden blow: the great wings beating still
Above the staggering girl, her thighs caressed
By the dark webs, her nape caught in his bill,
He holds her helpless breast upon his breast.
How can those terrified vague fingers push
The feathered glory from her loosening thighs?
And how can body, laid in that white rush,
But feel the strange heart beating where it lies?

A shudder in the loins engenders there
The broken wall, the burning roof and tower
And Agamemnon dead.

                    Being so caught up,
So mastered by the brute blood of the air,
Did she put on his knowledge with his power
Before the indifferent beak could let her drop?

CONSTRUCTING A PRELIMINARY READING OF "LEDA AND THE SWAN"

1. Write, in your own words, what you think is happening in this text. Compare your paraphrases with those of your classmates, noting differing interpretations.
2. Once you make some preliminary decisions about the event that the

poem describes, try turning your attention to the question the poem raises about that event. To do so, follow the processes you have practiced: list gaps, think about the world to which the text refers, follow narrative perspectives, notice the genre, and so on.

3. Discuss some possible answers to that question with your group members.

You may remember from Patricia Mitchell's conversation with Howard Nemerov that W. B. Yeats has an "unlisted number" and therefore cannot be reached for comment about his intention in "Leda and the Swan." A number of scholars have rushed in to fill that void, however, and Yeats's poem has occasioned much speculation and disagreement. The articles that follow were written for academic journals by professors and scholars. Because you are not their intended audience, I've edited them for brevity and included some explanatory notes. As we read them together, let's assume that the context for our discussion is a conversation about "Leda and the Swan." The different participants in the conversation have different questions and agendas. Our agenda—unfocussed as yet—is to come to terms somehow with the last question: "Did she put on his knowledge with his power . . . ?"

One of the first things we notice about the scholarship is that it's not necessarily concerned with the question we're raising. So one of our first tasks, therefore, is to find or make relevance. What, if anything, does each of these scholars have to say about our concern with the last question? John Unterecker, the author of *A Reader's Guide to William Butler Yeats*, discusses this poem in a context of an extended examination of Yeats's view of history and myth. He believes that the poet saw the story of Leda and the swan as analogous with the angel Gabriel's annunciation to Mary: both events began a new "cycle" of history.

from *A Reader's Guide to William Butler Yeats*
John Unterecker

. . . Mary's real experience [Yeats] concludes was, like Leda's, an experience of horror—of terror at the violent arrival of the god, an experience that might, he suggests at the end of each poem, have been compensated for by insight (knowledge) gained in the violent encounter with the supernatural.

Explaining his poem and his system in *A Vision*, Yeats comments:

> I imagine the annunciation that founded Greece as made to Leda, remembering that they showed in a Spartan temple, strung up to the roof as a holy relic, an unhatched egg of hers; and that from one of her eggs came Love and from the other War. But all things are from antithesis, and when in my ignorance I try to

> imagine what older civilisation that annunciation rejected I can but see bird and woman blotting out some corner of the Baylonian mathematical starlight.

The annunciation he refers to is, of course, the rape of Leda by Zeus who, disguised as a gigantic swan, had in that remarkable conception begotten not only Helen but as well the whole consequence of Helen: the fall of Troy, the death of the Greek heroes. . . .

[I]t is . . . a nearly perfect sonnet. If we visualize the division between octave and sestet as a kind of fulcrum, we can see how carefully Yeats maneuvered into lines 8 and 9 a point of balance. For one instant, the instant of Helen's conception, the opposing flows of passion intersect. Zeus at the beginning of the poem had been passionate, Leda helpless and terrified. At the end of the poem Leda is "caught up" in his passion, Zeus is "indifferent." But at the structural center of the poem a kind of communion takes place. Leda must feel, Yeats insists, "the strange heart beating where it lies" at exactly the instant that "A shudder in the loins" engenders the future.

Everything in the poem contributes to this design. Even rhythm itself underlines the shifting passions of the two characters. The five anapests literally move Leda through the poem staggering her, loosening her thighs, letting her be caught up and finally letting her drop ("the staggering girl," "her loosening thighs," "Being so caught up," "The indifferent beak"). The deliberately Freudian imagery (the white rush, the broken wall, the burning roof and tower, to name only the most obvious), the puns on such words as laid and lies, the ambiguities inherent in "those terrified vague fingers" (visually vague because buried in feathers or blurred from beating, emotionally vague because, in spite of the fingers' terror, thighs already loosen to the equally ambiguous feathered glory), the unanswerable question that ends the poem all serve to bind up into "a classical enunciation" a poem no part of which does not function in all other parts.

Like the reviewers of *Oleanna*, Unterecker begins by stating what he believes to be the theme of the poem. He develops his reading by discussing

"Leda and the Swan" is a sonnet, a lyric poem of fourteen lines that has one of several definite rhyme schemes. This one has the scheme ABABCDCD EFGEFG. (Robert Frost's "Design," which you read in Chapter Two, is also a sonnet.) An *anapest* is a poetic unit (or *foot*) that consists of two unaccented syllables (that Unterecker presents like this: –) followed by one accented syllable (/). One of the generic characteristics of sonnets is that (sometimes, but not always) the first eight lines establish a situation and the next six lines comment on that situation.

the poem's "form"—its genre, its rhyme scheme and rhythm, its use of figurative language—and his sense of the poem's meaning is based on the form that he perceives. He asserts that the first eight lines of "Leda" (the octet) lead up to the description of the sex act, ("A shudder in the loins"). That description is, Unterecker thinks, like a fulcrum that is the point of balance between the first eight lines—in which the mortal Leda and the God Zeus are separate—and the final three and a half lines in which they are together, combining Zeus's divinity with Leda's mortality. The rhythm of the individual feet, he thinks, recapitulates the divisions of the poem. He implies but does not specify a psychoanalytic reading of the poem's figurative language (which he calls "imagery"): the "white rush," the burning roof and tower," and the "broken wall" all (in a context of Freudian symbolism) connote sexual activity to Unterecker. He supports his reading with references to the poem: he quotes lines that he uses as examples of his assertion and as reasons for it.

Unterecker has at least one comment that might be relevant to our question: "Leda's . . . experience . . . of terror at the violent arrival of the god . . . might have been compensated for by insight (knowledge) gained in the violent encounter with the supernatural." On the basis of this sentence, we have some gaps: What kind of knowledge are we talking about and how might it compensate for violence? Why would someone believe that this is the case?

CONSTRUCTING A READING OF A READING

1. Do you and your group members agree that knowledge (of what) might have compensated Leda (for what)?
2. Unterecker does not explain his reading of Yeats's tropes beyond asserting that they are "deliberately Freudian." With your group members, try to decide how Unterecker reads Yeats's figurative language.
3. Talk with your group members about why Unterecker did not think it necessary to flesh out his reading, by, for example, explaining exactly how he reads the tropes. From that discussion, infer a description of Unterecker's readers.
4. What do you think in general about relations of knowledge and power? Most schooling involves an exertion of power over students, for example. Does the knowledge that a student derives compensate for the experience of being subject to the power? For Leda? For Carol? For John? For you?

Thomas Parkinson constructs a reading of "Leda and the Swan" by looking closely at Yeats's early drafts and letters. He assumes that, by noting the circumstances under which Yeats wrote, and the changes that he made as he revised, a reader can get a sense of the poet's intention. A corollary, commonsensical assumption would seem to be that the poem gets better as Yeats revises.

Here is an excerpt from Parkinson's book, *W. B. Yeats: The Later Poetry*. Even though we may not be particularly interested in Yeats's composing process, we might be able to learn something helpful from Parkinson's notion of what the finished poem says.

from *W. B. Yeats: The Later Poetry*
Thomas Parkinson

The swan of "Leda and the Swan" emerges from a supernatural realm, embodies a god, and descends upon the merely human circumstances of Leda. In the first drafts the stress is entirely on the godhood of the bird, and there is a marked difference between the octave of the drafts and that of published versions:

> Now can the swooping godhead have his will
> Yet hovers, though her helpless thighs are pressed
> By the webbed toes; and that all powerful bill
> Has suddenly bowed her face upon his breast.
> How can those terrified vague fingers push
> The feathered glory from her loosening thighs?
> All the stretched body's laid in that white rush
> And feels the strange heart beating where it lies.

Yeats's chief difficulty came from the opening two lines, and before getting the poem in publishable form he made at least two other versions:

> The swooping godhead is half hovering still
> Yet climbs upon her trembling body pressed . . .

> The swooping godhead is half hovering still
> But mounts, until her trembling thighs are pressed . . .

Gradually he came to stress the bird-like rather than the godly qualities of the swan:

> A swoop upon great wings and hovering still
> The bird descends, and her frail thighs are pressed . . .

Even the first printed version held some vestiges of his earlier stress on the godhood of the swan:

> A rush, a sudden wheel, and hovering still
> The bird descends, and her frail thighs are pressed
> By the webbed toes, and that all-powerful bill
> Has laid her helpless face upon his breast,

> How can those terrified vague fingers push
> The feathered glory from her loosening thighs!
> All the stretched body's laid on the white rush
> And feels the strange heart beating where it lies;
> A shudder in the loins engenders there
> The broken wall, the burning roof and tower
> And Agamemnon dead.
>   Being so caught up,
> So mastered by the brute blood of the air,
> Did she put on his knowledge with his power
> Before the indifferent beak could let her drop?

This version is still far from the masterful poem as it is generally known. The swan hovering and descending at once is a symptom of the halting descriptiveness of the poem that annuls the sense of immediate implication that distinguishes the final version. "Webbed toes" sounds like silly circumstantial detail, and "the bird descends" is portentous beyond any need. There is no necessity for making the explicit antithesis of "frail" and "all-powerful," which is certainly clear enough in the action itself, the use of "laid" exhibits a kind of easy carelessness, and the stretched body is simply awkward, especially when juxtaposed with the uncomfortably stifling image of Leda's face upon the swan's breast.

Even in this version, which Yeats was shortly to find inadequate, we can see a stress on the supernatural and natural qualities of the icon, their common superiority to the human. Caught up, mastered, conquered by this passion, the helpless ambiguous human state is defined.

At some time between August of 1924 and May of 1925, he rewrote the poem so that the stress on "bird and lady" occupied the entire scope of the octave. The bird ceased to be "all-powerful," and the manuscript versions reveal a willed insistence on physical qualities. Leda's "frail" thighs become "white" in contrast with the "sooty webs" of the swan, and with the deletion of "that all-powerful bill" he could try various phrases to underline the animal nature of Leda:

> . . . her nape is in his bill
> . . . her nape caught in his bill
> . . . that white nape in his bill
> . . . her nape caught in that bill
> . . . her nape caught in his bill

In his effort to specify and vividly envision the scene he fell into momentary absurdity:

> The bird has fallen but is hovering still
> Leda can run no more . . .

> And where can Leda run. . .
> And what can Leda do. . .
> And Leda staggers. . .
> Above the staggering girl. . .

But even the comical nail-biting of "What can Leda do?" turned his attention to the lady of the action and led to the special "carnal eloquence" that distinguishes the final version, with thigh, nape, and breast placed against toes, bill, and breast, the beating wings above the staggering girl:

> A sudden blow: the great wings beating still
> Above the staggering girl, her thighs caressed
> By the dark webs, her nape caught in his bill,
> He holds her helpless breast upon his breast.
>
> How can those terrified vague fingers push
> The feathered glory from her loosening thighs?
> And how can body, laid in that white rush,
> But feel the strange heart beating where it lies?
>
> A shudder in the loins engenders there
> The broken wall, the burning roof and tower
> And Agamemnon dead.
>   Being so caught up,
> So mastered by the brute blood of the air,
> Did she put on his knowledge with his power
> Before the indifferent beak could let her drop?

Tracing the swan through his various appearances, we can see in this poem an initial bald statement of his godhood and omnipotence that is then deleted until he becomes a bird with wings, webs, and bill. His potency is in his action and the consequences of that action, so that the single mention of his power accompanies his mastery, bruteness, and sexual satiation. What this poem does, in effect, is to compose the essential duality of the icon, making it at once a symbol of supernatural power and an image of natural force: ". . . the brute blood of the air." The tragedy of Leda is that she should be a battleground, that her descendants should also be helplessly caught between the natural and the supernatural, the human image being endowed with significance only insofar as it can participate in the life of nature and supernature. So she is at once dignified, exalted, and destroyed.

CONSTRUCTING A READING

1. Collaborate with your group members on a paraphrase and fleshing out of Parkinson's conclusion that Leda is "at once dignified, exalted, and

destroyed." In what sense is Leda exalted? In what sense dignified? In what sense destroyed?

2. Again with your group members, talk about what, if anything, Leda's being dignified, exalted, and/or destroyed has to do with the final question of this text.

3. In general, do you think that being destroyed can contribute to being exalted? Write in your journal for a few minutes about other circumstances in which people might hold that belief—for example, religious experience, war, love, schooling.

Bernard Levine, like Parkinson, writes about "Leda and the Swan" in the context of Yeats's development as a poet; like Unterecker, he addresses questions of knowledge and power in the context of the poem's form. In his book, *The Dissolving Image*, Levine describes his sense of the theme of the poem: "'Leda and the Swan' is undoubtedly the best example of that delight Yeats said he had 'in all that displayed great problems through sensuous images.'" Parkinson, then, can help us to show that the poem is not merely a description of a part of a myth but also a statement of some kind about a "great problem." What does Levine think the "great problem" is?

from *The Destructive Vision*
Bernard Levine

We may begin the explication of "Leda" by noting in "Leda and the Swan" the reflexive opposition of concrete and abstract imagery. Leda, "the staggering girl," is identified through concrete detail: "Her thighs," "her nape," "her helpless breast," "her loosening thighs." The swan, on the other hand, is never referred to in the poem itself as a "swan." He is described as an overpowering abstraction—"the great wings," "the dark webs," "that white rush," "the brute blood," "the indifferent beak." It may be the purely mechanical simplicity of the grammar that finally requires pronominal identification of the "swan," in the third, fourth, and thirteenth lines of the poem. But at these points the use of pronouns tends to humanize the essential action. The relationship of swan and girl is not only the relationship of god to mortal but of male to female, the notion of divinity momently converted into something human, albeit animalistically derived:

[3]   her nape caught in his bill,
[4]   He holds her helpless breast upon his breast.

[13]   Did she put on his knowledge with his power
[14]   Before the indifferent beak could let her drop?

In these last lines of the poem (13 and 14) we are reminded once again of the original separation between the personal and the divine, and the distinction between animal and spiritual energy.

What then about the intervening lines, 5 to 12, in which the climax of the sexual act is quite unforgettably described? In these lines there is not only a conspicuous absence of pronominal forms (only one pronominal phrase is used, "her loosening thighs") but more importantly the distinction between the concrete (or personal) and the abstract gives way to a profound ambiguity—the more astonishing because it is fully sustained throughout the second quatrain and for the first two lines of the sestet.

The middle section of the poem is best approached by returning briefly to the opening quatrain. Essentially what we find in the poem is a complex reversal of roles, and this is anticipated first by the phrase in line 2, "the staggering girl." Here the immediate meaning requires that the participle be regarded as intransitive (that is, the girl is literally staggering; the action is physical, concrete); but a possible, secondary meaning suggests the transitive form of the verb, making the swan, not the girl, the object that is affected (that is, the girl "staggers" the mind, imagination or willpower of the swan-god; the action takes on figurative meaning). The undercurrent meaning thus moves in a direction contrary to the direction of the apparent meaning, and makes the situation as described bilateral, with agent and recipient of the "action" potentially interchangeable. R. P. Blackmur explains this kind of interchange in "Leda" by citing Yeats's much-quoted doctrine of the unitive imagination. The doctrine would here apply to our organic perception of the poetic "action" in "Leda" rather than to the action of figures described in the poem: "That the borders of our mind are ever shifting, and that many minds can flow into one another, as it were, and create or reveal a single mind, a single energy. . . . That this great mind can be evoked by symbols." Commenting on the application of Yeat's words, Blackmur observes: "Copulation is the obvious nexus for spiritual as well as physical seed." Perception of a unity in the poem thus tends to break down the separation between elements constituting the tension, or dichotomies, in the poem.

A second example of the ambiguous play of current and undercurrent meaning in "Leda" occurs in line 4. The possibility here is perhaps harder to grasp.

He holds her helpless breast upon his breast.

The ambiguity arises from the provocative omission of internal punctuation. A semi-colon and two commas mark the caesura at the end of the second foot, the third foot, and the second foot, in lines 1 to 3 respectively. The reader is left in line 4 with an option as to where to pause, if he is inclined to pause at all. The line as written above follows through on the 2, 3, 2 caesural pattern previously established if we pause briefly after "helpless breast." But what if we mentally punctuate the line as follows:

> He holds her, helpless, breast upon his breast.

This reading possibly reverses the primary sense of the line. "Helpless" can be taken to modify "he" as well as "her." Our initial impression of the violence of the swan thus is countered by the suggestion of a quite different form of intimacy: the swan, "helpless," would seem to be arrested by his willful embrace of Leda.

No regular metrical pattern is to be found in "Leda and the Swan," but there is a pervading rhythmic base in which verbal stress displaces the accent-guided line. In the first quatrain one finds a counterbalancing of verbal and rhythmic movement. The rhythm pushes the action forward, while the words tend to hold back, delay the action. Lines 1 and 2 are run-on, indicating by linear separation a reluctance of the opposed images to merge, a reluctance which by line 3 is gradually relaxed:

> [1]   . . . the great wings beating still
> [2] Above the staggering girl, her thighs caressed
> [3] By the dark webs . . .

The counterpoint is furthered by the connotation of individual words. Most conspicuous is the word "still." As a form of enantiosis, coming at a pivotal point in the verse line, "still" implies both continuity and fixity. It is as if, as Leo Spitzer suggests, the great wings have never stopped beating as a mythic event. And yet the bird is described as having just dropped down upon the unsuspecting Leda. He is pictured balanced on her thighs, in movement and yet without moving, as he beats the air with his wings. Taken this way the image conveys a feeling of vibrant and timeless stasis. And in this connection the word "caught" in line 3 and the word "holds" in line 4 both serve to reinforce our impression of dynamic stillness.

Consider again line 4 in juxtaposition with the preceding clause in line three:

> [3]   her nape caught in his bill
> [4] He holds her helpless breast upon his breast.

To which of the two figures does the word "caught" apply? One's immediate response would be to regard the swan as having done the catching ("caught" read as a past participle). Presumably he is the agent. Considering the ambiguous syntax of line 4, however, line 3 may be read with reverse meaning: the girl may he construed as struggling in such a way as to have forced "her nape" into "his bill" ("caught" read as past tense), making *him* "helpless" even though "he holds her." This reversal of the apparent meaning suggests that Leda's role may be actively rather than passively submissive. As John F. Adams puts it: "While Leda—woman—is violated, in spite of herself her own passion draws her into a participation in the experience." It is possible then to regard the swan not as clutching Leda in a vise of brute strength but as coupling with her in mutual embrace.

Are these speculations about lines 3 and 4 at all borne out by the central section of the poem? Our approach will be facilitated by asking from this point on: Who of the two principals is acting and who is being acted upon? Consider first the opening of the second quatrain:

> How can those terrified vague fingers push
> The feathered glory from her loosening thighs?

Whose fingers are doing the pushing? It would seem most obvious that Leda's are. She is the one who appears "terrified." But is she? And how do we account for the fact that her fingers are vague ? They are "vague" in the sense that they are "wandering" (from the Latin root), but this suggests that she is not pushing to get rid of the terror the swan inspires in her.

Yet the swan may also be regarded as having the "vague fingers." The dark webs or the great wings terminate in what only imperfectly resemble "fingers." And this approximation is expressed by the word "vague." But then why should the swan be "terrified"? That word was once used to denote a sense of being irritated, tormented, teased. If this meaning is permitted, then we may make out the swan to be a creature who must vent his frustration, satisfy some natural longing. The girl, in turn, may be regarded as the innocent victim, or as the source for alleviation of an intolerable abstinence

If we consider the ambiguity of the action being described in line 5, we get some idea of the interchangeability of the emotion being expressed, and we can begin to appreciate better the psychological complexity which inheres in the sexual drama. Take now lines 5 and 6 together:

> How can those terrified vague fingers push
> The feathered glory from her loosening thighs?

This statement may he read at least four ways. How can Leda ever get free of the swan? How can Leda hope or even want to get free of the swan? How can the "terrified" swan, frustrated in accomplishing his will, succeed in begetting offspring (his "feathered glory") through Leda? And finally, how can Leda succeed in begetting issue worthy of the swan's natural or supernatural resplendence? The question in the poem is so phrased that we cannot tell apart the anxiety and the desire of girl and swan. The reading of the lines depends upon whom we take to be the subject of the statement, upon the kind of emphasis we place on the words "can" and "push," and thirdly upon how we interpret the phrase "feathered glory."

Consider in this context the last two lines of the quatrain:

> [7] And how can body, laid in that white rush,
> [8] But feel the strange heart beating where it lies?

Another question, and again a complementarity of meaning. The sense of struggle, urgency, or anxiety—however one may read it—implied in lines 5 and 6 is weakened rather than reinforced by lines 7 and 8. Here the ambiguity is substantially reduced, and even though it is still possible to posit a double meaning for the statement, the question implies a fusion of sensibility in relation to the experience of swan and girl. If the narrator is here speaking from the point of view of the swan the question would read as follows: How can the physical body, *her* body, exposed to this gathering of energy, but feel its imminent release giving life to her and me—as though her heart were mine and mine hers? And from the point of view of Leda the question posed would be: How can the physical body, *my* body, ravished, but feel the expended force of his will, and so transform my sense of being that I feel *his* heart? (It is quite immaterial whether the ambiguous "it" in line 8 refers to "body" or "heart"; whatever the reference, the interchange of meaning in this case signifies a mutual transformation through sexual embrace.) The lines imply that the sense of separation is what brings anxiety and induces struggle, and that such a feeling of separation can be ameliorated in sexual climax. The breaking of sexual tension described in the lines that follow (9 to 11) does not necessarily reveal portents of disaster; it can as well represent release from the feeling of fear or alienation, on the one hand, or relief from insatiable desire on the other.

In these lines (9 to 11) of the sestet describing what may be called "the ejaculation scene" one finds the ambiguity of the poem most striking:

> A shudder in the loins engenders there
> The broken wall, the burning roof and tower
> And Agamemnon dead.

"Engenders" where? we may ask. In the house of Priam or in the house of Atreus? In the womb of Leda? In the supernal consciousness of the swan? In the consciousness of a given culture? Perhaps none of these possibilities need be excluded.

What we have basically is a confrontation of the physical and the mental event. The speaker imaginatively participates in and yet obviously stands outside the situation. He witnesses Leda's rape as he would the tragedy at Troy and Argos, and understands how one event is implied in the other. From whose point of view does the speaker witness the sequel of Leda's rape? Is one partner or the other responsible for the epic situation at Troy? By the last two lines, certainly, the whole burden of the poem rests upon the disparity between the point of view of Leda and the point of view of the swan: "Did she put on his knowledge with his power. . . ?"

How is the physical event then—the sexual-historical relationship—to be regarded? Is there another way of looking at the ejaculation scene without having to fall back on a recapitulation of the historical irony? Can that scene somehow explain the myth as an illusion of the power expended in the sexual act? And this leads to our final correlation between textual and subtextual meaning. If the poem focuses intently on the rape of Leda, then the line and a half describing the subsequent fall of Troy and of the house of Atreus is in no sense a digression. The unity of the poem is not disrupted if we regard the mytho-historical reference in lines 10 and 11 at the same time as sexual imagery. The "broken wall" reminds us of the walls of Troy, but then again it rings up associations with "maidenhead" and "womb." The "burning roof and tower" reinforce our picture of Troy being destroyed, but then too it may suggest the burning effect following sexual climax. The swan's experience and knowledge is the kind which exempts him from further involvement in this fatal course of events at Troy. His wisdom replenished after the rape of Leda, he assumes again the indifference of a god. The implication, once more, is that the historical scene represents nothing but an extension of the willful violence that may be dissolved in the sexual act.

CONSTRUCTING A READING OF A READING

1. With your group members, consider Levine's assertion that the swan is first "described as an overpowering abstraction," then referred to with masculine pronouns, until finally "[t]he relationship of swan to girl is not only the relationship of God to mortal but of male to female, the notion of divinity momentarily converted into something human, albeit animalistically derived." Paraphrase this part of his reading and try to determine how he supports it. What, in other words, is Levine saying that Yeats is saying?

2. Levine writes of a "complex reversal of roles" in which the phrase "the staggering girl" can indicate both that Leda staggered from the force of Zeus's approach and that her beauty was staggering to Zeus. Later, he suggests that the word "helpless" in line 4 can be taken to refer either to Leda or to Zeus. What's up with that? Paraphrase his assertion that "the situation as described [is] bilateral, with agent and recipient of the 'action' potentially interchangeable."

3. If the action is potentially interchangeable, is it still a rape?

Although Unterecker calls the question that ends the poem "unanswerable," W. C. Barnwell offers three possibilities:

The Rapist in "Leda and the Swan"

W. C. Barnwell

Often read as a rape-poem, "Leda and the Swan" offers perhaps the clearest example of the extreme importance of Yeats's copulatory *personae* who act and are acted upon in various ways to learn certain lessons.[1] "Leda" is in fact a profound and provocative dramatization of the ambiguities of sexual encounter for Yeats, and questions as well as answers the major premise in his scheme of thought: the idea of a perfect order in the universe that supports, guides, and affirms all of man's endeavors in various ways. The question of the rapist thus acquires great significance. If the swan is the rapist, then man exists as mere object and is not himself an important actor in the cosmic drama of time and eternity; if Leda is the rapist, then man does play a major role in that drama; if a third party is the rapist, then both man and god are perforce victims; and if we as readers are seen as the rapists that repeat again and again the drama of sexual encounter through reading the poem itself, then the questioning involved becomes a truly universal microcosm of the human experience of mingled naturalism and supernaturalism.[2]

Previous readings of "Leda" have by and large concerned themselves with literal interpretation, the problems of visual influence, the measure of mythic identity, and the use of *A Vision* in its formation, or in rare cases the question of the degree of involvement of Leda in the rape itself.[3] I want to enlarge on the possibilities posed in the latter reading and suggest two further readings that throw light on the important final question of the poem. It will be necessary first of all to retrace the standard understanding of "Leda":

> A sudden blow: the great wings beating still
> Above the staggering girl, her thighs caressed
> By the dark webs, her nape caught in his bill,
> He holds her helpless breast upon his breast.
>
> How can those terrified vague fingers push
> The feathered glory from her loosening thighs?
> And how can body, laid in that white rush,
> But feel the strange heart beating where it lies?
>
> A shudder in the loins engenders there
> The broken wall, the burning roof and tower
> And Agamemnon dead.

> Being so caught up,
> So mastered by the brute blood of the air,
> Did she put on his knowledge with his power
> Before the indifferent beak could let her drop? (CP, 211)

In the first and most obvious reading, Leda is clearly a victim of the aggressor swan. She staggers under the impact of the sudden blow of his body and reels in a numbed daze while he works his will. She cannot fend him off and is unable to avoid the results of the act. Consequently in trying to answer the final question, "Did she put on his knowledge with his power," we can only answer, "No, why should she, she is the victim and victims receive nothing." Supernatural knowledge remains with the gods, and man (through Leda) remains ignorant of the cause-and-effect nature of history and time, the "broken wall, the burning roof and tower / And Agamemnon dead." In this reading, we see little to applaud from a human point of view; the gods are in control and man's fate will emerge with or without his own help or hindrance. At best this reading recognizes that God and man do interact, but in certain ill-defined if clearly violent ways, at least as far as man is concerned. Leda is being raped by a force unconcerned for her existence as a questioning entity.

There is a second possibility first explored in depth, as far as I am aware by Bernard Levine in his study of *The Dissolving Image*. And that is that Leda, not the swan, is the aggressor and that the god-swan may in fact be the victim. Zeus, the notorious womanizer is "staggered" by Leda's great beauty and cannot *not* attempt an assault upon her. Leda in turn has placed herself in a violent context presumably for a reason; perhaps to gain supernatural knowledge. At the risk of straining, we can read many of the lines in a different way. For example instead of reading "caught" in line 3 as a past participle, and Leda the one being captured, we read it as a simple past tense and "her nape caught in his bill" becomes entrapment on Leda's part. Just as a fish-hook catches in a fish's mouth, so Leda uses her neck to catch firmly in the bill of the swan. Similarly, the absence of punctuation in line 4 leaves open the question of a clearcut antecedent. Whom does "helpless" modify, the bird or the girl, when "He holds her helpless breast upon his breast"? Early drafts of the poem suggest that it is Leda. If a comma had followed "helpless," the swan would clearly be the aggressor; if a comma had preceded "helpless," then the swan would still hold something of the edge on being the rapist. But if "helpless" is seen in a grammatical zeugma in the way it now stands, Leda could well be the rapist as well as the victim: "He holds her helpless breast upon his [helpless] breast." It is not absolutely clear in the last published version, in the absence of pinpointing commas, just who is helpless and we may read that ambiguity as the basis of assuming interchangeable roles, both Leda and the swan being potentially the rapist. Moreover, lines 3 and 4 suggest an interchangeable set of fingers that try to "push" away the union of the two figures. The antecedent of "her loosening thighs" is obviously Leda; the antecedent of the "feathered glory" seems equally clear, although it could refer to a possible offspring. But who or what is the antecedent of "those terrified vague fingers"? In the first reading they belong to Leda, who vainly attempts to avoid penetration by the phallus of Zeus. But in our second reading, in which Leda is suspected of being the rapist, the terrified fingers become those of Zeus, and they are "vague" because they are webbed and therefore similar to, but not exactly like, human fingers. The swan cannot "push" Leda away; he cannot help himself; he cannot avoid the results of his act either; history will still unfold.

In lines 7 and 8 the uncertainty is more intense and more confused, concerned as it is with present and future. The body of a swan, "the brute blood of the air," is strange to that of a human and vice versa. Both hearts beat at a different rate and so on; the body of a god would be strange to that of a human and vice versa; also the human has a heart, the god may not. But sometimes it does, and this is what terrifies the Greek in *Resurrection*, that he felt the "heart of a phantom . . . beating."[4] Similarly, the "white rush" can be several things: the whiteness of the swan's plummage, the seminal flow of generative juices, or Leda's encompassing thighs. "Laid" here could also refer to the offspring of the union of the two, and it is then the heart of Helen that is "strange" to both mother and father, being between the two as she is, being both mortal and immortal. The poem thereby leaps from present (the conception) to the future (birth of infant, by egg), just as in the third stanza a leap is made from orgasm to the consequence of that orgasm and conception, "The broken wall, the burning roof and tower / And Agamemnon dead."

If the effects of their copulation is Greek history, and remains so whoever is the rapist, it seems clear that through verbal ambiguity the *persona* of Yeats casts some doubt on the exact roles of the two participants. The ambiguous statements (or pseudo-statements) of fact lead up to the final question, itself highly ambiguous: "Did she put on his knowledge with his power?" In the first reading the answer may be no, Leda is a victim. In the second, however, the answer may be yes: why should she so tempt Zeus but to gain something, gain knowledge of the future, of the course of history, and perhaps the knowledge to change and effect that course? In this second reading, Leda emerges as a human hero willing to tempt and plumb supernatural heights for human benefit. In fact Giambattista Vico had suggested to Yeats that man had created history and so was capable of understanding it; but not so with nature, which was created by God and so could be understood only by God (AV, 207). Did Leda put on the god's knowledge of history as well as his generative and mysterious power before the "indifferent beak could let her drop?" Indifferent because the supernatural, knowledge given or not, always has been and always will be above the human reality of the flesh into which Leda is dropped by Zeus after the momentary union of the two has passed.

There is a third reading of the poem that suggests that both Leda *and* the swan are victims and that a third party is in fact the rapist. The suggestive ambiguities that surround the act of Leda and the swan can lead us not only to interchange their roles, but also to question if either one of them is the aggressor. After all, if it is unclear who staggers or is staggering or in what capacity, active or passive; and if it is unclear whose fingers are terrified, or whose breast is helpless, then perhaps neither of the figures, bird or woman, is in control of the situation. Who then is the aggressor, and for what reason? Here we must turn briefly to Yeats's scheme of history and time. History revolves in 2,000 year cycles, one cycle violently followed by an opposite cycle, and so on for at least thirteen revolutions, at the end of which time may cease or it may begin all over again.[5] Pattern is behind history and its cycles and presumably dictates its motions. Therefore it compels history to come into being, to act and to cease. And in order for a cycle to begin there must be a coupling of the natural with the supernatural; that is, Mary with the Holy Ghost, or Leda with the swan. Since such sexual contact is necessary to get the cycle rolling and to keep it going for whatever reasons the perfect pattern may have for its existence, the supernatural as well as the natural is influenced by this force. Zeus or the Holy Ghost or whatever must copulate with Leda or Mary or whomever. Both man and god are forced into sexual union for the sake of a history that must move in certain prescribed grooves for certain destined ends. The pattern of history and its turnings, then, is the rapist in this reading and both Leda and the swan are its victims; they are manipulated into the sexual tableau pictured in the poem from the "sudden blow" to the "shudder in the loins" and then "engenders there," in the mortal loins of Leda, the future implied in the Greek cycle of history with its central episode the Trojan war and all its subsequent tragedies.

If we read pattern as the rapist, the answer to the final question may then be no; why should Zeus have any knowledge to impart if he, as much as Leda, is a victim? He may have no knowledge for Leda to put on; she remains as ignorant as ever and as unable as ever to control her own or mankind's destiny. The cyclic universe with its serial history is the infinite rapist; the gods may have knowledge of its inner workings, but an inability to act on it. Man endures such violations only because it is all he knows.

There is a final reading of the poem that places man squarely in the picture once again. Before arguing the point I must paraphrase what Ernst Cassirer has to say about the relationships of man, *animal symbolicum*, to his symbols and poems. For Cassirer, symbolic reality is the only reality man can know; he cannot know something if he cannot symbolize it in some way. The act of reading a poem, then, recreates a specific reality in symbolic space and time in which, for example, the "great wings are beating still / Above the staggering girl," and human history is repeated over and over again, rehearsed as it is in the symbolic arenas of the mind.[6] Since man's specific difference in the animal world is his ability to create a symbolic reality, he is literally cut off from everything else thereby. The only way he can now experience anything is symbolically. In this sense, then, it is the reader of the poem who is the rapist; for he manipulates the bird and woman through their paces again and again, through countless shudders and blows, through countless burnings and deaths, through countless conjectures and questions about life and time and their ultimate meaning. Man lives darkly in and through history, but he also tries to understand its nature and thereby affect it in certain meaningful ways; man is human in his errors, but tries to parallel godhood in his visionary scope. The result of this attempt is always problematical, a question mark, but it is one posed by man's own "resinous heart." This does not mean that man must exist purely as either an idealist or a realist, but rather as an explorer who has already traversed certain territories or forms, mapped them, and is yet unaware or ignorant of the *terra incognita* ahead. Certain things have happened in time that man understands; other things have happened that he does not understand, and his knowledge of future events can only be based on what he already knows or can fathom in his momentary sensings of the infinite. The symbology of the poem powerfully concretizes these sensings and in a sense creates them. Man rapes and is raped by his poems just as Leda rapes and is raped by the swan. Cassirer might ask, do we put on their knowledge with their power before their indifferent form can let us drop?

Rarely can one reading of a poem stand alone; divergent readings are usually taken as a form of health in a poem, a testimony to its vigor and its ability to stir readers into responding to it. This is true for "Leda." All four readings, I think, have their truth; moreover, all four operate together to project Yeats's attitude toward systematic order and meaning in the world of man. His tentative reaches in art are important whether any answer to his question is really there or not; their value lies in the hypothetical situations that they create. For example if the supernatural rapes man, still man is an object of attention and need; if man is the rapist, his pursuit of occult knowledge implies that he wishes a unified understanding in his world and that he has an active chance to get it; if unknowable pattern is the rapist, there remains a shred of free will in man's attempts at understanding it at all; if the rapist is that human cognition that intermittently imposes itself on chaos, there is the suggestion that ability to create such a drama entails potential divinity as well as profound humanity. In any case, the overall thrust of the poem, whoever the rapist, is that there is meaning in time behind mere complexities and behind man's necessarily limited vision in both his everyday life and the often violent convulsions of his sexuality.

Notes

1. Richard Ellmann mentions the "powerful ritualized" moment of "rape of Leda by the swan." He adds further that Yeats decided in the final version of the poem to focus the action "upon the rape itself." *The Identity of Yeats* (New York: Oxford University Press, 1964). p.176. See also John F. Adams, "Leda and the Swan": The Aesthetics of Rape, *Bucknell Review*, XII, 3 (December 1964) 47–58, who continues the tradition of seeing the poem as a dramatized rape. Allen R. Grossman reminds us that "sexuality in the cabala is the exclusive prerogative of God." *Poetic Knowledge in the Early Yeats* (Charlottesville: The University Press of Virginia, 1969),

p.56. But Yeats could and often did change tradition to suit his needs: it was precisely because sexuality was associated with divinity that Yeats came to praise the motions of sexual activity and to assert man's ability to create his own perfection through its right use. Yeats placed the poem in the "Dove or Swan" section of *A Vision*. He suggests that "Leda" had political implications but that politics gave way to "bird and lady." See "Notes" section of *The Variorum Edition of the Poems of Yeats*, ed. Alt and Alspach (New York: Macmillan, 1968), p. 828.

2.   Thomas Parkinson argues that the "tragedy of Leda is that she should be a battleground, that her descendants should also be helplessly caught between the natural and the supernatural, the human image being endowed with significance only insofar as it can participate in the life of nature and supernature. So she is at once dignified, exalted, and destroyed." *W. B. Yeats, The Later Poetry* (Berkeley and Los Angeles: University of California Press, 1964), p. 142. Parkinson also points out that "there is a marked difference between the octave of the drafts and that of published versions." The draft emphasis is clearly on primacy of the god-swan. But successive drafts and the final published version tend to support my thesis that ambiguity of roles came to be uppermost in Yeats's mind. In the later versions, according to Parkinson, the bird ceased to be all powerful and the physical qualities of "bird and lady" dominate. The swan becomes less and less the clear-cut aggressor and more and more a copartner in the sexual drama. See pp. 136–141.

3.   See John Unterecker, *A Readers Guide to William Butler Yeats* (New York: Noonday Press, 1959) for a standard reading of the poem; T. R. Henn's *The Lonely Tower*, for the role of visual influences and of *A Vision*; M. I. Seiden, *William Butler Yeats: The Poet as a Mythmaker*, 1865–1939 (Lansing: Michigan State University Press, 1962), for Yeats and the normative function of myth in his verse; and David R. Levine, *The Dissolving Image* (Detroit: Wayne State University Press, 1971), for a look at "Leda and the Swan" as I discuss it in this essay.

4.   *Collected Plays* (London: Macmillan & Co., 1963), p. 593. Speaking of the phantom of Christ after his resurrection, the Greek *persona* declares that "It may be hard under my hand like a statue—I have heard of such things—or my hand may pass through it, but there is no flesh or blood. [He goes slowly up to the figure and passes his hand over its side.] The heart of a phantom is beating! The heart of a phantom is beating! [He screams. The figure of Christ crosses the stage and passes into the inner room.]" Clearly the idea of a spirit being incarnate, having flesh and blood, is frightening to the Greek mind.

5.   Richard Ellmann, *Yeats: The Man and the Masks* (New York: E. P. Dutton, 1948), p. 282: "Only at this point [Yeats's discussion of the thirteenth sphere] do we realize that Yeats, after building up a system over three hundred pages, in the last two pages sets up that system's anti-self. All the determinism of *A Vision* is abruptly confronted with the Thirteenth Cycle which is able to alter everything, and suddenly free will, liberty, and deity pour back into the universe."

6.   Ernst Cassirer, *An Essay on Man* (New Haven: Yale University Press, 1962), p. 24: "Between the receptor system and the effector system, which are to be found in all animal species, we find in man a third link which we may describe as the *symbolic system*. This new acquisition transforms the whole of human life. As compared with other animals man lives not merely in a broader reality; he lives, so to speak, in a new dimension of reality."

Notice how Barnwell helps his readers to follow his argument. First, (like Unterecker) he states a "theme," but then immediately raises a question within that theme. If the poem is about relations between mortal beings and supernatural forces, and if "rape" is the trope for that relation, then the question becomes "who rapes whom?" That is the question that Barnwell proposes to answer—providing several alternatives and finally choosing the one that makes most sense to him. Notice, too, that he reprints the poem, so that his readers can immediately refer to the lines that he uses to support his position. Each of his three complete readings goes through the poem from beginning to end. Barnwell also attends to the work of others. He cites Unterecker, Parkinson and Levine, as well as Yeats's own writings and the philosophical speculations of Ernst Cassirer about human beings' uses of myth. Barnwell acknowledges his use of others' thinking in his lengthy footnotes, so that you, if you choose, can look at his sources to see whether you agree with the use to which he has put them.

CONSTRUCTING A READING OF BARNWELL'S THREE READINGS

1. The differences among Barnwell's three readings come from different understandings of crucial words: "staggering," "caught" "helpless," and so on. Make a chart or a computer graphic that represents these differences visually.
2. Summarize Barnwell's three readings, and, with your group members, talk about what's at stake in the differences among them.
3. With your group members, talk about Barnwell's "readability." Do you find him readable? Why or why not?
4. With your group members, discuss how Barnwell uses Parkinson, Unterecker, and Levine.

Conventions of Academic Writing: Taking Account of Others' Readings

After encountering these professional readings, you and your group members are part of the "conversation." To celebrate your enhanced conversational abilities, you may wish to expand or revise the gap questions you made earlier. Here are some possibilities:

- Consider the swan and Leda as tropes. What do you think they represent?

- Consider the question of rape. Has a "rape" occurred? What do you think? If it's a metaphorical rape, is it still a rape?
- Consider the question "Did she put on his knowledge with his power?" What does the question mean? How do you answer it?

On the basis of these questions or whatever other ones you and your group members devise, you'll almost certainly experience agreement and disagreement with other readers. Now you are ready to take account of the other readings. To *take account* is to consider the extent to which the other readings intersect with your own. Do you understand them or do they come from a world that you don't know much about? If so, do you need to find out about this world to do this assignment or can you safely ignore it? (You might not need complicated analyses of Yeats's revising process, for example, to use the conclusions to which that analysis has led Parkinson.) Do you agree with the other readers? Do you disagree? Do the other readers bring up aspects of the text that you hadn't thought about before? If so, do they change your reading? To *take account* is also to acknowledge the extent to which the other participants in the conversation you have entered have affected your reading. To *take account* is to decide on the relevance of other readings, to describe them as accurately as you can, to note the ways in which the other author (or authors) arrive at their readings, and to stipulate your agreement or disagreement while you explain your own reading of the text. Direct quotation, summary, and paraphrase are all ways of taking account of another's work.

Deciding What to Include and What to Leave Out

But how do you decide which parts of the conversation to take account of, and how to introduce them into your own writing? That decision must begin with your own reading, and emerge from the gap questions you formulate for yourself. For the sake of practice, however, we have made several assumptions: that you're interested in knowledge and power relations, especially in the final lines of this poem. You're not sure how you feel about that issue yet, mostly because you're still rather puzzled by some aspects of the poem itself. You've talked to your group members, and perhaps you've even come to some clarity about the event the poem describes, but you're still uncertain about how to respond to this particular poem's depiction of this particular event. Your assignment has specifically required that you take account of other readings.

You go to Barnwell first, let's say, because he gives a list of alternative readings that you think might be a good place to start. Early on, you encounter this sentence:

> . . . if a third party is the rapist, then both man and god are perforce victims; and if we as readers are seen as the rapists that repeat again and again the drama of sexual encounter through reading the poem itself, then the questioning involved

becomes a truly universal microcosm of the human experience of mingled naturalism and supernaturalism.

Perhaps, as you read this sentence, you feet a bit like Mamet's Carol. You're not at all sure what Barnwell means but you're pretty sure it's important. Many writers, when faced with a situation like this one, simply quote the sentence they don't understand. "After all, " they reason, "the teacher will understand what it means, and it would be better not to mess with it by trying to put it into my own words. Besides, quoting is faster and easier than paraphrasing." You write something like this:

> The "question of the rapist" in "Leda and the Swan," by William Butler Yeats, is the subject of much disagreement. W. C. Barnwell states:
>
>> If the swan is the rapist, then man exists as a mere object and is not himself an important actor in the cosmic drama of time and eternity,

and so on through all of Barnwell's alternatives. What does this paragraph tell your "authoritative reader"? That you can copy accurately? That you can type? That you have read (or photocopied or scanned) Barnwell's article? Yes, but does it tell your reader how you take account of Barnwell's reading? Or, what *you* think the poem means? Or, what is at stake for you in that reading? Does it matter who rapes whom? Why? Is it even a rape? Does it matter who knows or learns what? Why?

When you merely quote someone else, you leave the writing—and the thinking—to the person you quote and the reader you address. You—and your *difference*— disappear from the conversation. And that's unfortunate, because your opinion is valuable—and because *your* opinion is what the assignment sought. What your authoritative reader needs to see, in other words, is that you've read and understood your sources—but have come to your own conclusion. (Therefore, as you may already have noticed, papers that are heavily laden with direct quotations usually do not receive high grades.) Let's try again.

Incorporating Other Readings into Your Own

This time, you notice that Barnwell begins by making an assertion about the poem's theme: Leda is often read as a "rape-poem." Barnwell evidently agrees with that reading and asserts that Yeats's "copulatory *personae*. . . act and are acted upon in various ways to learn certain lessons." OK, you *summarize*, "Barnwell believes that the poem describes a rape from which somebody learns something." Here is an issue in which you have some interest. Do people learn something from rape? If so, what do they learn? Who does the learning? What could they possibly learn? Does learning something make rape OK? For whom? You now have a gap—in fact you have several.

Now, you have begun to take account of Barnwell's reading *and* you've found a focus for your paper. Your next step might be to decide whether to use

Barnwell's three alternative readings as a framework in which to compare answers to your question or to make your own framework. Let's say you're pressed for time, and you decide to use Barnwell's. Your next step might be to *paraphrase* Barnwell's alternatives. You easily paraphrase the first two and then you come to that third one.

> If we as readers are seen as the rapists that repeat again and again the drama of the sexual encounter through reading the poem itself, then the questioning involved becomes a truly universal microcosm of the human experience of mingled naturalism and supernaturalism.

Instead of just quoting this time, though, you go to p. 730 where Barnwell elaborates on that alternative: "The pattern of history and its turnings, then, is the rapist in this reading and both Leda and the swan are its victims." This articulation seems much clearer and you're now able to paraphrase the third alternative.

The next step might be to look at the other readings to see whether they fit into Barnwell's categories or require new ones. Let's try Unterecker. Two of his passages seem relevant:

> Mary's real experience he [Yeats] concludes was, like Leda's an experience of horror—of terror at the violent arrival of a god, an experience that might, he suggests at the end of each poem, have been compensated for by insight (knowledge) gained in the violent encounter with the supernatural.

[and]

> The annunciation he [Yeats] refers to is, of course, the rape of Leda by Zeus who, disguised as a gigantic swan, had in that remarkable conception begotten not only Helen but as well the whole consequence of Helen: the fall of Troy, the death of the Greek heroes.

OK, (you summarize again) Unterecker also thinks the poem is about a rape—of Leda by Zeus—and he does not take a stand on the question whether the rape is "compensated for" by knowledge. He does seem to fit into Barnwell's categories. You try Parkinson:

> The tragedy of Leda is that she should be a battleground, that her descendents should also be helplessly caught between the natural and the supernatural, the human image being endowed with significance only insofar as it can participate in the life of nature and supernature. So she is at once dignified, exalted, and destroyed.

What do you think? Does Parkinson fit into the categories? And should you summarize or paraphrase his position?

Next, you look at Levine again for the specific purpose of finding out where he stands on the "rape" issue—and you find that he emphasizes the ambiguity.

By now, I hope, you have begun to develop tentative answers to your gap questions—and you have done so by entering a conversation and taking account of what is being said. You're probably ready to start a draft. You might begin with your answers to the questions you've formulated, and then discuss (paraphrase, summarize and quote) the other readers as their readings are relevant to yours. As you begin each of these discussions, you need to decide how exactly you are going to use the other reading to form a part of your reading of this poem. What do you want it to accomplish in *your* conversation with *your* reader?

SHARING A READING—FINALLY

1. On the basis of the readings you've done so far, and any others that your teacher might assign, formulate your own question about "Leda and the Swan" and take account of at least two other readers as you offer at least one answer to your question.

TEXT FOR FURTHER READING

In each of the chapters so far we have read at least one poem by Robert Frost. Here is one more:

The Gift Outright
Robert Frost

The land was ours before we were the land's.
She was our land more than a hundred years
Before we were her people. She was ours
In Massachusetts, in Virginia,
But we were England's, still colonials,
Possessing what we still were unpossessed by,
Possessed by what we now no more possessed.
Something we were withholding made us weak
Until we found out that it was ourselves
We were withholding from our land of living,
And forthwith found salvation in surrender.
Such as we were we gave ourselves outright
(The deed of gift was many deeds of war)
To the land vaguely realizing westward,
But still unstoried, artless, unenhanced,
Such as she was, such as she would become.

SHARING A READING

Write a researched paper about the work of Robert Frost in which you take account of at least two other readers as you consider one of the questions that follow or one of your own. Your teacher will help you to find other scholarly readings in the library or on the Internet, but don't forget to attend to the readings of your fellow students. Like you, they already know how to read culture: everyone does it all the time.

1. Robert Frost often writes about such elements of the natural world as woodchucks, apples, spiders, and moths. Can you generalize about his use of these figures?
2. Write for an audience of elementary or middle school teachers, on why you think or do not think some of Frost's poems might be appropriate for younger readers.
3. Some critics have said that Frost is concerned with "metaphysical" issues—that is, with questions about such abstractions as the supernatural, the existence of God, and the possibility of an afterlife. Write an essay for

an authoritative reader in which you agree or disagree with this judgment.

4. Choose a few of Frost's poems from this book—or others that your teacher might suggest—and develop a generalization about Frost's treatment of human relationships. Explain your conclusions to someone with whom you have a significant relationship.

5. Use Robert Frost's work to explain one or more of the acts of reading you have practiced in this book to a specific audience of your choosing. It is not necessary for you to demonstrate every act of reading for every poem. In fact, one of your first tasks is to decide how to limit this assignment. You may want to limit yourself to one or more acts of reading—gaps, for example, or themes. Or you may want to do complete readings of just one or two poems.

Credits

TEXT SELECTIONS

Angelou, Maya, "Martial Choreograph," from *Just Give Me a Cool Drink of Water 'Fore I Die*. Copyright © 1971 by Maya Angelou. Reprinted by permission of Random House, Inc.

Atwood, Margaret, "The Loneliness of the Military Historian," from *Morning in the Burned House*. Copyright © 1995 by Margaret Atwood. Reprinted by permission of Houghton Mifflin Company, and McClelland & Stewart, Inc., The Canadian Publishers. All rights reserved.

Bambara, Toni Cade, "The Lesson," from *Gorilla, My Love*. Copyright © 1972 by Toni Cade Bambara. Reprinted by permission of Random House, Inc.

Barlowe, Jamie, "A Failure of Apology" is reprinted by permission of the author.

Barlowe, Jamie, "Hoosier-ettes" is reprinted by permission of the author.

Barnwell, W. C., "The Rapist in 'Leda and the Swan'," originally appeared in the *South Atlantic Bulletin* 42.1 (1977); 62–68. Reprinted by permission.

Beattie, Ann, "The Working Girl," from *What Was Mine*. Copyright © 1991 by Ann Beattie. Reprinted by permission of Random House, Inc.

Cardenal, Ernesto, "Prayer for Marilyn Monroe," from *Marilyn Monroe and Other Poems*, translated by Robert Pring-Mill (1975) published by Burns & Oats, Wellwood, Nort Farm Road, Tunbridge Wells TN2 3DR UK.

Carver, Raymond, "Cathedral," from *Cathedral*. Copyright © 1981 by Raymond Carver. Reprinted by permission of Alfred A. Knopf, Inc.

Chang, Lan Samantha, "The Eve of the Spirit Festival." Copyright © 1995 by Lan Samantha Chang. Reprinted by permission of the author.

Child, Christine, "Black Swamp." © Christine Child 1991. All rights reserved

Coover, Robert, excerpts from *Briar Rose*. Copyright © 1997 by Robert Coover. Reprinted by permission of Grove/Atlantic, Inc.

Cullen, Countee, "A Brown Girl Dead," published in *Color* © 1925 Harper & Bros., NY. Renewed 1952 Ida M. Cullen. Copyrights administered by Thompson and Thompson, New York, NY.

Dickinson, Emily, "A Narrow Fellow in the Grass," reprinted by permission of the publishers and the Trustees of Amherst College from *The Poems of Emily Dickinson*, Thomas H. Johnson, Ed., Cambridge, Mass.: The Belknap Press of Harvard University Press, Copyright © 1951, 1955, 1979, 1983 by the President and Fellows of Harvard College.

Dickinson, Emily, "I Like to See It Lap the Miles," reprinted by permission of the publishers and the Trustees of Amherst College from *The Poems of Emily Dickinson*, Thomas H. Johnson, Ed., Cambridge, Mass.: The Belknap Press of Harvard University Press, Copyright © 1951, 1955, 1979, 1983 by the President and Fellows of Harvard College.

Doyle, Sir Arthur Conan, "The Red-Headed League," from *The Complete Sherlock Holmes*. Reprinted by permission of The Sir Arthur Conan Doyle Literary Estate.

Dukes, Thomas, "Minerva, Ohio," first appeared in *Poetry*. Copyright 1993 by The Modern Poetry Association. Reprinted by permission of the Editory of *Poetry*.

e.e. cummings, "I sing of Olaf glad and big," copyright 1931, © 1959, 1991 by the Trustees for the E.E. Cummings Trust, Copyright © 1979 by George James Firmage, from *Complete Poems: 1904–1962* by E.E. Cummings, Edited by George J. Firmage. Reprinted by permission of Liveright Publishing Corporation.

Faulkner, William, "Dry September," from *Collected Stories of William Faulkner* by William Faulkner. Copyright © 1930 and renewed 1958 by William Faulkner. Reprinted by permission of Random House, Inc.

Fitzgerald, F. Scott, "Babylon Revisited," reprinted with permission of Scribner, a Division of Simon & Schuster, from *The Short Stories of F. Scott Fitzgerald* edited by Matthew J. Bruccoli. Copyright 1931 by The Curtis Publishing Company. Copyright renewed © 1959 by Frances Scott Fitzgerald Lanahan.

Francis, Robert, "Pitcher," from *Collected Poems 1936–1976*. Copyright 1976. Reprinted by permission of Wesleyan University Press.

Frost, Robert, "A Drumlin Woodchuck," from *The Complete Poems of Robert Frost*, Copyright 1936, 1942, 1951, 1956, 1958 by Robert Frost, 1964, 1967, © 1970 by Lesley Frost Ballentine, Copyright 1923, 1928, 1930, 1939, © 1969 by Henry Holt & Company. Reprinted by permission of Henry Holt & Company, Inc.

Frost, Robert, "Design," from *The Complete Poems of Robert Frost*, Copyright 1936, 1942, 1951, 1956, 1958 by Robert Frost, 1964, 1967, © 1970 by Lesley Frost Ballentine, Copyright 1923, 1928, 1930, 1939, © 1969 by Henry Holt & Company. Reprinted by permission of Henry Holt & Company, Inc.

Frost, Robert, "Fire and Ice," from *The Complete Poems of Robert Frost*, Copyright 1936, 1942, 1951, 1956, 1958 by Robert Frost, 1964, 1967, © 1970 by Lesley Frost Ballentine, Copyright 1923, 1928, 1930, 1939, © 1969 by Henry Holt & Company. Reprinted by permission of Henry Holt & Company, Inc.

PHOTOS AND CARTOONS

Index